Complete Guide to
Internet Publicity

Praise for Steve O'Keefe's *PUBLICITY ON THE INTERNET*

"This book is the most important marketing resource in print today!"

—*BBL Internet Media*

"This is, by far, the best nuts-and-bolts explanation of what goes into a successful online campaign I have seen to date. RECOMMENDATION: run to your local book store and buy a copy."

—*Richard Hoy, Moderator, Online Advertising Discussion List*

"Written in a lucid, engaging style and grounded by thorough research and the author's extensive real world experience, I can't imagine a better constructed guide to this dynamic and complex field."

—*Ken McCarthy, President, E-Media*

"(*Publicity on the Internet*) has been my Bible, survival kit, and warm teddy bear of security...Everyone here wants to use it and I won't let it go!"

—*Cindy Railing, Account Supervisor, DuDell & Associates, Inc.*

"I've read over 100 books on the Internet over the past four years, and *Publicity on the Internet* is one of my two favorites!"

—*David Scott Lewis, President, Strategies & Technology, The Internet Marketing Consultancy*

"*Publicity on the Internet* is a really excellent book, one of the best I have seen on any topic relating to the Internet. Not only is it well organized and comprehensive, it is written in a wonderfully clear and readable style. This book is a significant contribution to the literature about communicating on the Internet. I am recommending it to everyone I know, except for our competitors."

—*Bob Novick, Impulse Research*

"*Publicity on the Internet* is great. I have read the first 4 chapters but I can safely say I enjoy it so much I can hardly stand it."

—*Susannah Breslin, Postfeminist Playground*

"I learned more in the first fifteen minutes I spent with *Publicity on the Internet*—and not just raw knowledge but directly useful information—than in reading several other Internet business books all the way through. All I can say is, Bravo!"

—*Shel Horowitz, Author, Grassroots Marketing*

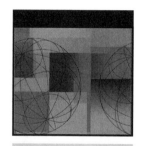

Complete Guide to Internet Publicity: Creating and Launching Successful Online Campaigns

Steve O'Keefe

Wiley Computer Publishing

John Wiley & Sons, Inc.

NEW YORK · CHICHESTER · WEINHEIM · BRISBANE · SINGAPORE · TORONTO

Publisher: Robert Ipsen
Editor: Cary Sullivan
Assistant Editor: Christina Berry/Scott Amerman
Associate Managing Editor: Penny Linskey
Associate New Media Editor: Brian Snapp
Text Design & Composition: D&G Limited, LLC

Published by John Wiley & Sons, Inc., New York

Published simultaneously in Canada.

This publication is designed to provide accurate and authoritative information in regard to the subject matter covered. It is sold with the understanding that the publisher is not engaged in professional services. If professional advice or other expert assistance is required, the services of a competent professional person should be sought.

Library of Congress Cataloging-in-Publication Data:

ISBN: 0-471-10580-5

Printed in the United States of America.

10 9 8 7 6 5 4 3 2 1

Dedicated to the memory of
Russell L. Eberlein, owner of the Internet

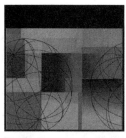

Contents

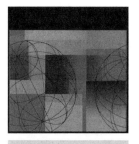

Acknowledgments

Throughout this book, I use the arrogant pronoun "I" when, in fact, a cast of thousands was involved. To list them all here—or even the major actors—would compound that arrogance, allowing me to bask in their brilliance. Yet, intellectual honesty requires that I share the credit while claiming all errors as my own.

First and foremost, I would like to thank my former employer, Cliff Kurtzman, at The Tenagra Corporation, and my staff, Christopher Lenois, Skye Wentworth, Gwendolynn Gawlick, Jeremy Hart, Mohammed "Taz" Tazehzadeh, Kate Bolin, Susan Diaz-Romero, Jesse Vohs, Tonya Lehner, Deborah Fairchild, and Bill Garnett.

Over the past seven years, I have been inspired by a group of mentors and colleagues who have helped me think through the problems of online communication and pioneer solutions of lasting value. I cannot thank them enough for their guidance, wisdom, and support. They include Jill Ellsworth, Alice Acheson, Glenn Fleishman, Richard Hoy, Daniel Kehoe, Ken McCarthy, Eric Ward, Paul Krupin, Ned Schumann, Janet Attard, Anne Papina, Mike Bayer, David Marriott, Don Bates, Richard Morris, Neil Gordon, Heather Stone, Gary Hardin, and Kelly O'Keefe.

I thank my clients for funding my research and providing the examples in this book. I thank all the Web masters, forum hosts, moderators, sysops, and chat hosts who worked with me and gave their venues over to the campaigns described here. And, I thank my fellow authors and instructors who have bravely attempted to describe the workings of this new world for the benefit of all who follow.

The Power of Internet Publicity

Five years ago, I put the finishing touches on my book, *Publicity on the Internet*, and shipped it off to the publisher. It was a good book. It became a bestseller at Amazon.com. It earned dozens of rave reviews from the media and one bad one. I received hundreds of letters from fans thanking me for writing the book. The ones I cherish most are from colleagues in the trade—marketers, publicists, and public relations professionals—who used the techniques in the book and reported that "it worked." But that's not why it was a good book.

Publicity on the Internet was a good book because money had nothing to do with it. Don't get me wrong; I'm an unapologetic capitalist. But I've been around the publishing profession long enough to know that good books aren't written for money. They're written because they *have to be*. They are written out of compulsion. And while we're used to thinking this way about great works of fiction, it applies equally to modest how-to books.

I wrote *Publicity on the Internet* in self-defense. At the time, I had a small business which provided online publicity services to book publishers and authors. When I started the business in 1994, I starved. But soon enough, like everyone else in the industry, I had more clients than I could handle. Analyzing my time sheets, I learned I was spending 25 percent of my working day turning away clients. Publishers thought they could do an end-run around wholesalers, distributors, and retailers and sell directly to the public. Authors thought they could do an end-run around publishers. They all thought the Internet was some kind of magic wand, and they wouldn't take no for an answer. So I had to explain how online promotions can only *supplement* traditional marketing, not *replace* it. It took time for the message to sink in, and some people still don't get it.

I wrote *Publicity on the Internet* because I realized that most people couldn't afford to buy these services. They needed to learn to do the work themselves. So, in the spirit of the free sharing of information (which is a hallmark of online communications), I spilled the beans. I didn't write platitudes about the potential for this new medium; rather, I wrote an instruction manual with detailed, step-by-step procedures for locating the target audience online, crafting promotions that appeal to that audience, and deploying them with near-surgical precision. With the book as my shield, protecting me from educating the public one at a time, I ducked back into the trenches doing the campaign work I love so much.

In the five years since *Publicity on the Internet* first appeared, I have launched campaigns for more than 1,000 books, several dozen Web sites, and a smattering of non-publishing clients. I graduated from a publicist to a manager of publicists, but I hated being even one step removed from the action. Ultimately, I burned out from the relentless pace of four launches every week. I took a sabbatical but couldn't resist the siren song of the dot.com startup. After skillfully avoiding several opportunities to become a millionaire, I hooked-up with the people at www.myjobsearch.com, who I felt had the right stuff to pioneer a whole new industry: personal career management. Myjobsearch.com gave me a palette and asked me to paint a picture of the company it wanted to become. They stiffed me on my fees, and my stock options are worthless, but I will forever be grateful to them for the opportunity to sketch a vision of the future.

This year, when my publisher asked me again if I might be interested in revising *Publicity on the Internet*, I said yes. A few months earlier, I had written reviews at Amazon.com and Barnes & Noble Online, advising people against buying my book. It was hopelessly out of date—so much so, in fact, that instead of updating it I rewrote the whole thing from the bottom up. What you are holding in your hands is a completely new book. Why my publisher would want to bring it out in the present market is a mystery to me. Why I wrote it is not. And it has nothing to do with money.

The Complete Guide to Internet Publicity is the culmination of a career spent in the trenches. Writing it has given me the opportunity to step back from the fray and reflect upon a large body of work, to tally my successes and failures, to extract what I believe are the core principles of online communication, to share my mistakes with my colleagues so they won't have to repeat them, and to share my small victories so they can surpass them. Although no one wants to talk about online marketing right now, they will again someday soon, and they will be glad that someone with as much experience as I have has bothered to step back, assess his work, and write honestly about what the Internet can and can't be expected to do.

Don't worry—I'm not about to drag you into another soul-searching, what-went-wrong memoir. As always, I remain obsessed with the minutia of *how to do it*. The remainder of this book is full of the nuts-and-bolts tips that my readers have come to expect. When I started in the publishing business decades ago, I was floored by the amount of detail in Dan Poynter's seminal *Self-Publishing Manual*. Instead of saying, "Pack your books carefully before shipping them," Dan expounded on the relative merits of three different types of strapping tape: how much they cost, how easy they were to use, and how they withstood a round trip through the post office. I relish that style of microscopic attention to detail that reeks of real-world experience, and I strive for it in my own writing. Others might wax philosophical about the advisability of using e-mail news releases; I tell you what font to use and the maximum number of characters per line.

But before I dive into the wonderful nitty-gritty of this *magnum opus*, I hope readers will forgive the indulgence of surveying the field and summarizing the lessons learned. In writing *The Complete Guide to Internet Publicity*, I have been forced to do a thorough inventory of the practices in our profession. I think my readers would be cheated to see only the trees and not the lush forest that contains them. Here, then, is a summary of where this profession all started, where it faltered and flourished, and where we are likely to go from here.

The Promise

Do you remember the moment the light bulb went on, when you first recognized the potential of the Internet to transform business practices worldwide? I do. I had been online for eight years, beginning in 1986 when I bought my first 300-baud modem and used it to explore local bulletin board services. In 1992, I joined CompuServe and The Well. I was working as editorial director at Loompanics Unlimited, a counterculture book publisher located in the quaint Victorian village of Port Townsend, Washington. The Internet was where my working day went to die.

In those days, I used the Internet for research and to participate in discussion groups, trolling for writers, graphic artists, and translators. The Internet was fascinating and frustrating. While I was able to locate people with similar interests, such as obscure jazz recordings, communicating with them was stilted and misleading. The Internet was limited to text messages in those days. As I writer, I felt comfortable in that environment, but the commands for communicating there were too confusing. I didn't think the Internet had the potential for mass appeal, and I resented how much of my time it took up.

In early 1994, my opinion changed. I was promoting a book called *Secrets of a Super Hacker* when a friend posted a favorable review online. I asked permission to reprint it, inserted ordering information, and posted the review to several Usenet newsgroups devoted to computer security. Within minutes, the fax machine started humming with orders for the book from Sweden, Japan, Saudi Arabia, and other countries. A U.S. spy agency bought a dozen copies of the book. I received an inquiry from a firm in South America about the Spanish-language rights to the book. In a few weeks, I sold those rights, negotiating the whole deal through e-mail. The day I posted that review was my magic moment. I knew the world of commerce would never be the same.

In the following months, I built one of the first book catalogs ever put on the Internet. It was housed at a gopher server on The Well. I remember telling my boss we could now compete on equal footing with Random House. Nothing they put online would look any better, or work any better, than our catalog. When I left Loompanics later that year to start Internet Publicity Services, Inc., I asked my boss to be generous with my replacement about time spent online. "This is the future of publishing," I wrote in a letter left on my desk.

This future was the promise of the Internet: All geographical barriers to the free flow of information would be eliminated; people would quickly be able to find material related to even the most obscure topic; that information would come with a purchasing opportunity, ending the disintermediation between the marketing message and the buying moment; people would be able to find other people with similar tastes and interests; the costs of delivering information would drop to zero; business intermediaries such as wholesalers, distributors, sales representatives, brokers, and even retailers would be cut out of the loop; and manufacturers would sell directly to consumers, reducing prices while increasing profits.

No longer would the world's brightest people be landlocked. The Internet would give everyone access to the best doctors, lawyers, teachers, and leaders. We would no longer be dependent upon the media for news, with its built-in biases. Now, we could go to the source and communicate directly with people of talent. The playing field would be leveled, and businesses would have to compete fairly for employees and customers. As the costs for storing, delivering, and retrieving information disappeared, a global agora would blossom.

I didn't buy all the hype then, but I was on board for plenty of it. To me, it seemed like the world had finally made a place where all voices could be heard, where the little guy had a chance, and where people with unusual interests would no longer be lonely or discriminated against.

When Mosaic debuted in the fall of 1994, leading to the modern World Wide Web, the promises shifted. Having come up in the world of book publishing, I was conditioned to the concept that color reproduction is expensive and should be avoided. Suddenly, color was free. And you no longer had to be a computer scientist to navigate the Internet. Documents could be displayed—not just retrieved—and a five-year-old could operate the point-and-click interface. It became clear that companies with bigger budgets would be able to produce better Web sites, so the playing field tilted a little bit. But the tradeoff was that ease-of-use would hasten worldwide adoption of the new medium.

After the Web came Java and application servers, and new promises were made. Now, we were told that content could be customized and personalized. Everyone would get *exactly* the information they wanted and wouldn't be bothered with stuff about which they couldn't care less. The consumer was in the driver's seat now, and marketers had the ability to focus their pitches with laser-beam precision. People logging onto the Internet would enter a world custom-tailored to their interests, tastes, preferences, and whims—a world designed by themselves, for themselves.

These were the promises.

The Problems

When every voice can be heard, it doesn't take long to get noisy. From the start, online discussion groups reminded us that there are a lot of voices in the world we *don't* want to hear. Usenet newsgroups erupted into arguments while mailing lists became bogged down in petty squabbles. With no cost for message delivery, marketers saw no reason to tailor their messages and unloaded a steady torrent of spam, choking discussion groups and e-mail.

People retaliated against spam with blacklisting and sabotage, and spammers responded with hacking and sabotage of their own. It seemed the only way to get merciless marketers to reconsider their behavior was to increase their costs of sending unwanted messages. It would soon cost plenty to defend a business against the repercussions of disregarding netiquette.

When the Web appeared, corporations began setting up Web sites with zeal. Hoping to cut out intermediaries while selling directly to the public, they damaged vendor relationships that had lasted for centuries, only to find that the public wasn't buying—at least, not directly. Still, companies worked harder to improve their content and search engine position, chasing a retail customer who wasn't interested while turning their backs on their best customers—those intermediaries who bought in bulk and sold to end users.

With the explosion in the number of Web sites, finding quality information online got harder and harder, leading to the rise of Internet directories and search engines. Today, these guides are flirting with uselessness, are hampered with broken links, and often lead to sites that don't contain the desired content or to sites that haven't been updated in so long that they're a waste of time. Today, with so many sites going out of business and search engines and directories starved for cash to maintain quality control, the situation is only getting worse. The rise in paid placements has reduced the value of these guides even more. Today, the results of search inquiries are more likely to contain ads than relevant leads.

The great free forum that is the Internet has exposed both individuals and companies to dangers never before imagined. Malicious hackers vandalize systems out of vengeance or just for fun. People are afraid to open e-mail even if they requested it, much less if it's unsolicited. Companies dependent on e-commerce and e-communication find that their systems are fragile and can be completely shut down. People online are reluctant to pay even the smallest subscription fee for access to information. And folks who would never shoplift from a store think nothing of duplicating and distributing copyrighted material.

The dream of a perfectly customized world has morphed into a nightmare of access restrictions and offensive, off-target advertising. Consumers say they want personalization but won't disclose the kind of personal information that makes it possible. They have good reason to be cautious, however, because private information about their identities, surfing habits, and purchases is being used by people to make their lives miserable.

Like the stock market's estimation of dot.com value, our own expectations for the Internet have crashed. From a free global marketplace, some now see a cesspool of pornography, crass commercialism, hackers, vigilantes, deviants, thieves, and saboteurs. No wonder companies have retreated to reassess their strategies toward this powerful but dangerous tool.

The Principles

What lessons can we draw from this seven-year experiment with the commercial Internet? From a marketing perspective, and with a view from trenches based on hundreds of campaigns, here are the attributes I consider when designing online promotions.

Transactional

For the time being, the Internet is still a transactions-based medium. With a few exceptions, it is not a good vehicle for entertainment. People have been conditioned by television to expect a level of quality that can't be delivered online—even with what passes for a broadband connection. People expect their entertainment to contain beautiful, clear video streams, backed with quality acting, writing, lighting, sound, music, animation, and graphics. In some future world where it is possible to deliver this level of quality to a decent-size screen/monitor, most companies won't be able to afford to produce this kind of programming. Perhaps only then will it become apparent that most companies should stay out of the entertainment business and focus on handling transactions through their Web sites.

Companies are spending most of their online budgets improving the efficiency of operations, and that's the way it should be. Rather than eliminate market intermediaries, the Internet makes it possible to economically serve trade customers and suppliers. Maybe seven years of experience has taught us the value of intermediaries in organizing markets? The number one missing ingredient on book publishers' Web sites was the *purchase order form*. The purchase order became a symbol for me, an example of how companies turned their backs on their biggest customers—those who already had a relationship with the firm (and in most cases, an account with a credit line). Instead, they chased a retail market they had little experience in serving.

The broad online audience follows a grab-and-go pattern, hunting for solutions, gathering documents, and heading home. Retail customers prefer to shop at stores where they can not only find good prices, service, and selection, but where they also have an account relationship. Money spent turning your e-commerce site into an entertainment site is largely wasted. If the Internet is a transactional medium, it makes sense to devote your online budget to serving the transactional needs of your business partners and to export your promotions to the high-traffic entertainment and information sites where your target audience gathers.

Filtering

In a world where every voice can be heard, nothing is so valuable as a good set of filters. From an unbridled infostream, we are entering an era of filtered content again. The public has learned to value the role of the media as judges of worth. They gravitate to sites where the filters are set to favor their tastes. They draw from a variety of sources to make sure they are getting the full story and the right spin, but they also demand access to source documents so they can make up their own minds about how well the media is doing its job. Finding these key media properties, and working together with them, is part of the publicist's agenda.

The public will use e-mail filters to lock the vast majority of online users out of their mailboxes. Journalists will use filters, too, to keep from having their e-mail clogged with the pitches of indiscriminate publicists. Filtration can be a death sentence for publicists, forever banished from the inboxes of the media. The trick for publicists is to learn to court the media in a way that doesn't trigger filtration. One method is to work through the Web sites where the press gathers. Another strategy is a return to printed publicity, where a poorly targeted news release doesn't carry a price tag of irrevocable shunning.

Targeting

Targeting is the natural reaction to filtering. Publicists need to be careful about what messages they send and to whom they send them. If they can't impose this discipline themselves, their audiences will impose it. Better targeting comes from knowing the detailed interests of the people with which you are trying to communicate. As we've seen, the public is leery of revealing these details of their private lives. It makes sense to export promotions to those sites that are able to capture enough information about their users to target effectively. For press relations, publicists have to do a better job of tracking the stories in which contacts are interested. They need to actually read the publications journalists are writing for, watch the programs that producers put together, and note changes in direction signaled by new jobs or job titles.

Layering

One of the unique hallmarks of online communications is the layered message. The marketing chain begins with a simple query to find people interested in a topic, with a button to press for more information. These initial salvos have to be brief and on target, so those who are not interested in one particular message will ignore it instead of filtering you out permanently or retaliating against you. Those who find the message of interest should easily be able to dig deeper for more information.

At each stage of the marketing chain, this pattern is followed by an easy opt out for those who are not interested in going farther and by a depth of information available for those who will follow. People drilling through this process expect a payoff at the end. Journalists expect to find good source documents, artwork, interview prospects, and contact information. The public expects to find detailed, relevant, up-to-date information.

Universal Access

Web surfers really don't care if you provide a variety of viewing options for your content as long as you provide the one that *they* want. Each format decision you make can shave a few percentage points off the audience. Make enough of these decisions, and you end up with an inaccessible promotion. The solution is to offer alternatives to meet the needs of different users: newsletters in text, HTML, and *America Online* (AOL) formats; streaming media optimized for three different speeds; artwork displayed in low resolution for fast browsing but available in high-resolution for the media; Web sites designed to look appealing with any browser; and promotions that don't require an arsenal of plug-ins to enjoy. Add foreign language translations and time-zone sensitivity to the list, and you have a set of variables that can overwhelm any Web master.

Universal access is another reason to partner with high-traffic sites on promotions. It could be prohibitively expensive for you to offer the features desired by your target audience. Take payment and shipping options, for example. If you buy books from publishers' sites, chances are your choices are very restricted. Go to Amazon.com and you'll find numerous ways to have your books shipped and a corresponding number of choices for how to settle the bill. The complexities involved in serving a large—and largely unknown—universal audience argue for a strategy of focusing your own Web site on a core audience of business relations and exporting promotions to sites capable of serving the diverse needs of the general public.

Self-Protection

Every promotion has to be examined through the lens of self-protection. People can no longer be expected to open unsolicited e-mail and will certainly resist opening file attachments. You also have to assess the likelihood of a promotion to result in criticism and/or an attack. One of the problems I have with calculations of *return on investment* (ROI) is that they seldom take into account the negative impacts of poor promotions. What price do you put on damage to a brand or strained relationships with consumers? Does ROI take into account the costs of repairing computer systems infected with viruses or installing and maintaining security software? I'll talk more about the problems of calculating ROI at the end of this book. Internet marketers need to do a better job of assessing the short-term and long-term risks to their companies from botched online promotions.

Sharing Value

Marketing messages by themselves are ignored online or retaliated against. A more successful strategy is to offer the public and the press something of value in exchange for accepting your promotional pitch. When you approach the media, you should offer a compelling story and back it up with documents, statistics, artwork, and interview subjects. When you approach the public, you should offer content that satisfies, in the form of articles, tip sheets, helpful files, and offers of expert assistance. When you approach high-traffic Web sites, you should offer programming that will help them attract and retain an audience.

Every company has something of value to share with the online audience. Usually, it is expertise in the field. One of the jobs of the publicist is to uncover the value locked inside a company and format it for online delivery. The knee-jerk route is to advertise—to pay to place the marketing message online and hope enough of the audience responds. The tactical route, with a more lasting impact, is to publicize—to create something of value and donate it to the online audience, letting your marketing message ride along for free.

Partnership

As the number of Web sites online explodes, the ability for small sites or standalone promotions to draw an audience dwindles. All of the characteristics of online communication point in the same direction: the need to promote products and services through high-traffic channels that the online audience has embraced. Filtered content has come to the Internet, and you need to get inside those filters by going to sites that are trusted. This book will show you how.

The Practice

From these principles of online communication, I have developed a set of practices for effective promotion. This book is a guide to creating, deploying, and measuring the impact of these campaigns. Here are some of the highlights of this new text.

Media Relations

E-mail has replaced print and telephones as the preferred way to pitch stories to the press. In order to have effective communications with journalists, you need to find the e-mail addresses they really use. Commercially available databases simply do not contain these personal addresses. In the chapter on news releases, I show you how to economically locate journalists' e-mail addresses and maintain them in a database. Also missing from most commercial media directories are new media contacts, including discussion group moderators, chat show producers, e-zine editors, and Web site content editors. I'll show you how to find these contacts (who can make or break an online promotion).

Once you have contact information, you need to write news releases that will not result in filtering. In painstaking detail, I will show you how to write and format news releases for e-mail delivery that will appeal to journalists interested in your story without bothering those who are not. In the chapter covering online newsrooms, I'll describe the content you need—and don't need—at your Web site. It's surprising how many online newsrooms lack the simple, cheap elements that journalists want while spending vast sums on features the press is unlikely to use.

Another way to reach the media (who either don't respond to e-mail or who have filtered you out) is to move your media relations to the Web sites that journalists use. In the chapter covering online newsrooms, I talk about two promotions that are suitable for export: online news conferences and online presentations. I'm particularly keen on this last item—bandwidth-friendly, narrated PowerPoint slide shows that can be easily updated and shipped out to media sites. In the online newsrooms chapter of this book, I describe how to build a small newswire service to increase your value as a source for stories, and in the syndication chapter I show how one company used this strategy to generate 10 times the coverage they garnered from press releases.

Web Site Promotions

Whether you are trying to attract an audience for your own Web site or lure browsers to a partner site, I'll give you the latest tricks of the trade. Web site registration techniques have changed a lot in the past year as several key sites have gone out of business and the survivors have started charging for position. I'll cover the well-worn turf of search engine optimization and hopefully prove to you that for most sites, anything more than simple META tag improvements is a waste of resources. Of much greater value is the linkage campaign. I'll not only show you how to generate far more traffic than search engine and directory listings, but also how to get *quality* traffic that comes to your site knowing what to expect and ready to buy.

Web site marketers will welcome a new chapter on using newsletters and direct e-mail, along with an updated chapter on tried-and-true discussion group postings. The chapter on syndication has a section on using affiliate programs to market a Web site. I believe this usage was the key to Amazon.com's phenomenal IPO (Initial Public Offering), though in the long run it hurt itself by losing control over affiliates. I'll show you how to build an affiliate program where you can update the content and design without relying on your partners' assistance.

Web site promoters will also enjoy the chapter on contests and other fancy promotions. Contests are one area of online marketing where there is ample room for improvement. If you've been disappointed using online contests, the problem is probably not the concept but the design. Most online contests are not structured to achieve the stated goals. I'll show you how to build contests that really work by making every facet of the contest reflect the marketing message: the prizes offered, the activities required to enter the contest, and even the sites recruited to host the contest. This chapter also covers traffic builders and stupid Web tricks, such as the dancing baby and a food-processed frog, along with cutting-edge viral promotions for films such as *The Blair Witch Project* and *A.I.*

Online Events

I've dusted off the instructions for producing a chat tour and revised the campaign for the increased competition over premium chat venues. I've also added instructions for online seminars and workshops. These campaigns are on the edge of the distance-learning movement and use a lot of techniques developed for the classroom. I cover a no-frills, low-tech seminar that can be exported to multiple sites as well as high-tech events that include streaming media.

In the syndication chapter, I follow chat tours through a logical progression, first as they develop into a chat *series* and finally into a recurring program syndicated to high-traffic Web sites. The Internet is ready for expert guides to come online with weekly programming to help people get the most out of the Internet. Locking up one of these expert slots today could be the smartest online marketing move you ever made.

Building a Department

As the Internet has become a critical component of publicity, marketing, and public relations, so has the amount of money spent on outside services. In prior years, companies either didn't have enough need for these services to warrant an in-house department or couldn't find the talent to staff one. The time has come for many organizations to take their online publicity efforts in-house. Thanks to the dot.com crash, experienced employees are easy to come by and high schools and colleges are turning out more Internet-literate graduates every year.

An important addition to this book is the chapter on building your own online publicity operation. It contains job descriptions and a training regimen for achieving competency in a hurry. You'll learn what skills are required, how to find and hire people with those capabilities, and how to integrate these services within the total *public relations* (PR) and marketing mix.

The Prognosis

New promises for the Internet have replaced the inflated dreams of the early years. Instead of compressing supply and distribution chains, the Internet makes them more efficient. Companies will deal with *more* intermediaries than ever before but will use them strategically, taking advantage of the unique capabilities of a wide variety of wholesalers, distributors, suppliers, retailers, and other vendors.

The online public is following a similar pattern. People are realizing they simply don't have the capacity or desire to hear every voice online, nor do they want to be dependent on a few powerful information providers. They will gravitate to a small group of key sites that do a good job of filtering the infostream, but they will also access alternative sites for different flavors of coverage (and ultimately, if they need it, they want to see source documents as a safeguard against bias).

We've seen this pattern before with television, though played out over a longer timeframe. From a few broadcast channels that had to satisfy the general public, we now have cable and satellite systems that offer hundreds of niche channels. The public will use a variety of channels depending on their moods and needs. In the news delivery business, for example, we have local channels for regional news, broadcast networks for national news, CNN for international news or breaking stories, and Fox news for a more irreverent slant. The challenge for news providers is not so much to compete as to define a specialty. We see this same scenario in business supply chains and in consumer Web sites.

As the Internet grows up from a free-for-all into a filtered medium, it is more important than ever for companies to forge partnerships with Web Sites That Matter to their target audiences. As the Web comes closer and closer to interactive television, the online audience will become even more concentrated around sites that have the budget to produce quality programming. Most companies will be unable to create Web sites that appeal to the masses or draw traffic to promotions on their own sites. Hopefully, they will realize that it is cheaper to export promotional programs to high-traffic sites looking for content. This strategy is inexpensive, flexible, and effective. This book is a guide to putting that strategy into motion. Let me show you.

E-Mail News Releases

E-mail has completely disrupted the relationship between public relations profession-als and the media. On the media side, e-mail has escalated the trend of outsourcing writing and program production because talented people can more easily work from remote locations. The people who write the news no longer see the faxes, letters, and packages sent to company headquarters. Phone calls are answered by voice mail and are seldom returned. Taking a reporter to lunch now means taking a flight to the city in which he or she lives instead of walking down the street to his or her office.

On the PR side, e-mail has made it possible to instantly send news releases to thou-sands of media contacts at a fraction of the cost of fax or mail. Stories can break in min-utes all over the globe, instead of slowly spreading out from media hubs. Pressured to generate coverage, publicists mercilessly spam the press, sacrificing their companies' futures in a desperate search for a few lines of ink today.

With the invention of e-mail, the sometimes cozy but always cautious relationship between PR and the media has become a war zone. Journalists have cut off all tradi-tional forms of communication while publicists overuse the one mode of contact left: e-mail. And now the war is news itself, with editors using their columns to lambaste the spammers and PR pros vowing to go directly to the public and cut the media mid-dlemen out of the loop.

How did we get into this mess? The answer is technology and greed—the ability to use e-mail to reach journalists divorced from the respect and manners that attended more personal relations. And how will we get out of it? The answer is technology and

greed—the ability of journalists to filter their e-mail combined with a growing awareness in the PR profession that coverage can't be demanded but must be earned with
solid story leads that are respectfully delivered.

In this chapter, I'll examine the shifting dynamics in the relationship between publicists and the press resulting from the growth of e-mail. I'll suggest grounds for a cease-
fire in the war of words over spam. I'll also demonstrate how technology is imposing
a solution to this problem that will force public relations professionals to mind their
manners when dealing with the press.

I'll also show public relations professionals exactly how to write, format, and distribute news releases and how to find and manage the e-mail addresses of the media.
Topics covered include the following:

Using and abusing e-mail news releases. What journalists like about e-mail news
releases, what they hate about e-mail news releases, and the three ground rules
of engagement.

Types of news releases. The purpose of a news release determines not only its
content, but also the method of delivery. I'll explore the differences between
releases promoting products, services, people, events, survey results, breaking
news, and routine announcements.

Writing e-mail news releases. Mark Twain once said, "If I had more time, I would
have written less." Here's my guide to accomplishing more by saying less and
saying it well.

Formatting e-mail news releases. I explore the different e-mail software
packages available and explain in minute detail how to design releases that
reporters will read.

Finding e-mail addresses of the media. I'll make recommendations on contact
management software, then show you how to fill those files with the personal
e-mail addresses of thousands of media contacts.

Sending e-mail news releases. How to choose media contacts for a release,
assemble the outgoing e-mail, and bypass restrictions set by your ISP.

News release follow-up. How to troubleshoot bounced mail, handle complaints,
and process requests for additional information.

Using and Abusing E-Mail News Releases

It's safe to say that the Internet has radically transformed the distribution of news
releases. But don't take my word for it. Take a look at the long series of *Media in Cyberspace* studies conducted by Don Middleberg and Steven S. Ross, which you can find
archived at www.middleberg.com. Middleberg is an online PR heavyweight, an early
adopter of Internet technology, author of the book *Winning PR in the Wired World*
(McGraw-Hill, 2001), and founder and CEO of Middleberg Euro RSCG, a public relations consulting firm. Ross has been a professor at the prestigious Columbia University Graduate School of Journalism for 15 years and is the author of 18 books. Together,

they began tracking the media's use of the Internet in 1994 and have now assembled an impressive history of trends.

According to the 2000 survey released in April 2001 and retitled *Survey of Media in the Wired World*, 98 percent of journalists check their e-mail at least once a day. Because the survey includes broadcast, online, and print media, the term "journalist" should be seen as any professional news gatherer—not just writers for print publications. Rounding the numbers slightly, I'd feel comfortable saying that virtually every journalist in all media in the United States is accessible by e-mail. But do they like receiving e-mail news releases?

The answer is "Yes." More than half the journalists surveyed like receiving story pitches via e-mail while three-quarters use the Internet to find news releases and to find sources and experts. When I began using e-mail to distribute news releases in 1994, the only media contacts online in significant numbers were technology reporters. By 1997, you could reach the average journalist via e-mail, but most of them were not comfortable receiving news releases that way. Today, everyone is online and the majority of them prefer e-mail releases to any other method.

The 1998 *Media in Cyberspace* study showed e-mail beating out all other news release delivery methods for the first time. For communications with known contacts, journalists preferred e-mail (38 percent) to phone (32 percent), in-person (21 percent), or fax (9 percent). For communications with unknown sources, in-person and phone pitches beat out e-mail in 1998. I don't have an update for these numbers, but I suspect today most journalists prefer to be pitched first by e-mail, even from unknown sources (it's a lot easier to delete an e-mail than to get out of an in-person pitch).

In five short years, e-mail came out of nowhere to become the preferred form of contact by researchers, writers, and producers in all media. So why is everyone complaining about e-mail news releases?

A Word About Spam

Everyone hates spam. More formally referred to as *Unsolicited Commercial E-Mail* (UCE), spam is the bulk e-mail you get that you didn't ask for, don't want, and wish would stop coming. And journalists *really* hate spam because they can't hide from it. Journalists rely on e-mail for communications with sources, colleagues, and their audiences, so they can't keep their e-mail addresses private. Even if they cut down on the number of "Make Money Fast" spams that they receive, they're still left with dozens— sometimes *hundreds*—of "legitimate" e-mail pitches a day seeking news coverage. The ease of locating journalists' e-mail addresses has created a real e-mail management problem for the fourth estate. According to the 2000 Middleberg/Ross survey, journalists spend an average of 15 hours a week processing e-mail. That's more than one-third of a normal 40-hour work week. And they aren't happy about it.

In the May 1, 2000 issue of *The Standard*, editor James Fallows kicked a hornets' nest with an editorial about press relations spam. "Ninety-five percent of incoming PR e-mail is completely inappropriate," says Fallows, and he's not referring to "Make Money Fast" spam but to communications from PR professionals. "The PR person has scraped every available name off a publication's masthead and blasted press releases to all of them, without the slightest idea of who writes what," Fallows complains. And this complaint echoes throughout the world of the media. Here's a line from a scathing guide to netiquette compiled by Esther Schindler and the members of the Internet Press Guild (www.netpress.org), a group of journalists who cover the Internet beat: "It's also important for you to figure out which writers care about what kind of information." And here are a few more choice morsels from a list of "Pet Press Peeves" found at www.Futuremedia.org:

- Being pitched by someone who hasn't looked at the newspaper and doesn't have an idea of what we cover and how we do it.
- Having story ideas pitched by people who do not know the publication.
- My number one peeve is getting pitched a story by somebody who doesn't bother to read the magazine.

And the beat goes on. Off-topic news releases—that is, news releases sent by people who do not read the publication, watch the program, listen to the broadcast, or know what topics are covered by the journalists whom they're sending to cover the releases —are the biggest complaint the media has about online public relations. When Fallows aired his gripes in the pages of *The Standard*, he got more mail than he's received on any subject in a long time—most of it applauding his stand and echoing his complaints. But PR flaks have their own list of offenses committed by journalists, among those being rudeness. I have frequently received form flames from journalists who asked to be put on my media list, then complained when I sent them a release about a topic they cover. There's a lot of animosity between the PR industry and the media, and yet neither functions very well without the other. E-mail has made both sides much more vulnerable. Faxes get shredded without comment. Stupid phone calls result in a quick hang-up. But errant e-mail seems to bring out the mean streak in people, and they retaliate with the worst sort of purple prose.

In the interest of easing tensions between PR and the press, I offer the following guide to E-Mail News Release Netiquette. If you follow this guide, you'll not only cut down on the number of complaints you receive, but you'll also dramatically improve the results from your releases.

E-Mail News Release Netiquette

All it takes is common sense, empathy, and perhaps a little experience to understand how to pitch media contacts via e-mail. Unfortunately, many publicists lack common sense, or abandon in it favor of expediency, or are being pushed so hard for results that they will try anything to get coverage. Unrepentant PR spamming has led to a backlash from journalists, and the Internet is now littered with op-eds disparaging our profession written by people who know how to cause serious injury with words.

The solution to this problem lies in filtering. Most e-mail software comes with filtering features, some of which are very advanced. One of the easiest to set up is a bulk mail filter: If the e-mail is not personally addressed to you, it gets deposited into a bulk mail folder instead of your inbox. This feature cuts down on the morning mail clutter and lets you deal with bulk mail when you find time. Most bulk mail divides into newsletters you've subscribed to and spam. The bulk mail filter is handy because you don't get fooled by clever subject lines that make it sound like you asked for this information. You can trash these messages unopened more easily than if they're seeding throughout your inbox. For the logic minded, here is the programming script for a bulk mail filter:

```
IF recipient
DOES NOT CONTAIN myemailaddress@company.com
TRANSFER TO bulk mail folder
```

Another simple, useful e-mail processing tool is the Bozo filter. Add someone's e-mail address to the Bozo list, and you'll never see e-mail from him or her again—it's automatically deposited into the trash. Many people ask me if Bozo filtering hurts my ability to reach the media. In fact, the opposite is true: The more journalists who use filtering, the better my response rate has been. Why? The answer is, if you are very selective about who you send releases to, you won't get filtered, and your releases will stand out because all the idiots taking up precious inbox space have been Bozo-filtered.

If you haven't tried Bozo filtering, I highly recommend it. There is a certain satisfying feeling you get dropping some moron's name onto a Bozo list, knowing they won't ever be able to bother you again. That feeling alone is worth experimenting with filters. Filters run in sequence, so you'll want to run your Bozo filter *before* your bulk mail filter or else mail from your Bozo list will get deposited into your bulk mail folder instead of the trash. Here's the programming sequence for the Bozo filter:

```
IF sender
CONTAINS bozo@company.com
TRANSFER TO trash
```

That's so simple, isn't it? But you need to exercise some care with these filters as with anything automated. When Hotmail first started giving away free e-mail addresses, I noticed a lot of spam coming from Hotmail accounts. So I Bozo-filtered anything coming from Hotmail. Some time passed before I realized that a few of my friends and clients were using Hotmail addresses, and all their messages to me were going into the trash unseen. It might take a little tweaking to get your filters set up just right.

So, my suggestion to the media is to learn how to use e-mail filtering. It is really very easy and has a dramatic impact on both efficiency and peace of mind. And my warning to publicists is that if you do not observe proper netiquette when e-mailing to the media, you will be filtered out, you won't know it, and you'll never be able to undo the damage unless you change e-mail addresses. What is proper netiquette? Here is my list of the three top rules for e-mailing the media based on a study of all the literature bashing the practice of online public relations.

Target Your Contacts Carefully

You only want to send e-mail to media contacts who are highly likely to be interested in the subject of the release. It's not good enough to rationalize that your Web site redesign is a technology story, and therefore everyone who writes for *Information Week* is a legitimate prospect because it is a technology publication. You need to do a little research to find out who at *Information Week* covers Web site redesigns. The easiest way to do that is to *read the publication*, think about where your story should or might run, find the e-mail addresses of the people responsible for those sections, and send them your release.

That might seem like a lot of work, but it's not that bad. Chances are, the companies or causes you are promoting care the most about a core group of media outlets. As we'll describe later in this chapter, after a single day in the library rifling through periodicals and directories, you could walk away with as many as 300 fresh, top-quality media e-mail addresses. If you work for a large PR firm or ad agency that serves a diverse client base, then one of your most important assets is a high-quality, broad-based list of media contacts and the subjects they care about. It's worth putting some money into building that list, adding e-mail addresses, and tagging every contact with appropriate subject codes.

Tagging contacts with subject codes is a tricky process. If you tune your coding too tightly, you will miss sending to contacts who could very well be interested in the story. Code too loosely, and you risk antagonizing people who couldn't care less about your release. I've found that a two-tier subject coding system works best for me. Each contact has a macro code, such as "business" or "computers," and a micro code, such as "personal finance" or "software." I've tried three levels of coding, but it's like splitting hairs. One level of coding (or none) is way too broad. I'll cover this process in more detail later, where I talk about contact management software.

In defense of my fellow publicists, I'll say the following: Journalists expect you to somehow divine exactly what story they are working on right now and only send them releases related to that story. You might have gotten an e-mail address from an article about kayak design and stupidly sent the writer an announcement about a revolutionary kayak paddle your client developed. You should have known that the journalist is writing for *Dance World* now and has no interest in paddles. Shame on you! My advice is to do a good job of coding your contacts, take your best guess when sending out releases, and then offer to refine your codes for any journalists who complain.

Another problem for publicists is the generic e-mail address. If you can find only one e-mail address for a talk radio station, such as feedback@WXYZ.com, what can you do? I think it's okay to send any release to that address if you have an interesting guest who is willing to talk on air, but don't hold your breath. Generic addresses such as "letters," "comments," or "info" are often just euphemisms for "trash can." You need to find the personal e-mail addresses of real people who make decisions about what stories get produced. With personal e-mail addresses, you can be much more careful in your targeting, coding them with the specific subjects covered by that person. For a talk radio station, you would ideally like to have the personal e-mail address for every show producer, coded with the subjects their shows are about. As we'll see, it's not that hard to find or guess these addresses.

As tempting as it might be to send e-mail to everyone on your media list, this strategy often backfires. I sent a poorly worded announcement to my media list once, and several prominent people asked to be removed from my list. For me, that's like losing members of my extended family. If I failed to honor their requests and kept mailing to them, my messages would likely be filtered out, deleted unopened, or they might publicly flame me or report me to a blacklist or legal authorities. To give you some perspective, for a typical e-mail news release, I mail to about 500 media contacts and get about 50 positive replies, 25 undeliverable messages, and one complaint. I have weeded many sensitive people off my list over the past seven years; it might take you a few releases to get your complaints down to zero.

Keep It Short

If you have to scroll to read it, your news release is too long. I have trained numerous online publicists, and length is enemy number one. This rule is the hardest for me to follow, too. Everyone thinks that their story is the exception, that it's so compelling it warrants breaking the rules, and that it simply can't be told in a shorter space. This problem is so bad that I think we should stop using the term "news release" to describe these documents. "Query" is a better word, and it more accurately describes the document and the process.

You can't send a conventional news release via e-mail. It's too long. What you're really sending is a query to see whether the media is interested in this story. In short, you're not sending a news release but instead are asking whether they want to see a news release. E-mail news releases follow the same pattern as Web site communications: They are layered. A good subject line will get your message opened. A good pitch paragraph will bring a request for a document. A good document might result in a phone call, a request for artwork, or an interview. But if you start with a lengthy news release, it will either be trashed or saved for later and then trashed.

I know several reporters who receive more than 300 pieces of e-mail a day. If it took one minute to read and process each message, that's five hours per day just opening e-mail. If you want to build any level of respect with the media, you have to get to the point fast. If you ask journalists what they want, they'll tell you "one paragraph." I can sympathize with them, but based on my results, one paragraph won't do it. Almost all e-mail news releases can be boiled down to a standard three-paragraph pitch.

First comes the news hook: What is the compelling news angle related to this announcement? Second is the credentials: What makes you the right person or company to talk about this item? And third, how do you get more information (contact names and numbers, a Web site address, an offer to send more information, and a request for coverage)?

If you are chafing under the length restrictions, maybe this information will help. Print is still a very effective way to communicate. You can make a case for coverage much better in a printed document than you can in e-mail. You get better design control with print. People will read a long printed document if it's good, but they won't read a long e-mail no matter how good it is (unless they print it out). Using e-mail to query and then following up with a faxed or printed news release is a great one-two punch. And once someone has responded to a query, the etiquette shifts. If they asked to see something, a follow-up phone call to see if it was received is appropriate. If they never asked to see anything, however, a follow-up phone call is seen as rude. Think of this process as seduction: Your e-mail is a tease. You don't want to reveal the whole story yet. You want to hold something back. You want them to beg for it. Learn to use e-mail news releases properly, and you'll have the media eating out of your hand.

Text Only and No Attachments

If you're looking for a sure-fire way to anger media contacts and get yourself Bozo-filtered, try sending an e-mail news release with HTML styles, embedded graphics, a VCF card, and an attached file. Do I need to depose the experts to make my case? From the Internet Press Guild comes this admonishment: "Let's make this clear: Unsolicited attachments merit the death penalty." From the Journalists' Pet Peeves site at Future-media, "I hate getting e-mail press releases in word processor formats." What journalists hate most about "rich e-mail" is the arrogance to assume that they can handle whatever you throw at them. It's rude, but that's not all that's wrong.

First of all, how an e-mail message looks and functions is dependent upon the receiver's equipment. While I was writing this chapter, I received an e-mail news release from a company inviting me to a seminar on "Advanced Email" design. I don't know how the e-mail looked on *their* screen, but on mine it was a nightmare of jagged line endings, broken URLs, and non-functional graphics. I think I'll pass on the seminar. You have no way of knowing the computer configuration of the people you send news releases to, so you're better off assuming incompatibility and just sending text.

Second, people are afraid to open unsolicited file attachments. You never know what disease they might contain or whether they will infect your computer, destroy your data, and ruin your life.

Third, attachments are often stored separately from your e-mail message. It's annoying to find files on your computer when you don't know how they got there and any e-mail message they were related to was deleted long ago.

Fourth, you don't need fancy graphics or design for a three-paragraph news release. Graphic design is good. It helps break up long documents, organize them, make them easier to read, and make them communicate better. And it goes against my training as a former typesetter and graphic designer to have to create the world's most ugly documents: ASCII text only. But until there is a universal standard that accommodates graphic design, I'm sticking with plain old text because *it works*. Everyone can read it, it almost always looks on the receiver's screen exactly like it looks on my screen, and I don't need fancy graphics for a brief query letter.

For these reasons, please don't use fancy formatting or file attachments for your news releases. Only send attachments upon request, and try to verify that your receiver has the equipment to view them before you send them. This practice works well with my seduction theory: You want to offer graphics, files, or documents and get your media contacts to request them. When *they* ask *you* for something, half the battle is won. But you must be prepared with those files, in the proper formats, to handle any requests promptly and professionally.

Types of News Releases

News releases are the workhorses of publicity and public relations. Before I launch into detailed instructions of how to format and deliver them via e-mail, I should describe the different purposes for these releases and how the purpose can determine the content and method of delivery. Here's a quick run-down of the most common types of news releases.

Promoting a Product or Service

Companies want to get attention for their offerings in the news media. Releases promoting products or services usually are built around new offerings or new features. The news hook is what is new or different about the product or service. This information should be stated up front, in the subject line and first paragraph. This information should be followed by a list of the target audiences for the new product or service and how they will benefit from the new features. A good response generator is to offer a free sample of products for review by the media or to offer a knowledgeable spokesperson for an interview about the product or service.

Many companies that want to make the news have approached me, but they have nothing new to offer. You can get coverage for old or existing products and services, but you have to come up with a good news hook on which a journalist can hang a story. An example might be a tax return service offering top tips on preparing returns or advice on recent changes in tax law. The service might be old, but the tips are new and timely.

Announcing Findings

A common form of news release is the announcement of the results of a study, survey, or some investigation. The news hook here is the findings; for example, teenage drug use has increased or decreased, or people use the Internet to rekindle old romances. A great response generator is to offer the full survey upon request. To gain credibility with the media, however, some note on methodology should be included in the release, such as the number of people surveyed, the dates covered, or any partnership with a polling firm or research group.

In early 2000, I worked on public relations campaigns for a career consulting firm. I spent five months brokering partnerships between the firm and Yahoo!, Lycos, CompuServe, Talk City, and World Without Borders. My client would provide live career coaching through chat facilities on these sites. I delayed the announcement of any partnerships until all deals were consummated; my thinking was that we would get more bang out of the announcement while keeping the competition in the dark by announcing all the agreements at the same time. A news release was distributed, and the reaction of the media was a great big yawn. Apparently, a deal the size of AOL and Time-Warner is required to break through with the press.

Roughly a week later, the same company announced the finding of a Web poll that more than 90 percent of resumes submitted online received no response—not even an acknowledgement. This story was covered by dozens of media outlets, picked up by a news wire service, and was syndicated to countless others. Television and radio interviews followed. I believe the final tally was more than 80 clippings for this release. I was shocked to say the least. The poll was a completely unscientific, voluntary Web survey. This research is junk research, but apparently a headline is more important to the media than a real story.

My attitude on Web polls has changed. If the press is going to cover these bogus stats as news, then by all means I recommend feeding them a steady diet until they lose their appetite. CNN has taken to including these stats in every newscast (shame on them). The broadcaster always announces that the poll is "unscientific" (I wish they would use the word "bogus"), but this line is no defense. It puts their news product in the same category as tabloid media, who trade in hearsay and rumors rather than research and facts. I'll talk more about using legitimate surveys and research later. For now, an important point is that the press loves surveys and stats and is inclined to ignore the process used to generate the numbers.

Offering an Expert or Opinion

When notorious hacker Kevin Mitnik was apprehended in 1995, I was able to offer journalists interviews with two experts who had followed the case for months. E-mail is a particularly effective way to reach journalists covering breaking news. Within two hours of Mitnick's arrest, my client had news releases in the in-boxes of journalists all across the country. Interviews were secured with numerous outlets, including *NBC News*.

One of the sharpest news hooks you can have is to tie-in somehow with a hot story. Publicists who track the media are in a good position to see stories as they break. They should be prepared to respond to current events with expert opinions from their clients. The focus of these news releases is the qualifications of the expert being offered, and the desired result is usually an interview. Timely release is critical, because you risk losing the spotlight to another expert or missing the moment altogether if you do not contact journalists promptly.

News releases offering expert commentary on current events are an excellent way of generating a continuous news stream for companies that don't have new products or services to hype. Stock biographical material can be collected in advance for leading company spokespeople and can be custom-edited to suit the demands of each story that unfolds. With good advance preparation and persistence, these spokespersons can become critical sources for media contacts who need an authoritative sound bite in a hurry.

Announcing a Web Site

Five years ago, you could make the news simply by announcing you have a Web site. Today, there has to be much more to the story than that to break through. Web site announcements have to stress new and innovative features to get press coverage. The focus should be on novelty, and Web site designers can be offered as interview bait.

One way to get attention for a Web site announcement is to couple it with an event. Consider hosting an "open house" at the site exclusively for the media prior to the public debut. A live celebrity appearance at the site should get media coverage. Contests or giveaways can generate consumer interest, but it's hard to get the press to fall for these come-ons (we will have more about this topic in the Contests chapter of the book). I'm fond of using charitable tie-ins for Web site openings. If you can do some good for your community while tooting your own horn, the media is more likely to play along, and the coverage you get is usually less critical.

E-mail news releases are not really the best vehicle for announcing Web sites. Media contacts get so many of these notices that they have grown immune to any pitch that asks them to visit a new site. You'd be better off faxing or mailing a release so that you can tell a longer story, and your contacts will have the URL handy when they're ready to evaluate the site. E-mail is an immediate-response product: Either they visit or the message gets deleted along with the Web address. Postcards and printed invitations are excellent for Web site announcements because they can be kept until needed.

Many media outlets review and rate Web sites, and the journalists working this beat will respond to e-mail pitches. There are also a number of outlets that bestow awards on top Web sites, such as *PC Magazine's* "Top 100 Web Sites" list. Any Web site announcement campaign should include soliciting reviews and ratings and submitting the site for awards. Some of this work is done by posting the release to Web site announcement services (such as *Net Happenings*) and by filling-out applications at Web sites. Of course, winning a major Web site award is grounds for yet another e-mail news release.

Promoting Events

E-mail news releases can be used to promote online and offline events, although the results are mixed. For online coverage, the release should be sent as close to the date of the event as possible. The Internet is the ultimate impulse medium; when people hear about something happening online, they either go immediately or forget about it. Event announcements appearing weeks before an online event are unlikely to draw any traffic. On the other hand, traditional media outlets won't use your announcement unless you give them adequate notice. Therefore, for event promotion, I suggest a two-pronged approach: faxed or printed releases to traditional media outlets well ahead of time and e-mail news releases to the online press no more than a week before the event.

Event announcements lack pizzazz unless they're coupled with a news hook. I handled online publicity for the @d:tech convention for four years, and we came up with a variety of methods to get media response—and, thus, coverage—for an ever-growing number of @d:tech events. Our first response generator was to offer press passes upon request. That sounds simple, but I've received dozens of event announcements that never explicitly offer passes. Other news hooks we used were a scholarship fund, a charitable partnership, an awards program, and online seminars leading up to the convention. Event announcements are fine if the only coverage you're looking for is a listing; if you want a story, however, you need to couple the announcement with a compelling news hook.

I had one client who wanted me to issue an e-mail news release from a printed version that was six pages long. The release promotes a news conference in New York City involving several non-profit organizations, sponsor organizations, educational institutions, and publicists on two continents. When I sent the e-mail version, I tried to get people to ask for the full news release. Here's the message:

Subject Line: Criminal and Antisocial Behavior

No, I'm not talking about spam. I'm referring to a new book that will be the subject of a major international news conference in New York City next Wednesday, January 24.

"Genetics of Criminal and Antisocial Behaviour" is a landmark study with serious legal and moral implications. The controversial issues surrounding this book will be explored in depth at a news conference chaired by Professor Sir Michael Rutter of the Institute of Psychiatry, London, and including Dr. Deborah Denno of the Law School, Fordham University, New York, and Dr. Gregory Carey of the Institute of Behavioral Genetics, University of Colorado.

You are invited to attend the news conference at the New York Academy of Sciences, 2 E. 63 St, New York City, beginning at 10:30 a.m. on Wednesday, January 24. You are also invited to request a copy of the news briefing, an interview with one of the speakers, or a review copy of the book. Simply reply to this e-mail with your RSVP or request, or contact one of the following people:

Events can also be promoted by uploading announcements to online events calendars. You'll find these at Yahoo! and other major portal sites, and the Web sites of trade associations related to the subject of the event or regional Web sites serving the city where it's held.

Routine Announcements

Companies and organizations issue numerous routine news releases that are unlikely to draw significant coverage. These include earnings reports and personnel changes. These announcements can be delivered via e-mail if you have the specific addresses used by media outlets for such announcements. They should not be sent to individual media contacts unless there is a substantial news hook, however (such as earnings greatly exceeding forecasts or the hiring of a new CEO). As far as writing style goes, it's best to avoid attempts to make routine announcements sound like major stories. Most of these announcements, if printed at all, will be printed verbatim if they were written in the standard style used by the media. In other words, these are filler items, not feature items, and the news release should use filler style.

News Wire Service

After my experience, described earlier, where a bogus ("unscientific") Web survey garnered more media attention than a legitimate news story, I recommended that my client build a news bureau to deliver branded news covering workplace issues to the media. The reasoning went as follows: We will get more media coverage as the source for news and information in our field than we'll get with news releases about our own activities. The idea was to become the Associated Press of workplace news. It's a sound approach to getting coverage that many companies are now adopting.

If you are paying attention to media coverage related to your field, you can turn your research into news coverage by helping the media. Simply by tracking stories appearing in other media, writing a short synopsis of each story, and providing links to sources, you can help the media who cover these subjects by cutting their research time. By feeding the press a wire of such stories, you magnify the chances that your own experts will be interviewed or that your company will be cited as the source of the information.

In the news wire service I devised for my career-services client, we sent a daily dispatch to workplace editors that had a feature story, several smaller story leads, a "fast stat," and a calendar of events. Bogus Web polls would be used to grab headlines, but these polls would be fleshed out by unearthing corroborating research and articles generated by other companies and linking to them in the feature story or story leads. We planned to include some legitimate, scientific polling work as well and to include news about the company itself. Finally, our news wire editors would be able to direct journalists to potential interview prospects: common folks who had stories to tell related to the topics of each day's news wire.

It's not that expensive or time-consuming to produce a daily news summary like the one described. This kind of news-gathering activity is very useful internally and is conducted to some extent by most companies. Delivering it as a news wire to journalists requires polishing the summaries with journalistic language and developing a reputation for dependability (daily or weekly service) and reliability (the story leads are solid). The hope is that every time a media outlet uses the "fast stat," your company will be cited as the source. The branding that can be achieved through such a campaign is incredible, especially when the cost of the program is compared with advertising expenses for a similar amount of brand penetration.

If you build a news wire service related to your field and deliver it to media contacts who cover that field, you will find your own coverage blossoming exponentially. In effect, you serve the highest goals of the public relations professional: to become a relied-upon source and conduit for the media, someone who can assist them with story ideas, leads to supporting documentation, and interview sources. If you can get 10 times the media coverage with a news wire than you get with news releases about your own company, maybe it's time to become a news provider yourself?

Writing E-Mail News Releases

So far, the only tip you've gotten about writing e-mail news releases is to keep them short. This section will help you make them memorable. We'll start with some overall strategies, then give suggestions for each of the three main elements of an e-mail message: the body text, the subject line, and the contact information.

Copy Writing Strategies

The typical strategy for writing a news release is to think of it as a script for the coverage you want to receive. If this were an item in your local daily newspaper, how would it read? If a local television station covered the story, how would they lead in? What visuals would they show? The standard style for most modern journalism is to start with a personal story ("Jim and Jane faced a real dilemma . . . "), then step back to talk about underlying principles affecting everyone ("Studies show that four out of five families have similar problems . . . "), and then zoom back in for the finish ("That's how Jim and Jane solved their problem . . . "). This style—from the personal to the general and back to the personal—makes for a good news release, too (but not an e-mail news release).

In e-mail, you simply don't have time for an elaborate setup. Trust me, I've tried repeatedly to get journalists to hang in there for a good story, but they won't. For one thing, e-mail written in this style starts out sounding like spam. Imagine you're a journalist, you've just opened this message about an "amazing new product," and it begins with "Jim and Jane faced a real dilemma." Your delete finger instinctively reaches for the keyboard, and the message is zapped.

Because you don't have time to tell the whole story in e-mail, you have to tantalize journalists. You have to do what TV shows do with their promos: Suggest a sizzling story, then tell people they must tune in to find out more. You want to set the table and make them request the meal. Your e-mail news release is not a news release at all but a teaser asking media contacts, "Are you interested in this story? If so, I'll send you the details." Your e-mail news release is like a survey, casting out to a broad audience to find the few who want what you have. Once you have them hooked, you can send the rest of the story via e-mail, fax, or phone.

A second major strategy is to try and hitch your news release to a major current event. In early 1996, I promoted the book *Finding Your Perfect Work* by Paul and Sarah Edwards. While I was preparing the campaign, AT&T announced the layoff of 40,000 employees. These soon-to-be-unemployed people would be surfing the Internet looking for job opportunities. In a section of the book dealing with subcontracting, the authors report that some of the most successful self-employed people got started when they were laid off and the companies they worked for had to subcontract for the same work. I had my hook. The news release read as follows:

Subject Line: Free Review Copy: Perfect Work

Two weeks ago AT&T gave pink slips to 2,000 employees, the first of an expected 40,000 layoffs as part of a major restructuring and downsizing effort. These people, and millions more like them, are looking for work. Paul and Sarah Edwards are helping them find something more.

Paul and Sarah Edwards are the self-employment experts. Authors of the best-selling book "Working from Home," they host CompuServe's Working from Home Forum and cable TV's "Working From Home" show. Where some see the clouds of corporate downsizing, they see a silver lining of self-employment.

To celebrate the release of their new book, "Finding Your Perfect Work," Paul and Sarah have contributed an article and resource list to the World Wide Web's JobCenter <http://www.jobcenter.com>. In the article, Paul and Sarah point out that workforce reductions often result in opportunities for former employees to become inde-

```
pendent contractors, thereby gaining more control over their work
and their lives.

For a review copy of "Finding Your Perfect Work" (Tarcher/Putnam,
ISBN 0-87477-795-X) or an interview with the authors, simply reply
to this e-mail.
```

A lot of journalists were writing about the AT&T layoffs. Most of the coverage was about how difficult it would be for the fired employees to find work. I gave them another angle—some optimistic numbers they could use in their coverage. When you find a newsy hook, you find one way to make your story valuable to the media.

Body Text

I use a three-paragraph template for e-mail news releases. The first paragraph is the news hook, the second is the credentials, and the third is the call to action. You see this style reflected in the Paul and Sarah Edwards release. The news hook is the announcement of large layoffs and that my clients offer assistance. The second paragraph presents their credentials. A third paragraph was added due to the need to promote partners who installed materials on their site. Whenever there is a chat tour or online seminar associated with a campaign, I expand on the e-mail news release to include the schedule of events. The final paragraph is a call to action: Please request a review copy of this book.

Next is another example, this time a promotion for the book *KidNet*. The news angle is an attempt to tap into the huge amount of media coverage warning parents about the hazards awaiting children online. In the second paragraph, rather than elaborating on the authors' credentials, I wanted to draw the media in with examples of the positive content available for kids online. The call-to-action paragraph offers both an e-mail option and a phone number.

```
Subject Line: Free Review Copy: KidNet


There's been a lot of talk lately about the dangers waiting for
children on the Internet and precious little discussion of the ben-
efits. If you're looking for balanced coverage, consider "KidNet,"
a new book by Debra and Brad Schepp that explores the wealth of
online resources available for children.

Subtitled "The Kid's Guide to Surfing Through Cyberspace," KidNet
offers pointers for parents and children aged 9-14. KidNet covers
the Web, America Online, CompuServe, Prodigy, the Microsoft Net-
work, and other online services. Subjects covered include parental
control, homework helpers, international pen pals, games, music,
sports, hobbies, ecology, TV and movies, among others.
```

```
For a free review copy or an interview with the authors, please
reply via e-mail or contact HarperCollins Publicity, (212) 207-7723.
```

Body text for e-mail messages should be broken up to reduce eye strain and increase response. We'll get into the nitty-gritty formatting details later. As far as writing style goes, try to keep your paragraphs to around 55 words. Think of the old universal speed limit: 55 miles per hour. Line lengths should be no more than 55 characters and paragraphs around 55 words. You can go as long as 100 words if you have to, but you risk message deletion with a paragraph that long. Bulleted items and numbered lists work well in e-mail news releases. They are particularly good for earnings highlights.

Subject Lines

A subject line on your e-mail messages is like answering a receptionist who asks, "Can I tell Chris what this call is regarding?" If you have the right subject line, maybe Chris will open your message. If you use the wrong line, maybe he will not. I can't imagine Chris taking a phone call from someone who "wants to show you how to get rich fast." Yet that's exactly the kind of subject line many bulk e-mailers use.

If you try to trick media contacts into opening your news release, you won't have much long-term success. The best suggestion is to be straightforward and build a reputation for honesty. Some publicists I know identify their messages as news releases in the subject line. They might start the line with the words NEWS RELEASE or just NEWS so the recipients know what to expect. Once journalists on your list know who you are, they'll have a good feel for the quality of your news releases. If you consistently provide timely information about the subjects they cover, they'll open your news releases.

Whether you're promoting a Web site or some other product or service, you should look for some unique characteristic to bring out in the subject line. Possibly the most worn out subject line on the Internet is "Check Out My New Web Site!" Just because your Web site is new or improved doesn't mean reporters will want to visit. You have to look for an angle that will help you stand out from the crowd. Your audience is the media, and what they're looking for is a story. Think of the subject line as a headline for a story, and you're well on your way to writing news releases that get opened.

A good way to get a feel for interesting subject lines is to look at the news ticker used by CNN or the Headline News channel on their telecasts. The ticker runs at the bottom of the TV screen and rotates through news headlines. CNN's writers have gotten very good at crafting these little zingers. Most of them are 10 words or less.

Another good way to get a feel for effective subject lines is to visit the Usenet newsgroup "Net Happenings" at news.comp.internet.net-happenings. It consists almost entirely of news releases, and there are dozens posted every day. Take note of which subject lines grab your attention. Why? Was it because they were clever or because they mentioned a subject of great interest to you? You'll notice people making beginner mistakes, such as using ALL CAPITAL LETTERS or very long subject lines.

There is a real art to writing subject lines that will motivate media contacts to open a message. Figure 2.1 shows a sampling of subject lines from Net Happenings with three of the lines highlighted. The first says "USA Today Hot Web Sites." That line caught my attention—I'd want to know who compiles their list. But look at the middle

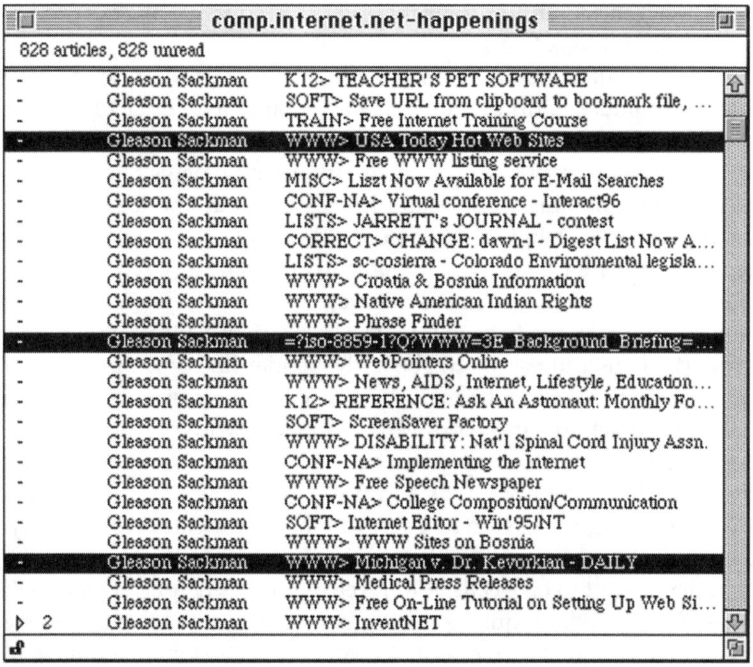

Figure 2.1   Sample subject lines from news releases archived at Net Happenings. Three subject lines are highlighted. Notice how poorly formatted the "Background Briefing" subject line is?

highlighted line. Doesn't it look inviting? It reads "=?iso-8859-1?Q?WWW=3E_Background_Briefing=..." It makes you want to jump right in. The third highlighted line, "Michigan vs. Dr. Kevorkian—DAILY" works very well. It's probably about the trial against the infamous "Dr. Death." The subject line isn't cute or clever, just accurate and brief.

There's no firm rule on subject line length. You should be aware that long subject lines will be truncated by some e-mail systems. In most cases, readers determine how much of the incoming subject line to display. Shorter isn't necessarily better, because you want to provide enough information for people to decide whether to open the message or not. You should look for ways to shorten subject lines that are longer than 25 characters and never exceed 55.

Contact Information

How much contact information should you include in an e-mail news release? Due to space constraints, I suggest the minimum amount necessary. A lot of people include signature files (sigs) with their e-mail news releases, but I recommend against them.

First, I like to see everything in the news release before I send it out. If you work with a sig file, you could have several blank lines at the end of your news release and never know it. Your sig file would be added after all the blank lines. Or, there might not be enough space between the end of your message and your sig. It's best to see exactly how your message will look to people receiving it.

Second, sig files usually contain way more information than you need, such as your mailing address and fax number. Journalists will always make first contact by either e-mail or phone; this added information wastes precious space. You can use your sig on follow-up e-mail with the press, but I wouldn't use it for e-mail news releases.

Third, signature files are sometimes sent as attachments and automatically deleted by certain systems. AOL used to eliminate signature files longer than six lines from incoming messages. I'm not sure that it's still possible to automatically screen out sig files, but I wouldn't take a chance on bulk news releases.

All the contact information you really need is your name, e-mail address, and phone number. Your name and e-mail address should be in the Sender line of the message. If you want responses to come to a different e-mail address, you should specify that with a "mailto:" link in the call-to-action paragraph. We must issue a word of caution, however: It's easiest for media contacts to simply hit the Reply button to request further information. If you make them go through the additional step of sending replies to a second e-mail address, they might just skip it or reply to the sending address anyway.

Your phone number can be added in the call-to-action paragraph. You can skip the phone number if you don't want to take calls. A toll-free number is helpful if you don't mind picking up the tab for media inquiries. I have seen publicists include a phone number in the Sender field of the message so that media contacts don't even have to open the message to locate the phone number.

Once a media contact has responded to your e-mail, all future correspondence can include a full signature file with your title, fax number, mobile phone number, and mailing address.

Formatting E-Mail News Releases

I get complaints every now and then about how obsessive I am concerning document formatting for online delivery. Does the line length really have to be limited to 55 characters? Can't I use indented text in my e-mail? If I err on the side of micro-management, I apologize. But my main complaint about the other books about online publicity and public relations is that they don't tell you *exactly* how to do things. They are long on theory and short on specific formats. In some cases, it's because the authors don't have a lot of practical experience launching campaigns. They have a different agenda than I do. Their job is to educate people about the potential of this new communications medium. My job is to give you the nuts and bolts.

How many people have sent more than 1,000 e-mail news releases without ending up on a blacklist? I have this kind of trench warfare experience from years of trial and error, and I report here the exact techniques that have produced the best results. I have received enough testimonials from readers who have followed my instructions *exactly* and report excellent results that I know it's not just me: These techniques work for others. When you finish this chapter, I don't want you to think, "E-mail news releases are an important part of public relations; I should start using them." I want you to know precisely how to write, format, and deliver those releases for maximum effectiveness.

Unfortunately, the details matter in an e-mail news release much more than in a fax or printed version. The audience is less forgiving. So I hope you will pardon me for harping on formatting issues, but the majority of e-mail messages I receive are so poorly formatted that it's obvious people need better instruction in this area.

Software Considerations

Anything I have to say about the capabilities of specific e-mail programs would be dated by the time this book gets printed. With rare exceptions, you can follow the instructions in this chapter regardless of the e-mail program you use. I have a personal preference for Eudora software; I've used it for many years, so it's comfortable, and I find its filtering capabilities superior to all competitors. Almost every innovation in Eudora's software has been adopted or exceeded by the competition, however, and you can expect this trend to continue. I recommend you use the program you are most comfortable with, buy the professional version, and upgrade as soon as new editions appear.

The dominant software programs for e-mail are Outlook Express embedded in Microsoft Internet Explorer; Netscape Messenger embedded in Netscape Communicator; America Online's e-mail service; CompuServe's e-mail service; Microsoft Outlook; Lotus Mail; and Eudora. I do not recommend using either AOL or CompuServe for e-mail media relations. You should invest in a direct Internet connection for this work. Someday AOL and CSI will make it easy to use your own e-mail client or upgrade their capabilities to make bulk e-mail management easier. For now, their services are so inferior and the cost of a direct connection so inexpensive that it is not worth explaining how to manipulate AOL and CSI software for bulk e-mail campaigns.

Other than AOL or CSI, the rest of the programs are close enough to equal that you should choose the one you're most comfortable with and learn to use all the features built into the software. There are many other good e-mail software programs, and I don't mean to endorse this list by omitting good software. Beware of free e-mail programs, though—they usually will not have the power features and controls you need for serious online media relations. That includes the light versions of Eudora and Outlook Express. The professional versions of these programs are well worth the added cost.

A new class of e-mail software has appeared since I wrote *Publicity on the Internet*: bulk e-mailing software. This software combines the features of sophisticated e-mail programs such as Eudora with contact management programs such as ACT! These powerful programs are popular mostly with spam artists: bulk mailers of *Unsolicited Commercial E-Mail* (UCE), although there are many legitimate uses for this software. Brand names include Emerge, Stealth, NetContact, and DirectMail. I've tried Emerge, and I like the program, but the contact management features weren't good enough to lure me away from NowContact.

Bulk e-mail software programs have one big advantage over conventional e-mail software: e-mail-merge capabilities. This feature enables you to send a personalized, custom message to everyone on your media list. For example, you could write three versions of your e-mail news release—one for print journalists, one for broadcast journalists, and one for online journalists—and the software will automatically send each journalist the proper release. Custom form letters have been around for decades, ever since someone married a word processor with database software. Now, the same capability is available for e-mail. If you work for a public relations firm or other high-volume e-mailer, I suggest you investigate bulk e-mail software.

In coming years, these merge features will be folded into e-mail software embedded in Web browsers. The muscle-bound Web browser of the future will include a database, word processor, spreadsheet, presentation software, calendar, media player, and so on. You can already create customized bulk e-mail with Eudora and other programs, but I would never recommend using Eudora, AOL, CSI, Outlook, Messenger, or any of the others for contact management. Their capabilities in database manipulation are so primitive you would be creating a nightmare for yourself.

Formatting Text-Only Releases

All Internet software has one common design flaw: The look of the message is determined by the receiver's software, not the sender's. While this "flaw" makes it possible for so many people to share the benefits of connectivity, it makes it difficult to provide every viewer with a quality reading experience. Figure 2.2 shows what some folks see when they open their e-mail—and that's after wading through a header that looks like the instruction manual for your VCR.

What looks like perfect prose on your screen might look like very bad poetry on the receiver's screen. Many e-mail programs force line endings on all outgoing e-mail. For Eudora, the default line length is set at 76 characters, although mail can now be sent wrapped and received that way on compatible systems. If the person reading the e-mail

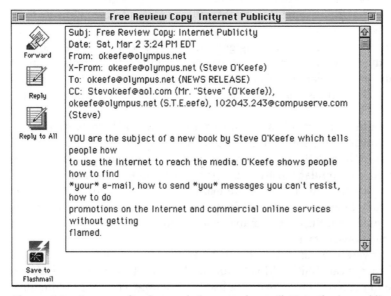

Figure 2.2   An example of a poorly formatted e-mail. Note the jagged line endings. Would you want to read e-mail that looks like this one?

has a default line length shorter than 76 characters (like most folks on AOL), they will get the kind of jagged line endings shown in Figure 2.2.

Another problem is non-standard characters, especially "smart quotes." Many word processors, such as Microsoft Word, default to using smart quotes, which are used to distinguish an open quotation mark from a closing one. They also change the character used for an apostrophe. When e-mail is sent with smart quotes, they are changed into ASCII equivalents; that is, into meaningless gibberish. Dashes are also problematic, often changed into underscores. Ampersands and bullets also cause problems. I receive one e-mail newsletter that always has smart quote problems. Many of the subscribers to the newsletter have complained, and the editor has responded that he is "working on the problem." Excuse me, but the solution is simple: Turn off the stupid quotes.

The way to deal with most formatting problems is to compose your message in a word processor before importing it into e-mail. You can use the template provided at the companion Web site for this book, which is shown in Figure 2.3. For a program

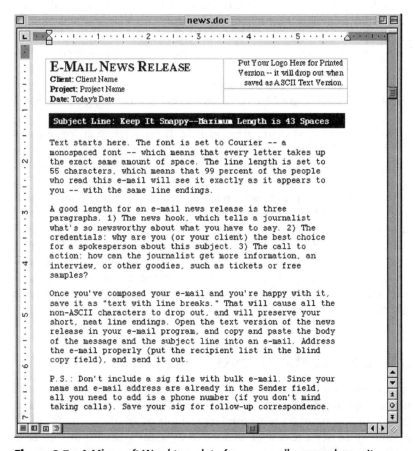

Figure 2.3   A Microsoft Word template for an e-mail news release. It uses a monospaced font and line length of 55 characters to generate a crisp, clean e-mail message when saved as ASCII text with line breaks. This template is available at the Web site for this book.

such as Microsoft Word, you need to disable all auto-formatting features. The process reminds me of a scene in the movie *2001: A Space Odyssey*, where astronaut Dave shuts down computer HAL by gradually pulling out all its circuits. In Word, you open your preferences and customization features and uncheck all the boxes until *you* regain control of your word processor. No more smart quotes, no more auto-correcting. Then, you change your font to a monospace typestyle such as Courier and set your right margin at 55 characters. After you've performed this task once, you can save the file as a template for future news releases.

After you compose and edit your news release and you're ready to send it out, save the document as "text only with line breaks." Now you will have two versions of the news release: one we'll call news.doc (the working version, which is a word processor document), and the other called news.txt (the final version, which is an ASCII text document). You can open the text version from your e-mail program, make sure that it looks good, then copy and paste into your e-mail message. If you decide to make changes to the final document, you should make the changes first in the .doc version, then save again as ASCII text. This procedure will ensure the integrity of your formatting. This process is more work than you'd want to go through for day-to-day e-mail, but for news releases going to a large media list, it's well worth the effort.

When you save as ASCII text, you lose a lot of formatting. Tabs disappear, often replaced by space bands. Italics and bold drop out; so do larger point sizes, ruling, colors, and unusual characters such as dingbats. To add emphasis to your message, you must be creative. You can use ALL CAPS, *asterisks,* or _underscores_ to highlight phrases. Uppercase is considered SHOUTING online and should be used carefully. One way to emphasize text is to surround it with extra white space, such as blank lines. But keeping the length down is important, so don't get heavy handed with the Return key. You might have to rewrite your news release so it works well as a text document.

When you open the .txt version of the news release in your e-mail program, you will probably have to clean it a little before pasting it into an e-mail message. Any headers or footers you use in the .doc version should be deleted. Figure 2.4 shows what the E-Mail News Release Template in Figure 2.3 looks like as a final e-mail document ready to be sent. The top part of the message contains all the headers: the addresses and the subject line. The bottom part contains the body of the message. Some people like to repeat the subject line at the top of the body of the message, and that's okay as long as you can afford the space.

Adding Graphics or Attachments

Do you want to impress your boss, or do you want to get media coverage? If you want to impress your boss, go ahead and make an HTML e-mail news release with beautiful graphic design (be sure to use obscure typestyles) and lots of graphics, and for kicks include a streaming video news release embedded in the e-mail. Send it to your boss and maybe you'll get a promotion. Send it out to the media, and most likely you'll get blacklisted—eliminating the possibility of anyone from your company ever communicating with the press via e-mail again.

```
        To: NEWS RELEASE <realnews@bellsouth.net>
      From: Steve O'Keefe <realnews@bellsouth.net>   [ News Release    ‡ ]
   Subject: Keep It Snappy--Maximum Length is 43 Spaces
        Cc:
       Bcc: Medialist
X-Attachments:
```

Text starts here. The font is set to Courier -- a
monospaced font -- which means that every letter takes up
the exact same amount of space. The line length is set to
55 characters, which means that 99 percent of the people
who read this e-mail will see it exactly as it appears to
you -- with the same line endings.

A good length for an e-mail news release is three
paragraphs. 1) The news hook, which tells a journalist
what's so newsworthy about what you have to say. 2) The
credentials: why are you (or your client) the best choice
for a spokesperson about this subject. 3) The call to
action: how can the journalist get more information, an
interview, or other goodies, such as tickets or free
samples?

Once you've composed your e-mail and you're happy with it,
save it as "text with line breaks." That will cause all the
non-ASCII characters to drop out, and will preserve your
short, neat line endings. Open the text version of the news
release in your e-mail program, and copy and paste the body
of the message and the subject line into an e-mail. Address
the e-mail properly (put the recipient list in the blind
copy field), and send it out.

P.S.: Don't include a sig file with bulk e-mail. Since your
name and e-mail address are already in the Sender field,
all you need to add is a phone number (if you don't mind
taking calls). Save your sig for follow-up correspondence.

Figure 2.4   An e-mail news release ready to go out. This release was made by saving the template in Figure 2.3 as text only with line breaks, then copying and pasting the text version into an e-mail.

If you want to get media coverage, do yourself a favor and forget about HTML e-mail for now. Send a simple ASCII-text news release with a compelling news story and invite inquiries or direct the press to further information available at your Web site (such as a streaming video news release). Yes, you can create an HTML news release that lets you use different fonts, styles, and sizes, but most of the people you are trying to communicate with will not appreciate it. Include graphics and your audience will want to shoot you. Include file attachments, and your receivers will go out of their way to send you hate mail, report you to the authorities, and blacklist you.

I could spend 20 more pages of this book describing in minute detail exactly how to create HTML news releases, but I'm not going to do it. I'll consider covering the subject in the next edition of this book if the vast majority of journalists have high-speed access, if universal standards have been worked out and embedded in all the popular e-mail programs, and if media contacts report that they now prefer HTML news releases. Today, HTML formatting and graphics ruin your e-mail news releases, and file attachments should never be sent without prior approval and agreement on format. Enough said.

Finding E-Mail Addresses of the Media

"Where can I find the e-mail addresses of the media?" That ranks as one of the top questions I have been asked in the five years since my book, *Publicity on the Internet*, was published. My answer always begins, "Check your Rolodex." Start with the media contacts you already know. Gather their e-mail addresses from their bylines, mastheads, and Web sites. If that doesn't work, try phoning the companies they work for to get their e-mail addresses, or guess what the addresses might be (which is usually very easy). Ask colleagues to share e-mail addresses. Search feedback threads at media Web sites to see whether journalists have posted messages related to their stories; if so, they probably revealed their e-mail addresses.

There's a saying that a publicist is only as good as his or her contact list. Most publicists hoard their contacts and treasure them like gold. I know I do. Am I going to share my media list with you? Not a chance. Will I teach you how to build one yourself that is even better than mine because it is custom-tailored for your market? You bet! Come in close, dear readers, because herein lie trade secrets you will not find in any other book.

Nearly every book I've read about online PR sings the same song: Don't send out mass e-mail news releases; ask media contacts if they want to be on your list; and give them an easy button to hit to opt off your list. This statement is admirable, but hogwash. Do you ask journalists if they want to be on your phone list before you call them, or whether they want to be on your fax list before you fax them, or your mailing list before you mail to them, or your pop-in list before you drop by to see them? My standard is very different: Don't send media contacts stuff they're not interested in, and don't e-mail them again if they ask to be taken off your list. Let's explore this point a little further because my brethren in the PR profession without a doubt consider this advice dubious.

Let's say you work in public relations for IBM. Should you e-mail journalists and ask whether they want to be on your media list for e-mail news releases? The answer is "No." Why? Who wants to give you blanket permission to spam them with news releases? I guarantee that most people you contact this way will not reply. Why should they? Now, do you send to the no-response people or not? Because you asked permission and didn't get it, I would suggest you are on unfirm ground sending them releases. Most of those who do reply will not want to be on your list. They don't know what they're saying yes to: one release a month or one release a minute? Are the releases applicable to the subjects that they cover or all over the place? If you're IBM, you're generating a lot of news in a lot of different areas appealing to different audiences. The people who want your earnings reports aren't the same people wanting tech briefs.

Therein lies the rub: People will decline to be on your media list who would want certain specific releases, but now you can't send to them. My feeling is that a journalist is a journalist. If they publish their e-mail address somewhere, it's fair game to send them a release. They are interested in the subjects they cover, they expect you to know what they write about, and if you guess wrong, you pay the price. So don't guess wrong, and take people off your list if you're a bad guesser and they complain. Almost all the good press I've gotten for my clients I would never have been able to get if I relied on getting journalists' permission to send them e-mail.

Let me give you an example to help make my case. I sent a news release to a journalist in my database who was tagged as writing about computers and the Internet. I received a flame reply asking to be taken off my list. I checked my records, and this journalist had responded positively to four e-mail pitches in the past. So I sent him e-mail saying, look, you responded to these previous four pitches. Are you sure you want me to take you off my list? I can be very specific about the kinds of releases I send your way. I've removed your name from my list, but I hate to lose you as a contact and will happily reinstate you if you desire.

This little scenario has been repeated more than 40 times in the last few years, and in every case except one, the journalist asked to stay on my list. Usually, they reply: "Sorry, Steve, that was my form flame. Didn't realize it was you. Keep me on the list, please." Some even marvel that they get a personal response to a "take off" request. In the case described earlier, the journalist replied that he only covers the software beat and isn't interested in general computer or Internet stories. My database was appropriately updated, and the contact was coded as "touchy" so that I would be more discriminating sending to him in the future.

If I had asked permission to e-mail these "touchy" media contacts, I wouldn't have received it. They wouldn't have gotten my e-mails, and I wouldn't have gotten their coverage. So instead of asking, I earn their respect by being selective about what I send them and responsive when I guess wrong. And I never e-mail to them again once they ask to be taken off. Try running a PR firm by getting permission from every media contact for phone calls, e-mail, mail, and faxing. In short order, you will be talking to yourself and all your clients will move to agencies that hire intelligent people who understand PR and know who to send a release to.

Contact Management Software

Good software will help you guess right about which media contacts to send your e-mail news releases to. If you work for a single company, as opposed to a PR firm or ad agency, you might be able to manage a small media list of a few hundred critical contacts without any special software. You can maintain your media list in a spreadsheet, an e-mail address book, a word processing document, or even a Rolodex-style card file. But if you work for a PR firm or ad agency, or if your media contact list numbers in the thousands, you will benefit greatly by using contact management software.

When I started doing Internet publicity, I had a few hundred media e-mail addresses and felt like it was a goldmine. Today, I have more than 10,000 contacts and

I feel like I'm falling behind. A lot of media outlets have only one mailing address, maybe a few fax numbers, and up to a dozen phone lines but perhaps *hundreds* of e-mail addresses. A few years ago, *The New York Times* distributed a list of the e-mail addresses of all staff researchers, writers, and reporters; it numbered more than 200 contacts.

My media list database started as a Word Perfect document. Once I had a couple thousand names, it went to an Excel spreadsheet, and quickly thereafter to NowContact, a contact management program. I have set up half a dozen media databases for companies since, using everything from FoxPro to ACT! Today, we are on the brink of having bulk e-mail software that functions as well as contact management software. But we aren't there yet. My recommendation for managing media lists of 1,000 or more contacts is either NowContact or ACT! I have created custom templates for both of these programs, which will help you get up and running in a hurry. You'll find them atwww.wiley.com/compbooks/okeefe.

ACT! and NowContact are very powerful database programs. Because they are so versatile, it can be intimidating setting up a good media list on them. You have a lot of choices and not much guidance. Because they are designed for contact management and not other database functions, however, they contain features that make them more intuitive for publicists, marketing, and PR personnel. For example, in NowContact I can select media contacts for an e-mail news release, extract the e-mail addresses for use in Eudora, generate a tracking report in Word, and print mailing labels in standard Avery formats for follow-up packages. All of these needs are anticipated in the design of the software and are accomplished with minimal fuss.

Large companies might consider developing a distributed Oracle database that can be easily accessed over an intranet by a dispersed team of users. You'd better break out the checkbook, though, because programming in Oracle is a spendy proposition. I've seen some attempts at Oracle contact-management solutions, and they have been uniformly bad. The main problem is that the people doing the programming and the publicists using the software don't speak the same language. For example, to a database programmer, the name of a business is put in the "company" field. But to a publicist, the name of the business is the publication or station, and the company that owns the publication or station is less important. Until Oracle databases have been debugged and perfected by marketing and publicity users, you're probably better off using a tried-and-true off-the-shelf contact management package.

In setting up a media list, you have to balance two conflicting needs. First, you want to collect as much information about each person on your list as possible. But your second goal is to be able to choose quickly whom to send releases to from among thousands of contacts. I use a two-pronged approach to choosing media for news releases: I add people to the list based on the topics they supposedly cover, and then I subtract people from the list based on my past experience with them. Figure 2.5 shows a selection from my media list in NowContact. This illustration shows how I view my list when picking media for a release. You'll notice that the first field is the "category" or media type: magazine, newspaper, radio, TV, and so on. Then come two subject fields: a macro subject and a micro subject. These subjects are my main method for sorting through the list to decide whom to send to. One subject classification doesn't provide enough information for me, whereas three subject classifications is too much to wade through when picking media.

Medialist in Now Contact

✕	Category	Custom 4	Custom 5	Company	Full Name	T	C	Custom 8
✓	Magazine/Jou	T1: Business	T2: Books	The Business Reader	Ted Kinni			Hit: *4* bplans, Si
✓	Magazine/Jou	T1: Business	T2: Consultants	Consultants Report	C. Sherman Severin,	Edi		Hit: *1* bplans
✓	Magazine/Jou	T1: Business	T2: Entrepreneur	NV Magazine		Edi		Hit: *1* bplans
✓	Magazine/Jou	T1: Business	T2: Entrepreneurs	Young Entrepreneur	Misty Elliott	Exe		Hit: *2* bplans, Be
✓	Magazine/Jou	T1: Business	T2: Finance/Law	The Daily Deal	Greg Storey	Co		Hit: * bplans
✓	Magazine/Jou	T1: Business	T2: Internet	Gartner Group	Kimberly Hiller		:: C	Hit: *2* bplans, Co
✓	Magazine/Jou	T1: Business	T2: Regional, State	The Kitsap Business Jo	Lary Coppola	Edi		Hit: *24* bplans, N
✓	Magazine/Jou	T1: Business	T2: Regional, State	Texas Business	Roy Adams	Ma		Hit: *2* bplans, Be
✓	Magazine/Jou	T1: Business		Harris Publishing	Deb Taylor	Int		Hit: *13* bplans, S:
✓	Magazine/Jou	T1: Computer	T2: Business	ComputerEdge Magazin	Douglas W. Welch	Co	:: V	Hit: *5* bplan, Jan
✓	Magazine/Jou	T1: Computer	T2: Industry	Amy D. Wohl's Opinio	Amy D. Wohl	Edi		Hit: *21* bplans, C
✓	Magazine/Jou	T1: Computer	T2: Industry	We Compute	Eric McMillan	Pul		Hit: *8* bplans, Si
✓	Magazine/Jou	T1: Computer	T2: Internet	OnTheInternet	Wendy Rickard	Edi	:: "	Hit: *7* bplans, Al
✓	Magazine/Jou	T1: Computer		Computer Book Cafe	David L. Rogelberg		:: C	Hit: *10* bplan, ao
✓	Magazine/Jou	T1: Computer		Information Week	Karyl Scott	Fea		Hit: *5* bplans, 3-
✓	Magazine/Jou	T1: Law	T2: Technology	The Lawyer's PC	Dan Harmon	Edi		Hit: *4* bplans, Ca
	Magazine/Jou			Resource Center for Cyl	David Silver	Dir		Hit: *7* bplans, Si
	Magazine/Jou			The Washington Times	Thomas Elias		:: N	Hit: *14* bplans, F
✓	Newspaper -	T1: Business	T2: Regional, State	Boulder County Busines	Jerry W. Lewis	Edi		Hit: *15* bplans, F
✓	Newspaper -	T1: Business	T2: Regional, State	Sacramento Business Jo	Joe Vanacore			Hit: *1* bplans
✓	Newspaper -	T1: Business		Business First of Colum	Laura Newpoff			Hit: *2* bplans, m
✓	Newspaper -	T1: Editor?		The Wanderer				Hit: *25* bplans, F
	Radio Syndic	T1: Business	T2: Entrepreneur	Let's Talk Business Net	Mitch Schlimer			Hit: *2* bplan, Vil
✓	TV Show	T1: Business		Economic Television	Daniel Hopsicker	Exe		Hit: *3* bplans, Er
✓	TV Syndicate	T1: Business	T2: Computer	Red Herring Communic	Courtney Heller	Bro		Hit: * bplans
✓	Web Site - Fc	T1: Business	T2: Books	Business Start Page	Frederick Pearce			Hit: *3* bplans, Cl
✓	Web Site - Fc	T1: Business	T2: Entrepreneur	Working From Home	Paul & Sarah Edwards		:: N	Hit: *20* Kappl, S
✓	Web Site - Fc	T1: Business	T2: Ethics	Spear-It Enterprises, LL	Dennice Boscoe	CO	:: N	Hit: * bplans
✓	Web Site - Fc	T1: Business	T2: Executive	CEO Refresher	Rick Sidorowicz	Ma		Hit: *2* bplans, St
✓	Web Site - Fc	T1: Business	T2: Finance	About.com Stocks	Michael Griffis	Ma	:: N	Hit: *2* bplans, Be
✓	Web Site - Fc	T1: Internet	T2: Marketing	WebSight, Inc.	Kevin Bramlett		:: V	Hit: *4* bplans, Da

40 of 40 Contacts

Figure 2.5 View of a media contact database in NowContact. I use this view of the database to quickly sort through media contacts by the subjects they cover when assembling a distribution list for a news release.

You'll notice in Figure 2.5 that one of the contacts is highlighted: Mitch Schlimer from the "Let's Talk Business" radio syndicate. Figure 2.6 shows Mitch's individual record in the NowContact database. The macro subject for Mitch is business, and the micro subject is entrepreneur. I wouldn't send Mitch a general business news release unless it had something to do with entrepreneurism. The field called "hits" has abbreviated notes on news releases Mitch has responded to in the past. After a journalist responds to several pitches, I can tell the kind of material they like, and I'll adjust the subject categories accordingly. For example, if I have a contact with a macro subject of computers and a micro subject of Internet, and they show a pattern of only responding to news releases related to Internet software, I'll move them into macro category Internet and micro category software so that I don't bother them with Internet-related news

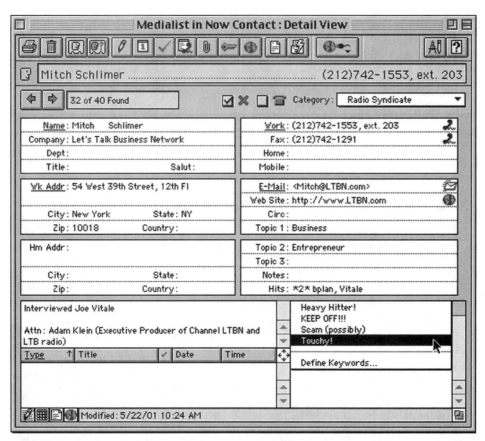

Figure 2.6 View of an individual contact's record from my media list in NowContact. The keywords in the bottom, right-hand corner are used to tag contacts who require a second look before sending a news release.

releases unless they have something to do with software. In the lower left-hand corner of Figure 2.6, there is a space where I can enter any special notes about this contact.

Now that you know how I work over a media list when selecting contacts, let me clue you in on my tips for excluding contacts. In the lower right-hand corner of Figure 2.6, you'll notice a series of keywords I can use to tag Mitch Schlimer: Heavy Hitter!, KEEP OFF!!!, Scam (possibly), Touchy! Once I've compiled a distribution list for a news release based on the subjects the journalists cover, I'll review the list by taking a closer look at everyone tagged with one of these exclusionary words. I might not want to bother Heavy Hitters with mundane releases, saving them for when I have really juicy material. I hate losing a Heavy Hitter from my list, so I'm careful not to wear out my welcome in their inbox. Journalists tagged with KEEP OFF!!! have asked to be taken off my list. As protection against accidentally putting them back on my list, I never remove them but simply delete their e-mail addresses and tag them as KEEP OFF!!! Contacts tagged as Scam (possibly) have a history of requesting freebies such as books, software, tickets, press passes, and so on but never seem to do stories on my clients. I treat them with suspicion until I get evidence of coverage. Finally, someone tagged as Touchy! has complained about getting an e-mail news release in the past but has agreed to remain on my list. For a typical news release, I might decide against sending it to half the Touchy! contacts because I don't think the release is a perfect fit for them. Figure 2.7 shows a record from a database in ACT! software program.

So that's my media list method: select contacts based on the subjects they cover, then cull the list based on the sensitivity of the contacts. It's easy to sort lists in contact management programs by subjects and tags, making this add-and-subtract method extremely efficient. At the bottom of the screen in Figure 2.7, you'll see an Exclude? field that gives me the choice of tagging contacts as Heavy Hitter!, KEEP OFF!!!, or Touchy! You'll find templates for both ACT! and NowContact at www.wiley.com/compbooks/okeefe. If you own the software, you can use my templates and import your contacts to get a versatile media list of your own.

Building Your Own Media List

To build your own media list, you should first determine what software you want to keep the list in and then design a template so that each record contains the kind of information you want. You can download the templates I have created for ACT! and NowContact available at the Web site or use them as a guide for deciding what fields to include in your own database. Once you have the database set up, start pouring in

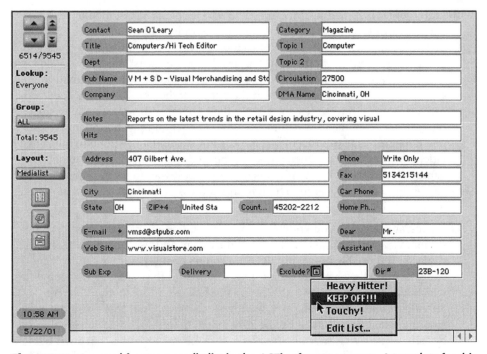

Figure 2.7   A record from my media list in the ACT! software program. A template for this database design—as well as one for NowContact—is available at www.wiley.com/compbooks/okeefe.

contacts from your existing files from a database you have purchased or through your own research.

To be successful in Internet publicity, you need to find the personal e-mail addresses of the people who create news: writers, reporters, editors, and producers. According to the Middleberg/Ross *Media in Cyberspace* study, journalists have on average two e-mail addresses, with some having up to 12. Which address do you want? I recommend the one that their bosses use to communicate with them, because that e-mail account is likely to be closely monitored. My point here is that try as they might, media contacts can't keep their e-mail addresses private because they need them distributed fairly widely in order to function. Here are my tips, then, for locating e-mail addresses of media contacts to add to your database:

Start with your own list. Begin by inputting all your previous media contacts into your database. You can glean e-mail address from business cards or phone the companies your contacts work for and ask for e-mail addresses.

Research print publications. The most fruitful way to gather media contact e-mail addresses is to go to the library with a portable computer, flip through every publication that reaches your target audience, and keyboard the e-mail addresses you find. Some publications list e-mail addresses on the masthead. If nothing else, the masthead should provide you with the domain name used for all e-mail addresses of people employed by the company, such as "nytimes.com."

Research broadcast media. You can use directories of broadcast media (such as Bacon's or Gale's) to get the domain names of radio and television stations, networks, and syndicates. Sometimes these directories will contain e-mail addresses for contacts at those outlets, but I wouldn't trust them. You'll mostly get generic addresses such as "news@" or "feedback@"—not the individual addresses you need. If you can, find the names of the news directors and producers in the directories, then guess their e-mail addresses. For television programs, I recommend watching TV with a paper and pen handy for writing down the names of producers that appear in the credits. I've gone so far as to videotape programs and then pause on the credits during playback to get the names of producers. This method is by far the best way to get current contact names, because turnover is so high in this profession that printed directories are out of date by the time they're bound.

Guessing addresses. If you know the domain name used at the publication or station, you can easily guess the rest of the e-mail address for your target contacts. You can be pretty sure they use some variation of their names for addresses that they actually monitor (as opposed to the ones they use in bylines, which are often opened by staff). For example, Walter Mossberg at *The Wall Street Journal* uses the public e-mail address mossberg@wsj.com. With the amount of mail he gets, you can be sure that mail sent to this address is filtered by staff. A review of *The Wall Street Journal's* Web site indicates that a wide variety of addressing formats are used, including firstname.lastname, initial lastname, firstname initial, and so on. So using poor Walt Mossberg as an example, you might try the addresses walt.mossberg, walter.mossberg, wmossberg, waltm, and walterm. Most publications or stations have one common addressing system, and once you unlock it, the media contacts are yours. So, I recommend that you pick a variation and try it; there is no penalty for guessing wrong. If the address doesn't work, your e-mail will bounce, and you can keep guessing until you get it right.

Finding addresses at Web sites. Using the Web to find media e-mail addresses is a hit-and-miss proposition. It's a good way to find the addresses of Web site editors and content producers, but the addresses of print or broadcast contacts are seldom revealed. Web sites for individual media outlets should, however, reveal the addressing system used by the outlet to help you make better e-mail address guesses. You can sometimes find e-mail addresses using online directories, but most of the sites I recommended in the past have either gone out of business or no longer give out full e-mail addresses (InfoSearch, for example). Figure 2.8 shows a search for Walter Mossberg's e-mail address using Yahoo!'s People Search that produced seven promising prospects.

Another very sneaky way to find e-mail addresses is to browse the message boards at Web sites for newspapers, magazines, radio stations, and TV stations. Reporters and producers often respond to comments and criticism on these boards, and their e-mail addresses are usually displayed along with their messages.

Finding addresses on America Online and CompuServe. America Online still has a handy mechanism for searching the membership directory by keyword. Figure 2.9 shows a search for the words "talk show producer" in the Occupation field that returned 65 matching members. You can also search the directory using a person's name. CompuServe doesn't have global profile searches like AOL, but

Email Basic Search Results

Showing 1 – 7 of 7
First | Previous | Next | Last

Name (click for details)	Location	Email
Walt Mossberg	Redmond, WA	waltm@msn.com
Walt Mossberg		wmossberg@msn.com
Walt Mossberg	Washington, DC	eww69a@prodigy.com
Walter Mossberg	New York, NY	walter_mossberg@yahoo.com
Walter Mossberg	Santa Monica, CA	twtechnews@yahoo.com
Walter S Mossberg	Washington, DC	71005.3303@compuserve.com
Walter S. Mossberg	Washington, DC	wmossberg@mcimail.com

First | Previous | Next | Last

Figure 2.8 Yahoo!'s People Search is one way to find e-mail addresses of media contacts. This search for Walter Mossberg's address produced seven promising alternatives.

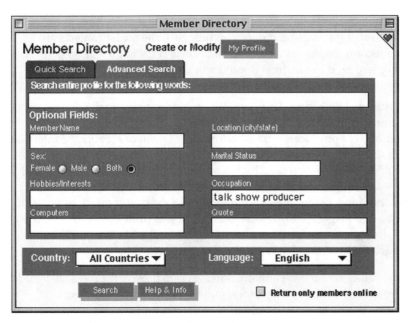

Figure 2.9 Using the Advanced Search option in America Online's membership directory, you can find people who have the words "talk show producer" listed as their occupation. This search resulted in 65 matches.

you can search for a person by name. If you are searching at a specific forum on CompuServe, such as the Media Professionals Forum, you can search profiles by keywords such as journalist, producer, reporter, and so on. AOL and CompuServe searches are good ways to find private e-mail addresses for media contacts at major outlets who have their corporate mailboxes screened.

Buying Media Lists and Distribution Services

An alternative to building your own media list from the ground up is to purchase a list from someone who has already done the research. This method sounds like a good strategy, but the lists available suffer from two major problems. The first is that they don't contain enough personal e-mail addresses. The use of e-mail by media contacts has escalated dramatically in recent years, and the major directory vendors haven't kept pace. Even as directory publishers scramble to add e-mail addresses, media contacts are switching to private addresses and withholding personal addresses from directory listings to spare journalists from inappropriate, excessive releases.

The second major problem is that most directories do not contain contact information for freelancers. This situation is a huge issue for several reasons. Media outlets have adopted leaner staffs over the past 10 years, maintaining a skeleton crew of managers and advertising sales representatives and contracting out for content. This situation is true not only of print publications, but also of television news programs. And these freelancers are usually much more stable and productive contacts than employees of the outlets they serve. Employee turnover ruins media contact databases. But freelancers seldom change the subjects they write about and keep the same e-mail addresses regardless of who they write for. You might find a freelancer's e-mail address in a trade newsletter and see their byline a month later in a major national magazine. Freelancers have produced most of the coverage generated by my own media list: They don't get hit often with PR pitches and are thus more receptive to my news releases. I've gotten many a client into major magazines and newspapers through the freelance back door after the client's in-house PR team failed to get through the outlet's front door. In short, the cultivation of an excellent list of free-lancers who cover topics important to your client is essential to modern day publicity and public relations success. But the major directories don't contain good freelance contacts.

You can still purchase a database of media contacts, but consider it a starting point for your own list or a supplement. These lists will have good mailing address and fax information, which can be helpful for traditional releases or supplemental materials. But you'll have to add the e-mail addresses yourself. Don't be surprised if you get fewer than 100 good e-mail addresses in a database of 10,000 media contacts. Here's a quick run down of some of the lists and services available:

Bacon's MediaSource www.bacons.com. Bacon's boasts a directory of more than 460,000 contacts representing more than 70,000 outlets. Just don't expect to see a lot of personal e-mail addresses. You can purchase the MediaSource CD-ROM and updates for $1,895 or buy smaller directories covering just print or broadcast outlets. For the same price, you can access the same contacts for a year over the Internet. For power PR users, I recommend you purchase the CD-ROM and import selected information into your own database. This action is completely legal, because the information contained in directories such as these is copyright free (only the *style of presentation* of that information is protected by copyright).

Gale Directory of Publications and Broadcast Media www.galegroup.com. Gale's directory is comparable to Bacon's with a claim of more than 63,000 print and broadcast outlets. Price for the print edition is $730. Gale is developing an online subscription version of the directory, but at press time I was only able to access advertising for it—not the site itself or pricing information. A CD-ROM version of the directory is not currently available.

Ulrich's Periodicals Directory www.ulrichsweb.com. Published by R.R. Bowker, Ulrich's directory does not include broadcast media. Still, it claims more than 250,000 entries. Online access to the directory is available for $1,195 a year. A CD-ROM of the directory is available for $850.

Gebbie's All-In-One Media Directory www.gebbieinc.com. Mark Gebbie provides an excellent product for the budget-minded PR professional. His All-In-One database covers about 20,000 print and broadcast outlets. You can purchase it on disk for $295 or buy a CD-ROM that includes news release distribution software for $540. I've used Gebbie products a couple of times, and I like them. Gebbie's list doesn't include the names and e-mail addresses for individual contacts at these outlets, but as Mark Gebbie points out, neither do most of the other directories (and when they do, those contacts are usually out of date).

MediaMap www.mediamap.com. I love these guys, but I hate their prices. The folks at MediaMap really understand public relations. They know it's a people game, and they know that what counts when you're looking for coverage is not the station or the publication but the *people* that work there. MediaMap provides the kind of nitty-gritty, up-to-the-minute contact information you need: the name, title, phone number, fax number, and e-mail address of the specific person who can get you coverage at a station or publication. Unfortunately, they charge through the nose for this service. Access to each module of their online database is more than $2,000, and there are more than a dozen modules in all. Ouch! Here's a tip for the budget conscious: Subscribe to their free MediaWatch newsletter. The newsletter tells you about personnel changes at every outlet MediaMap covers (without the corresponding contact information, of course). Then, go dig up the e-mail addresses yourself. It's time consuming but free, and half the work has been done for you by the MediaMap staff.

E-Mail Publisher and World Newspaper Database
http://emailpublishing.homestead.com/email.html. Here's a tip so good it will probably disappear soon. Phil Philcox is a freelance writer. He realized at some point that he could query dozens of editors at once via e-mail and sell a lot more articles a lot faster. Eventually, Phil accumulated more than 10,000 e-mail addresses of newspaper and magazine editors, and now he's selling the database for $50. That's right—$50. Several PR professionals I know overlooked this resource because it's being marketed to writers who are trying to pitch stories to editors. But those are *exactly* the contacts you want to reach with your news releases. Phil's list is still fresh, and he claims an 8 to 10 percent undeliverable rate on e-mail (most lists I've tried are about 25 percent undeliverable via e-mail), so I suggest you grab a copy while the getting is good.

All Media E-Mail Directory www.owt.com/dircon. This directory of media e-mail addresses so highly touted in my last book is sadly no longer available. Paul Krupin, the brilliant man behind the list, pulled it off the market after getting too many complaints from the media about the quantity of crap they received from thoughtless users of the list. Krupin now operates a service distributing news releases, which he calls iMediaFax and I call "Poor Man's Newswire." You can achieve the same results as PR Newswire or BusinessWire at a fraction of the cost. The catch is, the interface is tricky and takes some adjustment. For anyone with a regular need for news release distribution, it's worth going through the learning curve.

Other new release distribution services. For the sake of brevity, I'm going to lump together all the other news release distribution services: PR Newswire, BusinessWire, Media Distribution Services, and so on. These firms, and several others, have been issuing news release for companies for decades. They are professionals and offer top-tier services at matching prices. Most of them offer e-mail distribution as well as fax, print, and even video or satellite services. One advantage of using these services is that news releases are archived online and through file-sharing agreements are available from multiple news portals and search engines. I've received inquiries from news releases I uploaded years ago to the Internet, so I can vouch that old news releases still pull even if the traffic is very light.

In the future, I expect most media databases to be available only online and not on disk, CD-ROM, or print. By offering services online, these companies make it more difficult for you to build your own database from their contact lists. If they can keep the lists fresh and the prices down, it will make more sense to use a service rather than to build your own list. But I don't have confidence in their abilities to track individual journalists' e-mail addresses and make them available for a nominal price. So, I recommend that you search around for independent distributors such as Paul Krupin, Mark Gebbie, and Phil Philcox, who can provide you with a nice starter list of contacts at bargain-basement prices.

Sending E-Mail News Releases

I bet you thought I'd never get to this section. E-mail news releases are such an important publicity tool, however, that it's worth carefully describing each step of the process: writing, formatting, and finding media contacts. Once your operation is properly configured, releases can go out like clockwork with a minimum of technical difficulties or complaints. Let's see how we put everything together to get these releases out the door and into journalists' inboxes.

Assembling the Distribution List

Here is my method for preparing the distribution list for a news release. The steps you use will be dependent upon what software configuration you have for word processing, e-mail, and contact management—but it will be similar to these instructions.

First, open your media list, and if you're concerned about corrupting your main database, save it under a new name, close the original file, and work in the duplicate file. Unmark all contacts in the file just in case any of them are still marked (or selected) from the last time the list was accessed. Choose the media contacts who should receive the release, and mark them for inclusion. I make my selections based on the subjects they cover. Out of a list of 10,000 contacts, I typically send to between 500 and 700 media contacts. If I'm including the news directors of radio stations, that number can double. Once you have marked all the contacts who should be included on the final list, export the marked contacts into a new file and save it in a folder for this particular project. That concludes the selection process.

Now, you begin the exclusion process. You open the new, smaller media list and search for any contacts with exclusion tags. Start with your Heavy Hitters. Are you sure you want to mail to all of them? With every release you send, you risk having a contact ask to be taken off your list. Treat your Heavy Hitters with respect, and delete any contacts that aren't a perfect match for this release. Next, search for your KEEP OFFs and delete all of them. Next, find your Touchy contacts and decide whether the release is close enough to their interests to warrant including them on the final distribution list. When I make my selections for the media list, I almost never look at individual contact records; instead, I grab names fast and get through the list. But when I start excluding contacts, I look at their individual records to see exactly what kinds of material they want. For any contact tagged as Touchy!, there should be a note in the record as to what news release they complained about and why. Finally, you might want to search for any contacts tagged as potential scammers. If your release is offering something of value such as tickets, review copies of products, press passes, and so on, you might think twice about offering these freebies to dubious journalists.

You now have a streamlined media list, but it's not quite ready to go yet. A major problem with large media lists is duplicate contacts. For example, a string of regional weekly newspapers might all share an e-mail address such as news@weekly.com. For each contact, the name of the person and his or her mailing address will be unique, but the e-mail address will be identical. Because news releases sent using Blind Copy are not individually addressed, if you have six of these contacts, the one e-mail account will get six copies of your release. Needless to say, you don't want anyone on your list to get duplicate copies of the release because they will likely ask to be taken off your list.

Most contact management programs enable you to search for duplicates. You need to set the duplicate searching defaults to look at only the e-mail address when deciding whether contacts are duplicate (not the name, company name, mailing address, and so on). Some journalists might be on your list with two different e-mail addresses. That's okay. I would send to every unique e-mail address in the file. If journalists get two copies because they use two different e-mail addresses, they usually ask to have one of the addresses deleted. If you don't have automated duplicate searching in your software, simply sort the list by e-mail address and visually scan for duplicates—they are readily noticeable. Sorting the media list alphabetically by e-mail address also helps with dividing the list, as I'll explain in a moment.

Now, your list is clean and you can export the e-mail addresses into a text file. Use either tab-delimited or comma-delimited export—it makes no difference. These e-mail addresses will be put into the Blind Copy field when you address the e-mail.

Preparing the E-Mail Release

In your e-mail program, create a new message for the news release. See Figure 2.10 for an example of a news release prepared in Eudora and ready for delivery. In the To: field, insert your own e-mail address. You can use your own name in the To: field or put in any text you want, just as long as the e-mail address is your own. I use the text NEWS RELEASE in the To: field to alert journalists who receive it that it's a news release. The From: field should contain your name and e-mail address. If you want, you can add text here, too, such as a toll-free phone number for responses, but be careful that your message doesn't end up looking like spam.

Next, open the text version of the media list you created. It should contain only the e-mail addresses of the contacts. You can copy and paste these names directly into the Blind Copy or Bcc: field, or you can create a nickname for the group in your e-mail address book. Figure 2.11 shows my Eudora address book. I created the nickname

To: NEWS RELEASE <realnews@bellsouth.net>
From: Steve O'Keefe <realnews@bellsouth.net> | News Release   ⇕ |
Subject: Free Review Copy: entrepreneurship.com
Cc:
Bcc: **medialist1**
X-Attachments:

I'm writing to offer you a free review copy of a new book
by Tim Burns, MBA, CPA, JD, called "entrepreneurship.com,"
published by Dearborn Trade. The book is built around the
concept of an "e-plan" borrowed from guru David Cowan of
Bessemer Venture Partners. Burns argues that a modern
business plan should be presented as a series of 12
PowerPoint slides plus an Executive Summary. As the author
of five business plans myself, I can tell you this approach
is both unique and valuable. The e-plan pleases potential
investors by immediately getting to the point. It's easy to
update, and it helps entrepreneurs remember that a business
plan is wedded to a verbal pitch or presentation.

Burns is uniquely qualified to write this book. An
attorney, accountant, MBA, and college instructor, he
approaches the business plan from all angles in easy-going
style, without getting bogged-down in minutia. The book is
highlighted with examples from his own client roster of
dot.com successes and failures, and interviews with dozens
of investors, venture capitalists, angels, and
entrepreneurs. The book has earned advance praise from such
luminaries as the highly effective Stephen R. Covey and the
always entrepreneurial Bill Reichert, President of
Garage.com.

For a free review copy of "entrepreneurship.com" (Dearborn
Trade, ISBN 1-57410-136-6, $19.95) -- or an interview with
author Tim Burns -- simply reply to this e-mail. Thank you.

Figure 2.10 An e-mail news release in Eudora, addressed and ready for delivery. Note that the To: field contains the sender's e-mail address, and the Blind Copy or Bcc: field contains a nickname for the entire distribution list.

"medialist3" and copied all the journalists' e-mail addresses into that nickname, as shown on the right side of the image. I then put the nickname into the Bcc: field of the message, as shown in the completed e-mail in Figure 2.10.

When the release goes out, the text of the release and the address list are sent to your *Internet Service Provider* (ISP), where a copy of the release is then sent to everyone on the list. If you address each e-mail individually, for example using emailmerge software to customize each release, the releases are sent one-at-a-time to your ISP for

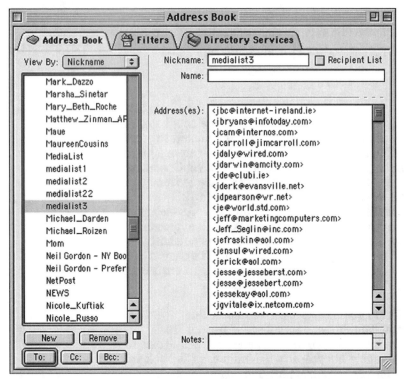

Figure 2.11   The e-mail addresses for recipients of the news release are dumped into a group name or nickname in the e-mail program. The group name is then put into the Blind Copy or Bcc: field, and the release will be delivered to everyone in the group.

delivery. If you have hundreds of individually addressed releases, just sending the e-mail to your ISP can take hours. When you Blind Copy everyone with an identical release, it only takes a few seconds to send it. Many ISPs have a limit on the number of recipients you can send an e-mail to, however. These limits are set to reduce the amount of spam sent over the Internet. Even if you are your own ISP, your software might be preprogrammed with a limit, and you'll have to disable this preference before sending out e-mail.

One way around the limit is to break the media list into chunks that are each under your ISP's limit of recipients. If the limit is 100 names, you'll have to break a media list of 600 journalists into six groups and send a release to each group. If your ISP's software is smart enough to catch this trick, you might have to vary each message slightly so they don't appear identical. You can perform this task by adding one space band at the end of the first bulk e-mail; two spacebands at the end of the second e-mail; and so on. The messages will still look identical to the recipients, but they will pass muster with any software looking for a large number of duplicate messages.

Once you have the addressing complete, you can open the text version of the news release itself and copy the subject line and the body of the release into your e-mail message. If you saved the news release as "text only with line breaks," it will appear similar to the release shown in Figure 2.10 with tidy, short line endings. Before you send it, you might want to double check that your distribution list is in the Blind Copy field and that you didn't accidentally grab an interim version of the news release. You don't want to make a mistake in front of hundreds or thousands of journalists. On one of my first e-mail news releases, I accidentally put the group name for the media list in the To: field instead of the Blind Copy field. Every recipient got my entire media list at the top of the news release. I won National Public Radio's Longest Header of the Month contest for that bonehead move, and the press had some fun at my expense. A quick, humorous apology—this time sent with the media list in the Blind Copy field—helped me reduce the damage caused and the Keep Off requests.

News Release Follow-Up

Within minutes of sending your release, you'll start to get responses. Most of the early responses will be bounced, undeliverable messages. Soon after, they should be followed by positive responses and requests for information. You should also expect a few complaints, too, especially if you are using a list you purchased for the first time or a large number of new and untested contacts. Let's look at how to deal with all these replies.

Processing Positive Replies

In the summer of 2000, I set up an e-mail news release operation for book publisher John Wiley & Sons. One goal was to issue a real news release at the end of training—not a practice release, but a genuine release to members of the working press. I spent a week working with Wiley's IT people to install a database of media contacts and another week testing and training. After two weeks of drilling the staff on the importance of formatting and netiquette, and giving them tools to handle complaints, everyone was extremely nervous as we prepared the first release for delivery. It was like we were potentially dropping a bomb, and we were prepared for the worst.

The news release went out. Everything worked as expected. Within five minutes, we got our first thank-you note and request for review copies of the books we were offering. A cheer went up in the office. By the next day, Wiley had almost 30 positive replies and no complaints. I was hoping they would get at least one flame so we could review the process for handling complaints, but no one ever squawked about the release. A similar scenario transpired at an insurance company in Seattle where I set up a news release service in 1997: lots of preparation and agonizing and then nothing but positive results. I recently received fan mail from a person who followed my instructions to the letter and reported that his inbox was "slammed" with requests for more information. It amazes me how consistently this program works. I have literally hundreds of testimonials from people who have put these methods to use in their own businesses and are delighted with the results. Yes, it's a lot of work to set up a good news release delivery service, and, yes, it's worth the effort.

For a typical release to about 500 journalists, I get about 50 positive responses. When you get a positive reply, you should check the e-mail against your media list database and update any new information. First of all, you should note in the database that the person responded favorably to this release. Then, check the person's name and contact information against what you have on file. About 10 percent of the media contacts replying will have new job titles or e-mail addresses. A common situation is that you sent the news release to a generic e-mail address, such as "editor@magazine.com," but the response came from a personal e-mail address, such as "joe.writer@magazine.com." You can now add Joe Writer to your database and keep the old "editor@" address, too, in case it gets answered by someone else next time. Many of the responses you get will contain signatures, and these often tell you what beat the journalist covers, who they write for (in the case of freelancers), and other helpful information that should be added to their records.

Be prepared to send the media anything they might need to build a story. Response times online are stunningly short; if e-mail doesn't get a reply in one day, people get upset. You should be prepared to acknowledge any requests immediately and follow-up with documents, artwork, and interviews as soon as possible. You might only have a journalist's e-mail address and need a mailing address. Don't worry about sounding ignorant; you'll sound thoughtful if you ask for a "preferred mailing address" in case they don't work out of company headquarters. In many cases, it's best to handle follow-ups by telephone. Using the phone helps you establish a closer personal connection with the journalist and is far better than e-mail for such things as scheduling an interview.

Dealing with Undeliverables

If you're using a brand-new media list for the first time, expect an undeliverable rate of about 25 percent. For a list of 600 media contacts, that translates into 150 bounces. That's a lot of messages to process individually, but you shouldn't just delete all those contacts from your database. There are many reasons for bounced messages, and there are different ways to handle them. Here are some common causes and remedies:

User Unknown. That means the e-mail address is no good any more. Delete the e-mail address from your database. If the contact is important enough, you might search online for a newer e-mail address.

Server Unknown. That means not only is the user gone, but so is the domain name associated with the e-mail address. Unfortunately, as a result of the Internet crash of 2000, you'll see a lot of these messages. The address should be deleted from your database.

WARNING Unable to Send. These are timeout warnings. You should not resend the release because the mail server is still trying to deliver it. If it doesn't succeed, you'll eventually get a Time Out message.

Time Out. That means there was a problem connecting with the mail server. The e-mail address is probably still good and should not be deleted from your database.

Mail Box Full. That means your contact is using an Internet service that limits the amount of unread mail he or she can accumulate. It usually indicates an address that has been abandoned or is no longer checked. You can keep the e-mail address on your list, but if the contact is important, you might want to find a better address.

Unlike positive replies, it's best to hold off dealing with undeliverables for a few days until all the stragglers come in. Then, you can spend a rainy afternoon updating your media list, cleaning out all the dead wood, and hopefully adding bright new prospects at the same time.

Handling Complaints

Complaints come in a colorful assortment of language and styles. The best way to handle most of them is to remove the e-mail address of the person from your database and tag him or her as a KEEP OFF. If you delete the entire contact from your database, you risk putting him or her back on your list someday when you run across an e-mail address in a byline somewhere. My experience is that people complain the first time you e-mail them, but they frequently attack the second time. You don't want to ever get a journalist into attack mode.

Sometimes angry people will complain to your boss and/or your ISP. When this situation has happened to me, I always try to soothe the waters by explaining to my boss and ISP exactly what I sent, why I sent it, and what steps I'm taking to eliminate future complaints (such as taking the complainer off my media list). After a few such incidents, both bosses and ISPs have decided I am handling the situation responsibly, limiting any potential fallout for them. After going through this routine about 10 times, I had one ISP ask me to please not bother explaining myself any longer; he understood my business, my methods, and just ignored any complaints related to my services. I wish all ISPs were so understanding. Some of them will discontinue your service if they get too many complaints. But you have to be a major league, unrepentant spammer to get to that level. Most ISPs don't have the time or resources to investigate complaints and won't even notice them until they start to receive thousands or even millions of angry e-mails. If you're running a responsible e-mail news distribution service, you'll most likely stay off an ISP's abuse radar.

If the complaining parties have responded favorably to e-mail pitches in the past, chances are you were a little bit off-target with your e-mail and they sent you form flames. As I described earlier, simply reply to their flames with a note reminding them of your previous contacts and offering to be more selective about what releases you send in the future. Nine times out of 10, they will consent to staying on your media list. Even if you don't have a track record of favorable interactions with a complainer, if he or she is an important media contact, it's worth attempting to smooth any ruffled feathers to keep him or her on your list.

It might take a few news releases to cull the sensitive media contacts from your list. After that, complaints should be few and far between. I was concerned for a while that my media list would gradually be whittled away by bounced addresses and people asking to be taken off. But actually, my list has grown in both numbers and responsiveness over the years. Journalists weren't sure what to make of e-mail news releases at first, and many complained about getting pitched that way. But now most of them have come to realize it's easier to breeze through e-mail pitches than fax or mail releases, and e-mail releases are more timely, often giving them the margin between a scoop and an also-ran. And because they hate phone pitches, there aren't too many ways left to gather original news. As the Middleberg/Ross survey shows, e-mail is now preferred by journalists for news releases, but they insist that the releases be on target, newsworthy, and brief. And they are learning how to use filtering software to keep people who don't play by the rules out of their mailboxes.

Top Tips

Start using e-mail news releases. If you haven't already shifted to e-mail news releases, what are you waiting for? It's easier and cheaper for you, and journalists prefer to be pitched this way.

Be selective. Sooner or later, media contacts are going to learn how to use those filters built into their e-mail software, and publicists who violate netiquette will be permanently locked out. So, learn what kinds of material each person on your list wants, and be careful to send only releases they're likely to be interested in.

Use the add-and-subtract method for picking media. Add contacts to your distribution list based on the subjects they cover, then delete contacts with a history of sensitivity to e-mail releases. This method is the fastest way to manage the large task of selecting contacts for a news release.

Buy good software and learn to use it. Spend the extra money for the professional version of free e-mail software, and use books and tutorials to learn how to tap its potential. Buy good contact-management software for maintaining your media list. Soon, these two software families will merge into one, and your work will get easier.

Avoid rich e-mail news releases. I know it's tempting to spice up news releases with HTML formatting and graphics, but the people receiving these releases have made it abundantly clear they want plain text. You've been warned.

Practice the art of seduction. You can't tell the whole story in an e-mail news release, so don't try. Instead, think of the release as a tease, giving journalists a glimpse of the story and asking whether they want to see more. Try to be the Mae West of media relations, turning heads with a good subject line while saying as little as possible to stimulate their imagination and lure them in.

CHAPTER 3

Online News Rooms

In the past few years, online newsrooms have become an essential public relations tool. They're like a media supermarket that is open 24 hours a day, seven days a week, where journalists can come and gather breaking news, background information, artwork, and even video news feeds. One-stop shopping is the goal of these sites, which put the media in control of what information they want, when, and how.

These media supermarkets present many difficulties for organizations that are used to the specialty boutiques of old, with separate outlets for media relations, investor relations, community relations, and human resources. These departments must learn to work together under one roof to better serve the customer. When a corporate crisis happens, the online newsroom looks like a supermarket before a hurricane with thousands of journalists clamoring for anything they can get their hands on. Management needs to decide whether to board up the store and flee or try to profit from the experience by offering all the competing brands of information to the hungry press corps.

This chapter is a guide to designing and stocking the media superstore. I'm pleased to include here some brand-new products that I believe will boost media coverage in the coming decades to new heights: corporate news wires, online presentations, and online news conferences. These products are still being test marketed, but so far the results are encouraging. Topics covered in this chapter include the following:

Newsroom organization. A guide to the competing interests of the departments and people involved in the newsroom and a discussion of whether to restrict access to the store (can't we all just get along?)

Newsroom architecture. Designing a workable Web interface and managing databases of news content, artwork, and multimedia

What should the site contain? Filling up the store shelves with enough content to lure the media and keep them happy, along with a few suggestions for items that should be discontinued

News wires and news feeds. If you follow the media covering your market, you can share your research with the press in exchange for coverage. This technique is a remarkably inexpensive and effective strategy for multiplying media coverage while building an image as an industry leader.

Online presentations. Another low-cost tool for public relations professionals to share perspectives with the press without hogging a lot of bandwidth

Online news conferences. Drawn by improvements in technology and pushed by fair disclosure rules, organizations are opening their news conferences to the general public with mixed results. I'll help you produce these events and prevent the problems that have plagued many wanna-be broadcasters.

Online crisis management. In a crisis situation, the newsroom becomes a war room. I'll look at how to change the chain of command, deal with the fight-or-flight syndrome, and decide what inventory to stock in a crisis center.

Newsroom Organization

Everyone wants an online newsroom. That's where the agreement ends and the arguments begin. Large corporations have well-established procedures for dealing with the media. Channels of communication between the corporation and the press have been groomed and refined for years. Thanks to the Internet, the protocol has changed. Different groups must unite to make the Web site work, not only for each other but also for the media contacts who will visit. In this section, I look at some of the core issues regarding how to organize the newsroom: whether to restrict public access or leave it open, how to accommodate the needs of all the different departments who contribute to the newsroom, and suggestions for handling sensitive contact information.

Restricted Access

The first question you need to address in building an online newsroom is whether to restrict access to verified members of the press. This decision should not be made lightly. Controlling access to the newsroom results in numerous difficulties, such as:

Processing requests for access. Staff time must be devoted to processing requests for entry. Are you going to verify the credentials of everyone who requests entry, or do they simply have to register using an online form, thus gaining access without verification?

Determining Press Credentials. What constitutes a legitimate member of the media? If you are going to verify credentials, you have to develop some guidelines for who is a member of the media, and that's not always easy. Does a Web site content editor count? How about a discussion group moderator or sysop? Freelancers are important media contacts, but their credentials are difficult to verify because they don't work for a single media outlet and e-mail from them won't come from a media domain.

Losing the moment. When the press is knocking at your virtual door, time matters. They have come for a reason and usually want immediate access. If you can't get them into the newsroom within seconds, you might miss your opportunity to be included in a story or to influence a story that is being written right now. Do you have the staff to handle requests for access on a timely basis, over weekends and holidays, or at night?

Lost passwords. If access requires a user ID and password, you're going to have to deal with a lot of requests for lost passwords. Many e-commerce Web sites have automated ways of handling these requests, but they require a more invasive registration process and more expensive software to handle lost passwords. Media contacts struggling to keep track of all their passwords and user IDs might decide it's not worth the fuss.

Disappointment. When you require registration for access, users typically expect to find some goodies in the newsroom that normally wouldn't be available to the public. If media contacts jump the hurdles required for entry only to arrive at a site that has nothing but stock information, your news operation could generate a negative impression that tarnishes news coverage.

The practical effect of restricting access to the newsroom is to restrict media coverage of your company. Most companies want all the coverage they can get, and even in a crisis situation they want to influence stories being written under tight deadlines. Any barrier you place between your news content and the media is unlikely to have a positive impact on news coverage.

The benefits of restricting access are twofold. First, you get contact information for the media (which can be stored in a database and used when you want to reach out to those media who have shown an interest in your company's affairs). Before you implement a restricted newsroom, however, you should have clear plans for how you will store and use the registration information you get. The second benefit is limiting general public access to potentially sensitive information or bandwidth-consuming presentations that could slow down your site for everyone.

Getting the media to identify themselves to you is an admirable goal. Rather than forcing them through a registration process that results in numerous logistical problems on your end, however, you could lure them into revealing contact information by offering them something of sufficient value. For example, you could keep access to your newsroom open but offer e-mail alerts on breaking stories, press passes to events, or access to online news conferences to members of the media who register or request such information. You'll catch more coverage with incentives than with barriers.

As to the bandwidth issues, you can make access to these features of your newsroom available by registration or request. The media will be more understanding if you grant open access to your stock information but restrict access to certain features that would be problematic to make available to the general public.

For these reasons, I think the trend of limiting access to a newsroom is waning. It defeats many of the great benefits of online communications: speed, access to information, and user control. It puts the company on a pedestal, deciding who to grant access to and who not to, generating a feeling of control and manipulation. It is undemocratic and will mostly work against the company. Some combination of an open newsroom, combined with restricted invitations to special previews or events, is a compromise that works well. Media contacts coming to your site won't feel like their use of the site is being supervised, yet they will appreciate being let in on stories ahead of the masses.

Interdepartmental Coordination

You should anticipate that your newsroom will be used by all the publics your company serves, sometimes for unconventional reasons. The main groups accessing your newsroom will be the media, shareholders and analysts, customers, consumer groups, community groups, and government agencies. But don't be surprised if you find your newsroom frequented by the general public, students, instructors, job seekers, salespeople, public relations professionals, authors, librarians, researchers, attorneys, vandals, suppliers, contractors, collection agencies, fundraisers, competitors, private investigators, and even spies. How do you develop a newsroom that serves all these groups while protecting your organization?

As online newsrooms began proliferating in the mid-1990s, noticeable rifts developed inside corporate hierarchies. At first, newsrooms were used for publicity only, and investor relations, human resources, and so on maintained their own online centers. But this piecemeal method for doling out information about the company did not find favor with Web site users and resulted in too much duplication of resources and effort. In recent years, the trend has been toward consolidation of newsrooms, spawning considerable bickering between departments who share in the joint venture. Let's look at some of the major participants in the company newsroom and their goals and fears concerning the Web site.

> **Public relations.** PR is usually in charge of a company's overall interface with the media and the public. PR people are a cautious bunch: Everyone else is interested in *promoting* the company, whereas PR is also charged with *protecting* the company. PR should manage the overall coordination of the newsroom, even if that means everything on the site will be scrutinized with an eye toward potential exposure and liability. Community relations and government relations are branches of the PR department and are so tightly controlled by PR that for the purposes of developing a newsroom, PR can represent them.

> **Publicity.** Pity the poor publicity department. Perpetually stuck between marketing and PR and chronically underfunded, publicity plays third fiddle.

While there's no clear line between publicity and PR, a good working definition is that the former is charged with generating media coverage and the latter is charged with avoiding it. Between marketing and publicity, the marketers get all the budget to squander on paid advertising while publicity gets the crumbs off marketing's table even as they generate 10 times the return on expenditures. Most positive news releases are generated by the publicity department, which often has the best writers in the company. Media relations is frequently the responsibility of the publicity department unless there is a crisis, whereupon PR steps in.

Investor relations. IR people tend to stay a little above the fray. Because they communicate with capital—the life's blood of the company—they are frequently treated like prima donnas with budgets larger than they deserve. My experience with IR is that while they are pleased to be able to court investors through the Web site, they are unhappy about losing control over some of the content and being dragged down into the mire with lower life forms on the PR ladder (publicity, human resources, and—God forbid—customer service).

Human resources. The primary goals of online human resources appear to be protecting the company from an onslaught of unsolicited resumes and limiting liability in a lawsuit-happy field. Human resources is very helpful in generating bios of key staff for the Web site. They also tend to preside over employee relations, although content in this area is more often delivered over private intranets than via a public Web site.

Marketing. For the most part, marketing could care less about the online newsroom. These are e-commerce folks. They usually dominate the company Web site and have an IT budget that makes the newsroom look laughable. They often have responsibility for the publicity department and might pay lip service to supporting news-generating activities online, but if PR wants to reign in publicity, hey, who really cares? Marketing is increasingly responsible for customer service (much to their displeasure), and the Web site is critical to customer service functions, so marketing might be reluctantly dragged deeper into the newsroom debate.

Customer service. Customer service is to the marketing department what internal affairs is to the police department: essential but despised. Everyone knows that customer satisfaction is the key to profitability and growth, but most companies are obsessed with quarterly profits. Sales, not service, calls the shots in marketing. Customer service and PR have usually been at opposite ends of the building, but this situation is where the Internet has totally changed things. Customer service inquiries will flow through any chink in the Web site, so PR has to work together with customer service to process these inquiries and protect the company from liability.

Information technology. IT has to work with everybody. Somehow, they're supposed to wave a magic wand that turns the statement "I want more media coverage" into a brilliant technological solution with no design flaws. IT often plays the mediator role for interdepartmental squabbles over the Web site and of course gets blamed by everyone when the results don't measure up to expectations. Fortunately, IT has now become so big and important that they can have moles planted in each department who are charged with translating those vague wishes and desires into workable code.

Like the previously mentioned IT wizard, I wish I could wave a magic wand and give you a clear set of guidelines on how to coordinate departmental contributions to an online newsroom. I've tried drafting charts to show various contributions and benefits, but they always end up looking like one of those "how the world works" graphs with lines going every which way. The specific implementation depends on the size and structure of the company, and there's so much variation in these factors that exceptions dwarf any clear rules. But I will attempt to summarize those few general principles that I think should govern development of an online newsroom:

1. PR should have overall responsibility for the online newsroom. PR should therefore serve as the coordinator among departments with different goals. Ideally, there should be an IT person in the PR department who will assist with design issues and be the first point of contact between divisions of PR and the IT department. PR should be responsible for developing a crisis plan for the site.

2. IT should be responsible for building and managing the site to the specifications of the PR department. IT should manage all databases, artwork repositories, and templates.

Handling Inquiries

There is no ideal way to handle the display of contact information in the newsroom. The main problem is that people will use the contact information for inappropriate purposes, such as consumer complaints. But you can't eliminate all contact information and serve the purpose of the newsroom, which is to communicate with the media. Journalists working on a story don't have time to hunt down contact information, and PR professionals don't want to risk having promising press leads processed by untrained staff answering generic feedback e-mail.

A second problem is that content archived in the newsroom might contain contact names, e-mail addresses, and phone numbers that are out of date. Again, you could eliminate contact information from archived news releases, and many sites have, but then you make journalists hunt for or guess the appropriate person to which they should direct their inquiries. Apple Computer's award-winning newsroom puts personal contact information on every single news release, on a contacts page, and even on the home page of their news section (see Figure 3.1).

The best strategy I've seen for dealing with contact information is to consolidate all the contact information on a detailed media contacts page. This page would have the names, phone numbers, and personal e-mail addresses of all the press relations people and their areas of responsibility. Within each news release, you can include the name of the contact person, the departmental phone number, and a generic e-mail address such as news@company.com. This generic phone number and address can be used in the boilerplate frame or navigational runner for the entire newsroom.

Figure 3.1 Apple Computer has an award-winning online newsroom. Right from the first page, journalists get personal contact information including names, phone numbers, and e-mail addresses.

Some sites restrict access to contact information to registered users to cut down on the number of customer-service inquiries directed to media relations staff. But that leads to the same problems described earlier, where journalists who need information immediately have to fumble for a password. Another solution is to avoid the mention of any e-mail addresses and instead provide a Web form that would be routed to the appropriate person.

Regardless of the solution you use, staff members have to be trained in the proper distribution of media inquiries. E-mail will be received at both personal and generic addresses that belongs somewhere else. Media inquiries will flow from other feedback mechanisms at the site, as well, and IT and other departments need to know how important it is to forward inquiries promptly. Mail coming to generic addresses should be processed every working day, and special care should be taken to insure coverage during vacations and holidays.

Newsroom Architecture

Designing an online newsroom that works for more than a few minutes is difficult. What happens when the contact person in media relations changes? If you include contact information in your news releases, the whole archive is out of date. What happens if the company logo changes? What about if your server or directory structure changes? The newsroom is not immune to all the headaches that plague Web sites as a company changes over time—and companies always change. Some simple design tips will help you minimize the trauma caused by the normal ebb and flow of personnel and systems.

Most newsrooms are served up inside a corporate shell. A good corporate shell will contain the company logo, a positioning statement, a navigational runner for content near the top of the page, a navigational runner for assistance at the bottom of the page, and a copyright notice. That leaves you with the middle of the page. You can put your newsroom navigational runner on the left side of the page, then pull your content into the middle of the page. This standard display grid is shown in Figure 3.2. You'll see this design mimicked in most of the screen shots of online newsrooms contained in this chapter.

There are two key databases that contribute content to the online newsroom: the news release archive and the artwork database. Let's look at each of these separately for some design tips.

News Release Archive

Designing a news release archive is a critical operation, because these releases are used in many different sections of most Web sites. Investor relations will want to highlight financial news releases; community affairs will have their own list of important releases; the e-commerce portion of the site will feature news about new products and

Home | News | Services | Clients | About Us | Search

News Home
News Archive
Investor Relations
Management Profiles   CONTENT HERE
Community Affairs
Pending Legislation
Company History

Site Index | Feedback | Help | Copyright Notice

Figure 3.2 Typical organizational grid for a newsroom Web page. The corporate shell contains the top and bottom navigational runners. Newsroom navigational links are on the left side of the page. Newsroom content is pulled into the center of the page.

services; and all sections of the site will want to tap into the full news release archive. The best way to accomplish this task is by adequately coding each release the company generates when it is added to the database. The codes should include the following:

- Date of issue
- Originating department
- Geographical tags ("all" or "country" or "city" or "region")
- Subject tags (could be the same as originating department)

You'll also want the database to have a separate field for the headline and a field for a brief description of the release. With a database properly set up, you can pull the latest news release titles and their summary paragraphs onto the home page of the site. In a similar fashion, each of the major subsections of the site can lead off with the top news release summaries for that section: Investor relations will have the most recent financial releases, and community relations will have the most recent outreach releases.

News releases typically contain the name and phone number of the contact person for that release. But in a Web archive, this format creates problems whenever the staff changes. You can solve this problem in several different ways. One way is to include a generic media relations e-mail address in the shell surrounding the release. Another is to include only generic e-mail addresses and phone numbers in the body of releases. Another is to completely eliminate contact information from archived news releases and instead include a link to the newsroom Contacts page, where up-to-date names, phone numbers, and e-mail addresses are provided.

For large news release archives, journalists appreciate an excellent search feature. I used the search feature at one site and got 1,701 matching entries. I tried to narrow the search several times by piling up more keywords in the search box but still kept getting 1,701 matches. That's too many documents for any journalist to wade through. I would have appreciated an advanced search mechanism that allowed me to narrow the search by date, subject, or geographical location. At the least, I would have liked to use qualifying phrases such as AND, OR, and NOT to limit the number of matches to my query.

Artwork Database

Artwork consumes a lot of bandwidth and is used all over a company's Web site. In order to minimize duplication and present a consistent company image, all the artwork used on the site should be maintained by the IT department. Ideally, IT should be responsible for retouching images, converting them to the proper formats, devising a naming regimen for images, and maintaining the database with updates and deletions.

The newsroom has special artwork needs that other departments might not have. Media contacts want artwork in formats suitable for reproduction in a variety of media: print, broadcast, and online. High-resolution artwork—especially video—can occupy massive amounts of file storage space and should not be used in most of the public portions of the site. When high-resolution artwork is offered to the media, the resolution and file size should be noted so journalists can decide whether the image will suit their needs and whether they're willing to initiate a potentially lengthy download. Figure 3.3 shows artwork offered by Apple Computer in its press room. The caption next to the artwork identifies the compression format (BinHex) and file size (2.5MB) but fails to include the resolution of the image. Is it 600 dpi, 300 dpi, or 72 dpi? Apple has won awards for its press room, but it can do better.

One of the things missing from most artwork archives is adequate captioning. It's my opinion that caption text should be embedded at the bottom of an image so that there's no chance of the identifying information getting separated from the image. Every image should contain a caption specifying what the image is and including a copyright notice. Beyond that, the caption should include a photography or design credit if there is a legal requirement to do so. Most artwork requires a credit to the artist even if all the rights are owned by the company that purchased it. When you embed this information into the artwork, the only way it can be removed is by intentional cropping, which is fine if the media outlet using the image includes the proper notices in its own caption for the image. Embedding copyright notices into artwork discourages unlawful duplication, protecting the company from legal claims by artists and giving the company added ammunition in legal action against pirates.

Along with the lack of captions embedded into artwork, the lack of clear captions on Web pages leading to the artwork is another problem. Look at Figure 3.3 from Apple Computer. The caption "Family of Apple Displays" is certainly scant; "Apple's revolutionary flat panel displays come in a variety of sizes and styles" would have been more informative and would likely get repeated verbatim in news coverage. Along with failing to mention the image resolution, the caption doesn't specify what type of image it is: TIFF, PICT, EPS, or PhotoShop?

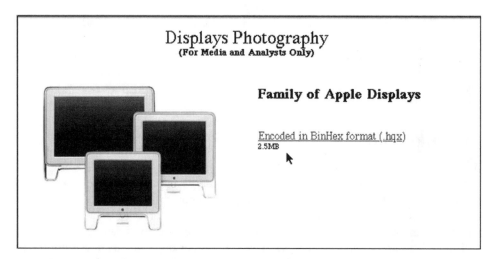

Figure 3.3   A page from Apple Computer's online press room offering high-resolution artwork to the media. This page has several problems, including a poorly worded caption and a lack of information about image type and resolution.

Multimedia Files

Most online newsrooms now contain multimedia files along with more traditional still photos. These files pose special problems because they are typically huge and the software used to access them is neither standardized nor seamless. In order to deliver audio and video files over the Web, a company needs a media server. The two most popular brands are RealMedia's RealServer, starting at about $2,000, and Microsoft's Windows Server, starting at about $1,000. In order for your visitors to access these files, they need to have media player software. Corresponding to the servers, the most popular media players are RealPlayer and Windows Media Player. Both of these programs are available for free download.

If you are going to offer multimedia from your newsroom, you should recognize that visitors will arrive with many different software and hardware configurations, and it's helpful if you can offer them a menu of choices to suit their needs. First of all, you will want to include links to sites where they can download free media players. Then, you'll want to give them as much information as possible for each file you offer, along with choices based on their connection speed. For any given file, the Web page should indicate what file formats are available (Windows Media Player or RealPlayer), what version of the software is required (such as RealPlayer 8.0), and what download speeds are available. As of this writing, the most considerate sites offer choices of three transmission speeds: 28.8 kps, 56 kps, and broadband (also labeled as T1, ADSL, or cable modem).

Audio files can be a compelling part of a newsroom operation. They are bandwidth friendly and offer authoritative quotes from company spokespersons, which can be used in print or broadcast coverage. Video files are currently less valuable. Streaming video is usually of poor quality, with a small image size, poor resolution, and few frames per second. This last feature gives online video that jerky look we've all seen. Figure 3.4 is a still image captured from a streaming video of Microsoft Chairman Bill Gates defending his company against attacks from the U.S. Justice Department. The

Figure 3.4 Microsoft Chairman Bill Gates responds to a U.S. Justice Department investigation using a streaming video presentation. The image resolution used in most streaming video is not suitable for print or television reproduction.

blurry quality of the photo is due to the low image resolution of the video feed and is not the fault of this book's printer. Still, streaming video, coupled with streaming audio, can provide authenticity and nuances that are meaningful for journalists—just not broadcast or print-quality graphics.

At the cutting edge of online media relations is using the newsroom to deliver broadcast quality video to media contacts. Video captured with a digital video camera can be offered for download over the Web. These files are too large to be viewed online through streaming video, but it's possible to offer them for download. Good netiquette here requires that you identify the video format, resolution, and file size. File sizes can easily run into gigabytes, putting a strain on your system if the files are popular. It's not unreasonable to require preregistration to access high-resolution images, audio, and broadcast-quality video, because making these files available to the public could cost the organization a considerable amount for hardware and software.

In the near future, it will become commonplace for companies to offer broadcast-quality digital video for download from the Web site. This function is a very effective form of public relations. If you can offer television stations, cable stations, and other Web sites high-quality video, you'll certainly expand the amount of coverage you get through these broadcast outlets.

Other Design Considerations

Events calendars can also be stored in a database and pulled into different sections of the Web site. Most companies will not have enough calendar entries to warrant database design. For those that do, one advantage of databasing these items is that the expiration date for each item can be part of the database, eliminating any embarrassment from past events appearing in the calendar.

When a corporation is involved in a crisis, the function of the online news room changes dramatically. The newsroom, in essence, becomes a war room. The difference is so important that I cover the subject in depth at the end of this chapter. For now, it is enough that you know that none of the normal operating procedures apply to companies in crisis and that a separate plan should be made for handling these situations.

What Should the Site Contain?

The newsroom functions as a guided tour to the organization through the eyes of a journalist. You have to first think like a journalist to be able to determine the content at the site. I've seen many ambitious newsrooms that make the assumption that journalists will be keenly interested in the activities of the organization and return every day for updates. This view is an unrealistic view of how the press operates. You can expect a visit by the media when they are working on a story, at which time they will want access to everything, neatly organized. Once the story is done, you probably won't see them again for weeks, months, or years—if ever.

For an excellent analysis of online newsroom content, I recommend an article in the August 20, 2000 issue of WebReview, which can be found at www.webreview.com, written by B. L. Ochman, president of www.whatsnextonline.com. Entitled "Creating an Online Press Room," the article is based on an analysis of 50 online newsrooms covering a wide spectrum of industries. Ochman argues for full disclosure, including detailed contact information and even links to unfavorable information about the company. I'll explore this last suggestion in the crisis management section later in this chapter. The article is well worth reading for the examples of interesting content offered in top newsrooms.

Let's take a look at a broad range of content you might want to offer a visiting journalist:

Current news. Headline news about the company; this news is usually prepared by the publicity department and is featured not only in the newsroom but also at the home page of the Web site

News release archive. An archive of news releases as far back as you care to go; preferably, this archive should be searchable by keyword, geographical location, and date

Staff profiles. Biographies of key staff, including management and the board of directors; profiles should include photos. These profiles are usually provided by human resources or investor relations.

Corporate history. A concise story of the company's history; this section of the newsroom can also include a mission statement and/or a statement of core values

Community activities. Information about the organization's philanthropic activities. This information is often presented as a combination of news releases covering current events and a newsletter archive chronicling the organization's efforts to improve the world.

Product and service descriptions. Information, including artwork, about the company's major products and services; this information is usually found elsewhere at the site but can be linked to from the newsroom

Calendar of events. This calendar would include things such as news conferences, shareholder meetings, public appearances, trade shows, and sponsored events. Any events that will be held at the Web site should be promoted.

Legislative initiatives. Position papers on pending legislation, providing both the media and legislative aids with detailed information to help them make the case for the company's position

Financial information. The company's current stock price; access to the latest annual report and an archive of previous annual reports; news releases for the latest earnings reports; and an archive of financial performance news releases. Much of this information can be accessed through links to an independent investor relations site.

Speeches and other transcripts. Many sites offer the full text of significant speeches made by company spokespersons. Chat transcripts can also be offered this way. Figure 3.5 shows transcripts offered at the Microsoft press room that appear adjacent to a news release. Microsoft offers hundreds of speeches and transcripts by dozens of the company's leading executives.

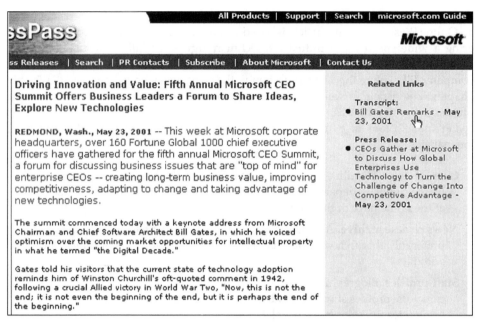

Figure 3.5 Microsoft does a good job of integrating news releases with related documents, such as speech transcripts.

Multimedia archives. Archives of news conferences, online presentations, and chat transcripts

Artwork. While artwork is seeded throughout the site, media contacts should be offered access to high-resolution artwork that is suitable for use in print publications and television broadcasts.

Press kits. For large companies with multiple products, services, subsidiaries, and/or brands, online press kits are a real time saver for journalists. Instead of having all the newsroom content in large, searchable databases, content related to specific products or companies is gathered together for the media into handy kits that contain all the news releases, product information, artwork, and contact information related to that product or company.

Contact information. A list of contacts and their areas of responsibility, with phone numbers and e-mail addresses, is very helpful for the press. If you are concerned about divulging this much information to the public and opt for generic feedback or inquiry e-mail addresses instead, you need to make a commitment to processing that e-mail promptly. An inquiry from a reporter on a tight deadline shouldn't be lost in a pile of feedback responses.

An opt-in news service. To assist those media contacts who are interested in following your company, you should offer an e-mail notification service to alert them to breaking stories and news of events. Some sites will have multiple newsletters, allowing press contacts to be more specific about the stories in which they are interested. It's a good idea to tell journalists what the alerts will contain and how often to expect them. For example, the release can be sent weekly or when there is major breaking news.

The content of online newsrooms has become fairly standardized in recent years. You can turn to one you admire and simply copy the format. A friend of mine, Jeffrey DeMarrais, developed an award-winning online newsroom for www.GE.com. He included an archive of past CEOs with photographs and was pleasantly surprised to see the images and information reprinted in a *New York Times* article. Barry Forward, executive vice-president of www.Reputations.com, a public relations firm, makes the point that journalists love calendars of events—but not when all the entries are ancient history.

This statement brings me to the topic of things you *don't* need in online newsrooms. You don't need anything you can't maintain, so if you have a small company, you have to think about whether it's really worth devoting much effort to an online newsroom. Perhaps all you need is contact information for a media relations person? Don't knock yourself out providing detailed art and graphics if the press has shown no interest in your site. You can accomplish your media goals with news releases, phone calls, and prompt assistance when requested.

You don't need feedback threads or discussion areas at your site. Trust me, the press doesn't need a forum on your site, nor do you want to police one, and you don't want the whole world to read reporters' critical comments about your operations. You don't need chat facilities unless you provide them in combination with access-restricted online events. You don't need to update the site every day to keep it fresh. When you've got news to share, add it to the site, and make sure any calendars are current.

News Wires and News Feeds

I had been a book publicist for many years when I first learned the secret to getting media coverage. My awakening resulted from a conversation with Steven Schragis, president of The Carol Group, a New York book publisher. A master at getting media attention, one of Schragis's titles got a front-page write-up in *The Wall Street Journal* that catapulted the book from obscurity onto bestseller lists everywhere and into translation in more than 50 languages. I commented on his good fortune, and Mr. Schragis sharply informed me that his coverage in *The Journal* was not a matter of chance. From that brief telephone encounter, I realized I needed to take my publicity efforts to the next level. Instead of giving the media an interesting story idea, I began to give them the whole enchilada: a complete story, not just part of it.

What does it take to give the media a complete story? Let's say you want to promote a new product. A traditional approach would be to issue a news release touting the features and benefits of the new product and offer a knowledgeable spokesperson as interview bait. The expanded approach is to offer a whole story: information about the product, a spokesperson, five ordinary people whose lives were improved by the product, five people who hate the product, government employees who have oversight on issues surrounding the product, members of academia for and against the product, plus still photos, video, historical background, and facts and figures.

It's a lot more work to assemble this kind of promotional campaign, but the results are amazing. For one thing, you don't have to worry as much about the media stealing your idea but leaving your product out of the story; you build the story around the product so it doesn't work without it. Another reason this strategy works is that so many media outlets have been reduced to skeleton crews of administrative staff; they welcome complete story packages that require little effort or expense on their part. If you want to get a client on a TV talk show, you don't offer the producer your client; rather, you script an entire program and offer the whole show. You'll see this strategy reflected throughout this book in the production of chats, seminars, and other online content. In this section, I'll focus on how you can increase your news coverage tenfold, not by sending out news releases, but by sending out news.

The Power of Becoming a News Provider

In 1999, before the Internet crash of 2000, I was on the advisory board of a career services Web site called www.myjobsearch.com (MJS). One of my projects there was to take the company's content on the road. Instead of relying on traffic coming to the Web site, we wanted to put our content and brand onto high-traffic Web sites. Seeing that www.Monster.com dominated the job postings business on most high-traffic sites, we offered a service that the monster had missed: live career coaching. It took three months, but I negotiated deals with five top venues: Lycos, America Online, CompuServe, Talk City, and World Without Borders. I delayed any announcements until I could promote them all at once, hoping for a bigger media bang. When the news release went out on November 1, it was greeted with a great big yawn. The coverage was minimal, just one more partnership press release of little interest in the megadeal dot.com world.

Three weeks later, myjobsearch.com issued a news release that more than 90 percent of resumes sent out over the Internet get no response from the employers soliciting them—not even an acknowledgement. The release was an attempt to show that in the job search, as in so many other areas, the Internet fails to live up to its hype. The numbers were based on a totally unscientific Web site poll. Even so, the release was widely covered, picked up by a wire service, syndicated to newspapers throughout the United States, and a TV news spot about it was syndicated by a major broadcast network. This non-story got incredible coverage, bringing the myjobsearch.com brand into U.S. households more effectively than anything else we had tried. That story launched a new venture: WorkWire.

If the media was going to cover this unscientific poll with such zeal, taking our brand to places it had never been, imagine what they might do with real news. Because the research department at myjobsearch.com was unearthing all kinds of stories about workplace issues, we decided to provide a synopsis of those stories to media contacts. We hired a graphics firm to produce a daily chart for us, similar to *USA Today's* front-page "Snap Shot." And we began negotiations with a legitimate polling firm to conduct surveys for us. The hope was that we could become the AP of workplace news. Instead of settling for the miniscule coverage we got from our own news releases, we would go for the brand penetration of being cited as the source in article after article. And it wouldn't hurt to slip news items about myjobsearch.com itself into the wire delivered daily to the media.

MJS spent months building WorkWire and was producing daily issues on a trial basis for several weeks. Then came the dot.com crash. The funding was pulled out, and I never got to see exactly how much media attention you could get with this strategy. But you don't have to be a rocket scientist to see the potential. Just run a search at Yahoo! for "newswire" and see how many companies are making this strategy pay.

The Tall Ship NewsWire (Figure 3.6) distributes news about sailing, wooden boats, and anything having to do with, yes, tall ships. Their terms of service make blatant the branding strategy behind such a wire service: "All photographs and those articles used 'as is' must carry the 'TSNW' (for Tall Ship NewsWire) identifier in captions and datelines. If you violate any of these terms, your permission to use the material automatically terminates and you must immediately destroy any copies you have made of the material."

The *Environmental News Service* (ENS) is a fascinating example of harvesting an important media niche. The service claims to be independently owned and operated, stating on the "About Us" page that "[ENS] is not affiliated with any business, industry, government or environmental group." But ENS sells a news release distribution service called "E-wire," charging companies a minimum of $325 to distribute a news release. In a paragraph explaining the service, ENS states that "E-Wire is affiliated with PR Newswire, the world's leading distributor of press releases." The company has a

Figure 3.6 The Tall Ship NewsWire is an example of a small niche news service. It builds brand awareness for the company through caption and byline credits in conventional media coverage.

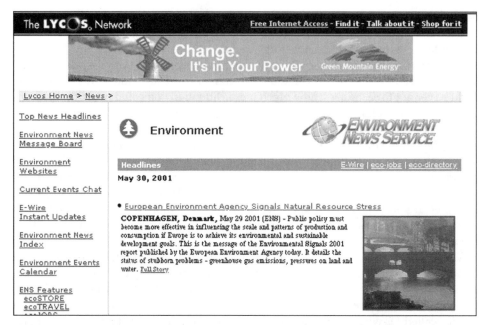

Figure 3.7 Environmental News Service distributes news about the environment to an impressive list of media outlets and Web sites. The site is supported by advertising, sponsorships, and a fee-based news release distribution service.

partnership with Lycos, which hosts the ENS Web site, and Lycos sells advertising on the site through the DoubleClick Network. On the day I visited, banner ads included a Doubleday book, WebMD, and the eco-friendly company shown in Figure 3.7.

In addition to the Lycos alliance, ENS feeds environmental news to MSNBC and the Wired news service. A look at E-wire's distribution list shows what amazing reach you can get with your own news wire: thousands of media outlets are listed, including television stations, radio stations, news syndicates, magazines, journals, newspapers, and newsletters—with a substantial number of international outlets. The E-wire archive indicates that numerous large companies—many with poor environmental track records—use the service to distribute news releases. I don't believe a company like this one could achieve the impressive media penetration they have without upholding high standards for the quality of their news service. Still, it shows that if you build a reputation for a quality news feed with the media, you can use that feed to build brand awareness for your own company.

Sometimes the chain of ownership on these newswires can be quite obscure. MP3newswire.net distributes news about the popular audio file format along with links for downloading software and purchasing MP3 players (Figure 3.8). There is no copyright notice or usage restrictions posted at the site. A feedback e-mail address is from the domain "optiline.net," which is a site run by Cablevision, the large telecommunications conglomerate. It's unclear whether Cablevision operates MP3newswire.net or whether it is the project of a Cablevision subscriber.

MP3_newswire.net_

Beginners - MP3 Links - Top Search Engines - Expansion Memory - Best Buys - Accessories

MP3 PORTABLE PLAYERS

Creative Nomad Jukebox - Review: 6GB player
Rio Volt Portable CD MP3 Player - Review:
plays MP3 and WMA CDs
Rio PMP 600 - Review: 32MB player
Nike PSA[Play 120] - Review: 64MB for the
gym.
RCA Lyra2 -Review: 64MB with an FM radio in
a brushed aluminum case
Rio 800: 128 MB player for $237
RaveMP2100 - Review: 64MB with voice
recording and electronic organizer.
RaveMP2200 - Review: 64MB player
Rave MP2300 - Review: 80MB Click! drive
portable.
Sony Memory Stick Walkman - Review:
ATRAC3 player

TOP MP3 STORIES

Review: Morpheus (Music City)
The closest clone to the Napster experience?

We Test Drive the Rio Volt MP3/CD
Portable Player

Winamp 3 Preview
Some info on the upcoming version of Winamp.

Review: Microsoft Windows Media Player
7.0

Universal Buys MP3.com
The record industry has now acquired most of the
major Net Music properties.

SINGLES

Price Drop! Creative's 6GB
NOMAD Jukebox can be ordered from
Amazon for $264. Available in Blue
and Silver.

Figure 3.8   MP3newswire.net distributes news about the popular audio file software. It's a mystery who owns and operates this site.

Designing a Good News Feed

When you think about it, most large companies are already doing all the research they need to create a good news feed. Just by keeping up on the news related to the subjects you are most concerned about, you are gathering information that could be very useful to journalists. If you have a clipping service or news monitoring service of some sort, you are gathering even more leads. All you need to do to become a news provider is organize that research, employ a good copywriter to turn it into a newsletter, and format it for online delivery.

The newswire I designed for myjobsearch.com had the following content elements:

Picture of the Day. A simple graphic illustrating the "stat of the day," usually drawn from the feature story

Feature story. The top news story of the day; the feature story was no more than a few paragraphs long and often cited multiple sources for supporting documentation

Story leads. Three to five story leads, each with a headline and summary paragraph written by a wire service copywriter. These were almost always summaries of news items unearthed from conventional media outlets, research organizations, think tanks, and colleges and universities. Our preference was to gather story leads related to the feature story so that the whole issue had a theme running through it, but you have to take what's available for a daily wire service.

Fast stats. Three to five "factoids," each one sentence long, with sources cited. These were often stats culled from the story lead articles or feature story sources, once again providing a continuity of theme.

Credits. More or less the "masthead," with writing and production credits, copyright and disclaimer notices, and contact information

Most of the niche wire services I've seen don't bother with a feature story and just go with one-paragraph story leads. I think the graphics and the factoids are fantastic elements for a newswire because they feed the media's insatiable hunger for tidbits and filler. Plus, the artwork is protected by copyright, ensuring that the wire service will be credited in the copyright notice any time the graphic is used by a reputable media outlet.

As far as writing style goes, it's important to have your own staff write the story leads, the feature story, the factoids, and the graphic caption. This process protects you from copyright infringement that would occur if you used someone else's summary verbatim, and it also protects you from unauthorized duplication. An original story in *The Washington Post* is owned by the *Post*, but your one-paragraph summary of that story is completely legal and is owned by you. We were blessed with a great headline writer at myjobsearch.com, Jeff Westover, who came up with humorous, snappy, succinct headlines for the story leads, crisp captions for the artwork, and ingenious turns of phrase for the factoids. Believe me, the media love getting carefully crafted copy in a newswire, and a good headline writer can double or triple the story pickup rate.

One of the services you are providing the media is research. The items are called "Story Leads" for a reason. They're meant to point journalists in the direction of a good story. All our story leads contained URLs to take journalists to source documents so they wouldn't have to fumble around to verify our numbers or expand on the story. Here's an example of a story lead from WorkWire:

```
=> Working Americans See Nothing But Net At Work

Rutgers University has published a new work trends survey showing
that American workers are enthusiastically plugging in computers and
logging on the Internet. Working Americans spend an average of 3
hours per day at work on a computer. One-third of all workers spend
at least an hour a day on the Internet at work and 14% report spend-
ing at least half of their work day online. An overwhelming percent-
age of workers from across all demographic groups report that they
need more computer skills to achieve career goals. Over 44% complain
that the computer training they require is not being supplied in the
workplace. For complete details of the survey, visit this link:

    http://uc.rutgers.edu/medrel/viewArticle.phtml?ArticleID=357
```

One of the great reasons for developing your own news feed is that you get to frame stories for journalists. For example, the Rutgers survey that we mentioned contained a lot of information about work trends. The WorkWire staff chose to focus on the importance of computers in the work place because, hey, the company is a dot.com. A major product of the company is online training, so naturally we felt that the statistic about employees wanting more training was compelling. Certainly, a journalist can visit the Rutgers site and take the story in a whole different direction, but the power of suggestion is impressive. Chances are that a journalist would not follow up on the lead unless they were interested in pursuing the story we framed—in this case, about the penetration of computers and the Internet into the workplace. Having your own wire service allows you to filter news through your own perspective of what is important and why.

If you don't abuse that privilege by flagrantly slanting your coverage, you will be able to subtly push your perspective through to the media, becoming a trusted source for story leads and getting great branding.

Any time we did Web site polling that had interesting results, it would make the WorkWire. While these polls are unscientific, they often tipped us off to stories we weren't aware of. For example, a poll showing that most employees would switch jobs for as little as a 10 percent pay increase put us on the search for employee dissatisfaction stories, and we found plenty of legitimate research that supported our Web poll. One story we broke this way was that long-time employees were upset about perks given to new recruits while loyal workers received only nominal raises. An unscientific Web poll put us onto the story, and U.S. Bureau of Labor statistics backed up the low rates of pay increases while major media outlets had plenty of stories we could cite about the tight labor market and outrageous recruiting bonuses. These stories got great coverage in the media, reaching hundreds of outlets and always carrying our brand name.

Another tactic used to bolster WorkWire was that we offered to put journalists in touch with "real people" who would share their personal experiences. I've seen many newsrooms offer a similar service. For example, Microsoft will hook you up with "real users" of its products for stories about PowerPoint or Office or Internet Explorer. This function is all part of the strategy of giving the media the whole story—not just a story idea. If you can consistently give media contacts story ideas coupled with research, easy access to source documents, graphics, and even "real people" to interview, you will soon become a trusted and reliable source and you can expect to see your agenda and your brand getting substantial media coverage.

Formatting News Feeds

There are several ways to deliver a news wire with corresponding formatting issues. The preferred way is to deliver it via e-mail. You should review the instructions in the chapter on formatting newsletters. The layout is similar to other e-mail dispatches: ASCII text, short line length, and brief copy. Hyperlinks to story sources can be embedded into the copy. Graphics should not be embedded or attached to the wire; rather, journalists should be given a link to the graphic on your Web site.

You can also deliver the service via fax. In this case, you should design a shell in either a word processing or page layout program. You can cut and paste from the e-mail version into the fax version or create the fax version first and save it as text for the e-mail version. For the fax version, you can use all the graphic design you want: fancy fonts, larger point sizes, bold, italic, and so on. If you are going to include artwork, make sure it looks good in black and white, because that's how it will be seen at the other end of the fax machine. You might test any color artwork on a photocopier first to be sure it reproduces well in black and white. The fax version should include a URL where journalists can find the artwork on your Web site so that they can grab a color version suitable for reproduction.

Faxing can be done through your own computer system, or you can contract with firms that will fax your release for you. These companies are often more economical than faxing yourself. You send them an e-mail message containing a list of fax numbers with the fax version of the document as an attachment, and they distribute it to the list. One such firm is CYNET, Inc. at www.cynetinc.com, although I'm sure you can find others.

For storage at the Web site, the formatting issues get a little tricky. If you want to produce a searchable archive of story leads, you have to database them, and that means tagging them with search parameter codes such as subject, date, city, state, industry, keyword, and so on. The artwork can also be databased. If you're really ambitious, you can database the factoids, sorting them by subject, but that might be more work than they're worth. One advantage of producing a news wire is that you generate news content for your own Web site, which can be pulled onto your home page or your newsroom or used in other areas of your site. Good databasing makes it easier to syndicate your news content to other Web sites, similar to the deal struck between Environmental News Service and MSNBC (mentioned previously).

Finding Contacts for Syndication

How do you get journalists to subscribe to your newswire? You can solicit subscriptions from your Web site, not only in the newsroom but also on your home page. You don't have to limit distribution to the media; other people who use your Web site might be interested in subscribing, including customers and suppliers. These subscriptions can be managed with off-the-shelf mailing list database software, covered more extensively in the chapter on newsletters. If your wire service is good enough, you might be able to charge a subscription fee or spin it off to a standalone Web site, but you risk reducing the media coverage you get by a substantial amount. For most companies, I think it's wiser to consider this cheap PR rather than a revenue-generating item.

You can also solicit subscriptions via e-mail. Using a database of media e-mail contacts, you can send a sample issue to people you think will be interested and ask them to opt-in. A better strategy might be to start sending it and include a link to opt out and just keep sending it until someone declines to receive it any longer. I describe in detail how to build or buy such a list of e-mail addresses in the chapter on news releases.

Your newswire is an excellent source of copy for a printed newsletter. You can include news items in an existing newsletter and solicit subscriptions that way. You can also use a direct mail campaign to solicit subscriptions. Because print communicates better than e-mail, you can produce a beautifully formatted printed sample copy and use it to lure e-mail subscribers.

As you get experience with the newswire format and build a reputation for quality, you can explore syndicating your content to high-traffic Web sites. There are many markets for niche news coverage, such as trade associations and organizations, trade journals, and regional or special-interest Web sites. If you can't persuade these outlets to pay for reprint rights to the wire service, you should be able to extract a decent amount of advertising in exchange for the news content. Places such as iSyndicate will broker your content for you, but for a narrowly targeted news feed, you probably know the players better than they do—and you'll be more persuasive making a case for your content.

A sophisticated online syndication program will require much more rigorous databasing than we hinted at earlier. Formatting issues will have to be resolved on a partner-by-partner basis. Many of your outlets might want a custom news feed, containing only stories on certain subjects or related to specific geographical regions. You might end up producing a daily news wire but syndicating custom versions only once a week. Designing an infrastructure for these advanced syndication operations is beyond the scope of this book. If you find your little wire service growing to such levels, you'll need to seek out a better instructor than me.

Online Presentations

Online presentations represent a new twist on existing technology, which I believe will have a significant impact on the field of online public relations. This technology lets people create PowerPoint presentations and upload them to intranets or to the Internet for streaming delivery to a remote audience. The technology involved isn't all that new, but the powerful public relations uses for it have barely been explored.

Probably everyone reading this book has been exposed to a PowerPoint presentation at some time. Part of the Microsoft Office family of software, PowerPoint allows users to create simple slide shows which are then projected onto screens during seminars, workshops, and other live presentations. PowerPoint presentations are ubiquitous at sales conferences, trade shows, and conventions. In their simplest and most annoying form, each slide contains an outline of material covered by the speaker. Imaginative presenters avoid this redundancy and use the slides to supplement the verbal presentation, not repeat it. In any case, it is a type of software and a style of presenting that is nearly universal; many PR professionals are familiar with creating and viewing these programs.

In 1997, PowerPoint added a feature to convert slides into HTML for uploading to a Web site. A search of the Web will turn up numerous university and college sites containing PowerPoint slides from class lectures. Without the accompanying speaker, however, these static slide shows fail to capture the vitality of a live presentation. If PowerPoint presentations are boring in person, how much more boring are they without a speaker?

Delivering PowerPoint Presentations Online

In approximately 1998, RealNetworks, the famous streaming media company, produced the first version of RealPresenter Plug-In for PowerPoint '97, allowing audio to be added to slideshows and allowing these presentations to be served over a network. Like all of this new technology, you had to be technically adept to create these multimedia presentations, refine them, store them, and deliver them. The required skills and knowledge limited users to IT specialists.

In 2000, a company called presenter.com introduced a product called Instant Presenter that offers compelling features for people wanting to distribute PowerPoint presentations over the Web. With Instant Presenter, you simply upload the PowerPoint presentation, phone in the narration, and presenter.com does all the rest. It's fast, simple, and requires no more technological prowess than browsing the Web. With Instant Presenter, creators of PowerPoint presentations can now distribute them without support from IT.

One of the things I like so much about these online presentations is that they are bandwidth friendly. While you have the option of incorporating streaming video into the presentations, I don't recommend it. The video is small, of poor quality, slows everything down, and distracts the viewer from the slides and narration. The best presentations incorporate a still photo of the speaker, a streaming audio soundtrack, and a sequence of PowerPoint slides timed to the narration. They are simple, fast, and compelling.

Who Uses Online Presentations?

The most enthusiastic adopters of this technology have been colleges and universities. PowerPoint presentations have been used for years to supposedly "spice up" classroom lectures. Universities with substantial computing faculties and staffs have pioneered much of the software related to the Internet, including putting PowerPoint presentations online. These presentations have become bedrocks of the distance-learning movement. The best tutorials for creating these presentations can be found not at the software manufacturer sites but at college and university distance-learning sites.

Online presentations received a second round of support from corporate trainers. Distributing training modules over networks is far cheaper and less disruptive than bringing the audience together at a specific time and place. Sales representatives were not far behind the corporate trainers. Salespeople are very familiar with using Power-Point software and embraced the opportunity to reach remote buyers with a powerful packaged pitch.

One company exploiting the capabilities of online presentations is Pricewaterhouse-Coopers, which uses them to distribute annual technology forecasts. You can sample these programs at the presenter.com library. AIMS Multimedia, a leader in distributed training programs, offers more than 8,000 programs for law enforcement professionals, government agencies, teachers, and others. Not all of these programs use the streaming PowerPoint presentation format. In the public relations arena, the well-known advocacy group Public Agenda uses Instant Presenter modules to distribute research and opinions on issues such as childcare and education (see Figure 3.9).

Public Relations Uses for Online Presentations

It doesn't take much of an imagination to see how useful this new technology can be for public relations professionals. Any sort of presentation can be quickly uploaded online, narrated, and modified as needed. Here are some ideas for incorporating online presentations into public relations practices:

Investor relations. In addition to business plans, PowerPoint presentations can also be created for annual reports or even quarterly earnings statements. They can augment prospectuses for new stock offerings or other capital-raising initiatives.

Crisis communications. Presentations can be made outlining the nature of a crisis and the efforts an organization is taking to handle the crisis. The presentation is one more way an organization has to relate its position, frame the debate, and provide factual data to those who need it. The voiceover communicates much

Figure 3.9 Steve Farkas, director of research for Public Agenda, presents the advocacy group's findings on childcare by using an online presentation at presenter.com.

better than silent Web pages that an organization is taking the crisis seriously and provides authoritative quotes that can be used in media coverage.

Media relations. A PowerPoint presentation is an excellent way to explain to the media what your company is all about, giving journalists the option of jumping around in the presentation along with the ability to capture slides for reproduction in print publications, on television, or on the Web. These presentations can be used to explain mergers, acquisitions, restructurings, or to introduce new products and services.

Government relations. A slide show is a fine way to present an organization's position on issues of the day and to give legislators and their assistants factual ammunition to support a stand on proposed policies or legislation.

Employee relations. Slides can be used to explain management changes, changes to benefit plans, new initiatives, or simply to provide sales representatives and others with information they can use to bolster their claims for products and services.

Speechwriting. Instant Presenter can also be used to help practice and refine speeches. There's nothing quite like hearing your narration played back for finding weak wording or bad timing in public presentations. After uploading the first draft of a speech, revisions can be made based on how the speech plays —not just how it reads.

How to Create Online Presentations

Instant Presenter is produced by presenter.com. You can create a slideshow for free and they will host it for one month. You simply upload the PowerPoint slides, phone in your narration, and you're done. Annual licenses start at $600 for 20 presentations with up to 100 viewers per presentation per month. The presentations are hosted at www.presenter.com, but you can link to them so that it appears that they are hosted on your own Web site. Paying customers get traffic reports and online account-management tools.

Alternatives are available from RealNetworks. Their RealSlideshow software allows you to create presentations with streaming audio, and the RealPresenter software lets you add streaming video (which I do not recommend). Both programs come in free demonstration versions with limited production control and limited distribution: The presentations can only be used on a private network, not online. The full-featured versions of RealSlideshow ($99) and RealPresenter ($199) give you more design options and the ability to upload presentations to a public server for delivery over the Web.

I should include a few caveats about the RealNetworks software. First, Macintosh versions are not available. Second, you can't offer your presentations from your own Web site unless you have a RealSystem Server, which starts at $2,000. Sites such as Yahoo! will serve your programs for you, but that's an unacceptable solution for many companies. Third, while the Real programs give you a lot more control over the design of your presentation, you will probably need assistance from IT or a designer to take advantage of those features. That's why I like Instant Presenter so much: You are limited to their design format, but it's so easy to use.

Microsoft PowerPoint 2000 incorporates the ability to broadcast presentations on intranets and the Internet. The instructions for using this feature are anything but clear, however. As with RealNetworks, it requires access to a server, in this case the Windows Media Services (formerly NetShow Services). You can find the rather confusing instructions at Microsoft's Web site. Microsoft will without a doubt improve this capability in future PowerPoint releases.

In the coming months, we will start to see more of these presentations in online press centers, and they will become important tools for communicating information about company products, earnings, and policies to a wide variety of interested people.

Online News Conferences

As careful readers have probably noted, I can be a bit of a curmudgeon when it comes to whiz-bang technology. Time and again, I argue for plain ASCII text documents, simple Web page design, and brevity. But online news conferences are one area in which I'm wondering what is taking people so long to get on the boat? Internet technology allows companies and other organizations to reach the global media market for a fraction of the cost of satellite broadcasts or in-person events. As more and more journalists work away from the main office, the Internet is becoming the *only way* to reach them. Why there aren't 100 online news conferences a day is a mystery to me.

There are many benefits of hosting online news conferences. As already stated, two motivational reasons are the relatively low cost and the ability to reach a geographical dispersed audience. Online news conferences increase media coverage by giving journalists an authoritative spokesperson who can be quoted in news coverage. They are terrific for responding to news events quickly, making sure your voice is heard while the story is still hot. They can be promoted easily, resulting in greater exposure for the company through event listings and other publicity. They're still cutting-edge, helping boost an image of technological savvy and possibly boosting stock prices, as well. And while they require users to have broadband access to appreciate the news conference, most of the people in the target audience have high-speed Internet connections.

Do you need another reason to start conducting online news conferences? The answer is two words: fair disclosure. New Securities and Exchange Commission regulations require publicly traded companies to share information about material events with all investors. No less of an authority than Fraser P. Seitel, author of the bedrock textbook *The Practice of Public Relations*, says that companies are using Webcasts to satisfy regulation fair disclosure requirements.

The main drawback to hosting online news conferences is that they can be technologically complex to orchestrate, and a botched event can result in a negative impression. Many different types of software are involved in broadcasting online news conferences. The software is not standardized, and many of the components are in version 1.0—barely out of beta. The hardware required—mostly servers—can be massive, especially if adequate backup servers are used. Finally, there are simply not enough people trained to produce these conferences. But all of these factors will change for the better in the coming months and years.

To illustrate how difficult it can be to pull off a full multimedia-quality news conference, consider that Ford Motor Company, Intel, Dell, and even Microsoft outsource these events. The reigning king of online conferences is Broadcast.com, acquired by Yahoo! and now called Yahoo! Broadcast Services (Figure 3.10). Yahoo!'s Webcast Studio claims a successful delivery rate of more than 99 percent, according to spokesperson C. J. Fretheim. He points to Yahoo!'s infrastructure as the main reason and claims that more than half of all the streaming that takes place online is served by Yahoo!

As far as costs go, hosting a live news conference on Yahoo! or on one of the other online broadcast services (Evoke, PlaceWare, Digevent, and so on) starts at about $5,000. It's difficult to get comparable quotes from these different services because there are so many variables involved. But when you compare the cost to conducting a satellite news conference, which starts at upwards of $10,000 and can run into six figures, you can see why companies need to get educated about this new technology.

Producing an Online News Conference

As you begin preparing to produce an online news conference, you'll have to make many decisions about the format. Here are the common variables you'll have to address, along with my recommendations:

Live or canned? A live news conference is a better news hook, because journalists know they will be getting the scoop when everyone else does. But this benefit

Resource Center

Yahoo! Broadcast Services

Tools

Yahoo! Broadcast Services can enable business webcasts with a variety of 'cool tools'. In order to enhance communications and create an interactive experience for viewers, any of these can be added to a product launch, shareholder meeting, or any other business critical broadcast.

- Flash Introduction
- 'Push' or 'User-Driven' Slides
- Phonebytes
- Question Manager
- Report Manager

- Presentation Manager
- Embedded Video Player
- Multicast in Windows Media Player
- Broadband Feed
- Tell-A-Friend

Figure 3.10   Yahoo! purchased Broadcast.com and merged its operations into Yahoo! Broadcast Services, which is now the largest provider of online conferencing services in the world.

comes with the risk of technological failure and potential embarrassment if events don't go according to plan (for example, a protester interrupts the proceedings). With an event that is recorded and archived, there is the potential for editing, but that reduces credibility. I would opt for the live event unless through experience you found that the problems outweigh the benefits.

Interactive or not? You have several options for adding interactivity to the Webcast. You can allow people to ask questions through a Web interface, which adds technological complexity to the proceedings. You can include a conference phone call with the Webcast, which substantially adds to the cost. My recommendation is to either hold the news conference in front of a live audience and only accept questions from that audience, or if there is no live audience, accept questions through a chat-style Web interface.

Video or audio? The advantage of using streaming video is that it communicates more powerfully than an audio feed, giving some sense of nuance that can be observed. Is the speaker hostile, relaxed, nervous, or lost? But using video effectively shuts out all but fast-access participants—it's definitely not suited for the consumer market. And streaming video is not broadcast quality, so you don't get the benefit of seeing clips used on the nightly news. Audio, on the other hand, is bandwidth friendly and makes the presentation much easier to understand. My recommendation is to use a still photograph of the speaker combined with streaming audio and to skip the streaming video unless there are unusual circumstances, such as a celebrity appearance or a crisis situation. Figure 3.11 is a still from a live online news conference sponsored by Ford Motor Company during the Firestone Tire crisis in 2001.

Slide shows and Web tours. If you plan to use visual aids during your presentation, you'll want to be sure that the venue can accommodate them. For audio-only presentations, these visuals are essential for keeping the audience

Figure 3.11 An online news conference featuring Jacques Nasser, president and CEO of Ford Motor Company, during the Firestone tire recall of 2001. Crisis situations are one instance where streaming video is recommended for online news conferences in order to better communicate leadership.

attentive. They also add value for journalists if you make broadcast-quality copies of the slides available from your Web site or upon request. The most popular visual aid is to stream a PowerPoint slide presentation during the news conference. Another popular option is a Web tour, where a portion of the screen is directed to Web sites either specified in advance or selected on the fly. My recommendation is to include a slide show of some sort with a streaming audio program and skip the streaming video.

Streaming speed. You'll want to provide a variety of broadcast speeds so that participants can optimize their experience. If you're using video, you'll want to offer a 56 kps stream along with a broadband stream (about 100 kps). You won't be able to successfully reach people with slower Internet connections. For an audio news conference, you can offer four rates of speed: 14.4 kps, 28.8 kps, 56 kps, and broadband. The more speeds you offer, the larger the potential audience but the higher the price. My recommendation is to offer a variety of speeds your first few times out, then delete speeds used by fewer than five percent of your audience.

File format. The two most popular choices today are Windows Media Player and Real Player. You should offer both formats. You should also tell people what minimum versions of these programs are required and provide links to free download sites for the programs. In the near future, these programs will be seamlessly integrated with Web browsers, making your job a little easier.

Number of people attending. Some of the online conferencing providers charge you based on the number of actual connections. Others charge based on the capacity of the facilities you use. Yahoo! Broadcast Services can accommodate thousands of users per event and doesn't price separately based on news conference attendance. If you require preregistration to attend the event, you can size the facilities accordingly. Otherwise, trial and error will help you estimate attendance for future events.

Duration of the event. Many service providers charge by the minute, so you'll want to set a limit on how long the event will last. If you aren't taking questions, you can time the presentation and purchase the smallest amount of time you need. If you're taking questions, allow for at least a half hour. Yahoo! Broadcast Services provides up to an hour with its basic package. The extra time is helpful because it can take five or 10 minutes for the audience to assemble, then you have introductions, a presentation, and Q&A. If you plan on taking questions, I recommend buying a one-hour time slot. Otherwise, try to keep your presentation to about five minutes to reduce the file size of the archived copy.

In-house or contract production. The expense for serving an online news conference can skyrocket if you have to hire a professional broadcasting team to stage and capture the event. With streaming video, you need to consider such things as staging, lighting, art direction, makeup, and camera angles. But because the result is not broadcast-quality video, you don't have to worry about seeing an ugly clip on TV. For audio, you need microphones and someone doing sound. The method you choose will mostly be dictated by your budget. If you plan to do a lot of these, you should try to hire in-house staff capable of producing an acceptable show. You don't need veteran broadcasting professionals for this kind of low-level event. You might want to contact local television stations to see whether they offer these services. Figure 3.12 shows how WWL-TV in New Orleans produces Webcasts of news conferences by a NFL football franchise, the New Orleans Saints.

Once you have decided on the configuration of the event, you can start thinking about exactly how the event should proceed. It helps to write some sort of script. If you use PowerPoint to script the event, you can save some of the slides for streaming during the news conference. You'll need to title and date the event and identify any speakers who will be used. Most online news conferences I've attended begin with an introductory speaker who then turns the microphone over to the featured speaker. The introduction gives latecomers time to connect to the proceedings. The main speaker should be someone who has the weight of authority; media contacts are not impressed by news conferences conducted by junior staff from the PR or IR departments. Hopefully, your main speakers will be well prepared and rehearsed and will know how to advance the slide show portion of the program.

Before you start entertaining questions from the audience, it's a good idea to plug ancillary resources that are available from your Web site. For example, you might let everyone know that an archived copy of the program will be available at the Web site, or a transcript, or the PowerPoint slides, or artwork suitable for print and broadcast

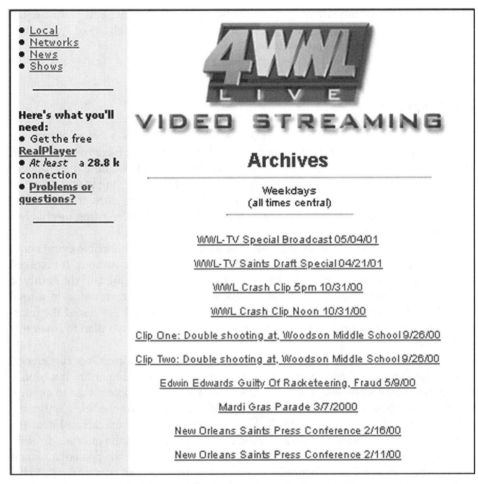

Figure 3.12 Local television stations have the production facilities and staff to produce video news conferences and might also have the resources to stream them online. This image shows how a television station in New Orleans hosts a news conference for the local football franchise.

reproduction. By offering these items upon request, you can flush out some of the important media contacts who might be lurking in the audience.

Handling questions can be tricky. You'll want a moderator for each method of sending questions, whether live, on the phone, or online. Taking questions online is easiest because you can simply ignore stupid or repetitive questions. With the phone, you'll want some way to cut off people who display inappropriate behavior or don't know when to stop.

After the program is over, you can edit the recorded version and archive it online. Every online conference provider I've dealt with records a copy of the event, and most of them will store it at their Web sites for a limited time. The copyright to the event adheres to the company sponsoring the event and not the broadcaster (though you'll want to check the boilerplate on any production agreements you sign). Because you own the copyright, you can store the presentation on your own Web site or syndicate it to other sites online, such as news bureaus.

Troubleshooting Online News Conferences

The best way to avoid difficulties with online news conferences is to test everything well in advance and establish emergency procedures. You don't have to run through an entire mock news conference, but you do have to make sure that the microphones are recording properly and that the digital streaming of the recording is working. You should test the mechanism for delivering slide shows and Web tours. If a telephone conference call is involved, test the phone numbers and the conferencing mechanism to make sure they work.

The chapter of this book covering online seminars describes a horrible event sponsored by Nielsen//NetRatings and produced by Evoke Communications. It involved a Web presentation with PowerPoint slides, a conference phone call, and the ability to ask questions online. The Web display never worked, however, resulting in a total meltdown of the seminar. I'm sure Nielsen//NetRatings must have tested the interface prior to the program, but they didn't have an adequate backup plan to cover this contingency.

The first option in a backup plan is to cancel or reschedule the news conference. That's what Nielsen//NetRatings should have done. If a vital element of the conference goes down, it's probably better to reschedule and fix the problem than to attempt carrying on without it. For an online news conference, I would reschedule if either the audio feed or the slide show failed. If the video feed fails but you can still hear the audio and follow the slides, that's not cause for abandonment. If the interface for asking questions fails, I would opt to proceed with the formal part of the presentation and take questions from a live audience if available. It helps if you can communicate to the audience when the rescheduled event will happen. For example, if you anticipate trouble and discuss it with your online conferencing supplier, you can plan that if technical difficulties force aborting the event, you will try again in one hour or one day. That way, if trouble strikes, you're prepared with an alternative date and time.

A large company such as Yahoo! Broadcast Services has experience in handling these events and dealing with trouble. They have backup servers for their backup servers. Still, this medium is relatively new, there are a lot of bugs, and no one can protect you from major Internet pipeline breaks or servers shut down due to hackers. You should quiz your online conferencing provider about what will happen if each element of the presentation breaks down. If they don't have good answers, you might want to pay a little more money and buy some peace of mind with a more experienced and prepared provider.

Promoting Online News Conferences

E-mail news releases are the best way to promote news conferences, especially if the conference is in response to breaking news. Consult the chapter of this book devoted to e-mail news releases for detailed instructions on writing, formatting, and delivering these documents. News releases promoting live news conferences should be sent very close to the time of the event—ideally, the day before. If registration is required to attend the event, you can send out news releases further in advance and then send a reminder the morning of the event.

For regularly scheduled news conferences, such as for earnings reports, you can promote the conferences well in advance by including the schedule in printed promotional materials, at the company's Web site, or by using online events calendars. Yahoo! and other portals maintain calendars of online events. You can usually find a form to fill out to add your event to the listings.

News conferences are often used to follow major news releases and product announcements. For example, a release can be issued stating a company's position on pending legislation with a notice that an online news conference will be held to discuss the issue. Most news conferences are intended for the media, not the public. But in the modern age, concerned members of the public, such as employees, suppliers, and shareholders, are likely interested in attending these events. I've heard a lot of buzz in the PR industry lately about bypassing the media and going directly to the public. While I don't think that strategy will be ultimately successful, here's an opportunity to test it. If you can get the media to tell the public you're having an open online news conference, you can see whether the public is interested enough to show up.

Online Crisis Management

We've been building up to a discussion of how to use the newsroom to handle a major crisis. I want to preface my remarks by saying that I am not an attorney or a crisis-management specialist. There are many better sources for consulting on this subject. Two of the best are Shel Holtz's book, *Public Relations on the Net* (Amacom Books) and Don Middleberg's *Winning PR in the Wired World* (McGraw-Hill). Both of these learned men have years of experience weathering crises with companies, they both have an intimate understanding of the new technology, and when they write about crisis communications, you can feel the veracity of their words. What I can offer you are my *opinions* about how to handle crisis communications and specific strategies for using the newsroom to facilitate a dialogue with the media and other concerned people.

Establishing Emergency Procedures

Planning for a crisis is an art unto itself. Good crisis planning is, unfortunately, considered a luxury at small and medium-sized companies that are struggling to build their operations and their profits. The sad truth is that the overwhelming majority of businesses and organizations will not prepare for a crisis and will deal with the situation when it is upon them. One problem with this lack of planning is that in a crisis, companies are often measured more by how they react to the crisis than the gravity of the situation itself. A small problem can turn into a public relations nightmare if the company appears weak or bullheaded in response to the problem.

An example of this is the famous Pentium chip fiasco that rocked computer giant Intel in 1994. A mathematics professor discovered a bug in the chip's calculating capabilities and posted a message about it on a Usenet newsgroup. Intel responded that it knew about the bug and had corrected the problem. They pointed out that the bug would have no impact on 99 percent of computer users, and they offered to replace chips upon request. This response was unsatisfactory to many people in the online community; they wanted Intel to recall the chip or at least notify users about the bug. Intel stalled, and it cost them plenty.

For weeks, online discussion groups crackled with criticism of the chip maker. Intel was in the midst of a marketing campaign touting its famous "Intel Inside" slogan. Online consumer advocates referred to the "Intel Inside" logo as a warning sticker. The controversy spread beyond the Internet as the story was picked up by the mainstream press. The technical details of the flaw were buried beneath the impression that something was wrong with Pentium processors. Intel eventually made further concessions to stanch the criticism, but it paid dearly for underestimating the gravity of the situation in terms of lost sales, marketing momentum, and stock price.

In a crisis situation, the normal rules of customer service and media relations change dramatically. A company needs to be prepared to alter its operations quickly to acknowledge the depth of the problem and to improve response time. For the newsroom, this situation means that inquiries usually handled by junior staff need to be brought to the attention of senior PR officials, legal council, and the rest of the company's top management. So, the first part of an online crisis plan is to reconfigure the chain of command.

A crisis plan should be developed between the company's legal counsel and the head of public relations. The plan should discuss how inquiries from the media will be handled. In most situations, junior staff will collect inquires and search for information online about how the crisis is playing out, preparing reports and forwarding inquiries to senior management. By using generic e-mail addresses at the Web site, such as news@company.com, programmers can easily reroute inquiries to senior staff or an outside PR firm hired to help manage the crisis.

Some companies go so far as to create entire crisis Web sites that are ready for launch in place of the normal Web site in the event of a crisis. Ford Motor Company followed this policy in its dispute with Firestone over problems with tires used on the Ford Explorer. I'll be referring to this incident throughout this section, because it not only gives a good idea of how companies are using the Web to handle crises but also involved two companies positioning against each other. We get to see different ways of responding to the same crisis. Figure 3.13 shows the home page for the Ford Motor Company during the crisis. Clicking on the Newsroom link takes people to a special news area built for crisis communications.

The main decisions you will have to make regarding online crisis communications are who should be handling the inquiries and whether you will dismantle your standard newsroom and replace it with a crisis news room or just communicate through the existing newsroom.

Figure 3.13 Ford Motor Company's homepage during the Firestone tire crisis of 2001. The word "recall" is absent from the page, which gives little notice to the issue. The Newsroom link leads to a special crisis newsroom and not Ford's traditional online newsroom.

Isolated versus Integrated Response

One problem with Ford's crisis communications newsroom is that it's not integrated with the storehouse of content available in the old newsroom. I tried for more than a half hour to find a profile of Ford President Jac Nasser at the crisis Web site and was unable to do so. Using the Search box at the top of the newsroom, I searched for "Nasser" and got the message that no matches were found. I eventually found profiles of dozens of Ford's senior managers, but Nasser wasn't on the list. I finally discovered a back door into the old newsroom, where I found the appropriate executive biographies, including one for Nasser. There is no access to the old newsroom from the crisis news-room—a major logistical mistake on the part of Ford.

In contrast to Ford's response to the crisis, Firestone integrated crisis coverage throughout its site. Figure 3.14 shows the Firestone home page during the crisis. The word "recall" is the first thing you see on the page. Breaking news releases related to the crisis are linked to from the home page, and a link is provided to the newsroom for more detailed crisis communications.

For many companies, the initial response to a crisis is to pretend it's not happening —at least, as far as the Web site is concerned. When that doesn't work, companies attempt to isolate the crisis with a crisis site that is segregated from the core Web site. As we shall see, this tactic often works against a company and results in media reports accusing the company of trying to bury the story. If you do employ a separate crisis Web site, you need to be sure that media contacts can access basic background materi-als such as executive biographies, artwork, and financial records that are normally available in the newsroom.

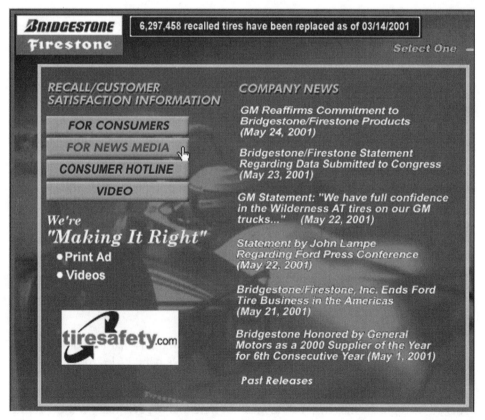

Figure 3.14 Firestone's home page during the tire crisis of 2001. The company's forth-right acknowledgement of the crisis is a stark contrast to Ford's attempt to downplay it.

Content Considerations for a Crisis Site

There is a major divide among public relations professionals between a proactive versus defensive response to a crisis. The media naturally want access to every scrap of information they can find—good and bad—about a company. Attorneys concerned with liability, on the other hand, frequently err on the side of caution, afraid that any information presented about a crisis could lead to claims made against the company. My personal preference is for full disclosure, and I'm pleased to see that Shel Holtz takes a strong stand in favor of providing thorough crisis coverage in his book, *Public Relations on the Net*.

The advantages of providing complete information at a crisis Web site are that the media will rely on your site as a source of information and that you can frame the way critical information is presented. When you present links to critical news coverage of your company, you get an opportunity to comment on the coverage, correcting any errors of fact, and offering company spokespersons who can respond to the charges. When you provide source documents, you earn the media's respect by not hiding from a story but by addressing the issues head-on. You have an opportunity to assist media contacts working through the story and to repeatedly offer your own opinions and experts to fill out media coverage.

The crisis coverage of Ford and Firestone in 2001 is a compelling illustration of the difference between the two main strategies for handling a crisis: caution versus full disclosure. After barely acknowledging it has a crisis, Ford provides access only to its side of the story: Ford news releases. Figure 3.15 shows a chart that Ford provided to illustrate how safe the Ford Explorer is. No link is provided to source documentation for this

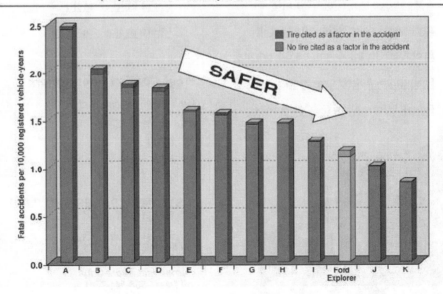

Figure 3.15 In response to concerns over tire problems on the Ford Explorer, Ford offers this simplistic chart in its newsroom with no source documents or links to source documents.

claim, although a source is cited in miniscule type at the bottom of the graphic. The only vehicle named in the graphic is the Ford Explorer: Which vehicles rated better or worse? A giant arrow indicating "SAFER" is slapped above the graphic. This display is the worst sort of crisis communications, attempting to divert the discussion from the problem at the heart of the controversy with cheap graphics that communicate little. If Ford is really confident of its safety performance, why doesn't it provide complete source documentation for its claims rather than an obviously company-generated safety chart?

In contrast to Ford's coverage, Firestone makes source documentation available from its newsroom (Figure 3.16). Coverage includes the full copy of an independent analyst's investigation, which is critical of Firestone, along with a complete copy of Firestone's own investigation. This later document includes artwork illustrating the problems with the tires that can be used to accompany stories and that does not contain the editorial bias of Ford's Safety Chart, illustrated in Figure 3.15. Firestone solicits media inquiries from its newsroom, whereas no direct contact information is provided at Ford's crisis center. At the Ford site, a link to "contact us" leads to consumer contact information, and

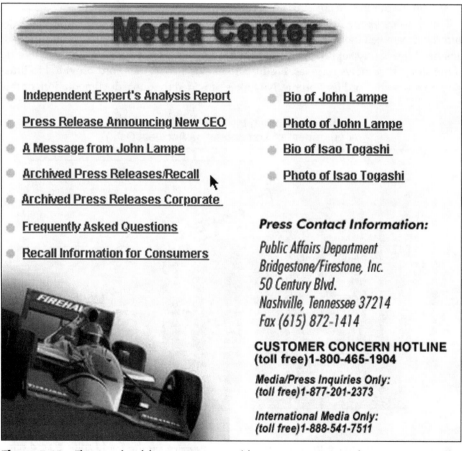

Figure 3.16 Firestone's crisis newsroom provides access to source documents as well as clear contact information for media inquiries.

consumers are advised to contact their local dealers first. A link from Ford's contact page is provided for shareholder inquiries, but nothing is provided for the press. This display is an unbelievable head-in-the-sand response from a major multinational corporation.

An excellent example of a company that began by ignoring a crisis, then acknowledging it, and finally actively managing it, is Microsoft. Journalists jumped on Microsoft for its lack of information about the U.S. Justice Department's investigation into non-competitive practices at the company. As of this writing, Microsoft's coverage is a model of good crisis communications (Figure 3.17). Still involved in the dispute, Microsoft's legal coverage provides complete source documentation for the dispute, including full transcripts of oral arguments and depositions, complete reprints of judgments rendered in the case, and other documents from both sides of the dispute. Microsoft is aggressive about presenting its own side of the story with each document and offering assistance to journalists covering the story. Yes, the entire site is presented from Microsoft's perspective, but they also provide journalists with all of the source documents necessary to come to their own conclusions.

Figure 3.17 Microsoft's "Press Pass" newsroom provides detailed information about the company's battle with the U.S. Justice Department, including full copies of source documents, depositions, and transcripts. This newsroom is a model of good online crisis communications.

In his survey article of online news room practices for *WebReview*, B. L. Ochman sites Monsanto as an example of a company that has learned how to deal with crisis communications. The company goes so far as to link to negative news stories, always presenting its own side to counter these arguments. Such openness and honesty takes courage and will hopefully prove a better model for companies than the attitude that forthright coverage makes a problem bigger than it needs to be.

Top Tips

Why bother? If you can't support and maintain a decent newsroom, don't even try. The most important feature you can provide the media is responsiveness to inquiries, and that only requires a commitment to service and a little contact information.

Open access. Restricting newsroom access goes against Internet culture and leads to administrative headaches. If an open site causes problems, cordon off the smallest amount of content necessary to solve the problem, such as personal contact information and high-resolution graphics.

Learn to database. To get a Web site that satisfies everyone from IT to PR, you need to tag and database content such as news releases, artwork, and calendar entries so they can be pulled into different areas of the site and exported to other sites, users, and devices.

Streaming video is out. It's expensive to produce, looks terrible, hogs bandwidth, and (thankfully) is not suitable for print or broadcast reproduction, which means that it's pretty useless for PR purposes.

Broadcast-quality video is in. You can't stream it from your Web site, but you can make it available for download to media outlets. In five years, the cassette-bound video news release will be extinct, replaced by online downloads of broadcast-quality digital video news releases.

Stop begging and start dishing. If you can generate more media coverage at a lower cost by distributing your own news wire, why are you still dumping money into news releases, press kits, and media events to which no one responds?

Exploit adversity. Online newsrooms are becoming the theaters where crisis communications play out. Are you going to watch the show or stage it? Rare is the chief executive who realizes that a company crisis brings unparalleled opportunities for favorable coverage.

Discussion Group Postings

Discussion groups pre-date the modern Internet, which is dominated by the World Wide Web. Prior to the Web, the Internet was used mostly for e-mail, file transfers, and discussion groups. I participated in my first online discussion group in 1987, using a 300-baud modem to dial into a local bulletin board. Bulletin boards—like the 300-baud modem—are part of the past. They have been replaced by online discussion groups, including Usenet newsgroups, Internet mailing lists, Web-based message boards, and forums on commercial services such as America Online and CompuServe.

Discussion groups have gone through periods of waxing and waning as the Internet has matured. With the Web's focus on visual presentation, text-based discussion groups lost appeal. But then, the commercialization of the Web saw many people returning to peer-to-peer groups, and their popularity rose. America Online had the liveliest discussion groups anywhere until it gutted them in an attempt to cut costs and redirect members to areas of the site run by paid advertisers who wanted to market to people, not empower them. In just a few short years, the Web has gone from having no decent discussion groups to hosting thousands of unregulated forums. Web sites inflate their hit counts, and thus advertising revenue, by giving spammers free access to their message boards. This glut of useless discussion boards will be trimmed in the coming years with the meltdown of traffic-based ad rates, and moderated forums will take their place at the Web's best sites.

Discussion groups might rise and fall, but they will never disappear and they will always be an important part of an online promotional campaign. These groups, along with chat rooms, are the real bastions of peer-to-peer interaction. People want to communicate with each other online, and they will seek out others with similar interests and join them in discussion away from the supervision of commercial interests. There are now hundreds of thousands of online discussion groups—possibly millions—usually focused on narrow, specialized, or arcane topics. Publicists who have something to contribute to these groups will be welcomed. Those that treat these groups as advertising vehicles will be shunned and even attacked.

This chapter will show you how to locate online discussion groups for any given topic, how to draft a posting that will be welcomed by members, and exactly how to distribute that message to a variety of venues. I'll talk a lot about spam and netiquette, how to defend your postings, and what to do if you're blacklisted or attacked. But I'll also focus on the positive results of a postings campaign and the benefits of forming lasting relationships with discussion group moderators who cover your beat. If you follow the instructions in this chapter, you will reap great rewards from online discussion groups and you will stay clear of the war between the spammers and the flamers that has tarnished these temples of discourse. Topics covered include the following:

The postings campaign. A quick tour of how this campaign works and the benefits that come from a net-friendly effort

Spam, spam, spam, spam, spam. The truth about posting commercial messages in discussion groups; it has little to do with the law and a lot to do with peer pressure

Writing effective postings. I cover content, style, and formatting—or what to say, how to say it, and how to keep your messages readable.

Posting to newsgroups. Usenet is one of the great experiments in human interaction. I'll help you find places where your message is welcome and show you how to use software to distribute and track your postings.

Posting to mailing lists. There are hundreds of thousands of these discussion groups. I'll show you how to quickly find the top dozen groups for any target audience and how to satisfy their strict standards of style.

Posting on America Online and CompuServe. Are you so successful that you can dismiss the more than 30 million people who use these services? I'll show you how to win over forum hosts and woo members with just the right touch.

Posting on Web site message boards. The new frontier in online discussion groups could use a few sheriffs. I'll show you how to find moderated boards that are spam-free and anxious to hear from you.

Defending your postings. No matter how good you are, there's someone in cyberspace ready to flame you. Even Mother Theresa would feel like Joan of Arc after posting online. I'll give you advanced techniques for defending yourself from verbal attacks, cancelled messages, and blacklisting.

The Postings Campaign

When you want to send a message to the media, you use an e-mail news release. When you want to send a message to the public, you use discussion group postings. There are hundreds of thousands of online discussion groups, each focused on the most miniscule of subjects. But if you send a message to all of them, Internet vigilantes will make your life miserable in a nanosecond. The best way to approach these groups is to create a message that has as little commercial content as possible, then diligently search for only those groups where the message will be welcomed. This section will show you the end result of a postings campaign, and then I'll work backwards to show you each step of the process.

There are four main categories of discussion groups online, each with different rules and procedures for postings:

Usenet newsgroups. Usenet is the Internet's informal news service. There are more than 40,000 Usenet newsgroups with names like *rec.arts.sf.announce*. Reading these groups and posting to them requires either newsreader software or a Web browser with news reading capabilities. Some of these groups are moderated, which means a moderator must approve your message before it's posted to the group.

Internet mailing lists. The term "mailing list" for these discussion groups is very confusing. They are called that because the discussion thread is sent to subscribers via e-mail, rather than stored online as with Usenet newsgroups. Mailing lists are used to distribute private newsletters as well as public discussion threads. You use e-mail software to join a group (subscribe), read the discussion, and post messages.

Commercial discussion groups. This category includes discussion groups on America Online, CompuServe, and other commercial online services. While commercial services have made more and more of their content available on the Web, posting to discussion groups is usually limited to paying subscribers. You'll need to subscribe to these services and use their proprietary software to participate in discussion groups.

Web site message boards. Many Web sites now host message boards where the public can engage in discussions. A Web browser is used to read these groups. Posting to message boards is usually accomplished with a Web-based form.

A Sample Campaign

When you embark on a postings campaign, your best strategy is to create a generic message in your word processor, then customize the content and format for each of the four types of discussion groups described earlier. What follows is a sample posting from a campaign I did promoting the @d:tech Convention and Trade Show. A template for a generic posting in Microsoft Word is available at www.wiley.com/compbooks/okeefe.

DISCUSSION GROUP POSTING

Subject Line: Standardizing Online Advertising

Last May, at @d:tech Chicago, Proctor & Gamble vice
president Denis Beausejour announced the formation of FAST
-- Future of Advertising STakeholders -- a trade group
charged with accelerating the development of online
advertising. FAST gained momentum with support from major
advertising trade associations and online publishers, such
as America Online, Wired Digital, Turner Interactive, the
Association of National Advertisers (ANA), the American
Association of Advertising Agencies (AAAA), and the
Advertising Research Foundation (ARF), among others.

Rich LeFurgy, chairman of the FAST Forward Steering
Committee, is holding a series of online chats to talk
about FAST's attempts at standardizing online advertising
terms and practices. LeFurgy was the architect of
Starwave's online advertising program, overseeing ad sales
at ESPN.com, ABC.com, ABCNews.com, Disney Online, NBA.com,
NFL.com, NASCAR Online and Mr. Showbiz. LeFurgy is now
Chairman of the Internet Advertising Bureau (IAB) and a
member of the @d:tech Advisory Board.

The schedule for LeFurgy's chats is below. If you are
unable to attend or prefer transcripts, please send me e-
mail with the subject line, "Send LeFurgy," and I'll reply
with a consolidated transcript as soon as it is available.
Rich LeFurgy's chat tour is sponsored by @d:tech New York,
which will be held at the Marriott Marquis, October 26-28.
@d:tech is the leading conference and trade show dealing
with online advertising and e-commerce. For more
information, please visit the @d:tech web site at:
http://www.ad-tech.com

CHAT SCHEDULE:

=> Wednesday, September 30, 7:30 p.m. Eastern Time
MSNBC <http://www.msnbc.com/chat/>

=> Wednesday, September 30, 9:00 p.m. Eastern Time
America Online Business Know-How Forum

=> Thursday, October 1, 8:30 p.m. Eastern Time
Talk City <http://www.talkcity.com/communities/business>

I'll talk more about how to write and format these messages in a moment. For now, I want you to get a quick understanding of the goals of the postings campaign and how it works. The goal of this campaign is to generate awareness of the @d:tech Convention and, hopefully, attendance. The target audience is people who are interested in the convergence of advertising and new technology. The message is crafted to appeal to this audience. The next step in the campaign is to locate online discussion groups that reach the target audience. Figure 4.1 is the distribution report for the message. It lists the discussion groups where the message was posted. I think the distribution report really explains the campaign in a glance. We wanted to attract people to the convention, and here's where we found our target audience online.

There is a template for the distribution report at www.wiley.com/compbooks/ okeefe. As you go about your business of sprinkling your message around the Internet, you add the names of the places where you posted the message to your distribution report. This report helps explain your work to employers or clients and helps you track any follow-up discussion in the groups. At the time of this @d:tech postings campaign, there weren't any decent Web-based discussion groups reaching the target audience. Because the campaign involved a chat tour, however, we did post messages about the chats to the online events calendars shown at the end of the distribution report.

The Value of Postings

A postings campaign provides a speedy vehicle for generating awareness of, and interest in, your activities. In short, it is a buzz machine. It can be used to distribute news about products, services, events, job openings, favorable media coverage, awards, polls, surveys—just about anything. But to be effective, the text of the posting itself must follow strict writing and formatting guidelines, and the places it is posted must be carefully selected. Let's explore this concept a little further.

One of the most powerful online marketing strategies you can follow is to cultivate good relationships with the forums that reach your target audience. Because online discussion groups are tightly focused on narrow topics, it's easy to locate your exact target audience. In the distribution report shown in Figure 4.1, I posted to 16 Usenet newsgroups out of a pool of more than 40,000. I would call that being selective, and it would hardly be considered "spamming" (although we'll get to that subject in a moment). I posted to 12 mailing lists out of more than 200,000. I posted to eight America Online groups and nine CompuServe groups out of thousands of forums at each service. And I posted to chat calendars on four Web sites out of millions.

For my client, these 50 discussion groups represent the core target market online. These are groups that @d:tech would want to court over and over again, building favorable relationships that span years and drawing speakers and registrants from the groups' members. When you approach these groups, you need to be thinking about long-term relationships. These are *discussion* groups, and quick hit postings that are off-topic are not appreciated and damage a company's reputation and ability to conduct business in the future. Cultivating the goodwill of these groups means that each posting must add something of value to the discussion.

DISTRIBUTION REPORT

Client: ConExMarketing
Project: @d:tech New York
Date:

~ Discussion Groups Where Messages Were Posted ~

Usenet Newsgroups

alt.business	comp.internet.nehappenings
alt.businessmisc	market.internet
alt.culture.internet	market.internet.free
alt.internet	misc.business.marketing
alt.internet.commerce	misc.business.marketing.moderated
alt.internet.guru	misc.news.internet
alt.internet.talk	misc.news.internet.announce
biz.misc	news.announce.conferences

Internet Mailing Lists

e-commerce- A moderated discussion of all aspects of e- commerce
Exposure - Internet advertising and marketing industry news
I-ADVERTISING - The Internet Advertising Discussion List
IAR - Internetcom'sInternet Advertising Report
I-SALES - Internet Sales Discussion List
ONLINE -ADS - Discussion of Advertising Online
uk-netmarketing - online marketing in the UK: visibility, advertising, etc.
Web Marketing Today - Monthly email newsletter by Dr. Ralph F. Wilson
EverydayBiz Online - weekly ezinepacked with news all about Business Online
WMO -ECOMMERCE - WMO E-Commerce List
WMO -INTERNATIONAL   - WMO International Online Marketing List
ZCOMMERCE - ZCommerceDaily

America Online

Forum Name> Message Folder Threads

Business Know How Forum>Adveritisng , Sales and Marketing>Internet Marketing
Advance Your Career> Career Aids/Resources
Computers, Internet & Technology> CI&T Important Notices
Consultant> Marketing your practice
Advertising forum> Advertising- Forum Business
Inc. Online Network>About Your Industry> Advrtising Agency
Business Talk>Small Business>Advertising Sales and Marketing>
Businssof the Web>Using Internet in Business
Rogue> Rogue Message boards.

CompuServe

Forum Name>GO Word>Message Folder Threads

Entrepreneurs Forum> Go: Smallbiz > Marketing Smarts
Building Your Business Forum> Go: Buildbiz > Promo and Advertising
Electronic Commerce Forum> Go: Ecommerce> Advertising methods
PR&Marketing Forum> Go: PRSIG> Advertising
International Trade Forum> Go: Trade> Marketing
Cyber Forum> Go: Cyber> The web
Internet World Forum> Go: IWForum > Ecommerce news
Business Web Forum> Go: BWEBFOR> Resources
Internet New Users> Go: Inetnew > Selling Online

Chat Calendars

Yack
Netguide
Yahoo!
On Now

Figure 4.1 A distribution report showing online discussion groups where the @d:tech message was posted.

I once handled a postings campaign for a scientific manual on polymers. If you can believe it, there were more than a dozen mailing lists devoted to just this subject. It doesn't matter how narrow an industry you are in, you can still find at least 20 places where that subject is being discussed online. One of the great benefits of the Internet is that it allows people who are interested in very arcane subjects to gather together and share information. You might have a subject that appeals to only one person in 100,000 on the planet, but that's 50,000 people, and a great many of them might be gathering together online in discussion groups.

A concrete example is a posting campaign I did for Random House publishing. One of the discussion groups was a moderated mailing list for acquisition librarians. The posting had to be approved by the moderator, and I had never won her approval for a posting before. Because the campaign involved a charitable partnership with Read Across America, the moderator approved the posting. This mailing list is made up of 9,000 acquisition librarians—9,000 people who control the budgets of libraries all over the world. There are few opportunities to reach a group like this one. Can you imagine the value of this group's support to a book publisher?

Another point I want to make about the value of a postings campaign is that it costs nothing. There is no charge to post on these groups, although some mailing lists might try to sell you sponsorships instead. Compare this situation to the cost to advertise to these people. Advertising to the general public is cheap on a *cost-per-thousand* (CPM) basis, but whenever a publication can deliver a highly targeted audience, the CPM skyrockets. If you are a pharmaceutical company, you can spend hundreds of dollars per thousand to reach physicians. Or, you can locate discussion groups where physicians gather—and there are dozens of them—and place a carefully crafted message for free.

I've trained many people to conduct postings campaigns. It's not particularly difficult work, although it can be time consuming and tedious. I remember one of my staff complaining that the postings were no longer generating enough response to make them worth doing. That afternoon, we received a response from a posting in a forum on CompuServe from a writer for the *San Jose Mercury News*. She was working on an article related to the subject of our posting and wanted to interview our client for publication. That single article was worth more to the client than the cost of the whole campaign. And this incident isn't isolated.

Journalists use the Internet to research stories. The Middleberg-Ross *Media in Cyberspace* survey shows that this use is the most popular use of the Internet for members of the media, with more than 70 percent of journalists researching stories online. When they research, they use search engines, and those search engines find our postings. I've gotten coverage for my clients in *People Magazine, The Washington Post, Harper's,* and *The Wall Street Journal* from discussion group postings. These postings are intended for the general public, but they reach anyone interested in the subject of the posting, including the media, potential business partners, suppliers, competitors, government agencies, investors, and so on. And because these postings in many cases remain online for years, they are out there when journalists are looking for leads. I've gotten inquiries off postings that are three years old! It's rare, but it does happen.

Part of the lesson for me about the value of a postings campaign is that I never know where the good hit will come from. For the *San Jose Mercury News*, it came from a CompuServe forum. My *People Magazine* hit came from an America Online posting. If I knew which discussion groups would be golden, I would skip the others. But you never know, and the forum you decide to skip could well be the one that would have coughed up the big hit. I've learned that virtually every campaign brings a couple of good hits that make the whole effort worthwhile. The only time you can be assured of getting no response is when you skip the campaign.

Discussion group postings are also very helpful in entering foreign markets. Everyone wants to go global these days, but how do you find contacts in foreign countries when you don't speak the language? Well, English is the language of business—for better and worse—and people working in foreign markets read English-language discussion groups devoted to the topics that interest them. They will make contact with you. I've uncovered international partnership opportunities for several clients through old-fashioned, low-tech discussion group postings, and I've seen those deals consummated. So, yes, you can reap extraordinary rewards using postings campaigns—*if* you follow the rules of netiquette.

One way of achieving success with discussion-group postings is to cultivate the goodwill of the moderators, forum hosts, sysops, and editors who manage these groups. You won't find their names in conventional databases of media contacts, and many of these people don't consider themselves "media," but they are. They should be courted like other media contacts: their names added to your database, invited to press events, sent review copies of new products, and offered articles and interview subjects for their forums. Once you have won these people over, all your future efforts to reach their members will go smoothly. And because they're not used to being treated like media contacts, the smallest gestures can have major impacts on your working relationships.

I came to know Janet Attard from her work as forum host for America Online's Business Know-How Forum. The first few times I posted there, I had to defend my postings and modify them to suit Janet. Today, Janet runs a whole family of business forums for AOL, her own successful Web site, and is the author of numerous articles and books about e-commerce. If I have something I want to run through her forums, I call her on the phone or send an e-mail and it's done. The same goes for Mike Bayer, sysop of the Advertising & PR forum on CompuServe. Mike's turf has grown to include many forums on CSI and the Web. He is a very powerful opinion-shaper in the world of online advertising, yet you're unlikely to find his name in any database of media contacts. In my early days online, I modified my postings to suit Mike's needs, made a friend, and today I'm able to place experts in his forums just by asking. Whatever your bag is, you would do well to court the dozens of people behind the scenes at online discussion groups who can make or break a marketing campaign.

Spam, Spam, Spam, Spam, Spam

There is more than one flavor of spam served online everyday. The most common is e-mail spam—unwelcome messages from anonymous strangers that clog your e-mail account. Another is discussion group spam—an endless sea of commercial messages surging into Usenet newsgroups, Internet mailing lists, Web site message boards, and AOL and CSI forums. If these messages have anything to do with the topic of the discussion group, it's purely by accident. Spammers will hit any and all groups they can get into, hour after hour, with the same slimy messages offering cheap phone service, cheap porn, low interest rates, or dubious work-at-home schemes.

There are many misconceptions regarding discussion group spam. The first is that no commercial messages are allowed in Usenet newsgroups. That is simply not true. Some newsgroups are specifically set up for commercial announcements, such as the *misc.forsale* family of groups that feature classified ads. Even in groups not devoted to commercial activity, commercial messages relating to the topic of discussion are usually welcome if properly worded. For example, participants in a newsgroup devoted to a piece of software are often interested in commercial products that extend the capabilities of that software. People participate in discussion groups to learn about everything related to the topic of discussion—including commercial products.

A ubiquitous form of advertising in online discussion groups is the signature file, or "sig." A sig is like a letterhead that appears at the end of your posting, providing contact information and sometimes a commercial message. People often advertise products and services in their sig files, and this behavior is accepted when not excessive. I see commercial sigs used all the time in postings complaining about spam, where the person griping about commercial activity is simultaneously engaging in it. In general, the rules of netiquette allow for commercial signatures if they aren't overly long (more than six lines), overly commercial (full of hard sales copy), and, most importantly, come at the end of a posting that is a genuine contribution to the group.

Commercial activity can be very subtle online. There's a gentleman named William L. Whipple who handles a lot of newsgroup support related to the Microsoft family of products. His sig file contains only his name, but his e-mail address contains the domain for his business, WLW.com, where you will find consulting services advertised. I would never accuse Mr. Whipple of advertising in newsgroups; rather, he is engaged in the most responsible form of marketing possible: assisting people free of charge. But there's no doubt that his postings pull traffic to his site, and his helpfulness combined with his domain name results in commercial activity. Of course, this kind of commercial activity—sharing advice with others for free—is not only welcomed but encouraged in all newsgroups.

Another misconception regarding spam is that non-commercial posts are welcome in newsgroups. Let me get to the point: No matter what you put into online discussion groups, there will be people in the audience who don't like it. It doesn't matter if you're friendly or mean, commercial or commerce-free, or helpful or a time waster. *Every* posting is apt to upset someone online. That's just the way the Internet works. If you plan to participate in any discussion groups, you should develop a thicker skin, because you are going to feel some heat.

Rampant hostility on the Internet is a subject worthy of sociological dissertations. It seems to stem from a combination of an unrestricted environment and the absence of the calming effect of human contact. Spammers and flamers have a difficult time seeing each other as human beings. In the detached world of cyberspace, tempers don't just flare, they spontaneously combust. As more and more discussion groups move to moderated vehicles, the hostility online is starting to ease. Still, you need to be careful what you say if you don't want to be targeted by Internet vigilantes.

Acceptable Use Policies

There are two basic types of discussion groups: *moderated* and *unmoderated*. Moderated means that someone is in charge and has the authority to block or remove posts they don't approve of. All discussion groups on commercial online services are moderated. They usually have two levels of control over postings. First, there are the Terms of Service you consented to when you opened your account. These describe acceptable and unacceptable behavior. Here is an excerpt from America Online's terms of service concerning commercial activity:

```
Advertising and Solicitation. You may not use AOL to send unso-
licited advertising, promotional material, or other forms of solic-
itation to other Members except in those specified areas that are
designated for such a purpose (e.g., the classified area).
```

The second level of control over commercial service discussion groups is exercised by forum administrators or sysops. They might have their own guidelines for the kinds of messages they will allow in their forums. There's really no point in trying to fight with these sysops about whether you can post your message or not. They have the authority to remove any posting they want for any reason. You might be able to negotiate with them, but they have the final say.

Many Internet mailing lists and Usenet newsgroups groups are also moderated. Your postings must be approved by a moderator before they are distributed to the group. If the moderator approves, your posting is acceptable. If the moderator doesn't approve, your posting doesn't go up. Moderated groups really cut down on spam and flame wars, which is why more and more people are forsaking unrestricted groups in favor of these moderated forums.

Unmoderated discussion groups are wide-open forums. There might be *guidelines* for postings but no *rules*. You are free to post whatever you want. Some people act like they own these groups and might flame you or retaliate against you if they don't like your postings. But they aren't owners and they have no legal right to restrict your contributions. The only laws that govern unmoderated discussion groups are those passed by various governments (prohibiting distribution of obscene materials, for example) and the rules set by your ISP.

Here is a relevant passage from the *Acceptable-Use Policy* (AUP) that my ISP uses:

```
Advertising may not be "broadcast" or otherwise sent on an intru-
sive basis to any user of the network or any directly or indirectly
attached network. However, when requested by a user of the net-
works, product information and other commercial messages are per-
mitted to be transmitted over the network.
```

You might want to check the boilerplate of your online services agreements to see what they say about commercial messages. If you end up with a legal dispute on your hands, these documents will probably determine the outcome. If you only provide information to those who are likely to want it, then you won't run into any disagreements you can't solve quickly and calmly.

At the end of this chapter, I have some suggestions for defending your postings. I don't want the discussion of flames to take away from the positive information in this chapter about how to distribute your message in an appropriate way. For now, let's just say you shouldn't post messages indiscriminately. Now, let's take a look at the kinds of messages you *can* post and how.

Writing Effective Postings

You can tell what works and what doesn't just by spending a few hours reading online discussion groups. When presented with a menu of subject lines to choose from, which ones attract your attention, and why? Have you ever opened a message and immediately closed it because it was too long or poorly formatted? When you're spending your own valuable time online, what do you like to see and what do you hate? If you write the kind of message you'd want to read, chances are other people will also find it worthwhile.

Reading discussion groups will also give you a good idea of the standards each group has concerning netiquette. Are there commercial messages in the group? If there are and they draw no complaints, chances are that your message will not draw any fire. Do people use commercial signatures regularly in the group? If so, you have an excellent basis for defending your posting from attack. Despite the efforts of Internet bullies to set a uniform code of behavior for online discussion groups, each group has its own tone and boundaries. If you fit in with the group, chances are no one will give you a hard time. In the following sections, I'll fill you in on important points of netiquette that will help keep you out of trouble.

Message Content

To me, the single most important aspect of a discussion group posting is that it offers something of value related to the subject of the group. Messages that just try to pull people to a Web site are unwelcome in most groups, even if the site has valuable free content related to the subject of the group. Sometimes it's hard to think up a good giveaway, so I'll give some examples to stimulate your imagination.

Product samples. When I promote a book online, I offer to send an excerpt upon request. For a new CD, offering to send a sample song in MP3 is recommended. For software, I've offered a demo copy—either a free "light" version of the program or a version that expires after a certain number of days. The difference between offering to send something and telling folks to get it at your Web site is the difference between getting thank you notes or flames.

Documents. Helpful documents of all sorts are good giveaways. Articles, product specifications, surveys, quizzes, help files, research, statistics, instructions—all of these make good giveaway files. If you are promoting a new product, what are the benefits of using the product, and how does it compare to competitors? Offering to send an article summarizing the benefits and features of a product is considerate. I never post news releases to online discussion groups, but I will post an offer to *send* a news release to those who are interested in the subject.

Access to experts. People need help with their problems, so if you connect them with an expert in their field, they appreciate it. I'm able to post news about events such as news conferences, chats, seminars, and workshops in part because I offer to send transcripts to those who can't attend. Sometimes, I'll offer to forward questions to the guest, then relay answers back (usually in the form of transcripts). These offers of assistance soften an otherwise commercial-sounding event promotion.

Services. Can you afford to offer some service that demonstrates the value of what your company sells? If you are selling domain name registration, you could offer to send people a list of domain names available similar to one they desire. You can always provide the URL of a Web site, but many people would rather reply to your message and let you do the work rather than drop what they're reading to visit your site.

Giving away something of value through your posting helps you measure the effectiveness of your efforts. Yes, you can measure traffic increases at your Web site and assume that sharply higher levels are the result of your posting, but you can get a better idea of the importance of each discussion group to your market by using giveaways. Giveaways also have the benefit of helping to keep your messages short. By holding something back and making people request it, you can keep your posting to the smallest amount necessary to lure a response.

Along with giveaways, creativity gets rewarded with discussion group responses. When I promoted a book by Gen-X author Douglas Coupland, his publicist said he didn't want a conventional campaign. I struggled to come up with something unusual when Mr. Coupland called and asked if I could do anything to promote a party he was hosting at the Tech Museum in San Jose. He spent a lot of money renting the space and hiring caterers but was afraid word hadn't gotten out, and the party was in one week. Within two days, I had cooked up a partnership with trendy Web site HotWired and spun out copy to promote the bash online. Here's the discussion group posting:

```
Subject Line: microserfs PARTY PAGE

Douglas Coupland is throwing a party and YOU'RE INVITED!

Coupland is the author of "Generation X" and "Shampoo Planet." The
party is a coming-out bash for his new book, "microserfs," which
documents the lives of fictional Microsoft employees.

The party will be held in a simulated clean room at The Tech Museum
of Innovation in San Jose, California, Wednesday, June 21 at 6:30
p.m. You'll be presented with a complimentary clean room jumpsuit
at the door so that you can mingle on a no-status basis with Sili-
con Valley luminaries and temp slaves.

Other party favors are included. There will be a rare showing of
"Close Personal Friend," Jennifer Cowan's short documentary about
```

```
Douglas Coupland. A six dollar cover charge goes to The Tech Museum
to support their efforts.

For more information, see the microserfs PARTY PAGE on HotWired at
the  following  URL:  <http://www.hotwired.com/Coin/WS/microserfs/
microserf.html>
```

When I placed the *microserfs* announcement, one person wrote to me and said, "You're obviously new to the Internet. Don't you know that humor is not allowed in Usenet postings?" His sarcasm is a sorry comment on the parched quality of most Usenet postings. Like a lot of people, I don't mind commercial announcements in "my" newsgroups; what bothers me is how unimaginative folks are.

You want to have a successful announcement campaign? Sharpen your cursor! Make the words dance! Pare down your prose, spike up the humor level, and enlarge your vocabulary. Just because you're using a computer to distribute your message doesn't mean it has to sound like a computer wrote it.

I know it's not easy to be creative on command. You might want to let your announcement simmer for a day before sending it so you can read it with fresh eyes. Printing your announcement sometimes helps you see how stiff it is. Reading your announcement aloud will alert you to poor phrasing. Ask a friend or coworker to look at your announcement before you send it out. Spend a little more time creating a clever posting and people will spend more time reading it and less time flaming you.

Most complaints about discussion group postings focus on the commercial content of the message. You will reduce these complaints by excising your message of any blatant or subtle sales pitches. You can include a complete sales pitch in a giveaway file, but your public postings should be carefully screened to remove anything that could be construed as a sales pitch. For example, when I post messages offering excerpts from books, I never mention the price of the book, the ISBN number, any toll-free order number, or even a URL where it can be purchased. If dollar signs or 800 numbers appear in your posting, they're warning flags that the message is commercial. It's important that your postings not only *are* non-commercial but also that they *look* non-commercial. That's another reason I never include a sig in my discussion group postings. If challenged, I can point to the hundreds of messages in the group containing commercial signatures and contrast that with my information-only posting.

Message Style

All discussion group postings, whether on commercial online services, Web sites, Usenet newsgroups, or Internet mailing lists, have the same basic structure: a header, a subject line, the body of the message, and a signature. Figure 4.2 shows a sample message from a Usenet newsgroup viewed with NewsWatcher software. We'll look at each part and see how to make them work for you.

The Header

The header identifies the sender of the message. It usually includes the sender's name, e-mail address, organization, the date, and the subject line. We'll deal with the subject

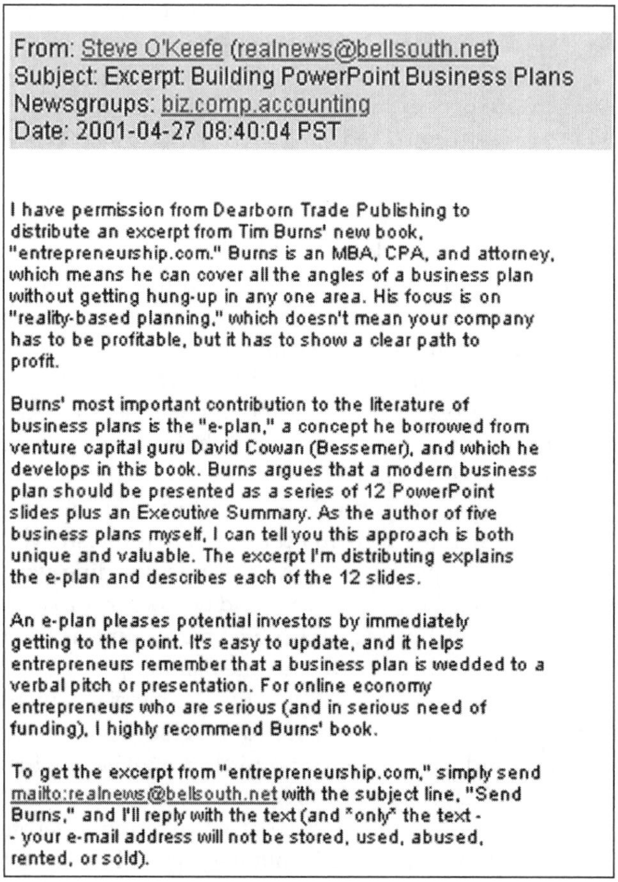

From: Steve O'Keefe (realnews@bellsouth.net)
Subject: Excerpt: Building PowerPoint Business Plans
Newsgroups: biz.comp.accounting
Date: 2001-04-27 08:40:04 PST

I have permission from Dearborn Trade Publishing to
distribute an excerpt from Tim Burns' new book,
"entrepreneurship.com." Burns is an MBA, CPA, and attorney,
which means he can cover all the angles of a business plan
without getting hung-up in any one area. His focus is on
"reality-based planning," which doesn't mean your company
has to be profitable, but it has to show a clear path to
profit.

Burns' most important contribution to the literature of
business plans is the "e-plan," a concept he borrowed from
venture capital guru David Cowan (Bessemer), and which he
develops in this book. Burns argues that a modern business
plan should be presented as a series of 12 PowerPoint
slides plus an Executive Summary. As the author of five
business plans myself, I can tell you this approach is both
unique and valuable. The excerpt I'm distributing explains
the e-plan and describes each of the 12 slides.

An e-plan pleases potential investors by immediately
getting to the point. It's easy to update, and it helps
entrepreneurs remember that a business plan is wedded to a
verbal pitch or presentation. For online economy
entrepreneurs who are serious (and in serious need of
funding), I highly recommend Burns' book.

To get the excerpt from "entrepreneurship.com," simply send
mailto:realnews@bellsouth.net with the subject line, "Send
Burns," and I'll reply with the text (and *only* the text -
- your e-mail address will not be stored, used, abused,
rented, or sold).

Figure 4.2 A Usenet newsgroup posting. The subject line is contained in the header information in the top part of the message. Beneath the header is the body of the message.

line separately. You can control the information in the header by setting the preferences in whatever software you're using. For example, you might choose to use your real name, a fictitious name, a company name, or some other name. The e-mail address included in each message is the one specified in your preferences. Don't think that using a bogus e-mail address will prevent people from tracking you down, however. All your postings will contain enough routing information to identify you unless they are sent through an anonymous remailing service. Using services that strip out your routing information is beyond the scope of this book and contrary to the spirit of my instruction, which is to help you generate positive responses to messages distributed in a net-friendly manner.

A note of caution is called for when setting your preferences. Many discussion group postings include a line in the header that identifies the organization the sender represents. You can put anything you want in this field. If you leave it blank, though, your ISP might just fill it in for you automatically with an ad for its services. It seems funny to me that in a world so critical of commercial discussion group postings, more than half of the postings I see online contain advertising for Internet firms that is *built into* the software used to participate in discussion groups. You've got to love the Internet!

Your e-mail address is always included in the header of discussion group postings, and that can create problems. Whenever you post a public message online, your e-mail address will be scooped up by extracting software used by spammers to collect e-mail addresses. Your e-mail address will then be sold and resold to merciless direct marketers, and your mailbox will quickly fill with spam. Because this situation is unavoidable, I recommend that you don't use an e-mail address you value for posting work. I use a special, dedicated e-mail address only for postings so that the spam I get doesn't clog my primary e-mail accounts.

Another reason not to use a valued e-mail address for your posting work is the potential for blacklisting. If you are blacklisted, postings from anyone at your company could be blocked. Sometimes even *e-mail* from your company will be blocked. It's a good idea to maintain a completely separate e-mail account (not just a screen name) to use for posting work as a way of shielding everyone else at your company from blacklisting problems. If you run into trouble, you can dump the blocked account and get another one without disrupting everyone else at your place of business.

The Subject Line

When people are following discussion groups, they often decide whether or not to read your message based on the subject line. Figure 4.3 shows a list of subject lines from the Usenet newsgroup alt.business.seminars. The first column shows the sender's name. The second column shows the subject lines. People use a lot of formatting gimmicks to get their messages to stand out. Which messages would you read first? The third column shows the length of each message. Notice the highlighted message at the bottom with the subject line, "$$FAST MONEY IN JUST WEEKS$$." This is a typical subject line for spam, using all capital letters—a big mistake. And look at the length of the message: 272 lines. Who would want to wade into that?

The best subject line is one that is irresistible for members of your target audience. That's an elusive goal. You'll usually have to modify your subject line to appeal to the audience of the particular group to which you're posting. For example, people in the newsgroup sci.life-extension are going to be more focused than those reading alt.misc. The highlighted subject line at the top of Figure 4.3 reads, "[Article] Smart Moves during an Economic Slowdown." While the subject line of this message is too long, resulting in being truncated in my newsreader, the content is good—telling me it's offering an article related to the subject of the group.

The most overworked subject line in all of cyberspace is "Check Out My New Web Site!" I've had my best results with subject lines that pose questions such as "Confused about Chat?" If you are giving away a help file as part of your campaign, then you can ask a question in the subject line and offer a solution in your message.

You should try to use "power words" in your subject line. You can find a list in any direct marketing manual. They include tried-and-true manipulators like "new," "fast," "hot," "save," "sex," "free," and so on—you get the idea. Keep your subject lines shorter than 55 characters to keep from having them truncated. DON'T USE ALL

alt.business.seminars			
# S Authors	Subjects	Lines	Date & T
Cindy Nemeth-Johannes	[article] Smart Moves during an Economic Slo...	10	4/1
sallyrob@beer.com	{{{{ WORRIED ABOUT YOUR JOB? ? ? ? }}}}}}...	73	4/1
sallyrob@beer.com	((((((((((((((((SECRETS OF WEALTH REVEALED)...	29	4/1
sallyrob@beer.com	#### WHAT HAPPENED TO YOUR DREAM.....#...	38	4/1
Marc	Network Marketing as a Real Business	11	4/1
Xavier LeMond	How to Retire Like A Millionaire (When You Don...	11	4/1
McMillions********@...	SEMINAR EVENTS NETWORK	5	4/1
Best Casino	A business online? You need this!	16	4/1
Samuel Wong	The Rules Just Changed!	12	4/1
Samuel Wong	Build Your Downline - FREE	26	4/1
Anthony Binder	Earn Loads of Money Fast	33	4/1
PQuasar22	Going Platinum - A Prospectors "DREAM SITE"	30	4/1
tagsuccess@hotmail.com	JOIN NOW AND EARN 40% Commissions!	5	4/1
Samuel Wong	Would you like to earn money for FREE?	27	4/1
Samuel Wong	Build your own Downline - FREE	27	4/1
Artie	people-commerce	35	4/1
Cindy Nemeth-Johannes	Visit ABCs For Small Business	12	4/1
JOE2118	- TWO WEEKS to Get FREE Fundraising Source	26	4/1
JOE2118	- Earn Equity Interest in WATKINS ONLINE	26	4/1
JOE2118	- FREE MLM Success Tips	25	4/1
JOE2118	- FREE Banners Make You $$	25	4/1
Garrett Sznyitar	$$$ get rich now $$$	4	4/1
Jonathan Altfeld	Linguistic Wizardry in Boca Raton, FL - April...	74	4/1
TOP INCONE	$$ Part-Time US$1500/mth from Home	10	4/1
Japan, Incorporated	Japan, Inc.	25	4/1
Senior Member	Seminars Net	6	4/1
People-commerce	your invited	18	4/1
AWEVHECLLGSK@spamm...	Optin Lightning Strikes 2011	37	4/1
joanne	EMAIL PROCESSORS WANTED!!	17	4/1
Basic420	This is what I am doing to make money come re...	5	4/1
Samuel Wong	Sharpen Your Internet Marketing Skills for Mor...	13	4/1
Nanker	Seminars Team Building, Company Days & Ince...	7	4/1
Jackie Nicholson	Join this free site	4	4/1
William Meyer	MAKE 10K PER MONTH	4	4/1
Kambar2	$$FAST MONEY IN JUST WEEKS$$	272	4/1
Mike H	Free eBiz Rotator-You'll love it!	38	4/2
Mike H	Free eBiz Rotator-You'll love it!	37	4/2
Artie	THIS WORKS IF YOU WORK	27	4/2
Recycleguy	Need Web Hosting?	6	4/2
LEONCITA19	OVER 7168 SITES TO PLCE YOUR FREE AD	6	4/2

Figure 4.3 Subject lines from a Usenet newsgroup. Which ones would you want to read?

CAPITAL LETTERS—it makes your subject line harder to read and is considered "shouting" and is bad netiquette.

In many cases, just getting people to open your message is more important than getting them to respond. If you're promoting a product or business, much of the benefit of an announcement campaign comes through the name recognition you get from your postings. A good subject line will get your target audience to open the message. After that, a message that's brief and to the point will help them remember your name.

The Body Copy

My main rule here is to keep it short! People don't read online; they scan. They open messages, read a few lines, close them, and then move on. You have to come to the point immediately, then provide a way of getting more information either by e-mail or at a Web site. This strategy is known as "layering"—giving people a way to find ever deeper levels of information. Instead of trying to present everything at once, you give them a little piece and a button to press for more.

More than a screenful is wasteful is my motto for writing announcements. You want to make an impression quickly. Three paragraphs are usually enough: the hook, the message, and the contact information. The hook grabs the people you're trying to target. The message tells them what you have to offer. The contact information tells them how to get all the details. Add a URL for your Web site, and you're done.

Many messaging systems allow people to see how large messages are before opening them. They might be told the number of pages or the size of the message in kilobytes. It doesn't take long for people to learn to avoid huge messages. I've opened messages on America Online and if my cursor spins from the upload, I bale out and move along. If you have a lot of information to share, you're better off enticing people into requesting it than packing it into a single message.

When you include an e-mail address or Web site address in an e-mail message, make sure you format it so that it will become a hotlink when the message is viewed. Most message readers recognize URLs and make them hot—but only if you include the full "http://" preface. I can't tell you how often I see this mistake made in postings, where the author has started a Web address with "www," leaving off those magical characters that will bring the link to life. With e-mail addresses, you need to precede the address with the word "mailto" followed by a colon and *no space* before the e-mail address. For most readers, the e-mail address will then become a hotlink that automatically opens a message to you. Using the "mailto:" format in postings significantly cuts down on the number of messages sent back to the discussion group or to a wrong address.

Some posting systems allow you to include even more formatting in your messages. With Web-based message threads, you might be able to embed a logo in your postings or at least a hotlink to the Web site. Formatting these messages requires a more advanced understanding of HTML. For example, you might have to use the <A HREF> tag to install a link in your message. For those who know what I'm talking about, look for the capability to add HTML when posting—but don't overdo it, because you don't want to ruin the posting for people with incompatible software. For those who aren't familiar with HTML tags, you'll need to consult a basic Web design book or Web site.

The Signature

A signature is a short piece of information automatically appended to your announcements. It usually contains the same information as your letterhead: name, address, phone numbers, URL, and so on. Here is a signature file from a posting to a Usenet newsgroup. The author has included a notice that he charges for spam sent to his e-mail address (nice try):

```
Steve Thompson
OSP LLC
330/335-9907 office
330/334-2097 fax
>>>                     NOTICE
```

```
>>> All UCE/BCE mail is subject to a US$95.00 handling charge
>>> per each one received for all OSP owned/operated accounts
```

You don't need a signature in your announcements. Your header should contain all the basic information people need to know: your name, company name, and e-mail address. People will almost always respond by e-mail rather than phoning. If you want to include a phone number, however, you can either try to embed it in the header or put it at the end of the posting.

When people go to the second level of your message, then you can give them your snail mail address and anything else you want to throw in your signature. By "second level," I mean when people respond to your message, either by e-mail or by going to your Web site. At that point, they're seeking more information—and it's appropriate to send them all your contact information.

Message Formatting

The formatting instructions for a discussion group posting are similar to e-mail. First, I recommend that you write your posting in a word processing program where you have better tools for formatting, spell checking, and grammar checking. You can use the word-processed version to get approval from your boss or send to your clients; it will look much more impressive than the text-only version you will use when uploading the posting to discussion groups. A Microsoft Word template for a discussion group posting is available at the Web site for this book.

You should use a monospace font such as Courier for your posting. Set your line length at 55 characters, which will make your message easier to read and will guarantee that there won't be jagged line endings when people view your message. You can't use any non-ASCII characters in your message. That means no bold, italics, large point sizes, fancy typestyles, smart quotes, or unusual characters such as ampersands (&) or percent signs (%). You can indicate emphasis with *asterisks* or ALL CAPS, but use them sparingly.

Once you've made any final changes to the posting, save another version of it as "Text Only with Line Breaks." This action will strip out any unconventional formatting and will force the lines to break at no more than 55 characters, preserving your formatting. Be sure to take a look at the text version of the posting before you start using it. If it looks funky as text only, rework the word processor version of the posting and save it again as "Text Only with Line Breaks." One advantage of using the text version of your posting for uploading is that a text document can be opened in almost any software program, including e-mail, Web browser, news reader, America Online, and CompuServe, reducing the problems that come with cutting and pasting across platforms.

You might need slightly different versions of your posting to satisfy the needs of different outlets for the message. Based on the service used (AOL, CSI, Usenet, Web, mailing list, and so on) or the topic of the forum, you might have to change some of the language in your postings. You can usually do this on the fly as you post. If the required changes are extensive, however, you'll have to create different word processor versions of the posting and save them each as text files. It's a good idea to name these files with an extension denoting the service they correspond to: posting.aol for America Online, posting.cis for CompuServe, and so on.

Posting to Newsgroups

Usenet distributes discussion groups throughout the Internet. At this writing, there are more than 40,000 newsgroups available covering an astonishing range of topics. In communications history, there's never been anything like Usenet. Comparisons to party lines or APAs (alternative press associations) don't capture either the depth or vitality of Usenet newsgroups.

Imagine getting a daily newspaper with an article written by one person on every block of your city. What would that be like? Well, if there were a big event (like a fire or accident), you might get 20 or 50 or 1,000 similar reports on it. Some will be keenly written, and others will be barely literate. You'll get articles about the most personal feelings that you wouldn't find in a professionally edited newspaper. You'll get neighbors bringing their private wars online, sniping at each other through their columns. That's what Usenet used to feel like to me until it was overrun with spam artists.

People speak much more freely online than they would on the telephone, in person, or through the mail. The smallest annoyance is cause for reams of bombast. As more people crowded onto the Internet, the temperature in Usenet newsgroups steadily increased. The same folks who brought us telemarketing scams now jam newsgroups with a steady diet of "Make Money Fast" spam. Net vigilantes retaliate, and suddenly there's a flame war.

As Usenet has degenerated into a battlefield of spammers versus flamers, intelligent discourse has gravitated to moderated discussion groups. Usenet, "the world's newspaper," is getting editors, and that's a shame because the moderated groups just don't have the vitality of free-range newsgroups. When historians write about Usenet, will they tell us that for a brief moment communication was free, instantaneous, and completely unregulated and humans took the opportunity to blowtorch each other?

Newsgroups are still an important part of a publicity campaign—especially moderated groups. Announcements are welcome in newsgroups if they're on-topic, if they fit the tenor of discussion, and if they bring something of value to the group. Let's look at how you can find appropriate newsgroups to which you can post.

Finding Appropriate Newsgroups

Until recently, it was difficult to post to Usenet newsgroups that were not available from your ISP. ISPs subscribe to Usenet news feeds and are able to choose or reject certain groups, limiting your access. For a time, ISPs were selective about which newsgroups they would offer. Many of the newsgroups are used to exchange materials that some people might find objectionable. This situation is particularly the case with newsgroups used for swapping pornographic image files. But liability cuts many ways, and the Internet is a new legal frontier full of minefields.

When an ISP is selective about what newsgroups it will allow, then it might acquire the responsibility to be selective. ISPs cannot claim to be "common carriers" with no responsibility for the content that crosses their transoms and at the same time exercise selection about which newsgroups to offer based on the content of the messages. You can't have your cake and eat it, too. And because many innocent-sounding newsgroups are also used to exchange what some people might find to be objectionable material, isn't it incumbent upon the paternal ISP to censor those newsgroups as well? It seems that the legal pendulum has swung away from censorship in recent years toward full news feeds from ISPs anxious to preserve their common carrier status. My current ISP offers more than 32,000 newsgroups, and I suspect the reason why I don't get a larger selection is due to the removal of inactive groups, broken groups, and other technological considerations and not a result of content decisions.

Just two weeks before writing this chapter, a technological solution surfaced for those who get incomplete news feeds from their ISPs. Google, the company that purchased the giant Deja.com archive of Usenet messages, has reinstated the ability to post to newsgroups for free through the Google Web interface at http://groups .google.com. This news is great for Usenet lovers and promoters. Google has taken Deja's good but unprofitable service and turned it into a miraculous service that hopefully will make enough money to survive. In addition to offering the ability to search, read, and post to a news feed in excess of 35,000 groups, Google has indexed the entire Deja archive of 650 million past Usenet messages (Figure 4.4). This feature alone will haunt the politicians of tomorrow as their brash, youthful utterances are unearthed for the world to see.

Figure 4.4 shows the search function at Google Groups. I searched for the term "alternative medicine," and the search results page begins with three newsgroups that contain that phrase in their group descriptions followed by 14,700 messages contain-

Figure 4.4 You can use Google's "groups" feature to search through, read, and post to tens of thousands of Usenet newsgroups.

ing the phrase. Messages appearing at the top of the list had the search phrase in the subject line of the message. This example shows the importance of carefully wording the subject line of your postings. I try to include the client's company name or product name in subject lines, in part so that those messages will pop up during an online search for the company or product.

Using the Google Groups search engine, you should be able to easily locate groups where your message will be welcome. I recommend that you make a list of these groups, copying their names into your postings report. Investigate each one a little further to make sure your message fits with the tone of the group, then post your message. You can post directly from Google or use another news service. America Online and CompuServe both offer robust news feeds, and you can use either of these services for finding, reading, and posting to newsgroups. I recommend using them as backup services if for any reason you are having difficulty getting your messages out through your own ISP's news feed or through Google.

One advantage to using a dedicated news reader is that you get more functionality than Google Groups can offer. I use NewsWatcher software for reading and posting to newsgroups. With NewsWatcher, I can create a list of newsgroups related to the project I'm working on and save the list. Each time I open my project list, NewsWatcher retrieves any new messages in those groups. This feature is extremely helpful for tracking responses to my postings, which is cumbersome using Google Groups. Figure 4.5 shows a list of newsgroups I used for a discussion group posting about PowerPoint business plans.

The best way to determine whether your posting will be appropriate is to read the newsgroup and use common sense. Are there commercial messages in the group? Do they result in flames? If your message seems like it would fit in, post it. You can't decide by the name of the group alone; you have to get in there to see what people are talking about.

Most newsgroups have "charters," a statement of purpose drafted when the newsgroup was first proposed. UUNET houses them in an FTP directory, but unless you're a historian, they're pretty useless—which is why none of the other major Usenet resource sites archives charters. If you were trying to decide what political party to join, would you base your decision on party platforms written in the 1800s? Charters have a similar relevance to deciding what is appropriate discussion for a newsgroup.

Another tool for determining whether the group is appropriate is the FAQ file (or Frequently Asked Questions) that some newsgroups maintain. You can find many of these files at the Internet FAQ Archives Web site, www.faqs.org/faqs. But you shouldn't judge a newsgroup by its FAQ. Some of these FAQ files are longer than this book. I've waded through 20-page FAQs only to find that they never address the purpose of the newsgroup or provide guidelines for appropriate messages. FAQs can be entertaining and educational; they're just lousy resources for determining what sorts of messages are welcome in a group. Many of the FAQs were written by one member of the group a long time ago and don't come close to reflecting current standards in the group.

Common sense is your best guide, but some people lack it. A while back, a fellow posted an inquiry on one of the mailing lists I read. He wondered why he was getting flamed for a posting he thought was appropriate. He posted an announcement for his financial services in the newsgroup *alt.cancer.support*, reasoning that people dying of

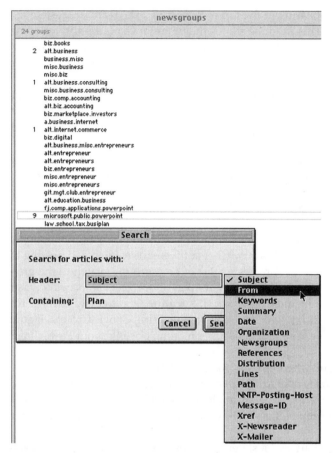

Figure 4.5 A list of newsgroups used for a posting campaign about PowerPoint business plans. NewsWatcher software allows you to easily track messages in a small batch of newsgroups and search those groups using a variety of parameters, shown in the bottom right-hand corner of the image.

cancer would need financial planning. I don't have to tell you his message was not appreciated. He should have been sensitive to the purpose of the discussion group. If cancer victims are looking for information on estate planning they'll go to discussion groups dealing with financial services.

If the group is moderated, all postings must be approved by a moderator before being released to the group. If the moderator approves your posting, it is de facto appropriate. You can locate moderated groups by using Google Groups or other news reading software and searching for the word "moderated." For unmoderated groups, anyone can post any message they want. There are no restrictions. If your message is out of sync with the group, you'll hear about it, either through flames or retaliation. If you were wrong (and I've been wrong many times), admit it and cancel out your posting. If you were right, defend your posting. We will close this chapter with some suggestions on why you should defend your postings and how to do it.

Uploading Usenet Postings

The mechanics of posting to Usenet newsgroups are fairly simple. With whatever news reader software you're using, compile a set of newsgroups where you think your message will be appropriate. You can post to all the newsgroups at once, but you risk waking up the "Cancel Moose." The Moose automatically detects identical postings to large numbers of newsgroups and issues forged cancellation notices to wipe the postings out. The Moose will then visit your mailbox to tell you about it. You don't want to wake up the Moose or any of his pyromaniac friends, so you should cross-post to no more than five groups.

Cross-posting means posting to multiple groups at the same time. The idea is that people don't want to run into the same message in every group they read. When you cross-post, people will see your message the first time they open it, but they will not see it in the groups to which it was cross-posted. Cross-posting is welcome to a degree. Every time someone responds to your message in one group, however, the response is sent to ALL the groups in the cross-post, so folks don't like it if you cross post to dozens of groups. You have to strike a balance, cross-posting to similar discussion groups and avoiding cross-posts to very different groups.

You might want to sort your newsgroup list by the way you intend to cross-post. The newsgroups in Figure 4.6 are sorted by topic, with bunches of business groups, entrepreneur groups, software groups, and so on. When you create your messages, address them to small batches of similar groups. Figure 4.6 shows a posting for a book called *Get a Financial Life* that is addressed and ready to go. This message will be cross-posted to three groups shown in the first line: alt.books.technical, misc.books.technical, and alt.books.reviews.

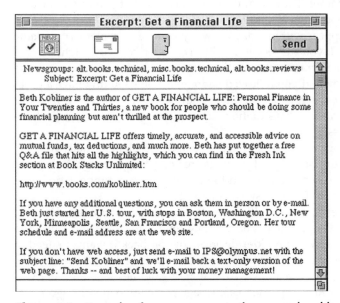

Figure 4.6 Example of a newsgroup posting properly addressed and ready to go. Note that the message is cross-posted to the three groups listed in the Newsgroups field.

You might need to vary the subject line and content of your message depending on the newsgroups to which you're posting. Sometimes it helps to tailor the message more closely to the readership to avoid flames and improve results. Varying the subject line and content also helps you stay out of the clutches of the Cancel Moose and his friends, who might be looking for identical postings. One way to fool the Cancel Moose is to add one blank space at the end of the subject line for the first batch of postings, two spaces for the second batch of postings, and so on, continuing until all messages are sent. In a similar fashion, you can add blank spaces at the end of the body text so that each batch of messages has a different character count. This action will help defeat canceling software. Avoiding cancellations is a cat-and-mouse game, with spammers and vigilantes outsmarting each other all the time. By limiting your postings to no more than 20 newsgroups and varying the subject lines and body text slightly, you should be able to stay out of the fray.

You should never cross-post to moderated newsgroups. If the posting is not approved by the moderator, it won't show up in any of the groups in that batch. You should also post individually to groups such as comp.infosystems.www.announce—a popular newsgroup for announcing new Web sites—that have strict message formats to which you must adhere. They might want your subject line to begin with WWW, or whatever, or they might want your e-mail address in the body of the message.

Follow-Up on Usenet Postings

Depending on the service you use, your postings might appear in a matter of seconds. I've done postings from America Online, however, that took more than three days to appear. America Online used to have terrible delivery problems with anything going to, or coming from, the Internet. They've improved a lot since, but you can still wait a long time for your Usenet postings to appear.

If your postings don't appear within a day or two, you have a problem. A vigilante might have canceled them. If you suspect you've been canceled out, you might want to visit the newsgroup *news.admin.net-abuse.sightings* and see whether someone is bragging about shutting you down. If you followed netiquette, you shouldn't have a problem. But you never know when some clever vigilante is going to find a message offensive and have it removed. If this situation happens, you can carefully repost different versions of your message.

If your postings don't appear, you could have a technical problem. Contact your ISP to see whether there's some reason Usenet postings are not getting through. You might have to find another news server from which to post. If my Usenet pipe is broken, I post from America Online and if AOL is slow, I go to CSI.

Once your message appears, you should follow the newsgroups for a few days and respond to any feedback. People often ask me how long a message stays up. The answer is, "Forever." Each service provider decides how far back it wants its feed to go. At some point, old messages are removed from the feed and archived. Realistically, you'll get any responses within three days. After that, it's old news. (Note: As I was writing these words, I received a response to a message posted two months ago.)

In contrast to the horror stories you've heard about flames, most people are very pleased to receive helpful information related to the subjects of the groups they follow.

That's why they participate in the groups. I received e-mail recently from the moderator of a Usenet newsgroup devoted to science fiction, where I offered to send members of the group an excerpt from a new sci-fi novel. If you follow my guidelines, you'll soon be receiving mail like the following:

```
Your submission for rec.arts.sf.announce has been received. Due to
your previous history of submitting on-topic articles to the group,
you are being promoted to fastpath posting status. What this means
is that future submissions by you from the same e-mail address will
be processed automatically and posted to the group without human
intervention.

    Scott Hazen Mueller,
    Moderator, rec.arts.sf.announce
```

My NewsWatcher software has the ability to search multiple newsgroups looking for responses to my postings. I can search for subject lines containing words I used in my posting (see Figure 4.5 for an illustration of a search), and NewsWatcher delivers a set of messages that meet that criteria. This search feature makes follow-up a snap. You can also use Google Groups to search newsgroups looking for your name, company name, or any other keyword. At this writing, there's no charge to use Google Groups.

At the end of this chapter, there's information on defending your postings. Flames are not always a bad thing. They can generate additional interest in your messages and give you an opportunity to talk more about whatever it is you're promoting. Before you add more fuel to the fire, though, you should calm down, read the relevant passages in this book, and respond strategically.

Posting to Mailing Lists

Newsgroups live on the Internet where anyone who wishes can come and read them. Mailing lists are delivered via e-mail to subscribers. Mailing lists tend to have much smaller audiences than newsgroups. Subscribers are more dedicated to participation than their newsgroup counterparts who might make one posting and never come back. In general, I have found mailing lists to be much more responsive to announcements than newsgroups but also much more sensitive about commercial postings.

Finding Mailing Lists

There are many places to find information on mailing lists, and you will probably have to use multiple services to find a good number of lists that exactly match your criteria. The resources chapter of this book and www.wiley.com/compbooks/okeefe contain excellent resources for finding mailing lists. I'll cover my top three picks here.

Yahoo! Groups at http://groups.yahoo.com: Yahoo! purchased two services that used to be on my top 10 list for finding mailing lists: eGroups and OneList. The result is an amazing service with information on hundreds of thousands of groups. The service is almost too good; searching for the term "e-commerce" produced more than

1,300 matches—far too many to sift through for a postings campaign. With no advanced search option as of this writing, you'll have to get good at using Yahoo! Groups' one search box to narrow your results. Nice features at Yahoo! Groups include the ability to join groups without having to switch to e-mail and an easy mechanism for unsubscribing. Their search results page tells you how many members each group has and whether it's public or for members only.

Topica at www.topica.com: Topica bought another one of my favorite mailing list finders, called Liszt. Topica has a much smaller archive than Yahoo! Groups, but you can find good lists here you can't find elsewhere. A search for "e-commerce" matched 48 groups, a manageable number to sort through. Unfortunately, you can't determine how many members a group has or whether it is moderated from the search page. If the list is hosted at Topica, you can subscribe right from the Web site.

L-Soft at www.lsoft.com/lists/listref.html: L-Soft is the parent to the former CataList search engine. It is a directory of mailing lists that use Listserv software. Because there are more than 180,000 such groups, it will lead you to many good mailing lists. In my experience, many of the most responsive mailing lists use Listserv software, so it's a quality crowd. The problem with L-Soft is that you can't easily determine how many people subscribe to each mailing list, and you have to drill down to find out whether the list is moderated or not. A search for "e-commerce" produced 10 matching groups.

The best strategy I can recommend is to start at Yahoo! Groups, try to work the search mechanism to get a reasonable number of lists to sort through, then move on to other mailing list finders to fill out your list. Ideally, you want groups with large, active memberships, but realistically you're just going to have to take your best guess and see which ones are responsive.

Mailing lists range from completely private affairs to wide-open discussion groups. I've classified mailing lists into five types. These aren't official terms or categories—just the way the lists seem to be structured to me:

Private/read only. Many companies use mailing lists to distribute news about their products. These lists aren't discussion groups and are not open to contributions from the public.

Private/read and write. You must apply for membership before being granted rights to participate in discussion. For example, an accounting list might limit membership to those who can prove they passed the CPA exam.

Moderated. Membership is open to anyone, but postings must be approved before being released to the group.

Subscription required. Not moderated, but you must be a subscriber before you can send messages to the list.

Completely open. Unmoderated and no subscription required. You can post messages without even subscribing to the list.

Using Yahoo! Groups and the other resources, you should be able to get the addresses for mailing lists where your posting might be appropriate. It's difficult to tell from the name of the list alone whether your message will be welcome. You can browse some of the lists on the Web, and that will give you an idea of how much activity they get. When you subscribe to the lists, you'll get an introductory message that

should help you further determine whether the group is an appropriate place to post
your message. Subscribing is covered next.

Uploading Postings to Mailing Lists

Mailing lists are a little more tricky to post to than newsgroups. When I do announcement campaigns, I like to make a list of groups I think are appropriate and then subscribe to all of them. I read the information that is sent upon joining and unsubscribe
from lists that seem inappropriate. I post messages to the remaining lists, follow the discussion for a few days, and then unsubscribe from all of them. Here's a group of mailing lists I used to promote a Web site for kids that was based on a fictional book series:

```
BOOKTALK - Children's literature and classroom use
KIDLIT-L - Children and Youth Literature List
ffk - Families for kids & Kellogg Foundation Project
KIDS-PT - PreTeen discussion list
KIDS-TE - Teen discussion list
KidsPeak - Announcements
KIDZMAIL - Kids Exploring Issues and Interests Electronically
FICTIONCHAT-L - Fiction Chat List
world-design - Forum on Designing Fictional Settings/Worlds
YAFICT-L - Young Adult Fiction Writers List
HSJOURN - High School Scholastic Journalism
```

For every mailing list, there are two important addresses: the address of the server
and the address of the list. Membership commands such as "subscribe" and "unsubscribe" are sent to the server. Announcements and other postings are sent to the list.
For example, here are the addresses for the mailing list Market-L, a popular marketing
discussion group:

```
The Server: listproc@mailer.fsu.edu
The List: market-l@mailer.fsu.edu
```

To subscribe to a list, you send e-mail to the server with the word "subscribe" in the
body of your message and the name of the list to which you're subscribing. You might
also need to include your name, depending on the type of software used to manage
the list. There are three major types of mailing list software: Listserv, majordomo, and
listproc. They each use slightly different commands, but the following format should
allow you to subscribe or unsubscribe from any of them. Just substitute the name of
the list for *listname* and your own name for *yourname*:

- ■ To subscribe, send e-mail to the server address with the following text in the
  body of the message: subscribe *listname yourname*.
- ■ To unsubscribe, send e-mail to the server address with the following text in the
  body of the message: unsubscribe *listname yourname*.

When you subscribe to a mailing list, you'll receive an e-mail acknowledgement and
a set of instructions for communicating with the list. SAVE THESE INSTRUCTIONS!

Mailing lists can generate an enormous amount of e-mail, and it's very frustrating trying to stanch the flow if you've lost the instructions for getting off the list. A good suggestion is to set up a separate e-mail folder for mailing list activity related to every postings campaign. In this e-mail folder, you can store all subscribe and unsubscribe requests along with the instructions that come with each list.

Once you've subscribed and you're confident that your message will be appropriate, send your announcement to the list. You will want to adjust the wording of your announcement to match the preferences of each group. Many mailing lists are moderated, and your announcement won't be distributed unless the moderator approves. Several times, moderators have asked me to adjust my phrasing slightly before they'll release my message. The most common request is to include an e-mail address in the body of the message, because asking people to "reply via e-mail" might result in people replying to the list rather than to the sender.

Follow-Up in Mailing Lists

Once you've sent your message, keep an eye on the mailing list for a few days to gauge a reaction to your message. If your message never appears, you might write to the moderator and ask why. The address for the moderator should be in the instructions you received when you first subscribed. Some lists are not very active, the moderator might be on vacation, and it could be weeks before your message goes up.

If you're getting heat for a posting, you should be able to defend yourself. If the list is moderated, the malcontents should be flaming the moderator, not you. If it's an unmoderated group, then you're free to post what you like. If you think the message conformed to the guidelines for the group, say that. People are entitled to have different opinions about what messages are appropriate. If you blew it and posted a message totally out of character with the list, apologize.

In case you are concerned that distributing information this way is considered foul play, let me share some results with you. I have handled more than 1,000 online promotional campaigns involving postings to more than 10,000 mailing lists. I can count the number of flames I've received from mailing lists on my fingers. Because many of these groups are moderated, I almost never get complaints. Unlike Usenet postings, where I will draw at least one complaint no matter what I post, for most mailing list campaigns I post to a dozen lists and get no complaints. Lately, I get a lot of e-mail like this response to the campaign on PowerPoint business plans:

```
Speaking in behalf of the WVEF steering committee, we are very
appreciative of identifying good resources that others can use to
improve their chances of success... Thanks again for sharing this
with others.

    Regards,
    Jan Berkow
    West Virginia Entrepreneurs Forum
```

Posting to mailing lists, like other online promotional activities, can be tedious, but as long as you offer something of value, your message will be welcome and has a chance of generating amazing results. For a typical campaign involving a dozen mailing lists, two of the lists will be highly responsive—but there's no way to tell which two until after you post to them all. In general, mailing list response has slowed in recent years as people gravitate to the fancy graphics and interactivity of the Web. But many professional and academic groups still rely on these lists and participate vigorously. If these groups are important to your success, you would do well to cultivate the goodwill of online mailing lists and their moderators.

Posting on America Online and CompuServe

The process for posting on AOL and *CompuServe* (CSI) is similar to Internet postings: You search for discussion forums related to the topic of your posting, examine the group to see whether your message fits in, open the text version of your posting, copy and paste the content of the message into the form at the forum, tweak it to make it fit in better with the group, and then post it. On both AOL and CompuServe, your message will appear within seconds. This situation is different than moderated discussion groups on the Internet, where prior approval is required to post. If the forum staff finds your message objectionable, they will remove it, usually sending you a form e-mail that your message violated service standards and was taken down.

As to the value of posting on these services, that's a complicated issue. AOL has dramatically reduced the number of its message boards in recent years, and the ones that are left can be hard to find. AOL used to be a happening place, where a relatively young and free-spirited crowd interacted with each other and contributed content to the forums in which they participated. But AOL has sold out its membership in the search for revenue. AOL wants to sell the privilege of communicating with its members and has accordingly reduced the ability of members to communicate with each other. Not only message boards are disappearing, but also chat venues and file libraries. AOL has decided it doesn't want to empower you—it wants to advertise to you.

The up side of AOL is that it's so darn big. In January 2001, the service had 26 million subscribers. That's a huge percentage of the online audience. The majority of these people simply use AOL as a gateway to the Internet and don't participate in AOL's proprietary forums, which are shrinking and disappearing at an alarming rate. But postings in the forums still pull responses in large enough numbers to make it worth including AOL on the postings campaign.

CompuServe, which is owned by AOL, has also been migrating its content to the Web. Unlike AOL, however, that content still contains a serious commitment to user participation. Most of the action on CSI happens in the forums, and all of the forums have message boards, chat facilities, and libraries where you can upload and share files. CSI still has a very professional disposition and reaches an important audience that is serious about getting value from time spent online. Even as CSI's importance in the overall scheme of things has faded, it is still a responsive group and pulls as well as AOL postings despite having only a fraction of AOL's membership.

In preparing postings for delivery on AOL and CSI, there are two important issues of protocol to observe. First, never solicit replies to an e-mail address outside the service. This action makes you look like a poacher and will result in your messages being removed. If your posting says, "E-mail me for further information," that's fine; people will reply to the e-mail address in the header of the posting, which is always native to either AOL or CSI.

The second point of protocol is that if your posting is offering some form of give-away file (and most good postings are), it's considered courtesy to upload that file in a library on AOL or CSI and point to it in your posting, rather than solicit e-mail requests. This situation is less important on AOL, where forum libraries are hard to find. It's essential on CSI, however, where each forum has a library and the sysops like it if you upload the file in the library and point forum members there. Here's a message that I received from a CSI sysop, making obvious the value of following this protocol in winning over sysop support:

> I read your post and I just can't pass it by without commenting. As you know, advertising and soliciting are not permitted in the forum. However, uploading a file that advertises in accordance with forum policy, and then making a post that gists the file and directs people to where it is for downloading is perfectly acceptable.
>
> This is what you have done, and you have done it so superbly that I would like to ask permission to use excerpts from your post as an example to others who post solicitations and advertisements here without realizing they're breaking the rules because they're not familiar with forum policy.
>
>   Carl Burch
>   Sysop, CompuServe Internet Resources Forum

There are other commercial online services that could be important to your market. Some of the better known ones are MSN (The Microsoft Network), MindSpring, and The WELL. I used to conduct promotional campaigns on seven different services, but as more and more of the audience have gravitated to the open Internet, I no longer stay in touch with these other services. Most smaller online services have a regional base. If your target audience is primarily regional, you should explore the message boards on these smaller services.

Finding Discussion Groups on AOL and CSI

The easiest way to find message boards on AOL is to log onto the proprietary service and go to Keyword: message boards. This action will take you to the message board search engine shown in Figure 4.7. Type a subject into the search box, and you'll get a list of recent postings about that subject. These postings will lead you to actual message boards, but not necessarily the best message boards. Another way to find message boards is to go to Keyword: Keywords. There, you'll find a list of all AOL keywords related to certain subjects. When you open the keyword list (which is *huge*), use the Find command to search for the word "forum." This action will take you to

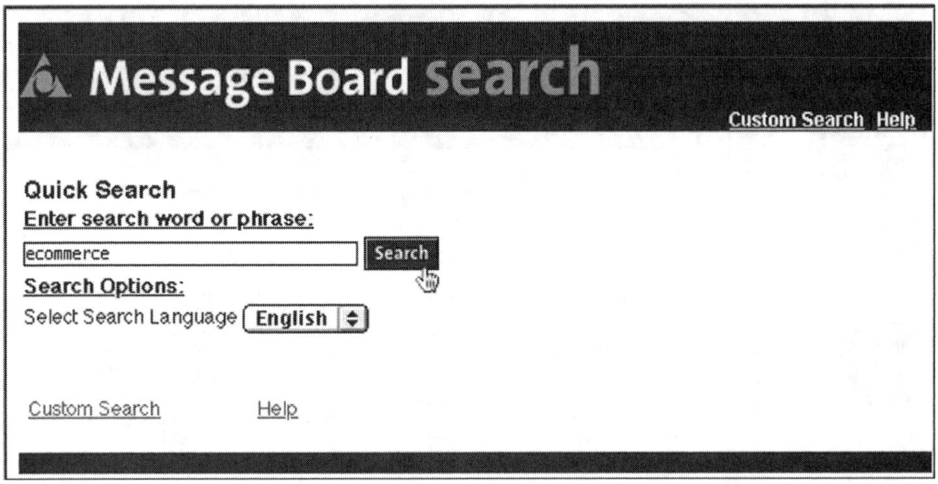

Figure 4.7 The fastest way to find discussion groups on AOL is to use the Message Board Search feature found at Keyword: Message Board or on the Web at http://mbsearch.web .aol.com.

keywords associated with forums; because most forums have message boards, you'll be able to quickly find discussion groups related to your topic.

CompuServe's message boards are a lot easier to find. Simply go to the CompuServe.com Web site and click Forum Center. After providing your CompuServe ID and password (or an AOL ID and password), you'll be taken to the easy-to-use forum directory shown in Figure 4.8. Almost every CSI forum has a message board, so you don't have to wade through all of them searching for a place to communicate with other members the way you do on AOL.

CompuServe has a quirky little feature that before you can post a message in a forum, you have to "join" that forum. This practice dates back to when CSI charged a premium to use certain forums. To the best of my knowledge, all the forums are now free. It costs nothing to join, so hit the Join button at each forum, post your message, and be on your way.

Uploading Messages on AOL and CSI

Posting on both America Online and CompuServe is fairly easy once you find the message boards. Figure 4.9 shows the home page for the Doing Business Online forum at AOL. A menu of forum content is provided. The second item, which is highlighted, is a link to the Online Business Message Boards. AOL always uses the "thumbtack" icon to indicate a public message board. These icons are your links to success.

Due to message board consolidation and a concerted campaign to eliminate user interaction on AOL, working the message boards can be quite confusing. The message boards listed at many forums are actually maintained at other forums, so when you drill down into the message boards, you could end up in a forum different from where

Figure 4.8 Finding discussion groups on CompuServe is a snap. The Forum Center is a directory of CSI forums, and almost every forum has a public message board where you can post.

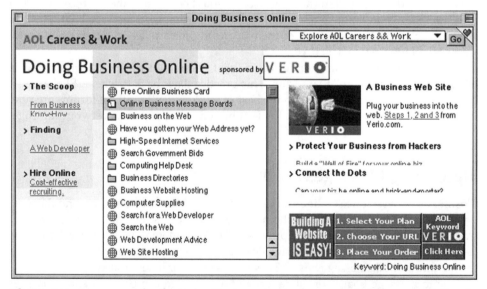

Figure 4.9 Home page for the Doing Business Online forum at AOL. The second item in the content menu is a message board, which is where you'll go to place your discussion group posting.

you started. Also, the message boards are hierarchical, nested inside of message folders, and you might have to drill down five or six times to get to a place where you can post your message. At the end of your drilling, you will arrive at a window that looks like Figure 4.10. Here, you see a familiar discussion group index with the subjects of messages, their authors, and the message date. At the bottom of the screen, there is a Create Subject button. That's what you'll use to post your message.

When you activate the Create Subject link on an AOL message board, you'll get a window like the one shown in Figure 4.11. Copy the body of your posting out of the text version of the file and paste it into the AOL message window. Add the subject line

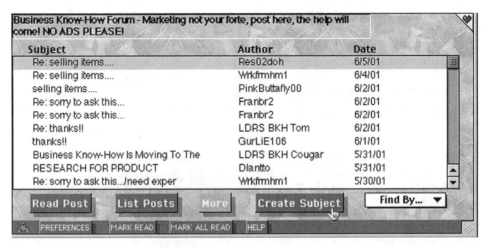

Figure 4.10 It might take some deep drilling, but the message boards at AOL eventually lead to message threads like this one where you can add your posting.

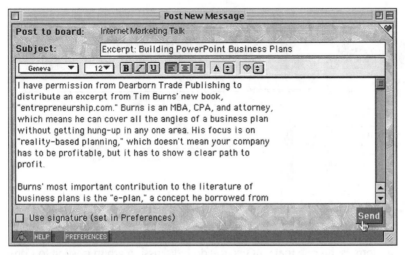

Figure 4.11 This form is the one that you use to add a discussion group posting to a message board at AOL.

at the top, and press the Send button. Your message will almost always appear on the board within seconds and will remain there until removed by a forum host or archived. You don't need anyone's approval to post to message boards on AOL, although your message will be removed if the forum hosts groom their boards and find your posting objectionable.

Posting on CSI is quite a bit easier. All forums have the same basic architecture, which is a blessing compared to the confusing variety of configurations found on AOL. When you enter a forum at CompuServe, you'll see navigational buttons at the top of the page identical to those shown in Figure 4.12 for the Media Professionals Forum. The Messages button takes you right into the message boards. The Files button will take you to the forum library, where you can upload any files referred to in your discussion group posting. The Search Forum button is handy for finding the proper library or message board for your upload.

Once inside a forum's message boards, you can upload your posting by hitting the Create Message button at the top of the page, as shown in Figure 4.13. Copy the body of your message from the text version of your posting, paste it into the message window, and add a subject line. CompuServe requires that you "Choose a Section" for

Figure 4.12   All CompuServe forums have the same navigational runner, shown here, that gives you quick access to message boards, file libraries, and forum searches.

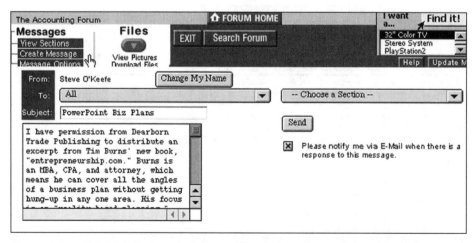

Figure 4.13   This form is the one that you use to add a discussion group posting to CompuServe's message boards. Make sure that your message is addressed to "All" people in the forum, and I suggest that you request e-mail notification for any replies to the message.

your message by using a pull-down menu of about a dozen discussion threads available at each forum. Please resist the urge to post your message to multiple threads in the same forum, because doing so will invoke the wrath of sysops. You have some additional choices for your CSI message, including whether to send the message privately or to everyone. Always choose to send to everyone by making sure the word "All" appears in the To: field of the message. You can also change your name in each forum, but there's seldom any need for that.

In Figure 4.13, you'll notice a checkbox asking if you want to be notified via e-mail if anyone responds to your message. Be sure to check this box; if you don't, replies will be held for you inside the forum, and you'll have to visit every forum you post to every day to find out whether someone has flamed you or responded favorably to your message.

Follow-up on AOL and CSI

As you post messages on AOL and CompuServe, be sure to record the names of the forums and message boards on your distribution report. Refer to Figure 4.1 at the beginning of this chapter to refresh your memory about how to format your list. In order for you or your client to find your AOL postings, you might have to record the whole long chain of nested folders in which each message is stored. For both CompuServe and AOL, you'll want to record the GO word or Keyword associated with each forum, which are shortcuts that will reduce follow-up time.

Positive responses to your posting will usually arrive at the e-mail account you have for each service. You can forward all your e-mail to a central account or program your e-mail software to check your e-mail addresses on different services. It's OK to respond to e-mail using your preferred e-mail address; you don't have to reply from an e-mail address native to each service. Be careful sending file attachments with your replies, however, because most people on these services block file attachments from non-native e-mail addresses.

Negative responses to your message will also arrive via e-mail. When I get flamed for posting to a Usenet newsgroup, I might argue with the complaining party about whether my message was appropriate or not. With AOL and CSI, there is little point in arguing with the forum hosts because they have absolute authority when it comes to managing their message boards. Because there are only a handful of forums on each service that are important to any given target audience, you can't afford to burn your bridges with forum hosts if you plan to conduct campaigns on these services in the future. So take a deep breath, swallow your pride, and try to work out a solution with the forum hosts.

If you get complaints from forum hosts, explain why you thought your e-mail was appropriate and ask if there is any way you can modify the message to suit their standards. Forum hosts are easily won over if you make a commitment to adding value to their forums. By providing timely news and support files and posting messages that contain little or no sales language, you are contributing in a way that makes the forum more valuable for everyone involved. Forum hosts welcome such contributions, in part because the more people who use the forum, the more money the hosts make. Once you have come to a compromise with a forum host, you'll find that your messages and files are suddenly welcome and the hosts will soon be asking *you* for files and chat guests.

In addition to e-mail responses to your postings, many people will respond on the message boards. Their responses can be both positive and negative, so you need to follow the boards for a few days to see whether you get any heat or stray requests. Even if the message says, "Please send me e-mail for more information," lazy or inexperienced posters might respond publicly in the message boards instead of privately via e-mail. A lot of activity on the message boards indicates that this group is an active group where people pay close attention to the boards. You should court the forum hosts of active groups that are important to you and keep the forum on your priority list for places to involve in future campaigns.

At the end of this chapter, I provide detailed instructions on how to respond to serious flames or attacks by people who don't like your postings. On AOL and CSI, you mostly have to worry about the sysops and forum hosts, because the public will never get a chance to flame you if the hosts don't allow your messages to go up in the first place.

Posting on Web Site Message Boards

Welcome to the Brave New World of Web site discussion groups. When I wrote my last book, *Publicity on the Internet*, there were almost no public discussion threads on the Web, and the few that existed were not worth posting to. Today, it is common practice for large Web sites and portals to have threaded discussion groups. But there's still the problem of finding ones that are worth posting to.

Haven't we learned anything by observing Usenet newsgroups over the years? Discussion boards are *worthless* without cops. Look at the message boards at Yahoo! at http://messages.yahoo.com. They are choked with spam. Why in the world would anyone follow a message thread there? As near as I can tell, the only reason most sites include unmoderated message boards is that they get to serve several ads for every visit. It's true, the only people visiting are spam artists, but the site pumps up the visitor count and ad revenues by providing a spot for spam artists to dump their commercial messages. Yahoo! has a usage policy for its message board, but if it is enforced at all, you wouldn't know it.

The story is much the same everywhere you look on the Web. Even venerable MSNBC lets spammers run amok on its discussion boards (see Figure 4.14). As long as advertisers are paying by the impression, you can expect to see the red carpet rolled out for spammers at Web site message boards. Perhaps if Web sites started charging for exclusive sponsorship of the message boards, they would see a revenue stream that is tied to having quality content at the site, not just a quantity of hits.

Another reason why Web sites do not police their message boards is because it's expensive. Managing a good message board takes a lot of staff time. First, there's the issue of keeping spam off the board. Because 99 out of 100 messages at an unregulated board are spam, it can take a great deal of time to find that one good posting. Second, even good postings have to be trimmed of excessive commercial content, poor formatting, or long quotes. Third, moderators have to handle numerous complaints about censorship from both legitimate participants and spammers. Some of these complaints can escalate into attacks in the unhinged world of online communications. Fourth,

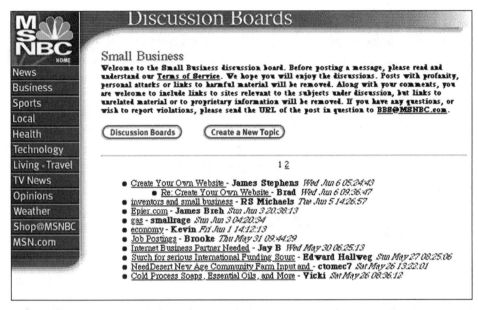

Figure 4.14   The problem with unregulated Web-based message boards is that they are wastelands of spam. Even MSNBC, a jewel among Web media outlets, has let spam artists take over its discussion boards.

good moderators not only protect the message boards but also strive to eliminate repetitive messages, suggest new topics, and get conversation unstuck from terminal loops.

AOL and CompuServe know all about policing message boards. Their efforts demonstrate an amazing commitment when compared to the laissez-faire attitude on most Web sites. The cost of policing these boards, however, has driven AOL to sharply curtail the number of message boards on its site, much to the detriment of considerate members who use the boards to communicate about their favorite topics. There is no solution to this problem except to police the message boards, and that means staff time (which costs money). I expect the next wave of Web commerce to result in a curtailing of Web-based message boards, accompanied by an increase in the number of quality moderated boards where you will be able to post intelligent messages.

Finding Web-Based Message Boards

It's difficult to find good message boards on the Web because you end up visiting so many lousy sites for every moderated board you come across. My suggestion is to visit the top Web sites where your target market congregates and search for message boards. Bookmark any good boards that you find, and keep an eye out for moderated message boards in your day-to-day Web browsing or while conducting promotional campaigns other than the postings campaign. Soon enough, you should be able to gather a handful of outlets worth posting to. Another tip is to go to sites with strong brand names in the hopes that the parent companies will want to protect their brands by keeping their message boards free of spam.

Figure 4.15 *The Wall Street Journal's* Discussion area is moderated but still active. Boards can quickly generate 100 intelligent entries and can run for months without losing steam.

A good example of a moderated message board is *The Wall Street Journal*'s Discussions area, shown in Figure 4.15. *The Journal* runs a pretty tight ship, and the boards can feel a little bit parched as a result, but they keep the site free of spam and they keep the discussion on topic. *The Journal* won't let you start a topic of your own; you can only respond to the topics they set up. But participants have a way of taking the discussion where they want it to go, and as long as that doesn't lead to abusive behavior or spam, *The Journal* is inclined to let the discussion wander.

The Wall Street Journal allows the use of a limited amount of HTML coding in messages. You can code your e-mail address as a hot link in a posting, although I've never seen a hotlink to a Web site. Using *The Wall Street Journal*'s message board can help you get noticed by influential people, especially if you have something intelligent to contribute to the discussion. I've seen a lot of senior executives using the boards to share ideas with colleagues or put forth their own agendas.

Another good place to look for moderated Web-based discussion boards is at trade publication Web sites. These sites usually derive revenue from membership dues or subscription fees and don't generate enough traffic to sell ad space on their sites. Because they aren't focused on getting more hits, they have good reason to keep their message boards clean. Also, because these boards generate far fewer postings than portal sites, monitoring the boards takes minimal staff time. Figure 4.16 shows a message board for the Fluid Power Society. The board is free of spam, yet it generates about five postings a day, which indicates a decent amount of participation.

Another method for finding good boards is to use a search engine and search for the words *moderated message board*. You'll generate a lot of matches for that phrase, but you can narrow the search by using keywords related to the subjects about which you are

The Fluid Power Society Discussion

[Start a New Message Thread] [FAQ] [General Rules]
[E-Mail a question about this Board] [Search the Site]

- WANTED: LOOKING FOR REXROTH VALVE SUPPLIER. CONTACT US FOR ENQUIRY LIST - **SUPERMAR** *08:2*
- Looking for Cartridge Valve and Manifold Mfr's to Represent - **Sales Manager** *23:56:55 6/04/101* (0)
- Hydrostatic Transmission Valves (Hot Oil Shuttles) ????? - **Dave Matson** *23:48:46 6/04/101* (2)
  - o Re: Hydrostatic Transmission Valves (Hot Oil Shuttles) ????? - **Sylindersam** *12:11:19 6/06/101* (0)
  - o Re: Hydrostatic Transmission Valves (Hot Oil Shuttles) ????? - **Sylindersam** *11:23:33 6/06/101* (0)

Figure 4.16   The discussion threads at the Fluid Power Society Web site. Specialized trade sites are promising prospects for finding moderated discussion groups.

posting. Unfortunately, this search string will miss Web sites that call their message boards "discussion groups" or "threads" or other variations. With some practice, you should be able to find quality boards that reach your target audience. When you find them, *bookmark them* so you don't have to repeat the process for subsequent postings on a similar theme.

Uploading Messages to Web-Based Boards

The mechanism for posting to Web-based message boards is not universal and depends on the software employed at the site. Fortunately, most sites are intuitive, and posting usually is done by using a Web-based form. You create a new message, cut and paste from the text version of your posting, and send the message.

The majority of Web sites with message boards insist that you register with the site to use the boards. This process will require extra time on your first visit. Depending on your level of paranoia, you might want the site to "remember your name and password" so that you don't have to re-enter it every visit. For security purposes, I prefer not to do that. Rather, I've established a dedicated e-mail address that I only use for posting work, coupled with a generic screen name and password that I only use for posting. The password is eight characters long to satisfy almost every site's minimum or maximum password length, and the user ID is strange enough that it's unlikely to already be claimed. Using this strategy, I only have to write down my ID and password for sites where my generic one is rejected.

Many Web-based message boards allow you to use sophisticated HTML formatting in your discussion group postings. E-mail addresses can become *mailto:* links, URLs can become hotlinks, and so on. Formatting this way requires knowledge of HTML and can take time, but if the forum is important to you, it could be worth the effort. One little secret that the message boards seldom reveal is that if they allow *some* HTML formatting, you can probably include *any* HTML formatting. That means you can put such things into your postings as a company logo, a thumbnail photo, even a text-entry box for signing people up to a promotion or mailing list. While I argue against using special formatting in your newsgroup and mailing list postings, formatting in Web-based posting is platform independent: Almost every browser will see the message the same way. So take advantage of adding interactivity and graphics to your Web-based postings if the audience warrants the extra effort.

Follow-Up on Web-Based Message Boards

The hardest part about tracking Web-based message threads is remembering where you put the messages. In the heat of a postings campaign, it's hard to remember to bookmark the sites where you posted and then to use those bookmarks later. When you bookmark a Web page, the title of that page is what appears in your bookmark list. Most sites don't put a lot of effort into page titles or pull pages into frames that all have the same title. Consequently, when you look at your bookmarks after a postings campaign, you'll probably see something like the following:

```
Message Board
Message Board
Discussions
Message Boards
Discussions
```

You'll have no idea which message board leads to the Journal of Oncology Web site and which leads to the Oxygen health threads. One way to deal with this situation is to annotate the bookmarks, either as you're posting or after you finish putting messages up. You accomplish this task by opening your bookmarks window and adjusting the name and/or description for each bookmark. Annotating your bookmarks takes time but saves time later when you're preparing a distribution report and doing follow-up work. Annotating bookmarks is worth the effort if you plan on doing continuing online promotion related to the same subject. Time invested now will save you time down the road.

If the moderators of the boards complain about your message, you should follow the standard operating procedure of apologizing and asking if there's any way you can modify the message to make it acceptable. Positive responses to your message can help build a relationship with the people who run the Web site. If you are offering a help file and are getting good feedback and numerous requests, you might ask the Web site staff if it wants to feature the file at the site. Getting a reputation for contributing value on the message boards at media Web sites can lead to offline print or broadcast coverage. The message boards can be a back door to increased coverage or a partnership when the front door seems closed. More and more media properties are pulling content from Web message boards and running it as feedback in print and broadcast properties. And writers who work for trade journals, newspapers, magazines, and television programs are pulling story ideas from hot threads at the Web site.

Be prepared to take advantage of positive Web thread responses by having artwork, text files, and multimedia files ready in the proper format for online delivery. One excellent reason to offer some sort of giveaway in your posting is to measure the responsiveness of Web-based message boards so that you can skip the quiet boards next time and roll with the winners. Without some form of measurement, you are essentially clueless as to whether Web-based postings are worth the work involved.

Defending Your Postings

I started this chapter with a discussion of spam, and I'm going to end there, too. Because so many people have gotten themselves and the companies they represent into serious trouble through thoughtless discussion group postings, I will provide here the lessons I've learned in the School of Hard Knocks.

If you notice funny things happening with your computers shortly after a postings campaign, there's a possibility that the two events are related. You might be the victim of high-tech hanky panky, which can take many forms including viruses, e-mail bombs, or hacks. I don't want to scare you off from doing legitimate postings campaigns, and if you follow my advice you are unlikely to have any problems. But cyberspace can be a strange place, and you never know how people will react to a posting.

The tendency in dealing with flames is to go with your gut reaction and either ignore the insult or flame right back. Both responses are poor choices, because they aren't taken with a clear understanding of your objectives. When you receive complaints about your postings work, the first thing you should do is assess your position.

Assessing Your Position

When formulating a response to a flame, consider what would be the best possible outcome not only for you but also for the companies you represent. You don't want to inadvertently cause harm to yourself or your clients. Ideally, you would like to get past this incident and continue to do promotional work online without encountering trouble. A thorough understanding of your position vis-à-vis the complainant will help you understand how to respond. I tend to divide complaints into different categories, each with a corresponding course of action.

   Complaint from a moderator. If you get a complaint from anyone with real authority over the discussion group, such as a moderator, sysop, forum host, discussion leader, or Web master, there is little point in arguing. You should apologize for the posting even if you think you were in the right. If the group has an active, valuable membership, it's worth taking time to try and win the moderator over. First, you can explain why you thought your posting was appropriate. Second, you can suggest modifications to the posting that might help it win approval. Third, you can ask the moderator what changes he or she would require to approve the posting.

   Moderators are often surprised to get apologies and offers to modify postings after they've issued a rebuke. They're used to dealing with spammers who could care less. By taking yourself out of the camp of the spam artists, you put yourself into the category of people who value a relationship with the forum.

This gesture helps broach the wall of anonymity and make both you and the moderator real human beings trying to communicate and achieve similar goals. This method is how friendships are formed, and working relationships, and maybe even partnerships that smooth the flow of all future promotions.

On two occasions, I felt mistreated by moderators and, when all efforts at conciliation failed, I went public with my complaints. In one case, it resulted in a stimulating discussion on censorship and netiquette, and I felt like forum members were sympathetic to my cause. In the second instance, I was unable to rouse any support from the members. In hindsight, I really did not help my cause or the cause of my clients in either case. Yes, it felt good to be able to defend myself against tyrants, but I should have acted in the best interests of all concerned and quietly accepted defeat.

Private complaint from a member. If I get e-mail objecting to a posting, I resist the urge to fire back and I just ignore it. You have no idea who is on the other end of that e-mail or what they're capable of. There are a lot of people in cyberspace who are wound very tightly and looking for a target. You don't want to put a bullseye on your forehead. Quietly ignoring private flames is the best response, although you might need to develop a thick skin. One of my favorite flames came from a person who said they wished Steve O'Keefe was enclosed in Styrofoam, because they would love to set me on fire and watch little pieces of me explode and melt down. Do I want to provoke such a person further? I think not.

Public complaint from a member. If a complaint appears in the discussion group and not in e-mail privately addressed to me, I decide on a case-by-case basis whether to reply or not. I consider a public flame to be an attack, and I tend to defend myself, but if the person sounds like an obvious nut, I won't reply. Don't argue with fools lest you be confused for one. If the complaint sounds rational and not hysterical, I'll defend my posting publicly. Oftentimes, I don't have to defend my posting because someone in the group steps up to my defense. In moderated groups, the moderator will often step in and defend approved postings, relieving me of the responsibility and taking some of the heat.

Attack from the Internet. If I've been attacked by someone, I will naturally take defensive maneuvers. A humorous anecdote will help prepare you for this unlikely event. I was doing a postings campaign aimed at married couples where one partner is starting a business. The posting offered a guide to help resolve issues in entrepreneurial relationships. I posted the message to groups dealing with entrepreneurship or marriage. One of the mailing lists I posted to was called something like "marriage-L," but I got a message back saying that "marriage-L is now BBGG," so I just posted my message to the new group. That's when all hell broke loose.

One of the members of BBGG didn't like my posting and started mail-bombing me: sending me dozens of hateful e-mail messages an hour. I investigated and found out that BBGG stood for Boy-Boy Girl-Girl—a discussion group about same-sex marriages. Even though the attack was private, I posted a public apology to the group. Then, the discussion began.

People in the group argued that there was no reason they should be excluded from getting this information. After all, gay and lesbian couples engage in entrepreneurship, too, and the issues dealt with in the file I was distributing pertained just as well to same-sex relationships. I would have worded the message with more sensitivity if I knew it were going to a same-sex group, but that was water under the bridge. In the end, the members of the group welcomed my posting, and suddenly the mail bombs stopped.

One lesson here is to investigate groups before you post to them. I was caught off guard by the name change of the group and posted without thinking. Another lesson is that an apology can cool things down fast. A third lesson is to make sure and follow-up your posts so that you know if trouble is brewing and you can take defensive measures before it explodes into an attack.

Handling Usenet Flames

There's always someone who thinks they own the newsgroup. They will flame anyone for posting anything they don't like. These pyromaniacs ruin newsgroups by chasing away intelligent discussions. I used to be intimidated by these folks until I realized that most of them are just bullies. If you get flamed for posting to a newsgroup, follow these steps:

1. Double-check the newsgroup. Did your posting fit with the current level of discussion in the group? Are there similar messages in the group?

2. Read the charter or FAQ. Does your posting seem appropriate? Resources for finding Usenet charters and FAQs can be found at www.wiley.com/compbooks/okeefe.

3. If you posted inappropriately, apologize to the flamer and cancel your posting. Most services allow you to erase a previously posted message, although sometimes you can't do it yourself and have to ask a sysop for assistance.

4. If you feel your posting was appropriate, defend it. Don't let bullies drive you out of a discussion group. They have no more right to determine appropriateness than you do.

If you are using a giveaway file and your posting simply tells people how to get the free file, it is not a commercial announcement. Here's a flame I got for a posting about the book *Everyday Cooking with Dr. Dean Ornish*:

```
This posting is blatantly commercial, and is totally off-topic. The
sci.life-extension group is for discussions about vitamins, life
extension, etc; not for services or commercial businesses.
```

Here's an abbreviated version of my reply:

```
Perhaps you don't care for my posting to sci.life-extension, but it
is neither off-topic nor commercial. As a reader of life extension
literature, I'm sure you're aware of how important proper diet is to
```

life extension, particularly a diet low in animal fats. Dr. Ornish
has done pioneering work in this area. Secondly, my posting was not
commercial. I am not selling anything, nor asking people to buy anything. I'm simply informing them of the availability of an excellent
article about Dr. Ornish and his new book. I would have posted the
article in its entirety, but such long posts are considered bad
netiquette. This is an open discussion group and the information I
provided was clearly within the bounds of the charter.

The flamer then sent me an apology, admitting that my posting was appropriate
and that he didn't examine it carefully before turning on his torch. He then confessed
to spending many hours each week scanning his favorite newsgroups and flaming
anyone who made "inappropriate" posts. After a few encounters like this one, I've
become a little hardened. If my post is inappropriate, I apologize and remove it. But if
it is appropriate, I vigorously defend it.

Cancelled Messages and Blacklisting

If you conduct a postings campaign but never see your messages appear in the discussion groups—or they appear only briefly—you probably have a problem, and a potentially serious one. To combat the glut of spam in Usenet newsgroups, Internet
vigilantes developed methods for removing posts they didn't like. This procedure is
called "canceling," and it began with the Cancel Moose (now retired) and has been
refined over the years through the diligent efforts of volunteer programmers.

The way canceling currently works is that programs sift through Usenet newsfeeds
searching for multiple identical postings, then forge cancellation notices to remove
those posts. In a hilarious twist on the power of technology, spammers who are irate at
having their postings blocked have used cancellation software to eliminate legitimate
Usenet postings, and in some instances, to completely shut down newsgroups favored
by their enemies. So it goes in the world of cyberspace, as spammers and flamers try to
outprogram each other in battles over territory.

If you suspect that your messages were cancelled, you should immediately consult
newsgroups in the family of *news.admin.net-abuse*. If your messages were cancelled,
you'll usually find a posting there by a vigilante explaining why and how your postings were removed. The generally accepted criteria for cancellation is always changing, but the latest version I've seen targets identical messages posted to more than 35
newsgroups. I've never posted a message to more than 20 newsgroups, and I've never
had my messages cancelled. By making subtle changes to the subject line and body
text of your postings, and posting to a limited number of groups, you should never
find yourself drawn into the war between spammers and flamers.

A persistent pattern of spamming will lead to blacklisting. The most common form
of blacklisting today is to submit your IP address or domain name to a list of known
netiquette violators. Many ISPs subscribe to this list. The list is automatically run
against the Usenet news feed, and messages by anyone on the list are deleted. Obviously, this strategy doesn't stop determined spam artists, because unmoderated newsgroups continue to be flooded with spam. But blacklisting could have serious
repercussions for your company or clients.

One company I worked for had a major blacklisting problem. The company's servers were hacked by a spam artist who used the servers to distribute millions of commercial messages in a matter of hours. Although the company itself was not the source of the spam, the company was blacklisted—and for a time could not communicate with the Internet by using e-mail or postings. Better server software was installed, and the company had to switch IP addresses to get back in the favor of the online community. Messages were then posted in the net-abuse discussion groups, explaining what had happened and the steps taken to rectify the situation. If you follow good netiquette and still run into trouble, you can usually make your case in front of the net-abuse newsgroups and win parole. But if you keep getting cancelled, you could dig yourself a technological hole that will be difficult to climb out of.

Commercial Service Encounters

There are two things that AOL and CompuServe forum hosts frequently object to. The first is a blatant commercial advertisement. If you post a message that says, "I'm selling widgets for $15 each. Please send e-mail for a product description," the host is not going to like it. It's not that they want to spare the members commercial announcements—on AOL, there are commercials on every screen. They would prefer that you *paid* for the privilege of commercial announcements like other paying advertisers.

The other thing forum hosts hate is when you aren't contributing to the discussion. If you're promoting a product, you should be ready to engage in discussion about it. You don't have to post ads—let your signature do the selling. When you contribute to the discussion, you're joining a dialogue with equals, not marketing to sheep. There's always a way to phrase your announcement so that it sounds like a news item rather than an ad.

You can satisfy some forum hosts by moving your announcements or giveaway files. Some forums have special places for commercial announcements. Rather than remove your posting, they'll ask you to put it in the commercial area. Some forums have special threads for announcing Web sites so that the message boards don't get cluttered with these announcements. If you have a posting removed, it might just be a matter of finding a more appropriate thread in which to put it.

The most successful online marketing is done by people who get involved in the discussion groups. They respond to other people's messages. They answer questions and offer advice. They don't push their business but let their signatures do the selling. Their participation is not only tolerated but also welcomed by forum hosts and members alike. It's known as the "soft sell," and it's very effective. If you plan to market online, then you should get close to the forums that are important to your success and become an active participant. People always welcome someone who makes valuable contributions to the group.

Top Tips

Postings work. Discussion-group postings are an excellent vehicle for getting close to a highly targeted audience. Identify those groups that are important to your market, and court their goodwill.

Share value. Postings are only effective if you offer something of value directly related to the topic of the group. Share something of value, and you'll increase the value of your company's shares.

Be selective. Even if your message relates to hundreds of discussion groups, pick your top 10 for each service and stop there. You can hit another 10 next time, slowly locating responsive groups that should be included in all future campaigns.

Don't forget AOL and CSI. AOL and CompuServe represent a third of the market. By including them, you increase market penetration for every campaign.

Calm down. Before you respond hastily to a flame, determine what is in the best interests of the companies you represent and respond strategically. The best response is often no response.

Know your rights. You have as much right to post in discussion groups as anyone else. Let current standards exhibited in the group be your guide to good behavior. Consult your terms of service in the unlikely event of a legal challenge.

Build relationships. When you reach past the anonymous screen names and connect with the real people who manage these groups, you smooth the path for future promotions and open doors to profitable partnerships.

Newsletters and Direct Marketing

Visit almost any Web site and you'll find an invitation to "sign up for our newsletter" along with a little box for inputting your e-mail address. Online newsletters are one of the great cultural phenomena unleashed by the Internet. They give voice to thousands of non-mainstream points of view as well as allow companies to communicate more directly and inexpensively with customers, investors, and suppliers. But is there a point where enough is too much?

If you're like me, you suffer from newsletter overload. Most of my subscriptions go unread, routinely jettisoned and finally cancelled. I might like to hear from a company once a month, but twice a week is just too much. And many of the newsletters I get contain precious little news and a whole lot of self-aggrandizement. This chapter will help you set up a newsletter operation with a realistic perspective about what it takes in terms of staff time, hardware, and software and what it will give in terms of revenue, sales leads, promotional presence, and prestige. You'll find concrete suggestions about content, style, format, and frequency. And I'll suggest an alternative strategy of partnering with already-popular newsletters.

One client told me they had a database of people who joined a notification service, but they had never used it. They were afraid of getting complaints or having people retaliate against them. That's the kind of environment in which we work. While there's good reason to be careful when handling bulk e-mail, companies should not fear to send direct mail to those who have asked for it. I'll cover responsible direct e-mail operations in this chapter, including how to reduce complaints and properly deal with those you get.

There are thousands of people who have used online newsletters and direct e-mail to generate revenue, build their businesses, and achieve positions of prominence in their industries. I'll share several good stories through detailed case histories of people who have set a standard of excellence. You can follow their wisdom and examples to make these marketing channels work for you.

Subjects covered include the following:

Hardware and software. I'm not an information technology specialist, but I do know what you need to set up a small operation reaching a few thousand people, and I know who you need to talk to for larger systems.

Direct e-mail. After distinguishing between spam and legitimate bulk e-mail, I'll show you how to collect e-mail addresses, write and format compelling messages, deliver them to your target audience, and deal responsibly with any complaints.

Online newsletters. I'll introduce you to Richard Hoy, veteran of ClickZ and the Online Advertising Discussion List, who knows more about using online newsletters than just about anyone on the planet. Then, I'll show you how to design and manage a newsletter and what revenue streams you can expect to flow from it.

Case history: *Publishers' Lunch.* I've subscribed to thousands of newsletters in the past seven years, and this one gets my vote for the best I've ever seen. I'll talk with editor Michael Cader about the benefits, drawbacks, and day-to-day responsibilities of running a successful online newsletter.

Hardware and Software

To answer the question, "What hardware and software do I need?", I need to ask a question: What do you want to do? Or, more precisely, how many people do you want to do it to, and how often? The core software involved in direct e-mail and newsletter marketing is called list-management software, and solutions run the gamut from freeware to systems that cost tens of thousands of dollars. The main factor determining the system you need is the volume you want to handle. A second important consideration is the level of technical expertise you have. Let's begin by looking at hardware for direct e-mail and newsletter management.

Hardware Issues

If your needs are limited, such as a monthly newsletter or managing a database of up to a few thousand names, you can probably get by with whatever computer you're currently using. A PC running Windows 98 or a Macintosh using System 8 can handle the job nicely as long as your processor speed is higher than 250 MHz. You need this configuration to comfortably surf the Web nowadays. Therefore, if you are having trouble with basic Web surfing, you'll need to upgrade your computer before you add newsletter management and bulk e-mailing to your load.

For a small business solution, you'll need a personal computer with a Pentium II, 486 processor or better, at least 128MB of RAM, 2 Gigs of storage space, and a T1 Internet connection. This equipment will allow you to manage a newsletter subscriber base in excess of 10,000 members and handle bulk e-mailing up to several thousand pieces at a time. When you start working with databases of this size, you need to maintain a constant connection to the Internet, 24 hours a day, 7 days a week, and you can't do that reliably with either a cable modem or DSL—the two high-speed connections available below a T1 level.

Large commercial installations are simply beyond my level of expertise, and you'll have to consult with an IT professional for advice. These systems involve running servers I know nothing about. There are businesses that process millions of pieces of e-mail a day, operating their own mail server software. While the issues raised in this area are not outside the scope of this book, they *are* outside of my knowledge base. I am just a publicist in geek's clothing, and while I know enough about computers to get applications to work for me, I know very little about setting up complex networks and servers. Sorry.

Database Software

I currently use ACT!, a contact-management program, for handling my databases. I'm sure my tech-savvy readers are rolling their eyes, wondering why I'm not using Oracle, SQL, or other sophisticated database solutions designed with the Web in mind. I don't manage a large Web site, I don't host a mailing list, and I don't do bulk e-mail marketing, so I don't have need for a workhorse system. Many of my readers are in the same position. My largest database has about 10,000 records, and ACT! does the job quite nicely. While it doesn't interface with the Web very smoothly, it has benefits that most Web-oriented databases don't. For example, it interfaces with the print world beautifully, generating form letters, mailing labels, envelopes, and reports. It also has a user-friendly interface that satisfies my need to put my finger on someone's phone number quickly. Phoning people, or sending out letters, are old-fashioned forms of communication that haven't been retrofitted very well into trendy new database software.

If your situation is similar to mine, working with a small number of contacts over a variety of different media, then you can use ACT!, NowContact, Lotus Organizer, Microsoft Outlook, Lotus Notes, Eudora Pro, Microsoft Access, Filemaker Pro, dBase, or even FoxPro—in short, whatever you are comfortable with. I know a lot of lightweight users who have regretted giving up their familiar, outdated software for the headaches of unfamiliar, buggy new programs. Just because you work with the Internet doesn't mean you need the latest software. Those who have huge databases that they work with frequently know more about the software they need than I do, and my attempts to guide them in this regard would be worse than useless.

E-Mail Software

Once again, for lightweight users of databases with up to 10,000 contacts, you can use whatever program you feel most comfortable with. Eudora Pro, Microsoft Outlook, Lotus Mail, or Netscape Messenger all handle bulk mail for a list of this size. I like to keep my contacts in ACT! and port them into Eudora when I need to send bulk mail. You can store your contacts right in your e-mail program, but so far I haven't been impressed enough with the databasing capabilities of any e-mail program to lock up my contacts there.

For more intensive users, there is a brand of software that combines e-mail and database functions specifically for the purpose of bulk e-mailing. Brand names include Emerge, Stealth, NetContact, and DirectMail. I've used some of these programs, but I haven't been willing to give up the contact management features I like in my present configuration. If you plan on sending mail to tens of thousands of people or mailing on a daily or weekly basis, you'll have to upgrade to this level of software.

Newsletter Software

Software for managing an online newsletter goes under the heading of mailing list software. List management features include subscribing and unsubscribing, mailing the newsletter, processing bounced mail, and archiving the content. There are literally hundreds of different programs available, ranging from freeware that works very well to systems costing tens of thousands of dollars that work rather poorly.

The kind of program you need depends on the size of your list, the number of lists you're offering, and your level of technical sophistication. Mailman is a freeware program that is based on Python and that many people swear by, but you'll need help from an IT professional to install it and operate it. PostCast is an inexpensive program ($300 for the full-featured version) that will let you serve a small number of subscribers (under 5,000) comfortably over a DSL or cable modem connection to the Internet. Post-Cast includes bulk e-mail, newsletter services, autoresponders, and so on. It's a hybrid between an e-mail program and a Microsoft Access database—just one example of this new brand of software that will get radically better in the coming years. Right now, you have to be technologically savvy to install and run PostCast and deal with the bugs.

For high-volume users, with lists reaching more than 10,000 subscribers, Lsoft produces what is probably the most popular program, called Listserv. Other popular programs are ListBot, ListProc, and Lyris, the last of which seems to be the program of choice for many Internet marketing professionals due to its advanced features and reasonable price. Be forewarned that none of these programs is very satisfactory, however. According to no less an authority than John Audette of the MultiMedia Marketing Group, a heavy user of list management software, there isn't a reliable, full-service program on the market. Expect to spend between $2,000 and $5,000 for software that can handle a list of 10,000 to 50,000 contacts.

Newsletter operators want list software that does everything. They want a Web interface for pulling in subscriptions, managing unsubscriptions, archiving past issues, giving users format choices (text, HTML, AOL, and so on) and delivery choices (per message, daily digest, weekly digest, and so on). Managers want to have all list administration automated so that people can easily change configurations, go on vacation, and get on or off the list without human intervention. They want a program that will automatically send subscribe and unsubscribe confirmation notices and process confirmation replies. They want to automatically detect and weed out bounced mail. They want tracking features to determine whether the newsletter gets opened, whether readers click through to full-text articles or sponsor sites, and whether they buy anything at those sites. And they want to be able to view these statistics in a friendly format. There's a lot more to this newsletter business than you might think, and every newsletter manager I've talked with complains about buggy software. This business is one area of software development that is rapidly improving, so watch for reviews of new releases.

One alternative to expensive software installation and technical support is to contract with a firm to host your list. SparkLIST will host a 50,000-subscriber list for a $100 setup fee, plus $50 per mailing. An even cheaper solution is to use a free service, such as Topica or Yahoo! Groups. Both of these sites let you set up a full-featured newsletter for free. They run ads on every dispatch from the group. You can purchase a no-ads option at Yahoo! Groups for $60/year, however. I've seen groups on these sites with more than 100,000 subscribers, and I've heard very few complaints about technical problems. Another inexpensive solution is to see whether your ISP offers free list-management services with your account; many do. The disadvantage is that if you change ISPs, you lose your newsletter service, and relocation can be painful. Better to host the list yourself or go with a site like Topica or Yahoo! Groups that will host your group, no matter how many times you change ISPs.

You'll find contact information for the companies and services mentioned here at the companion web site for this book at www.wiley.com/compbooks/okeefe.

Direct E-Mail

Those of you who are looking for a discussion of how to best collect millions of e-mail addresses and then set up hardware and software to spam them need to look elsewhere. There are legitimate ways to conduct mass e-mail marketing, using opt-in lists collected by firms such as Postmaster Direct, but these activities are definitely outside the scope of this book. There are dozens of books available on e-mail marketing written by people with more experience than me. Seth Godin and Don Pepper's *Permission Marketing* (Simon & Schuster, 1999) is essential for its keen insights into the dynamics of electronic relationships. Add Kim MacPherson's *Permission-Based E-Mail Marketing That Works!* (Dearborn, 2001) for a how-to course on implementing Godin's principles. MacPherson held down the e-mail marketing desk at ClickZ for two years, and you can find an archive of her columns there. My one caveat about MacPherson is that she seems to never have experienced a dial-up connection to the Internet. She's overly fond of "rich e-mail" with its fancy fonts and graphics, which might pull higher response rates but which non-respondents hate with a passion.

Readers looking for a hard-core, direct marketing stance toward using the Internet should consult *Internet Direct Mail: The Complete Guide to Successful E-Mail Marketing Campaigns,* by Stevan Roberts, Michelle Feit, and Robert W. Bly (NTC, 2000). The authors are long-time direct marketing professionals who expound on how to milk the new medium. Also highly regarded is *The Engaged Customer: The New Rules of Internet Direct Marketing,* by Hans Peter Brondmo and Geoffrey Moore (HarperBusiness, 2000). I have issues with the direct e-mail marketing crowd, mostly over their definition of *return-on-investment* (ROI), and while I'd prefer to keep my thoughts to myself, I feel I owe it to readers to warn them about some of the problems they might encounter if they follow this marketing strategy.

While the concept of getting someone's permission to send advertisements is sound, in practice it's extremely difficult to implement. Through experience, I have learned that many people who opt-in to lists will nonetheless complain about the mail they receive. As state laws against spam proliferate, you can expect to receive many threats of legal action. Although you might be on safe legal ground, dealing with these threats (and in rare cases, lawsuits) siphons time and money away from more productive marketing activities. There are hidden costs of direct e-mail marketing that are seldom included in calculations of ROI, such as the percentage of people who form negative impressions of you, the number of people who filter you out of their e-mail permanently and who you can no longer reach with more innocuous or targeted messages, the time spent dealing with electronic attacks such as mail bombs and viruses that often result from e-mail marketing campaigns, or the cost of improved defensive software to keep out malicious hackers.

Most of the advocates for direct e-mail marketing take an ROI approach, with calculations such as "list rental, message creation, and message delivery cost us $5,000, and we generated $8,000 in revenue." But this view is a narrow view of the costs and doesn't take into account the time and effort spent dealing with problems. With response rates lower than 5 percent on direct e-mail, 95 percent of the people getting the message probably didn't want it (even if they opted-in). And while this response rate is acceptable for direct mail promotions, where people simply trash unwanted pitches, it's courting disaster online where a significant percentage of people complain about spam and a small percentage retaliate.

I use direct e-mail, but I use it much more cautiously than my direct marketing colleagues. I never rent lists, for example, but only use lists that are self-generated. I'm hyper targeted about whom I send to, and I avoid mailing more than once a quarter (not including newsletter subscriptions). For most online marketers, there are better strategies that might generate a lower ROI on the surface, but over the long run—when hidden defensive costs and brand damage are factored into the equation—produce better results. Not surprisingly, I think a key strategy overlooked by many marketers is to put your marketing message into other people's documents (such as list sponsorships or even ads in other people's direct mail). Let other folks deal with the technological headaches, the complaints, and the threats of lawsuits while you protect your sanity and your brand.

My focus here is on the publicity uses for direct e-mail, and my experience is with five-figure mailing lists, not millions. Publicity uses for direct e-mail include news releases targeting the media, investor relations, community outreach, and to some degree opt-in mailings from registrations at your Web site or in response to promotional campaigns. My techniques for managing a contact database, formatting messages, sending messages, and handling follow-ups are covered thoroughly in the E-Mail News Releases chapter of this book. What follows are comments on the differences between e-mailing news releases and other types of direct e-mail.

Collecting Names

Names gathered from Web site opt-in lists or registrations are stored in a database where they can be retrieved for direct marketing efforts. I've always relied on IT people to set up the mechanics of this process and can't guide you on hardware and software beyond the advice given at the beginning of this chapter. Instead, I'll focus on how you decide what information to send to contacts gathered in this way.

Some sites default to adding your name to an opt-in list when you register as a member or user of the site although you never consented. Using lists generated this way will increase the percentage of complaints you get. It infuriates me that my AOL membership defaults to opt-in, and every time they add a new way of annoying me, I have to track down the opt-out triggers in the software. The process of disabling AOL's advertising machine is daunting, making you go to separate pages to turn off logon announcements, pop-up ads, Instant Messenger ads, e-mail ads, and so on. Does this situation give me a negative impression of AOL? You bet. Does it reduce AOL's ability to contact me with news I really care about? Absolutely.

A second method of collecting opt-ins is to use checkboxes that default to activated status and make users uncheck them to opt-out. While this method provides a way to opt-out during registration, many sites try to hide the checkboxes as much as possible or try to slip one by you with a row of unchecked boxes and one checked box. Once again, using opt-in methods that result in a significant percentage of people unintentionally giving you permission to e-mail them will increase the number of complaints you get. I think the ethical high ground in this regard is to require a positive action to opt-in—not the absence of a negative action.

One feature that will help cut down on complaints is to tell people up front how often you plan to e-mail them. The phrase "from time to time" appears on many Web sites and of course tells you nothing. You might indicate that you send announcements about once a month, daily, or weekly. Several times I've passed an opt-in I would have joined if I knew I would get only one monthly announcement. I refuse to give Web sites carte blanche to spam me at will, although I will register if the purpose is narrow enough and the frequency is rare enough.

There are many other good ways of collecting e-mail addresses of people interested in hearing from you on a regular basis. Some ideas include the following:

Discussion group postings. Offering a newsletter or notification service through discussion group postings

News releases. Including opt-in choices for journalists at the bottom of e-mail news releases, such as investor news, human resources news, local news, or breaking news

Seminars. Collecting the e-mail addresses of people who have participated in online seminars or workshops. Sometimes these addresses are collected by seminar partners who will share them with you upon request.

Chats. Collecting the addresses of people who participate in chats that you sponsor. Sometimes these can be gleaned from transcripts.

Banner advertising. I've used opt-in boxes on banner ads in the past with good success. My favorite design for a banner ad allows people to input their e-mail address right into the banner, as shown in Figure 5.1.

Figure 5.1 A banner advertisement used to collect names for an opt-in list. I like banner ads that don't require you to click through to a site to get what you want.

Message Content

Once you've collected names, what should you send them? Naturally, if you've specified the purpose of the opt-in, you should stick to it. If you promise news of new products or services, then don't send anything but that. Every time you send to a list, you risk opt-off attrition, so your reasons should be good. One of the catch-22s of direct e-mail is that people expect you to read their minds about *exactly* what they're interested in without providing you enough of their minds to read. Intrusive registration processes that would give you this kind of intelligence turn off too many good prospects. As in all matters involving Internet marketing, experience is the best guide.

To pull myself down from any ethical pedestal, I should mention right now that I'm not opposed to sending bulk e-mail to people who have not asked for it. When people subscribe to seminars that I sponsor, I will keep their e-mail addresses and notify them of any future seminars on the same topic. I will gather e-mail addresses from chats that I host and ask people if they want a transcript. As explained in the chapter on news releases, I will never ask journalists whether they want to be on my media list, although I'll promptly and permanently remove them if they ask to be taken off. I have a different perspective on this whole permissions marketing thing, which for lack of a better term I'll call *clairvoyant marketing*.

Clairvoyant marketing means somehow divining the subjects that a person is interested in and sending them messages related only to those subjects. Whether or not someone has given you permission to talk with them, they are interested in what they're interested in. If you guess correctly about their interests, you will be rewarded, and if you guess incorrectly, you will be punished. And, frankly, most people won't voluntarily provide enough information for you to clearly know their interests. I guess, and I modify my behavior based on a pattern of successful and unsuccessful guesses.

I'm guilty of using my own attitudes as a guide to the preferences of others (that's part of being clairvoyant). I don't mind getting spam if it's something I'm interested in, and I don't like time-wasting messages even if I opted-in. I have a sister-in-law who sends me every sappy chain letter that hits the Internet, and while I'd like to strangle her some days, she's definitely staying on my opt-in list. And I admit to buying cheap toner cartridges from a spam artist who guessed my printer correctly. For me, the rule is to send people what they want and don't send people what they don't want, whether they opt-in or not. The cost of guessing wrong is high enough to keep me from erring on the side of indiscretion. Many people who use opt-in marketing delude themselves into thinking that there is no penalty for guessing wrong because they have permission.

Clairvoyance can be cultivated. I carefully track the replies to all news releases I send so I can zero-in on a journalist's beat. Just because someone writes for a computer magazine doesn't mean they want every news release related to computers. I need to know whether they cover hardware or software, business news or consumer news, or operating systems or applications. When sending to the public, I'll capture any information that comes back, such as zip codes in signature files or job titles, and add it to my database to more correctly code people's interests. If I get more than a few complaints on any mailing, I'll analyze my copywriting for errors of judgment. Unlike ROI guys who are looking for a small percentage of positive responses, I formulate my messages and choose my lists to generate *no complaints*. How many permissions marketing people have that as a goal?

So the content of your message needs to be as microscopically targeted as possible to the interests of the people on your list. One way to help generate clairvoyance is to offer something of value in a message that will allow you to measure response. I dislike announcements that have no feedback loop. The simplest method is to code URLs in a direct mail piece so you can tell exactly where your Web traffic is coming from. Giant bulk e-mailers will test a variety of different announcements to discover which wording pulls best and then roll out a campaign. For the kind of small-list marketing discussed in this chapter, that's not practical—but you can learn a lot about message content from analyzing the spam you get every day. For example, contrary to those who tout rich e-mail, almost all of the big-league professional spam I get is text. I know that if these sharks perceived even a one-tenth of one percent increase in response rates for rich media, I would be inundated with rich spam. And that brings me to my next topic.

Message Format

As you can already tell, I'm not keen on rich media in e-mail messages. I prefer to write and format messages in a word processing program using a monospace font such as Courier and a fixed line length of 55 characters. Once I'm happy with the message and it has been approved by clients and superiors, I'll save it as "text only with line breaks" to preserve the right-hand margin. All the non-ASCII formatting will drop out, such as bold, italics, and tabs—with a few important exceptions. Characters such as smart quotes, dashes, and ampersands will look fine in a text document on your computer screen but will be converted to ASCII equivalents by the receiver's e-mail software and will look like the alpha-numeric gibberish seen so often in spam messages. You might have to disable all automatic formatting features in your word processor to catch these gremlins.

E-mail messages should be kept short. This advice should go without saying, but considering the number of 24-page bulk e-mails I receive, some people still don't get it. Three paragraphs usually suffice: 1) the hook, 2) the pitch, and 3) the call to action. The hook establishes a bond between the sender and the receiver. A typical hook is, "Here is the information you requested," which lets me know I supposedly asked for this information. The pitch is where you explain why your news is so important to warrant a spot in my inbox. The call to action is a request for me to take a measurable step, such as replying to the message or visiting a Web site. Amazon.com has been cited by many direct e-mail marketing gurus as a masterful mailer, and I agree. Let's look at one of the company's pitches:

```
Dear Amazon.com Customer,

   As somebody who's purchased CDs by Bill Evans in
   the past, you might like to know about the new
   reissue of his long unavailable second
   collaboration with Tony Bennett, "Together Again."
   For the next few days, you can order your copy at a
   savings of 30% by following the link below:

   http://www.amazon.com/exec/obidos/ASIN/B00002MZ3D

   Longtime admirers of one another, Tony Bennett and
   Bill Evans finally recorded together in 1975; the
   low-key "Tony Bennett/Bill Evans Album" has taken
   its place as a classic in both men's catalogs. But
   their second and final disc, "Together Again," was
   made for the small Improv label in 1977 and never
   appeared on CD-until now. The duo demonstrate
   their musical bond on standards ("A Child Is Born,"
   "You Don't Know What Love Is," "You Must Believe in
   Spring") and a number of deserving lesser-known
   tunes. The Rhino label's remastered version
   includes the bonus tracks "Who Can I Turn To" and
   "Dream Dancing" along with many alternate takes.

   To learn more about "Together Again," please visit
   the following page at Amazon.com:

   http://www.amazon.com/exec/obidos/ASIN/B00002MZ3D

   Happy listening,

   Rickey Wright
   Music Editor
   Amazon.com

   P.S. We hope you enjoyed receiving this message.
   However, if you'd rather not receive any future
   notices of this sort from Amazon.com, please visit
   your Amazon.com Subscriptions page:

   http://www.amazon.com/subscriptions
```

Notice the hook in the first sentence: "As somebody who's purchased CDs by Bill Evans in the past, you might like to know about the new reissue . . . " They've got my number. What's important here is not so much that Amazon knows what I've bought but that they explain up-front the reason why they're writing to me. In a similar fashion, I start all news releases with wording as follows: "As a freelance journalist covering software development issues, I'm writing to inform you about . . . " For opt-in mail, I always begin with, "You requested information about . . . ," and for non opt-in, I'll start with something like, "You attended the chat I hosted for . . . " or "As someone who participated in the Dearborn Financial Planning Seminar, I thought you would be interested in . . . " These hooks help make an immediate connection by demonstrating that the e-mail is not random.

Amazon's second paragraph elaborates on the selling proposition. The fact that this CD is a new release is important, perhaps justifying interrupting my day and making the announcement newsworthy. The call to action is to visit the Web site for a limited-time, 30 percent discount. The pitch would have been more compelling if they told me I could listen to some of the tracks at the site. I might have gone for a listen and been unable to resist the "add to shopping cart" button. Putting the name of an editor at the end of the pitch is a nice touch and warms up this bulk mail, although I don't believe for a second that a reply to this message would reach Rickey Wright. Finally, Amazon provides opt-off instructions, which is good, although it would be better if I could opt-off via e-mail rather than having to visit the site, log in, and drill down to unsubscribe.

Amazon follows classic formatting in this e-mail: ASCII text, dashes rendered as two hyphens, song titles enclosed in quotation marks instead of using italics, no smart quotes or smart apostrophes, and line length forced to about 55 characters. They also used full Web address protocol, including the "http://" preface, which turned the URLs into hotlinks in my e-mail program. You would be surprised by the number of e-mails I get with URLs that don't include the "http://" tag, forcing me to cut and paste the address if I want to visit the page. Repeating the URL for the target page was unnecessary, but this feature is a small flaw in an otherwise excellent document.

If you feel you have a compelling story to tell that takes more than three paragraphs, then make the e-mail a teaser and offer to send the full story via e-mail or make a case for visiting a Web site. Bulk e-mail is best seen as a notification service, surveying a large number of prospects to find those interested in the item. Brief e-mail reduces complaints and take-off requests from those not interested and provokes a measurable response from those who are interested. Constantly challenge yourself to say less and entice more. Try to cultivate an attitude that by leaving things out, you're adding to the mystery and lure of your message.

As for rich e-mail, I recommend that you forget about using graphics, fancy fonts, animation, multimedia, or—heaven forbid—file attachments. Recently, I received bulk e-mail that included a pitch for a seminar on e-mail marketing. The rich formatting on the message was a nightmare when viewed in my e-mail program, with borders breaking horribly, graphics strewn everywhere, broken images, and dysfunctional links. I decided not to take instruction from this guru. If you really want to experiment with these features, then ask people when they opt-in on your list if they prefer text or rich media.

Delivery and Follow-Up

I still send my bulk e-mail the old-fashioned way, exporting the e-mail addresses from my database and piling them into the Blind Copy field of an e-mail message. Due to the anti-spam software run by many ISPs, you might have to chop your distribution list into smaller pieces and send several copies of your message out. A better solution is to invest in one of the new bulk e-mail programs described at the beginning of this chapter. Most of these programs have mail merge features now so that you can personalize and customize each e-mail message. Using e-mail merge will improve the results of your bulk mail while helping you get past anti-spam software.

You should try to send your messages at a time of day when they're most likely to be opened immediately. Avoid sending messages on Friday, Saturday, Sunday, and Monday mornings. If your target is home computer users, you'd like your message to arrive between 6 p.m. and 11 p.m. in the user's time zone. If you are trying to reach people at work, send your message so that it arrives between 10 a.m. and 4 p.m. It's tempting to send messages at night, because there's less demand on computing resources at that time, but mailboxes that fill overnight are usually purged in the morning. Many people use alerts to notify them when e-mail is received, and if your e-mail arrives after the morning purge, it will probably get immediate attention and a fair chance to get opened.

If you don't have sophisticated bulk mailing software to handle replies and bounced messages, you should at least invest in e-mail software that has good filtering features. I use Eudora Pro specifically for its filtering capabilities. Here are some filtering suggestions for handling replies:

Bounces. Create a mailbox for undeliverable mail. Then, set a filter that if <subject line> includes <returned mail> or <delivery failure> or <warning> or <undeliverable>, then <transfer message> to <undeliverable mail>. You can pile bounced messages into this mailbox until you have time to go back and clean your list. One note of caution: This filter will catch all undeliverable messages, not just bulk mail bounces, so if you sent an important personal message that bounced, you might never know that your message didn't get through.

Replies. Create a mailbox for replies. Then, set a filter that if <subject line> includes <Re: original subject line>, then <transfer message> to <replies>. This action will segregate your bulk mail replies from your other e-mail to keep from swamping your inbox.

Requests. If your bulk mail message offers a document, coupon, instructions, or other file, you might be able to automate the processing of the requests. For example, when providing book excerpts, I ask people who want the excerpt to send mailto:myaddress with the subject line "Send ??? Excerpt," where ??? is the book name or author name. Then, I set up a mailbox for ??? Requests and a filter as follows: if <subject line> contains <Send ??? Excerpt> unless <subject line> contains <RE:>, then <reply with ??? Excerpt> and <transfer message> to <??? Requests>. The filter sends people the document they wanted, then stores their requests in a separate mailbox where I can find them if there's trouble. The portion of the filter that excludes "RE:" messages prevents me from sending the file to someone twice because they responded the first time with a comment or a thank you. This filter functions much like an auto-responder—a feature commonly found in listserver software. If you have listserver software, you can use an auto-responder in place of this e-mail filter.

When you get flames—and no matter how clairvoyant you are, you *will* get complaints—try this unique approach: apologize. In all the years I've been online, I've never received an apology in response to a complaint or a take off request. Perhaps that explains why my form apology is so effective—it catches people by surprise. Here's a generic wording you can use as a template:

```
You complained about the e-mail I sent you and asked to be taken off
my list. I apologize for soiling your In box and have removed your
name from my mailing list. I am not a spam artist; some time ago you
asked to be put on my notification list for announcements about
_____. I hate to lose anyone from my list, and I can be quite
discriminating about the kind of news I send you. If you would like
to remain on the list, please let me know, and I'll note any sub-
jects you prefer to get news about-or prefer *not* to receive.

Sincere Apologies,
STEVE O'KEEFE
```

I've had great success with this apology letter. More than half the people getting it have asked to remain on my list. Often, they've issued form flames without realizing it's a list to which they subscribed. Sometimes they give me clues about the kinds of material they don't want, such as new site announcements or financial news releases. Other times they will specify more clearly the subjects in which they are interested. If you offer a menu of list options in your apology letter, they might choose to narrow the number of lists to which they're subscribed.

It's not efficient to look at every contact on my list to determine whether they are right for a mailing. So I select people based on broad criteria, then deselect people who have a history of complaining. For example, anyone who complains but asks to stay on my list gets tagged as "touchy" in my database, and their particular preferences are noted in their record. After making selections for a mailing based on broad subject criteria, I'll search for all the *touchy* people on the list and examine their preferences one-by-one. Unless the mailing matches perfectly with their expressed interests, I'll delete them from the distribution list. As I said before, clairvoyance can be cultivated, and I view complaints as an opportunity to fine-tune my powers of perception. It takes time to market this way, but trust me, the goodwill it generates will pay dividends in the long run.

Online Newsletters

Newsletters are critical elements of online marketing efforts. They establish permission to talk with people who are interested in a company's products, services, and news. They're used by readers to gather information about special interests that are not covered well in the mainstream media. Newsletters allow for the dissemination of information more quickly than traditional print publications. For Web site hosts, newsletters provide a way to contact people between site visits, and the content of a newsletter will often give people a good reason to return to the site. Online newsletters are inexpensive to produce and distribute; unlike print publications, where delivery costs increase with the number of recipients, it's just as cheap to send an online newsletter to 10,000 people as it is to 500 people. No wonder so many Web sites offer newsletter subscriptions and so many readers have flocked to these special-interest publications.

That's the good news. But the bad news isn't so bad. Many people online have maxed out their capacity for online newsletters. If you're like me, you subscribe to many of these periodicals but rarely find time to read them. I'll subscribe to a newsletter, read an issue or two, and then start archiving them for a rainy day. Pretty soon, I'm dumping the archive once a month. Finally, I get honest with myself that I'm never going to read this publication, and I unsubscribe—or try to, at least. Getting off subscription lists can be frustrating, especially if you've changed e-mail addresses or forgotten a password.

Newsletter publishers all want to establish a "one-to-one" relationship with their readers. Many readers have no desire for a one-to-one relationship with Web sites or companies, however, and certainly they don't have the capacity for a one-to-one relationship with very many of them. I eat Campbell's soup, but do I want a one-to-one relationship with Campbell's? No. And think about that for a minute: How can you have a one-to-one relationship with a corporation? Do I want a one-to-one relationship with every person that works at Campbell's? Absolutely not! There must be tens of thousands of products in my home, many of them the collaborative effort of dozens of manufacturers. Do I want one-to-one relationships with all of these companies? And realistically, does Campbell's have the resources to handle one-to-one relationships with all the people who buy their soup?

My point here is that while I agree for the most part with marketing pundits who insist that every site should offer a newsletter, I think there's a little backlash against these periodicals, and you shouldn't put too many marketing resources into this basket. You have to ask yourself whether your subscribers are the people you'd hoped to reach or if those people must be courted in other ways. You can't delude yourself about the number of people subscribed to your publication. If 90 percent of them never read the newsletter, your subscription base means little. And you have to be realistic about the true costs of operating a newsletter. I've talked with many newsletter editors over the years, and a majority say that the effort involved was not nearly compensated for. For this reason, so many newsletters that started with high ambitions end quickly in disillusionment. I'll talk about some good alternatives to hosting your own newsletter at the end of this section.

On the positive side, newsletters are effective at increasing Web site traffic. They can help you build brand recognition and grab mindshare. They're good at establishing a person as an authority in a field, and even when not lucrative, they can lead to better gigs, such as a syndicated column, radio show, or TV show. They help a company maintain a dominant position in an industry. For many marketers, such as Richard Hoy, newsletters work because they make the cash register ring.

Richard Hoy is the president of Booklocker, an e-book publisher and vendor. With his partner, Angela Adair-Hoy, he produces the e-zine *The Write Markets*, which contains job prospects and tips for freelance writers at www.writemarkets.com. "Every time we send out an issue, sales jump," Hoy told me. More than the Web site or any other marketing tool they use, the newsletter is what gets people to buy. *The Write Markets* is crammed with sales copy: announcements of new products, paid advertisements, Web site bestseller lists, and plugs for books authored by Angela. Look at this snippet, which is just one page of a 30-page weekly newsletter:

```
P.S. Don't miss these new releases!

   HOW TO READ/WRITE A DIRTY STORY
   http://www.writersweekly.com/index-orderform.htm
   The how-to bible for erotica readers and writers. Susie
   Bright is the foremost expert in American erotic literature
   and publishing, and offers her candid advice on everything
   from getting ideas to writing a bestseller, all the way to
   transforming your erotic life through personal sex writing.

   HOW TO PUBLISH AND PROMOTE ONLINE
   by Angela Adair-Hoy and MJ Rose!
   http://www.amazon.com/exec/obidos/ASIN/0312271913/
thewritemarket00A
   "Anyone interested in e-books or e-publishing should
   read this informative - and ground-breaking - guide."
   -Publisher's Weekly

   THE COMPLETE GUIDE TO WRITING & SELLING MAGAZINE
   ARTICLES by Peggy Moss Fielding and Dan Case.
   http://www.writersweekly.com/magart.htm
   I predict this book will quickly become one of our best sellers!

   NEWSPAPER EDITOR EMAIL DIRECTORY
   http://www.writersweekly.com/index-orderform.htm
   Email your query to 2,000+ editors!


   =========================================
   BOOKLOCKER'S #1 BEST SELLER!!
   How to Make & Market Gel Candles That Sell Like Wildfire!
   http://www.booklocker.com/bookpages/lathomas01.html
   =========================================
```

Why would anyone wade through all of this marketing hype? The answer is, because the content in-between is so good and so on target. While half of every issue of *The Write Markets* is promotional, the other half contains legitimate tips for freelance writers about paying markets. Without that content, which is extremely valuable for freelance writers (as well as up-to-the-minute accurate), no one would read this zine. Because almost all the ads are for products directed at freelance writers, readers listen to the drumbeat of the marketing copy and go to the Web site to purchase the books and manuals that will show them how to take advantage of all those sales leads. *The*

Write Markets claims almost 55,000 subscribers, which means little because many if not most readers probably never open it. More useful are the Web site statistics, with 250,000 page views per month. Another important statistic is the amount of click-through, which is critical to advertisers and gives an impression of how active the list membership is. The best statistic is sales; the newsletter goes out, the sales go up, and the revenue more than compensates for the labor in producing the zine.

It's no surprise that Richard Hoy is at the helm of such a successful online newsletter. Hoy was the moderator of Tenagra's highly regarded Online Advertising Discussion List for many years at www.o-a.com. Not only did he learn how to manage a successful list there, but the active subscriber base is also made up of online marketing professionals sharing their secrets and opinions with each other. Hoy also ran ClickZ's list for years, and you'll find archives of his articles at that site. A personal friend and former coworker, Hoy has made no secret of his desire to write a book about e-mail marketing. He's probably too busy making money with Booklocker and *The Write Markets* to collect his wisdom between two covers. I'm indebted to Hoy for many of the concepts in this chapter, from the technical how-to to the incredible depth of experience he has with newsletter content.

Designing a Good Online Newsletter

Let's begin with the purpose of your newsletter. What do you want it to do? If you want the newsletter to bring people back to a Web site, then load it with good reasons to do so, such as contests, incentives, events, and new features. If you want the newsletter to sell, then load it up with easy buying links and surround it with compelling sales copy. If you want to lure prospects for a product or service that can't be sold with a simple link, then offer something to flush out potential buyers, like an article or seminar. If you're hoping to earn money by selling ads on the list or selling services, then you'd better have amazing content, flawless formatting, and terrific technical support. If you're trying to establish yourself as an authority in a field, then offer advice or answers to subscribers' questions. If you are trying to fulfill regulatory obligations by informing investors of material news, then stick to the facts and don't try to build your newsletter into a community.

Once you understand the purposes of your newsletter, research the market and see what else is out there. Visit Yahoo! Groups and Topica and search them by keyword for sample lists. Figure 5.2 shows the results of a search at Topica for newsletters about agribusiness. There were nearly 40 newsletters available, not including the 16 separate dairy science zines. If you haven't already, subscribe to a variety of newsletters and keep a list of good ideas, both in terms of content and design. How easy was it to subscribe and unsubscribe? What formats look appealing? What features would make good additions to your newsletter?

Voice

The tone of your newsletter will go a long way toward determining how well it fulfills its purpose. A formal, objective tone lends itself to news distribution, financial announcements, legal notices, and so on—in short, pieces you are required to distrib-

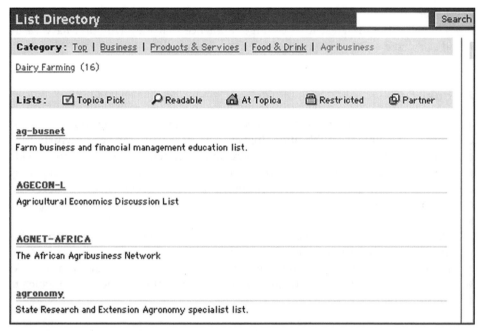

Figure 5.2 When designing a newsletter, sample the competition. This search at Topica for agribusiness zines turned up more than 40 publications.

ute where you don't want to engage readers so much as fulfill obligations. If you're trying to engage readers, you need a more biased approach. "People build relationships with other people, not with faceless corporations," says Richard Hoy in an article for ClickZ. "So your newsletter needs to be written by a real person. And the personality of that individual needs to come through in the writing," Hoy says. If you're trying to establish yourself as an authority, then you need to express strongly felt opinions. People who like your opinions will stay on as avid readers, and those who don't will look elsewhere.

Many newsletters are composed largely of comments by readers. These discussion groups can have the most loyal following of all zines, building a real sense of community among subscribers. That doesn't mean you take a hands-off approach. In fact, user-contributed zines require a great deal of moderating and hand-holding to keep the discussion from melting down into arguments. As a moderator of such a group, you can expect to deal with a lot more complaints and requests than you get with a producer-driven publication. Sometimes just a small letters to the editor section in your zine will help foster a strong sense of community.

The worst style for a newsletter, in my opinion, is the self-congratulatory drivel that passes for news at many corporate Web sites. Are your subscribers really interested about new deals you've cut, awards you've won, or good deeds your CEO has performed this week? Maybe you can slip this kind of information into a truly informative newsletter, but if that's all you have to report, why bother? The problem is that most newsletters need a strong, personal voice to thrive, and most corporations do not allow or reward that kind of presence. If you can't achieve this personal style in your newsletter, then you need to make up for it with extraordinary research to unearth news items of keen interest to your target audience that they wouldn't have easily found elsewhere.

Frequency

The main determinant of frequency is how often you have something worth saying. A daily dispatch is suited to publications that are user-driven but can be an awful burden on staff, especially if there is no revenue stream to compensate for the effort. Weekly publications are more typical but can tire subscribers if you don't have compelling content. A monthly list is about as far as you want to go between issues; otherwise, cautions Hoy, people will forget that they subscribed and will complain that you're spamming them.

Most listserving software gives users some control over how often they receive the publication. User-contributed newsletters will send out each message as it comes in. Subscribers can usually choose to receive either a daily or weekly digest instead. As with all things Internet, it's best to give subscribers a variety of options from which to choose.

Content Elements

I've seen the following content elements used in newsletters. You might want to mix and match from the list:

News briefs. Opinionated summaries of breaking news events carefully tailored to your target audience; should include URLs to full-length articles available on the Web.

Company news. Includes such things as earnings reports, stock performance, awards, community service, new product or service announcements, staff changes, and new features at the Web site. In my opinion, these announcements should be kept to the minimum and buried in a newsletter or strategically dropped into other stories unless the newsletter is an internal house organ.

Feature stories. You might have space for one feature story in each issue. I've seen many newsletters that give you a few paragraphs of a feature story, then a URL to a Web site where you can read the rest. This practice is annoying and defeats the point of having newsletters delivered. It's a better idea to just explain what content is available at the Web site than to start a story and abort.

Calendar of events. This calendar is a very useful item but is rarely included in newsletters. Events can include online items such as chats and seminars as well as offline events such as trade shows and speaking engagements. Having an events calendar can lead to advertising or sponsorships from event producers.

Interviews. Brief interviews with leaders in the field about subjects in the news are popular newsletter features and help establish you as an authority without having to toot your own horn.

Chat transcript snippets. Newsletters are great for hawking chat transcripts. A carefully selected tidbit or two from a chat will drive traffic to your site for full transcripts, which should contain complete marketing and promotional information. Chat appearances are undercovered by the mainstream press, so this content is unique for online publications.

Letters. Including a few short letters to the editor really perks up interest in a newsletter. For one thing, it lets subscribers know who else is getting the publication. If folks see a letter to the editor from a respected leader in the field, they'll pay more attention to the publication and probably pipe up with their own comments more often. You'll need to articulate a clear policy of being selective about letters and reserving the right to edit for space unless you plan to cede control of your publication to subscribers.

Polls. To draw out readers, you can bait them with a question of the week or a poll. I think the love of polls will fade soon, but for now folks can't seem to get enough of them.

Factoids. Factoids make good filler if used judiciously. In zines that are used to distribute news briefs, factoids will get the most reprint mileage and your publication will often be cited as the source, improving branding. Some publications have a running stat or metric that they examine each issue.

Format

It's no surprise that e-mail marketing guru Richard Hoy recommends a plain-text format for newsletters with a forced 50-character line length. He also advises against URLs that contain more than 80 characters, because they will likely break over two lines when the newsletter is sent out and the editor will get numerous complaints that the link doesn't work. Figure 5.3 shows a portion of a newsletter that suffers from bad design, with tabs and a long line length that make reading difficult.

Nowadays, it's common to offer a choice of formats including text, HTML, AOL, or reading at a Web site. If you're using commercial listserving software, it will probably have an automatic process for generating these multiple formats, although each version will require some tweaking.

Length is less critical than you might think. If the content is good, readers will hang in there for 10- and 20-page newsletters. Rare is the newsletter that is that good, however, and short newsletters have a better success rate and require less work to produce. One factor against long newsletters is that navigation is difficult. In text newsletters, you can't include a hyperlinked table of contents to help readers jump around. Scrolling is the only way to move, and people tire of it quickly. If your newsletter has grown into a monster, consider splitting hydra-like into multiple newsletters that address targeted segments of your audience.

Managing a Newsletter

In 1995, I interviewed Glenn Fleishman, moderator of the Internet Marketing mailing list, for an article in *Internet World* magazine about his experiences as an influential

```
┌─────────────────────────────────────────────────────────────┐
│                          Winning with Web Conferencing E-sales and │
│ E-learning                                                    │
│                          Smart Sales Force and Channel Partner Training │
│                          Every Tuesday, 11 AM PDT/2 PM EDT    │
│                                                               │
│                          This seminar is for sales or training professionals │
│ who want to keep their sales team and partner channel up-to-date and ready to drive revenue quickly. │
│                                                               │
│                          Register Now:                        │
│ http://www.placeware.com/seminar/esales1.html?167.NA.US.01.MA.11.7.CC01.1.4.25.0 │
│                                                               │
│                               ***                             │
│                                                               │
│                          E-marketing with Web Seminars        │
│                          Generating Sales Leads and Increasing Return on │
│ Investment through Web Seminars                               │
│                          Every Wednesday, 11 AM PDT / 2 PM EDT │
│                                                               │
│                          If you're in sales or marketing and are interested in │
│ getting the most return on your marketing dollars, you won't want to miss this presentation. │
│                                                               │
│                          Register Now:                        │
│ http://www.placeware.com/seminar/websem.html?167.NA.US.01.MA.11.7.CC01.1.4.25.0 │
│                                                               │
│                          Back to top                          │
└─────────────────────────────────────────────────────────────┘
```

Figure 5.3 Excerpt from a poorly designed e-mail newsletter. The tabs and line length make it difficult to read.

newsletter editor. Fleishman articulated the litany of woes that fall upon any high-volume list operator: technical gremlins in the software creating numerous problems; dozens of duplicate messages informing him about those problems; hundreds of unsubscribe requests directed to him personally or sent out as part of the newsletter instead of using the unsubscribe address; people on the list constantly rehashing the same, tired topics; people complaining about censorship; people complaining about not enough censorship; trying to keep the newsletter spam-free; and trying to steer discussion to fruitful new topics and away from personal attacks. One of the more humorous but difficult problems to fix: people who go on vacation and set up an e-mail autoreply. Every time the list sends a message to that person, the autoreply sends a vacation notice to the list, leading to an infinite loop of hundreds of vacation messages going out to everyone on the list. What a nightmare.

Glenn spent many hours every day working on the list. It was one of the most important forums covering the commercial uses of the Internet and had a Who's Who of digital marketing gurus as subscribers. Some months later, with list membership hovering at about 10,000 people, Glenn instituted a voluntary subscription fee of $30/year. *Three* people subscribed—an early example of the maxim that people won't pay for online content. Shortly thereafter, Glenn closed the list and called it quits.

If your newsletter is going to be any good and your subscriber base reaches a respectable volume, you can expect to spend a lot of time managing your list. For starters, you should expect to use the services of two people: one writer and one tech expert. Sometimes you get lucky and can find an individual with skills in both departments, but these people will usually have better job offers than newsletter editor. For publicity or marketing departments, you'll either need someone inside the department with great tech skills or someone from the IT department who will work closely with you. Mistakes in newsletter operations can cost the entire corporation. If your company gets blacklisted for spamming violations, e-mail from anyone at the company to anyone outside of the company could be blocked. And this situation can happen even if you aren't spamming, but some hacker is using your company's servers to dish out spam.

For a weekly company newsletter, I've had good success working with one writer and having that person interview the staff of other departments once a week. My experience is that if I ask department heads for a weekly summary or news item, I won't get it. But if the newsletter editor calls them or makes an office visit, he or she will get plenty of content for the company newsletter. After writing, spell checking, and final approval, the newsletter can be dispatched and archived on the Web site.

If you're planning to generate revenue from your newsletter, you'll need to budget staff time for selling ads and sponsorships. You can do some selling through the newsletter itself with a rate card at your Web site, but profitable newsletters usually employ sales representatives who use direct mail solicitations and work the telephone to sell ads. This statement brings me to the next topic for discussion: revenue streams.

Revenue Streams

Getting revenue out of an online newsletter is like getting blood from a stone. Many have tried, and a few have succeeded. While my focus is on the promotional benefits of newsletters, I'll share a few revenue-generating strategies that might help cut the costs of your operation.

One reason why Glenn Fleishman couldn't get paying subscribers for his excellent Internet Marketing group was that few people on the list recognized the value of his contributions. He labored behind the scenes, keeping the list free of spam and vitriol. His contribution was largely unseen and therefore undervalued. Glenn should have given us daily statistics, such as how many hours he put in or how many messages he removed, so that we could better appreciate what he was doing for us.

The Write Markets newsletter makes money through a variety of revenue streams. First and foremost are the sales of books, articles, and other products from the Web site. The second source is advertising and sponsorship sales. Ads in the newsletter cost $50 per line, and there are several slots available per week. The newsletter also sells classified ads, buried at the end, for $10 per line. I've not subscribed to any other newsletter that sells classified ads.

Ad prices for most periodicals are based on circulation, but pricing advertising for online newsletters this way is misleading. The *circulation* of a free newsletter and the *readership* can be leagues apart; a high percentage of issues never get opened. Sponsorship rather than ad space is probably a better way to sell advertising. Sponsorship packages are usually exclusive and include branding opportunities in the newsletter, on the Web site, and even through direct e-mail. The Online Advertising Discussion List—a successor to Fleishman's list—sells exclusive sponsorships for $4,875 per week.

Other revenue-generating schemes include pricing ads according to how many people click through to the advertiser's site. This situation gets around the issue of inflated circulation figures, but the money in such deals isn't worth chasing for the vast majority of newsletters. Another method is to sell direct e-mail solicitations, spamming your subscribers for a fee. As long as there's an opt-in on the solicitation list (and an opt-out), it's fair game. Many newsletter subscribers will give you permission to send them information on products and services related to the topic of the newsletter, and several newsletter editors I know have made a reasonable sum this way. For lists that reach highly targeted professionals, such as doctors or IT managers, advertisers are willing to pay outrageous costs-per-thousand to advertise this way.

If your newsletter content is good enough, you might be able to generate revenue by selling it or syndicating it to other sites. As the dot.com crash sinks in, many news sites have disappeared and the survivors have reached out to form partnerships to aggregate content and cut costs. Founded in 2001, Web site Plastic.com features content gathered through a dozen different partnerships, including *SPIN*, *New Republic*, *Wired News*, and *NetSlaves*. You don't have to be on the level of *SPIN* to syndicate your content online, although the benefits might be more promotional than financial. For more information, consult the Syndication chapter of this book.

For most newsletter editors, the benefits are not direct revenue but more sales leads and a higher profile in the industry. You might have to scale back your newsletter ambitions to match the reality of their bottom-line impact. Or, you could take my favorite approach, and instead of building a newsletter yourself, you could channel your content to newsletters that are already serving your target market.

Promoting through Other People's Newsletters

Promoting through other people's newsletters is perhaps the most underused marketing tactic on the Internet. Unlike Web advertising, which has consolidated around a few advertising networks that can coordinate payments and creative deployment through thousands of sites, the newsletter advertising market is fragmented and underserviced. Prices for advertising in these periodicals are rock bottom, and while many subscribers don't read their issues, those that do form an active and attractive audience.

A coordinated campaign of list sponsorships can have a far greater impact than a similar amount spent on Web site advertising. Marketers should make an effort to get rate cards from newsletters that appeal to their target audiences and see for themselves the benefits of list sponsorship. And there's a market out there for advertising agencies to develop a network of lists and broker ad placements for clients. These newsletters deserve financial support, and heaven knows they could use the money.

With a glut of newsletters on the market, companies should look hard at the benefits of partnering with existing projects rather than launching one of their own. News briefs can be fed into popular newsletters, reducing the editorial burdens on newsletter staff and increasing the readership for company news. Feature articles can also be syndicated this way, along with statistics and news about chats and other online events. If your goal as a publicist is to increase the profile of your company and its products and services, your best strategy might be to scrap the company newsletter and cut deals to send the content where the target audience reads.

Case History: Publishers' Lunch

Naturally, my favorite online newsletter is one that covers a subject of interest to me: the book publishing industry. But the attraction goes beyond subject matter; I've subscribed to literally thousands of online newsletters over the past seven years. For each promotional campaign I do, I might subscribe to 20 different publications, make an announcement, and then unsubscribe. I've been exposed to every zine format imaginable, and I think *Publishers' Lunch* is the finest example of an online newsletter I've encountered. So I interviewed editor Michael Cader to give you a behind-the-scenes look at what it takes to run a top-flight online publication.

Publishers' Lunch, at www.publisherslunch.com, is a daily news summary for the publishing industry written by editor Michael Cader, president of Cader Books, a book packaging firm with headquarters in Manhattan. Cader Books mostly works with household-name franchises to develop books and calendars around brands. They've created books for *Saturday Night Live* and its many spin-offs, calendars for Disney and Tom Clancy, and "Recipeasels" for the Moosewood cookbook and a few famous chefs. Michael Cader had a strong relationship with Seth Godin back when Seth was just a hard-working author and not a new economy guru. Michael has a fascination with electronic publishing, and in particular, e-books, and has become an oft-quoted authority on these matters.

Publishers' Lunch began publication in e-mail format in the summer of 2000. The initial circulation was most likely to Michael Cader's e-mail list of clients, friends, and publishing insiders (we didn't discuss this point), and the subscriber base has grown through prominent promotion at the Cader Books Web site and through strong word-of-mouth. Today, the newsletter has about 10,000 subscribers and is published every working day, delivered at about noon New York time—just in time for lunch.

Content and Format

Publishers' Lunch is a breezy read. Each issue contains between five and 10 news summaries, written in a casual, snappy style by Cader. Here is the newsletter's mission statement, if you will, from the Web site: "Publishers' Lunch is the industry's 'daily essential read,' gathering together stories from all over the web and print of interest to the professional trade book community, with a little perspective and the occasional wisecrack added in." The target audience is very focused—a good feature for an electronic newsletter. Here is a sample news brief that gives a taste of Michael's writing style:

```
Advance Look at Tina and Harry Bio

Judy Bachrach's book about Tina Brown and Harry Evans has a pub
dateof July 31 but books are already shipping and conceivably will
be instores any day now. Inside says the book is embargoed, but it
soundslike everyone's already got a copy--Michael Wolff is writing
about it on Monday, the NYTimes "will weigh in before publication.
"Inside, too, has read the book "and is happy to pre-emptively pee
all over it for you." Far be it for me to characterize it any dif-
ferently. The extensive story is billed as "exclusive," yet at the
```

```
same time Sara Nelson wonders, "will anybody west of the Hudson
care?" S&S has announced a 25,000-copy first printing.

   Inside on Tina and Harry
   http://link.ixs1.net/s/link/click?rc=al&rti=443039&si=d9211395
```

Cader has a good nose for news, an instinct from years of experience about the stories that matter to his readers. He name drops a lot, careful to include such information as an author's agent, a ghost writer's name, an acquisitions editor's name, or a publicist's name. These details are relished by industry insiders. He uses the jargon of the trade, such as "pub date" in this particular example. His comment that the book is "embargoed, but it sounds like everyone's already got a copy," is a typical Cader zinger, pointing out the hypocrisy of publishers who claim to be withholding review copies of a book from everyone while leaking some to media heavyweights or people they favor. Cader does most of his cut-up work with judicious selection of quotations, letting *Inside* magazine cut loose in this excerpt. This point is important for newsletter editors: When you write news summaries, you get to frame the story.

Publishers' Lunch is gossipy, and I asked Michael Cader if he ever got in trouble with readers for his sharp cursor. He said that subscribers have responded positively to the frequently sarcastic tone. "Everyone likes it when I say something nasty about someone else." Indeed, part of the fun of reading *Publishers' Lunch* is to see who Michael is going to skewer today, although he's really a reporter and most of the damage is self-inflicted by the people he covers. Richard Hoy's criteria that a newsletter needs a strong personal voice to succeed is evident here, but if you're representing an organization and can't afford to be too opinionated, you can still engage readers by framing news stories from your own perspective.

Publishers' Lunch uses standard online newsletter design: text only, a narrow column width, lots of white space to separate stories, and links to sources or longer articles. Each issue begins with a table of contents, formatted in ASCII-friendly characters as follows:

```
**************************************************************
   Table of Contents
**************************************************************
- Today's Meal
  + Top Stories
  + The Basics
  + Cry the Beloved Oprah
  + Random Finalizes Mondadori Joint Venture
  + Fodor's Launches e-Books With Free Title
  + Poll Says Teens Love Reading
  + Advance Look at Tina and Harry Bio
  + E-Books and Libraries
  + Baker and Taylor Develops e-Book Initiatives for Libraries

- A Good Day for Jobs
  + Both Seekers and Employees
```

In addition to the text version, subscribers have their choice of HTML or AOL. Subscribe and unsubscribe instructions are included in every issue, although people obviously have trouble understanding how to cancel their subscriptions. Michael Cader has taken to YELLING at them in all capital letters to "PLEASE do not tell me" about address changes. "Instead, interact directly with the system," he says. All newsletter editors should brace themselves for the fact that no matter how easy and clear the mechanics are for getting onto and off of the list, you'll still get many e-mails a day asking for assistance—some of them employing the most repugnant language. This constant vitriol over simple matters has soured many an editor toward online publishing.

As *Publishers' Lunch* has grown, Cader has spun off two other publications: *E-Publishers' Lunch* and *DealLunch*, the later covering mostly big money book publishing contracts. This strategy is important for all newsletters editors to tune into. If your membership is getting large and satisfying everyone starts to get difficult, consider refining your focus with splinter publications. You'll develop an instinct for when readership declines (even if subscriptions are going up), and that can be a warning signal that it's time to re-evaluate your focus. After you've operated a newsletter for a while, you'll get a good idea of the concerns of your readers, and you can even migrate the membership over to a more tightly focused zine then kill off the parent publication.

The links in *Publishers' Lunch* to source documents have a unique format that allows Michael Cader to measure the number of people clicking through to any story. I haven't seen this linking style used in many newsletters, but it's extremely helpful. Tracking links helps give you an idea of how active the list membership is. For example, the most active story on *Publishers' Lunch* generates between 150 and 300 clickthroughs a day. The highest clickthrough ever was about 1,000, which at that time represented 15 percent of the subscriber base. By tracking the clickthrough to the subscriber ratio over time, you can more closely estimate the number of subscribers who don't read their issues.

Cader cautions against putting too much emphasis on clickthrough, because he believes that if his summaries tell the story sufficiently, there is no need to click through to the full article. That's part of the point of the publication—to spare readers the chore of locating these stories and wading through them for the meat. Cader believes he delivers the meat, and failing to do so can artificially increase clickthrough. He has a better method for estimating active participation: He can tell whether HTML subscribers have opened their newsletters. More than half of them do every day. Then, he can apply the same percentage of unopened issues to the text and AOL versions to arrive at an active readership rate.

Cader uses eWayDirect software for managing his mailing list, formatting issues, and distributing them online. I'm impressed by eWayDirect's services, especially the tracking feature. There are bugs, just like any listserving software, but Cader says that the staff is attentive to his concerns (a rarity in this business). eWayDirect at first provided its services free in exchange for being able to run ads in each issue of *Publishers' Lunch*. After the dot.com crash, eWayDirect needed revenue, just like everyone else, and began charging for the service. The Web site for eWayDirect, www.ewaydirect .com, doesn't quote prices and Cader didn't elaborate, but I got the impression that it's an affordable solution. Cader considered using Lyris but wanted to buy the service and get good support instead of installing software himself.

Revenue Streams

Publishers' Lunch is a labor of love. Cader sells advertising and sponsorships, but the money they bring in is negligible. A new feature of the zine that's quite popular is a job board. Employers can post openings there for $199 and get a full refund if they aren't happy. But the money isn't going into Cader's pocket. The job board is operated by MediaBistro, and they keep 100 percent of the posting fees. Cader sees it as an important service that he's able to provide readers at no cost to himself.

Cader also partnered with BoardHost to maintain a set of message boards for *Publishers' Lunch*. The boards are lightly used, averaging about 10 postings per week, and many of the postings are commercial hustling. Michael told me that he suspected that his readership of industry heavyweights wouldn't have much interest in the message boards, "and I was right." But the boards cost him nothing; the company that maintains them sells advertising on the boards and does not share the revenue with Cader.

One of Cader's goals with *Publishers' Lunch* is provide the content his readers want without busting his budget. His partnerships have been formed more with an eye to reducing costs and administrative responsibilities than generating earnings. This function is a clear application of my philosophy to look for partners who are strong where you are weak. If you want to publish an online newsletter, you can get all of the infrastructure you need for free and focus your attention on the content.

I asked Michael Cader the killer question: How many hours do you spend a day on *Publishers' Lunch*? I almost hate to ask that question, because most newsletter editors coldly analyzing the ROI will cease publication immediately. Cader replied that it takes one-and-a-half to four hours per day on average, and I got the impression that the four-hours-a-day figure was closer to the truth. With no real revenue stream, I asked him whether the newsletter helped bring in business. "Actually, it's hurt my business," he said, explaining that the publication hadn't really flushed out a higher number of quality prospects and that his editorial duties cut into the time available to handle paying work. I asked whether *Publishers' Lunch* helped him land his paying gig covering electronic publishing for *Inside* magazine. "I had a relationship with the people there already," he said, but acknowledged that it didn't hurt.

Conclusion

With all the hours that *Publishers' Lunch* takes and all the frustration dealing with technical issues, the relentlessness of a daily publishing schedule, and no material revenue stream, why does Michael Cader continue to publish? "It's exhausting," he said, "but it's great fun. It certainly gives me a high profile." I got the impression that Cader is a news addict, and *Publishers' Lunch* gives him an excuse to indulge his hobby and the satisfaction of sharing his opinions with the leading figures in the industry. Ultimately, ROI has nothing to do with it. He'll keep publishing as long as it makes him happy.

For those considering online newsletters, the lesson here is that you have to bring some passion to the proceedings; you won't be able to justify the work involved in terms of financial performance. If you don't have that passion, perhaps you should consider supporting the efforts of those who do with sponsorship dollars or content partnerships. And if you do have that passion, perhaps your publication *will be profitable* someday, although it might be difficult to measure exactly how. Successful newsletters, like successful small businesses, always look like a bad idea when they start—but if the passion is there, it's amazing how often they beat the odds and succeed.

Top Tips

ASCII nicely. Plain text is still the preferred format for both direct e-mail and online newsletters, with line lengths no longer than 55 characters. You can offer HTML or rich media on an opt-in basis, but default to text.

Cultivate clairvoyance. You'll increase the results of your mailings and reduce the number of complaints you get by honing in on subscriber interests. Consider narrowing the focus of your newsletters based on experience. Carefully track reactions and reading patterns for better clues as to what your audience wants.

Put honey on your burns. When you get flamed for spamming, don't just take those people off your list. Try apologizing and offering alternatives. You might retain half or more of them, and you'll create a lasting impression of attentiveness and thoughtfulness.

Use someone else's server. The easiest way to reduce the costs and administrative headaches of running an online newsletter is to use someone else's server. Yahoo! Groups and Topica will handle the infrastructure for free, or you can hire an inexpensive service such as eWayDirect or PostCast.

Don't hide your bite under a bushel. The most successful newsletters convey the personality of a strong editor. You have more to lose from appearing objective than from letting your opinions be known.

Publish or cherish? With so many newsletters out there, does the public really need yours? You might be able to achieve your objectives with less work and expense by sharing content with, and financially supporting, the best newsletters that are already serving your target audience.

CHAPTER

6

Chat Tours

The Internet is alive with chat. On ESPN.com, boxer Oscar De La Hoya boasts about an upcoming bout. At MSNBC, the Dave Matthews Band shares stories with groupies. At MedSupport, multiple sclerosis caregivers learn new ways to ease the pain. At Oprah.com, Gary Zukav helps people find meaning in their lives. From the banal to the profound, from silly entertainment to life-saving skills, the Internet is buzzing with a crazy wave of interactive indulgence that we call chat.

In the past seven years, I have booked hundreds of tours for chat guests. I watched as children used the Internet for the first time to ask innocent questions of the Berenstain Bears. I cried at stories of abuse streaming across my screen during a Talk City chat with a family therapist. I laughed at the stupid tricks suggested by David Pogue, author of *Magic for Dummies*. I sat alone in a building design forum, feeding questions to a famous architect just to get a good transcript. I've seen everything that chat has to offer, enough to understand that chat is unlike any other form of human communication and enough to know that—like it or not—chat is here to stay.

A lot of people hate chat. It's confusing, they say, hard to use, and frustrating. Or it's shallow, vacuous, and lame. And they're right, chat is difficult to use and often results in noisy, primitive, disgusting interaction. But chat also fulfills one of the promises of the Internet: that the common people will be in charge, that regular folks will get to interview superstars, and that famous people can talk to fans without a mediator. While chat fails to live up to this mission, the magic happens often enough to keep people coming back.

Chats are one of the only reliable vehicles for Internet-acceptable promotions. Produce a chat program, and you can post messages to discussion groups, pad a portal with promo copy, and get listings in event calendars online and offline. There are two barriers to making chat tours pay off. The first is booking top venues, an exercise in frustration if there ever was one. The second is tapping the publicity potential of public appearances, which takes a great deal of preparation and hard work. This chapter will help you get your guests on the hottest sites and use those gigs to generate a maelstrom of media coverage.

Topics covered include the following:

Can we talk? An excursion into the wild world of online chat. You'll learn why people love chat, why people hate chat, and how marketers use chat to push products. You'll also visit the dark underbelly of the chat world and see how it is completely different from the moderated world of celebrity chat.

Preparing for chat. The way to get top bookings is to do all the work for your chat hosts and serve them a program on a silver platter. I'll show you how to use the Chat Profile to make hosts an offer that they can't refuse, how to pump-up your appearances with support files, and how to prepare your guests.

Booking chats. It can take months to book a chat tour if you don't know how to pitch your programs like a pro. I'll show you how to find power players on top Web sites, AOL, and CompuServe and how to seal deals in record time.

Promoting chats. A chat without promotion is a waste of good electricity. Learn how to turn a 45-minute appearance into a month-long installation and how to use discussion group postings, news releases, and events calendars to magnify the impact of your events.

Conducting chats. A look behind the screens at what happens at a chat. You'll learn how to handle hosts and manipulate moderators and how to deal with ghosts (typists), gremlins (technical difficulties), and goofy guests.

Chat follow-up. It's not over until it's over; how to buff transcripts and distribute them online and how to suck-up to hosts and turn your successful chat into a syndicated program

Can We Talk?

I don't know if you've visited many online chats, but I've always found them kind of lame. You park your cursor in this auditorium and wait for the main guest to show. Maybe you kill time conversing with other members on your "channel" or in your "row." This small talk is often more fun than the main event.

Finally, the moderator shows up. The guest is introduced and you get a plug for his or her new book or CD or movie or whatever, and then the chat begins. You've always wanted to know what the guest thought about working with so-and-so. You type your question and send it to the moderator. Now, you wait for your question to be asked. You see all the other questions go by, and they all sound so similar:

```
CyberDude22: I've been a fan of yours since the very beginning.
What is your favorite [book, record, movie, movie star, color,
song, hairstyle, scene, character, outfit, instrument, pet, lip-
stick, etc.]?
```

Isn't someone going to ask an intelligent question? In the long pause between question and answer, as the guest furiously types a reply, the moderator slips in another ad for Chevrolet or some online event or another plug for the guest's latest release. Finally, your question gets asked—the moment you've been waiting for. All these years, you've wondered what it was like working with so-and-so, and now the answer comes:

```
Guest: Interesting.
Moderator: Our next question comes from...
```

Huh? That's it? "Interesting." No detail? No follow-up? I'm outta here! And so you log off and once again the lure of the Internet fails to live up to its promise. You swear to never come to an online chat again. But a month later, you see an ad for a chat with Tweak, the drummer from Zappa's Ghost, and you just have to find out what it was like working with so-and-so. And so you go . . .

Does Anyone Like These Events?

The answer is, "No."

I did an informal poll on a couple popular mailing lists asking people what they thought about online chats. If they had been a chat guest, did they like it? Did they find it a good way to promote their products or services? If they sat in the audience, was it a rewarding experience? I was a little surprised at how overwhelmingly negative the responses were.

For those who sat in the audience, the responses were 100 percent negative. The main complaint was the stilted nature of online chat. It's not like talk radio where you can ask a question and follow up, get a clarification, interrupt, or the guest can ask you to rephrase the question or engage in dialogue with you. In online chat, you have to write a good question, send it to the moderator, and wait for it to be asked. There's no way to engage *discussion*. Answers to questions are often brief, partly due to the interface and also due to the lack of true dialogue. There's seldom an opportunity for follow-up questions. And so, chats seem shallow.

Then, there are the technical problems. If the guest is well known, you might never get into the auditorium. Many online auditoriums tap out at 300 visitors. If you put a TV star on CompuServe, thousands of people will try to attend. More people will be shut out than actually get into the chat. For the lucky few who make it inside, chances are that their questions will never get asked. That's assuming that you can figure out how to ask a question. An online chat is very confusing the first time you join one.

On the other side of the screen, chat guests were not thrilled about the results, either. The number one complaint was technical difficulties. They couldn't connect to the service. They logged on, but then the connection was dropped. They couldn't get into the auditorium. Their computers crashed. They spent hours setting up software for a lame, half-hour chat. They couldn't figure out how to reply to questions. Chats are just as confusing for first-time guests as they are for first-time audience members. They're getting messages from the moderator that no one else sees, and people in the audience are making comments that the guest can't see. What a mess!

But does it move the product? Once again, chat guests were not pleased. Very few sales or inquiries resulted from their appearances. In many cases, the moderator or host failed to mention that the guest had something to sell: no plugs for their new book or CD and so on. In some cases, no moderator was provided and rude people dominated the discussion.

Even some moderators hate online chats. They know from experience that both the guest and the audience are likely to be disappointed. The host takes the flak when someone's question doesn't get asked. They have to hype the guest's latest release or post other plugs. Often, the guests don't show or are late and the host has to improvise. They get to deal with all the lovely technical problems. What a headache!

So Why Are Chats So Popular?

Chats are popular because we live in a celebrity culture. People simply can't resist the opportunity to meet their favorite performers, whether they are movie stars, CEOs, authors, recording artists—anyone who is known beyond their immediate family. Why do people attend concerts or sporting events in giant stadiums where you can't see or hear the performers? Because it's a scene—there's just something about being there.

People will attend chats even if they hate chats—even if they know that they won't be able to ask a question and even if they could just swing by and pick up the transcript the next day and read it for free offline. There's always the chance that lightning will strike, that the guest will say something interesting, intelligent, and original, and that *your* question will result in some startling, shocking, headline-grabbing utterance from the guest.

Chats are popular because they're interactive, even if it is the most feeble sort of interaction. They take advantage of the most powerful lure of the Internet—the potential that the user might have some impact on the event. We've all seen Mary Hart on *Entertainment Tonight* or Barbara Walters on *20/20*; now *we* want to ask the questions, and *we* want to interview the guests. Chats hold out that promise although they seldom deliver.

Despite the technical difficulties, chats *are* popular with guests. For an author, a terrible chat session is usually better than a typical bookstore signing. You don't have to be publicly humiliated by low turnout, and it costs almost nothing to do an entire tour online. Actors and celebrities like chats because they don't have to get made up and they don't have to worry about stalkers the way they do at in-person appearances. Chats are safe.

Publicists like chat because they actually *do* move the product. Even if the chat is a disaster, so what? Millions of people might have seen the announcement for the chat on their login screens, building name recognition for the guest and his or her latest release. That recognition will help all of the other marketing work better: TV ads, interviews, newspaper ads, and point-of-purchase displays. The Internet is a fantastic way to get a "buzz" going about something. If the product is any good, the buzz will help it sell.

More than anyone else, online services *love* chat. Chat gets people to register with sites, opening the door for direct e-mail marketing. Chat gets people to spend time at a site, improving time-spent-per-visit numbers that are used to determine ad rates. A lot of stuff can be done quickly online: logging on, grabbing your mail, downloading software, and logging off. But if you visit a chat, you might be there for hours. During that time, you might be exposed to thousands of ad impressions. Most chat software causes a participant's screen to refresh every few seconds to keep up with the chat. Every time the screen refreshes, it's another hit in the Web log, boosting a site's traffic numbers (and thus, ad revenues). One person sitting in a chat room can generate thousands of hits in a Web log. No chat, no hits. No hits, no sponsors. No sponsors, no money.

Finally, there are some really positive results that can come from chats. For authors and other creative artists, it's a chance to hear from fans when your following doesn't warrant a real tour. A good chat tour can boost their self esteem and help them build an audience. Educational chats are often rewarding. For example, the Mayo Clinic hosted a series of chats with some of its best-known doctors. Employers can use chats to coordinate big projects. In the poll that I conducted, the only people who had positive chat experiences were those involved in small, educational chat sessions where there was an opportunity for follow-up questions and deeper discussion.

For all these reasons, online chats are here to stay. They will likely improve with the technology. In fact, as online video and audio become commonplace, online chats will look more like TV talk shows (sorry about that). But those days are still a ways off. No matter what technology is available, you can dramatically improve your chat results with careful preparation. That's what this chapter is all about.

The Two Worlds of Chat

When I mention "chat" to a new client, the first reaction is often disgust. They imagine a dingy den of iniquity with people using screen names such as "ImSoHorny" and obscene messages scrolling by at an almost-unreadable pace. They're sure the first question they'll get asked is, "What are you wearing?" and that the chat will go downhill from there. They don't want anything to do with this subculture.

Yes, that's a popular form of online chat, but it has almost nothing to do with the other style of chat, which is held in brightly lit auditoriums with hosts and moderators and protocols. For the sake of simplicity, I'll refer to these two worlds as "moderated" and "unmoderated." Those terms mask the similarities and differences between these styles of online discussion. Chat is a completely new phenomenon that is unlike anything that has come before. It's not the same as chatting on the phone, talk radio, or instant messaging. It's worth a brief side trip into the culture of online chat to help understand its potential and the differences between these two worlds.

When I was a teenager, my sister told me about a phone number I could dial and tap into a conversation with all kinds of people in the area. I called this mysterious party line, and sure enough there were eight or ten people all talking at once, asking questions such as, "Where do you live?" and "What's your favorite band?" I spent many an evening calling this exotic phone number and other similar numbers I learned about on the party line or from friends. There was a fascinating, hidden world on the other end of the phone, made up of people my age, free of parents and supervision. It didn't take long for me to realize that the goal of most people on the party line was to connect in person with a member of the opposite sex. I played the game, but I never got a date out of it, although I did get girls to call me directly a couple of times. The whole experience was a little bit naughty, occasionally thrilling, but ultimately unfulfilling.

When I bought my first modem in 1986, I found a flyer on a telephone pole advertising a local bulletin board. I dialed in with my computer and found a stilted equivalent of the teenage party line. Hidden behind obscure nicknames, people left messages for each other on these boards. A few of the messages were about local happenings or political arguments. But most of them focused on trying to connect in person with a member of the opposite sex. It was all a little thrilling, a little naughty, but ultimately boring.

Bulletin boards in those early days lacked the vitality of the telephone party lines. You couldn't make small talk back and forth but had to leave messages and dial in later to see whether anyone responded. You couldn't judge people by the sound of their voices, to know whether they were being sarcastic, mean, teasing, or dull. You couldn't even tell what sex people were—they might be pretending. The lessons learned about communicating online in those early days helped me adapt to the Internet immediately—lessons such as how you write is more important than how you speak and that you can never be sure about the identity of someone else online.

When I logged on to America Online in the early '90s, I wasn't at all surprised about the sex talk there. What was new, for me, was that some of the vitality of the telephone party line was back in the form of chat rooms. Twenty-four people could be in the same room at the same time, and the flow of conversation was nearly instantaneous. You could engage in real-time discussion, and if you connected with someone, you could slip off somewhere private. But unlike a telephone party line, all the dialogue was text. In a crowded room, it was nearly impossible to keep up with the verbiage spilling past on the screen. You could try to focus on just one or two other chatters, but picking out their messages from the flow was difficult. People learned to communicate in as few words as possible, using acronyms and emoticons to cut down the text. The need for brevity is a hallmark of online communications.

When I first started putting authors into chats, this environment was the one that we entered. It was a free-for-all, and the author had to do the best that he or she could to keep up the pace and ignore or fend-off rude behavior. But the poor manners of a small number of people in the audience were ruining events for everyone, so the first improvement came with the host's ability to disconnect someone from the chat, quickly followed by the ability to keep them out once you kicked them out. In response to the chaos of questions, answers, and side talk, protocol was developed. If you wanted to ask a question, you had to "raise your hand" by typing an exclamation point, then wait to be called on by the host. I produced dozens of chats that began with the words, "We'll be using protocol tonight."

Over the years, these attempts at controlling behavior during online chats led to improvements in software and procedures. Today, we have software that can restrict entry to those who are invited, require people to pass questions to the host who then chooses those that will appear on the screen, keep the guest in a private "green room" where they see only the messages sent by the host, allow people in the audience to block messages from certain chatters, and highlight messages from others. Today, we can use color-coding to distinguish hosts from guests or one audience member from another. We have the ability to include visuals in chats, such as PowerPoint slides or Web page tours. We can stream a portion of the chat in audio or video. Today, in addition to the hosts of old, we have chat producers, chat coordinators, moderators, and typists—all of whom work to create a rewarding event. In short, we have created a controlled environment that almost guarantees that malcontents will not spoil a chat. And that's what I call *moderated chat*.

In some ways, these new controls have taken the life out of chat. For all its problems, there was something real and gritty about unmoderated chat. It was performance art. Guests were tested for their ability to handle themselves under the intense pressure of an endless stream of questions and stupid comments. Some rose to the occasion like gladiators proving themselves in battle. Others buckled and were mercilessly booed. I had to gird myself before entering chat rooms in those days, and I got an adrenaline rush from a fast-paced chat that was unlike anything I had experienced as a publicist.

Today, when I put a guest on a chat tour, it is nothing like the wild days of old. There are no surprises anymore. Everything goes according to plan, nice and smoothly. My biggest concerns are the turnout and being stood up by the guest. Some promoters with weak ethics will let a publicist or assistant fill in for the guest, letting the audience believe that it is chatting with a real celebrity. The spread of broadband will bring more audio and video chats in its wake, and it will be harder to fool the online audience. But then, chats will lose even more of their character. Guests will have to put on makeup and get in front of a camera, events will be more carefully produced, and the blunt confrontation between a star and his or her public will be all but gone.

The world of unmoderated chat hasn't disappeared. In fact, it has gotten much bigger— but it has gone underground. AOL wants to present a nice, wholesome face to the public, so it has cut back on unmoderated chat rooms and shunted them into a dark corner of the service. AOL feels that by providing members access to the larger Internet, those who want to engage in dirty talk can do it somewhere outside of AOL. Web portals that first embraced chat in a lust for traffic are now cutting back. Their revenue is coming more from sponsorships based on reputation rather than raw numbers, and they don't want to soil their brands. Lurking under the surface of the commercial Internet is a secret world of unfettered communication financed by low-brow advertisers who don't have brands to protect. One of the tricks of the modern marketer is dipping into that enormous pool without getting pulled into the muck.

For mainstream publicists, the venues for moderated chat have been shrinking of late. But that's a temporary condition. Once unmoderated chat has been purged from all branded media outlets, moderated chat will return in its place. It's irresistible. Why? The answer is, "Because it operates just like a television talk show." The Web sites get free content in the form of celebrity appearances. These appearances draw traffic to the site, which increases advertising and sponsorship revenue. The appearances generate sales of the product, increasing e-commerce revenue for the site. And sites use chats with recording artists, movie stars, and authors to pressure media companies to advertise CDs, movies, and books on their sites. Here, we have three revenue streams and no direct costs. Yes, the future will be full of moderated chat opportunities.

The Benefits of Chat

After years of producing chat programming, I still have trouble convincing clients of the benefits of promoting through chats. I've already handled the first objection: that chat rooms are dens of iniquity. The second major objection is that chats are poorly attended. I didn't address this issue adequately in my book, *Publicity on the Internet*, and it raises its head nearly every time I do a tour. So, for the record, here's my response:

Attendance has nothing to do with a successful chat.

That's correct. It doesn't matter how many people show up. Virtually the entire value of a chat comes from the amount of promotion you get for the chat and not how many people turn out for the gig. You'd think advertising people would understand this concept, but they don't. In 1998, I was hired by ConEx marketing to do an online promotion for the @d:tech Convention. I had worked with @d:tech for several years, and it was our custom to put a headliner from the convention on a chat tour to build awareness for the show. @d:tech offered Andrew Jaffe, a living legend in the advertising world, who had agreed to participate. When I contacted Jaffe to go over the details, he responded something to the effect of, "Why would I want to do a chat tour? That's a complete waste of time."

It took a while for me to articulate the value of a chat tour to Mr. Jaffe, but he finally got it. Here's the gist of my remarks.

A chat tour gives you something on which to hang an online promotion. No one buys a product that they've never heard of. No one attends an event they don't know about. The primary objective of all marketing is to *make the target audience aware that the product exists.* Beyond awareness, you hope to be able to give the target audience enough information to make a buying decision. To get product awareness online, you have two choices: you can either buy advertising or you can engage in publicity efforts. For publicity, you need something newsworthy. @d:tech could have sent a news release out with the dates of the convention and the names of featured guests, and the announcement would get picked up by a few publications and Web sites. But if the company posted an announcement like that to online discussion groups, it would have gotten flamed and damaged its reputation. Much of @d:tech's core audience participates in online discussion groups.

That's where my promotional strategy comes in: Give the audience something of value in exchange for listening to the commercial pitch. By hosting a series of chats with a leading figure in the advertising world, @d:tech is giving something of value to the online community. The announcement for the chat tour will be welcome in groups devoted to advertising and technology. Through the announcement, *the target audience learns that the event exists.* So, the first level of publicity is that, because you are producing the chat tour, you get to distribute your message about the tour *and* your conference to a broad-based audience, creating awareness. Look at Figure 6.1. This page is the home page for Yahoo! Events, which gets tens of thousands of visitors a day. The first item on the page says "Uncle Kracker . . . discusses his friendship with Kid Rock, the stories behind his music, and his new CD, *Double Wide.*" Bang! The name of the artist and the title of his new CD on the homepage of Yahoo! Events—not because he paid for the spot, and not because he issued a press release, but because he agreed to do a chat and promoted it properly.

The second level of publicity comes from the venues hosting the chats. That's why you look for host sites that reach large numbers of your target audience. For @d:tech promotions, we've secured chats on MSNBC, America Online's Business Know-How Forum, CompuServe's PR & Marketing Forum, Talk City's Business Center, and other top venues. Typically, these venues provide one or two weeks of publicity before the

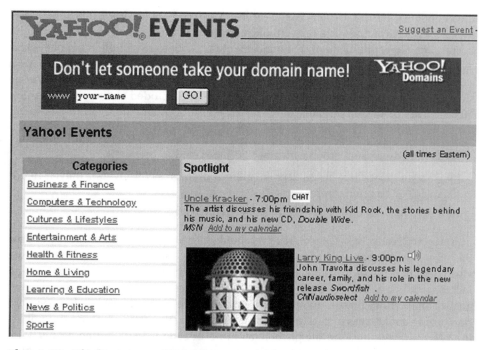

Figure 6.1 The homepage of Yahoo! Events. The lead item is for a chat by Uncle Kracker on Yahoo! competitor MSN. The listing plugs Kracker's new CD. Chat tours are a great way to generate awareness for new products, services, and events.

event and chat transcripts after the event, plus direct e-mail announcements to people who have opted-in or registered. In the case of CompuServe in 1998, if you got an announcement into their *What's New* newsletter, every member of the site had to drill through that to get to their e-mail. We're talking about millions of impressions a day for an entire week. Thanks to a good relationship with Anne Papina, we *always* got our announcements into CompuServe's *What's New* newsletter (which, by the way, was not crowded with other events).

This topic brings up another benefit of conducting chat tours: You build relationships with the forums that matter most to your target audience. For reasons already articulated, forum hosts love having good chat guests and programs. When you bring this content to their forums, they often reward you by plugging your products or events in a personal way to the forum membership. And these hosts become receptive to additional marketing efforts, such as letting you store product information in their libraries, letting you post announcements on their message boards, giving your products premium exposure in their affiliate stores, and cooperating on future campaigns. If you posted a standard news release in these forums without the chat, it would be removed and the hosts might be prejudiced against you in the future.

The first level of awareness, then, comes from postings for the chat tour. The second comes from the promotion you get at the venues. The third level of awareness comes from alerting the media to your chat tour. Today, every major metropolitan daily newspaper contains some place for notifying readers about online events that might interest them. Some papers have calendars of online events; others leave it up to section editors. A news release about a convention might make it in the daily paper of the city hosting the convention, but an announcement of a chat tour will often get picked up by dozens of daily papers. News of the chat tour can also be uploaded to online events calendars, including high-traffic sites such as Yahoo! Events and to lower-traffic trade sites. In the case of @d:tech, news of the chat tour was included at many of the largest Web sites devoted to advertising.

OK, let's take a tally of the results and see what we have:

- Online discussion groups: maybe 50,000 targeted impressions

- Promotion at chat venues: tens of millions of impressions overall, maybe 10,000 to 50,000 targeted impressions

- Daily newspapers: hundreds of thousands of untargeted impressions

Instead of issuing a news release that would get precious little coverage, by adding the educational chat tour component you get widespread coverage—generating awareness that the event or product exists. Most of the coverage you get online will include a link to a Web site. So in addition to awareness, you achieve the second major goal of marketing: providing enough information to make a buying decision. You don't get instant access to in-depth information from radio, television, or print publicity: People have to pick up the phone, go online, or send mail to get the details. With the Internet, more information is one click away. And thanks to e-commerce, the buying transaction itself is only two clicks away, achieving the ultimate goal of all marketing: closing the deal.

How many people actually attended the @d:tech chats? In most cases, fewer than 25 people showed up for each chat, and fewer than 100 total were present for each tour. On MSNBC, we had 300 people for a single chat, but that was the exception, not the rule. If you were counting on the bang for this campaign to come from chat attendance, you'd be sadly disappointed. If you were measuring the amount of media coverage against the cost of the campaign, you'd be ecstatic. Many companies are turned off to chat due to poor attendance. Time and again, book publishers have told me that they tried chats, but no one showed up. I would ask, "What did you do to promote the chat?" Silence. They thought their job was done when they booked someone on AOL or Yahoo! That's where the real work begins.

As I approached chat day on one campaign, a client asked, "Do you think the tour will be successful?" I responded, "It is successful. All the promos are in place and we got the publicity we wanted. We don't know if anyone will show up, but that has nothing to do with the success of the campaign." People don't like to hear that attendance doesn't matter, and it is stretching the truth a bit. I always want to draw enough of a crowd that the guest feels like the chat was time well spent. I want to draw a large enough crowd to keep the host happy, too, or they'll sour on future events. For reasons of ego and integrity, turnout matters. But from a strictly marketing point of view, attendance means nothing.

I am hammering on this point because if you are a publicist and you put people on chat tours, you must know how to deal with this issue. Guests are always disappointed at low turnout. They think it means that no one loves them when most of the time it's because few people participate in moderated chat. You have to prep the guest about what you hope to accomplish and what's likely to happen at each chat. Then, if the turnout is average (about 20 people for a non-celebrity appearance on a smaller venue), they're happy, and if the turnout is low (five people or fewer), you'll have to console them with the value of the promotional exposure. And it's not just guests who you have to comfort; sometimes your boss will attend the chat and see how few people are there and decide that this form of marketing is a waste of company resources. You have to condition your superiors, too, by documenting the promotional coverage you get and saying, "Base your budget allocation on this, not attendance."

Now that you are convinced about the benefits of online chat tours, let's look at how to produce them.

Preparing for Chat

The effort required to put together a good chat tour has waxed and waned over the years. When I started doing these tours in the mid '90s, I had to beg to get my authors into chat venues. Good venues were few and far between, and forum hosts didn't understand that they were in show business. By the late '90s, the number of venues exploded, and the forum hosts did a 180-degree turn—now begging me for guests. It all had to do with money. Chat was a cash cow for America Online because fees were based on time online, and only gaming exceeded chats in the ability to glue someone to a computer screen. Web site advertising was sold based on impressions, and chat could deliver thousands of impressions per hour. Venture capital flowed to sites that could show high-traffic numbers, and these sites gravitated to chat. Those were the glory days of online chats, when you could get your pick of venues and demand high-profile promos from the hosts.

Then came the dot.com crash of 2000, and chat venues contracted dramatically. The bottom fell out of the impressions-based advertising market, and more sites moved to section sponsorships and e-commerce revenue streams. Talk City started charging to host chats. America Online switched to flat-rate pricing, and many chat venues disappeared overnight. CompuServe began moving all its content to the Web, where the chat interface didn't work as smoothly. Web sites and forums slashed payrolls, and chat hosts and moderators were among the first casualties. These were the dark days of chat, where booking a tour could take two months and you had to take whatever venues you could get.

The pendulum is starting to swing back. Let's face it, you can't have an entertainment site without celebrities, and celebrities like tours to promote their new releases. For many Web sites, live events are the only reliable way to motivate an audience to come back. Browsers can drop by anytime for files or software, but for a baseball game or a concert or a chat, you have to come back *now*. The latest generation of Web serving software has made it a lot easier for smaller, niche sites to hold quality chats. And that's good news, because the further that broadband penetrates the market, the more people will gravitate to audio and video programming. When that happens, it will cost a fortune for small sites to compete with the production values available on large sites. Producing chats will become a lot like producing talk shows, requiring lighting, makeup, sound, wardrobe, hair stylists, a popular host, music, whiz-bang graphics, writers, multiple camera angles, and so on. A few powerful sites will dominate the top talent, and people like me who promote authors that are not household names will be limited to smaller niche sites running text-based chat.

My secret for getting second-tier talent onto first-tier chat programs is a ridiculous amount of preparation. The idea is to remove every possible barrier to acceptance. And the main vehicle for doing that is the chat profile.

The Chat Profile

A chat profile is a Web page that is used to book a tour and provide the hosts with everything they need for a successful program. The public never sees this Web page; it's sales literature, and the target customer is a chat host. The hosts will look at the page and decide whether or not to host the program. If they decide to go ahead with the show, they'll grab whatever artwork and text they need from the chat profile and repurpose it for their sites. Figure 6.2 shows the top of a chat profile for Ray Kurzweil, famous inventor and author of the book, *The Age of Spiritual Machines*.

Like the other campaign materials described in this book, it's usually a good idea to draft the chat profile in your word processing program and then convert it to HTML once it has been approved and any final changes have been made. At the companion web site for this book, you'll find both a Word version and an HMTL version of a chat profile template that you can use to prepare these documents. The full chat profile contains the following sections (we'll explore each one in more detail):

- Guest
- Subject
- Related links
- Promo
- Introduction
- Sample questions
- Artwork

The Guest

"The Guest" means the name of the guest and his or her claim to fame. Some guests have many claims that could be put forth here, such as "Winner of the Nobel Prize" or "President and CEO of XYZ Corporation." Pick *one* item—either your best shot or something related to the subject of the chat—and save the rest of the official designations, accolades, and honors for the introduction later in the profile.

The Subject

Picking a good subject for a chat is critical to getting quality venues. Most chats suffer from having either too broad of a topic or no topic at all. You need a subject that will appeal to a niche audience rather than a generic audience, and you'd like a subject that

Chat Profile for Ray Kurzweil

GUEST:

Ray Kurzweil
Author of the New Book
The Age of Spiritual Machines:
When Computers Exceed Human Intelligence

Ray Kurzweil

RELATED LINKS:

Companion Web Site for The Age of Spiritual Machines
http://www.penguinputnam.com/kurzweil

SUBJECT:

Are Humans Beings Obsolete?

PROMO:

Are Humans Beings Obsolete?

What will happen when human beings are replaced by machines as the dominant species on the planet? If this sounds like science fiction to you, then we invite you to join a lively chat with Ray Kurzweil, author of *The Age of Spiritual Machines*. Kurzweil is one of the most decorated scientists, inventors, and visionaries of the 20th Century. He has developed software and devices that enable computers to see, read, talk, and make music. Now he says that computers can think, too, and will soon exceed human intelligence. Don't miss this opportunity to chat with one of the great thinkers of our time: Ray Kurzweil!

Figure 6.2   The top part of a chat profile for Ray Kurzweil, used to book a tour in support of his book, *The Age of Spiritual Machines*. A template for a chat profile is available at www.wiley.com/compbooks/okeefe.

has a chance of being adequately covered in a 30- to 60-minute chat. For example, a chat about "Online Marketing" is way too broad; it's better to focus on subjects such as "Designing Banner Ads that Pull," "Managing a Direct E-Mail Database," or "Hot Issues in E-Commerce Security."

There's a dual purpose for defining the subject of a chat. The first is to hit on something irresistible to the chat host. They will want something new and unique that isn't already being covered at their sites. If you understand your target audience and stay close to the sites that are important to them, you'll have a good idea of what generic topics to stay away from. The second purpose of the subject is to draw in the target audience. The subject of the chat will be used in your discussion group postings and news releases and needs to stand out in order to capture attention. Don't worry about being limited to that topic during chat—you chat about whatever the audience wants to chat about. The subject of the chat isn't a straight jacket; it's a siren's song.

For the Kurzweil chat profile shown in Figure 6.2, we used the subject, "Are Human Beings Obsolete?" That's provocative, and I like using a question as the subject, suggesting that people tune in for the answer. The title of Kurzweil's book, *The Age of Spiritual Machines*, is too open and broad for a chat. A subject line is your chance to hook into current events or narrow your focus to recent trends. A CEO will want to talk about the company's latest innovations, not the whole history of an enterprise. I promoted a book by Dr. David Simon of the Chopra Center for Well Being entitled *Return to Wholeness*, which was about dealing with cancer. The title of the book is too vague for a chat subject. One of the best chapters in the book dealt with humor therapy, so I went with a subject of "Laughing at Cancer." Believe me, that got attention from the target audience. We got a few complaints about the subject line, but not from people who had cancer or were caretakers for those suffering from the disease. The target audience understood the seriousness of our efforts and appreciated the idea that people dealing with cancer need a little levity now and then.

Another good reason to pick narrow topics for your chats is that most chats promote something, and you don't want people to think that they got it all in the chat. If you're promoting an event, you want people to attend the event. You might want them to buy a book or a CD, visit your Web site, call a toll-free phone number, or get involved with a charity. A chat that focuses on one small aspect of the product being promoted has a chance of successfully making the case for seeking out the rest of the product. A chat about how the Girl Scouts changed one person's life will inspire more participation in the organization than an overview of its history and roots.

Related Links

You should include at least one link in this section to a site that you hope people will visit as a result of the chat. A link is one of the promotional benefits of conducting a chat tour, and almost every host will grant you that courtesy. This link will often be broadcast during the chat, usually at the conclusion.

You can include links to multiple sites in this section, but be careful. If you include a link to a site that competes with the site that you're pitching, you might lose a gig. Links to educational resources on sites run by non-profit organizations are acceptable, but avoid more than one commercial link in the chat profile. You can always negotiate with each chat host for additional links *after* they've committed to the chat.

Promo

The promo gives you one paragraph to sell the chat. In this case, you're looking to sell it to the target audience, not to the chat host. Your hope is that this paragraph will be so good that the chat host will use it verbatim to promote the chat on the host site. If chat hosts think that the subject of the chat, the guest, and this promo will pull a crowd, they'll run with it. It's a good idea to repeat the subject line at the top of the promo paragraph, because the two items work together to explain the chat.

There's a tendency to load the promo copy with the accomplishments of the guest speaker, but you don't have room for that. When writing this paragraph, really focus on how you see a host site promoting this chat to its audience. This copy is what you want on the homepage of the host site. There isn't a lot of room on the homepage for fluff, so the promo should be enticing, hard-hitting, and brief. In 90 percent of the hundreds of chats I have booked, the promo copy I wrote was used without changes at the host site. In the remaining 10 percent, it was modified slightly by the hosts to suit their needs.

Introduction

Now, you can unload with all the great things your guest has done in his or her life. The introduction provides a more complete biography of the guest, explains the focus of the chat, and plugs whatever product, service, event, or organization the chat promotes.

Your goal in writing the introduction is to provide the chat host with copy to use at the beginning of the chat. You can be a little long-winded here. About three or four paragraphs is good, which is still far less than most celebrity bios. The host will usually edit this copy down, picking and choosing what to use on chat night. If the host site sells a product related to the guest, they won't plug a competing e-commerce site. The introduction also gives you room to make a stronger case for your guest in the hopes the host will agree to sponsor the chat.

Some sites will use the full introduction on a promotional page for the chat and an abbreviated version to start the chat. Many sites will limit the advance promotion to the promo paragraph, and some are so stingy they'll only plug the guest's name and the title of the chat. The design of the chat profile helps you write copy that will work for all different sites.

Sample Questions

I enjoy writing the sample questions for a chat show. Choosing a subject and writing a promo can be agonizing work, but writing the sample questions is fun. There are several goals for the sample questions, but the funny thing is you hope that they never get asked. If the chat draws a good crowd, you want the guest to answer the audience's questions, not yours. That's the whole point of having a chat: People get to ask the questions that are important to *them*. I get furious at chat hosts that monopolize the guest's time when there's a good crowd in the room. I've attended chats with 50 people in the room, and the host didn't allow an audience question until 30 minutes into the chat! If there are people in the room, the host should run the introduction, then immediately open the floor to questions.

The sample questions are written to give the host something to use to break the ice or if the chat slows down. They also help both the host and the guest focus on the topic of the chat instead of wandering all over the place. They keep the chat from deteriorating by providing a well-thought-out question at just the right moment. People attending the chat might be hard-pressed to come up with questions in the heat of the moment as good as the sample questions prepared with plenty of time for contemplation. Sample questions can be used to steer the chat away from murky subjects and to spark the audience's imagination.

I also use the sample questions to convince potential chat hosts that this chat will be an interesting, thought-provoking chat. I like to play hardball with some of the chat questions, to throw in zingers I know the guest will be uncomfortable with. Chat hosts don't want to put on programs where the guest does nothing but plug his or her product for 45 minutes. The hosts might be suspicious of your motives, and the sample questions help convince them that your guest is ready to educate and entertain, not just promote. I use sample questions to challenge the guest.

For a chat with a chef about *foie gras*, which is made from fattened goose livers, one of the sample questions was about cruelty to animals. If the guest isn't prepared for a question like that, they shouldn't be doing a live chat. I'll ask CEOs about marketing mistakes or poor earnings reports; I'll ask homeopaths if they're really quacks; I'll ask athletes what they plan to do when their careers end at age 40. The chat profile is approved by the guest before the tour is booked, so they have a chance to delete or reword sample questions they are uncomfortable with. By including hard questions in the profile, I'm putting guests on notice that they need to be prepared to handle tough questions, even if we delete them from the chat profile.

In accordance with the style of online chat, sample questions should be specific and lead to answers that are succinct. In training several chat coordinators, I've discovered this disposition is not intuitive. I still see questions like, "Tell us about your new movie," or "Did you always want to be a writer?" in chat profiles. These questions lead to long answers or are too vague to be addressed in a chat. Great questions come from an intimate understanding of the product being promoted and focus on very minute details. Instead of asking, "How can humor ease the burden of cancer?", a better question is, "In your book, you describe a woman whose tumors shrunk after she started doing stand-up comedy. What makes you think the improvement was related to humor and not other factors?" Details are always fascinating, and generalities are boring. If you focus on details, it will inspire the audience to ask better questions and it will feed a desire to buy the product promoted at the chat to get the rest of the story.

The guest should be able to answer each sample question in a couple of sentences. There's no time in chat for verbal excursions. The guest is there to answer the audience's questions; to the extent that sample questions are used, they should provoke short answers so that the chat stays focused on audience concerns. Good sample questions are a backup plan. They help convince the host that the chat will be lively, they put the guest on notice to prepare for tough questions, and they provide a security blanket so that even if no one shows up, you'll get a good transcript from a dialogue between the host and the guest. You hope to never need the sample questions, however, and most of the chats I've done haven't used more than two of them.

Artwork

The chat profile should have artwork formatted to be used by the host site. A photo of the guest is essential. A lot of celebrities will provide a black-and-white head shot, but you should get a color photo if at all possible. One of the benefits of the Web is that it's as cheap to run color art as black and white. Sometimes you can find photos at the guest's personal Web site or at a site promoting their work and use those. Be careful, however, not to violate the photographer's copyright. Most publicity shots are owned by the subject of the photo, not the photographer, and can be used with the subject's permission. But you need to ask first. Photos used on book jackets and CD covers are often owned by the photographer, who has granted limited reproduction rights to the product's manufacturer. You need to inquire whether the photo can be used online and whether a photo credit must appear next to it.

Captions and photo credits should be embedded into the artwork and not sent separately. It's easy for a photo to get separated from the credit and then be circulated all over cyberspace. The caption should be viewed as another selling opportunity, containing not only the guest's name but also the title of his or her latest release or a URL for a Web site. The photography credit can also be embedded in the image if required. Embedding the photography credit in the image means that if the image appears anywhere online without the credit, someone intentionally removed it. Embedding the credit will help you in any legal action taken by the photographer and will hurt whoever intentionally removes that credit.

The guest photo should be sized to no more than 1.5 inches wide and saved as either a GIF or JPEG file. I used to use larger images, but the chat hosts shrunk them, resulting in poor image quality. It's better for you to shrink the image to the smallest reasonable size than to let the host do it. You should, of course, prepare larger versions of the photo to handle requests for bigger artwork, but don't include them in the chat profile. Figure 6.3 shows a head shot for a guest prepared in PhotoShop with the guest's name and URL embedded inside the image. The image is a color photo, but because this book is printed in black and white, the color has been removed.

In addition to a photo of the guest, the chat profile should contain other artwork related to the chat. If the guest is promoting a book, movie, CD, or other product, a shot of the product is recommended. Formatting should follow the same guidelines as the guest photo: caption embedded, small size, and saved as JPEG or GIF. A company logo can also be used in a chat profile. Chat hosts are less likely to use it because it

Figure 6.3   The guest photo in a chat profile should be no more than 1.5 inches wide. The guest's name and a marketing message can be embedded in the photo. This image was used to promote Heather Stone, president of myjobsearch.com.

looks like advertising, but it doesn't hurt to try. Other artwork can be prepared to support the chat, but it shouldn't be used in the chat profile.

Support Materials

The chat profile, as important as it is, does not have everything you need to pull off a good chat program. One of the arts of the publicist is to open a chink in the wall around premium Web sites, then drive a semi-truck full of promotional materials through it. Here are some ideas for stocking the truck:

Artwork

You should try to prepare in advance as much artwork as you think you'll be able to use for a chat tour. Preparing artwork starts at the top, with full-size photographs, and works its way down to thumbnail GIFs. After scanning the photos, save them in high-resolution versions of 300 dpi, so you can offer them to print and or broadcast media who might use them to fatten listings for the event or in related stories about the products being promoted through the chat tour. From there, save the photos in a large size (no more than three inches wide) and a small size (no more than 1.5 inches wide) at 72 dpi. as JPEGs or GIFs for use online.

Articles

For every chat booking, I offer the hosts an article or op-ed piece to feature at their sites. Sometimes I give them text files and let them do the HTML to turn the pieces into Web pages; other times I'll prepare the HTML myself. The advantage of offering a text file is that no matter how you do the HTML, it is unlikely to work on host sites and will have to be recoded. The advantage of using HTML is that I can show them what the article looks like by pointing them to a Web page, increasing the likelihood of acceptance for a good-looking article.

Along with articles, you can offer surveys, quizzes, checklists, excerpts, or other documents. This content is welcome by chat hosts, and it often will draw more traffic than the chat itself. Plus, these documents have staying power; the chat tour will be over in a week, but the support materials might stay around for years. You should include a proper copyright notice in these materials, and you can usually get away with a substantial amount of marketing copy, including endorsements, toll-free phone numbers, prices and product descriptions, and links to purchasing opportunities.

Multimedia

For recording artists, support materials should include an MP3 clip or a full song that has been approved for free distribution online. For film promotions, a movie trailer can be offered in support of the chats. You can even provide software in the form of mortgage payment calculators or other gimmicks. Streaming media files should be optimized for different connection speeds, the most common being to offer at least one slow version (14.4 kps, 28.8 kps, or 56 kps) and one broadband version (100 kps or 300 kps).

Preparing the Guest

My interactions with chat guests have mirrored the development of the Internet. When I started booking chat tours, the guests were mostly geeks who understood the technology. I would book them into chats, and then it was up to them to connect to the service and conduct the chat. If I booked a guest on AOL, CompuServe, or Prodigy, the host would provide me with a temporary user ID and password to give to the guest. I had boxes full of those ubiquitous AOL diskettes, along with CompuServe and Prodigy, in Macintosh and IBM formats. The guests had to install their own software if they didn't have accounts with each service. Because there weren't good chat venues on the Web then, most tours involved one stop each on AOL, CSI, and Prodigy. That's a lot of software to install, and the guests had difficulties.

Realizing that the technical requirements were too difficult for most guests, I took an old portable computer and loaded it up with software, passwords, IDs, and toll-free phone numbers for all the online services. I would then FedEx the computer to the guest with instructions to plug one cord into a power outlet, the other cord into a phone line, and start chatting. At the end of the tour, the guest slapped a return label on the package and I got my computer back. But the problems continued. Online services were pretty unreliable in those days, and the guests didn't know what to do if the connection dropped. Plus, the guests were intimidated by chat: The questions came too quickly, they couldn't type fast enough, and they didn't understand protocol. Thus was born the *ghost typist*.

The ghost typist is a person who logs into the chat under the guest's name and types for them. In the early days, I was the ghost typist. I put on a headset phone, called the guest on one phone line, and logged into the chat on another phone line. I would read questions to the guest and type his or her responses. I'll talk more about the fine art of ghost typing a little later. Ghost typing made it possible for non-techies to have trouble-free chats and reduced the responsibilities of the guest to a phone call. Today, the work involved in prepping a guest is pretty easy.

The Chat Tour Q&A

I like to fax a Q&A sheet about the tour to the guest, then follow-up by phone to establish a working relationship and to answer lingering questions. I don't recommend e-mailing the Q&A because it's too long and the guest probably won't read it. Here's the text of a Q&A form that I use for author tours. You can modify this form for any type of guest.

```
Q: Give me a quick rundown on what you're doing.

A: Your chat tour usually consists of three appearances: one on
America Online, and two on high-traffic web sites. It's our job to
make sure these chats get booked and promoted, that you are pre-
pared for your chat, and that technical problems don't spoil your
presentation.

Q: How do you use the "Chat Profile" and what should I look for when
reviewing it?
```

A: In order to get the best chat bookings, we create a "Chat Profile" to entice hosts into holding the chat. The Chat Profile is a web page that is viewed by chat hosts -- not the public. It contains your photo, a subject for the chat, a promo announcement, an introduction, and sample questions. Chat hosts view this page and, if they decide to do the chat, usually copy the art and text and use them for the chat.

When evaluating your Chat Profile, make sure you feel comfortable with the subject of the chat, your introduction, and the sample questions. In most cases, you'll see the same exact text being used the night of the chat. Of course, some questions are designed to be uncomfortable; that is, to provoke discussion and keep the chat lively. But you don't have to live with the questions we provide -- we welcome your suggestions. It's important to ask for changes quickly, because we can't book your tour until you approve the Chat Profile.

Q: How do you schedule the chats?

A: We ask the hosts for suggested dates and times. Prime time for chats is Tuesday through Thursday, between 8-11 p.m. Eastern Time. Each chat lasts for one hour. When a host responds with a suggested date & time, we run it by you for approval. Once all chats are booked, we send you a complete schedule including contact names, phone numbers, and e-mail addresses. Then we start promoting your tour.

Q: How long will all this take?

A: It should only take a few minutes to review your Chat Profile and to respond to booking requests (dates & times). Each chat requires a little more than one hour of your time.

Q: Do I have to install any software?

A: No! We provide a "ghost typist" for each chat, so you don't even have to be near a computer -- just near a phone. Of course, you may keyboard your own answers -- and we will help you prepare -- but we highly recommend you take advantage of our professional ghost typing services.

Q: What is a "ghost typist"?

A: A person who keyboards your answers to chat questions. The ghost typist eliminates any technical worries you might have about doing online chat. They log in under your name, then phone you about five minutes before the chat. The rest of the chat is similar to a telephone interview for a radio talkshow: the ghost typist reads the questions and keyboards your answers. They are trained to deal with technical problems that can arise during chat. They will also guide you to give shorter or longer answers. Chat is very confusing for the uninitiated; our ghost typists let you concentrate on your answers while they handle all the technical issues and "chat noise."

Q: What is the style and tone of most chats?

A: Chats are very informal and very fast. After the initial intro- duction and some opening remarks by you, chaos reigns supreme. Questions come quickly, overlapping one another. Your answers should be short -- usually only a sentence or two. Have you ever participated in two or three conversations at the same time? Multi- ply this three or four fold and you have some idea of how confusing it can get. Your ghost typist will help sort things out and keep the momentum going in a positive direction. At the end of the chat, you usually get time to sum up or add closing comments.

Unfortunately, chats tend to be superficial. That's why our ghost typists are trained to remind people that there is a book behind this appearance, and if they find the subject interesting, they might want to get the book for a calmer, more thorough approach to the issues being discussed. Our typists have all the information people will need to order your book.

Q: Do chats really sell books? Are they worth the effort?

A: Sometimes attendance at online chats is so low, and the level of discussion so shallow, that you have to wonder why you're doing this? But when you compare the results to, say, a bookstore sign- ing, the answer is clear. Even a bad chat tour is better than most bookstore signings. You don't have to leave home or dress-up or put on makeup. Each chat only takes an hour, and if no one shows up, it's not like you're sitting at an autograph table looking silly. Properly publicized, most chats draw an audience of at least ten people, which is a nice size for a reasonable discussion. We always hope for a rewarding chat experience: intelligent, educational, and entertaining. But the real value of a chat, from your publisher's perspective, comes from the promotion.

If we posted messages online announcing your new book, we would be shunned as "spammers." However, most online discussion groups welcome announcements about chats, if the subject of the chat fits the purpose of the group. Our messages promoting your chat tour may be seen by thousands of people, getting your name and the name of your book in front of the target audience. Transcripts of your chat are stored online and usually double the number of people reached with the chats. Finally, the chat hosts often promote your chat with banners, log-in announcements, and forum messages that reach thousands of people. Purchasing ad space with the same reach would cost far more than the chat tour.

If you have any other questions about your chat tour, just ask. We're here to make sure your tour goes off without a hitch, so let us know if there's anything we can do to make you feel more comfortable.

Who's Running This Show?

You are. Even if you're working directly for the guest, you're the producer and you have to take charge or you'll never pull it off. I don't ask a guest what they want to talk about; I should know enough about the guest and the goals for the tour to pick a good subject for the chat and write the chat profile. Left to their own devices, guests will come up with overly broad topics and softball sample questions or won't do anything at all. So *you* pick the topic, *you* write the chat profile, and then you fax it to the guest for approval. If you included any controversial sample questions (and you should), that will get the guest's attention.

After faxing the chat profile, I'll modify the copy based on the guest's reaction. Usually, the profile has a sample question or two that wakes the guest up and makes them realize that this chat is for real. Poor Karen Southwick at *Forbes ASAP* was so concerned about her sample questions that she really studied for the chats, afraid about what she might be asked. She had crisp answers the entire tour, although she seldom saw any of the sample questions. One client had three members of his staff draft detailed responses to each of the sample questions so he wouldn't be caught off guard. I try to tell the guests not to sweat the details, but if the guest is in a position of authority, his or her responses to chat questions could have political or financial ramifications, and the transcripts could be out there for years. A little forethought about how to handle the chats is called for. If a guest doesn't respond to the profile in a week, I'll start using it to book the chats and hope that I can make any last-minute changes before the promos go public.

You need the guest to give you a target week in which to book the tour. It's best if all the chats on the tour happen within a one-week span so that you can promote them all together. When talking with guests, you have to impress upon them the importance of making themselves available for the chat phone calls. If the guest doesn't show, you ruin your reputation with the hosts. I did a chat with a sports superstar who didn't show for his chat on ESPN despite numerous promises and reminders. He ruined my credibility with the producers there and probably didn't help his own prospects for editorial coverage. Chat is still in its formative stages, and you can overcome a bad outing, but as more dollars and air time are devoted to plugging live chats, the consequences for no-shows can be severe.

At the same time you're convincing the guest of the importance of showing up, you have to let them know that if no one else shows up, the tour will still be successful.

Dampening attendance expectations is an important part of guest relations. You want them to feel good if only 10 people show up. Ten people should generate enough questions to keep the chat flowing. You have to focus the guest's attention on the promotional value of the tour. In today's celebrity culture, most chat guests understand how the system works. Big-name guests will always draw a satisfactory crowd, and smaller-name guests are usually grateful that someone is trying to build an audience for them. It's rare when I get a guest who is furious with low turnout, but it does happen.

Booking Chats

Putting together a good chat tour can be a frustrating experience, even for a veteran chat coordinator. Persistence is the key, along with cutting down the approval layers. I've had chat tours that had three layers of approval on the client side: a corporate publicist, the guest's personal secretary, and the guest herself. Add two layers of approval on the venue's side—the chat host and a supervisor such as a sysop—and you've got gridlock. You could spend months booking a three-venue tour. Most of the trouble centers around the difficulty of scheduling appearances by using e-mail.

Let's say that I e-mail a host asking for a chat date, and they offer February 19 at 7 p.m. Eastern time. I send the date back to my contact for approval, it goes to the guest's personal assistant, and two days later I get an e-mail that the 19th is no good, how about the 20th? That message goes back to the chat host, who runs it up the flagpole on her side, and I get back a message that says "No the 20th won't work for us, how about the 22nd?" And so it goes, on and on. The most frustrating moment comes when you have two chats booked and can't nail down the third one. Let's say that by February 1st, you have chats set for the 22nd and 23rd. If you spend two weeks nailing down that last chat, you've got only one week to promote the tour. What a headache!

So, here are my tips for booking a tour in a reasonable amount of time:

- Start booking the chats two months ahead of time. That means you need final approval for the chat profile two months ahead, and you need the guest to give you a target week in which to book the chats (which they are promising to keep open for you).

- Complete the bookings one month ahead of time. That gives you adequate time to promote the chats, and hopefully it is far enough in advance that the chat guest will not make any other commitments that conflict with the tour.

- Pitch the chat hosts first via e-mail, then *switch to telephone* the minute they show any interest in the chats. On the phone, you can negotiate a date and time much more quickly than through e-mail.

If you work as a publicist for a single company or celebrity, you'll quickly develop relationships with the chat hosts who matter in your subject area. Once these people know you on a first-name basis and you have a track record of delivering good programming, you'll have a much easier time booking subsequent tours. If you work for a large advertising agency or public relations firm handling diverse clients, you've got your work cut out for you, building working relationships with dozens of hosts.

Turnover is so high in the field of chat hosts that you could find yourself starting from scratch every time out. I'll give you my best tips here for pitching chat hosts and completing a tour without losing your sanity.

The Chat Schedule

The chat schedule is the key document used in organizing a chat tour. Fill out the schedule and the booking is done. The schedule is used to create news releases, discussion group postings, and other promotional materials. It's faxed to guests so that they know exactly where they are supposed to be, when, and who to call if there's trouble. It is sent to the guest's publicist, or parent company, for inclusion on the company's Web site or in other marketing materials, such as newsletters or media alerts to wholesalers and trade buyers. The chat schedule replaces dozens of e-mails that were used to build the tour. If you were to rely on the guest sifting through all those e-mails to figure out where they're supposed to be, you'd have a lot of no-shows at your chats.

A sample chat schedule is shown as follows for a four-venue tour for Ray Kurzweil, author of *The Age of Spiritual Machines*. A template of the chat schedule, in Microsoft Word format, is available at www.wiley.com/compbooks/okeefe.

```
CHAT SCHEDULE
   Guest: Ray Kurzweil
   Client: Ray Kurzweil
   Date: Updated January 27, 1999


   America Online
   Date: Tuesday, February 9
   Time: 9-10 p.m. Eastern Time
   Location: Book Central Spotlight (Keyword: BC)
   Software Needed: Ghost typist provided. AOL for visitors.

   Hosts: Book Central
   Contact: Christie Mack <BkCnZoe@aol.com>, Phone: (972) 555-1212
   Address: 1234 Main Street, Anywhere, TX 70000
   Contact: Jenny Lee <jlee@spier-ny.com>, Phone: (212) 555-1212
   Address: SpierNY, 460 Park Ave. S., Fl.7, New York, NY 10016


   CompuServe
   Date: Wednesday, February 10
   Time: 7-8 p.m. Eastern Time
   Location: Stein Online <http://www.compuserve.com/cir/>
   Software Needed: Radio (audio) interview, simulcast in chat room
on CompuServe. They provide ghost typist for guest. RealAudio
needed for audience.
```

Contact: Eliot Stein <EliotStein@compuserve.com>
Address: 3727 W. Magnolia Blvd. #803, Burbank, CA 91505
Phone: (818) 555-1212

MSNBC
Date: Thursday, February 11
Time: 7:30-8:00 p.m. Eastern Time
Location: http://www.msnbc.com/chat/
Software Needed: They provide ghost typist for guest; Java or IRC
for visitors.

Contact: Chris Donohue <Chris.Donohue@MSNBC.com>
Address: MSNBC, 1 Microsoft Way, Bldg. 25-2216, Redmond, WA 98052
Phone: 425-555-1212 or Page: 1-800-555-1212 PIN: 5551212

ZineZone
Date: Thursday, February 11
Time: 9-10 p.m. Eastern Time
Location: ZineZone <http://www.zinezone.com/events/> --or--
Chat at Talk City <http://www.talkcity.com/calendar/>
Software Needed: Ghost typist provided. Web browser or IRC for
visitors.

Contact: Sue DeMarco <sdemarco@zinezone.com>
Address: ZineZone.Com, 2 Gill St.; Suite X, Woburn, MA 01801
Phone: (781) 555-1212

For each venue listed in the chat schedule, you record the day and date of the event, the time, and the location. You'll notice that all of the Kurzweil events happen in a three-day span. That's a nice, compact schedule, with two events on Thursday, February 11. When scheduling, you like to give the guest enough time between chats to compose himself or herself, to get a drink of water, to hit the restroom, or whatever. It's sometimes easiest for the guest to get as much done in a night as possible, and you can schedule events back-to-back and let the hosts know that you have to duck out from each event five or 10 minutes early (so you can connect to the next one in time).

Time is a major issue when booking chats. Time zone miscommunications have ruined almost as many chats for me as technological problems. I shy away from overseas guests because I've had so much difficulty coordinating time zones. I try to use Eastern time in all my communications with hosts and guests and in all my promotional materials. I also include both a starting time and an ending time for each chat. These little organizational details will save you a lot of grief down the road.

The "software needed" field dates back to the days when guests would type for themselves. Nowadays, even my most tech-savvy guests don't do their own typing, so the "software needed" field just tells them whether I'll provide the ghost typist or the venue will. It also tells what software is required for visitors in case the guest is telling friends about the chat or if the company the guest represents is promoting the chat.

The second half of each entry in the chat schedule provides a contact person in case of problems. I always include a phone number, e-mail address, and physical address. Many chat hosts are freelancers who don't work out of corporate headquarters. You need their personal phone numbers, and their addresses can be used for sending support materials, thank-you notes, Christmas gifts, bribes, and so on. If anything goes wrong during the chat, that's the person who's going to get the call.

Now, let's see how you go about filling up the slots in the chat schedule.

Pitching Chats

When pitching a chat to a potential host, the question you have to answer is, "What's in it for them?" If you already have a working relationship with the chat host and a track record of putting on a good show, you should be able to refer them to the chat profile and then seal the deal in a phone call. But if the host is new to you, you'll have to use those publicity skills you have to persuade them to get involved. The initial pitch is done by e-mail and should contain the following three elements:

Content. You want to make the topic and guest sound irresistible.

Preparation. You want to sound like a pro and demonstrate the depth of your preparation with a reference to the chat profile. Basically, you're letting them know that you'll do all the work.

Promotion. Let the chat host know that you will be doing a major promotional campaign to attract an audience to the site.

What chat host can resist an appeal like this one? First, you are providing free content for their site. Second, you are willing to do all the work to pull off the event—all you need is a staging area. Third, you will be promoting the host site both online and off, generating good publicity and traffic. If the site has chat facilities and the topic of the chat matches the site's audience, you're in.

Next comes the question of when the chat will be held. I used to ask hosts for their suggested dates and times, but I've learned that it saves time to suggest a preferred date and let them give you alternatives if they don't like it. Settling on a date and time can take forever, so you want to do whatever is in your power to speed up the process. Figure 6.4 shows the body of an e-mail chat pitch for the Kurzweil campaign.

In the chat pitch shown in Figure 6.4, I hype the chat by letting the host know that the book is Viking's lead title for the season, that it will be in the news thanks to a large promotional campaign by Viking, and that it recently made the cover of *The New York Times Book Review*. Obviously, the book is hot. Because this forum is a venue dealing with books, this event should be a slam dunk.

Next, I tell the host the topic of the chat, I suggest a date, and I refer her to the chat profile. Then, I let her know exactly how I intend to promote the chat if she decides to host it: with news releases, discussion group postings, and listings in events calendars.

Jenny,

I'm writing to see if you would be interested in doing a chat with Ray Kurzweil, author of the new book "The Age of Spiritual Machines" at the Book Central site on AOL? The book is Viking's lead title for the new year, was part of the cover story in the New York Times Book Review Jan. 3, and is just rolling out a national tour.

We'd like to do a chat about "Are Human Beings Obsolete?" We are hoping for a chat date in early February if possible (the 10th would be great). Kurzweil's Chat Profile contains an intro, promo, artwork, and sample questions. It's at the following URL:

http://www.tenagra.com/chat/rkchat.html

If you host the chat, we will do a full promotional campaign in support of it, including news releases, postings to online events calendars, discussion group postings online, and more. We have permission to use an excerpt from the book, which I can send to you as a text file.

Please let me know if you're interested in hosting this chat, Jenny, and if you have suggestions for date and time. Thanks for your consideration.

Sincerely,
STEVE O'KEEFE
Director of Internet Publicity Services
The Tenagra Corporation
504-529-4344
~~~~~~

Figure 6.4 Pitching chat hosts starts with an e-mail that makes the chat sound irresistible, demonstrates your professional preparation, and tells the potential hosts how much promotional exposure they'll get from the chat.

Finally, I let the host know that I have supplemental materials to offer in the form of an excerpt from the book. That's more content for her site, sweetening the deal.

One mistake I've made pitching chats is telling too much in the initial e-mail. The longer the e-mail is, the less likely you are to get a quick response. When I started using chat profiles, that helped cut down on the e-mail pitch. Also, I've learned through experience that the hosts are more interested in what's in it for them than they are in the chat guest and topic. If you can find the host's real name (not an easy task), using it will warm up the e-mail and make it harder to ignore.

Many companies have business relationships with the parent companies of chat sites, and you can use those relationships to your advantage. AOL is part of Time Warner. If your company does any advertising with Time Warner properties, you should ask your ad people for a contact name, then ask the contact to help you set up the chat. Lots of businesses have relationships with niche trade sites that cover their industry, and these sites are prime targets for chats. Sometimes you have to marshal all your resources to book a tour, including memberships in professional or trade organizations, advertising and marketing connections, friends, and so on. In theory, there might be a "Chinese Wall" between advertising and editorial, but in practice, you will get better results on the editorial side (where chats are held) if you invoke an advertising relationship.

Once you get a response from a chat host, try to get a phone number to seal the deal. You can work out dates and times over the phone. One strategy I've used to speed the process is to book the whole tour before running any of the dates and times past the guest for approval. If I can send the guest the schedule for the full tour and then make adjustments, I avoid dozens of e-mails back and forth. I can usually get the whole tour approved at once.

One detail you need to clear up in your negotiations with the chat host is who will provide the typist. If the venue routinely provides a ghost typist, you need to know who that person is and how contact will be made on chat night. The typist will need a set of phone numbers for the guest, including backup numbers such as a mobile phone. You should be prepared to offer ghost typing services if the venue doesn't provide them. In that case, the chat host will need contact information for your ghost typist for sending instructions on connecting to the chat and other details. Your offer of a typist might turn an otherwise reluctant host into an enthusiastic supporter for the chat.

Now, let's see how to find chat venues and contact names for each of the major online services.

Web-Based Chats

The easiest way to locate chat venues on the Web is to go to the major online events calendars and search them with keywords related to your tour. Figure 6.5 shows the results of a search for "sports chat" at Yahoo! Events at http://events.yahoo.com. Because Yahoo! lists all kinds of events, including video, audio, and archives, searching for a topic plus the word *chats* will return a set of chat-only events.

In Figure 6.5, five different venues for sports chat are listed just for "Today's Events." They are as follows: ESPN.com, SportsLegends.About.com, The Sporting News, CNNSI.com, and Booknotes. Following the link to ESPN.com leads to a description of the chat along with a picture of the guest. The text describing the chat could have come from a good chat profile, and the picture of the guest had a photo credit embedded in it—so you see that publicists are catching on to this chat profile thing. Now comes the tricky part: finding the name and e-mail address of a chat host to whom you can send your pitch.

My first stab at ESPN.com was to check the transcripts of past chats to see whether I could find the name of a host or moderator. But ESPN removed all that information from the transcripts. Next, I tried the site map, which just took me on a loop back to the homepage for chats. Then I tried the "Contact Us" section, which of course contained no contact information whatsoever. It did lead to a feedback form, and you can pitch a chat through these forms, but the response rate is low. If you have to use a feedback form, a smarter approach is to ask who to contact about booking celebrities into chat at the site. Maybe you'll get a response, or maybe not. Finally, as frustration began to set in, I visited the Advertising Information section of the site, where I found e-mail addresses and phone numbers for ad reps. These aren't the best contacts for booking a chat, but they're better than generic feedback forms. I would e-mail an ad rep and ask who I contact about booking celebrities into chat. If possible, I would mention that I represent an ESPN advertiser. If that didn't bring a reply, I would try phoning one of the ad reps and ask to be connected to the person who is responsible for booking chats.

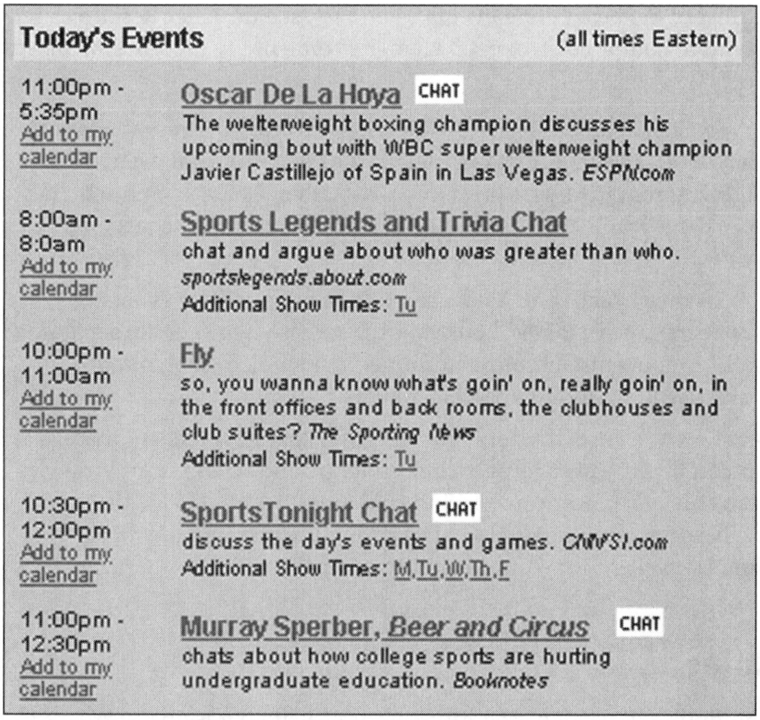

Today's Events (all times Eastern)

11:00pm -
5:35pm
Add to my
calendar

Oscar De La Hoya CHAT
The welterweight boxing champion discusses his
upcoming bout with WBC super welterweight champion
Javier Castillejo of Spain in Las Vegas. *ESPN.com*

8:00am -
8:0am
Add to my
calendar

Sports Legends and Trivia Chat
chat and argue about who was greater than who.
sportslegends.about.com
Additional Show Times: Tu

10:00pm -
11:00am
Add to my
calendar

Fly
so, you wanna know what's goin' on, really goin' on, in
the front offices and back rooms, the clubhouses and
club suites? *The Sporting News*
Additional Show Times: Tu

10:30pm -
12:00pm
Add to my
calendar

SportsTonight Chat CHAT
discuss the day's events and games. *CNN/SI.com*
Additional Show Times: M,Tu,W,Th,F

11:00pm -
12:30pm
Add to my
calendar

Murray Sperber, *Beer and Circus* CHAT
chats about how college sports are hurting
undergraduate education. *Booknotes*

Figure 6.5 To find good venues, do a keyword search at the major online events calendars. This image shows the results of a search for "sports chat" at Yahoo! Events.

This cumbersome process of finding chat hosts is unfortunately commonplace online. Sometime in the near future, chat hosts will be as important to a program as Stone Phillips is to *Dateline NBC*; that is, the hosts will start to get reputations for producing good programming, and their names will be promoted instead of hidden. You still won't be able to contact the host directly, but it will be easier to track down assistants or producers who are the decision makers regarding guests. When chat shows have credits, publicists will fly.

Any large portal will have an events calendar, but few of them will list events on other sites. I tried to find the name of a chat host for Lycos by going through the chat calendar at the site. The transcripts had been cleaned, of course, and contained no contact information. Drilling into the site, I never found any contact information—only feedback forms. The chat section of Lycos is part of the Communities section, however, which includes message boards. Inside the message boards, I found Lycos staff responding to questions, and the responses revealed their names and e-mail addresses. Because these people work in the Communities section, they are either involved in chat production or know who is. Contacting one of these staff members should lead to a direct contact for a chat host. Another sneaky way to pitch a chat at Lycos is to use the "Volunteer with Us" section, which lets you indicate what section of the site you want to help with, including chat. You can be pretty certain that a chat pitch sent using the volunteer form will go to staff in the chat department. Because most chat departments don't have a lot of staff, your message will probably go directly to the top chat coordinator at the site. Bingo!

For an updated list of the best online events calendars, see the Chat Resources section of www.wiley.com/compbooks/okeefe. Here are some of my favorites, with tips on how to use them:

LookSmart at www.looksmart.com. I really like this directory because it lets you search for chat *venues* by subject, as opposed to a calendar of chat events. You have to drill down from the home page into Chats, then Chats by Subject. Then, choose a subject and you'll get a list of all the Web sites that host chats on that subject. Very nice!

Yack at http://looksmart.yack.com. Yack used to be a major online events calendar. It appears to have joined LookSmart, but these two sites are separate. Yack now lists fewer events and more multimedia than plain chat, but this directory is still useful in finding top chat venues.

Chatsearch.net at www.chatsearch.net/. For the guerrilla marketers out there, this site will lead you into the peer-to-peer chat underground where edgy, viral marketing can still take place. You can find chat areas devoted to all kinds of subjects, but these are unmoderated venues and you won't find any hosts to pitch. This site is excellent for word-of-mouth campaigns.

America Online

It is much easier to find chat host e-mail addresses on AOL than it is on the Web. AOL is currently organized into 15 communities, covering broad subject areas such as "Career and Work" and "Learning." Each of these communities is host to numerous subcommunities, most of which offer both message boards and chats. Begin your search for chat venues by typing Keyword "Chat." That will take you to the People Connection welcome screen shown in Figure 6.6.

Once you are at the People Connection screen shown in Figure 6.6, you have two different ways to locate chat venues. With the "Find a Chat" button, you'll be taken to a menu of open chat rooms. These are mostly for peer-to-peer chat, although you can find some special-interest chat areas that are supposedly moderated. These are *not* good forums for conducting serious chat. Events here get no promotion (which you should know by now is the main reason for doing chats), and the environment is not controlled. Figure 6.7 shows a schedule of chats for this area. Note that each chat lists a host, and the host names always begin with the letters PCCL. Those stand for People Center Chat Leaders—the people you would want to contact about hosting special events in their chat areas. Each host's name is also their e-mail address: send your chat pitch to PCCLjudy@aol.com, and it will reach host Judy.

A much better way to find venues for your chats is to explore AOL's communities looking for chat areas. Figure 6.6 shows the pull-down menu for the different communities at AOL. Click the community of your choice, and you'll be taken to the Web site home for that community. As an example, I chose Careers & Work from the list of communities and was taken to the homepage for the community. There, I found listings for more than 100 chat rooms, most of them devoted to individual professions such as accounting or engineering. I selected the Broadcast Media chat area and got a weekly schedule for chat programming in that area (shown in Figure 6.8). In addition to the

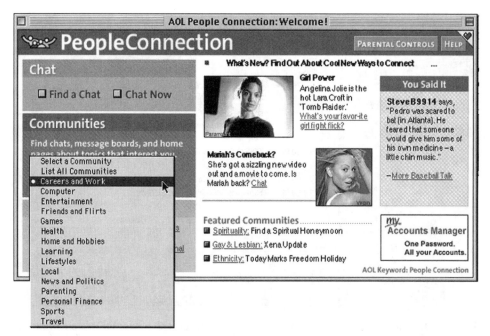

Figure 6.6 AOL's "People Connection" is your gateway to hundreds of special-interest chat venues. Use Keyword "chat" to locate the main board shown here, then click "Find a Chat" or browse the communities to locate promising chat venues.

chat schedule, you get the names of the hosts, all of which begin with the letters WPLC, which I believe stands for Work Place Leader Chat. To pitch the host with your chat idea, send e-mail to WPLCrick@aol.com, for example, and your e-mail will go to chat leader Rick.

When pitching chat hosts on AOL, it's a good idea to send the initial e-mail from an AOL account rather than from your Internet address. It makes you look local, and many AOL hosts will not accept e-mail coming from the Internet. After you establish contact with a host, you can switch to your preferred e-mail address. The host will likely have a preferred e-mail address, too. Oh, the little games we play to keep from getting e-mail from people we don't want to deal with.

Once you have done a chat on AOL, you can use your contact person there to help you find venues for other chats. Many times, AOL chat hosts have come to my aid, suggesting good forums for chats, providing contact names, e-mail addresses, phone numbers, and even letters of introduction to other hosts saying something like, "This guy really knows how to put on a good show—you should listen to his pitch." I can't overestimate how much time I've saved booking tours using this informal networking approach. Just be sure to remember your hosts with thank-you notes, Christmas cards, and other goodies.

AOL has a large chat venue called AOL Live. This venue is capable of holding 50,000 people at one time—far greater capacity than any other live forum online. When AOL Live first started operating, you could pitch the hosts in that area directly. Now, however, they are hermetically sealed off from the public. These hosts only work in

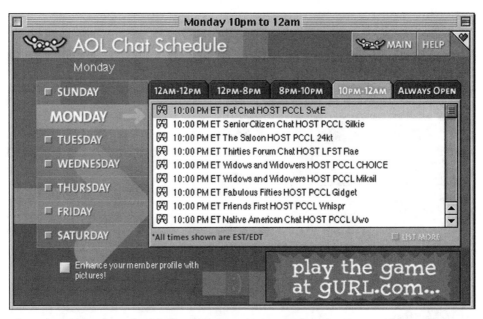

Figure 6.7 The chat schedule for AOL's People Connection chat rooms. This environment is not the best for hosting chats, but you can find host names here that will lead you to other opportunities. These rooms could be useful for an ongoing talk show produced by you.

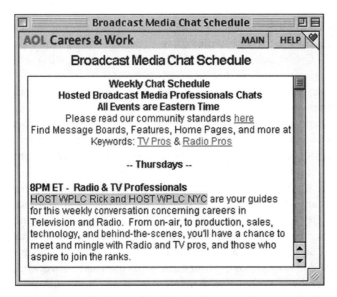

Figure 6.8 The chat schedule for the Broadcast Media forum on AOL's Careers & Work channel. The e-mail addresses of chat hosts are simply the host's name plus @aol.com.

cooperation with large sponsors, and your chance of getting through to them is virtually nil. Fortunately, the producers of AOL Live search through the event schedules for all the forums at AOL, and if they see a promising chat, they will pull it out of the forum and into the AOL live area. This situation has only happened to me once, and it's something over which you have no control. It's a good thing when it does happen, though, because the promos reach a huge audience of hundreds of thousands of people a day.

CompuServe

Finding chat venues and chat hosts on CompuServe is even easier than AOL. Every forum on CompuServe has a chat room, and every forum provides a roster of the forum's staff. So, all you have to do is use GO Word "Forum Center," choose a forum, and then search for "staff." Figure 6.9 shows the staff roster for the Build Your Business forum on CompuServe. The staff profiles include names, e-mail addresses, and job descriptions. Look for a job description that includes being a chat coordinator, producer, or host, and then send your pitch to that person.

BUILDING YOUR BUSINESS STAFF

Mike Bayer

(Chief SysOp)
[76710,3114]
- Mike Bayer is the President of the BusinessFor.Com Forum Group which operates seven CompuServe Forums. He writes CompuServe's twice monthly @Work column which is published on the Business Channel, Keyword: Business.

Kathy Henderson

(Wizop)
[112764.237]
- Kat is the owner of SmartMarketing Business Network, which provides customized traditional marketing and website services to small businesses and non-profits. Kat has over 25 years experience as a freelance writer and independent marketing consultant. www.smartmarketingnetwork.com.

Brad Anderson

(Asst Wizop)
[110364,2375]
- Brad is an attorney with 20 years experience in business, technology, intellectual property and litigation law. Much of his private practice is devoted to serving small inventors as they move from idea to market.

Figure 6.9 Finding chat hosts on CompuServe is a snap. Use the Forum Center to locate a promising venue, and then search for "staff" to find a roster of the forum's staff. You should find a file like the one shown here in every forum, with staff names, e-mail addresses, and job descriptions.

Just as with AOL, you should send your pitch from your CompuServe e-mail account so that it looks native, then switch to using your preferred e-mail address once you have established communications.

Promoting Chats

A chat tour without promotion is a waste of good electricity. If you're going to go through all the trouble of booking a tour, please go the distance and make sure that it gets promoted. Let's take a look at how to do that.

Promotion at the Venues

Once you have the venues on the hook for the chat tour, it's time to push the promotion. You want as much publicity as you can squeeze out of them. Ask the chat hosts right away if there is anything they need to promote the chat: better artwork, support files, and so on. Then, keep checking back to see that the promotions are put in place. Some chat hosts have very little control over the amount of promotion you get. This situation is true especially on AOL, where I have resorted to temper tantrums to get the promotions up in time. Here's a list of some of the promotional support you'd like to get for the chat:

Homepage of the site. At the beginning of this chapter, Figure 6.1 showed the kind of promotion you'd like right on the homepage of the site: the name of the guest, the name of their latest release (or product they are plugging, corporate affiliation, and so on), along with the date, time, and location of the chat. A thumbnail photo of the guest is nice, too. This listing should be linked to a full description of the chat.

Homepage of chat area. On AOL, CompuServe, or major sites like MSNBC, you're unlikely to get homepage coverage, but you can certainly push for a plug on the main page of the chat area. This page is where the chat schedule is located, and all sites will highlight a few of their upcoming chats with nice little promos. Many of those guests *paid* to be featured there or have a large enough advertising relationship with the site to get this preferential coverage.

Homepage of the forum. On AOL and CompuServe, you should get a promo on the homepage of the forum that is hosting the chat. You might not get it until a few days before the chat, but if you push you might be able to get a week or more of coverage there.

Write-up in the site newsletter. CompuServe has a weekly newsletter that gets sent out system-wide. I've had several chat listings in there. AOL has a newsletter for the AOL Live forum, and you can sometimes get chat listings in there. Most Web sites have one main newsletter, and you want to be included.

Write-up in the forum newsletter. Each of the forums on AOL and CompuServe will have one or more newsletters or news flashes, and you want to be included in all of these. Web sites will have opt-in newsletters for different subject areas, and your chat should be included in the newsletter for the corresponding subject area. You might have to gently suggest to the chat hosts which newsletters you think the listing should be included in.

E-mail notification or reminder service. Several sites I have worked with have an e-mail notification service for events. It really builds attendance for an event if an e-mail reminder is sent to the list the day before the event.

Listing in chat schedule. You might think this item is a no-brainer and that the chat should be listed in the site's chat schedule, but you'd be surprised how many chats get left out. On many services, the chat schedule will list only regularly scheduled chat programs, such as every Wednesday at 10 a.m. we talk about breastfeeding and won't include notices about special events. I feel that anyone opening a chat schedule should see a listing for my chat, and I push to get such listings.

Chat description page. Beyond a mere listing, it's essential to have a link to a page that gives a full description of the chat, including artwork. Very often, these pages are created verbatim from the chat profile. The sooner a chat description page appears on the site, the better.

Link to Web site. As a courtesy, most chat venues will include a link to a companion Web site. This site could be a book companion site, a movie site, a music site, a corporate site, and so on. It's nice if they make it a logo link, and you should have logo artwork available to offer.

Support materials. I always offer support files with a chat appearance, such as a book excerpt, an article, an MP3 track, a movie trailer, and so on. Most sites are more than happy to have this extra content and will install it in time. Gentle offers of assistance might help the chat hosts realize the importance of installing these files *before* the chat.

E-commerce links. If the chat hypes a product that can be purchased online, you'd like to have buying links installed throughout the chat promos for impulse shoppers. If the site has affiliate or associate programs with online vendors, this situation is an opportunity for the site to earn a little e-commerce revenue. I have gone so far as to offer to set-up an affiliate or associate program for sites that don't have them.

For Ray Kurzweil's chat tour, MSNBC took our pitch and ran with it. MSNBC used an excerpt from Ray's book, plus it requested an op-ed piece on a subject of its own choosing. MSNBC assigned a graphic artist to the chat, who came up with wonderful custom graphics for the promotion. They opened up a message board for continuing discussion about topics raised in the chat. Then, it gave the chat homepage plugs on MSNBC. A simple chat turned into a major installation over night. That's the kind of treatment you'd like to get from every host.

Keep checking back with your venues regularly to make sure that the promotions get installed. When they do, *document it!* Take screen captures of the promotions, crop them, and print them using a color printer. I wish I had collected screen shots of some of my early chat victories. Those screenshots are very important to demonstrating the value of the chat promotion to clients and bosses, and they look great in your portfolio.

For me, they have become important training materials in classes that I teach about online promotion. You'll never regret documenting these events, because chat promos are fleeting and if you try to recapture them a week later, they'll be gone.

Web Site Promotion

You should be able to get some promotion for the chats at Web sites beyond those belonging to the chat venues. The first place is on the sponsor or corporate site. If you're doing a chat for a Paramount Pictures release, you'd like to get the chat schedule and a promo on Paramount's site and on the companion site for the movie. If you're doing a chat for ERA Real Estate, you'd like to get some promotion not only from their home site, but also from ERA affiliate sites. I've done chats for many book publishers who don't promote the tour on their own sites. It's a little frustrating to hammer venues to install promotions when the parent company paying for the chat tour won't even promote it.

Some chats involve partnerships, and the partners are prime targets for chat promos. I once did a chat series for Random House Children's Publishing that was held at Talk City, ParentSoup, and iVillage. Target Stores paid for the chat series, which was a benefit for Read Across America Day. Both Target Stores and the American Library Association installed promotions for the series at their Web sites. You can see how a chat promotion spreads out like the arms of an octopus radiating from a central event, with tentacles reaching all over the Internet.

Banner advertising is actually an effective way to draw an audience for a chat—if the banners appear within a half-hour before or after the start of the chat and link people directly to the auditorium. Talk City was always able to pull a good crowd by running announcements through all its chat rooms that a certain guest was now online chatting. There might be 10,000 people chatting at Talk City at any given time, and announcements like these can easily pull dozens of people. The same is true at America Online, where announcements about a chat in the People Connection chat rooms will pull an audience to a special event chat.

Chat is an impulse buy, and the low-hanging fruit is people who are already online chatting, followed by people who are online somewhere. Banner ads can be purchased for a specific time of day. It's not worth buying banner ads just to support a chat tour, but if you are already paying for banner ads, it's worth creating custom banners that include a chat promo and running them only while your guest is chatting. The pull of a message such as "Chat NOW with Cher" will be irresistible to Cher fans on Yahoo! or Netscape or MSNBC. You might be able to get the venues hosting your chats to give you site-wide promotion for free or a discounted rate. If not, you'll need to consult with an ad network such as DoubleClick about buying timed banner ads.

News Releases

News releases promoting the chat tour will help you push beyond the boundaries of online publicity into print, broadcast, and other coverage. Unless you are a much more disciplined event planner than I am, you won't have your tour booked in time to get coverage from long-lead media outlets. Magazines and TV news magazine shows require months of lead time. I like to have a tour completely booked one month before the chats start, but I often have as little notice as two weeks. Realistically, you're looking for coverage in daily and weekly newspapers, and online media.

The chat tour can be tacked onto the end of a conventional news release. Here is the release for Ray Kurzweil's tour. The release offers a review copy of the book to the media, and the tour is tacked on the end in hopes of being used as a sidebar or in a calendar of online events.

E-MAIL NEWS RELEASE

Subject Line: Free Review Copy: Age of Spiritual Machines

I am writing to offer you a free review copy of what is already becoming one of the most talked-about books of the decade: Ray Kurzweil's "The Age of Spiritual Machines" (Viking). Kurzweil argues convincingly that computers will soon equal the processing capabilities of the human brain -- indeed, that machines will become appear to be "conscious." The practical and ethical ramifications are staggering.

It would be easy to dismiss such predictions as "science fiction" were it not for the author's impeccable credentials. Kurzweil is one of the most decorated scientists, inventors, and visionaries of the 20th Century. The recipient of nine honorary doctorate degrees, honored by two U.S. Presidents, the "restless genius" (Wall Street Journal) Ray Kurzweil has spent a lifetime teaching computers how to act like human beings. He developed software and devices that helped machines to see (the first CCD scanner), read (the first omni-font OCR software), listen (the first commercially marketed large vocabulary speech recognition), talk (the first print-to-speech reading machine), and make music (the Kurzweil digital piano). In "The Age of Spiritual Machines," Kurzweil says that computers can *think,* too, and will soon exceed human intelligence.

If you would like a free review copy of "The Age of Spiritual Machines" (Viking, ISBN 0-670-88217-8) -- or an interview with author Ray Kurzweil, simply reply to this e-mail. If you publish a calendar of online events, we would appreciate listings for Ray Kurzweil's chat tour:

CHAT TOUR
Ray Kurzweil, author of "The Age of Spiritual Machines"
Subject: Are Human Beings Obsolete?

```
=> Tuesday, February 9, at 9 p.m. Eastern Time
Book Central on America Online <Keyword: BC>

=> Wednesday, February 10, at 7 p.m. Eastern Time
Stein Online <http://www.compuserve.com/cir/>

=> Thursday, February 11, at 7:30 p.m. Eastern Time
MSNBC <http://www.msnbc.com/chat/>

=> Thursday, February 11, at 9 p.m. Eastern Time
ZineZone <http://www.zinezone.com/events/>
```

You'll notice that there's not even enough room in the news release to use the promo paragraph for the chats. E-mail news releases have to be kept short. Detailed instructions for preparing and distributing e-mail news releases are covered in a previous chapter. If you work for a public relations firm or other publicity services vendor, it is worth your while to cultivate a list of e-mail addresses for events calendar contacts and send chat tour schedules to them. For those who don't make publicity their profession, it's enough to send the release to your normal media contacts with a pitch at the end to use the chat schedule in any online events calendar that they maintain.

Discussion Group Postings

Announcements about chat tours are usually welcome in online discussion groups related to the topic of the chats. These groups include Usenet newsgroups, Internet mailing lists, Web site message boards, America Online Forums, and CompuServe forums. Instructions for writing, formatting, and distributing discussion group postings are covered in an earlier chapter. There are a few caveats concerning announcements about chat tours.

Chat tour announcements fall in the gray area between commercial spam and genuine contributions to a discussion group. People participating in discussion groups about computer security want to know about online events related to computer security. But chat tour announcements will always draw some complaints. You can soften these complaints by offering extra services with your posting. For example, I usually prepare some sort of file as support material for the chats. I will offer to send this file upon request in my discussion group postings and then tack the chat tour on the end of the posting for those who are interested. That softens the commercial tone of the announcement.

Another nod to netiquette is to offer to send transcripts of the chat to those who can't attend. This feature is a nice service, and people appreciate the courtesy. Because I have to clean up the transcripts anyway, it is not much more work to send them to those who requested. Another nice gesture is to offer to forward questions to the guest. These questions can be collected and sent to the chat host, who will decide whether to use them or not. Then, I send a transcript back to everyone who sent questions. This relay service is helpful if the chats take place on proprietary services such as AOL and CSI (to which many people online don't have access).

Finally, you have to show some sensitivity when posting messages in forums on America Online and CompuServe. AOL forums don't like to see you promoting chats on CSI and vice versa—even although they're both owned by AOL Time Warner. Some AOL and CSI hosts get upset if you promote chats taking place in other AOL or CSI forums. In these cases, you simply promote the support file and mention that the author will be on a chat tour soon. Then, you include the entire chat schedule at the beginning of the support file. That seems to keep everyone happy.

Discussion group postings on Usenet newsgroups and Internet mailing lists should go out a couple of days prior to the events. If you send out messages too far in advance, people will forget about attending. For America Online and CompuServe, if you are putting the chat schedule in a giveaway file rather than in the posting itself, you'll need to upload the file at least a week ahead of time.

Online Events Calendars

There are thousands of Web sites that maintain event calendars. The trick is finding those related to the subject of the chats. You can start by hitting the main online events calendars, listed earlier in this chapter, and found in the Resources section at www.wiley.com/compbooks/okeefe.

The next target is special-interest media sites, such as trade journals, trade associations, professional associations, and so on. Most of these sites maintain calendars, and they are usually very cooperative about including online events. The linkage chapter of this book has instructions on creating a good map to top online sites related to any given subject. If you have a map left over from a linkage campaign or a good set of bookmarks in your Web browser, making the rounds with your chat schedule won't take too much time.

Regional publications and business journals are also good prospects for calendar listings. Figure 6.10 shows a typical events calendar from the Indianapolis Business Journal. If you're having difficulty locating these calendars, you can try a search at Yahoo!, Google, or HotBot by using the terms "local events calendar" or "medical

Figure 6.10 An events calendar for the Indianapolis Business Journal. There are thousands of these calendars online where you can upload the schedule of a chat tour.

events calendar" if the subject of your chat is health-related. A clever use of search engines should yield a manageable number of good prospects.

The easiest way to approach these calendars is to create a text version of your news release or discussion group posting, then keep it open on your desktop, cutting and pasting information into calendar submission forms. Most calendars give you only 10 to 25 words to describe the event. It helps to have a short description prepared in advance.

Conducting Chats

It's chat day, and you're a little nervous. You can relax a bit knowing that the attendance at the chat isn't that important. If you are the guest for a chat, most likely you'll be working with a typist, and your responsibilities will be limited to being by the telephone when chat time comes. If you're the publicist for the chat, you might be handling typing duties yourself or supervising the typing arrangements. You should have received a set of instructions from the chat host about how to connect to the event. For Barnes & Noble Online, you'll be given the URL for a "green room" where you will wait for the chat to begin. For CompuServe, you might have a special screen name and password that you use to access a "stage."

You should check out the facilities for each of the chats ahead of time, especially if you are using a venue with which you're not familiar. Some chats require that you install software and plug-ins or that you upgrade your Web browser. The typist will have to take care of these details in advance and test the chat facilities to make certain that the connection is smooth. All guests require a user ID, password, and screen name, and these all need to be established between the hosts and the typist in advance of the chats. I've heard many publicists complain about technical difficulties chatting online, but most of these are self-inflicted. The publicist will book a chat on America Online, inform the guest about it, and consider his or her work finished. On chat day, the guest informs the publicist that he's not a member of America Online. No one set up an account, created a screen name, or tested the connection. Chat time comes, and the host and the audience are assembled and wait about 15 minutes for the guest to show up, then everyone leaves, and your standing as a publicist with that chat venue is ruined.

Hosts and Moderators

Let's take a look behind the screens at some of the producers of chat programming. A *forum host* is a person who makes content decisions at online forums and is likely the person who authorized the chat. A *chat host* or chat coordinator might run the entire chat operation at a venue or run a specific chat room. For smaller venues, the forum host and chat host are the same person, but for larger venues you might never deal with the forum host after pitching the chat.

The chat host usually welcomes the guest to the chat, signals the start of the chat, and runs the introduction. After that, the chat host will choose which questions to give to the guest and will often add follow-up questions to clarify an answer. Many chat hosts hog the cursor, monopolizing the guest's time with their own questions instead of letting the audience participate. This action defeats the whole point of the chat. We'll look next at how to handle that situation.

Most chat venues provide *moderators* in addition to hosts. The moderator tries to maintain order during the chat and let the host concentrate on the content. A moderator welcomes people into the chat room, runs announcements about who the guest is, runs product promos, and reminds people of the protocol for asking questions. The moderator will also chastise people who are disrupting the chat and bounce them out of the room if a warning doesn't suffice.

If there is no moderator, the host does double duty, interacting with the guest and also policing the room. It can be a tough job. A trained ghost typist will help ease the burden.

Ghost Typists

Ghost typist is one of the most intriguing job titles to come out of the Internet revolution. On the surface, their job is to read questions to the guest over the telephone, then keyboard the guest's answers. But a good ghost typist does much more and can make the difference between an extraordinary chat and a dud.

A good ghost typist is a model of advance preparation. These people tend to be Internet warriors, with dozens of software programs for connecting to every conceivable style of chat. They have to be fast typists—at least 50 words per minute—but speed is less important than composure. A ghost typist enters an arena of chaos and shapes it into a lucid discussion. A good ghost typist will be prepared with a text version of the chat profile and *paste bombs* ready to launch at a moment's notice. A paste bomb is a piece of text prepared in advance and dumped into the chat flow. It might be the introduction for the guest, a promotional announcement, or a file related to the chat, such as Top Ten Tips or a recipe.

The ghost typist is responsible for setting up the guest account, including the user ID, password, and screen name. The typist tests each venue ahead of time to be sure that any technical difficulties are solved in advance. Ten minutes before each chat, the typist connects to the venue and logs in under the guest's screen name. The typist introduces himself or herself to the hosts or moderators. The host will then invite the typist back stage or into any special waiting area, and the host and typist will discuss how the chat should play out. Then, the typist slips on a headset telephone, calls the guest at a prearranged number, and reviews procedures with the guest while waiting for the chat to begin.

Once the chat starts, a trained ghost typist can make all the difference. It's common for typists to smooth the verbal responses of guests into good text bites. If the guest refers to a question as "stupid," the typist will usually ask for another question instead of insulting an audience member. If the guest says, "In the movie I play a con man . . . " the typist will keyboard, "In 'Secret Games' (Paramount Pictures, in theaters August 1), I play a con man . . . " I'm frequently astonished at chat transcripts where the name of the guest is not used past the introduction and the product they are promoting is never mentioned. A typist should make sure that the promotional part of the chat doesn't get lost, rephrasing answers to get the name of the product out there or using paste bombs with ordering information.

There is a fine line between cleaning up a guest's remarks and misrepresenting the guest. Ghost typists need to be able to dance around that line. Sometimes they do it verbally by suggesting an alternate wording or by finishing a sentence for a guest who gets stuck in mid-thought. Small mistakes are usually cleaned up on the fly. The goal is to have a quality chat that accurately reflects the guest's remarks. I've typed for hundreds of guests, and most of them are grateful to have a buffer between their stream of consciousness and the online audience. And if a guest insists on shooting his or her foot in a live chat, I am more than happy as a typist to help pull the trigger. Ghost typists coach the guests to either stretch an answer or wrap up a long response that is sapping energy from the chat.

Where a ghost typist really earns his or her pay is in the behind-the-scenes interactions with hosts and moderators. In most venues, the typist will have two chat screens open at the same time: one with the audience and another for private messages to the hosts. Private messages fly by such as, "Do you want me to ask one of the sample questions?" and the typist has to respond to the right question in the right window. I've gone into chats where the host was completely unprepared. I would ask the host to use one of the sample questions and get a reply, "What sample questions?" At that point, I will feed the sample questions to the host through the private message window while typing the guest's replies in the public message window. You have to keep your wits about you to be a ghost typist.

There are other times where a typist has to usurp the authority of a host and take control of the chat. If hosts are monopolizing the guest's time, you privately tell the host you want questions from the audience. If the host is queuing the questions too slowly, you tell them you want two questions at a time or not to wait until you respond to queue the next question. Sometimes the typist needs to call on the next person in the queue instead of waiting for the host to do so. Typists might have to run introductions or even explain the protocol to the audience if the host fails to do so.

I've handled ghost typing for several high-tech superstars who are perfectly capable of handling typing for themselves. But after they've tried a ghost typist, they like it. All those messages flying across the screen—public and private—are extremely confusing. Having a typist allows them to focus on answering the questions and not the background noise that fills the screen. One of my least favorite typing scenarios, however, is when I'm ghost typing, but the guest is watching the chat on their computer. All of a sudden, they'll start answering questions that are not in the queue, and I have to explain that we have to wait for the host to send the next question or the chat will break down into total chaos. Once I typed an art history chat, and the guest would say names of artists I had no idea how to spell. After he saw the poor spellings spilling across his screen, he realized he needed to spell unfamiliar names to me over the phone. That slowed things down.

The chapter on building an online publicity operation has information about where you can find trained ghost typists. One route is to use online temp agencies or freelance services such as eLance at www.elance.com and post a notice seeking experienced chat typists. The going rate for this sort of thing is $50/hour. You should be able to find three or four people who have just the right qualifications and enough computing power to work around any obstacle. An excellent way to find good ghost typists is to recruit chat hosts. If you've done a chat where the host was exceptional, consider offering him or her a job. Many chat hosts, moderators, and typists are volunteers, and they will probably jump at a paying gig.

Prime time for online chats targeting North America is similar to peak television viewing hours: Monday through Thursday from 8 p.m. to 11 p.m. Eastern time. Any later and you miss the eastern audience; any earlier and the west coast audience won't be home from work. These hours don't match well with standard business hours, which is one reason why companies might want to use freelance ghost typists. A lot of ghost typists are stay-at-home parents with great computers and ample experience working online. They can be a godsend, especially after you've established a good working relationship and they know what you want to achieve during the chats. For promotions aimed at a business audience, you can conduct daytime chats, but my experience is that turnout is better at night.

Chat Style

There is a certain style for chatting online that is unlike anything else. One of the great thrills—and dangers—is that you never know what questions will pop up. You get to see how guests react under pressure. Someone asks a question, and the clock is ticking away while you type as fast as possible. There's no time to check spelling or verify a URL or even to make sure you don't sound like a complete moron. Responses are very casual, and most guests do not sweat the details—realizing that poor spelling and inappropriate responses can be cleaned out of the transcripts.

There will be a limited amount of room to type an answer (about two lines). If you want to type more, you have to send the first part of your answer and then continue typing the next part. Communicating this way can be very frustrating. It's best to keep your answers short and refer people to your Web site (or elsewhere) for more in-depth information.

Short is one thing, but some guests clam up in chats, providing one-word answers and forcing the moderator to draw the responses out of them. Here are some snippets from an America Online chat with author Robert Jordan:

Question: Have you written any books previous to the WHEEL OF TIME set?
RJordan2: Yes.
Question: Where did you get the concept for Perrin?
RJordan2: Out of my head.
Question: Your plots are so detailed and intricate. Do you ever get confused about what should happen when?
RJordan2: No.

Compare this clipped style with the responses of Eric Tyson, author of *Personal Finance For Dummies*, also from a chat on America Online:

Question: What is the best credit card? How can I transfer to it?
Eric Tyson: If you carry a balance, there are a number of cards with rates less than 10 percent. Try Consumer's Best Bankcard or Wachovia. Phone numbers and a longer list are in the book.
Question: Something I did not see in your book was stock options or index options...could you briefly explain this?

Eric Tyson: Options are a gambling type vehicle that payoff or not based on short term price movements of a security. I recommended avoiding them in chapter 10.

It's handy to have some resources at your fingertips to which you can refer people. You want to keep a list of your favorite Web addresses nearby and any other reference materials that you think will help. Your host will appreciate it if you plug his or her forum as a good source of information. If you're a guest on Lycos, for example, you should recommend the using the Lycos search engine if the subject comes up during chat, rather than a competing service such as Yahoo!. I've had authors on chat who mention that their books are available at Amazon when the host venue has a partnership with Barnes & Noble. That's embarrassing.

Just like radio and TV interviews, if you connect with the host, you tend to connect with the audience. It's hard to get any chemistry going online, though. Try to personalize the chat by using people's names. The host's name might appear as "Moderator" or "BJenks213" on the screen, but you can call her "Betty" (or whatever her real name is) in your replies. Another tip is to use humor; it will help you relax and enjoy the chat.

After ghost typing for many years, I realized that the pace of the chat had a major impact on the audience. If the pace flags, you'll notice attendance dropping with each passing minute. On the other hand, if you keep the pace at the boiling point, people will stay for the entire chat. One key to controlling the pace is to get two main discussion threads going simultaneously. While you are answering one question, the host should be displaying the next question so you can immediately respond to it. By the time you're done answering that, there might be a follow-up question to your previous answer. It's like you're bouncing back and forth between these two extended Q&A threads. When you get that rhythm going, it can be magical, and the audience will get inspired and stay engaged. If the host is not passing through questions quickly enough, ask him or her to give you two questions at a time or take charge and start calling on people yourself.

Dealing with Problems

Technical difficulties plague many chats, but most of them can be avoided with good equipment and advance preparation. If your ghost typist can't connect to the chat, he or she should call the emergency phone number for the host included on the chat schedule. The host can often provide a direct phone link between the guest and forum staff, taking the ghost typist out of the loop. If the connection is dropped mid-chat, the typist should be able to log back on quickly or find an alternate route to the service. For example, you can connect to America Online by using a local dial-in number, a toll-free 800 number (which is not free—it's billed to your AOL account instead of to your phone bill), or through an Internet connection (TCP/IP). The same is true for CompuServe.

If you're having trouble connecting to a Web chat, try accessing the chat via America Online's Web browser. By having multiple software programs open on your computer at the same time, you can usually get back into a chat before anyone except the host knows you left. When I used to ghost type, I would have two computers in the office connected to the chat under different screen names. If the connection dropped on one, I would switch to the other and let the host know that I was now using my backup screen name.

People in the audience demonstrating bad manners can spoil your chat. You can usually work around them, and most venues have the ability to kick them out and keep them out. Bad manners on the part of the *guest* are harder to fix. I did one chat where the guest had 10 employees attend, asking stupid questions like, "Why is your company the best in the world?" I suffered through the chat, but when it was over I gave them hell. They thought they were engaging in "viral marketing." I let them know in no uncertain terms that what they were doing was unethical, ruining not only their own reputation but mine as well.

One of the most humorous chat experiences I had was with *Wall Street Journal* reporter Kara Swisher. I had booked a tour promoting her book, *AOL.com,* and Kara insisted on typing for herself at the chats. After all, she is a technology reporter and she certainly has the hardware and software to assure a good connection. The first chat went well, although Kara takes no prisoners, online or off, and did not suffer fools gladly in her chats. Some of those transcripts are hot and might have benefited from a benevolent ghost-typing buffer. The second chat was on CompuServe, and when it came time to start, Kara wasn't there.

I was logged in on CompuServe to observe the chat, and as chat time approached and no guest appeared, I sent a private message to the host asking her to stall while I tried to locate our guest. I called Kara's first phone number and got voice mail. I tried her second phone number and got no answer. Finally, I tried her mobile phone and Kara answered. The conversation went something like this.

> **Steve:** Hi Kara, this is Steve O'Keefe. Did you forget our chat tonight on CompuServe?
> **Kara:** That's tonight? I thought it was tomorrow.
> **Steve:** No, it's tonight. There are about 20 people in the room waiting for you. Do you have access to a computer?
> **Kara:** No. What should we do? Can we reschedule it?
> **Steve:** I'd rather not. All the promos would have to be changed. We have an audience in the room now. I can log off, log in under your name, and we can do this right now.
> **Kara:** Okay, let's go for it.

I slipped on my headset, let the host know what was happening, changed my screen name, and entered the chat as Kara Swisher about 10 minutes late. I was reading the questions to Kara, keyboarding her answers, and I heard a horn honking. "Where are you," I asked Kara. "Driving home." I smiled. Here I was, in suburban Seattle, dialing into CompuServe's computers which were probably in Virginia or somewhere, with a host who was in L.A., chatting with Kara Swisher, who was talking on a mobile phone as she navigated her car through Silicon Valley. You have to love the Internet! I heard Kara pull into her driveway, get out of her car, and go in the house where she was greeted by her dog. Then she started cooking dinner, all the while shooting back sharp answers to tricky questions to an audience on CompuServe reaching all corners of the globe.

I did one chat tour where the guest, a famous day trader, conducted a chat on a cell phone in the bleachers of his son's baseball game. As a ghost typist, you have to tell the difference between the answer to a question and an argument with a referee. I did a chat tour promoting the book *Pregnancy for Dummies,* where the author was on call and might have to deliver a baby during the chat. Fortunately for the mother, that didn't happen, although secretly I was salivating over the PR we could have generated with *that* story. You never know what's going to happen with live events, but if you're a good publicist, you come prepared to deal with problems and to spin them into gold if you have to.

Chat Follow-Up

Time in chat passes incredibly quickly. It will seem like you just got started when the host thanks you for a rewarding chat. Once you have time to reflect on the chat, you might wish that you had told people about some other resources. You can contact the hosts and ask them to install links to Web sites or other resources. You might want to upload a file on the service, perhaps putting another article or excerpt in the library for people intrigued by the chat. You can also ask to have material added to the transcripts.

Chat Transcripts

Most services provide transcripts within a few days after the chat (see Figure 6.11). As mentioned earlier, these transcripts can reach more people than the chat itself. Transcripts vary tremendously in quality. Most services clean the transcripts, removing extraneous comments, correcting spelling, and pasting replies together that were posted in bits and pieces.

As soon as the transcripts are available, you should download them and check for mistakes. Here is a piece of a transcript from a chat I promoted on Delphi. Who would want to read such a horrible file?

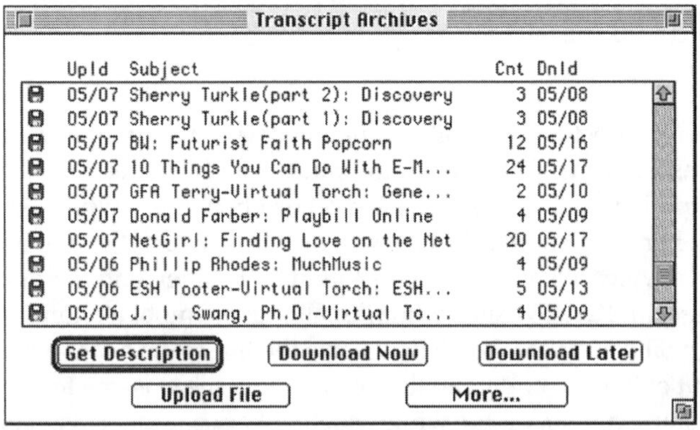

Figure 6.11   A chat transcript archive on America Online, showing the title of the chat, the date it was uploaded, and how many times the file has been downloaded. Popular transcripts will reach far more people than the chat itself.

```
/noxl xlon
XLON>  what is your favorite Elvis song/album?
BILLY_SMITH> It may sound like a cop out but all of them
how about you, Allanna?
QUEUE from XLON> 2 lines, 96 chars, subj: ?
BOOKSTORE> how about you, Allanna?
BILLY_SMITH> ALANNA-_ The early rockabilly stuff like "That's
BILLY_SMITH> Alright Mama".
BILLY_SMITH>
Thanks very much, to both Billy and ALANNA--.
BOOKSTORE> Thanks very much, to both Billy and ALANNA--.
If you are looking for the book Elvis Aaron Presley, and
BILLY_SMITH> ALANNA--It was fun.
```

Compare this text to a transcript of author Dean Koontz' appearance on Prodigy. The transcripts were cleaned, corrected, and put into an easy-to-read format with a short line length:

> **TSAbrams** (PRODIGY Member)
> I'd like to say that your books are great
> and that ever since The Bad Place I have
> been hooked. Where do you get your flare for
> wording or do you sleep with a thesaurus?
>
> **Dean Koontz** (Speaker)
> Actually, I don't own a thesaurus. But I've
> always loved the language and when you are
> raised reading Ray Bradbury, Charles
> Dickens, and Lovecraft, you become a walking
> thesaurus.
>
> **bumblebeebz** (PRODIGY Member)
> Here's a loaded question... Are you
> satisfied or slightly happy with the way
> your work has been modified in the movies?
>
> **Dean Koontz** (Speaker)
> Thus far, filmmakers have behaved with me in
> such a fashion that I feel comfortable
> calling them jackbooted thugs. Lately, I've
> been working with people of a higher talent
> level than was often the case in the past,
> but none of those projects is filming yet.
>
> **Moderator** (Speaker)
> Dean's literary successes have propelled
> him into the world of Hollywood. He has
> written the screenplays for the film

```
adaptations of his novels "Midnight,"
"Phantoms," and "Mr. Murder." In addition,
"Dark Rivers of the Heart" will soon be a
CBS TV movie, and last year, the film
version of Dean's "Hideaway" was released,
starring Jeff Goldblum.
```

I didn't attend the Koontz chat, so I don't know if the information about his movie projects was inserted into the chat transcript or if he was just blessed with an exceptionally knowledgeable moderator. I know that the chances of two people spelling "thesaurus" correctly in a live chat are remote. If the transcripts for your chat aren't up to snuff, you might ask the service to fix them or do it yourself.

When evaluating your transcripts, here are some things to look for:

- Is there a good introduction at the beginning of the file telling people who the guest is and when and where the chat was conducted?
- Is there information at the end of the file telling people how to get more information, buy your book, visit your Web site, and so on?
- Is there a proper copyright notice in the file?
- Have "noise messages" been culled out? These include logon and logoff messages and any debris that disrupts the flow of the chat.
- Has the file been spell-checked?
- Is the file in ASCII text so that anyone can read it?

Transcripts are usually owned by the service that hosted the chat, and this fact is reflected in the copyright notice. You need to request permission to use the transcripts from the copyright holder. This situation is true even if you are the guest! It's unlikely that your request would be denied, especially if you make it clear that the transcripts will include the proper copyright notice and a statement about where the chat was conducted. I ask for permission to use transcripts *after* a site has committed to doing the chat but *before* the chat runs. Usually I get an informal approval, and that's good enough for me. I don't want to get lawyers involved or sign a legal agreement to use transcripts if I don't have to. E-mail authorization from the host gives some defense in case I'm challenged. As sites have begun to realize the value of these transcripts, reprint authorization is getting harder to secure.

Once the transcripts are cleaned to your satisfaction, you can mail them to people who couldn't attend the chat. You can also put the transcripts on your own Web site and make them available by e-mail upon request. You can post another message on newsgroups and mailing lists notifying people that the transcripts are available at your Web site.

Chat transcripts can grow to become a major content source for companies and can be repurposed in a variety of ways. They can be used to build FAQ files for a Web site. They can be edited for use in sales literature or product support documents. They can be run as interviews in newsletters or circulated as Q&As in press kits. Transcripts accumulated over a year from a weekly chat program can even be published as books: *Everything You Ever Wanted To Know About _____, or 100 Common Questions about Your _____.*

If there's something controversial that came out during the chat, you can issue a news release about it and make the transcripts available to reporters. The Web site Salon is very good about marketing its discussion groups. If two authors are mixing it up at Salon, the Web site will issue an alert to subscribers or a news release to the media. Soon, we'll have the online equivalent of a World Wrestling Federation *Smackdown* taking place in chat rooms. I can hardly wait.

Host Relations

After a chat tour is over, it's time to bolster relationships that will serve you for many years to come. I try to send written thank-you notes to all the chat hosts who participated. Everyone knows that thank-you notes are effective—because few people will actually send them. They are even more impressive in online public relations; so much communication takes places through computers or over the phone that a hand-written thank-you note is a startling anachronism.

You should add all of your chat contacts to your media database. That way, you'll be able to find them when you start booking your next tour. Also, these people are media contacts—they control online programming and can have a major impact on the success of your promotions—but they aren't usually treated like media contacts, and you won't find their names in any directories of media contacts. These people should be invited to press events, sent news releases, offered review copies of new products, and courted in the same way that you would any other media contact reaching the same size audience.

After a successful chat tour, you can work with the hosts to design your next promotion or turn your chat appearance into a chat series or a chat show. Extended chat runs, such as a series or show, really cut down on the overhead related to individual tours. It's like you're booking six or 12 chats at once. This kind of chat programming results in better branding, because the focus for individual chats is on the guest, but the focus for a series or show shifts to the company providing the guests. Finally, chat series and shows have one huge benefit over one-off chats: Instead of getting a few days or weeks of promotion at the host venue, you get continuous promotion for as long as the series runs. Instead of taking promos down after a chat, the promo for the next chat goes up.

I'll describe the steps in building chat shows in the Syndication chapter. Now, let's recap the lessons of producing chat tours.

Top Tips

Attendance doesn't matter. The number of people attending a chat is about as relevant as the number of people attending a news conference. It's not the quantity that counts, but it's the coverage you get. And chat tours are a fantastic tool for generating name, product, and brand recognition.

Get organized. Use the two main templates I provide to assemble and book a tour: the chat profile and the chat schedule. The profile gives the venue everything it needs to produce the chat, and the schedule helps everyone involved know what's expected of them.

Get sneaky. Chat venues like to play "Hide the Host"; you have to be a detective to find the contact information you need to book a tour. If you want to succeed in this business, you have to be relentless in your pursuit of top venues, and you must be willing to use back doors when the front entrance is blocked.

Turn your 15 minutes into 15 days. Booking a tour is only the beginning of your work. You should be able to get about two weeks of promotion at each venue, but only if you push. A chat without promotion is a waste of good electricity.

The ghost in the machine. Ghost typists are essential to making chats celebrity-friendly, but a good ghost does much more than that—ensuring that a chat fulfills its marketing mission. Finding and retaining good ghost typists is a priority for online publicists.

Play hardball. People don't attend chats so that they can hear promotional fluff. Challenge your guests with difficult questions. And if a chat host or rude visitors are ruining your chat, be prepared to take control for the benefit of everyone involved.

Work those transcripts. Cleaning and distributing transcripts will multiply the reach of your chat. Chat transcripts represent substantial assets that are currently under-recognized and under-used.

CHAPTER

7

Online Seminars and Workshops

As high-speed access to the Internet has spread, so has the use of online seminars and workshops. Dr. Susan Love uses them to educate people about breast cancer treatment. Cisco Systems partners with the U.S. Small Business Administration to offer online courses for budding entrepreneurs. I've seen promotions for seminars on selling real estate, finding a job, playing the guitar, dancing—even improving your pet's behavior. In 1999, online seminars were cutting-edge; today, they're almost cliché.

The term *seminar* encompasses everything from a text tutorial to a full-blown multimedia circus. Most seminars include some form of interaction between the audience and the guest. As more people get high-speed access to the Internet and software companies develop clever ways to use that bandwidth, more seminars will feature streaming video and audio, PowerPoint presentations and Web tours, polling, gaming, and chats. But bigger isn't always better, and we'll learn about the perils of loading too much technology into a Webcast. I'll also show you a stunningly cheap and effective way of delivering a no-frills, text-based seminar that gets results.

At the high end of the online seminar spectrum is a field called *distance learning*. Colleges, universities, and corporate trainers have spent years experimenting with the online delivery of educational products. While they have developed many of the tools and techniques that we'll cover in this chapter, a discussion of distance learning is beyond the scope of this book. I'm going to focus on the publicity uses for online seminars and workshops, not their commercial uses. In other words, we'll be looking at how to give these programs away in exchange for promotional exposure, rather than how to turn them into a revenue stream. Topics covered in this chapter include the following:

The benefits of online seminars and workshops. What results can you expect from using these promotions? What distinguishes them from other campaigns, and what kinds of subject matter are they suited to?

Formats for seminars and workshops. We'll explore the attributes of a compelling presentation, the types of software used, and the most common configurations for online seminars and workshops.

Creating pitch pages and other set-up materials. Detailed instructions for assembling all the documents you'll need to produce and promote a seminar or workshop.

Finding and securing partner sites. Learn how to multiply your attendance and magnify your results by exporting your seminars and workshops to high-traffic Web sites.

Promoting seminars and workshops. How to get attention for your program by using news releases, discussion group postings, direct mail, online event calendars, and other tricks of the trade.

Conducting seminars and workshops. How to manage registrations, prepare a seminar guest, produce a live program, and handle a total tech meltdown with emergency backup plans.

Follow-up operations. How to measure the bang for your buck (ROI) and increase it through intelligent use of transcripts and registration databases; how to turn your little seminar into an ongoing, syndicated show.

The Benefits of Online Seminars and Workshops

The main reason why companies want to deliver online seminars and workshops is because they make an excellent vehicle for promotion. This statement might sound obvious, but if you look at the actions of companies—not their rhetoric—you'll see that my main theme of giving the audience something of value in exchange for tolerating a promotional pitch is not exactly standard practice.

Most companies are so focused on their own objectives that they fail to consider what the target audience wants and will respond to. These companies seek to generate more traffic, more sales, more media coverage, higher stock prices, and so on and therefore engage in variations of a diet of spam: Direct e-mail, discussion group postings, and news releases that simply say, "Check out our site. Buy our products. Write about our company." For most members of the target audience, these messages are unwelcome. The issuing company is jeopardizing its relationships with consumers and the media and risking permanent damage to the company's reputation and ability to communicate with constituents.

Promoters need to turn the marketing equation around. They need to ask, "What does our target audience want? Can we deliver it to them in a way that is both affordable and leads to greater traffic, sales, and favorable media coverage?" Online seminars and workshops offer just such a campaign: a way to affordably deliver something of value to the online audience, thus generating more traffic, sales, and media coverage.

A Good Basis for a Promotional Campaign

When a company produces an online seminar or workshop, the benefits reach far beyond the attendance at the event itself. If partner sites are involved in hosting the workshop, the company gets the benefits of promotion on those sites for weeks or months. Because most partner sites don't charge to host seminars, this promotional presence is *free*. Compare the value of the promotional presence with the cost of purchasing an equivalent amount of advertising space on the partner sites, and you'll quickly realize that the return on investment in these programs is huge.

Second, holding an online seminar is a valid reason for posting Internet-acceptable messages to online discussion groups. Without offering something of value, postings that say "Come to our site" or "Buy our products" are regarded as spam and are treated with hostility. But a discussion-group posting touting a free online seminar on a subject of keen interest to members of the group is welcome in almost all online forums. Courting the goodwill of these special-interest groups is one of the most powerful online marketing strategies that a company can use. Holding online seminars and promoting them to these special-interest groups helps engender an image of the company as a contributor, not a leech.

Third, sponsoring an online seminar is an excellent basis for a news release. Hosting an event that is educational, free, and open to the public is a legitimate news item. Many newspapers run calendars of online events, either in their technology sections or in the section of the paper devoted to the subject of the event. Personal finance seminars will get mentioned in the Money section, a workshop on child care might get listed in the Living section, and a fitness class might get a nod from the Sports editor. There are many online events calendars where information about seminars can be posted. When these event listings mention the company sponsoring the event, the promotional value of the listings alone can exceed the value of the attendance at the event.

Seminar sponsorship can also be included in company newsletters, on the company's Web site, in trade journals—even in TV spots. In March 2001, I received a piece of printed junk mail from Nielsen//NetRatings that included an invitation to an online seminar. It gladdened my heart, both for the confirmation that the use of online seminars as a marketing tool is growing and for the intelligence to send a printed invitation, which can be saved until needed (unlike an e-mail invitation, which would most likely have been deleted immediately).

Exportable to High-Traffic Sites

Online seminars can be hosted on your own Web site or exported to high-traffic sites frequented by the target audience. The text-based seminar I describe later in this chapter has great benefits over live Web broadcasts: It can be exported to multiple sites that participate in the seminar simultaneously—and not just Web sites, but also moderated news groups, mailing lists, and America Online and CompuServe forums. It's extremely difficult to have multiple partners for either chat programs or streaming seminars. If you hold a live, streaming seminar, you should consider the benefits of conducting it on a high-traffic partner site rather than on your own site; you will usually achieve greater results exporting the seminar.

High-traffic sites such as Yahoo, MSNBC, America Online, and NBCi depend on advertising to offset production costs. This situation isn't true of most corporate Web sites, which are too small to generate money from advertising. Because high-traffic sites rely on advertising, they need traffic. And in order to generate traffic, they need an unending stream of fresh, interesting content. At the same time, they want to spend as little as necessary to get that content. By offering these sites a seminar or a program, you are potentially reducing their production costs while increasing their traffic. They get free content, and you get eyeballs. And they also benefit from any promotion you do to attract an audience for the seminar, which will be hosted on their site. So, by offering them seminars and workshops, you are solving their problems while solving some of your own. It's a win-win-win situation, benefiting the consumer, the host site, and your company—the program's producer.

Database of Contacts

All the online seminars that I have produced have required registration to participate in the program. The registration process results in a list of people who signed up for the seminar and their e-mail addresses. Sometimes other information is also gathered, such as mailing address, occupation, and so on, although the more invasive the registration process, the fewer the people who will complete it. These names and e-mail addresses represent people who are keenly interested in the subject of the seminar. These people are often core constituents for a company. Their e-mail addresses might be used repeatedly in the future for online marketing activities. When you conduct chats, which usually don't require preregistration, you don't get this potential database goldmine at the conclusion of the event.

Many Seminars Aren't Live Events

The text-based seminars I've conducted are not live events. Questions are collected and sent to the featured guest, who replies sometime in the next 12 hours. The guest's answers are then formatted as a Q&A thread and are sent back out to participants along with the next topic for discussion. This format eliminates a lot of technical problems that plague live chats and streaming broadcasts. There is little fear of the guest not showing up, lost connections, the inability to use the software, and users having too slow a connection speed to enjoy the presentation.

Text-based seminars do not penalize people located in remote time zones. Try holding a chat at 4 a.m. Eastern time and see what kind of attendance you get. Text-based seminars are open to everyone around the world who can participate at their convenience. They are particularly well suited to marketing people trying to reach a global audience.

A More Serious Level of Discussion

All live online events where the audience is invited to participate (chats, streaming seminars, Webcasts, and so on) suffer from the same stilted level of communication. If there is a large audience, there is no chance that the featured guest will be able to handle everyone's questions in the time allotted. Answers are necessarily brief, and follow-up questions are hard to follow because the featured guest has often already moved on to the next question in the queue. Even talk radio allows for a better give-and-take conversation than online chat.

With text-based seminars, the guest is free to answer each question at whatever length it warrants. While it's true that follow-up questions might have to wait until the next day, the benefits of a well-thought answer far outweigh the lack of direct interaction with the guest. To answer questions properly, guests often consult resources that they would have no time to access during a live chat, such as company catalogs, directories, or even (heaven forbid) a dictionary.

Another benefit of this text-based seminar model is that similar questions can be consolidated and rude or offensive remarks can be eliminated before they even reach the guest, much less the assembled audience. Live chats can turn ugly with hecklers, stupid with repetitive questions, and confusing with logon messages, advertising, and other chat noise. Text-based seminars are, by comparison, a model of clarity.

Better Transcripts with Extended Value

When you hold a chat on America Online, MSNBC, or on most other major venues, the host site owns the transcripts. You can't post your own chat transcript on your own Web site without getting permission from the copyright holder, which is usually the venue. To be technically accurate, you can't even quote from these transcripts without permission, except in the case of "fair use," such as the transcripts excerpted in this chapter for educational purposes and editorial comment. I always request permission to reprint chat transcripts from my hosts, and I usually get it, although more and more sites are tightening up on these permissions for fear of giving away valuable content that they could sell.

With the text-based seminar I describe later in this chapter, the producer of the seminar owns the copyright to the transcripts, not the venues or partner sites on which the seminar runs. These transcripts are of a much higher quality than most chat transcripts. They can be repositioned as articles or training materials, collected into binders and books, published, given away, or sold. Salon, a cultural oasis on the frequently-sterile World Wide Web, will often issue news releases about spats between authors taking place on its message boards. The same approach can be used with seminar transcripts. They can be excerpted in company newsletters, or hyped with news releases to the trade press.

Generate a Feeling of Community

After a seminar series I conducted for John Wiley & Sons, several of the partner sites commented that the series had resulted in the first sense of community they had experienced at their sites. For all the talk about "many-to-many" communications made possible by the Internet, surfing the Web is still a pretty lonely affair. You visit a site, look around, maybe grab a document or two—even watch a program. There might be a lot of interaction with the site but precious little with your fellow browsers.

Chat is one way to develop a community, but most Web sites don't have chat facilities (and many that do wish they didn't). Chats can be ruined by people in the audience who care nothing about the presentation or the sensitivities of others. Many sites have message boards, but have you seen how poorly trafficked most of them are? I frequently see message threads that are lucky to get one message every six months. On high-traffic boards, many of the messages are commercial spam. A lot of the messages are pleas for help that never get answered.

It is easy to keep text-based seminars free of spam and rudeness. And the featured guest is somewhat obligated to answer those pleas for help—that's the whole point of the seminar in the first place. Because the seminars aren't open-ended but have a definite structure and ending date, people feel like they're not making a big commitment to join in. When I started experimenting with this form of online marketing, my main question was, "Will users find this form of communication valuable?" I wasn't sure at all, but the results of many seminars have convinced me that it is, indeed, enough of a quality experience to make participants want to repeat it.

What I wasn't prepared for, however, was the cross-chat that erupted in the seminars. We had professional chefs in the same city connecting with their peers through the seminar Q&A. By about the fourth day, they were talking to each other instead of the guest, asking about working conditions and job prospects at other restaurants in the city. What started as a teacher-student style presentation turned into networking almost overnight. It is a wonderful thing to see people who have surfed a site side by side for years finally recognize one another and start talking with each other to solve their own problems. That's why every site I've partnered with has asked for more once a seminar was over. If you follow the programs described in this chapter, they'll be asking *you* for more, too.

Formats for Online Seminars and Workshops

What does it mean to say that you will be holding an online seminar? The term *seminar* encompasses a wide variety of activities and formats. You can hold informal seminars on public Usenet newsgroups without any planning, preparation, prior notice, or even permission. You just say that you're going to hold a seminar, and then you do it. At the other end of the spectrum, a full-blown, live seminar can include a live audience with the action captured by a digital camcorder and streamed over the Web and combined with a telephone conference call. The technology for online seminars is improving rapidly, and combined with the ingenuity of seminar producers, we can expect many flavors of this type of programming in the near future.

In this section, we will start with simplest seminar format—an online presentation—and advance through increasing levels of sophistication from a text-based seminar to a multimedia seminar and conclude with distance learning courses. More sophistication, however, does not necessarily lead to better results, as we shall see. So, before we focus on how to produce a seminar in each of these formats, let's take a quick look at the attributes of a good seminar and some of the software and multimedia choices involved.

Attributes of a Good Online Seminar

When I first started producing online seminars in 1998, I was confident of their promotional value. Very few people were doing seminars then, so it was novel, and novelty translates into publicity. I was certain I could generate good buzz using this format, but I was very uncertain about the value of the format to participants. Could I deliver an online program that satisfied the people who attended? The answer, as we'll see, is yes!

Since those early days, I have learned many tips and tricks about producing online seminars in a way that adds value for participants. Here is my short list of the qualities that make an online seminar attractive:

Accessible. Accessible means that you don't want to exclude members of the audience due to technological or time zone limitations. Ideally, people should be able to enjoy the seminar no matter what connection speed they have, what platform they're on (Windows, Macintosh, Unix, and so on), what software they use, or what screen colors or screen resolution they have. The time zone issue argues against live seminars that exclude many people in the international audience.

Interactive. This feeling might be my own prejudice, but to me it's not a seminar or a workshop if the people participating can't ask questions. If you want to reach the masses, you're better off using chats that can accommodate tens of thousands of people. For a rewarding seminar experience, participants need to have a realistic chance that their questions will reach the featured guest and maybe even get answered. Most people in a seminar will lurk rather than ask questions, so you can usually handle as many as several hundred people without disappointing anyone.

Compelling. The combination of seminar guests and discussion topics should be timely. For example, a seminar with a recording artist should be timed to the release of a new recording and should focus on a hot subject, such as changes in the band's personnel or direction. Many companies err on the generic side when choosing a theme for the seminar: It's about our company or what we can do for you. If you're successful tying into a topic that is in the news and is likely to stay in the news until the seminar is over, you'll pull a larger audience and get greater press coverage.

Specific. Which would you rather attend, a workshop on buying a new house or a workshop on negotiating tactics for a home purchase and sale agreement? It is difficult to tackle broad issues in online seminars. For most participants, it's much more helpful to focus on one important aspect of the subject that can be adequately addressed in the time allotted.

Promotable. Because most of the marketing value of holding online seminars comes from the promotional exposure rather than the actual attendance, it's important to design the seminar to maximize coverage. One way of performing this task is to hold the seminar on a high-traffic site rather than on your own site. Another way is to partner with multiple sites. You need to budget adequate setup time so that you have time to promote before the workshop starts. For example, in order to get magazine coverage of a workshop announcement, you need to begin developing the workshop at least six months in advance, and you need to send out announcements four months in advance. Having a compelling topic and speaker will help generate media coverage, and tying into other marketing activities will broaden your impact. Charitable partnerships are always promotable.

Software and Multimedia Issues

The software choices for online seminars can be perplexing. Many online presentations require a battery of programs to run smoothly. Four years ago, that was true of chat software, too. Today, most chat software is seamlessly built into the Web browser program, and you can expect the same adoption curve for seminar software in the near future. When you are designing your seminar, please keep in mind that the more complicated the software configuration required, the smaller the potential audience and the greater the likelihood that technical difficulties will spoil your carefully planned event. If your seminar requires special software, you might mention that in your promotional materials and include links to download sites. Here's a run down on the most common types of software used:

Web browser. Explorer and Navigator dominate the market. Both of them allow users to view slide shows delivered by seminar or workshop hosts. Slide shows are the most common visual components of online seminars. Support materials for seminars are usually stored on Web sites, where they will be readily accessible to anyone with a browser.

E-mail. Virtually everyone online has access to e-mail. E-mail is used in registering for seminars, confirming registration, and delivering agendas and support materials. The text-based seminar I describe later can be conducted entirely through e-mail without access to any other software.

News reader. Seminars can be conducted through Usenet newsgroups. To participate, the audience must have access to news reader software. This capability is built into Explorer and Navigator, although some people prefer an independent news reader. In any case, there should be no problems reaching an audience with one caveat: Many libraries, schools, and other institutions (including private corporations) block access to some or all newsgroups, and filtering software (for example, AOL's parental controls) is often set to block access to newsgroups. Because educational institutions are primary target audiences for online seminars and workshops, you might want to offer additional ways to access the program besides newsgroups.

Multimedia players. The market here is dominated by RealPlayer and Windows Media Player. Both programs work as plug-ins integrated with the Web browser, but they are not always bundled with Web browser software—and users might have to download and install them first. Both programs are available for free download online. Many workshops require recent versions of these media players, so even people who already have the software might need to upgrade to participate.

Flash. I've seen a few online programs that require Flash software to participate. This software is another plug-in for Web browsers that usually is bundled with browser software and is available for free download.

Java. Many chats and online seminars require Java-enabled browsers, and the majority of browsers in use today have Java already built in. Some users have disabled Java due to concerns about security, but if that blocks them from participating in your program, they will get an error message giving them the option to activate Java and participate.

Acrobat Reader. This very popular software program and plug-in is not often used in conjunction with online seminars or workshops. Because it is the leading format for e-books, however, I expect its use in seminars and workshops to grow—especially for reading support materials. Acrobat Reader is available for free download online.

PowerPoint. PowerPoint is a ubiquitous presentation software program, part of the Microsoft Office line. It's understandable, therefore, that many online presentations are based on PowerPoint slide shows. These slide shows can be served over the Web now and are therefore accessible to anyone who has a fairly recent Web browser and plug-ins. To broaden the reach of your program, though, you might make the actual PowerPoint slides available to the audience, taking advantage of the huge installed base of PowerPoint users.

Telephone. OK, so a telephone is not a piece of software, but it is a multimedia tool. I've attended several seminars that involved a streaming Web presentation combined with a conference phone call. While the installed base of telephones is huge, the number of people who have two phone lines at home is not. If your program targets home computer users, you'll limit your audience if you require a phone call while the user is also online.

Connection speed. The vast majority of the online audience does not have high-speed access to the Internet. No matter what you hear to the contrary, it's very difficult to enjoy a live, multimedia presentation using a dial-up connection. Heck, it's difficult to enjoy them *with* a high-speed connection. Remember that a major goal is to deliver an experience that a user would want to *repeat*, not just something that he or she can *access*. If your target audience is extremely narrow and highly likely to have high-speed access—or you have prequalified the audience by telling them that participation requires high-speed access—then you can get away with a fancy seminar containing all the multimedia bells and whistles. But be forewarned: The more technology incorporated into your presentation, the greater the chance that Murphy's Law will rule.

Server software. If you're planning on delivering multimedia seminars and workshops from your own site, you will need some relatively expensive server software along with help from the IT department. You will need both Windows Media Service (sic) and RealServer to deliver streaming audio, video, and PowerPoint slides through your Web site. You might also need chat server software to allow for dialogue between the speaker and the audience. You should have these programs installed and operational long before you start advertising seminars, or you will regret the day you decided to try this marketing approach. The software and expertise required to deliver sophisticated online multimedia presentations explains why even powerhouse technology companies host their online seminars at specialist sites such as PlaceWare, Evoke, and Presenter.com.

Online Presentations

Online presentations are Web versions of PowerPoint presentations. Because they lack interactive discussion, they aren't really online seminars or workshops, although they can be used in conjunction with interactive programs. Some sites I've visited refer to their archive of PowerPoint presentations as "seminars" or "workshops," so beware of the confusing terminology.

I cover the subject of online presentations thoroughly in the chapter of this book devoted to Online Newsrooms, so I won't go into detail here about how to create them and deliver them. I will mention that many multimedia seminars are built around a PowerPoint presentation that is served through the Web, accompanied by live, streaming audio or video, and interactive chat capabilities for dialogue between the speaker and the audience. If you want to include online presentations in your seminar or workshop, please refer to the instructions presented earlier in this book.

Text-Based Seminars and Workshops

Despite the lust for fancy technology, these simple text-based programs are still my favorite way to conduct online seminars and workshops. While the setup instructions are a little complicated, the user interface is remarkably simple and nearly crash-proof. Plus, these plain seminars deliver every bit as much value—if not more—than their sardonic multimedia siblings.

The easiest way to conduct a text-based seminar is to go out, find a receptive discussion group, and offer your guest for a week of questions and answers. The discussion group could be a moderated Usenet newsgroup, an Internet mailing list, a Web site discussion thread, an America Online forum, or a CompuServe forum. I've had CompuServe sysops set up a special "room" (message board) for the seminar to keep it from interfering with the normal flow of discussion on other message boards. And America Online hosts have also arranged for special message boards exclusively for my clients' seminars.

Another good design for a text-based seminar is to start your own Internet mailing list for this purpose. There is information in the Newsletters chapter of this book about how to use Listserv and similar software programs to set up your own mailing list. It's so easy to use Yahoo Groups to create a custom mailing list, however, that I recommend it for those uncomfortable with listserver software. The instructions for building a seminar this way are covered later in this chapter.

Adding venues onto a text-based seminar is like adding rooms onto a house. You can easily partner with multiple sites on the same text-based seminar. For example, you could recruit a partner forum from America Online and one from CompuServe, add a Usenet newsgroup or two, include an Internet mailing list, and even get a Web site or two involved. It's very difficult to recruit multiple partners for live, multimedia presentations, but it's a snap with a text-based seminar.

These seminars all follow a similar format, covered in more detail later. You prepare an outline, a topic for discussion for each day, and any support materials that you think might help. You distribute these to the partner venues and anyone who has registered for the seminar. Then, each day you accumulate questions from all the partner sites, send them to the guest, format his or her answers into a neat little Q&A file, and distribute it back to the partners/members along with the next topic for discussion.

Text-based seminars are democratic, open to everyone who has e-mail, available in all the world's time zones, and ideal for the bandwidth-challenged. They are extremely easy to install, ultra low-cost, and thus a perfect guerrilla marketing tactic because they eschew glitz in favor of delivering true value.

The only real drawback to these seminars is that they don't allow for live give-and-take discussion. Initially, I thought that deficiency would make them less attractive for participants than live chat, but the market proved me wrong. As we will see, not only do participants find the level of discussion superior to chat, but they also actually found ways to extend thoughtful discussions across the chasm of daily dispatches, resulting in greater interaction with their peers than they experienced through chat.

Live Multimedia Seminars and Workshops

The simplest format for live seminars is chat. Because I more than adequately cover that subject elsewhere in this book, I won't repeat the instructions here. When does a *chat* become a *seminar*? When you call it one, I guess. On a more practical level, I would expect a seminar to include some supplemental materials, such as a syllabus and reading assignments. I also think of seminars as multi-day events, but they don't have to be. So go ahead and follow the instructions for producing chat programs elsewhere in this book and just graft the term "seminar" or "workshop" onto the promotional materials.

The number of people using multimedia seminars and workshops is exploding online, and I'm glad to see it. In the past few months, I've received a fair amount of spam touting free seminars and workshops. This situation shows that the concept is gaining cachet, although it is unfortunately leading to a glut of poorly designed programs and a bad connotation in the minds of consumers. Have you ever been solicited to attend a seminar in order to get a free vacation to someplace exotic? Online seminars might be going the way of condo and insurance sales; you'll have to work hard to distance yourself from the scam artists using this device to locate and sheer sheep.

Multimedia seminars are usually held in a single venue, often at a site specializing in such presentations. They most often incorporate a guest speaker using streaming audio to narrate a visual presentation: a PowerPoint slide show or a Web tour. Sometimes they include streaming video, and this feature is important if the point of the seminar is to demonstrate a technique, such as a medical procedure. They usually have an interface that allows members of the audience to ask questions. This chat interface is almost always text-based, rather than audio and/or video based.

The audience reach for live multimedia seminars is limited to those with the technology to participate. For any program involving streaming video, a high-speed Internet connection is required. With streaming audio, a dial-up modem connection can deliver acceptable results. Regardless of connection speed, participation almost always requires an up-to-date version of Web browsing software loaded with recent versions of the most popular plug-ins. All of these factors limit the audience for these seminars to people who have high-speed access at work. The technologically challenged are locked out, which includes most home users, government agencies, school systems, libraries, the poor, and institutions dependent upon tax dollars and the kindness of strangers.

Multimedia seminars are almost always live events, which limits the audience to those in nearby time zones—making it a poor choice for reaching a global audience. Even for those in near proximity to the event, if they forget or get busy or miss it for one reason or another, too bad. Many live events are saved and archived on Web sites and can be enjoyed later without the interactive dialog. And these canned seminars are often accompanied by feedback or info links that let you send in questions, but this style of presenting doesn't have the same energy as an ongoing seminar (either live or text-based).

On the positive side, multimedia seminars are cutting-edge, and for companies that value style over substance, something as dowdy as a text-based seminar will never do. It's not called the cutting-edge for nothing, so beware the high tech extravaganza that cuts your reputation to shreds. The Nielsen//NetRatings seminar I mentioned earlier was a disaster and reflected poorly on the sponsor although the fault was probably with the host presentation site. I've participated in dozens of multimedia seminars, and I have yet to see a single one go well—and I have a high-speed connection and all the latest software and plug-ins.

Distance Learning Classes

There is a slim line between online seminars and the distance learning movement. The focus of this book is on promotional campaigns, and that's how I use the seminars and workshops described. But you can expand on these offerings and turn them into distance learning vehicles, either charging paid enrollment or partnering with educational institutions to offer classes. It would be relatively easy to get college professors to include your online seminars in their courses. If the educational market is important to you, this strategy can be an excellent promotional opportunity. And there is value in sharing your expertise with future generations.

Most distance learning programs are built around the online seminar/workshop model, with added resources. A fully outfitted distance learning class would include most or all of the following elements:

- A syllabus and/or class schedule
- PowerPoint slides or a streaming PowerPoint presentation
- Online chat sessions
- Threaded message boards
- Links to online resources
- Archive of support documents and articles
- E-mail support for students

This list is very similar to the materials involved in online seminars and workshops. You'll find that the distance learning movement has pioneered a lot of this technology and that the best guides to creating PowerPoint presentations and other seminar support materials can be found not at the software manufacturers' sites, but at college and university distance-learning resource centers. The companion web site for this book lists several of these sites.

Creating Pitch Pages and Other Setup Materials

Once you have decided to use online seminars and have selected a willing guest and a suitable theme, the next step is to create campaign materials that will help you sell the seminar to partners, entice registrants, and promote the event. I'll start by covering text-based seminar setup, then move to a Web-based show and then cover the documents needed to launch your event.

Text-Based Setup Instructions

To build a text-based seminar, you need to start a mailing list. If you understand how to do this task and have listserver software in-house, you just set up a list dedicated to the seminar. If you want to do it in-house but don't have listserver software, please see the chapter of this book on Newsletters for descriptions of listserver software packages and instructions on how to use them. The strategy that I highly recommend is using Yahoo Groups instead of hosting the seminar in-house (see Figure 7.1).

Yahoo Groups is the successor to both eGroups and OneList, two Web-based services that allowed anyone to set up a listserver for free. You have to be a member of Yahoo to start a group, but membership costs nothing and signing up takes only a few moments. To start a mailing list, simply go to http://groups.yahoo.com and click "Start a new Group" (Figure 7.1). This action takes you to a page that asks you for the following items:

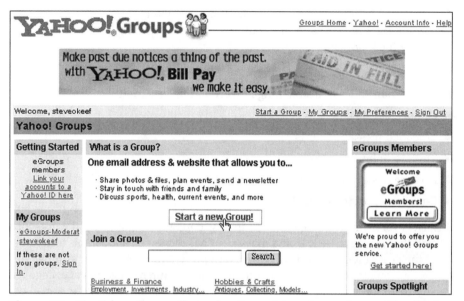

Figure 7.1 Use Yahoo Groups (formerly eGroups) to set up a free mailing list for your seminar. The list is easy to set up and has numerous useful features that aren't found in even expensive listserver software packages.

- Name of the group
- E-mail address for the group (must end with @yahoogroups.com)
- Description of the group

You'll be able to pull all these items off your seminar description sheet, which we cover a little later. Next, you have some choices to make regarding how your group will function. You can choose to have your group listed in the directory at Yahoo Groups. One of the benefits of using Yahoo Groups to host your seminar is that you will pick up registrations from people who search the directory there. This site gets an enormous amount of traffic (both eGroups and OneList were very popular services, and all their members automatically migrated to Yahoo Groups when Yahoo acquired these two high-traffic properties).

You have your choice of allowing anyone to join the group, requiring approval for all memberships, or operating a closed group that is limited to those you invite to join. For promotional seminars, I recommend you open the group to all comers. Your group can be moderated (all postings must be approved) or unmoderated (anyone can post to the list). I highly recommend a moderated group. That allows you to control the messages flowing through the group and remove anything commercial or offensive.

That's all you have to do. You now have a Web page on Yahoo for your seminar, along with a mailing list that has many control features not available in commercial listserver packages. You can change the settings and description of your group any

Figure 7.2   A list of the features you get with Yahoo Groups. In addition to a mailing list, you can host chats, store files, and build a calendar for your online seminar.

time you want, although you're stuck with the name of the group and the e-mail address associated with it (unless you decide to close the group and start over with a better name and address). Figure 7.2 shows some of the other features you get with a group on Yahoo Let's review them and see how they can be used to enhance your seminar.

The Files section of your group allows you to store supporting documents for your seminar, such as PowerPoint slides, Word documents, or Web pages. If you want to include a set of links to online resources as part of the seminar, I recommend that you build it as a Web page and store it in your Files section rather than use your group's Bookmarks area (it's easier that way).

The Calendar section of your group lets you specify which days the seminar will run and what topics will be covered each day. Using the Calendar, you can have reminder messages sent to the group automatically. I recommend sending only one reminder—the week before the seminar starts—to remind people who might have signed up weeks ago and forgotten about it. If you send reminders every day of the seminar, you will antagonize your subscribers.

The Promote control takes you to a page with subscription buttons and HTML coding that you can use to solicit subscribers for your seminar. Here's a sneaky trick: The subscribe buttons contain graphics with the Yahoo logo. You can easily replace Yahoo's logo with your own logo. See Figure 7.3 for an example. There is no need for anyone to know that this list is hosted at Yahoo Groups. With proper preparation, it will appear that the entire seminar is hosted at your own site—the mechanism can be invisible to subscribers.

One drawback to using Yahoo Groups for your listserver is that all outgoing messages contain advertising. What if you can't accept the idea of circulating someone else's ads? Simple: You purchase the "no ads" option from Yahoo Groups. Very few people know that this option exists, and Yahoo is quiet about it, but if you search the help files at Yahoo Groups for "advertising," you will find this statement:

```
For group owners who do not wish to have ads on their group mes-
sages, we offer  a "No Advertising Option." For an annual payment
of $59.40, we will exclude ads from the messages for your group.
(Banners on web pages of your group will not be removed.)
```

Further instructions for the "no ads" option, such as where to send your check, are in the help files at Yahoo Groups. As far as I'm concerned, $60 is cheap to protect the integrity of a seminar. It can cost thousands of dollars to hire a company to produce these seminars, so a small fee to keep the seminar ad-free is money well spent. You can't block the advertising on your group's Web page, but you don't ever need to send people to the Web page. You can use Yahoo's listserver mechanism and run the entire seminar without ever referring a single person to your Yahoo Groups Web page. If you want to offer support documents but you don't want to refer people to your Yahoo Groups site, simply make the files available from your own Web site or as e-mail attachments.

The Settings control takes you to a page where you can fine-tune the promotional copy and operation of your group. You can change the group description, select the heading you want to be under in Yahoo's directory, add a company logo or picture of the seminar presenter to your group's home page, and change all of the initial settings for the group. If you decide to retire the group after the seminar is over, just hit the "delete this group" button on your Settings page.

If you want to use your own listserver software to create the mailing list for your seminar, I suggest that you make it a moderated list, requiring your approval for all messages posted to the list. If you don't, you run the risk of having your list taken over by spam artists and malcontents.

Web-Based Setup Instructions

As with a text-based seminar, you can set up a Web-based seminar using Yahoo Groups. You get a free Web site when you start your group, and you can use the site to store files for the seminar or use the Chat function to host a live chat or Q&A session. When I think of Web-based seminars, however, I mostly think of streaming events: streaming audio or video, PowerPoint presentations, videoconferencing, and so on. You can't host these multimedia events through your Yahoo group. I recommend that you work with one of the Web services that specializes in this type of online programming.

Presenter.com at www.presenter.com allows you to upload a PowerPoint presentation, phone in a voice-over, and stream the presentation online. You can create one free show, and they will host it for a month. Annual licenses start at $600. For more information, see the Online Newsrooms chapter or visit the Presenter.com Web site.

PlaceWare at www.placeware.com is a Web conferencing provider. Through them, you can host an online seminar that incorporates pretty much anything you want: streaming video, simultaneous telephone conference calls, PowerPoint slide presentation, and so on. They offer many different flavors of services, but their two main sellers are Meeting Centers and Conference Centers. Meeting Center licenses start at $900/quarter for a 10-person room, plus a $3,000 set-up fee. Annual Conference Center licenses cost $600 per seat plus a $3,000 setup fee. For a 100-person-capacity conference center, that's $63,000 per year. PlaceWare offers free trials, and they have event-management services that could reduce your costs for a one-time seminar.

Evoke Communications at www.evoke.com is another Web conferencing provider. Like PlaceWare, it offers a wide range of multimedia services, including phone conferencing, PowerPoint presentations, Web tours, audience interaction, and so on. Most of its pricing is per user minute. For example, Web conferencing is 27 cents per minute, per user. If you had 100 people in an hour-long seminar, that's 6,000 people-minutes, or $1,620. A free trial for up to five people is available. For other variations and fees, please visit Evoke's Web site.

Digevent at www.digevent.com specializes in producing online events. It divides these into five communities: Communications, Technology, Music, Finance, and Business. Its service specialties include online news conferences, investor-relations products, and distance learning courses. Prices aren't discussed at the Web site. Clients and partners include Polaroid, Ingram Micro, and the Public Relations Society of America.

There are *dozens* of companies providing online conference hosting services, and dozens more will likely start offering services soon. This market is a growing Internet market that should experience a great deal of consolidation in the coming years, so please check your favorite Web directory for the latest listings. Also coming soon will be the ability for you to host your own conferences without having to install nearly as much hardware and software. With the proper servers, you can host your own videoconferences today by sticking a digital camera or Web cam in the back of a room, streaming the audio and video signals onto the Web and adding a chat or phone interface that allows remote participants to ask questions. Today, that technology is fairly complex to set up and is buggy, which is why even large technology companies such as Nielsen//NetRatings prefer to use the facilities of online conferencing experts.

Seminar Description in Text and HTML

Once you've decided how you're going to structure your online seminar (text-based mailing list or Web-based multimedia), the next thing to do is write a description of the seminar. This important document will be used to recruit host sites for the seminar, to market and promote the seminar, and to create other pitch materials. At www.wiley .com/compbooks/okeefe, you'll find templates for Seminar Descriptions in both Microsoft Word and HTML formats. Here's an example from an online advertising seminar that I produced:

```
FREE!!!

Online Advertising Seminar

with

ROBBIN ZEFF, President of the Zeff Group, a firm specializing in
strategic Internet advertising and marketing, research, training,
and consulting

and

BRAD ARONSON, President of i-frontier, a leading Internet advertis-
ing agency
Co-Authors of the new Second Edition of "Advertising on the Inter-
net" (John Wiley & Sons, ISBN 0-471-34404-4, 435 pages, $24.99)

WHEN:
Monday, Nov. 15 through Friday, Nov.19

WHERE:
Online -- of course -- at these host sites:
America Online:
CompuServe:
Mailing List:

HOW:
To participate, please visit any one of the host sites. Or you can
receive the seminar via e-mail by sending mailto:seminars@tena-
gra.com with the subject line: Join Advertising Seminar

FORMAT:
For each day of the seminar, a topic for discussion will be pre-
sented along with a supporting excerpt from "Advertising on the
Internet -- Second Edition." Feel free to ask any questions you
like -- you don't have to stick to the topic of the day. Your ques-
tions will be collected with those of participants all over the
world. The next day, you will receive a complete Q&A thread, along
with a new topic for discussion.
```

This "threaded discussion" format leads to more thoughtful answers than online chat, and allows you to participate at your convenience rather than at a specific time. Online seminars can be dynamic, feisty, educational and entertaining. They're a great opportunity to consult with industry experts (at no charge) as well as network with colleagues. We invite you to join and see.

TOPICS:
The topics for this seminar have been chosen to appeal to both buyers and sellers of online advertising. Here is the topic list -- but remember, you can ask any questions you want:

Monday, Nov. 15: Effective Ad Models/Designs
There are many different ways to advertise online -- here's your chance to ask the experts which ones work best for what purposes, and why? We invite questions about banner ads, buttons, links, sponsorships, advertorials, e-mail marketing, animation, banner size and location, clickthrough rates, etc.

Tuesday, Nov. 16: Pricing Online Advertising
Online advertising rates are wild, ranging from $2 to $200 per thousand exposures. Here's your chance to learn tricks for paying less (if you're an advertiser) or charging more (if you're a publisher). We welcome thorny questions about rate shaving, inflated traffic stats, package pricing, and other financial shenanigans.

Wednesday, Nov. 17: Issues in Ad Management & Measurement
The online advertising industry has made great progress establishing standard measurements for site traffic and advertising exposure, but there's still a long way to go. Robbin and Brad will give you the real dope on ad management software packages and ratings services that measure site traffic.

Thursday, Nov. 18: Buying and Selling Site User Data
The most controversial issue in online advertising. Is it legal to collect data about site users, then sell it to third parties? Is it ethical? If you're an advertiser, is the data good enough to warrant paying a premium? If you're a publisher, how much more money could you make selling "targeted" ads? Let's talk about cookies, site registration, psychographic profiling, and other cutting-edge issues.

Friday, Nov. 19: Wrap Up and Final Comments
Brad and Robbin review the main issues raised in the seminar and synthesize a few key insights that magically solve all our problems. Amazing!

REGISTER TODAY!

```
To register for the seminar, send mailto:seminars@tenagra.com with
the subject line: Join Advertising Seminar, or visit one of our
host sites today.
```

This seminar description follows the standard news release format of who, what, when, where, why, how, and so on. The "Where" portion is left blank because the venues had yet to be determined. There's always a way for people to subscribe directly, however, in this case by sending e-mail to seminars@tenagra.com. This service is not an automatic subscription service; the e-mail is processed by hand, and people are subscribed to the mailing list once it has been set up.

The "Format" section quickly tries to explain how a text-based seminar works while helping overcome fears that the mechanism is funky. Based on experience, people really like these text-based seminars even if they sound a bit less than dynamic, lacking live interaction with the guests. One major selling point for online seminars is that they give people a chance to communicate for free with guests who normally charge hundreds of dollars an hour in consulting fees. It's important to make that benefit explicit in your copy.

You'll notice that the "Topics" for each day are quite specific. For each topic, try to give a one-sentence explanation of what will be covered or what benefits the participants can expect. We found that it was helpful to plant suggestions about the types of questions we hoped participants would ask. People tend to lurk in these seminars unless you draw them out, and soliciting questions helps.

Figure 7.3 shows a Web page version of a seminar description, this time for the Wiley Culinary Seminar Series. You can post a page like this one to your Web site (or to any cooperating Web site) and use it to solicit registrations for the seminar. The HTML is kept very simple to make it easy for Web masters to pull content off the page and redesign it for use on their own sites. Earlier, I mentioned that you could set up a mailing list at Yahoo Groups, remove Yahoo's logo from the marketing materials, and insert your logo in its place. The subscription box at the top of Figure 7.3 is just such a cut-and-paste job. We took out Yahoo's logo and inserted Wiley's. Yahoo is not mentioned anywhere on the page, although if you type your e-mail address and click the "subscribe" button, you'll immediately get a Welcome Letter from the mailing list at Yahoo Groups.

The Web version of the Seminar Description page communicates better than the text-only version because you have the ability to use graphics and interesting formatting. I always create a Web version to use recruiting partner sites so they can decide whether they want to get involved in hosting the seminar or not.

Welcome Letter and Instructions

When someone registers for a seminar, you need to acknowledge their registration immediately and send them any instructions for participating, such as how to unsubscribe. So, before you start promoting the seminar and soliciting registrations, you should have the Welcome Letter written and approved. Here's a welcome letter that we used for the Wiley Culinary Seminar Series:

Wiley Culinary Seminar Series

Begins August 30 - Register Today!

Subscribe to Wiley Culinary Seminar Series

Enter your e-mail address:

| your e-mail | click here to join! |

~ Series Description ~

The Wiley Culinary Seminar Series is designed for professional chefs, restaurateurs, students in food preparation courses, and gourmet cooks. It is part of the Wiley Online Seminar Series, bringing experts and authors online for intelligent, educational discussion. This series features four new books for professional cooks:

Aug 30 - Sep 4:

Foie Gras: A Passion

Michael Ginor, co-founder and president of Hudson Valley Foie Gras and New York State Foie Gras, dubbed "the king of foie gras" by The New York Times, shares his passion (and secrets) for preparing the "ultimate guilty pleasure." Supplemented with some of the 75 recipes from world-renowned chefs that grace this gourmand's guide to gras.

Figure 7.3 This seminar description is produced as a Web page. It will be used to recruit host sites and to give those hosts good marketing copy and graphics to use when promoting their participation in the seminars.

WELCOME LETTER:

Welcome! You have subscribed to the Wiley Culinary Seminar Series. The series has four courses, running the first week of the month from September through December. You will get an e-mail reminder before the start of each course. Tell a friend about the series: instructions for subscribing and unsubscribing are at the end of this message.

SERIES DESCRIPTION:
The Wiley Culinary Seminar Series is designed for professional chefs, restaurateurs, students in food preparation courses, and gourmet cooks. It is part of the Wiley Online Seminar Series, bringing experts and authors online for intelligent, educational discussion. This series features four new books for professional cooks:

Aug 30 - Sep 4: Foie Gras: A Passion

Michael Ginor, co-founder and president of Hudson Valley Foie Gras and New York State Foie Gras, dubbed "the king of foie gras" by The New York Times, shares his passion (and secrets) for preparing the "ultimate guilty pleasure." Supplemented with some of the 75 recipes from world-renowned chefs that grace this gourmand's guide to gras.

Oct 4 - Oct 8: The Making of a Pastry Chef
Andrew Maclauchlan, Executive Pastry Chef at the Coyote Cafe in Santa Fe, NM, will inspire you to new heights of artistry and ecstasy with this seminar on sweet, flaky treats. This course, like the book, will combine recipes and professional development tips from the world's great pastry chefs. Find out why the dessert menu is the fastest growing area in the restaurant industry.

Nov 1 - Nov 5: Garde Manger: The Art and Craft of the Cold Kitchen
Join Chef Timothy Rodgers, Associate Dean of the prestigious Culinary Institute of America (CIA), and Mary Donovan, the CIA's Senior Cookbook Editor, for a comprehensive course in cold food prep. It's not possible to cover the full range of this book, but we'll do our best with sessions on hors d'oeuvre, cured & smoked foods, condiments & cold sauces, and cheeses.

Dec 6 - Dec 10: Chocolate Passion
Warning: The photos in this book are suitable for mature audiences only! We'll share some of these passionate pictures with you, along with recipes and commentary from Timothy Moriarty, features editor for Chocolatier Magazine. Learn to make holiday desserts with all the grandeur due the millennium!

SERIES INSTRUCTIONS:
Each course in the Wiley Culinary Seminar Series begins on Monday with the distribution of a topic for discussion along with supplemental materials (such as recipes and photos). Participants then send questions or comments to our featured guest. The guest answers as many questions as possible, and this Q&A is distributed to all participants on Tuesday -- along with the next topic for discussion. This process continues on Wednesday, Thursday, and Friday -- when the course wraps-up with some final comments by our guest author. There is no requirement to purchase the books, though you will certainly enjoy the seminar more with these lovely volumes at your side.

We have chosen to avoid a live chat format in favor of more considered, educational discussion. Feel free to ask as many questions as you like, and keep discussions going over the full length of the seminar. The guest will sometimes consolidate similar questions.

```
Through this format, our guests are able to give the kind of
thoughtful replies you don't normally find in live chat.

~~~~~~~~~~~~~~~~~~~~~~~~~~~~~~~~~~~~~~~~~~~~~~~~~~~~~~~

To subscribe, send mailto:
To unsubscribe, send mailto:


Copyright John Wiley & Sons, Inc. All rights reserved. The Wiley
Online Seminar Series <http://www.egroups.com/wiley> is a produc-
tion of The Tenagra Corporation <http://www.tenagra.com>.
```

The Welcome Letter is just a modified version of the Series Description document. This letter is a little different than the model used for a single seminar, because registrants are subscribed to *four* seminars each a month apart. A welcome letter for a single seminar would have a list of the daily topics and would do a better job of suggesting questions the audience should be thinking about.

You might be soliciting registrations for these seminars months in advance. It's important to send the welcome letter immediately. You could add a feature requiring e-mail confirmation, but I think the unsubscribe instructions adequately protect you from people who were subscribed to the seminar without their knowledge. Once you send the welcome letter, you can leave the person alone until the seminar begins.

If you use Yahoo Groups for your seminar headquarters, you can install the welcome letter at the group Web site where it will be automatically dispatched to new subscribers. You can also automate this process if you are using your own listserver software. Either way, be sure to test the formatting of the document by subscribing to the list yourself and seeing how the welcome letter looks when it gets sent back. You might have to force the lines to break at shorter lengths to get a document that looks appealing to subscribers.

Preparing the Guest

Text-based seminars are just about the easiest thing you can ask a guest to participate in. They don't require travel, they aren't live events that can be spoiled by technology or hecklers, and it's easy for guests to fit their seminar responsibilities into their own schedules. That doesn't mean that things always go smoothly with guests. Here are some important tips for preparing your guests for the best seminars possible.

It's the promo that counts, not the attendance. Guests need to understand that the main value of these seminars is the promotional exposure you get from partner sites, news releases, and discussion group postings—not the number of people who attend. Many seminars have fewer than 20 participants, and that's OK. Big seminars can get overwhelming. The guest gets a promotional bang no matter how few people attend. And a small audience can lead to better transcripts, which will usually reach more people than the seminar itself and can be important assets for the guest.

Explaining how the seminar works. For a text-based seminar, you (the producer) will collect all the questions from partner sites, consolidate them into one e-mail, and send them to the guest, usually at about 5 p.m. The guest then replies to your e-mail, answering as many or as few of the questions as he or she wants at whatever length he or she chooses. You must receive the guest's reply by 10 a.m. the next day. Then, you will put the questions and answers into a tidy format and distribute them to the partner sites and registrants along with the next topic for discussion. (You can adjust the sending/receiving times to suit your needs, your time zone, and the guest's time zone). Live Web seminars are often done as phone interviews: The guest is on the phone, talking and taking questions, and his or her responses are either streamed back to the audience or keyboarded by a typist. These seminars can be done from any telephone, but they are live and the guest must be available at the appointed time.

It's better for the producer to pick the topics than the guest. In my experience, guests are relieved when you (the producer) decide what topics should be discussed. They might ask you to remove or add certain topics, and that's great, but it's a bad idea to ask them to come up with a list of topics. You need crisp, specific topics that inspire people to register. Most guests, left to their own devices, will come up with the broadest, most boring topics imaginable.

The producer should set the dates of the seminar. You should approach the guest with suggested dates in mind. You usually start preparing a seminar at least three months in advance. Many guests won't have their personal calendars filled out that far ahead, so they will usually agree to the dates you suggest within a week or two. You want the guest to make a commitment to seminar week. You can't go out, sign up four major partner sites for the seminar, start your promotions, and then have the guest ask for a schedule change. That is a nightmare to avoid at all costs. A text-based seminar is very guest-friendly: They can participate on the road, on vacation, and around their personal schedules just as long as they commit to answering some questions every night or morning.

The Pitch Letter for Recruiting Partners

The next document to produce is a short pitch letter you will send to entice hosts of online forums to participate in the seminar. Here is a sample e-mail I used for my initial contact with potential Web site partners for the Wiley Culinary Seminar Series:

```
David & Tracy,

I am working with John Wiley & Sons to produce an online seminar
series around four books for high-end cooks: professional chefs,
gourmet cooks, restaurateurs, etc. I'm writing to see if you would
like to be involved?

Tenagra (the company I work for) will be producing the series.
We've already recruited the authors and set-up what I feel is a rea-
```

```
sonable format. But we'd prefer to partner with a high traffic site
such as Cooking.com. You will get the benefit of lots of additional
content for your site (excerpts, author seminars, artwork) and all
the revenue from book sales, and Wiley will get recognition and
awareness for its new releases.

I'd love to discuss the details over the phone, if possible. Is
there a good time for me to call you? Thank you so much for consid-
ering this request.

   Sincerely,
   STEVE O'KEEFE
   Director of Internet Publicity Services
   The Tenagra Corporation
   504-529-4344
   ~~~~~~~~~~~~~~~~~~~~~~~~~~~~~~~~~~~~~~~~~~~~~~~~~~~~~~~
```

First of all, notice how short the e-mail is. I've tried longer pitches, explaining how the seminar works, and so on, but through experience I've learned that it's best to just ask whether they want to be involved, point out the benefits for them, and see whether they respond. We'll talk more about this topic in the next section. For now, it's enough to create a simple e-mail message like the one shown. Now, let's look at how to use it.

Finding and Securing Partner Sites

From a promotional perspective, one of the great benefits of producing online seminars is that you can partner with multiple sites on the same event. Chats have to be held at a single site. You can string a group of chat appearances into a tour, but each event is separate and held at one site. The same is true for most multimedia, Web-based seminars: The audience has to come to the event. But with text-based seminars, you can hold the event simultaneously on numerous sites, collect all the questions at one central point, and distribute materials back out to the satellite locations. It's like broadcasting to a network. And like a broadcast network, your audience magnifies with each outlet you add, but your production costs don't increase at all.

Locating Venues and Contact Names

Text-based seminars can be offered to a wide variety of online forums, not just Web sites. Let's take a look at how you find these forums and the decision-makers who can say "Yes" to your pitch:

Usenet newsgroups. These popular online discussion groups can't participate in chats or multimedia presentations, but they can in text-based seminars. My two favorite tools for finding partner newsgroups are Google (Formerly DejaNews) at http://groups.google.com and Tile.Net at www.tile.net/news. Simply type a keyword and you'll get a matching list of groups. It's easiest to partner with *moderated* newsgroups because there's a contact person who controls the group and can say "Yes" to your pitch. You can find moderators either by searching through the messages in the group looking for the boss or by going to a site called "Internet FAQ Archives" at www.faqs.org, where you can find newsgroup charters and descriptions—most of which contain the name and e-mail address of the contact person for the group.

Internet mailing lists. These popular online discussion groups also can't host live chats or seminars, but they make great partners for text-based seminars. Unlike newsgroups, all mailing lists have owners, and most of them are moderated. The best place to find compatible lists used to be OneList. But because it was bought by eGroups and eGroups was bought by Yahoo, the new top resource for finding these lists is—you guessed it—Yahoo Groups at http://groups.yahoo.com. Either search by using a keyword or browse through their directory. Once you find groups you want to approach, you might have to join the group to get the contact information for the owner or moderator.

America Online forums. Still healthy after all these years, most America Online forums are not open to the public through the Web but can only be accessed from the proprietary AOL service. AOL memberships are cheap (as low as $4.95 a month, with something like 700 hours free). You're making a mistake if you exclude AOL from your promotional campaigns because you've got an Internet connection and you don't see the point. The point is that more than one-third of the online audience is on AOL. Use the search mechanisms on AOL to find forums to partner with, and then look for staff rosters for contact names. The people you want to connect with are usually called "editors" or "producers."

CompuServe forums. While these are typically smaller than AOL forums and less dynamic, they're still good for reaching a professional audience. A lot of executives started with CompuServe and have stayed with CompuServe because they find less spam, noise, and stupidity there than on either AOL or the Internet. CompuServe has an index of forums, and each forum has a "sysop roster" that lists contact names and e-mail address of forum staff. I suggest that you start with the highest-ranking staff member listed in the roster.

Web sites. I'm sure you know how to find Web sites. When looking for partners, I always begin my search at The 100 Hot Web Sites at www.100hot.com, which lists the top 100 sites by traffic in several different subject categories. The sites you partner with don't need any special facilities to participate in the seminars; all they have to do is put your registration box on their site. So your objective is to find a site that is maintained (otherwise, your pitch will fall on deaf ears) and look for a contact to whom you can send your pitch. A great place to find contacts is the "advertise with us" information; in fact, it's often the only place on some Web sites where you'll find names, phone numbers, and e-mail addresses that get checked regularly. The ad people will usually forward your pitch to someone in editorial.

Pitching and Follow-Up

It's easiest to have your little e-mail pitch letter handy as you go searching for partner sites. When you see a site you like, address the pitch letter and customize it so it doesn't sound like a form letter, then send it. Notice in my pitch letter that I try to set up a phone call to go over the details. It will take a little convincing to get sites to partner with you, especially if they're unfamiliar with the concept of online seminars. Your potential partners will likely have lots of questions about how the seminar will work, and e-mail is not a good medium for this kind of back-and-forth discussion. It will take you weeks to accomplish through e-mail what could be settled in a matter of minutes on the phone. For this reason, my advice is to *get on the phone* as soon as possible.

When someone expresses interest, whether through e-mail or telephone, try to focus your pitch on the benefits for them. Everyone wants to know, "What's in it for me?" Here are some of the major benefits of hosting a seminar:

Free content. They get the benefit of the content generated by the seminar at no cost, including the Q&A transcripts, support materials, advance materials, artwork, and an event worth promoting.

Free promotion. You will promote the seminar and their participation with news releases, discussion group postings, on your Web site, and in calendars of online events. You will help get their brand in front of a large audience.

Traffic. These sites want traffic; many of them are advertiser-supported, and more traffic means more revenue. Through your promotion, you will generate traffic for their site and the seminar will give people a reason to keep coming back to the site.

Sales. If there is a product being promoted through the seminar, it's possible for the partner sites to get cut in on a piece of the action. If the guest is an author or a musician and the site has an associate or affiliate store with Amazon or Barnes & Noble, they'll generate revenue from product sales. Even if the product is rather obscure, arrangements can be made to sell the product through the site and give the hosts a portion of the revenue.

E-mail addresses. You will, of course, share the e-mail addresses of all those who register for the seminar. These addresses can be used for direct e-mail campaigns.

Community. These seminars help grow a feeling of community at a site. For many participants, the seminar might be the first time they participated in any program at the site or connected with other people who use the site. I've seen this situation happen time and again in seminars. It might be hard to convince your host ahead of time, but they will see a new vitality in their core membership once the seminar is over.

Once you've got a potential partner interested, you can often close the deal by referring them to the Web page with the seminar description. This page will explain the seminar at a glance. It also provides them with all the artwork and promo copy they need to start promoting the seminar as quickly as possible.

Another way to think about the task of pitching partner sites is to ask yourself, "Why wouldn't they participate?" If you remove every objection or obstacle they have, why wouldn't they sign up? You want to make it as easy as possible for them to say yes, by producing and promoting the seminar yourself, by having all the materials they need to participate ready in the format they need, and by insuring the quality of the program. Several sites have agreed to host seminars for me because they simply couldn't find any reason to say no. And once they try it, I guarantee they'll want to do it again. Pitching these sites might be a one-time investment for you that pays off with a beautiful partnership that lasts for years.

Complications and Delays

The biggest impediment to partnering with multiple sites is the desire for exclusivity. If you get *Forbes* to partner with you, *Fortune* won't touch it. If you land Microsoft as a partner, you can forget about Oracle. If a site asks for an exclusive, it's just a business decision: Are they big enough for you to forego other opportunities? Are they important enough to your business objectives? If so, cut the deal. If not, thank them and keep looking.

One of the ways I combat the desire for exclusivity is to partner with sites whose audiences don't overlap. My ideal seminar lineup includes one Usenet newsgroup, one Internet mailing list, one AOL forum, one CompuServe forum, and one Web site. That's five venues, and none of these groups typically objects to any of the other partners. It's when you try and partner with four Web sites, all serving the same target audience, that you run into trouble.

Another potential complication is setting the date of the seminar. Let's say that you're out to recruit five partners and you get three of them the first week. If you started recruiting partners two months ahead of time, you feel pretty confident. But things slow down, and it takes two more weeks to land the fourth partner. Then, after another week, you've got the fifth partner on the hook. By now, you are only one month away from seminar week. What if partner number five is a major player and he or she wants to change the dates of the seminar to better fit his or her schedule? What do you do?

Anytime you run a promotion that involves multiple partners, you run into this problem. I always have scheduling problems on chat tours. But with chats, I have a window of a week or two in which I can schedule the chats. With seminars, the dates are set before I start approaching partners. You have to get the partners to agree to your timetable. The most graceful way out is to say that the timing won't work for this seminar, that you're already committed to the schedule, and it would be a major problem to change the dates—but that you'd like to partner with them on the next seminar you do.

At some point, you have to settle for the partners you have and start promoting the seminar. For the culinary seminar series I produced, Wiley set major obstacles in front of me. Instead of partnering with a newsgroup, a mailing list, an AOL forum, a CompuServe forum, and a Web site, they told me they wanted to partner with four major Web sites. They further requested that one site be located in each of their four major

Wiley Culinary Seminar Series

Partners List

The Global Gourmet
http://www.foodwine.com
An excellent gourmet cooking site. Cookbooks comprise the most compelling content on this site, and the editor of the cookbooks sections is also the executive editor for the whole site. They have an Amazon associate bookstore. They promise to "promote the heck out of" the series.

Culinary Institute Of America
http://www.ciachef.edu
This is the premiere culinary institute in the United States and a partner with Wiley in one of the books in the series: Garde Manger. The CIA's online bookstore is an Amazon associate. At first, they didn't want to partner on the whole series with us — just the Garde Manger book. But they have kindly installed a registration link (with Wiley logo) for the entire series on their site.

On The Rail
http://www.ontherail.com
This is a site for serious, professional chefs — a perfect target audience. Look at the amazing level of promotion we are getting: prominent homepage coverage, book featured at the top of their bookstore, info page for the entire series — all carrying the Wiley brand. With a hardcore following of more than 500 professional chefs, this partnership should lead to good sales figures.

FoodLines
http://www.foodlines.com
A site for people who have a passion for food. Recently redesigned, FoodLines is a Canadian-based culinary supersite. We have asked for the Seminar to be staged in their "Books for Professional Chefs" section, which includes bookstore partnerships with both Amazon.com and Chapters.ca (the giant Canadian bookseller).

Figure 7.4 Partners for the Wiley Culinary Seminar Series. How much more valuable is it to partner with four major sites in your niche than to run a seminar on your site alone?

territories: the United States, Canada, the United Kingdom, and Australia. I was able to convince them that this geographical requirement made no sense online—you can reach more Australians through a partnership with The Global Gourmet than you can through an Australian cooking site. See Figure 7.4.

The requirement for four Web sites was a major bottleneck. Because of exclusivity, most of the sites would not participate if their competitors were involved. I pitched dozens of sites but landed only three by the time the series started. A fourth site joined us after the first seminar and participated for the last three months. Figure 7.4 lists the partners that worked with Wiley on this seminar series. A pleasant surprise was that the fourth site turned out to be Canadian (not that it matters in cyberspace, though).

Promoting Seminars and Workshops

As I've mentioned several times, the real value in doing online seminars is not the attendance but the amount of promotional exposure that you get. So how do you get that exposure? By making a joyous noise, of course. Once you have your guest, dates, and venues set for the seminar, you can begin promoting it mercilessly. This section will show you how.

Installing Promo Materials at Partner Sites

The first and most important promotional task is to make sure that your partner sites promote the seminar. Call their attention to the Web version of the Seminar Description page that you created at the beginning of this process (Figure 7.3). Simply send an e-mail to your contacts at the partner sites, reminding them that they should feel free to take the materials directly from the Seminar Description Web page and install them on their sites. The Seminar Description page includes the following elements:

Artwork. Usually, a headshot color photo of each featured guest for the seminar; also, any logos for the companies represented by the featured guests. Often, the artwork will include a book cover, CD cover, or other images for products being promoted by the guest. All this artwork should be in JPEG or similar format, appropriately sized and ready for online installation.

Registration box. The box consists of a graphic element and HTML coding that allows a person to enter his or her e-mail address in the box and click a button to register for the seminar. All registration requests arrive as e-mail to the address specified and are replied to with the Welcome Letter containing seminar instructions. Registration replies can be automated or processed manually.

Promotional text. A description of the seminar that your partner hosts can simply cut and paste onto their own sites

Other promo materials. If you want, you can design banner ads to promote the seminar and offer them to partner sites. If you do, you'll want to be sure to include the partner site's name and logo in the banner (otherwise, they are unlikely to use the banners).

It can take some cajoling to get partner sites to install promotional materials. If you have prepared well, there is little for the partner sites to do to participate in the seminars. They don't have to think up the topics or the questions, prepare introductions or promotional copy, or generate graphics. But one thing you can't control is whether they actually install the promo materials. In many cases, the person who agreed to partner on the seminar (a content editor, for example) is not the same person who installs the promo materials (usually, a Web master). So you need to put pressure on your editorial contacts to get them to hound the Web master until the promos are installed. The sooner they get installed, the better the results expected from the seminar.

Try to approach your contacts with offers of assistance rather than criticism or threats. Ask whether there is anything you can do to speed up the process. Ask whether there is anything more they need or whether they need the graphics in smaller or different formats. Try to eliminate every reason they might have for delaying the installation of the promotional materials.

News Releases and Events Calendars

With your program and venues set, it's time to alert the media to your activities. Follow the instructions in the News Releases chapter of this book for preparing an e-mail news release. A sample news release is shown as follows, taken from the campaign for the Wiley Culinary Seminar Series.

E-MAIL NEWS RELEASE
Client: *John Wiley & Sons*
Project: Culinary Seminar Series

Subject Line: Wiley Launches Culinary Seminar Series

John Wiley & Sons, Inc., today announced a delicious new online marketing strategy for their professional cooking guides. Wiley is partnering with major cooking sites on the web for a four-month Culinary Seminar Series. The series schedule is:

Aug 30 - Sep 4:
Book: Foie Gras...A Passion
Guest: Michael Ginor, Hudson Valley Foie Gras

Oct 4 - Oct 8:
Book: The Making of a Pastry Chef
Guest: Andrew MacLauchlan, Executive Pastry Chef,
Coyote Cafe in Santa Fe, NM

Nov 1 - Nov 5:
Book: Garde Manger: The Art and Craft of the Cold Kitchen
Guests: Chef Timothy Rodgers and editor Mary Donovan,
Culinary Institute of America

Dec 6 - Dec 10:
Book: Chocolate Passion
Guest: Timothy Moriarty, features editor, Chocolatier

"Our strategy is to build relationships with the premier cooking sites online by providing them with a steady stream of content and guests," said Carmela DellaRipa, Wiley's publicist for the series. "In addition to the seminars, our partner sites will be using

```
excerpts, recipes, and artwork from the books. They get content and
sales through their bookstores, and we get exposure for our new
releases. It's a win-win situation." Partners for the series
include:

The Global Gourmet
http://www.foodwine.com/food/special/
A gourmet cooking site with an emphasis on cookbooks.

The Culinary Institute of America
http://www.ciachef.edu/geninfo/getasty.html
The premiere culinary institute in the United States.

On The Rail
http://www.ontherail.com/
A site for serious, professional chefs.

FoodLines
http://www.foodlines.com
A Canadian-based culinary supersite.

In addition to the partnerships, Wiley is promoting the series with
Online Bookstore Displays installed at the world's largest online
bookstores and special-interest cookbook stores. The seminar series
is being produced by The Tenagra Corporation, an Internet marketing
firm with five years' experience promoting books and authors online.

If you would like review copies of the books in the Wiley Culinary
Seminar Series -- or an interview about this new marketing strategy
-- just reply to this e-mail. More information about the series can
be found at the partner sites. Your audience can subscribe to the
series simply by sending mailto:wileycooks-subscribe@egroups.com
```

This news release is designed for delivery to the trade—that is, publications covering the book industry and the Internet industry. The release emphasizes the novelty of the seminar program and the partnerships involved. A release to media covering the food industry would put greater emphasis on the subject matter of the seminars and less on the mechanics of it. A release going to people who compile online events calendars would stress the dates and locations of the seminars, with only the briefest description of the subject matter and guests. You can format releases for different media audiences by editing down a trade news release like the one shown here.

Online events calendars are a major source of publicity for seminars. On the Internet, you can find such calendars at Yahoo! and at other larger portals. You should also try to get listed in Web calendars maintained by industry groups and associations that cover subjects related to your seminars. In many cases, you can get your event listed in calendars like these simply by filling out a form at the Web site. Have your news release file open while browsing for these sites, and when you find an appropriate calendar, either e-mail the news release to the Web master of the site or add the calendar listing yourself by cutting-and-pasting into an online form.

Chances are you will not be able to get coverage for your seminars in monthly magazines and newsletters. Their lead times are long, and you probably won't have your partners lined up in time to get coverage. The Web sites for these publications might have more up-to-date news, and you should be able to get coverage that way. For daily and weekly newspapers, however, the story is different. Many of these publications include calendars of online events. You should be able to get coverage for your seminars in weekly business newspapers and from the appropriate section editor at daily newspapers. For example, a seminar on personal financial planning is more likely to get listed from a news release sent to the "money" editor of a newspaper than one sent to a "technology" editor.

Discussion Group Postings

News about online seminars will be welcome in most online discussion groups devoted to the topic of the seminar. These discussion groups include Usenet newsgroups, Internet mailing lists, America Online forums, CompuServe forums, and Web site message boards. For detailed instructions about how to locate online discussion groups related to any given topic, please see the Discussion Group Postings chapter of this book, where you will also find meticulous instructions for formatting and delivering these postings.

The following is an announcement for a seminar about participating in clinical trials, hosted by the Web site HealthTalk.com. This announcement is a good example of one that cuts to the chase, giving you an idea of why you would want to attend and what credentials the featured guests have without wasting a lot of verbiage.

```
Wednesday, May 2nd at
5:30 p.m. Pacific / 8:30 Eastern
http://www.healthtalk.com/live/

"Understanding Clinical Trials"

Please join us to learn the latest about participating in a clini-
cal trial. Can they give you "tomorrow's medicine today?" Or are
there risks? Does your doctor have a "hidden agenda" about you par-
ticipating or not participating?

Hear from the experts on this important topic:

Joseph C. Avellone, M.D., M.P.A., president and chief executive
officer of VeritasMedicine.com, a leading web site for people seek-
ing information on clinical trials.

John Yee, M.D., vice president for clinical affairs and chief med-
ical officer of VeritasMedicine.com
```

```
Mary McCabe, R.N., director of clinical trial promotions at the
National Cancer Institute.

Clarence Braddock, M.D., bioethicist and Vice Chairman of the
Department of Medicine at the University of Washington School of
Medicine.

Branimir I. Sikic, M.D., director of two clinical trial programs at
Stanford University School of Medicine.
```

There are several ways to make your discussion group postings more palatable, thus resulting in greater registrations and fewer flames. The first is to offer to send transcripts to anyone who can't attend or who prefers to get their information that way. This generous gesture helps you build a database of e-mail addresses of people interested in the subject of the seminar. The second is to offer to forward questions to the guests for those who can't attend.

As far as timing goes, if you are promoting a seminar that requires attendance at a live event, the closer your postings appear to the start of the event the greater attendance you'll get. Messages sent weeks ahead of time will be forgotten or deleted before the seminar starts. If you have a live event and want to start promoting it well in advance, you should require registration. That way, you can send a reminder the day before the event to all those who registered. If your company spends money buying banner advertising, consider using the banners to solicit registrations for the seminar. It's possible to purchase banner ads that run at a specific time on a specific date so that you can promote a live event the moment it starts to an audience you know is online now. Banners that run at the beginning of an online event are very effective at drawing an audience for that event.

Direct Mail and Other Promotional Materials

Just because your event takes place online doesn't mean you have to limit your promotional activities to the Internet. People who work in cyberspace often forget the power of the printed word. A postcard containing the Web address for either the registration page or the event itself is very effective; people will hold onto the card if they plan to attend, whereas they are likely to either act on e-mail immediately or delete it. The most effective seminar promotion I received came from Nielsen//NetRatings. They sent a piece of direct mail with the following text right on the outside of the envelope:

```
Join us for our free online marketing ROI seminar.
Your reservation number is 33932-NTR1
Save this envelope for later reference!
```

I did, actually, save the envelope for the six weeks between when I received it and when the seminar was scheduled. I registered only three days before the event. One advantage of promoting this way is that it allows you to track the source of registration and to determine which mailing lists were most effective. I'm guessing my "reservation number" contains a source code showing that I am a Bell South customer. I wouldn't be surprised if Nielsen//NetRatings sent this mail only to people with cable modems, ADSL, or other high-speed Internet access—people most likely to be able to have a positive experience with a broadband-intensive online seminar.

Newsletters and other printed communications are also good ways to promote online seminars. If you are planning to promote to targeted audiences this way, you'll need to have your seminar schedule set far enough in advance to make the deadlines of most newsletters. To reach out through monthly publications, you would want your seminar schedule set at least two months in advance.

You can also promote online seminars through live appearances. For example, you can announce at a shareholders meeting that senior management will be available for online discussion at a future date and time. If you commit yourself to a regular seminar schedule, such as the first Wednesday of each month, you can promote your seminars in all the forms of communication between your company and the target audience: on radio shows, in TV ads, with catalogs, newsletters or other mailings, at live appearances, and so on.

Conducting Seminars and Workshops

The actual mechanism of conducting an online seminar or workshop is relatively simple compared to the work that goes into setting them up, finding partners, and promoting them. For text-based workshops, conducting the seminar is similar to running a mailing list, and I refer readers to the Newsletters chapter of this book for detailed instructions on using listserver software. For live, multimedia events, the issues get much more complicated. You are dependent on the capabilities of your broadcaster, whether that is your in-house IT department or a third-party service such as broadcast.com. I'll cover some of these issues at the end of this section.

Managing Registrations

Registrations for text-based seminars arrive as commands to subscribe to a mailing list. If you are using listserver software or a free Web service such as Yahoo Groups, you can automate the process of managing registrations. People subscribe by sending their e-mail address to the subscription address. Upon subscribing, they are usually asked to confirm their desire to subscribe by replying to e-mail. This action protects the subscriber from being unknowingly signed up for a group in which he or she has no interest. Confirmation is especially important for seminars dealing with controversial or potentially embarrassing topics.

Once people subscribe, they should be sent a welcome letter explaining the mechanics of the seminar, the subjects covered, the dates, and providing instructions for unsubscribing. Sample text for a welcome letter is covered earlier in this chapter.

Instructions for unsubscribing from the seminar should be embedded in every dispatch to registrants. Unsubscription is usually accomplished automatically by sending e-mail to the unsubscribe address.

If the anticipated number of participants is small enough, the registration mechanism does not have to be automated. It's sometimes easier to use e-mail filtering to segregate registration requests from other e-mail and then reply to subscribe and unsubscribe requests individually. The advantage here is that many people ask questions or make comments in their registration requests that are lost with automation. For example, a person might ask to be notified about future seminars although he or she can't participate in this one. Some people also use signature files in their registration e-mails, which contain valuable direct-marketing contact information.

In many cases, your partner sites will want to handle all the registrations generated through their sites. They won't want to share the e-mail address of participants with you or give you direct access to their audience members. In these cases, you will have to transfer the welcome letter and daily dispatches to your partners for distribution to their lists. You should at least ask for a count of how many people participated through their sites, and I always ask for e-mail addresses although I don't always get them.

You can also use a Web form for registrations, allowing you to collect a greater amount of information about each participant. An example is Figure 7.5, showing the registration form used by the Small Business Administration in partnership with Cisco Systems for a series of business seminars offered online.

Data collected from Web-based registration systems is offloaded to a database. Managing these kinds of databasing operations is beyond my level of expertise. For more information, you'll need to consult with an IT professional or experienced Web design person. I will caution you, however, about one common problem with Web-based registration forms: People frequently register two or more times, uncertain whether their initial request was processed correctly. Before starting a seminar, I suggest that you search for duplicate e-mail addresses in your database or list of participants. Otherwise, people will be sent two or more copies of all the seminar materials, and if they try to unsubscribe one address, they could very well delete themselves entirely from the database.

Support Materials Required

In addition to the Q&A that is the backbone of most online seminars, you might want to provide the audience with a variety of support materials. In the case of the Wiley Culinary Seminar Series described earlier in this chapter, we used excerpts from four books, recipes, artwork from the books, and even a quiz for chocolate lovers. Supporting documents are very helpful for online seminars, and quizzes, tests, Top 10 lists, forms, and other giveaways are always popular online.

Supporting materials should be stored at the companion Web site for the seminar, whether that is your own site or the file storage space provided by Yahoo Groups or another free Web site service. If you don't want or don't have a companion Web site, support files can be sent to participants as attachments via e-mail. Please be considerate of your audience. People have different computer systems and software and might not be able to use the files that you send. A lot of people are suspicious of any file attachments and are reluctant to open them for fear of unleashing a virus. I would only send files as attachments once I had permission from the receiving party and knew what format they preferred.

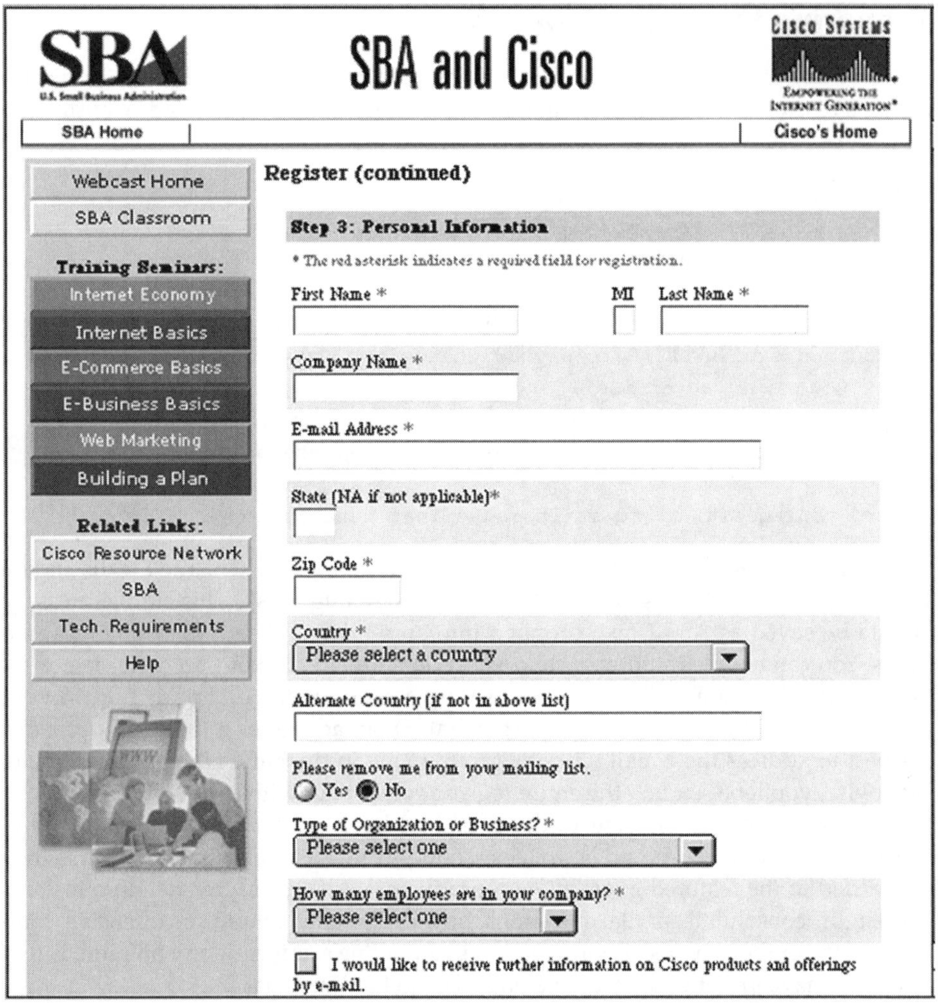

Figure 7.5 This Web-based registration form collects detailed information from people joining online seminars sponsored by the Small Business Administration and Cisco Systems.

Support materials should also be distributed to all your partner sites. You'll find that you can get more traffic for the supporting documents than you get for the seminar itself. Support files are often featured on partner sites and then archived indefinitely. Be sure that you have permission to distribute anything that is copyrighted, and include a copyright notice in all materials sent out online. It's smart to include full contact information in all these materials, too; you have to assume that they will be viewed and used independently of the seminar.

Preparing the Daily Dispatch

The first day of a text-based seminar, I suggest distributing a simple topic for discussion. Here is an example from an online advertising seminar with Brad Aronson and Robbin Zeff:

```
Tuesday, Nov. 16:

Topic: Pricing Online Advertising

Online advertising rates are wild, ranging from $2 to $200 per
thousand exposures. Here's your chance to learn tricks or pay less
(if you're an advertiser) or charge more (if you're a publisher).
We welcome thorny questions about rate shaving, inflated traffic
stats, package pricing, and other financial shenanigans.

Send your questions to mailto:adseminar@tenagra.com
```

As we discussed earlier in this chapter, you need to draw lurkers into the discussion by baiting them with suggestions of questions they might ask. This simple message should be saved as ASCII text, dropped into an e-mail, and sent to seminar participants. You can handle it through your listserver software, or you can do it via e-mail. For distribution via e-mail, you should set up a group name or "nickname" in your e-mail software, then dump all the participant e-mail addresses into the group name. It's best to address the e-mail with the group name in the blind copy or "Bcc:" field; otherwise, you'll be sending the entire registration list out with each e-mail.

Audience questions are sent to the e-mail address specified by the seminar producer. These questions should be collected and put into a single e-mail, which is then forwarded to the featured guest(s). As a producer, I would feel free to edit questions for length, consolidate similar questions, and delete silly, stupid, or offensive comments. One of the benefits of participating in an online seminar, in my opinion, is that you don't have to put up with all the noise you get at live chats.

Once the guest replies, his or her responses should be cleaned and integrated with the questions in such a way as to produce a readable Q&A thread. When things go back in forth in e-mail, they end up looking pretty rough sometimes; quote markers and forced line endings can lead to a nearly unreadable document. You want to create a clean, inviting Q&A thread out of this mess before sending it off to subscribers. Here's a portion of the thread from the online advertising seminar discussed earlier:

```
Online Advertising Seminar
with Robbin Zeff and Brad Aronson

TUESDAY, 11/16/99,
"PRICING ONLINE ADVERTISING":
_____--


[AngeliaLyn, from the Business Know-How Forum, AOL:]
Advertisers benefit from pay-per-click advertising, but
```

does it ever pay for web sites to accept cost-per-click
ads?
*****
ROBBIN SAYS: The only time it pays for an advertiser
to accept cost-per-click ads is if: 1) you're a small
site willing to take any ad revenue you can get; 2) you
have so much ad inventory you might as well sell it as
pay-per- click (PPC) rather that over-deliver huge
amounts; or 3) the request is coming from one of your
best customers, and you're willing to do a PPC campaign
because of all the money they already spend on your
site.

BRAD SAYS: The problem with accepting cost-per-click
(CPC) advertising is that you need to trust that the
advertisement will work. If you know your site well
enough, you should be able to pick out the
cost-per-click deals that will generate revenue for
your site. CPC is also good when you haven't sold your
inventory, because you can get some revenue for the ad
space.

[Peter Ferland, from the Online Advertising Discussion
List:] I'm responsible for increasing advertising sales
for an ISP. I'm doing a lot of cold calling and
prospecting to major companies and organizations, and
I'm doing a lot of follow-up -- I think my prospecting
ideas are great, but I haven't had a lot of sales
responses. The most frequent objections are "we don't
have the budget," "our budget for this year has been
spent already," etc... I know that a lot of money is
spent on banner ads. How can I close these prospects?
*****
BRAD SAYS: You need to reach the person in charge of
making purchasing decisions. If you're a national ISP
with significant traffic, I would make sure you are
listed in the places advertisers look for ad rates --
http://www.adknowledge.com/website/index.html
(AdKnowledge, AdPlanner) and
http://www.srds.com/get_listed/index.html (SRDS) are
two good places.

Also, it is worthwhile to advertise to media buyers.
ClickZ (www.clickz.com), ICONOCAST (www.iconocast.com),
I- Advertising List (www.interentadvertising.org), and
the Online-Ads Discussion List (www.o-a.com) are good
places to advertise.

```
You should try to focus on getting into year 2000
budgets instead of end-of-the-year spending, which (for
the most part) is already allocated.

Online Advertising Seminar
with Robbin Zeff and Brad Aronson

Tomorrow's Topic:
Issues in Ad Management & Measurement

The online advertising industry has made great progress
establishing standard measurements for site traffic and
advertising exposure, but there's still a long way to go.
Robbin and Brad will give you the real dope on ad management
software packages and ratings services that measure site
traffic.

Send your questions to mailto:adseminar@tenagra.com
```

From my early experiments producing online seminars, I learned that one real benefit for participants was networking with other participants through the Q&A thread. In this transcript, you'll notice that we include the name of the person asking the question and the partner site from which it originated. This feature helps participants get to know each other and provides branding support for partner sites. We also gave people the option of asking questions anonymously, in which case we would strip out any identifying marks (such as e-mail addresses) before sending the questions to the featured guest(s).

This same format is followed every day of the seminar: sending the previous day's Q&A thread along with the next topic for discussion. On the final day, the Q&A thread is sent with concluding remarks from the featured guest or producer. It's a good idea to include a copyright notice and contact information in all the dispatches that are sent.

Conducting Live Seminars and Workshops

Live events are much trickier than text-based seminars. There are many opportunities for disaster, and you need backup plans in case something doesn't work. Regardless of the multimedia used, you need to test everything in advance. Does your streaming PowerPoint presentation work? Is the chat room functioning properly? Did you test the conference call hook-up and make sure everyone on the phone could hear each other? I suggest a thorough dry run with a controlled audience, such as friends and/or employees, before going live with a program.

Even after a complete test of the facilities, I'd want some emergency procedures in place. If the featured guest's connection fails, can he or she phone an emergency contact person and have that person type for them? If the PowerPoint presentation or Web tour crashes, is the guest prepared to ad-lib the program? Is there a mechanism to handle hecklers or expel rude people?

For most live programs, the audience gathers at a Web site or chat room. It's a good idea to start a few minutes late so that people who need to register or sign in have time to complete that process. A moderator should be present to introduce the guest, manage the flow of questions, silence or eject hecklers, and deal with any technical difficulties. The moderator should be prepared with text to either recite or paste into the proceedings at appropriate points, such as the introduction for the guest, sample questions, and contact information. It's nice if the moderator has a way of exchanging private messages with the guest so that he or she can coach the guest on when to cut an answer short, stretch, or wrap up.

Let's take a look at a live seminar where pretty much everything went wrong so that you understand what kinds of risks you're taking and what sorts of backup plans you need.

Nielsen//NetRatings Nightmare

On April 12, 2001, Nielsen//NetRatings held an online seminar about Web marketing ROI. I was excited about this seminar because the producers put a considerable investment into marketing the seminar. They did everything right. They sent me direct mail that arrived six weeks in advance (roughly March 1). The direct mail piece included an envelope, a form letter, and a slick brochure. All three pieces plugged the seminar. You only needed to keep the envelope to have all the information required to register. Even so, that information was repeated at the top of the form letter and even in the brochure.

Nielsen//NetRatings used an elaborate multimedia live format for the seminar, hosted by Evoke Communications (www.evoke.com). Evoke provided an online forum where users could ask questions as well as a telephone conference call hookup. A PowerPoint presentation would be streamed over the Web site while the audio portion of the program was delivered via the conference call. Participants were expected to have Internet access (probably high-speed) as well as a separate phone line for the conference call.

The trouble began when I registered at the Web site three days in advance. I was told to expect e-mail with instructions on how to connect to the seminar. On the day of the seminar, I still hadn't received any e-mail, and I had to make three phone calls to track down someone who could provide me with the username and password I needed to access the program. I was told to call a phone number that was not toll-free and provide a code to get access to the audio stream for the seminar. I called, was put on hold, and waited for the presentation to begin. On the Web, I logged into the site for the seminar and waited there, too, for the presentation to begin. The login screen is shown in Figure 7.6.

As a participant, it wasn't clear at all how the conference call was supposed to function. I couldn't tell whether anyone could hear if I spoke. I suspected that I could hear the guests, but they couldn't hear me. Why they didn't just stream the audio online is unclear.

The presentation began, introductions were made, and then the speaker started referring to the PowerPoint presentation supposedly appearing on the Web site. Only there wasn't anything appearing on the site. After a few minutes, I tried reloading the screen, then asking through the phone whether the presentation had a problem, then using the "ask a question" feature on the Web site to plead for help. Finally, someone broke into the conference call to explain they were having technical difficulties and

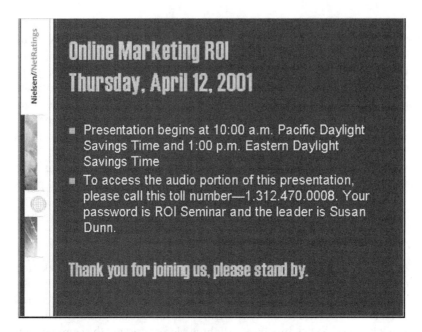

Figure 7.6   The login screen for the Nielsen//NetRatings Online Marketing ROI seminar. The message "Please Stand By" never went away.

were trying to get the PowerPoint presentation to work. At first, I thought the problem might be with my software; now I realized that no one could see the presentation.

And on and on it went. The first speaker finished, and we got another announcement about technical difficulties. Then we were told the PowerPoint presentations were being e-mailed to all those who registered, and we should check our e-mail for them. But nothing came via e-mail. I sent several e-mails as well as Web questions, saying I hadn't received the slideshow and providing my e-mail address again, just in case. In my ear, the next speaker read from his script, referring to slides no one could see. Distracted by the technical difficulties, how could any of us in the audience concentrate on the information in the verbal pitch?

Finally, the presentation ended, and the Q&A session began. People could indicate through their telephones that they wished to ask a question, and they would be patched into the audible portion of the conference call. I asked a question via the Web interface, just to see if it was working. When my question was recited, I knew that they must also have seen my pleas for assistance sent earlier. The second person to ask a question on the phone conference call said he never received the slides via e-mail, so I knew it wasn't just me. After about a half hour on the phone, I bailed out. Six days later, the PowerPoint presentation arrived via e-mail.

I don't know where the fault lies for this failed seminar. I suspect that Evoke had problems delivering the PowerPoint portion of the presentation. But Nielsen// NetRatings could have done a better job of processing registrations, testing the delivery, and following-up via e-mail. In the face of disaster, they just marched right through the presentation rather than postpone it or reschedule. Just hearing someone rattle on in your ear about online marketing stats is a less-than-motivational form of communicating.

Nielsen//NetRatings could have done a number of things to improve on this program. First, eliminate the telephone conference call—a streaming PowerPoint presentation with audio track would have been just as effective and can be easily produced by using RealSlideshow or Presenter.com or PowerPoint 2000 with Windows Media Service (see the Online Newsroom chapter for more details). They could have delivered a modest-bandwidth, canned presentation over the Web that could be coupled with chat for the Q&A session. And a presentation made this way can be stored online and used over and over again. There was no need for the live audio portion of the program, because it wasn't interactive until it got the Q&A session, which would have been better handled through a chat interface. By loading up the seminar with so much overlapping technology, they narrowed their potential audience while increasing their potential for technical difficulties several fold. It's embarrassing for a company delivering a seminar about intelligent online marketing strategies to demonstrate that they don't know how to use this technology to good effect. And it's mortifying to do such a good job promoting the seminar—and to spend so much money on that promotion—to have the event come off so poorly. What was Nielsen//NetRatings' ROI on the *Online Marketing ROI* seminar? Not very good, I suspect.

Follow-Up Operations

The results of an online seminar or workshop can be magnified several fold through good follow-up procedures. Let's start with using the transcripts generated from online seminars.

Cleaning and Distributing Transcripts

At the conclusion of an online seminar, you should be able to generate a very nice transcript that includes the topics for discussion and the Q&A threads. Like chat transcripts, these should be cleaned and consolidated, removing superfluous messages, spell-checking, and reformatting for readability. This document can then be distributed to the partner sites for archiving and/or converted into a Web page and installed on your own site. In most cases, you can expect a transcript on America Online, CompuServe, or a Web site to get more downloads than the number of people who attended the seminar.

If you conduct multiple seminars, over time you will get a large set of transcripts that can be repurposed. They can be bound together and sold as books or strung together into e-books. Recently, *The Wall Street Journal* began collecting articles on similar subjects into anthologies and selling them as e-books at its site. These Q&A files can also be culled and used for FAQs on your Web site or included with customer support materials, such as manuals. If there is enough value locked in the transcripts, they can be databased as help resources.

Some enterprising sites, such as Salon.com, have gone so far as to issue news releases about controversial topics that have surfaced on their discussion boards, luring the media and the public to download documents to get the full story. If your seminar has resulted in some newsworthy pronouncements, you can try this tactic to get extra mileage from them.

Using Registration Lists for Direct Marketing

One benefit of holding seminars that require registration—as compared to anonymous communication through chats—is that you end up with a database of contacts interested in the subject of the seminar who can be approached with other offers. You have to exercise some care in direct e-mail marketing, for example, only sending offers directly related to the interests of your list and giving them an easy opt-out mechanism. Responsible use of your registration list should generate continuing returns.

The first thing you can do with these lists is invite people to participate in future seminars you hold. You can also send them offers for products or services you produce related to subjects covered in the seminars. If you collected mailing addresses through your registration procedures, you can use them for direct mail marketing. People are much less sensitive about direct mail solicitations than they are about e-mail solicitations.

If you conduct an ongoing seminar program, you should soon accumulate a database of contacts that can become one of your company's biggest assets.

Measuring Reach and ROI

How can you measure the impact of an online seminar? The first number I would look at is how many people registered for, or participated in, the seminar. You can add the number of direct registrations you received and then ask any partner sites to share data with you on the number of people who participated through their sites. You might find this number to be quite small. In the case of seminars held on a single site that is not a major Web portal, I would expect between 10 and 25 registrations. For a partnership with a major portal, maybe double that, or up to 50 registrations. If you run the text-based seminar that I recommend, partner with several sites, and promote it, I would expect more than 100 registrations. For the Wiley Culinary Seminar Series, we had well more than 200 registrations plus an unknown number from one partner site that would only tell us "several hundred" people were participating through their site.

The number of people participating partly depends on the topics discussed. Some topics appeal to a very narrow audience. And for some marketing activities, you need only a small audience to be successful. For example, I have one client that is trying to reach out to neurosurgeons in the United States, of which there are fewer than 10,000. This client would be delighted if he could get 10 of these surgeons involved in an online medical seminar. So, you have to look at what your objectives are, what you're selling, what your average cost of customer acquisition is, and what revenues you derive from that average customer before you can calculate the ROI for an online seminar program.

The next measure is the number of people exposed to the seminar. If you partner with a mailing list that has thousands of members, all the members of the list are exposed to the seminar even if they don't register to participate. For example, we partnered with the *Online Advertising* (O-A) discussion list for the seminar on online advertising described earlier in this chapter. O-A ran promos for the seminar several times before it started, then carried the entire Q&A transcript each day of the five-day seminar. O-A boasts more than 20,000 subscribers, and because it is a tightly moderated list, the level of discussion tends to be quite high. You can't say that all 20,000 subscribers heard about the seminar anymore than you can say all the subscribers to *Time* magazine read a certain article. But it is one measure of reach.

The next measure of reach is the amount of promotion at the partner sites. This promotion can be documented with screen captures made once the partners install the promo materials. I look for both quantitative and qualitative coverage. When I partner with The Investors Forum on CompuServe, I usually get front-page coverage for the events hosted there. Furthermore, I get a little blurb in CompuServe's "What's Happening" newsletter that every one of CompuServe's millions of members has to get past to retrieve their e-mail. The Investors Forum always installs support files on their site, and some of these get downloaded hundreds of times, giving another measure of reach.

On America Online, it's a different story. It's difficult to get front-page coverage from any of the forum hosts. They seem to have much less control over their high-traffic pages, and so promotions for seminars are often buried three or more pages into the site. I've seldom gotten notice in AOL-wide areas, such as AOL Live, which have an audience in the millions. And it's getting harder all the time to find libraries on AOL where support files can be stored and easily located by people who want to download these documents. Still, AOL has some very active forums with audiences much larger than CompuServe, and I would always want an AOL partnership on any seminar.

One measure of reach is the number of times promotional materials for the seminar were served. It is very difficult to coax this information out of Web masters, AOL hosts, and CompuServe hosts. People are reluctant to release traffic statistics without a compelling reason to do so. If you are hosting seminars at your own Web site, you should definitely examine the number of times seminar promotions were served and compare it with the number of registrations, the number of times transcripts were accessed, and the number of times support files were downloaded. These figures will not only give you an idea of reach but also conversion ratios that you can use as benchmarks of comparison with future seminars.

Another measure of reach is the number of publications that ran news or information about the seminar. If you subscribe to a clipping service, you should be able to catch mentions of the seminar in print publications such as daily and weekly newspapers and on radio or TV stations. You also can do searches online at AltaVista and Google to see whether you can locate Web sites that mentioned the seminar. You can sometimes find the number of subscribers for mailing lists that ran your discussion group posting for the seminars. It is impossible to accurately estimate the number of people seeing your postings in Usenet newsgroups. Some of these numbers are difficult to churn, but these audiences are being exposed to your message and shouldn't be left out of any discussion of ROI. Another measure is increased traffic at your Web site. If your promotion points people to your Web site and traffic increases can't be attributed to other promotional activities, you'll have some measure of the effectiveness of your campaign.

Next, in my calculations I would want to know the advertising value of all the promotional exposure that the seminar received. For partner sites that have advertising rate cards, you can put a dollar value on a week's worth of prime Web site real estate. For mailing lists that sell sponsorships, you can put a daily dollar value on the exposure you get. You can calculate the dollar value of newspaper, radio, and television coverage the same way, and many advertising agencies that handle online events will perform these calculations and provide you with a numerical ROI.

But there's more to ROI than mathematical analysis of ad rates and coverage. You have to have an instinct for some of these things. If you could buy a banner ad on a Web site you partnered with for $20,000, was your exposure at that site really worth $20,000? It's easy to lie with these numbers, and I've seen agencies claiming that campaigns that cost $10,000 resulted in millions of dollars worth of coverage. Beyond ROI is an instinct as to whether a program was worth it or not. And that instinct is assisted not only with numbers calculating the value of coverage, but also with a sense about how much activity has increased at the office. Every good business person I have worked for can smell the difference between a successful campaign and a waste of resources, and they don't let the numbers fool them (nor do they ignore them).

When I started producing seminars, I had one big, gnawing question: Can I deliver a user experience that is good enough to make people want to come back? Will they be satisfied? Would they register for future seminars? Would they tell their friends about it? I was skeptical, but I've seen the results and the answer is yes, a quality program can be delivered this way. As a client, I would expect to see not only quality programming, but also a measurable increase in prospects, sales, memberships, subscriptions, or whatever quantitative measures of success I could surmise. Without these, I would not be swayed by the advertising value of the coverage I received to continue pouring money into these programs.

From Seminars to Shows

For the Wiley Culinary Seminar Series, we went beyond a single seminar to offer one seminar a month for four months. The power of this strategy is enormous. If you hold a week-long seminar, you can expect a couple of weeks of promotion at the partner sites, maybe more. The promotion is focused on the seminar: the guest and the topics. But when you host a seminar series spanning several months, you get continuous promotion from your partners. As soon as one seminar is over, they begin promoting the next one. And the focus of the promotion includes not only the guests and topics, but also *your brand*.

When someone asks me about the ROI from a seminar series, I have to reply, "What is it worth to have a major, branded presence on four or five of the key sites your target audience visits?" Running an online seminar will hopefully open the door for you to begin a seminar series. And that seminar series could easily turn into a regular monthly program. In a few months, you could find yourself with a high-profile de facto partnership with key, strategic Web sites. Many companies pay dearly for such partnerships, but because you approach these sites with programming they need to generate traffic, you will likely pay nothing for the partnership. That's smart marketing.

The costs you face are in developing programming, not paying the venues. With experience, these costs should drop. Through these seminar programs, you can build valuable partnerships with "Web Sites that Matter," exchanging your content for their audience. Once these partnerships are established, it is so much easier to push content through the pipe. You have relationships with all the key people, you have procedures for transferring promo materials, you know the drill, you fix the bugs, and the programs come off better and better all the time. Through these partnerships, you can improve and innovate, taking advantage of new technologies to offer ever-better user experiences, hopefully at lower costs to you. For all these reasons, I am confident that if you try seminar programs and your gut tells you that they are generating the right kind of buzz at the home office, then you can build upon them to form beautiful relationships that will pay off for many years to come.

Top Tips

Yahoo! Groups. What can I say—Yahoo! Groups offers a *free* staging area for your seminars that includes a mailing list, a chat area, automated membership processing, file storage, Web space, and even promotion through Yahoo! It's like having a full-service IT department without paying a cent. You would be foolish not to explore this excellent vehicle for delivering seminars.

Recruit partner sites. It can be hard dragging traffic to seminars on your own site. Consider partnering with multiple venues (including your own site). There are high-traffic forums that are anxious to get this kind of programming; they usually don't charge anything, you'll get much more exposure, and your seminar could be the beginning of a beautiful, long-term relationship.

Make it simple. You don't need to deliver streaming video to have an excellent online seminar. In fact, it can be a distraction, and it limits your audience to people with state-of-the-art hardware, software, and Internet access. A seminar with a streaming PowerPoint presentation and streaming audio can be enjoyed by most people online. A text-only seminar is accessible to everyone on the Internet and almost never breaks down.

Make it big. You can magnify the impact of your online seminar several fold through aggressive promotion. Budget enough time in your schedule to launch a complete publicity campaign, including news releases, discussion group postings, Web site promotion, listings in events calendars, and even direct mail solicitations. An online seminar is a great opportunity to toot your own horn. The value of the publicity you get will exceed the value of the seminar attendance.

Narrow your focus. My number one gripe with most online seminars is that the topics they cover are too broad to be handled well in the time given. Resist the temptation to offer programs on huge topics such as buying a house, starting a business, financial planning, or raising a child. When you narrow the topic, you actually increase interest in the seminar. Sometimes less is better.

CHAPTER 8

Web Site Registration and Linkage

Web site registration and linkage build the infrastructure upon which all online marketing depends. They are the first stage of Web site promotion, creating a network that makes it easy for people to find your site. With strong initial campaigns and ongoing maintenance, these gateways will help you achieve a dominant position in your industry.

The world of directory registration was thrown into chaos with the dot.com crash of 2000. In a frenzy of consolidation, major directories disappeared, changed names, and merged so that many seemingly independent sites ran off the same database. The desperate search for revenue has pulled us into the era of the paid placement. Directories now charge for admission, search engines charge for position, and cheap registration robots are no longer a viable option.

The role that linkage plays in the marketing mix is stronger than ever thanks to search engines using inbound links as a measure of popularity and relevance. Low-profile linkage campaigns are still undervalued by marketers, however. Companies spend a far greater portion of their online marketing budgets on search engine optimization than linkage, although a few well-placed links bring more and higher-quality traffic than search engines.

This chapter will show you how to conduct low-cost, common-sense registration, search engine optimization, and linkage campaigns. By the time this chapter is over, you'll probably rearrange the priorities for your online marketing budget, and you'll have more of that budget left for the kinds of advanced promotional campaigns that will make your listings and links crackle with traffic.

Subjects covered include the following:

Who do you want at your site? The answers might surprise you. I'll roast some sacred cows, such as "one-to-one marketing," and suggest less-ambitious, more effective strategies for online marketing success.

How people find your site. Shouldn't you know how your target audience will locate your site before you start spending money to lure traffic? We'll penetrate the Web wilderness, stalking the mysterious surfer to study its browsing habits.

Search engine optimization. Learn why search engine optimization is the most overrated game in cyberia, and learn the simple techniques you can use once a year to strengthen your position without losing your sanity.

Web site registration. You have to pay for listings and position, but otherwise the techniques remain the same. I'll show you how to prepare a registration form that collects all the information you need and then how to handle a campaign yourself or hire a pro.

The linkage campaign. The turtle in the race for online dominance, the linkage campaign is slow and not very glamorous, but it lasts a long time and will help you pass your rivals at the finish line. Learn how to find the best sites online and write a linkletter that Web masters can't refuse.

Who Do You Want at Your Site?

If only more people seriously addressed this question, how many billions of dollars in Web development costs could have been redirected to more profitable pursuits? For years, the knee-jerk reaction to the Internet was first, "We need a Web site," followed quickly by "We need more traffic." That last edict has led to millions of dollars squandered in fruitless search engine optimization efforts. So before I explain how to use registration and linkage techniques to bring more people to your site, let's examine the question of whether you really want them to visit.

The Public

In answer to the key question posed earlier, many people think they want everyone to come to their sites. Really? If your goal is traffic, then you should put pictures of naked people on your site. Most Web masters do not want to become purveyors of porn; in truth, they want a certain *kind* of traffic. Once you begin this process of narrowing the target audience, you'll arrive at intelligent strategies for bringing *selected* people to your site.

For some sites, raw traffic is important. These sites are supported by banner advertising, and more traffic translates directly into more dollars. Or does it? Banner advertising rates vary based on the characteristics of the audience that surfs your site. While generic banner ads can be purchased for fewer than $5 per 1,000 impressions (CPM), I know of medical specialty sites that get between $200 and $300 CPM. The amount of money you can make from banner advertising is more dependent on the perceived demographics of your audience than on your traffic numbers. With the crash of the banner advertising market in the past couple of years, sites that earn revenues based on traffic alone are disappearing.

There are still sites that would like to appeal to the largest general public possible, within reason. That last caveat means these sites aren't willing to install content that could damage their ad rates or jeopardize their long-term viability (by attracting lawsuits, for example). The main contenders in this department are search engines and directories. Half of the top 20 high-traffic domains are sites that help you find things online. They aren't destination sites so much as intermediaries. While it's difficult for any new site to get a foothold in this market, there are some lessons to be learned.

First, high-traffic sites are extremely useful to browsers; if your site is extremely useful, you can expect strong repeat traffic. Second, there is a market for special-interest directories that is underserved by the major general-interest directories. If you can develop and maintain a quality directory in a niche area, you cannot only generate substantial traffic, but that traffic will also be concentrated around the topic of your directory, enabling you to command a higher CPM for advertising. Many companies are trying this strategy, so the competition is intense and the costs of maintaining quality are high. One of the great experiments in this area is About.com, a Web site composed of niche subject guides/directories. If you survey the field and don't believe you could do a better job than About.com or a similar competitor, you should stay out of this market.

Consumers

Narrowing your focus from the general public to consumers seems like a good idea, but do you really want consumers of your products to be frequent visitors to your Web site? Think about your answer carefully. A lot has been written about companies developing one-to-one relationships with consumers, but I'm willing to bet most big companies want no part of that trend.

How much staff do you need to have a one-to-one relationship with all the people who consume your products and services? Hopefully, you won't need a literally one-to-one relationship. If you promise that level of personalized service but can't realistically deliver it, you'll generate more disappointment than good will with your effort. Perhaps that's why Southwest Airlines doesn't provide *any* e-mail addresses at its Web site: Southwest doesn't want one-to-one relationships with consumers; it wants to sell tickets as cheaply as possible and as quickly as possible.

Why do consumers want to visit the Web sites of producers? In many cases, it's to get help using products. But the Web sites of producers are often unable to handle the volume of requests. Have you tried the "Help" button at Yahoo! lately? You won't get an e-mail address. Instead, you'll get a catalog of FAQs (frequently asked questions). One of those FAQs is, "Why isn't there an email address I can use to ask support questions?" The real answer, of course, is that Yahoo! can't deal with the volume of e-mail. If you drill down far enough, you will find a Customer Care Form, but Yahoo! warns that you'll get an auto reply. If you respond to the auto reply, they'll consider answering your question. Don't hold your breath.

Another big reason for a consumer to visit a producer's Web site is to complain about a product. Again, most companies don't have the staff to handle these complaints. What's more, the *Federal Trade Commission* (FTC) has regulations requiring companies to respond to complaints within a reasonable period of time. It didn't take more than a few FTC inquiries for automakers to disable the feedback links on their Web sites. Today, it's rare to find feedback links at manufacturers' Web sites, and most inquiries result in a form e-mail acknowledgement that satisfies regulatory requirements without specifically addressing the consumer's needs. These e-mails usually direct the consumer to toll-free phone numbers, dealer outlets, and other established channels for handling customer-service inquiries.

Some companies really do want consumers of their products to visit. Consumers can provide vital feedback about how a product is used, any bugs it might have, or ideas for improving products. Software makers, for example, typically encourage the formation of user groups to help reduce the costs of product development, testing, and customer service. Microsoft not only encourages such behavior but rewards the best guides that surface in its user groups.

Customers and Prospects

Now we're getting somewhere. Many companies want to use their Web sites to reach customers and prospects directly. While there are still problems handling service inquiries over the Internet, these companies are willing to absorb the costs for the privilege of communicating with customers. Part of the planning process for the Web site involves figuring out who your customers are. It's harder than you think.

For many companies, customers are not consumers of the product. Rather, they are wholesalers, distributors, and retailers. When the Web first appeared, a lot of manufacturers thought they had finally found a way to sell directly to consumers, cut out the intermediaries, and keep a higher portion of the retail price for themselves. They built Web sites to attract retail customers. And they wasted an enormous amount of money with this strategy.

A lot of retail customers don't want one-to-one relationships with manufacturers. I don't want a relationship with Colgate, and I don't plan to ever buy directly from them. If I had to shop separately for every product in my household, I would go nuts. I want to go to big stores that stock lots of products where I can buy everything all at once. Let the stores have a relationship with the manufacturers. Possessed with greed, many manufacturers built Web sites to court consumers who don't want to shop there while simultaneously angering and ignoring trade customers who *do* want to shop online. Let me give an example that hits close to home.

The response of many book publishers to the Internet was to build Web sites designed to get readers to buy books directly. Of course, this situation upset wholesalers and retail stores. The public, however, is having no part of it. They want to shop at Amazon.com or Barnes & Noble Online, where they get good prices, service, and selection. Publishers spent millions on fancy entertainment sites to court consumers who don't want to shop at publisher stores while turning their backs on retailers and wholesalers who buy hundreds and thousands of books from them every month.

Yes, it's a good idea to build Web sites that serve your customers. But you need to know who your customers are. In many cases, the same purchasing chains will exist in a post-Internet world as existed before. They'll just be more efficient.

The Trade

Besides retail and wholesale outlets, there are many other trading partners who should be attracted to your site. A big category is suppliers: people from whom you buy products and services. As the initial entertainment phase of the Internet has cooled, the infrastructure phase is heating up. There's more than one way to increase profits. Companies are realizing that they have more to gain using the Internet to reduce costs rather than increase sales.

"Supply-chain management" is a trendy term you've probably heard a lot recently. That's because the Internet is streamlining procurement processes, helping companies reduce inventories and overhead costs. At least some of your online marketing efforts should be devoted to communicating the advantages of using your Web site to suppliers and other trade contacts. If nothing else, online trade directories should be included in both your registration and linkage campaigns.

Investors

We're really getting down to the nitty-gritty now. Investors are owners of the company, and naturally they would like to have their needs met at the Web site. That doesn't mean you want to attract them to your site, however, because you still have the problems of dealing with more feedback than you can handle. Disgruntled shareholders can make processing Web inquiries a nightmare. But you can satisfy the needs of most investors and potential investors without the kind of handholding that consumers often require.

Just as there are two kinds of customers (the retail customer who buys one of an item and the trade account who buys thousands), there are two kinds of investors: individuals with a few shares of stock and institutional buyers who might hold substantial stakes. The Web site should focus on the needs of analysts and large stakeholders while satisfying regulatory requirements for the fair disclosure of material news. By moving some investor relations operations to the Internet and communicating those capabilities to the target audience, you can reduce costs and improve results for this important department.

An understanding that investors are an important audience for the Web site leads to clever ideas such as including your stock ticker symbol in online directory listings and in the META tags on your Web site. You might also want to register the Investor Relations portion of your site separately from the main home page and include IR sites in a linkage campaign.

The Media

The media is an important target audience for most Web sites. A site that does a good job serving customers and suppliers will likely satisfy media contacts as well—as long as there is adequate contact information for press inquiries at the site. Some sites have gone overboard building newsrooms and press centers when all they really need is an up-to-date list of press contacts and to make sure that media inquiries are processed quickly. This situation is another area of overspending on Web sites that the target audience (the working press) doesn't really use.

If you want the media at your Web site, it's a good idea to reach out to them with Web site registration and linkage campaigns. There are many directories online that appeal to journalists and other media contacts. GuestFinder is an example. GuestFinder is a directory of potential talk show guests marketed to radio and TV producers. Figure 8.1 shows the results of a GuestFinder search for cancer experts. The directory is searchable by keyword, month, or area code. There are other directories that list experts on any given topic for the benefit of journalists looking for an authoritative quote or trade show organizers looking for a talented act.

How People Find Your Site

Now that we've examined the kinds of people you want to attract to your site, let's look at another piece of the puzzle: how do people find your site? The answer might change your whole approach to Web site marketing.

Figure 8.1 GuestFinder search results. GuestFinder is an example of a Web site directory that services the needs of media professionals.

Search Engines and Directories

There's a misconception that most people find sites by using the major search engines and directories. While statistics are hard to come by, I've heard enough anecdotal evidence in online marketing discussion groups to feel comfortable saying that less than a third of the traffic at most sites will come from these search engines. And the numbers I've heard are for large sites that have pursued aggressive search engine optimization techniques. For the vast majority of sites that do not engage in search engine optimization, the amount of traffic generated by these sites will be insignificant.

A second point is that the traffic coming from search engines tends to be the least focused of all incoming traffic to your site. People typing in your domain name, using a URL on a business card, responding to an advertisement, or following a link from another site are looking specifically for your site, whereas most people coming through search engines are looking for content they *hope* to find on your site. Once they see your site, they're likely to immediately return to the search engine and look for a better match. So not only is the volume of traffic generated by these listings small, it's also of poor quality.

While it's important to be included in major online directories so that people looking specifically for your site can find you, it's not important for most companies to have a prominent position. If one-tenth of the money squandered on search engine optimization were spent improving content, most of those sites would not only have more traffic, but the traffic would linger for more than a few fleeting moments. For Internet-based companies in aggressive competition with other online businesses, search engine rank is important. For 99 percent of the world's businesses, it means *nothing*.

Domain Name

A lot of folks will first try typing your company name into their Web browsers and see whether that works. The importance of a good Web address fueled the domain-name boom of the late 1990s, culminating in the sale of a single domain for more than $10 million (business.com). For better branding, many corporations changed the company name to the Web address, and this method might have been a good strategy for Internet-only companies. Now that dot.coms are out of favor, companies are scurrying to change their names again so they aren't stigmatized as non-revenue-generating businesses.

The reality for most companies is that the domain name doesn't matter. What does the name "Amazon" have to do with books or the name "Yahoo!" with searching? If what the company offers is in demand and the company has a quality Web site, it can work with almost any name. One of my clients, Book Stacks Unlimited, had the coveted URL "books.com," but that didn't stop Amazon.com from rolling over them. The URL was subsequently sold to Barnes & Noble Online. Another client called me one day and asked whether I thought they should spend a million and a half dollars on a certain domain name. That's when I realized I was in the wrong business. I should have been buying up domain names years ago, like some of my friends. I advised my client to put the money into building a quality site and marketing, making their brand name synonymous with the category as Amazon.com and Yahoo! had done.

As more domain name extensions come online and more dot.coms file for bankruptcy, the prices of good domains are coming down. It might be worth investing in a perfect name if the price is right. Some companies have successfully sued to get ownership of domain names for their brands. Another route is to buy "pseudo domains." For example, a company called "Johnson Plumbing" might be able to buy "johnson.plumbing.com" or "johnsonplumbing.business.com." These tricks greatly expand the number of good domain alternatives, though some suffer from not being acceptable to search engines. Sites such as Search Engine Watch provide a much more in-depth analysis of domain name issues than I can cover here.

Stationery and Collateral

This simple marketing vehicle is the most important and least-expensive way to generate Web site traffic. Printing your Web address on business cards, letterheads, statements, invoices, packing slips, mailing labels, reports, faxes, envelopes, and so on will lead to the highest-quality traffic at your site. Why? The answer is, because all these documents go to people who do business with you on a regular basis. This audience is the core audience for your Web site: people with whom you already have a relationship. Printing your URL on everything lets them know you're open for business online. And people will often have one of these documents nearby when they're ready to visit your site or will be able to put their hands on one quickly.

Think of your own behavior. When you get a bill you don't like, do you log onto the Internet, go to a search engine, type in the company name, and sift through the search results looking for the right link? I doubt it. You probably either pick up the phone or take the offending invoice to the computer and copy the URL into your browser. When I want to make changes to insurance policies, review my cable TV options, or bank online, I don't go to a search engine to find the site. If you want to buy something from a catalog over the Internet, do you go to a search engine to find the vendor? I'm guessing 95 percent of my spending is with companies I have a relationship with and whose URLs I either know, can guess, or have near me on a document of some sort.

Of course, I use search engines and directories to do research, to find information about subjects of interest to me, to get price quotes, or to comparison shop. But even then, most of the sites that turn up as matches to my search will not get a visit from me, much less any business. Sites that I visit in response to an ad, a recommendation from another site, or a business card in my hand are much more likely to get a fair hearing and eventually some of my hard-earned dollars. The intimidating number of matches to search engine queries and the high number of disappointing or broken links has led me to use these services as a last resort. While it's dangerous to project my own surfing habits on the general population, I've seen no evidence in online marketing discussion groups that search engine rank has had a significant impact on many businesses. Some companies, such as sex-related sites, travel services, and lenders, do benefit from search engine positions, which is why they purchase premium positions on these sites.

Links from Other Sites

More valuable than search engine position are links to your site from other compatible sites. At my own Web site, I generate more traffic from a well-placed link in an AOL forum than I do from all the search engines combined. Traffic coming from links on other sites is prefiltered; they have some idea of what I offer, and they're interested. Having a site that other influential sites link to is now a major factor in search engine rank, so not only do you benefit from the links, but you also get a better position in search engines. An ongoing linkage campaign should be part of every Web site's marketing efforts. I'll talk much more about this topic in the Linkage Campaign section next. For now, just keep in mind that linkage is the second most important source of traffic after stationery and collateral.

Media Coverage

Any media coverage of your company—good or bad—is likely to increase your Web site traffic. You don't have to limit yourself to campaigns to announce a new Web site. You can hang a news release on any kind of event, whether it's the launch of a new product or a chat tour you are sponsoring. Calendar listings for online events are productive, reliable ways of getting your URL out to the public. Many Web sites offer free event listings, such as regional city sites, trade publication sites, Internet access portals, and online event calendars. When you get a calendar listing at these sites, you usually get a link as well, thus improving your rank in search engines that tally linkage. The importance of linkage demonstrates the value of planning a continuous stream of online events, such as a quarterly or monthly workshop or seminar series, keeping your links active in all those calendars. The events don't even have to be hosted at your site; many media outlets will use your URL for more information about events taking place on third-party sites.

It goes without saying, I hope, that every news release you issue should include the URL of your Web site. It's a good idea to offer something extra beyond the news release that can be found at the Web site. You want to provide a reason for the media to include your URL in their coverage and a reason for the target audience to visit the site. For example, if announcing a news conference, you'll want to mention that transcripts or the full text of speeches will be available at the Web site.

One problem with most media coverage is that people watching television, listening to the radio, or reading a newspaper or magazine will forget your URL. In the early days of the Internet, broadcasters would recite URLs over the air, sometimes even spelling them out. Thankfully, this trend has abated as the public expects every company to have a Web site now and expects the site name to be somewhat intuitive. This issue of discontinuity between hearing about a site and visiting it argues in favor of an easy domain name as well as good directory registration procedures.

Active Promotion

The key to driving the target audience to your Web site is to first build an infrastructure through stationery, directory registration, and linkage, then to get your name out there with regular promotions. Promotions usually focus on new or temporary features at your site, giving the target audience reasons to return to the site. This book is filled with ideas for different Web site promotions, most of which can be pulled off on a modest budget. They include chats, seminars, workshops, news conferences, online presentations, offering documents, contests, and stupid Web tricks. While many companies take the lazy route of putting these promotions on their own Web sites, a better strategy is to seed the Internet with promotions on partner sites that are attractive to your target audience. Not only will these syndicated promotions draw more traffic to *your site*, but they will help you form lasting promotional partnerships and lead to better search engine positions through a higher linkage rating.

Active promotions provide reasons to issue news releases, increasing media coverage for your site. They generate calendar listings for additional media coverage. Most of the promotions I suggest in this book are Internet-friendly, too. Unlike direct e-mail marketing, which will increase traffic but is also fraught with danger, these campaigns are unlikely to lead to legal problems, complaints, or retaliation.

Analyzing Site Traffic

When I built my first Web site, I got a Hit Report every week from my Web master that gave me all kinds of information about activity at my site. You should contact your Web master and see whether you can get the same kind of report. If the tracking reports you get from your Web master are confusing, you should consider purchasing software that will render the raw numbers more meaningful. You can also find information on the Internet by searching for "Web site traffic analysis software" or similar terms. The main online marketing supersites, such as ClickZ, www.clickz.com, and the Online Advertising Discussion Group, www.o-a.com, are loaded with articles about traffic analysis and discussions of the significance of these findings. You'll find links to these sites and other online marketing supersites at the companion web site for this book.

You can learn a great deal about the kinds of people that come to your site, their reasons for coming, and where they come from by analyzing your own traffic statistics. Figure 8.2 shows the source domains for traffic from an old Web log of mine. For the week shown, I had 135 hits from South Africa. If nothing else convinces you of the amazing international reach of the Internet, your own hit report should do the trick.

Figure 8.3 is a portion of my hit report by subdomain. You really have to love the way computers can crunch these kinds of numbers. After "unresolved," my next highest hit source is "com.aol.proxy," otherwise known as AOL. CompuServe is right up there, too. A lot of marketing people ignore the commercial online services, thinking they've got the Internet covered if they have a Web site. But the numbers do not lie. Ever since I did a live chat on America Online, I get thousands of hits from AOL every month.

The subdomain report is very useful. When I see one, two, or three hits, I figure someone just wandered into my site or is mildly curious. When I see double-digit hits, I know I'm being seriously scoped. I usually get a phone call or e-mail soon after.

```
Total Transfers by Client Domain

Bytes Sent   Requests   Domain
------------ ---------|----------------------
      69520        20 | au    Australia
     377982        72 | be    Belgium
      84611        27 | br    Brazil
     501603        92 | ca    Canada
     184214        39 | ee    Estonia
     100487        23 | il    Israel
     100483        22 | it    Italy
      26186        12 | se    Sweden
     256760        61 | uk    United Kingdom
     912781       135 | za    South Africa
    6182285      1213 | com   US Commercial
    3116009       706 | edu   US Educational
    6644833      1170 | net   Network
    7366762      1513 | unresolved
```

Figure 8.2 A portion of a weekly traffic report from my Web site showing the originating domains for the traffic. Analyzing the countries of origin can tip you off to global marketing opportunities, among other things.

Traffic reports will tell you what pages people viewed on your site, how much time they spent at your site, the average number of pages viewed per visit, and so on. You can analyze these numbers to death, and sometimes the results are misleading. For example, a high number of pages viewed per visit could be a good sign that visitors like your site or a bad sign that your site is so poorly designed it's hard to find the content they came for. But the logs will certainly give you a good idea of the sources of your traffic and persuade you of the value of linkage and site partnerships.

Search Engine Optimization

While I think the emphasis on search engine position is totally out of proportion to its value, there are many simple things you can and should do to improve your ranking. For serious guidance on this matter, there is no finer authority than Search Engine Watch at www.searchenginewatch.com/. Started by arachnophiliac Danny Sullivan, a relentless student of "spiders" and "crawlers," as search engines are known, the site is now part of the Internet.com family of resources. The site contains dozens of useful articles on both a free and fee basis and newsletters with an impressive subscriber base of more than 150,000.

While I'm sure Danny Sullivan would disagree with the low value I place on search engine rank, he recognizes that the real beneficiaries of this practice are a small group of highly competitive companies. At the bottom of the core article on Search Engine Placement Tips at his site—after explaining all the rules for improving search engine position—Sullivan writes, "Also, remember that while search engines *are* a primary

Total Transfers by Reversed Subdomain

Requests	Bytes Sent	Reversed Subdomain
1513	7366762	Unresolved
361	1740399	com.aol.proxy
107	533768	com.compuserve
2	4684	com.gwis
3	12780	com.netcom.ix
14	99731	com.netconnect-inc
15	81375	com.prodigy
18	89499	edu.berkeley.cs
2	6324	edu.colorado.cs
22	103885	edu.dcccd.201.144
1	2729	edu.harvard.student
8	29438	edu.utexas.ots
2	5460	net.bluefin
14	29673	net.charm
13	80547	net.micron.boi
105	504616	net.olympus
56	113033	net.slip
6	24410	net.usa.den1-annex
1	2733	net.uu.ms.ma.boston.max5
3	12159	net.uu.ms.ma.boston.max7
5	26834	net.wis.vcr
4	20216	uk.ac.lancs
35	191278	za.co.global

Figure 8.3 A portion of my Web site traffic log showing the sites (subdomains) from where my traffic is originating. These reports can help you identify potential customers while evaluating the impact of various promotional campaigns.

way people look for web sites, but they are not the *only* way. People also find sites through word-of-mouth, traditional advertising, the traditional media, newsgroup postings, Web directories and links from other sites. Many times, these alternative forms are far more effective draws than are search engines."

Let's examine, then, how these search engines operate and see whether we can come up with a good strategy for optimizing search engine position without losing your sanity.

Myths and Realities

There are about a dozen important Internet search tools, and they break into two main groups: the directories and the search engines. Directories are compiled more or less by human beings and work a lot like business phone books: They organize sites into topical categories, such as Florists or Bakeries. The mother of all online directories is

Yahoo! Other directories include LookSmart, Lycos, AOL Search, NBCi (formerly Snap), and Open Directory (dmoz). These directories list the sites submitted to them, after staff review, and sometimes include staff-written site descriptions. While some search engine optimization techniques apply to directories, the techniques for courting these sites are more directly covered in the Registration section later in this chapter.

True search engines are called spiders or crawlers because they move out onto the Web every night and every day, indexing the content they find to provide you with a list of matching sites for any query. Popular search engines include AltaVista, Excite, Google, Ask Jeeves, All The Web (FAST), and Inktomi. These search engines have a set of criteria they use to match a query to relevant sites. Learning the secrets of this indexing criteria, then exploiting that knowledge for better positioning, is the science of *search engine optimization* (SEO).

As a result of the dot.com crash of 2000, there are major changes happening in the Web searching infrastructure that you should be aware of. These changes will make some of the information provided here obsolete in short order while other tips will gain in relevance. Last time I polished my crystal ball, in the book *Publicity on the Internet* in 1997, I predicted that, "In the future, you can expect to pay for everything except the tiniest little listing buried way down deep in Yahoo. You'll pay for listing, for position, for frequency, for formatting, for space." Well, friends, today is the future, and that's our first major caveat: the era of the paid placement is upon us.

As I write this book, all of the major catalogs, directories, and search engines are either selling premium positions on search results pages (see Figure 8.4) or plan to

Figure 8.4 The results page for a search at LookSmart begins with four paid listings. Almost all the online directories and search engines have started selling premium positioning.

start selling them soon, with the exception of the Open Directory Project (also known as DMOZ). And Yahoo! is now charging even for that buried listing in its business sections. In many ways, charging for inclusion and premium position has made life easier. Before, you had to wait months to get into Yahoo!; now, your payment results in 48-hour service. And paid positioning is putting an end to the cat-and-mouse game between SEO artists and the search engines they try to manipulate. Instead of spending thousands of dollars outsmarting AltaVista's programmers, these companies will spend that much or more to guarantee a top spot in AltaVista's listings.

There will be problems implementing these revenue schemes. People conducting searches will routinely avoid the paid placements at the top of the list the same way they ignore the banner ads at the top of the page. If search engines and catalogs attempt to exclude those who don't pay for placement, their databases will eventually become useless and people will gravitate toward comprehensive catalogs and search engines that rise up to take their places, such as DMOZ. For these reasons, basic SEO techniques will still be valuable in getting your site near the top of the non-paid listings.

The second major result of the dot.com crash relevant to this discussion is the consolidation among search engines and directories. Deals are being cut and names are changing faster than you can say AOL Time Warner. If it seems like you get identical results at five different directories, it's because they're all powered by Inktomi or LookSmart. What is my prediction for the future? There will be three survivors: AOL, Yahoo!, and MSN—and they will have a stranglehold on 90 percent of the searching with just enough non-profit, renegade, geeky sites to satisfy the independent spirits among Web browsers.

Top SEO Techniques

Search engine optimization is mostly a matter of common sense and attention to details. Spiders and crawlers search a site looking for standard indexing information. This information is contained primarily in three "tags" at the top of HTML documents: the Title tag, which contains the title of a page; the Description tag, which has a short description of the contents of a page; and the Keywords tag, which contains keywords related to the content on a page. Next, the crawler checks these tags against the content of the page to make sure the tags accurately reflect the content. Keywords are important elements in all three tags, so let's start there.

Keywords Tag

When choosing keywords for a site, try to think of words or phrases that the target audience would use when looking for your site. Obvious keywords relate to the content of your site: the industry you're in, brand names for products you sell, and content you feature at the site. You'll also want to include proper names, such as the name of a well-known company president or spokesperson, your stock ticker symbol, or any nicknames or anagrams for your company name. Another approach is to include words associated with the target audience for your site. Let's take a look at the keywords tag used by Search Engine Watch to see how the pros do it:

```
<meta name="keywords" content="listings search engine watch web site,
danny sullivan editor internet.com using meta tags improving place-
ment, how to submit urls to major internet search engines webmaster's
guide, rankings search engine registration tips for searching better
reviews, tutorials technology report free newsletter, news articles
placement engine submission online help www.searchenginewatch.com">
```

I don't follow SEO techniques closely enough to know all the nuances contained in this keywords section. You might wonder why you don't include every word in the dictionary as a keyword. As with most elements of SEO, if you overdo it, you will be penalized by the crawlers and possibly excluded from their indexes. This list is exactly 50 words (the URL counts as three words), so I would suggest that as a limit for your own efforts.

I'm guessing Sullivan "wasted" two keywords on *web site* because people using search engines will often include this qualifier in their search strings when they're looking for a specific *site* and not documents. Most of his keywords relate to activities his target audience is interested in: improving placement, submit URLs, and so on. A couple terms relate to the target audience: webmaster, editor. Three important buzz words—*free, help,* and *news*—are also included.

The biggest lesson in the keywords tag is how often the site's most important words are repeated. The words *search* and *engine* each appear five times. Other repeated words include *internet, news, watch,* and *submit.* The commas breaking up the tag appear to be strategically placed about every six or eight words and have little to do with grammar. The phrasing is awkward, but I know that one of the goals of SEO is to focus on *phrases* people will use when looking for your site, rather than *words.* You have almost no chance of holding onto a high search engine rank for single words such as *car* or *hotel,* so you're better off focusing on phrases.

Some things you don't see in the Search Engine Watch keyword tag are the proper names of competing services. You can get in legal hot water for using the trade names of competitors in your META tags. You also don't see words like *sex* or *contest* that many people use search engines to find. First, there isn't any content on this Web site to justify those keywords, and a crawler would penalize the site for that. Second, Danny Sullivan wants to attract his target audience to the site; he's not interested in pumping up his traffic numbers with people coming to the site expecting to find something that's not there.

It's worth brainstorming a fair amount on your keywords, because they'll be used for multiple activities. For example, when exporting content to other sites, you'll often be asked for keywords. Using the same keywords in content laced around the Internet will help strengthen your search engine position. One trick is to blurt out any word that pops into your head, using random association, and then cull the list. I frequently spew 100 keywords before whittling them down to the 10 words used in the Registration Form (described later in this chapter). The more fun you have with this process, the more likely you are to come up with clever keywords that work.

Description Tag

This tag should contain a brief description of the content of the page on which the tag appears. You should tweak the tag to more accurately reflect the content on each page of your site while still using most of your critical keywords. Let's take a look at the Description tag for the home page of Search Engine Watch:

```
<meta name="description" content="Search Engine Watch is the
authoritative guide to searching at Internet search engines and
search engine registration and ranking issues. Learn to submit
URLs, use HTML meta tags and boost placement.">
```

The word *search* appears four times, *engine* appears three times, and other important keywords such as *meta tags, submit, placement, registration,* and *rankings* got in there. The prose isn't exactly lucid, but the sentences are not just a slew of keywords. The description is relatively short at 31 words. Probably of greater importance is the number of characters. This description is 199 characters, which suggests that 200 characters is Danny's limit. Many search engines will return the Description tag along with the title of the page for each item on a search results page. If the description is too long, it will be truncated. If it's a jumble of keywords, it won't communicate well with people deciding which link to follow on their search results page.

Title Tag

The Title tag provides the text that appears in the Title Bar at the top of every Web page. It's amazing how many people do not use the Title tag on their pages or use it very badly. When you bookmark a site, the title of the page becomes the name of the bookmark. Have you ever bookmarked a Web page, then looked at your bookmarks to see an entry for <no title> or <order form>? That's so irritating! When building pages, I always include either the name of the company or the name of the Web site on every page of the site. Then, I'll use the rest of the tag to tell people where they are on the site. If someone bookmarks any page on the site, the name of the bookmark will include the name of the company or Web site.

Danny Sullivan and other SEO pros take a different approach. The contents of the Title tag are important to search engine position, so they use the tag strategically to improve their positions. They pile as many keywords as they can into the title of each page. Here's the Title tag from the home page of Search Engine Watch:

```
<title>Search Engine Watch: Tips About Internet Search Engines &
Search Engine Submission</title>
```

There are those magic keywords again: *search* and *engine* three times each and *Internet* and *submission* once apiece. The title is 12 words and 82 characters. When people first learned how important the Title tag is to search engine position, they started filling them with reams of concrete poetry. Of course, the crawlers retaliated and started penalizing sites that had excessively long tags. I don't like long tags because they don't display fully in the small space provided at the top of Web pages, but I like them better than no tag at all. And generic titles such as *order form* or *articles* or *help* should be changed to include the company name or site name.

Other Simple Tips

Search engine spiders will compare the content of your tags with the content on the page, starting at the top of the page and working their way down. Therefore, to improve your search engine position, it's good to use a lot of your keywords in the text on the page, and it's particularly important to use them near the top of the page. Let's look at an example.

If you have a business selling SEO services and your site contains sections called *articles, resources, services,* and *prices,* you might want to change them to read *search engine optimization articles, search engine optimization resources, search engine optimization services,* and *search engine optimization prices.* With each page of your site, you want to squeeze in those keywords as often as possible while also making sure the tags reflect the content on the page.

Other things that can hurt your search engine position are pages with no content (splash pages) and content that is contained in graphics. Image maps mean nothing to Web crawlers. Every time you put important keywords inside a graphic, as is often done with navigational buttons, you hurt your search engine rank. As I've said, however, I don't think search engine rank is worth sacrificing the editorial integrity of your site or your site design. If you can easily accommodate SEO techniques, great, but with rare exceptions you shouldn't sacrifice your style or tone for minute gains in search engine position.

You will hear many stupid ideas for improving your search engine rank, and you should treat them all with caution. When people realized the importance of keywords, they started embedding them like wallpaper into the backgrounds of their sites. By making the text color the same as the background color, these words would be invisible to people visiting the site but very visible to search engine crawlers. So the search engines retaliated by locking out sites that use this technique. It's easy to get caught up in this battle for search engine position. Take a deep breath and remember to focus your energy on content first and marketing second. Use the easy SEO techniques described here, and leave the battle tactics for others.

Learning through Surveillance

One of the nice things about the web is that you can easily see what the professionals are doing with their META tags as I've done with Search Engine Watch in this chapter. It's a good idea to survey some of the top sites that depend on search engine position for their traffic. When visiting a site, pull down the *View Source* tab in your Web browser, and the code for the site will pop up. These pages can be intimidating to decipher. The META tags are always right at the top of the page, however. Figure 8.5 shows what the source code looks like for the META tags at Search Engine Watch. The three most important tags—Description, Keywords, and Title—are slightly highlighted in

```
<!DOCTYPE HTML PUBLIC "-//IETF//DTD HTML//EN">
<html>

<head>
<meta http-equiv="Content-Type" content="text/html; charset=windows-
<meta http-equiv="Content-Language" content="en-us">
<meta http-equiv="PICS-Label" content='(PICS-1.1 "http://www.rsac
<meta name="description" content="Search Engine Watch is the authorit
<meta name="keywords" content="listings search engine watch web site,
<title>Search Engine Watch: Tips About Internet Search Engines & Search
<base target="_top">


</head>

<body bgcolor="#FFFFFF" link="#0000FF" vlink="#000080" alink="#FF0(
<center>
```

Figure 8.5 Source code for the home page of Search Engine Watch. You can view the source code for any page on the Web for clues about how to improve your own META tags.

the graphic. The text inside these tags will extend beyond the edge of your window, so you might want to copy them into a word processing document where you can see them better and analyze the word count and character count.

One way to improve your META tags is to go to search engines and search by using the kinds of phrases your target audience would use when searching for your site. See which sites come up near the top of the non-paid listings, then visit those sites and look at their source code for clues on improving your META tags. You might not be able to improve your rank enough to dethrone these sites from their positions, and you probably shouldn't even try. But you should be able to substantially increase your position to get close to the top in the results.

Another trick is to visit the sites of your competitors and check their META tags. Not only will you learn a few things, but you'll also be able to see whether they are illegally using your brand names in their tags. I recommend performing an annual SEO check-up, with a quick survey of your search engine rank, the rank of your competitors, a little snooping into the tags other people are using, and brushing up with articles on the latest in SEO techniques. After surveying the field, you can freshen the META tags on key pages of your site and update the tags on any templates you are using to generate pages for your site.

The Importance of Linkage

In recent years, search engines have added another tool in their efforts to return top-quality results for online searches. As a measure of a site's popularity, they now tabulate how many links to your site they find on other people's sites. Now, it's less important how good your site is and more important how other people perceive it—or, at least, how readily other people link to it. This change in search engine strategy has given a big boost to the importance of linkage campaigns as a marketing strategy.

Because I cover linkage techniques in great detail later in this chapter, we'll pick up this discussion there.

Web Site Registration

Web site registration is the active process of getting your Web site listed in online catalogs, directories, and search engines. Search engines will find your site on their own, and you'll get a decent position in them just by using good tagging and design format (as described earlier). You will get your site listed more quickly, however, and be included in companion directories, if you submit the site for review at the major search engines.

The first rule of registration is to *make sure your site works* before submitting the URL to directories and search engines. This advice might sound obvious, but I've been employed several times by companies that insist I proceed with a registration campaign before their sites are finished or tested. In one case, a Web site was stored on a temporary server until testing was complete, but the company wanted me to register the final URL for the home page of the site. If you used that URL, you were automatically redirected to the test site. Most of the major directories rejected the listing, however, because there was no content at that specific URL. The campaign was a waste of time and money. Other times, sites were dysfunctional on the days directories went to verify the listing, and the registration was rejected.

You don't have to register a site the day it appears online. You can wait for weeks, months, or even years before conducting a registration campaign. It's a good idea to plan a grand opening for your site about a month after it goes online. That gives you time to work out all the bugs in the site and plan promotional activities in advance. Once you are confident the site is working fine, you can begin the registration campaign, starting with preparing the registration form.

The Registration Form

The registration form is a document I create for every registration effort that organizes all the materials I need for the campaign in one convenient place. A template for this form in Microsoft Word format is available at the Web site for this book, www.wiley.com/compbooks/okeefe. You can download this form and use it for your own efforts or create your own version by using the outline shown in Figure 8.6. Creating this form before you begin the process of registration will save you hours of time. Let's take a look at each element of the form and see how you should prepare it.

Company Information

The company's name and address should be the company that owns the site, not the company that manages it. This information is collected for telephone directory-style Web sites. The contact name is the person to contact if there is a problem with, or a question about, the site. This person is usually the Web master or the marketing person who is conducting the registration campaign.

REGISTRATION Form
Name: Company Name
Site Name: Name of Site
URL: http://www.url.com
Date: Today's Date

EXAMPLE

Each directory has its own way of listing your site. The most common listing consists of the site name (hyperlinked to your site) and the 25-word site description:

Internet Publicity Resources
Steve O'Keefe's award-winning site packed with help resources for anyone interested in Internet publicity and promotions. Updated weekly.

The rest of the data on your Registration Form may apply to only a few sites. If you have any questions about any of the material on the Registration Form, please ask.

INFORMATION ABOUT YOUR COMPANY

This information is used to register your company in online business directories. Some sites want the name and email address of the webmaster in case there are technical problems connecting to the site. The contact person might get e-mail confirming registration, or containing passwords needed to update a listing, or soliciting advertising. Most of these stock notices can be ignored and/or archived for later use.

Company Name, Address and Phone Numbers:
Company Name
Mailing Address
City, State, Zip
Toll Free: 1-800-555-1212
Voice: (212) 555-1212
Fax: (212) 555-1212

Contact Name, E-mail Address, and Phone Number:
Web Site Administrator
E-Mail: webmaster@ mysite.com
Voice: (212) 555-1212

INFORMATION ABOUT YOUR WEB SITE

50-Word Description of Service:
Steve O'Keefe's award winning site packed with help resources for anyone interested in Internet publicity and promotions. Updated weekly. O'Keefe is the author of the "Complete Guide to Internet Publicity" (Wiley). Includes articles and resources for web site promotion, news releases, chat tours, online events, and other Internet publicity campaigns.

25-Word Description of Service:
Steve O'Keefe's award winning site packed with help resources for anyone interested in Internet publicity and promotions. Updated weekly.

10-Word Description of Service:
Award-winning site packed with free publicity resources.

Keywords for META Tags (Limit 50):
internet publicity resources online promotion marketing publicize web sites, steve o'keefe okeefe, online media relations email news releases, chat show production online seminars workshops, linkage campaigns web site registration search engine optimization, events tours contests promotions, awards submission postings, publicist webmaster ad agency communications resources, syndication brokering partnerships strategic planning

Keywords for Search Engines (Limit 10):
publicity, promotion, marketing, advertising, online, internet, resources, o'keefe, okeefe, media

Cataloging:
Path 1: Internet / Marketing / Resources or Consultants
Path 2: Online Resources / Business / Internet or Marketing
Path 3: Business / Marketing / Online Resources

Figure 8.6 The registration form organizes all the information you need for a registration campaign in one convenient location. A template of this form in Microsoft Word format is available at www.wiley.com/compbooks/okeefe.

Site Descriptions

The 50-word description is for directories that give you a little room to stretch out. You should start by writing the 50-word description, then pare it down to 25 words and then to 10 words. The description has a different purpose than the one used in your

Description META tag. This description is intended for a directory listing and should be composed for readability. The META tag description is designed to appeal to spiders and crawlers and is loaded with keywords, repetition, and convoluted phrasing.

The point of your listing is *not* to describe your site. This lesson is the hardest thing for Internet novices to understand (which means it took me a long time to figure out). The point of your listing is to entice your target audience into activating that hotlink. You have to think about who the target audience is. You have to write something that pushes their hot buttons if you want them to push yours. Let's look at a couple examples.

Figure 8.7 shows some Yahoo! listings for freelance writers. "Dial-A-Speech" is a bare link, wasting an opportunity to lure browsers to their site. "Ah! SpeechWriters," on the other hand, mentions social, business, and sporting events and tells you that it delivers by e-mail. If I were looking for a speech writer, I'd start with Ah!

In registration, words are precious. If the title of your Web site is "My Site," then you don't want to start your description with the words, "My Site is a . . . " You also don't need to duplicate words found in your URL. If the URL for "My Site" is www.company.com, then you might not want to use the word "company" in your description or keywords. This situation is unlike META tags, where you want to repeat keywords as often as possible.

Rare is the Web site that benefits from a lot of traffic. The more visitors you have, the more server space you need, and that can get expensive. Unless you're an entertainment site looking for advertising revenue, it's probably best to attract qualified browsers. Do you use your site to give out introductory information or to serve existing customers? Tailor your registration to narrow the audience to your best prospects. Let's look at a few more Yahoo! registrations.

Figure 8.8 shows partial results of a Yahoo! search for "piano retailers." Carl's Music qualifies their entry with the geographical area served: northern Delaware. This constraint should cut down on the number of hits from unlikely customers across the planet. M. Steinert & Sons does the same thing, attempting to attract an audience in eastern Massachusetts while specifically mentioning the Steinway brand.

None of the piano listings are particularly lyrical or clever. It's worth taking some time to think about who you want to attract to your site and then writing some powerful prose to draw them in. You can look in any direct marketing book for a list of

- Absolute Communications, Inc - ACI develops content for business and consumer information systems, proposals, strategic plans, and Net sites.
- Ah! SpeechWriters - Speeches for all social, business and sporting occasions e-mailed straight to you.
- Apposite Systems - we also translate from English into foreign languages.
- Bill Walthall - a freelance consultant in the areas of design, writing, and training.
- Communication Strategies NEW! - provides corporate writing, publication planning, and communications counsel for businesses, including: annual report writing, employee and customer publications, company profiles, and internet training.
- Dial-A-Speech

Figure 8.7 Sample listings from Yahoo!'s directory of freelance writers. You can learn a lot from viewing competing listings in directories, then fashioning your site description to stand out.

- <u>Carl's Music</u> - Piano tunings in the northern Delaware area by a professional pianist/singer.
- <u>Immanuel Piano</u> - Featuring finest names in piano, synthesizer, organs, and digital piano.
- <u>Ito Piano Atelier</u> - selling and maintaining pianos.
- <u>M. Steinert & Sons</u> NEW! - Steinert sells some of the world's finest accoustic and digital pianos. We are the exclusive Steinway dealer in Eastern Massachusetts.

Figure 8.8 Sample listings from Yahoo!'s directory of piano retailers. By narrowing your focus to people in a certain region or mentioning the brands you carry, you are more likely to attract the exact target audience you're hoping for.

power words that trigger a response: new, hot, fast, free, low-fat, sex . . . these words can be overdone, but you get the general idea. Just remember you are trying to entice, not describe.

You need to exercise care that your description doesn't include some temporary feature of your site. If you're running a contest offering a free trip to China, you'll have to change your registration as soon as the contest is over. It can take weeks if not months to update or correct a listing.

Once you have a 50-word description, cut it down to 25 words, then 10 words. The 25-word description will be the one you use most often, so focus your efforts on getting it just right. It's a good idea to browse Yahoo! and other directories for ways to stand out from your competitors and find ideas you might not have thought of. The 10-word description is for stingy directories.

Keywords and Cataloging

The keywords used for META tags should be repetitive and should focus on phrases people will use when looking for your site. From this 50-word list, you pare down to 10 essential keywords that you use when submitting your page to sites. This list is not repetitive and focuses on single words rather than phrases. Both keyword lists should start with your best words and work down from there. That way, if the list gets truncated, you won't lose your best words. So not only are the words themselves important, but their order is also important.

The science of choosing keywords and categories involves guessing exactly how your target audience is likely to search for your site. If you are a manufacturer of cooking utensils, you don't have a chance of competing with other sites for a match on the word *cooking*. Premium positioning for that word will be sold to numerous sites willing to pay the price, and non-paid listings will go to aggressive SEO artists who are willing to pay someone to constantly fine-tune their page design and META tags to achieve a top listing.

Anyone with much experience searching online is not going to search for *cooking* nowadays, because the resulting matches are too numerous and unfocused. Concentrate your effort on appropriate phrases, such as *retailer of cooking utensils* or *stores selling cutlery*. If your Internet business is miniscule and your focus is increasing sales at the retail outlet, then include geographical keywords such as *northeast, Maine*, or *Portland ME*.

When choosing categories, it's best to think about how someone who is *unfamiliar* with your business would look for you. People who regularly do business with you should be able to find your URL on your business cards, letterhead, or in ads. You'll mostly attract new prospects from your directory listings. For important directories such as Yahoo!, you should look over the categories carefully and try to find a way to stand out from the crowd.

Some sites allow you to register in multiple categories. But go easy; I've heard on the grapevine that registering your site in more than six categories will get your submission placed at the bottom of the queue. Other sites allow only one listing and eradicate duplicate URLs. If you try to put your site in several places, the registrar might eliminate your preferred categories and leave you stuck in virtual Siberia.

Registration Procedures

Once you've completed your registration form and it's been approved, you can embark on the registration campaign. Expect to spend about two afternoons visiting the major directories and search engines, uploading the information off your form. I have created a registration report Web page to help you with this process. It has links to the submission pages at the top 20 directories and search engines. You'll find it at www.wiley.com/compbooks/okeefe. Either download the page and open it in your Web browser or just click the page and work directly from it.

A do-it-yourself form that is far better than mine can be found at Words In A Row, www.wordsinarow.com/wheretogo.html. It has an orderly set of links to each of the major search engines and directories, with links to their submission forms and tips on how to complete each registration. I provide my form as a backup in case Words In A Row disappears by the time you read this book. The entire registration process is in upheaval right now, with sites changing policies, disappearing, and merging so fast that no one can keep up. I'll talk about this problem a little later in the section on Paid Registration Services. For now, let's stick with the do-it-yourself procedures.

With your registration form open, visit each directory and search engine, go to the "Submit Your Site" page, and copy the information from your registration form into the site's submission form. Then, make any changes you need to tailor your submission to the standards of the directory. You might need to cut down your site description to 20 words; you might be allowed 15 keywords instead of 10; or you might have to choose categories other than the ones on your registration form. You should also consider the tone of each directory. Galaxy is much more scholarly than LookSmart, so you might want to appeal to the users of each directory. You can get an idea of the tone and style of each directory by browsing its listings.

Another item you'll need besides the registration form to complete your campaign is a credit card. With most of the major players now charging to list your site, it can get quite spendy. Yahoo is charging $200, and so is LookSmart. You can expect to spend about $1,000 for a basic site registration campaign. Search engines are charging for premier listings, but I recommend you stay away from them because you will still show up in search results without paying. Some sites will benefit from these premium spots, but most will not. It's certainly not worth paying for anything beyond the top three positions. As of this writing, sites beyond the top three are not always syndicated to search engine partners. Because the major search engines partner with up to hundreds of sites, it's important to find out whether your paid listing appears on partner sites.

After you hit the major directories and search engines, move next to the phone book style directories, such as InfoSpace. At these services, you'll just be entering the corporate contact information and a URL and selecting a business category under which you want to be listed. These directories are used a lot by vendors and investors, so it's important to be included in them. You'll find a good list of business directories at About.com's Web Search forum at http://websearch.about.com/. There are a lot more of these than you might imagine, including sites for exporters, importers, manufacturers, retailers, the Dow Jones directory, the Forbes directory, and so on.

Next, you want to approach any niche directories related to your business. For any subject you can think of, there is a special-interest directory out there cataloging all the Web sites related to that subject. A good place to look for these special-interest directories is About.com's Web Search forum at http://websearch.about.com. The Linkage portion of this chapter, which follows, will go into more detail about locating these sites. Once you find them, it's important to bookmark them for future use. In the coming years, these directories will gain in importance as the sheer amount of content on the Web forces people to abandon global directories for ones that cover their interests more closely. Also, as advertising degrades the usability of major catalogs and search engines, people will gravitate to these smaller, less-commercial sites.

One-Stop Registration Services

I've always questioned the value of one-stop registration services that submit your site to multiple directories for free or for a nominal fee. The major directories and search engines are so important that it's worth custom-tailoring your submission to each one by hand. And beyond the top 20, who really cares? Do any of these smaller directories and search engines generate any traffic?

Today, with the major sites charging listing fees and so much consolidation in the industry, the whole one-stop industry is pretty much dead in the water. Submit-It used to let you submit your site to the top 20 directories and search engines for free. As of this writing, they are charging $60 for the service. Because that won't even get you into Yahoo!, however, what are they selling? I'm afraid their business model is in jeopardy. So many of the sites I visited while preparing this chapter are out of business or are no longer maintained that I'm reluctant to recommend any of them.

In my last book, *Publicity on the Internet*, I endorsed a "sane strategy" of submitting by hand to the top directories, then paying for an inexpensive service to hit the next 200 or so sites. I've used such services myself on several occasions, and I've been sorely disappointed. Most of the lower echelon directories are scams. They're advertising ploys, generating traffic from people submitting sites but never from people searching. Once online advertising rates started to crumble, many of these sites went out of business and the remainder switched over to spam machines. To register at their sites, you had to give them an e-mail address, and then they would sell the address to marketers targeting Web masters or charge those marketers to spam you themselves.

Another big problem with one-stop services is that many directories now refuse submissions that come through them. The major sites want you to do your own registration. It increases traffic at their sites and gives them an opportunity to market goods and services to you. Just recently, AltaVista announced that it would no longer accept submissions from one-stop sites, making public what many of us suspected all along: that directories and search engines are ignoring these submissions.

Paid Registration Services

You can pay professional marketers to handle your registration work for you, but it doesn't come cheap. As we mentioned earlier, any inexpensive service that promises 500 registrations for $50 simply will not be able to produce the results you're hoping for and will likely produce a stream of advertising you can do without. Because you're looking at about $1,000 in registration fees for a basic campaign, I wouldn't trust anyone who is charging less than $1,500 for registration services. For most sites, you can expect to spend between $3,000 and $5,000.

There are only two services to which I can give unqualified recommendations. The first is NetPOST, Eric Ward's registration service at www.netpost.com. Eric is the master of Web site launches. He gets results because he's obsessive about the details. He writes the Link Building column for online marketing magazine ClickZ, and you'll find plenty of good traffic building tips there. Eric is fussy about the assignments he'll accept, and his calendar is full well in advance. But if you have the right site and the money, his service is the way to go.

The other vendor I recommend is The Tenagra Corporation—my former employer. I never liked doing registration work and would only include it as part of a much larger Web launch campaign. But after I left Tenagra in 1999, they hired people who have fine-tuned the registration process and really know their stuff. Tenagra is host of the Online Advertising Discussion Group, and the staff is privy to the secrets of the best Internet marketers around. You'll find their services described at www.tenagra.com.

There are others who perform this work, such as Danny Sullivan's Calafia Consulting at www.calafia.com, but I haven't seen his results firsthand. Most of the firms that do this work will throw in Search Engine Optimization; however, I would avoid spending a significant amount on that—especially until the current shakeout has run its course. SEO is a never-ending game. The minute you get good positioning, someone works a little harder and knocks you out. So, you can run up big bills in a hurry, and the second you stop paying, your rank plummets. I'd focus on someone who will get you into all the major directories and niche directories and then monitor your listings on a monthly basis. Every year, you might want to reconsider your position, evaluate your traffic logs, and perhaps freshen your META tags and listings to keep up with the times. If you follow the simple procedures in this chapter, you'll have a solid foundation for your site and you can spend your marketing budget on promotions rather than chasing your tail with SEO.

The Linkage Campaign

Linkage is one of the most important and underrated ways to generate Web site traffic. My own traffic logs consistently show that a well-placed link will pull more traffic than even prominent search engine and directory listings. And the traffic generated from links is higher quality.

Linkage has gotten a big boost recently because it is now a major determinant in search engine ranking. Search engines, such as Google, use the number of people linking to your site as a measure of quality and popularity. Unfortunately, there are very high-quality sites that don't generate a lot of incoming links, either because they don't engage in linkage campaigns or they're unwilling to install reciprocal links. Such sites are now being penalized for their parochialism. And other sites that are worthless scams rank high in linkage because they get fellow scammers to link to them in a mutual lovefest that boosts search engine ratings. Ahh, will the search engine wars never end?

Beyond search engine rank, linkage is an important and worthwhile activity. Perhaps the easiest way to start this discussion is at the end, showing the results of a linkage campaign. Figure 8.9 is the linkage report from a campaign I did for a CPA exam review site. The target audience is people studying to take CPA certification exams. We targeted college and university sites heavily but also approached major accounting firms, because they employ many people who have not passed the exam yet (and the firms will often pay for study materials—an economic reason for linkage). We also focused on the major accounting resources sites on the Internet. The linkage report shows the name of each site and the URL for the page on which we requested a link.

The linkage report in Figure 8.9 is pretty impressive. In fact, every time I see a completed linkage report, I'm reminded of what an excellent campaign it is. Of course, not all the sites will install links. My success rate hovers at about 25 percent in the first two weeks after the request is made. Links trickle in after that date, but not many. I've reached highs of 90 percent acceptance (my Seussville campaign was a hit) and lows of 10 percent (for a poorly designed site that wouldn't link back). But there are many benefits to a linkage campaign besides links.

First and foremost, a linkage campaign is a great way to find the Web Sites That Matter in any given subject area. Stored as an HTML file, the linkage report becomes a road map to the key sites in your industry. These sites represent potential partners for programs and outlets for promotional materials. Almost all the campaigns in this book involve working with partners, and the linkage campaign will give you a ready list to consult before every campaign.

Second, the linkage campaign is like a crash course in Web design. You'll get great ideas not only for navigation and graphics from these other sites but also for content you might want to add on your site. If more sites had conducted linkage campaigns, they would have avoided adding message boards to their own sites. These boards seldom get any traffic, and when they do it's usually from spam artists trying to promote their services. A linkage campaign would have opened a lot of eyes to the fact that an "upcoming events" calendar that is actually a historical record is an embarrassment, and you shouldn't put a calendar on your site unless you plan to maintain it (in which case it is extremely useful).

Third, a linkage campaign requires that you make contact with someone who is responsible for content at each site. These contact names can be easily stored in the linkage report and can be exported to your e-mail address book or contact-management software. The people you contact are very often "The People That Matter at The Web Sites That Matter." In other words, they are important industry connections and are, in fact, *media contacts*, although they're not often recognized as such. Your letter requesting a link is an introduction to these people, and beautiful relationships can blossom as a

```
Web Site Linkage Report

  Site Name:        CPA Exam Review Site
  Site URL: http://www.wiley.com/cpa.html


  Arthur Anderson
          <http://www.arthurandersen.com>
  Coopers & Lybrand
          <http://www.colybrand.com/>
  Deloitte & Touche
          <http://www.dttus.com/hometext.htm>
  Ernst & Young
          <http://www.ey.com/us/>
  KPMG
          <http://www.us.kpmg.com/>
  Price Waterhouse
          <http://www.pw.com/us/>
  Rutger Accounting Resource On The Internet
          <http://Anet.scu.edu.au/mirror/anet/raw.htm>
  SDU Accounting Society
          <karenb@acusd.edu>
  Printed Resources In Accounting
          <http://www.cob.ohiostate.edu/dept/jobs/account.htm>
  SBAA
          <http://www.sbaa.com/link.html>
  ICON World  Accounting Courses page
          <http://galaxy.einet.net/galaxy/Oklahoma.html>
  OSCPA
          <http://www.bus.orst.edu/cob/acctng/prof_org/oscpa.htm>
  UACPA
          <http://www.uacpa.org/>
  College of Business, Oregon State U.
  Accounting and Finance On-Line Resources
          <http://www.bus.orst.edu/tools/acc_fin/acc_fin.htm>
  Carol E. Brown (Webmaster to a number of accounting sites)
          <http://www.bus.orst.edu/faculty/brownc/vita/home.htm>
  The Academy of Accounting Historians
          <http://weatherhead.cwru.edu/Accounting/>
  Andersen Consulting
          <http://www.ac.com/>
```

Figure 8.9 A linkage report documenting a campaign to garner links for a CPA exam review site. For most sites, linkage is a greater source of traffic than search engines or directories, yet the amount spent securing links is far less than is spent on search engine optimization.

```
Washington Accountants Network Home Page
        <http://www.eskimo.com/~earl/>
Rutgers Accounting Web
        <http://www.rutgers.edu/Accounting/raw.htm>
Filo List of Accounting Resources on the Internet
        <http://www.hiline.net/~dden/>
Kent Information Services
        <http://www.kentis.com/index.html>
James Madison University's School of Accounting
        <http://falcon.jmu.edu/~fordhadr>
Anthony T. Muscarella, CPA
        <http://www.tiac.net/users/tonymus/index.html>
Arthur Naman, CPA
        <http://www.ccsi.com/~anaman/>
Karen Cope Bachman , CPA
        <http://summit.clever.net/cpa/>
Chapski & Chapski, CPAs, LLP
        <http://www-personal.umich.edu/~chapski/>
San Francisco State University CPA, CMA, and CIA:
Exams and Licensing
        <http://www.sfsu.edu/~acct/Welcome.html#EXAMS1>
The CPA's Weekly News Update
        <http://www.hbpp.com/weekup/weekup.html>
Accounting Net
        <http://www.accountingnet.com/vendoring/arm.html>
Barry Rice of Loyola University Accounting Page
        <ftp://pacioli.loyola.edu/pub/ricemark.html>
Jagdish S. Gangolly School of Business
State University of New York at Albany
        <http://www.albany.edu/~gangolly/>
Coker and Company, CPA
        <http://www.cpa-coker.com>
CPA WebLinks
        <http://www.ice.net/~kstevens/CPAWEB.HTM>
Spark Web Services
        <http://spark.superlink.net/users/index.htm>
Allen Pretzl (Accounting-Web Main Menu)
        <http://www.eskimo.com/cgi-bin/mailback>
The Accounting.Com Home Page
        <http://www.accounting.com/>
Computerized Accounting
        <http://www.accounting.org/library.html>
AuditNet Resources
        <http://users.aol.com/auditnet/karlhome.htm>
```

Figure 8.9 Continued.

result. Sometimes a linkage request can lead to a job offer and possibly even—dare I say it—*love* and a richer form of linkage. I'm not supposed to talk about such things in a book about technology, but when you connect with peers in the same industry, many good things can happen. That's one of the things the Internet was supposed to help us do: build a sense of community among people with similar interests who are geographically dispersed. The linkage campaign, in short, can open many doors.

Figure 8.10 shows a more modern version of a linkage report, this time as a Web page. I developed this form so that clients could track the progress of extended linkage campaigns. This work was done for the career Web portal www.myjobsearch.com. For the initial campaign, 50 sites were approached. Then, each month 10 to 20 more links were sought, and we followed up on old requests. Each entry in the report contains detailed notes about who was pitched at the site, when, and what action resulted. Once links were installed, the entry was tagged as a linking site. The information contained in this report became a valuable asset for the company in finding partners for future efforts.

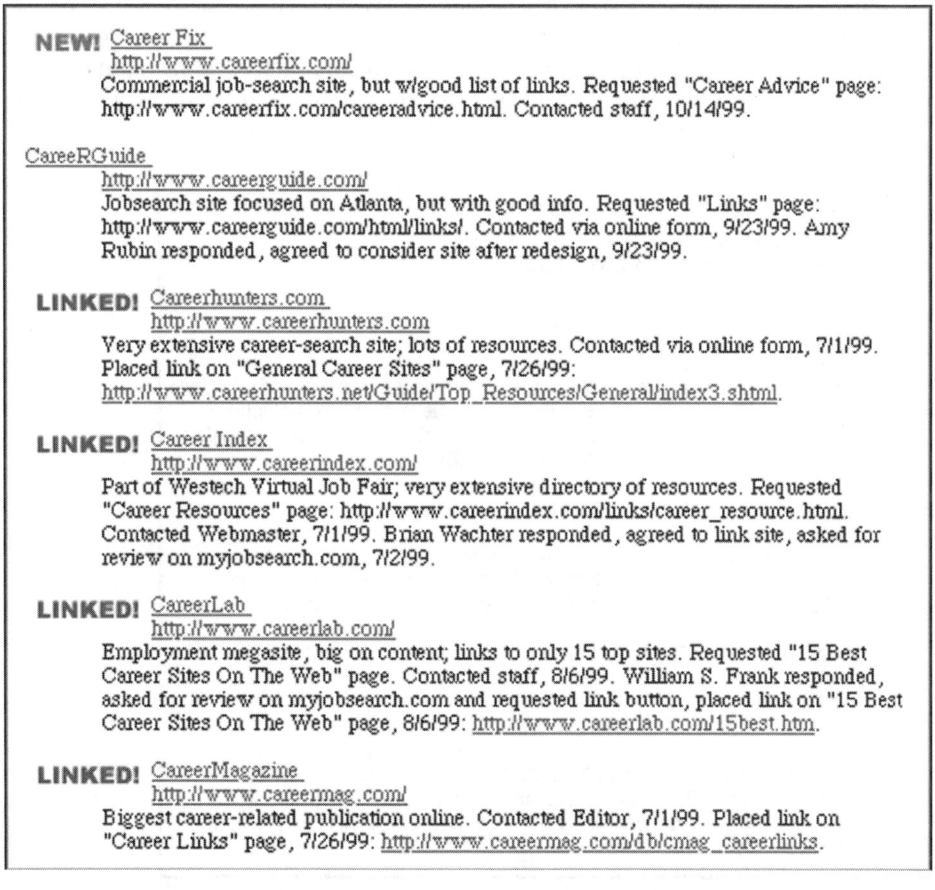

NEW! Career Fix
http://www.careerfix.com/
Commercial job-search site, but w/good list of links. Requested "Career Advice" page: http://www.careerfix.com/careeradvice.html. Contacted staff, 10/14/99.

CareeRGuide
http://www.careerguide.com/
Jobsearch site focused on Atlanta, but with good info. Requested "Links" page: http://www.careerguide.com/html/links/. Contacted via online form, 9/23/99. Amy Rubin responded, agreed to consider site after redesign, 9/23/99.

LINKED! Careerhunters.com
http://www.careerhunters.com
Very extensive career-search site; lots of resources. Contacted via online form, 7/1/99. Placed link on "General Career Sites" page, 7/26/99: http://www.careerhunters.net/Guide/Top_Resources/General/index3.shtml.

LINKED! Career Index
http://www.careerindex.com/
Part of Westech Virtual Job Fair; very extensive directory of resources. Requested "Career Resources" page: http://www.careerindex.com/links/career_resource.html. Contacted Webmaster, 7/1/99. Brian Wachter responded, agreed to link site, asked for review on myjobsearch.com, 7/2/99.

LINKED! CareerLab
http://www.careerlab.com/
Employment megasite, big on content; links to only 15 top sites. Requested "15 Best Career Sites On The Web" page. Contacted staff, 8/6/99. William S. Frank responded, asked for review on myjobsearch.com and requested link button, placed link on "15 Best Career Sites On The Web" page, 8/6/99: http://www.careerlab.com/15best.htm.

LINKED! CareerMagazine
http://www.careermag.com/
Biggest career-related publication online. Contacted Editor, 7/1/99. Placed link on "Career Links" page, 7/26/99: http://www.careermag.com/db/cmag_careerlinks.

Figure 8.10   A linkage report for www.myjobsearch.com, a career Web portal. The report is created by annotating bookmarks in a Web browser, then exporting them to an HTML file to create a Web-based tracking system.

The Linkletter

You should prepare a "linkletter" in advance of your search for sites from which to request links. Trust me, if you build your site list first and then go back and ask for links later, you will have a very hard time relocating the contact information you need to ask for a link. Several clients have asked me for a site list in advance of a linkage campaign, but it doubles the work involved, so I would have to charge twice as much. You'll understand this concept better once you start doing linkage work yourself. As you find sites you want to request a link from, you should have your linkletter ready, pitch them on the fly, and move along.

Figure 8.11 shows the linkletter I used to promote the Dr. Seuss site called Seussville. I like to start my linkletters with a compliment. Look for something on the site that genuinely stands out. Web masters put a lot of effort into their sites and seldom get any recognition. If you can say something honestly praiseworthy about their site, so much the better.

When you ask for the link, it's important to specify the page where the link should go. You should identify the exact URL to make it as easy as possible for the Web master to comply with your request. The site might have been built by an expert, then turned over to a novice for maintenance. If you tell them exactly where to put the link, you're more likely to get a successful placement. It also proves that you visited the site and you aren't just spamming the planet with link requests.

```
        To: Webmaster
      From: okeefe@olympus.net (Steve O'Keefe)
   Subject: Dr. Seuss Would Like a Link!
        Cc:
       Bcc:
Attachments:
..........................................................................................
You have a terrific page of links on your site and I wonder if you wouldn't mind
adding one for Dr. Seuss? The site is called Seussville (www.seussville.com)
and it has information about Dr. Seuss's books and other educational materials.
The link would work perfectly on your Lots-a-Links Page:

http://www.yoursite.com/lots-a-links.html

I've written some HTML linking text, below, which you can use or cut as you
wish. I also have a cute Seussville button GIF which I can send attached to
e-mail or FTP to your site. It's only 8K and features The Cat in the Hat.

Please let me know if you'd like to link -- or you want the button GIF. Thanks!

STEVE O'KEEFE


<a href:"http://www.seussville.com/>Seussville</a><br>
<p>The digital home of Dr. Seuss is a great place for learning or just hanging
loose. It's got stories and contests and fun things like that. You can even chat
with the Cat in the Hat!<br>
```

Figure 8.11 A linkletter requesting a link to Seussville, the official Dr. Seuss Web site. You should prepare your linkletter before looking for target sites so you can send it on the fly as you do your research.

After you make a suggestion about where to place the link, give them the linking text marked-up in HTML and ready for installation. Doing the HTML is oh-so-easy and makes it a snap for the Web master to install the link. I like to provide them with both the site name and a brief description, in case they have room for an annotated link. Here's what the HTML looked like for Dr. Seuss:

```
<a href:"http://www.seussville.com/">Seussville</a><br>
<p>The digital home of Dr. Seuss is a great place for learning or
just hanging loose. It's got stories and contests and fun things
like that. You can even chat with the Cat in the Hat!<br>
```

The top line is the link with a simple HREF to the URL for the site. By providing the Web master with the HTML, you can direct people to the proper page. If the Web master had to choose, he or she might link to a secondary page instead of the page where you want people to start their visit.

The art of the linkletter is to make the connection with the right person and give them everything they need to say "yes" to your link. I get hit with e-mail all the time asking for links. Sometimes they forget to tell me where their site is. I've learned you'll get a lot more links when you provide the text, the HTML, a cute button, and the exact location where the link should go. Some people think this effort is too much work, and maybe they're right. But one quality link that brings the target audience to your site is worth 500 links in all the scam directories cluttering up the Web.

Link Buttons

It helps to offer a small, graphical button for people to use when linking to your site. The button is a logo and builds name recognition, strengthens a brand, lifts the visual presentation of a page, and helps you stand out in a sea of hotlinks. It makes it harder for competitors to unseat your links because there's only so much space a Web master has for graphics like these. Whatever you do, however, *don't send the artwork attached to the link request*. It's considered rude to dump a file on someone without permission.

What are the characteristics of a good link button?

Small. Keep the file size under 10k and keep the dimensions as small as possible.

Simple. Try for brand recognition. Don't try to cram too much information into one tiny little image.

Universal. The button should look good against any background color.

Timeless. Try to avoid text or images that won't age well.

I've seen 100k buttons that are bigger than banners. Pare those buttons down to the bare essentials! Simplicity is easier said than done. Figure 8.12 shows an old version of Yahoo!'s logo on the right and a new version on the left. Yahoo!'s first button, while distinctive, is too busy. Both buttons have a distinctive shape. Shape is part of the "universal" strategy: the buttons are "transparent" graphics. Transparent graphics allow whatever background they're on to show through. For this reason, transparent buttons often have a cookie-cutter quality: they look shaped, not square, adding to ease of

Figure 8.12   Two versions of the Yahoo! logo. The older version, on the right, is too cluttered. The new version, on the left, while a little plain, communicates the brand and won't go out of date.

recognition. Transparent graphics can backfire, though, if they get lost in the background color. Successful transparent buttons always include a border to ensure that they're set off from the surrounding color.

Timelessness is tricky, and any image will look dated at some point. But some people actually build obsolescence into their buttons! Years ago, Netscape put a "2.0" banner across their popular button; Figure 8.13 shows before and after shots of the button. I don't have to tell you how silly the "2.0" button looks on Web sites today, as Netscape is in version 6.0. Creating buttons for contests, events, and other short-term projects is only going to clutter the Web with debris. If you change your logo or look, you have to find all those old buttons out there and ask the Web masters to update them. There's only so much patience a Web master has for such requests.

Figure 8.14 shows some of the buttons I created for linkage campaigns. In most cases, the artwork was taken from the client's Web site. The Seussville button works well because the Cat in the Hat is universally recognized and is the main character at

Figure 8.13   Two versions of the Netscape logo button. The one on the right, with the 2.0 banner, was guaranteed to go out of date. Don't build obsolescence into your buttons.

TM and © by Dr. Seuss Enterprises, LP.

Figure 8.14   Buttons created for linkage campaigns. The distinctive shape on the Book Stacks and Seussville buttons comes from saving the graphic as "transparent" files. The Crestar and @d:tech buttons are guaranteed to stand out against any background color.

the Web site. We had to clutter up the image with a trademark notice in order to please the attorneys. The Book Stacks button is shown at double its final size.

Building the Road Map

One of the hardest parts of a linkage campaign is finding quality sites for requesting links. This process shouldn't be hard—after all, there are an abundance of Web sites from which to choose. It's difficult to know before you visit a site, however, whether it has a page of links to other people's sites, whether it's professionally run, and whether it's even devoted to your subject area. I've wasted a lot of time working my way through Web sites only to decide not to request a link. Even with a fantastic site list, I only request links at about half the sites I visit. The other half either have no links to outside sites, or are inappropriate, or the site is no longer maintained. Let's start the road map discussion, then, with what you're looking for.

Evaluating Sites

Following the format of the linkletter, there are five things you're looking for at a site before you request a link:

- Is this a good place for a link to my site?
- If so, what page should the link go on?
- Who is the person responsible for maintaining that page?
- What is his or her e-mail address?
- Has the site been updated in the past two months?

The first question seems unnecessary. After all, you want as many links as you can get, don't you? Not always. Some people are fussy about the sites they're associated with. They don't want links from places that contain sexually explicit imagery or that otherwise reflect poorly on them. You also don't want to request a link if the site is a fee-based service or if you suspect it's a scam. Some people use their Web sites to build mailing lists, then hound you with solicitations. You might not want to ask a competitor for a link, and it's not always evident from the surface that the site belongs to a competitor.

The next question is, "Do they have a page of links to other sites?" If so, that's probably where they'll put a link to your site. Link pages can be called many things. Common names include "links," "cool sites," "resources," and so on. Figure 8.15 shows a typical links page called "Cool Links." Some Web masters sprinkle the links throughout the site, so be on the lookout for any page where a link to your site would be appropriate.

Once you've found the page, note the location (URL) and look for the e-mail address of the person who is responsible for maintaining that page. This person is usually the Web master on smaller sites, but it's a lot nicer to get the person's name and individual e-mail address. Some pages will tell you how to submit requests for a link. Other pages will have a copyright notice or credits at the bottom of the page, and you

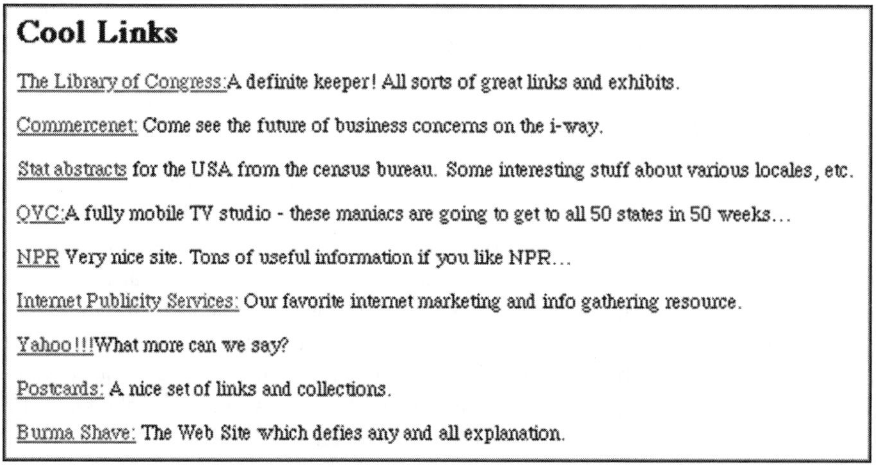

Cool Links

The Library of Congress:A definite keeper! All sorts of great links and exhibits.

Commercenet: Come see the future of business concerns on the i-way.

Stat abstracts for the USA from the census bureau. Some interesting stuff about various locales, etc.

QVC:A fully mobile TV studio - these maniacs are going to get to all 50 states in 50 weeks...

NPR Very nice site. Tons of useful information if you like NPR...

Internet Publicity Services: Our favorite internet marketing and info gathering resource.

Yahoo!!!What more can we say?

Postcards: A nice set of links and collections.

Burma Shave: The Web Site which defies any and all explanation.

Figure 8.15 A typical links page found at a Web site. These are called annotated links because they contain a short description of each site. Some sites use bare links, and some use graphical links (with or without annotations).

can often find contact names and e-mail addresses in these stock notices. If you can't find a contact name or address, you can try webmaster@sitename.com and hope it gets forwarded to the right person. You should be careful about using a bare Web master e-mail address, however. Many Web sites are built by companies that have no say in the content. Sending e-mail to webmaster@home.com is not likely to get you a link on one of the sites they've built.

If there is no evidence that the site has been maintained in the past two months, don't waste your time requesting a link. Unfortunately, a lot of the sites you visit will fall into this category. If you're unsure, go ahead and send the link request. The quicker you leave a site and move on in search of the next one, the faster your campaign will go. A linkage campaign approaching 50 sites might take a week of work, including preparing link buttons and link letters. Maintaining the campaign should only take a few hours each month.

Annotating Bookmarks

As you visit sites, you'll want to build your road map by noting which sites you approached, who you contacted, the date of initial contact, and the page on which you requested placement. The easiest way to perform this task is to bookmark the page you requested a link on and then write your notes inside the bookmark. This process is called *annotating bookmarks*, and it's one of the most time-saving Web surfing skills you can learn.

Figure 8.16 shows an annotated bookmark in Netscape. It includes the name of the site, the URL, and a description. This bookmark was used in an article placement campaign, but the process of creating the bookmark is identical for a linkage campaign. Figure 8.17 shows the window you use in Netscape to enter the annotation.

When you are about to embark on a site search, you should open your Web browser and view your bookmarks. Create a new bookmark folder for the linkage campaign,

Figure 8.16 An annotated bookmark as seen in Netscape. Note that unlike most bookmarks, it displays the URL as well as the name of the site. It also contains notes on the site.

Figure 8.17 This window is what you use in Netscape to create the annotated bookmark in Figure 8.16. To get this window, you first have to view your bookmarks in Netscape, select the bookmark you want, and then use the *get info* command (usually the Command key plus "i" pressed together).

and set this folder to the "New Bookmarks Folder." When you bookmark a site, it will be added to this folder. To annotate this bookmark, you view the bookmarks folder again, select the new bookmark, and use the *get info* command to edit the bookmark. In Netscape, the *get info* command is invoked by holding down the Command key and the letter "i" together. The window in Figure 8.17 will pop up.

For Internet Explorer, the process is very similar. On my version of Explorer, bookmarks are called *favorites*. You use the "Organize Favorites" command from the pulldown menu, then select the bookmark you want to annotate. Use the *get info* command (the Command key plus i) and the window shown in Figure 8.18 will pop up, allowing you to add notes to the bookmark.

At the end of a day's linkage work, your linkage folder in your bookmarks (Netscape) or favorites (Explorer) should be fat with information about the key sites in your industry and who runs them. This folder can easily be exported into word processing documents or uploaded to a company intranet for everyone to use.

Some readers will find this discussion of annotating bookmarks a bit labored. I'm sorry about that. But have you seen the bookmarks or favorites folder on most people's computers? They're a mess! Things are bookmarked willy-nilly, there is no organization, and after a few months folks stop using their bookmarks because it's easier to

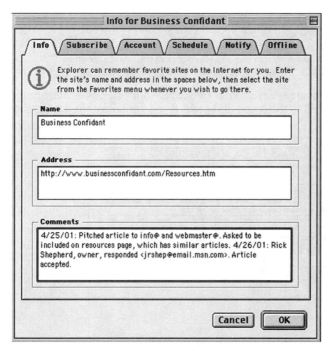

Figure 8.18 This window is used in Internet Explorer to annotate bookmarks. You get it by using the Organize Favorites pull-down menu, then selecting the favorite you want to annotate and using the *get info* command to get the window shown here.

find sites at Yahoo! or AltaVista. But going through AltaVista or Yahoo! whenever you want to return to a page is a huge waste of time.

The solution to this mess is to organize your bookmarks on a regular schedule (say, once a week or once a month) and to create folders for every major campaign. Perhaps we should have a global Organize Your Bookmarks Day? Quite seriously, companies might want to make time every Friday for employees to organize their bookmarks. Good bookmark habits will save a minimum of 10 percent of time online. They also are company assets that will aid greatly in the training of new employees.

Frankly, it's a pain to clean up bookmarks. If it weren't for linkage campaigns, I probably would be like everyone else and have a completely useless set. But now I tweak my bookmarks every day, inserting notes about why I found a site useful and changing the name of each bookmark to the name of the site. If you bookmark anything other than the homepage, chances are the name of the bookmark does not contain the name of the site—a result of poor Title tag usage that ruins bookmarking for many people. About once a month, I put the bookmarks into their proper folders: searching, shopping, clients, competitors, and so on. Call me obsessive, but in exchange for a few minutes at the end of each day, I have a set of thousands of annotated bookmarks that people drool over. I've taught dozens of people how to annotate bookmarks, including my college-age daughter. She thought her old man was ridiculous, but now her friends come to her when they want to find something online, and she's passed along annotating secrets to many other students, teachers, and coworkers.

The bottom line for this discussion is that good bookmarking habits are essential to successful linkage and syndication campaigns. Now, let's look at how you can quickly find the best sites for link requests and bookmarking.

Finding Sites

The secret to keeping your time down during a linkage campaign is to *find the supersite*. For any subject you can think of, there is a site somewhere on the Web where someone has painstakingly cataloged all the resources available online related to that subject. These supersites are often assembled by volunteers, individual fanatics, and educational institutions. If you find the supersite, the rest of your work will be much easier.

The best starting point for finding the supersite, in my opinion, is the Open Directory Project (also known as DMOZ). This site is a human-edited Internet directory maintained by thousands of volunteer editors. It does not charge to submit links, and it rates sites according to quality. DMOZ's catalog is so good that it is used by Netscape Search, AOL Search, Google, Lycos, HotBot, DirectHit, and hundreds of others. I suggest you begin your search here by looking for "resources" or "directories" related to a specific subject. For example, Figure 8.19 shows the results of a DMOZ search for "accounting resources."

The Open Directory Project page in Figure 8.19 begins with the top five categories that match the search string, followed by the top 20 sites in their catalog that match. Rutgers Accounting Web is given a star by its editors. Unlike other sites, where that might mean Rutgers paid a fee for preferential treatment, at DMOZ it is an editor's stamp of approval —and it's significant that it's the only site listed that has earned that accolade. I would immediately see whether Rutgers Accounting Web is the supersite I'm looking for.

My second pick for finding the supersite is to begin at Google. The results of a search for *accounting resources* at Google are shown in Figure 8.20. After a paid listing, the top item is a Google category that might be useful. In this case, it offers directories of accounting *firms*, which might be useful later in the campaign but is unlikely to lead to a directory of *resources*—the kind of supersite we're looking for. The first non-paid listing is for *Rutgers Accounting Web* (RAW). Next to the listing, the finger/cursor is pointing to a link that says "Similar pages." This link helps reorganize the search around sites like RAW and returns a very nice set of links to accounting supersites. The *Similar pages* feature at Google makes it a good second choice for locating a supersite.

Another good starting point for finding a supersite is About.com's Web Search forum run by Kevin Elliott, an SEO expert. Elliott organizes his supersites into 10 categories, such as Business/Money and Science/Technology. These groupings are way too broad, but through them you will find major directories and catalogs that will then lead you to the niche supersites you're after. With the DMOZ and Google, you can often find the supersite with one search. At About.com, it takes two steps. You can be pretty certain Google and DMOZ will survive in some form for years, but I get nervous recommending About.com because many of the best hosts have departed and a lot of the sites there aren't well maintained.

Yahoo! is really a poor choice for this kind of work. One nice thing about Yahoo! is that it has a classification in its cataloging specifically for supersites, called "Web directories." You can search for Web directories related to any subject at Yahoo! and get a matching list of supersites. Unfortunately, however, the sites aren't so super. Many of

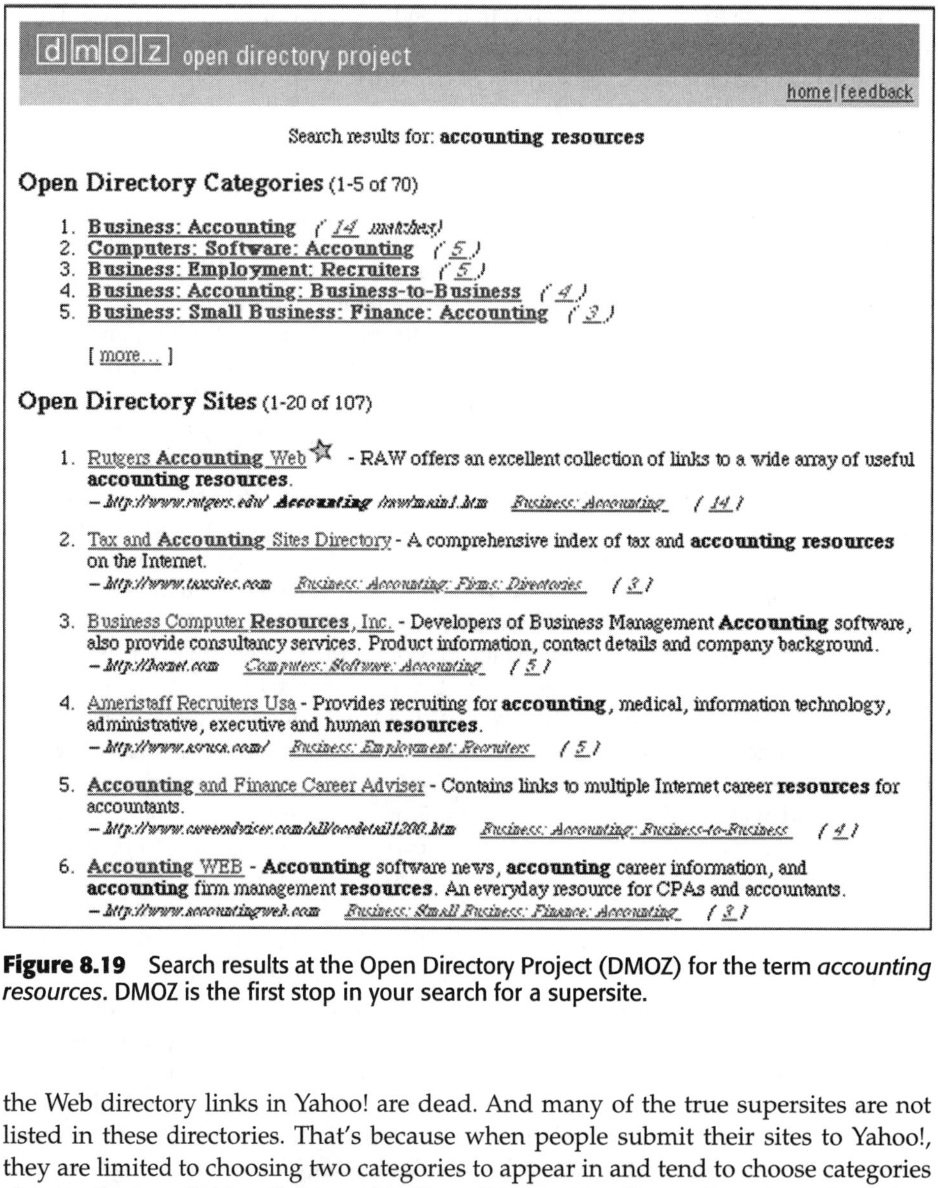

Figure 8.19   Search results at the Open Directory Project (DMOZ) for the term *accounting resources*. DMOZ is the first stop in your search for a supersite.

the Web directory links in Yahoo! are dead. And many of the true supersites are not listed in these directories. That's because when people submit their sites to Yahoo!, they are limited to choosing two categories to appear in and tend to choose categories close to the top of Yahoo!'s hierarchy. Open Directory's editors place sites where they belong, without limiting the number of categories a site can be in, making its directory much more useful. They also weed out dead links on a regular basis—certainly more often than Yahoo! does.

Figure 8.21 shows a portion of RAW. This site is truly a supersite, with links to everything you need for conducting a linkage campaign. In the left-hand margin of the image is a list of content areas, including professional associations, journals and publications, professors, and so on. One of the RAW categories is called "other sites" and includes the list of General Resources shown on the right-hand side of the image. What are these General Resources? Other accounting supersites, of course! Many

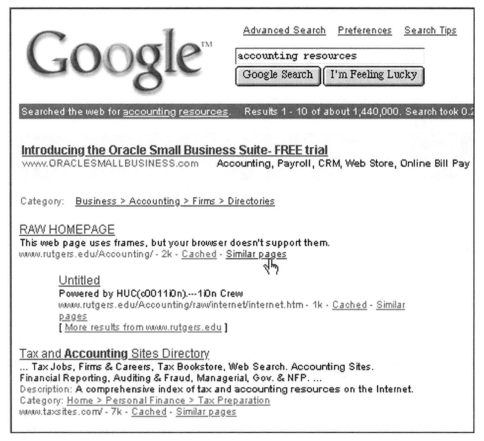

Figure 8.20 Search results at Google for the term *accounting resources*. One nice feature at Google is the "Similar pages" link, which helps you zone in on supersites.

supersites contain lists of related supersites, and these lists are usually much more pertinent and better maintained than you can find by searching Google or DMOZ or Yahoo! or any other directory or search engine. For a linkage campaign in the field of accounting, RAW is the only site you'll ever need.

Once you find the supersite, you simply work through it until your linkage campaign is complete. One trick to speeding the process is to save pages of links as *source* in your Web browser. For example, every time you visit one of the sites listed in Figure 8.21, you have to go through RAW. Because RAW is a popular site (most supersites are), it could be slow going. By saving the General Resources page as source, then opening the saved document in your Web browser, all the links are native on your computer and you don't have to keep coming back to RAW.

Other Sources for SuperSites

Magazines and newsletters that cover your industry probably have run articles about interesting sites on the Internet. These articles can provide a good starting list for your

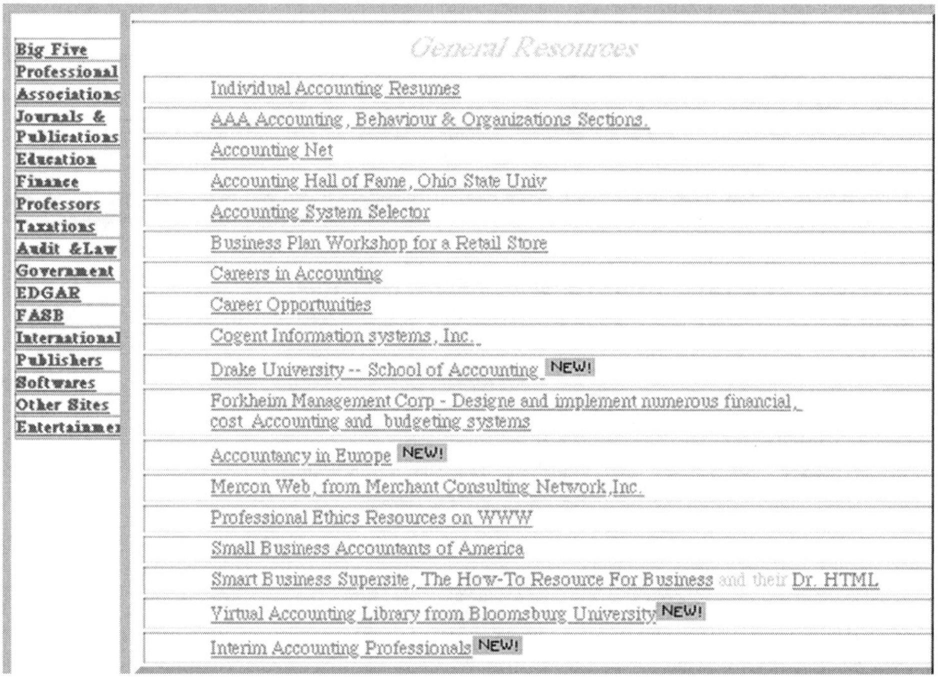

Figure 8.21 A portion of the Rutgers Accounting Web, a supersite of online resources related to accounting. Many supersites contain a good list of other supersites in the same topic area. The right side of the image is just such a list of other accounting supersites.

linkage campaign. Using print publications cuts down on your research time. Magazines and newspapers hire professional researchers to do the grunt work for you. If these articles are archived at the periodical's Web site, you might be able to call up a nice set of hotlinks. Sometimes these articles and resources are available only to subscribers, so if you are subscribing, get the full benefit of your subscription and take advantage of these hot lists.

You can also search computer magazine and Internet magazine Web sites for articles about your subject area. These articles usually include hotlists of good sites with descriptions of what you'll find there. The advantage of using magazine articles is that they've made value judgments about the quality of the sites they cover. Most online directories don't give you a good idea of what to expect when you finger that link. Many Internet magazines and books come with CD-ROMs that contain hotlists of Web sites sorted by subject area. Pop these into your CD-ROM drive and hit the information highway at full speed.

You can also find excellent site lists in books. Visit your library and photocopy the appropriate pages from the many Internet directories that have been published recently. You can use these as your starting lists. Or, there might be a book that covers Internet resources specifically related to your industry, such as *The Widget Maker's Guide to the Net*. These books always contain tightly focused, annotated site lists that can cut your linkage time and improve your results. Many books now have Web site companions that contain good resource lists. For example, the book you are reading has a companion

Web site with an updated list of top online publicity resources (www.wiley.com/compbooks/okeefe). The list includes Registration and Linkage Resources.

Follow-Up on Link Requests

You can expect a wide variety of responses to your link requests. Some people will be enthusiastic and will install the link immediately. Most people will remain silent whether or not they install a link. Others will tell you how lousy your site is. It's tempting to bury such bad news or defend the site. Resist that urge! These people are doing you a big favor. How many other people encountered problems with the site and didn't bother to send e-mail? How many people left the site with a bad impression and will never return?

When someone tells you about trouble at your site, you need to investigate and determine the cause of the problem and whether it's worth fixing. But the first thing you should do is thank your critics profusely and let them know you're investigating. When you pay someone to build a Web site, whether it's an employee or an outside firm, they don't always tell you the truth about your site. You could have a disaster in the making, and no one says anything except what a terrific site it is. When an outsider comes along and gives you an unsolicited evaluation of your site, you'd better listen closely because that's your market talking.

Other responses are easier to handle. If someone asks for a link button, send it to them along with a repeat of your HTML for the link. Figure 8.22 shows a typical letter I sent in response to a button request. You want to make it as easy as possible for people to install the link. Repeating your HTML helps keep everything in one place.

```
         To: Webmaster
       From: okeefe@olympus.net (Steve O'Keefe)
    Subject: Seussville Link Button Attached
         Cc:
        Bcc:
Attachments: :MAX:778:SeussHot.GIF:
..........................................................................................
Thanks for taking a link to Seussville, the official Dr. Seuss web site. I'm
attaching the link button you requested in a file called "SeussHot.GIF". If you
have trouble opening the file, please let me know and we'll try again.

The linking text is shown below, in case you need it. Thanks for your help!

STEVE O'KEEFE


<a href:"http://www.seussville.com/>Seussville</a><br>
<p>The digital home of Dr. Seuss is a great place for learning or just hanging
loose. It's got stories and contests and fun things like that. You can even chat
with the Cat in the Hat!<br>
```

Figure 8.22 An e-mail response to a linkletter reply asking for a link button. The HTML that goes with the button is repeated here so that the button and the text stay together. The button itself is sent as an attachment.

Your linkage campaign should generate many quality placements and some good feedback about your Web site. Many people will not respond at all. Check their Web sites in two weeks; if they haven't installed a link, resend your linkletter with a gentle reminder note. One of the responses you'll see frequently is, "I'll install your link if you install mine." That brings us to our next topic.

Reciprocal Links

A lot of people will not install a link to your Web site unless you install one for them. This situation is only natural, and you should be prepared for such requests. In the business, this situation is called "reciprocal linkage" and is a variation on "You scratch my back and I'll scratch yours." It's the Web's little referral system, and it can work wonders for your site.

You might want to plan on reciprocal linkage when you build your Web site. It will come in handy if you have some sort of "cool links" page at your site. If you don't have a links page, consider adding one. You can take your road map and use it as the basis for a ready-made links page for your Web site. If you're planning on asking other people to install a graphic link to your site, you should design your own links page to accommodate graphic hot buttons.

An Alternative Linkage Strategy

The process of linkage has gone through several waves. When the Web first appeared, link requests were commonly granted in a spirit of camaraderie among the small community of Internet users. As commercial interests came to dominate the Web in the late 1990s, people began to get stingy with links to other sites. Search engines helped reverse the trend early in the millennium as they added linkage to the criteria determining the quality of a site.

Just as it looked like a golden age of linkage had arrived, the dot.com crash changed everything. The climate for link requests is still good, thanks to their importance in search engine rank, but more and more sites are now asking for money to install links in a desperate grab for revenue. The problem now is exacerbated with directories and search engines charging for listing and positioning, with a potential backlash against these services. Between the number of directories that have closed down or merged and the declining quality of directories such as Yahoo! that contain so many stale links and the worthless commercialism of sites such as the corpse of Go/InfoSeek, searchers are looking for alternatives. If they move away from the big search engines, then Web masters will be less interested in installing links for the purpose of improving search engine rank.

If you find that straight link requests are not generating a high enough number of placements to continue the work, allow me to suggest another strategy. By offering something of value to the target sites, you can slip in a link through the side door. When you offer news items, articles, chats, workshops, or presentations, you will almost always get a link back to your site. Just like any other link, these links embedded in editorial content will improve your ranking with search engines. An offer of a reciprocal link might be considered a weak bribe nowadays. Content that you can produce rather cheaply, however, such as articles, could lead to very valuable links indeed.

There are many chapters of this book devoted to alternative campaigns that will get links onto other people's sites. In particular, the syndication chapter describes a systematic campaign to colonize the Web with content and inbound links. One of the more interesting case histories in this regard is the Amazon Associates program. Amazon could never have gotten all those graphical links from other sites just by requesting them. So they offered revenue instead—a share of sales generated by associate bookstores. For the vast majority of associates, the stores never earned enough revenue to meet the threshold for getting a check. Amazon got thousands of people to install graphic links to its site without paying a dime. So, if your link requests fall on deaf ears, try offering content. And if that doesn't work, maybe you should try an affiliate program?

Top Tips

Put naked people on your site. If traffic is all you want, nothing brings it faster than porn. Most sites want a *certain kind* of visitor—not just anybody. Before you start marketing your site, do some deep thinking about *exactly* who you want to attract, then tailor campaigns accordingly.

Traffic statistics don't lie (much). It's worth paying for Web site traffic-analysis software and reports. These reports show the source of traffic and help measure campaign results. They should convince you that linkage is much more valuable than search engine rank.

Stationery first. The best strategy for building traffic is also the cheapest: Include your URL in every printed item and advertisement your company produces. The traffic that results is high quality, consisting of people who have a business relationship with you or who are good prospects.

Just say no to SEO. For 95 percent of all Web sites, search engine position means *nothing*. Use easy and inexpensive techniques for improving your rank, such as drafting good META tags, but save your budget for better content and quality promotions.

Linkage—now more than ever. Linkage is the second most important source of traffic after stationery. Now that search engine rank is based in part on how well liked and linked your site is, conducting ongoing linkage operations is more valuable than ever.

Find the supersite. Linkage campaigns are frustrating and time consuming until you find the supersite. For every subject you can think of, someone has already located, organized, and ranked the top Web sites in the field. Find the supersite, and save yourself a lot of time and grief.

Learn to annotate bookmarks. The secret science of super searching starts with building better bookmarks. You need this skill for linkage campaigns, syndication, and other online promotions. If you make flossing your bookmarks a daily habit, you'll save 10 percent of your time online and be the most popular person in the office.

Bring your Visa card. We've entered the era of the paid placement. You have to pay to get listed in top directories and pay for position in others. And you can't hire robots anymore to do the work for $49.95; you have to do it yourself or hire a pro at prices of $1,500 and up. There's no such thing as a free launch.

Contests and Other Fancy Promotions

At this point in the book, you're probably sick of hearing about text-only promotions, netiquette, and proper formatting. What about the Big Show—the gala annual awards program, the breakthrough movie campaign, or the breathtaking product launch? You can't pull off any of these mammoth events without a solid understanding of the basics. But now that you're well versed in news releases and netiquette, discussion-group postings, and chats, let's go for the limelight!

Fancy promotions are part of any major marketing campaign, and they work especially well online. Instead of passively watching a show, people can participate. We can play trivia challenges, interview celebrities, and engage in Web treasure hunts. We can win P.T. Cruisers, bonus miles, or even a *billion dollars* in cash! For a break from workday stress, we can watch silly online animations or nuke a cartoon gerbil in an online microwave oven.

A big event always attracts a lot of attention. "The Blair Witch Project" set a new standard for online promotions, but it has been eclipsed by the elaborate game for *A.I.* (Artificial Intelligence). Everyone loves a parade, and the Web has become an endless stream of marching bands, floats, and hot air balloons.

Some of those balloons have burst, however, and that's part of the fun and danger of major online promotions. Imagine spending millions of dollars on TV and magazine ads promoting your Web site, only to fail to launch before the ads appeared? Sometimes pulling off a big promotion can seem like "Mission Impossible."

This chapter will help your promotions soar. I'll examine some of the greatest achievements and biggest blunders in interactive marketing history. You'll learn how to plan for success and how to avoid the triple threat of partnership problems, legal hassles, and technical glitches. And because creativity and novelty are essential to break-out promotions, I'll include plenty of examples to spark your imagination. Now, on with the show!

Topics covered include the following:

A tale of two promotions. DealerNet gave away a car online, and the Internet went nuts. Melissa offered $10,000 cash, and the Internet yawned. We will take a look at what went right and what went wrong with two early Internet promotions.

Designing good promotions. Everything you need to create a campaign with sizzle, not fizzle; covers the characteristics of a good promotion, establishing objectives, understanding the target audience, and planning the campaign.

Partnerships. To pull off a major online event, you need partners. But with partners come problems. This section presents instructions for recruiting and working with partners, highlighted with success stories and horror stories.

Contests. Sweepstakes and other giveaways are a well-worn path for promotion. With all that experience, why are most online contests so poorly designed? Learn how to structure a contest and pick prizes that will not only turn your promotion into a media miracle worker, but also will keep you out of legal hell.

Games and quizzes. When you challenge your audience, they will reward you with good consumer behavior and advice. Learn how to build entertaining, interactive promotions and how to syndicate them online.

Traffic builders. Sometimes you just need a Stupid Web Trick to boost traffic and relieve stress. Dancing Baby, Frog in the Blender, Dilbert, and Dolly the Cloned Sheep are all here, along with some warnings about copyright and trademark infringement.

Major events. From the Michael Jackson SimulChat to the fictional universe built for the movie *A.I.*, big events come with big headaches. Follow these tips for coordinating major online events, and you'll soon be the P.T. Barnum of cyberspace.

A Tale of Two Promotions

It was the winter of 1994. The online community was all abuzz about a new "killer app" called Mosaic. *Business Week* had just run a cover story about "The Internet: How it will change the way you do business?" Then, one company stepped forward to demonstrate that the old business models still work pretty well: If you want to get people's attention, give away something big. They gave away a car over the Internet.

The company was DealerNet, the virtual showroom selling new and used automobiles (Figure 9.1). DealerNet represented a new way of doing business. Now you could shop for a car from the comfort of your home (more likely from work) without the

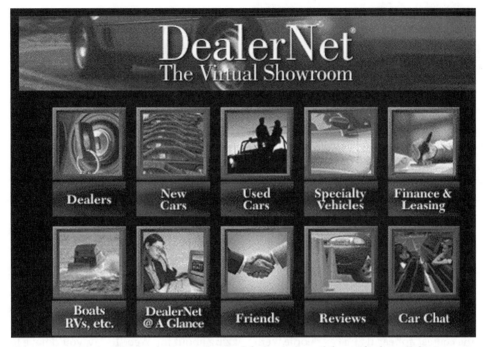

Figure 9.1   DealerNet ran the most successful promotion of the early days of the Internet.

pressure of a salesperson. You could visit dozens of dealerships without having to get out of your chair. You could easily prepare a list of the makes and models available and compare features and prices throughout the country. It was going to revolutionize the way cars were sold.

To promote its service, DealerNet relied on that tried-and-true marketing gimmick: the contest. It gave away a brand new Nissan Sentra. The Internet went nuts. Usenet newsgroups hummed as people swapped the URL for the online entry form. The contest was written up, not only in Internet trade journals, but also in newspapers and magazines from coast to coast. The DealerNet home page was getting thousands of hits a day. It was the first big, successful promotion on the World Wide Web.

It was the winter of 1994. The online community was all abuzz about a new "killer app" called Netscape. Microsoft just announced that it would be building its own commercial online service. Then, one company stepped forward to prove that greed was still the strongest marketing tool, or so it hoped. Carol Publishing announced it was giving away $10,000 cash. The Internet yawned.

I was the publicist for the $10,000 giveaway. It was promotion for the book, *Who Should Melissa Marry?* The book was an unfinished romance novel. The contest was to see who could write the best concluding chapter answering the title question. The promotion resulted in negligible media coverage and only a couple hundred requests for the rules. It was a disaster.

I take solace in the fact that the Melissa contest was not my idea. It had been running for several months offline. The media had not responded to Melissa's plea for help. Her prose was rotting on bookstore shelves, moving closer to the recycling bin as the contest deadline approached. The idea to put the contest online was a last-ditch effort to take advantage of the Internet's ability to reach a large audience quickly. It didn't work.

I must admit I was a little surprised at Melissa's poor results. When DealerNet gave away a car, the Internet exploded with activity as people burdened the bandwidth with entry forms and the press ran interviews with the geniuses behind the promotion. Melissa was giving away $10,000 cash, which could be considered more valuable than the car and certainly was costing the sponsor more. So why was response so lackluster? It was not a good promotion.

What Went Right

The DealerNet promotion was near perfect. The giveaway—a car—was in total keeping with the client's product line. If it had given away, say, an all-expenses-paid vacation to Ireland, the contest would not have resonated with the public. The contest was compelling for the target market: adults with ready access to the Internet. The point was to get people with automotive purchasing power to visit the site. It worked.

The scope of the contest was just right. A car giveaway is nothing new. In a magazine ad, it might draw only a modest response. But it was an order of magnitude larger than anything previously given away on the Internet. The timing was flawless, with the contest appearing just as people were buzzing about the Web. Today, you'd have to give away something more interesting than a car to get the media coverage that DealerNet received.

That brings us to perhaps the most important ingredient for success: novelty. Giving away a car is nothing new; giving it away over the Internet, however, made it fresh again. It's not easy coming up with a perfect hook for a promotion. The best you can do is delve deeply into the product being promoted, research the target market, and look for some thunderbolt linking the two.

If you find the lightning, you have to be ready for the ride. DealerNet had a professional team of publicists in place that knew how to ride the lightning. Once they caught a journalist's attention, they were ready to roll out the tale of a new company revolutionizing the way cars are sold. They were prepared for the jokes: How can you test-drive a car online? They were prepared for the questions: How many people have bought a car using your service? The contest was a bolt that punched a hole in the media's tough crust. DealerNet's publicity team used the opening to turn a news item about a contest into a feature story about a whole new way of selling cars.

What Went Wrong

Now, let's look at poor Melissa. The product was a book, and the contest asked readers to become writers and provide the final chapter. That has some integrity. But the prize —cash—worked against it. A date with Fabio, the famous book cover hunk, probably would have resonated more with the target market: people who read romance novels.

The scope of the project was off. For a cash giveaway, it was too small. Thanks to lotteries, factory workers become millionaires on a nightly basis. In 1999, Grab.com ran an online contest with a grand prize of *one billion dollars*. Yes, that's *billion* with a "b." If you're giving away cash, anything less than a million bucks just isn't newsworthy on a national scale. As for timing, do you think a title like *Who Should Melissa Marry?* is in keeping with the times?

It's interesting to look at the origin of the Melissa promotion. Bill Adler, the contest's creator, caught lightning in 1984 with a book called *Who Killed the Robins Family?* The publisher gave away $5,000 then. The contest was a sensation, capturing the imagination of the general public. With more than 100,000 entries, the book with a built-in expiration date became a best seller. But lightning wouldn't strike twice. Even the novelty of putting the contest on the Internet and giving Melissa an e-mail address was not enough of a twist to command media coverage.

One of the only things Melissa had going for her was preparation. We set up an autoresponder and were ready to handle the thousands of requests for information that would pour in every day. Fewer than 200 people responded, and only three entries were submitted using the Internet. Just as the contest was a recycled idea, so have copies of Melissa's unsold story probably been turned into newsprint.

Designing Good Promotions

A good promotion is like harnessed lightning. It rips through the heavy atmosphere of routine living, crackling with energy. It commands our attention with its sudden brightness. "Did you see that?" people ask, spreading the word. The media hear the buzz and move in. A lightning strike is a good story. Then, just as quickly as the powerful bolt appeared, it's gone.

DealerNet caught lightning in a bottle. Melissa caught nothing but heat. It's not easy catching lightning, but it's not completely up to chance. There are certain shared attributes of any great promotion.

Characteristics of a Good Promotion

Here is my short list for the features of a successful promotion. Consider this list a checklist: If you can design a promotion that has all six of these features, you're ready for development and deployment online:

1. *Integrity*—A promotion grows out of the product being promoted.

   This feature is the top one on my list, and yet it is the one most frequently absent from online promotions. A good promotion comes from an in-depth understanding of the product or service being promoted. If the product is a movie, it's not enough to have a promotion encouraging film viewing, such as a trailer. You need to drill down and find the soul of the product, its reason for being, and its unique selling proposition. You have to understand the smallest details of the product and then fashion a promotion that reflects and reinforces those characteristics. Integrity isn't as superficial as selecting a prize that matches the product. Every aspect of the promotion should be in harmony with the unique features of the product, including the design of the promotion, the marketing campaign, the behavior people are asked to engage in, the prizes, the way winners are chosen, and the conclusion of the promotion.

The online promotion for the film "The Blair Witch Project" was effective because it had integrity. The soul of the movie was whether it was fact or fiction and included a raw, gritty process of discovery. The film achieved this feel in part because even the actors and filmmaker didn't know what was going to happen; much of the script was improvised, along with the acting. So the making of the film reflected the subject of the film. The online promotion played on these characteristics with a Web site that reinforced the fact-or-fiction question and required a process of discovery and improvisation similar to the film. And the promotion of the Web site—using word of mouth rather than media hype—sustained the indie-edgy spirit of the project.

There are several reasons why promotions lack integrity. Having too much money is one of them. When you have a small budget, you have to be creative. With a large budget, you can appeal to greed, a reliable but dull motivator that delivers less bang for the buck. Another problem is hiring an outside firm to create your promotion. These companies understand *their* market, not yours, and the gimmicks they come up with reflect that. I can understand using outside firms to *execute* your promotion, but I would never give a stranger control over the concept or design. Other reasons for a lack of integrity include laziness that causes people to imitate successful models rather than look within, cowardess in backing away from innovation in favor of the tried-and-true, and a push for quick results that smacks of desperation.

2. *Focus*—The promotion is irresistible to the target market.

Just as integrity flows from an understanding of the product, focus is derived from a clear understanding of the target audience. Great promotions are relentless in their obsession with a clearly defined target audience. If anyone else is interested in the promo, who cares? I don't play online games; I don't like them; I consider them a waste of time. Nintendo couldn't care less about me. Their promotions aren't aimed at overcoming my dislike at gaming; rather, they want to reach a specific demographic (mostly young boys) who live for these challenging games. Promotions that are overly broad don't satisfy anyone: not the people who sponsor them, the people who participate in them, nor the companies that design them.

3. *Novelty*—The concept has a unique twist to it.

A contest that has integrity is likely to have novelty, because the promotion is not based on a generic formula, but on the totally unique characteristics of the product itself. Novelty is highly desired in part because it's so difficult to generate and is rarely seen. One of my favorite sources for inspiration in designing promotions is the "Quirky" page at Contest.com (hint: look in the "Best Bets" section). I don't find myself stealing these good ideas so much as whacking stale ones out of my head and bolstering my courage to dig further into the product looking for lightning. When thinking outside the box isn't working, don't retreat! Make yourself *more* uncomfortable. Blow up the box. Start thinking evil thoughts, ideas you dare not utter, and try to subvert your own goals. Why not charge a million dollars to enter a contest and offer *nothing* for a prize? When you find the hidden connection between a thing and it's opposite, you are on the path to enlightenment (and a good campaign, too).

4. *Timing*—The right gimmick at just the right time

Timing is hard to build into a promotion. If you see a trend coming and you incorporate it into your plan, by the time your campaign launches it will be old news, or you'll look like a copy cat. It's almost as though you have to be clairvoyant. Your promotion has to be out there already when synchronicity strikes. You can build timing into your campaigns, however, by building in trap doors that let you shape the promotion as you go. Part of my work as an online book publicist is to take something that was written a year ago and connect it with events in the news today. You need to leave a portion of the campaign open so that you can capitalize on current events. A good example is to specify a grand prize for a contest, but choose runner-up prizes at the last possible minute to accommodate new sponsors or to freshen your appeal. Sometimes what looks like luck is a combination of trap-door design, advance preparation so you can turn on a dime, and keeping your nose in the air so you can smell an opportunity coming.

5. *Scope*—The scale is perfectly suited to the product and the audience.

A lot of good promotions are ruined by attempting to do too much. Examples include Web sites that don't work, press conferences that no one attends, parties that no one knows about, and more replies than can be handled. Usually, these troubles occur when the target audience is not clear and a shotgun approach is taken rather than a laser beam approach. There's a certain elegance in knowing exactly who your audience is and what they want and giving them no more or no less. If you're giving away cash, you probably don't need a huge prize that will attract all comers but an amount that's just enough to get your target audience over the hurdle of registration without causing an avalanche of entries that you can't handle. When you have an ambitious campaign that involves multiple partners, you risk overwhelming your resources and running out of time. Better to have a smaller event flawlessly executed than an extravaganza that flops.

6. *Preparation*—You must be ready to ride the lightning.

Every big promotion is launched with a sense of uncertainty, but it's surprising how many people are caught off guard as much by success as failure. When I promoted the *RealAge* quiz, the traffic shut down the site for three days. I've offered giveaways where the client wasn't sure what the package contained until after people started asking for it. If you're giving away a trip to Disneyland, what exactly does that include? If the media picks up the story, you want to be ready to turn a blurb into an article and an article into a full-blown feature.

Advance preparation can take a small promotion and spin it out into major event. You need to be prepared to use the data you collect, to capitalize on the interest of the press, and to work around a crisis of too much success.

Defining the Audience and Objectives

If your promotion is successful, what will the results be? We all want to be successful, but would we know success even if we were basking in it? To design a good promotion, you need a better goal than a vague feeling of accomplishment. You should have a clear, detailed vision of the results you hope to achieve before launching an online promotion.

Setting Goals

Site traffic is certainly one measure of success. The fact that a lot of people were drawn to the promotion is usually a good sign. But don't lie to yourself about what those numbers mean. For example, consider iChat, a very cool conferencing tool that could be part of a successful online event. In order to follow the discussion in iChat, the screen reloads every few seconds. One person could easily account for thousands of hits during a single event. Some sites get more hits because they are poorly designed and require a lot of searching to find information.

Most online contests have a goal of building a marketing database through contest registrations. In this case, you probably have a target number of registrations you're hoping for. Does the registration form ask for enough information to pre-qualify the person as a likely prospect? Do you have a way to database the results, analyze them, and employ them in future marketing activities? You might realize what so many other sweepstakes sponsors have: that the quality of the registrants is so poor it's not worth marketing to them. You have to wonder whether this method is a cost-effective way to build a database.

Sales are another measure of success that's hard to argue with. If your goal is to generate sales from your promotion, the amount of traffic you get means little. Inquiries, prospects, or leads could be more important measures than sales, especially if you're marketing big-ticket items such as appliances, cars, or real estate. Inquiries are also important if you're selling services, not products. It's hard to buy a service over the Internet without making some inquiry first.

A more sophisticated approach to measuring results involves the use of ratios. Compare the traffic you get with the inquiries or sales you generate. How does the ratio change over time? If you are consistently converting 1 percent of traffic into sales, what can you do to improve the sell-through? Either the hit count or the sales level alone could be misleading, but their ratio is a number you can work with. What percentage of inquiries do you convert to sales? When people buy, how much do they buy? How can you increase the sales per customer?

In my work promoting books online, I've found that the best results (other than media attention) come from one or two big trade customers. A single foreign distribution agreement could be worth tens of thousands of dollars. A bulk sale to a statewide library system could be worth thousands. A movie rights deal could be worth more than a million. You have to service an awful lot of retail customers to equal one big trade deal. And guess what? The foreign agent, the librarian, the Hollywood producer —they're all online, whereas the home consumer is not online in huge numbers yet and is bandwidth-challenged with low-speed connections. If success for you means the overall financial health of your enterprise, then I suggest you focus your promotions on business-to-business accounts and leave the entertainment to Sony and Starwave.

Another facet of online success is presence, that most mercurial of measures that includes such intangibles as brand recognition, goodwill, and cachet. It's hip to be online and it's embarrassing to be absent from the scene. It's true that holding a high-profile online promotion can improve your standing with stockholders and customers. If you have a substantial marketing budget, it makes sense to allocate a decent portion to online activities. Your presence online will help your traditional marketing activities work better.

Understanding the Target Audience

You have to immerse yourself in the target audience if you want to be successful reaching them. For many online promotions, the real audience is the media. You're hoping the promotion will catch fire and you'll make the evening news and the morning paper. The media is a tough crowd, though, and when you invite their attention, you might be inviting disaster. If the promotion is a flop, the press can be merciless.

If the goal is to get media attention, then be prepared to handle the press. You should offer some sort of press packet to flush them out. It's hard to schmooze a journalist if he or she is an anonymous lurker, so you want to entice them into making contact. Have materials ready to turn a short news item into a feature story. Have artwork prepared in advance and a spokesperson who can anticipate and answer media inquiries.

If your target market is the general public, a completely different approach is called for. If you're looking for nothing but numbers—reaching the most people possible—then your promotion must be accessible as well as compelling. You might want to partner with someone who has a server powerful enough to handle the traffic. To estimate traffic demands, try to get advertising information from popular Web sites; they will often tell you how many hits they get for popular events.

To reach the masses, you want to design your promotion so that you don't exclude people from America Online or CompuServe, people who have out-of-date Web browsers, people who use Macintosh computers, and so on. Of course, a text-based promotion has the widest possible audience, but it's unlikely to captivate must interest. You might want to offer several alternative versions of your promotion for people with different software and/or hardware configurations. Your clever creations will not reach the masses if enjoying them requires a T-1 line and a 21" monitor.

If your goal is to reach potential customers, you might want to design your promotion for utility instead of entertainment. Too many promotions are geared to get traffic and nothing else. If you have 100,000 people a week coming to your site to play some silly game, you're probably making it more difficult for potential customers to get through. When customers arrive, does the site help them make a buying decision or provide them with ready access to your customer support team?

Is the Target Audience Online?

Maybe you have a good idea of whom you're trying to reach. Are they on the Internet? I've done a lot of work promoting items for kids on the Internet. I have to keep reminding my clients that it's not easy to reach young children online. If you're promoting a product for children on the Internet, you have to design the promotion for parents or teachers or the press.

In order to participate in an online promotion, people need two things: a computer and an account with an online service. Those criteria exclude 95 percent of the world's population. The characteristics of the remaining 5 percent look nothing like demographics of the population as a whole. You can have a crystal-clear image of your target audience and design the perfect promotion to attract them, but if they aren't online, it won't work.

One way to learn about the target audience online is to study the advertising rate cards of popular sites. Many sites require registration to access their best features, and the registration database is a goldmine of marketing information, especially when mapped to psychographic profiles based on residential zip codes. Online advertising networks are good places to hunt for such information. The DoubleClick network has a list of major online publishing outlets along with demographics and patterns for each site (www.doubleclick.com). Figure 9.2 shows the User Profile for *Esquire* magazine's Web site. It includes such important statistics as average age, median income, and gender. Some sites in DoubleClick's database have much more detailed information based on registration and surveys, including the percentage of the audience making certain purchases in the past 12 months. Studying rate cards will help you determine whether your target audience is online, where they like to hang out, and what kinds of activities you can expect them to engage in as a result of your promotions.

Typical User Profile*

- Median Age: 38.3
- Average Income: $61,528
- Male/Female: 64.6/35.4%

Purchasing Habits:

- Spend freely on clothing
- Likely to buy in the luxury and mid-luxury car classes
- Avid fans and consumers of high-end home entertainment and home computer equipment
- Buy pre-recorded music in quantity
- Chose the latest in portable technologies
- Shop extensively on-line, from retail to music

Interests:

- Attend cultural events
- Pursue charitable interests
- Participate in a wide variety of sports
- Travel frequently for business and pleasure

* Sources: MRI Doublebase Adults 1999; MRI Doublebase Men 1999

Figure 9.2   A user profile for *Esquire* magazine's Web site from the DoubleClick ad network. Analyzing site statistics will help you craft promotions that reach the target audience and motivate them to register or buy.

Many moons ago, I worked in politics. The most painful lesson I learned was that people who don't vote don't vote. You can't run a successful campaign for public office based on getting non-voters to cast ballots. The only way to win an election is to get the majority of the people who *do* vote to vote for your candidate. There might be millions of people with access to the Internet, but it's a mistake to think that you can tap that consumer buying power through an elaborate online promotion. Unless your target audience has shown a tendency to engage in the types of activities you hope to motivate with your contest, you have little chance of getting them to significantly alter their behavior.

Planning the Campaign

There are two important dates for a major online promotion. The first is the *launch date* when you want the promotion to begin reaching the target audience. The second is the *media date* when you need to tell the press about your promotion if you hope to get media coverage. To get coverage in major national print publications or on television news magazines or talk shows, the media date will be at least three months before the launch date. Let's look at the full planning calendar, working backward from the end to the beginning.

Follow-up. Results of the promotion are tallied and databases are exploited.

Launch date. The promotion is available to the target audience.

Media date. The media is told about the promotion.

Testing. A trial run of the campaign reveals any bugs.

Production. All elements of the campaign are assembled.

Design. The exact features of the promotion are determined.

Partners. Any partnership deals are consummated.

Planning. Includes timelines, budget, goals, and resources needed.

Concept. Idea for a promotion and analysis of the target audience.

This chart of activities should help you realize that holding a major online promotion is not something to enter into lightly. Many online events fail, not as a result of underfunding, but due to lack of time. For annual events, including something as grand as the Academy Awards or as simple an annual earnings report, planning begins as soon as last year's event ends. Promotions for major movies, CDs, and book releases often start a year prior to launch date and seldom less than six months in advance. For most companies, I recommend that you focus on one major annual event, rather than attempting quarterly or even monthly promotions. Pick a spot in your annual calendar where you think your promotion will have the best chance of success, and try to hit that spot every year. You'll get better as you go.

Good examples of major annual events are the exhibitions at the *University of California Irvine* (UCI) bookstore at www.book.uci.edu, shown in Figure 9.3. The bookstore's Web master has teamed up with content providers to create lavish exhibits that educate as well as entertain. Their first project was called "The Big Island of Hawaii," sponsored

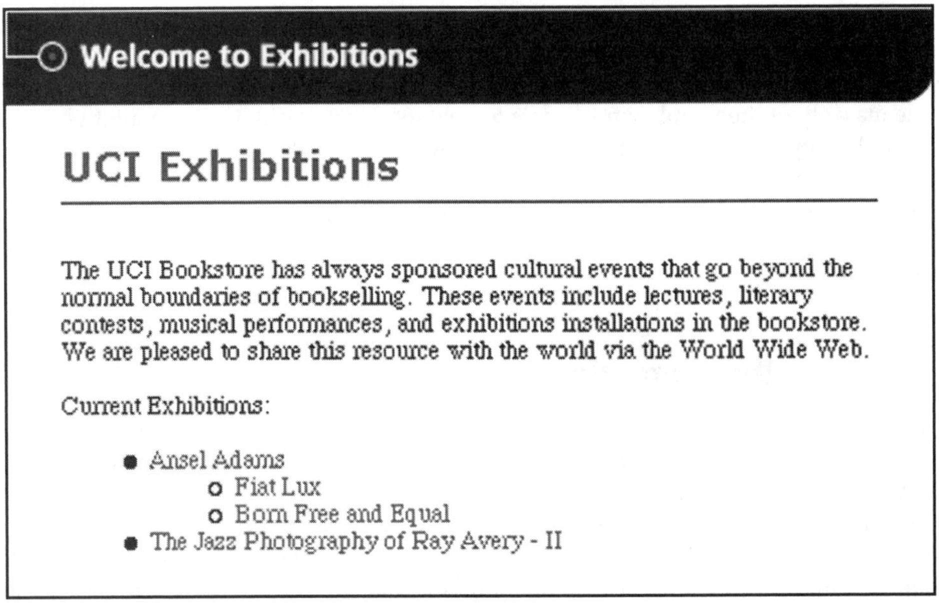

> ─○ **Welcome to Exhibitions**
>
> ## UCI Exhibitions
>
> The UCI Bookstore has always sponsored cultural events that go beyond the normal boundaries of bookselling. These events include lectures, literary contests, musical performances, and exhibitions installations in the bookstore. We are pleased to share this resource with the world via the World Wide Web.
>
> Current Exhibitions:
>
> - Ansel Adams
>   - Fiat Lux
>   - Born Free and Equal
> - The Jazz Photography of Ray Avery - II

Figure 9.3 The UCI bookstore conserves its marketing resources by developing major annual Web exhibits tied to store events. The installations are entertaining, educational, newsworthy, and connected with buying opportunities.

by Moon travel handbooks. Subsequent exhibits have included the Jazz Photography of Ray Avery and a feature on Ansel Adams. UCI's exhibitions include offline and online events, with an opening night to which the media is invited, readings in the store and audio archives online, and store displays matched by Web displays—all coupled with buying opportunities from the store's collection of music and books.

When you do an annual promotion like this one, you have time to plan. You can iron out the legal details of contests or quizzes. You have time to look for partners, sponsors, and advertisers. You can develop artwork, audio files, video clips, and databases that mesh together for a premium browsing experience. You have time to test the event to make sure it works before you open it to the public. Best of all, you have plenty of time to promote the event.

Instead of chasing after the media every week or month, you're asking them to visit just once a year, and you're hopefully providing an event with enough pizzazz to warrant coverage. You can promote the show with printed invitations to customers, suppliers, investors, and the press. You can buy print ads or get the event written-up in magazines and journals that have long lead times. Once the show is over, you can leave the exhibits on your Web site. UCI keeps its exhibits up for years.

Possibly the biggest advantage of holding an annual event like this one is preserving the sanity of your Web master and staff. I've seen many a programmer burn out trying to be the latest, hippest, coolest thing on the Internet. With an annual event, there's a schedule—a plan. As the deadline approaches, people will be stressed trying to get everything in place. But afterward, they can relax, take some time off, and start thinking about next year's show.

You'll notice in the timeline that the Media Date comes after the testing phase. If you want to get long-lead media coverage in magazines and on television, you should be testing the entire promotion about four months in advance of the launch date. Many promoters don't test until well after alerting the media to the promotion, which is a big mistake. If the promotion doesn't work as advertised, you will not only get blasted in the press, but you will also lose credibility for future announcements. You don't need to have everything in place by the time you announce your promotion to the press, but you should have enough of the work done to be able to invite them to visit. A media preview is a great opportunity to court the press and learn about any bugs in the installation. You can assure the media that the bugs will be fixed; if you have enough time to make repairs, they might even believe you. You can invite them back after improvements have been made so they can make changes to any stories in progress.

Also notice in the timeline that the design phase comes *after* securing partners. This sequence gives you the opportunity to customize a promotion based on the partners involved. In many ways, it eases the burden of planning because you don't need to work out all the details of a promotion before finding partners. You can go to your partners with a concept and a general plan and then tailor the details based on who jumps on the bandwagon. I'll talk more about partnerships in the next section.

If you want to run promotions more frequently than once a year, you might want to set up an annual schedule in advance. For example, if you want a monthly or quarterly program, you can plan for the whole year, secure an initial set of partners, and each session out will give you the testing experience you need to improve the program next time.

Case Study: LEGO Mindstorms RoboTour

I have been privileged to sit on the judging committee for the Tenagra Awards for Internet Marketing Excellence for two years (http://awards.tenagra.com). From this vantage point, I've been able to see detailed information on the creation and execution of some of the Internet's most successful promotional campaigns. I'll describe two of those campaigns in this chapter. If you're working on building a major promotion, I recommend consulting the Tenagra Awards site as well as these other sites where you can find examples of world-class efforts:

The Webby Awards at www.webbyawards.com. Given by the International Academy of Digital Arts and Sciences, the Webby Awards are among the most coveted in the industry.

Cool Site of the Year at www.coolsiteoftheday.com/awards.html. These awards are based on rankings at the Cool Site of the Day Web site combined with online voting by the public. Past award winners provide a treasure-trove of promotional ideas.

ChannelSeven.com—Ad/Insight (Case Studies) at www.channelseven.com/adinsight/case_studies/. Supplied by Ad/Insight, the case histories at ChannelSeven are a superb resource for promotion planners. They give behind-the-scenes looks at successful campaigns, although you'll have to wade through a lot of bragging to find the real lessons.

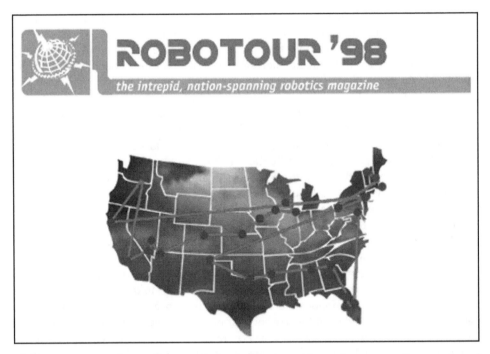

Figure 9.4 The LEGO Mindstorm RoboTour visited 25 cities on its way to a Tenagra Award for Internet Marketing Excellence. The campaign is an example of good planning.

The winner of the 1999 Tenagra Award for Online Public Relations Success was the team behind the LEGO Mindstorms RoboTour (Figure 9.4). The tour was organized by Switzer Communications, a San Francisco Bay-area public relations firm. The firm was hired to build interest in LEGO Mindstorm's Robotic Invention System, in which the famous interlocking blocks were coupled with a microprocessor core and various gears, motors, and sensors enabling buyers to build their own robots. Let's take a look at the objectives, timelines, and methods used in this campaign.

Switzer had an interesting problem on its hands with the Mindstorm promotion: no product in the stores. The product would appear in stores in fall for the upcoming Christmas shopping season. LEGO debuted the line at the Electronic Entertainment Expo in May and thought it had a hit on its hands. So Switzer was charged with building buzz for the product between June and October, and results would be measured first in the amount of media coverage the promotion generated, second in the sales of the toys, and third in building a long-term relationship with the core audience.

The core target market for this campaign was 12- to 15-year-old male teenagers. Switzer's research showed these boys didn't trust typical media outlets such as television and magazines for their news. More important to them was word-of-mouth, the Internet, and schools. School would be out during the summer months, so Switzer concentrated on getting media coverage, building a Web community, and basically going where the boys are with a grassroots, local media road tour.

Switzer took a young LEGO robot designer and prototypes of the product line on the road to 25 cities in the United States. For each city, the team connected with an expert in robotics or a celebrity associated with the subject and interviewed them. These dispatches made up the core content on the Mindstorm Web site. The LEGO team filled the time between interviews with stops at kitschy roadside attractions such as the World's Largest Ball of Twine and the Future Birthplace of Captain James T. Kirk, where they held photo-ops with the robots. Local media coverage was sought in each city, inviting journalists to join the interviews or see demonstrations of the robots.

I liked this campaign a lot because of the focus on the target audience and the integrity with the product being promoted. LEGO went to the heart of the matter by interviewing leading scientists and researchers as well as cultural figures associated with robots. The tour fostered a spirit of scientific inquiry and exploration among the audience and resulted in a promotion that was educational as well as entertaining. The timeline for the campaign is not enviable, but here Switzer made the best of it by focusing on short-lead media such as newsweeklies, local newspapers, local radio and television stations, and the Web. If they got coverage from long-lead magazines, it would appear as the *coup de grace* at the height of the Christmas buying season—not early enough to influence teens' Christmas wish lists. Stops in major media centers such as New York, Los Angeles, and Chicago were scheduled near the end of the tour, with hopes that grassroots coverage would lead to bigger media hits in these cities (and, of course, that the road team would have perfected its schtick by then).

The RoboTour began at the end of July and concluded at the end of September. It was a hit and generated great local coverage and some national attention including a feature article in *U.S. News and World Report*. The Web site generated millions of impressions (I won't quote the numbers, because impressions are such a meaningless measure of traffic) but more importantly fostered a community of youngsters who couldn't wait for the product to hit stores. When the line appeared in retail outlets, it sold out, which is certainly the best measure of a job well done.

While the RoboTour was an amazing campaign and more than anything shows the importance of local publicity, I have a few problems with it as a model. First, I'm sure it wasn't cheap, with all the travel, hotels, meals, and advance work in each city. No budget information was provided by LEGO. Second, it generated a lot of coverage from media outlets (which research showed were not that important to the target market). But the biggest omission was not involving the target market more closely in the campaign. It would have been nice if teens could have used the LEGO Web site to interview the scientists themselves or at least been able to forward questions to interviewers. And when the new school year started after Labor Day, LEGO should have included stops in school classrooms where kids could meet and interview the experts while getting to play with the robots. The interviews collected by LEGO could have been used in grade school and high school science classes, and teacher guidelines could have been made available at the Web site. Still, this campaign contains a good mix of offline and online activities, and Switzer should be applauded for taking the high road in favor of educational activities over the low road of glitz, gimmicks, and celebrity endorsements.

Partnerships

Partnerships are key to increasing the size of a promotion to breakthrough levels while keeping the costs manageable. The first type of partnership you should look for is a Web site to host the online promotion. It is far easier and much more valuable to find a high-traffic site to host the promotion than it is to drag the audience to your own site. The next step is to find prize partners. Promotions usually work better if third parties contribute any prizes given away, if for no other reason than to resist the temptation to give away the product being promoted—a bad sales strategy. Promotions that partner with a charity, educational institution, or non-profit organization can count on a media boost and a feeling of goodwill. Finally, a goal for large promotions is to find partners in areas where you are weak, whether that's money, technology, or practical experience.

A Partnership Success Story

In early 1996, Random House Juvenile Publishing launched an interactive Web promotion called *The Lurker Files* (Figure 9.5). They created a fictional online college complete with a chat room called "The Ratskellar," where The Lurker laid in wait. Behind the site was a professional writer (Scott Ciencin) who would spin out stories about the Lurker and other fictional characters attending the university. Visitors to the Web site would comment on the stories in the chat room, then see their comments turn up in the next episode as some plot twist. In other words, Random House's writers would work material from the chat room into the story.

This rather elaborate Web site was a big gamble. You never know whether people are going to come, whether they'll participate, and whether the chat room will work.

Figure 9.5 The Lurker Files was a joint effort between Random House and Yahoo!

But Random House had a couple of things going for it. First, the graphics were amazingly good. Someone at that company understands that you can't take good graphics from offline and put them on the Web. You have to create graphics that work in this environment. They have to load quickly, yet look sharp. It's not an easy balance, and few Web sites have done as good a job with their graphics as Random House.

Secondly, they co-branded the project with Yahoo!, the giant Internet catalog and one of the top 10 traffic sites on the Internet. Yahoo! was just beginning to segment into a series of special-interest catalogs. The first one to roll out was Yahooligans, a catalog for kids (Figure 9.6). Yahooligans became a co-sponsor for *The Lurker Files*. Debuting almost simultaneously, *The Lurker Files* got a premium link spot off Yahooligans' entertainment page.

Random House included a contest with the launch of *The Lurker Files* Web site. It asked kids to write a fictional account of what it's like being online. The prize was not money, which isn't much of a motivator, but fame: the chance to be published online or in print by Random House. The contest was positioned for teachers to use it as a writing assignment to get kids to talk about their online experiences.

Although *The Lurker Files* involved dragging the audience to a new Web site rather than working through a high-traffic site, it succeeded well beyond initial expectations. The site drew so much traffic that Random House decided to spin off a line of books, clothing, and other merchandise and shop the concept to television producers. The gamble paid off because the site was well constructed and Random House did a good job of co-branding with Yahooligans and marketing the site to educators and not just kids.

A Partnership Horror Story

Whenever you are dependent on a co-branding partner, there is the potential for trouble. The biggest problem I've had with co-branding is the time lag. Everything has to be approved by two companies, and it really slows down your ability to roll out a promotion and adjust it as necessary. You should plan extra time into your schedule. Just ask Apple Computer.

Apple partnered with Paramount Pictures on a Web site for the movie "Mission Impossible." Apple's product line is prominently displayed in the film. Its mission was

Figure 9.6 Yahooligans is a catalog of Internet resources for kids. The site partnered with Random House for a joint opening of Yahooligans and *The Lurker Files*.

to build a fancy Web site that demonstrated the value of its products. Apple should have turned down the assignment.

Apple launched the site with a series of television commercials and expensive print ads all built around the URL for the Web site: http://mission.apple.com/ (Figure 9.7). But the site wasn't up in time. Millions of dollars in advertising, and the only thing people connecting to the site saw was a "coming soon" graphic. I don't think many browsers came back soon.

The site was six weeks late according to the buzz on a mailing list for computer journalists. But things went from bad to worse for Apple when the site finally appeared about a week after the TV spots started running. To enjoy the site, you had to have an up-to-date browser and four plug-ins that most people didn't have. Those requirements eliminated a large portion of the potential audience, including everyone on America Online and CompuServe. (There's nothing like alienating millions of people.)

But the story gets worse. Even if you had an up-to-date browser and installed all the plug-ins, the site still didn't work. One wired journalist I know reported that the site crashed his system every time he tried to visit. First it was late, and then it was broken. That's not the kind of PR that Apple was hoping to achieve with its multi-million dollar investment.

Who knows whether the delays were caused by the co-branding relationship or by the difficulty of the programming or what? Certainly, whenever you are in a partnership, things will slow down. Time and again, I have been hired by companies to promote sites that are not ready. You don't want to invite millions of people to a site that is broken. So, give yourself enough time to make absolutely certain that the site works before you tell the world about it.

Finding, Recruiting, and Working with Partners

For locating partner sites, I use several different strategies. The first is to go where the traffic is. The Resources area of the companion web site at www.wiley.com/comp-books/okeefe has a section called SuperSite finders that will help you. I start with The

Figure 9.7 Connecting to Apple's partnership site with Paramount turned out to be a mission impossible.

Hot 100 at www.100hot.com, which lists the top Web sites by traffic in a dozen different categories. *PC Magazine* also has a good list of top Web sites; however, it's based on the opinions of editors rather than traffic. For every special interest you can think of, there is a Web site devoted to cataloging all the online resources related to that interest. Find these SuperSites, and you're well on your way to finding the best potential partners in your field. The Linkage chapter of this book explains how to build a map of the top sites in any given field. You can use that map to navigate the Web in search of partners.

Once you've located a promising partner site, finding the proper contact person for an inquiry can be difficult. The "about us" section of the site might yield contact names but seldom personal e-mail addresses or phone numbers. If the site has a rate card or an "advertise with us" section, you'll usually find a phone number there and perhaps the names of marketing people who can be good contacts for partnership inquiries. If you have any relationships with offline people at the target sites, use them to get an introduction to someone who has the ability to negotiate online partnership deals.

When pitching potential partners, I make an initial inquiry via e-mail. The biggest mistake in pitching potential partners is to reveal too much about the nature of the project. This reason is why I suggest you don't design your promotion until after you have your partners lined up. Use a brief e-mail with a message such as this one: "We are launching a new product this fall and are planning a major promotion to get print, broadcast, and online media coverage. I wonder if you would consider partnering with us on this campaign?" The more open you leave the query, the more room you have to customize it to satisfy your partner. The goal in pitching is to get either an e-mail address or phone number of someone who has the power to cut a deal for the partner company. As soon as you find that person, try to switch to phone communication. The phone lends itself to a give-and-take conversation, and it's harder to turn down someone on the telephone than it is in e-mail.

I use throw-away Web pages a lot in recruiting partners. The page is designed specifically for luring partners—not for the public—by showing them the concept for the promotion. I've used throw-away pages to rope in *Playboy,* MSNBC, Yahoo!, Lycos, and other major partners. Having a Web page demonstrates that I'm serious about pushing this project through and that I'm willing to do whatever it takes to make it happen. In many cases, I've lured partners with the Web page only to see that the final project looks nothing like the original concept. The partners take the ball and run in their own direction, and I try and hang on for the ride.

With partnership comes problems. The first is exclusivity. Some potential partners will be interested only if they can get an exclusive. If the value of the partnership is large enough and limiting yourself to one partner site does not work against the spirit of the campaign, go for it. Sometimes you can bring in other partners if they don't compete directly with the lead partner. For example, you might get Yahoo! to host the promotion and a manufacturer Yahoo! approves of for prizes. Sometimes your partners will bring their own partners, helping expand the reach of the promotion. *Playboy* did this on one partnership, bringing Amazon to the table.

Another problem with partners is losing control of the operation. You should prepare a list of everything you need to pull off the promotion and divide the list between the different partners. As long as you're clear about who is responsible for what, you'll have few control problems. Every partnership has the potential to bog down in bureaucracy. To the greatest extent possible, the partners need to be free to execute their portion of the project without the supervision of the other partners. As long as the results are achieved, the methods shouldn't be examined too closely. The larger the decision-making teams, the greater the likelihood the promotion will be late. If possible, you should limit your dealings to one counterpart at the other company and vice-versa. With individuals spearheading the project, more will get accomplished in a shorter time period. Sometimes you need to sacrifice prior approval of everything that goes into the campaign in the interest of getting it launched on time. If the promotion goes well, a working relationship will develop for future promotions. If the promotion flops, it's time to find better partners.

Case Study: Paper Mate

The Paper Mate promotion is another one that came to my attention through the Tenagra Awards for Internet Marketing Excellence. This assignment had to be tough: promoting writing instruments on the Internet—a medium that has no use for pens or pencils. I was completely impressed with what public relations firm Cone, Inc. did with this assignment. It's a textbook example of using partnerships in online promotions.

Cone first found a vehicle to hitch the promotion to: *Absolutely Incredible Kid Day* (AIKD), a program started by the Camp Fire Boys and Girls asking adults, one day a year, to write and send a letter to a child. Obviously, this vehicle is excellent for Paper Mate, but how do you spin it on the Web? Cone decided against building a standalone site and instead ran the entire promotion through partner sites. Using the feel-good hook, Cone forged partnerships with iVillage, Warner Brothers Online, Marvel Comics, and Sportsrap. Each site hosted a different AIKD promotion that encouraged the use of a pen. iVillage offered a contest to coax young writers with a prize of uniting penpals (Figure 9.8). Warner Brothers gave parents coupons to fill in and use as rewards for children, entitling them to escape chores or earn perks. All four sites were crosslinked to each other. Cone then secured donations of more than $11 million for banner ad impressions from sites such as Discovery Online, Excite, GeoCities, Infoseek, The Mining Company, and Women.com.

In the Paper Mate campaign, you see a classic example of the partnership strategy. First, partner with a charity or build in a public service hook. Second, look for high-traffic sties that reach the target audience to host the promotion. Third, bring in partners where you are weak (the banners donated to promote the partner sites). With each level of partnership, the reach of the promotion grows by an order of magnitude: The four partner sites probably delivered 10 times the audience Paper Mate could have gotten with a standalone site, and the banner ad partners delivered 10 times the reach of the four content partners.

Another thing I liked about this promotion is that Cone kept the exact nature of the project loose until partners were recruited. Cone must have gone to the four partner sites with a pitch like, "Do you want to be in on this Absolutely Incredible Kid Day promotion—it'll be great publicity." Once he had them hooked (and how can you say no to kids?), he helped design promotions that served each site's needs while fitting the loose guidelines of Paper Mate (the promotion had to require using a pen). Some

Figure 9.8 A promotion for Absolutely Incredible Kid Day unites host iVillage and sponsor Paper Mate to benefit the non-profit Camp Fire Boys and Girls. Put together by PR firm Cone, Inc., this endeavor is a textbook example of the power of partnership promotions.

of the partner sites recruited their own partners for prizes, thus gaining another layer of reach.

On the down side, I don't have any numbers about the effectiveness of the Paper Mate campaign. I know that Cone was given only four weeks from start to finish, which is not enough time to generate adequate media coverage for the promotion. Taking this campaign to the next level would mean getting the press to cover it, thus increasing by ten fold the number of people exposed to the message. Another problem is that the partner sites don't appear to be an ideal match for the target audience: women and parents. I suspect that Cone had to take the partnerships they could get quickly and that sites such as iVillage probably insisted on being the only women's site partnering on the promotion. Still, I couldn't ask for a better example of how the partnership game can be played to perfection.

Contests

Contests and sweepstakes are ubiquitous components of online promotions. When I preach my sermon of giving something of value to the online audience in exchange for them sitting still for a promotional pitch, what most people think of first is a prize. Because a prize is something of value, I won't dump on this strategy, but it's not a particularly clever idea (and in many cases, the contest is executed with so little creativity and forethought that many companies are disappointed by the results).

Like everything else online, sweepstakes might have had some novelty when they were first introduced, but they have been used so often that the online audience has a healthy skepticism for these clichéd events. In an article in online marketing magazine ClickZ, Chuck Hildebrandt describes the difficulties of breaking through to the target audience with a contest. When he wrote this piece in 1998, Hildebrandt was the director of marketing for CoolSavings, a company that specializes in opt-in promotions. "Don't rely heavily on contests and sweepstakes," writes Hildebrandt, who says that while sweepstakes can generate greater visibility, they "rarely work as a means of getting you qualified business." He cites poor clickthrough on sweepstakes banner ads and poor conversion ratios for those who do click through. "Most clickers perceive immediately that the sweepstakes are merely a manipulative device to get them to the site . . . They tend to resent them and split without enrolling."

On the positive side, contests and sweepstakes can be very popular. iWon, the Internet portal that is built around sweepstakes, is one of the most popular sites online. Forrester Research predicts that more than half of total Internet marketing budgets will be spent on promotions in the next three years. Contests and sweepstakes are familiar promotions for many companies, reducing the risk and expense of trying something new. Legal issues related to contests are well known, standards are clearly established, and there's less chance of running afoul of the law. And contests can be a great way of building an initial database that can be exploited with more refined techniques in the future.

If you're going to do an online contest, you should do it right. This section will help you design a contest that achieves your goals while steering clear of legal difficulties.

Designing a Good Contest

Take a look at the characteristics of a good promotion listed earlier in this chapter and apply them to your contest idea to see whether it measures up. A great contest will have integrity with the product or company being promoted, will be irresistible to the target audience, and will immediately command attention because of its novelty. Every aspect of the contest, from the rules to the registration process to the selection of the prize, should reflect these goals. Because the prize establishes the character of the contest more than any other element, let's examine that first.

Choosing a Good Prize

Choosing the wrong prize is a major problem with online contests. Companies spend far more money than they need to if they would only be a little more creative. According to Adam Posman, a media planner with BAM Solutions, an interactive ad agency in Canada, "What a lot of people do not know is that very often how impressive the prize is doesn't matter." In an article for ClickZ, Posman describes a contest with a $500 product voucher that got better results than another contest giving away two airline tickets *every day* for three months. And he goes on to describe a contest that gave $500 cash away every day that flopped. So I'd say that rule number one for picking prizes is that cash is not a great motivator.

Cash fails to motivate because it is not original or in any way identified with a given product or service. It's neutral, adding nothing to the spirit of the contest except greed. And cash prizes result in the least-targeted registrations. For companies that are concerned only with the volume of entries and no other consideration, a huge cash prize might work. Publishers Clearing House has become synonymous with a large cash prize, and the strategy works for them. But most people can't afford to play that game. And a cash prize seldom generates any media attention for the contest, eliminating one of the major goals of the promotion.

The second rule is not to give away the product you are promoting. This situation is a knee-jerk reaction at many companies, thinking first, "Let's have a contest," and second, "Let's give away what we make." The problem here is that people will not buy what they think they might win. I saw a contest on the Web promoted by a publishing company where the prize was a copy of the book they were trying to sell called *One Degree Beyond*. The description of the contest informed readers that "Everyone who enters the contest, whether they win or not, is also eligible to order a copy of the book . . . with free shipping and handling (a $3.00 savings)." What a deal! Let's say that 10,000 people enter the contest. Are they going to buy the book, too? No, at least not until they find out they didn't win. Is the publisher going inform all of them, "Hey, you didn't win the book. Would you like to buy it?" Disappointment is a poor sales hook. Who knows how many sales were lost by people who entered the contest instead of buying the book.

Not only is it a bad idea to give away what you sell, but you're also missing a golden opportunity to expand the scope of your contest by bringing in a prize partner. If you are going to do a contest, it makes sense to recruit prize partners who offer something that will motivate your target audience. You can recruit separate partners for the grand prize and runner-up prizes. Every time you add a partner, you magnify the reach of the promotion. Now the prize partner is involved and will likely promote the contest and your company. The prize partners piggy-back on your publicity and don't have to deal with the hassles or expense of managing the contest themselves. So, the next rule is to find prize partners and extend the reach of your promotion.

In analyzing the prizes offered at contest portals on the Web, I have to say that I'm disgusted with the sorry lack of creativity and the stunning loss of opportunities for so many contest sponsors. More than half the prizes are cash, and most of the other prizes are merchandise sold by the company sponsor. Office.com gives away office equipment, a sex toys site gives away condoms, and The Knot offers to pay for your wedding (don't they realize that this contest will postpone purchases of goods and services by contest entrants?). The list goes on and on. Add to it the number of companies who use a prize that has absolutely nothing to do with the target market or their products, and I think we have an epidemic of stupid, lazy promotions.

I've talked about what you shouldn't give away. Let's look at some ideas for things you should give away. For inspiration, I searched through the listings at Contest.com, a directory of online sweepstakes, to find good examples. Here are some that satisfy the prize criteria:

Southern Living Readers' Choice Awards. No, they don't give away free subscriptions to *Southern Living* magazine. Rather, with a prize partner, they give away a free vacation for two to a southern city.

FreeAdvice.Com. This legal advice Web site offered a trip for two to visit the U.S. Supreme Court in Washington, D.C. Other prizes included WillWriter software from prize partner Quicken.

Famous Amos Taste of Fame Contest. The well-known cookie maker offered to make the contest winner famous by putting his or her face on a Famous Amos billboard. That's a clever promotion that reinforces the brand name and is inexpensive.

College.com Full Ride Sweepstakes. This college portal avoided the temptation to give away merchandise available for sale at the site and instead gave away a full, four-year college scholarship and a wardrobe from prize partner Tommy Hilfiger.

Choosing a Good Activity

What do you have to do to enter the contest? Some contests ask for an essay, a recipe, you to name a new product, and so on. You should try to come up with an activity that reinforces the product and brand message. But beware, you cannot require people to engage in this activity in order to enter the contest. We'll cover this topic in more detail in the discussion of Legal Requirements, but you should know that chances are most people who participate in your contest will not do anything beyond completing an entry form.

While you can't require people to engage in anything beyond providing a minimal amount of contact information, you can *ask* them to jump through additional hoops. In many cases, the spirit of a contest comes from the theme behind it, often embodied in an optional activity and spun with clever copy writing into something that captivates the imagination. Here are some examples that might heat your creative furnace:

Slick Times. You have to guess the date that either Bill or Hillary Clinton will first file for divorce. Slick Times is a political satire Web site.

Sure Fit. This manufacturer of slip covers holds an annual Ugly Couch photo contest. The prize is cash, so it doesn't deter people from buying slip covers. A charitable partnership is also included in the promotion.

MovieThing.com. This site has a weekly movie review-writing contest with a nominal $25 prize. I like this contest because through the contest, MovieThing accumulates content for its site. I wonder what it would cost to hire writers to match the number of quality reviews they get from members for free?

If you want to require an activity of some sort for your contest, try to pick something that resonates with the target audience and gets them to think about why they need your products or services. A contest describing your dream kitchen would be great for a company like Williams-Sonoma or describing a dream vacation for a travel agency. Yahoo! Careers asked people to describe their dream jobs after research showed that many job seekers didn't have any concept of a dream job and were therefore not inclined to look for one. The prize they offered was a day in a dream job, contributed by prize partners. One prize job was an ice cream taster contributed by Ben & Jerry's. That's a well-designed contest.

Contracting with a Contest Management Firm

There are many companies that provide comprehensive contest services and will help you launch a contest and stay out of trouble. Two of the sources I used to prepare this chapter are Raffle.ca and Flying Aces at www.flying-aces.com. Another that I've heard good reports on is Marden-Kane. These firms can help pull in prize partners for you and help you market your contest on multiple Web sites. They will purchase or gather the prizes, write the boilerplate, set up the entry form, administer the contest, and award the prizes. The fees can be quite reasonable—just a few thousand dollars (not including the prizes).

One reason to hire a contest-management firm is to make sure that your contest satisfies the prevailing rules and regulations. It's a lot cheaper to hire contest professionals than defense attorneys. Let's look at some of the legal issues dealing with online contests and sweepstakes.

Legal Requirements

Nothing slows down planning a contest as much as lawyers. It seems like they're paid to think up novel reasons why you shouldn't do a contest instead of helping you launch one quickly and legally. I'm not an attorney, and my opinions here aren't meant to be legal advice—just suggestions about some of the issues you will have to deal with. If you're thinking about doing a contest with a prize worth anything, I suggest that you contact experienced legal counsel.

At the Web site for LawMaster, www.lawforinternet.com, you'll find an excellent article titled "How to Organize and Operate an Internet Sweepstakes." The key elements of a sweepstakes are that it has a prize, that winners are chosen by chance, and that no *consideration* is required. This last element can be particularly sticky. Let's say you're holding a contest for the purpose of building a database of people who would be good prospects for a sales pitch. To enter the contest, they must complete a survey giving you the demographic information that you want: contact information, household income, the brand of toothpaste they use, and so on. Well, according to the law, requiring people to provide more than the minimal contact information necessary for prize notification might be construed as "consideration." After all, you're forcing them to give you something of value to enter the contest.

Trust me on this matter: There are thousands of contest addicts who know the law and will use it against you. These people have a stack of 3-inch-by-5-inch index cards preprinted with their contact information, ready to mail off to any and every contest they find. They won't complete your invasive survey or engage in any activities not required by law. And they will sue you if you attempt to run a contest that doesn't follow guidelines of the jurisdiction you're in. This topic brings up another sticky point: jurisdiction.

There are four federal government agencies that regulate games: the FTC, the FCC, the Post Office, and the Justice Department. Then, you have state governments, attorneys general, district attorneys, and so on. Reading between the lines of contest boilerplate suggests that Florida, California, and New York have particularly stringent state requirements. But all states have some regulations, and they're often very different. States such as Rhode Island require that you register with the state if you plan to have a sweepstakes. Washington State says you can't make people pay postage to get a copy of the complete contest rules. As you can see, lawyers are the real winners of most contests, because their fees to keep you safe can easily exceed the value of prizes.

Your legal obligations include providing a set of rules for the contest, which can run for pages. The rules are filled with disclaimers to shelter you and the prize partners from liability while explaining what the prizes are, how much they're worth, and how they'll be awarded. I once entered a HotWired t-shirt contest and was notified that I won. A month later, I got a package from HotWired, but instead of my T-shirt it had a pile of legal documents I had to sign and return: pages and pages of boilerplate. Three months later, my shirt showed up in the mail.

On one of the Internet marketing discussion groups I participate in, an anonymous person posted a list of problems they had when setting up an online contest. Some of the items included the following:

- A requirement to get a bond to ensure performance
- Failed to get a special license required in Quebec
- Needed to get a lottery license in one of the states

I don't want to scare you off from doing a contest or sweepstakes. My point here is that if you need legal advice, *factor it into your timetable*. I've spent a lot of time working on contest design for clients, only to have the legal department pull the rug out from under us. You might want to consult with lawyers *before* any other planning to see whether you can get a list of demands up front. Then, you can build the contest around the boilerplate. It doesn't sound very inspiring, but neither is a subpoena.

Games and Quizzes

If all the legal issues related to contests scare you, consider using a quiz, survey, or game for a promotion. These are some of the most popular giveaways you can offer online. Without prizes, they don't carry the same risks as contests. I've had some of my best promotional results distributing quizzes and surveys all over the Internet. Judging from the number of personality profiles and trivia tests people forward to me via e-mail, these promotions are well suited to the viral marketing techniques in vogue right now.

Building Quizzes and Games

A quiz, test, or survey can be an excellent giveaway if it focuses the user's attention on subjects that demonstrate the value of your products and services. An Internet security checklist, for example, might help people realize that they need to devote more of their IT budget to this important issue. A survey on how to tell whether your boyfriend is cheating on you can be a good come-on for a background check service. No matter what field you work in, you probably have expertise you can share with your target audience in the form of a quiz or survey.

One of the hazards of designing quizzes is that you can be sure someone in the audience is smarter than you. I built my first online quiz as part of a campaign for the book, *The Seinfeld Aptitude Test* (Figure 9.9). An online quiz was a perfect promotion for a trivia book. I didn't even have to think up the questions—I just copied them from the book. One of the questions was, "What color was the defective condom George used?" We thought the answer was "blue," but an astute student of "Seinfeld" informed us that the condom was not, in fact, defective—George just thought it was. There were several other question/answer combinations that people took issue with. If we had been awarding prizes based on performance, we could have gotten into trouble. Without the prizes, it was all harmless fun.

If your quiz is popular, there's a good chance you can export it to a high-traffic Web site. When I built the "Seinfeld" quiz, I paid to place it at Bookstacks Unlimited, which was at that time the top online bookstore. The programmers at Bookstacks liked the quiz so much they offered to make it more interactive at no cost. My version of the quiz was self-scoring, with the correct answers at the bottom of the page. The turbo-charged version kept the answers hidden and let users hit a button to calculate their scores. Partner sites will not only help extend the reach of your promotions, but they often lend a hand with improving presentation and functionality. I'll go into more detail on this point in the following case history.

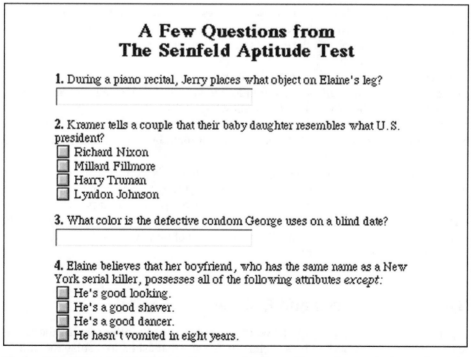

Figure 9.9 The Seinfeld Aptitude Test was the first online quiz I worked on. The main problem with quizzes is that someone in the online audience is always smarter than you.

The "Seinfeld" quiz was a lot of fun, but it didn't sell any books. We registered only 10 sales at Bookstacks in the first month of the promotion. I was crushed by the low sales numbers. One of the pitfalls of online quizzes is that just because people enjoy taking the quiz doesn't mean they'll buy the product. For the "Seinfeld" quiz, most of the hits were coming from colleges. That's great if college students are your market. But if they're not your market and they're not buying, do you want to spend thousands of dollars on programmers to entertain non-customers?

The "Seinfeld" campaign actually turned out well in the end. The quiz caught the eye of a *People* magazine reporter, and the book got a nice write-up there. The coverage in *People* was worth more to the publisher than the cost of the whole online campaign. When you design any online promotion, you should keep one eye on the media, building good stories into the design of the quiz. One way to perform this task is to ask people who take your quiz if they'd be willing to be interviewed. If you get an inquiry from a journalist, you can then offer someone who took the quiz as interview bait. I distributed a quiz on Internet privacy once, showing how much information is available about people online. In a news release promoting the quiz to reporters, my client offered to do an online background check on the journalists themselves as the basis for an article about Internet privacy. The media ate it up, curious to see what my client could dig up on them with a cursory search.

Games are very popular online because they take advantage of one of the Internet's unique characteristics: interactivity. Games can be very tricky to build, however, because they require both good graphics and good programming. You might consider hiring a gaming specialist to see whether they can devise a game that will be entertaining while driving home your marketing message. For a good example of simple but popular online games, check out the Boxerjam Web site at www.boxerjam.com. Figure 9.10 illustrates one of Boxerjam's most popular games—an exercise in pairing called "Strike the Match."

Boxerjam provides games for America Online and other portals. The games can include advertising as well as a chat window to keep the audience in place. Many of the games have multi-player interfaces, allowing site members to compete with each other. Boxerjam won the coveted Cool Site of the Year Award in 2000 and in 2001 partnered with Diet Coke on movie trivia games that include sweepstakes elements and are part of an Oscars ad campaign.

Another highly regarded producer of online games is FunnyGarbage.com. Their work is featured at The Cartoon Network and the Independent Film Channel's Web site. You can pay tens of thousands of dollars to develop a proprietary game. A much wiser strategy, and far less costly, is to license one of these games and replace the trivia-type questions they contain with your own set of mind teasers that relate to your products and strengthen your brand.

Syndicating Games and Quizzes

A popular game or quiz is a product worth exporting. Months after creating the "Seinfeld" quiz, I was approached by a "Seinfeld" fan site that asked to display the quiz at their site. The quiz remained on the fan site for another two years, linked through an associate's program to a buying opportunity for the companion book. I created a *Digi-*

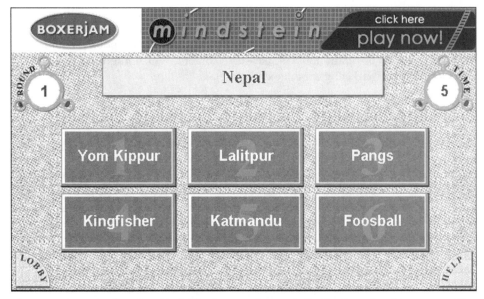

Figure 9.10   Boxerjam is a leader in the creation and distribution of online games. They can create games that help reinforce your company's marketing message.

tal Literacy quiz to promote Paul Gilster's book of the same name. The quiz was designed for use in college courses about the Internet and was syndicated to more than 20 college and university Web sites.

The way to find sites that might be interested in hosting your promotion is described in both the Linkage chapter and the Syndication chapter. The process basically involves building a road map of the sites that are critical in your industry or profession, then making contact with content editors at those sites. For quizzes, surveys, and tests, however, there's a reverse way to approach the matter. Instead of building the quiz or survey and then exporting it, you can partner with sites prior to development of the survey.

Many companies have research partnerships with educational facilities. By approaching department heads, surveys can be developed that help companies understand their markets and help students work on real-world problems and solutions. Some of the best Internet companies have grown from academic projects, and many of them maintain ties with those schools. The Ross-Middleberg *Cyberspace in Media* study is co-produced by the Columbia Graduate School of Journalism. Partnering with schools on surveys and studies will help lend legitimacy to your efforts while reducing your development costs. And the educational institutions serve as one more outlet when it comes time to syndicate the results.

Games are also popular items on the syndicate circuit. I don't have much experience producing online games and syndicating them, but I have plenty of secrets to share about animations and similar traffic builders later in this chapter. One of the benefits of the game format for promotions is that they always contain an area for advertising, and the online audience has accepted ads in their games as part of the deal. Unlike surveys or quizzes, which are static installations, the interactivity of online games brings opportunities to refresh the advertising space several times a minute. Sponsors can deliver sequential messages, building a case for their products, or test reactions to different ad designs to see which will pull best. Plus, the ads can be updated with teasers for current events or promotions, unlike static content (which might be archived for years without the marketing message changing).

Case Study: RealAge

In 1999, I promoted a book called *RealAge: Are You as Young as You Can Be?* by Michael F. Roizen, M.D. with Elizabeth Anne Stephenson. The book was based on a computer analysis of mortality data from over 25,000 medical studies. Roizen was able to develop a common currency for how different—and often conflicting—behaviors affected longevity. For example, smoking cigarettes might make you up to eight years older than your calendar age, while flossing your teeth could take as much as six years off your calendar age. Roizen and a team of programmers created a RealAge Test that took into account your genetic predisposition, age, and medical history, then superimposed questions about your diet, work, and lifestyle to determine not only your RealAge, but also how much you could reduce it by changing certain behaviors. This quiz became the cornerstone of the marketing campaign for the book.

My first instinct was to try to seek placements for the RealAge Quiz on high-traffic Web sites. Roizen had licensed the test, however, to a company he was involved in that hoped to exploit it on the company's own Web site. They saw the test as an important diagnostic tool with market value, and they didn't want to risk diluting the brand by making the test available everywhere. So I had to confine my efforts to distributing an abbreviated version of the quiz while driving traffic to the full version being programmed for the RealAge Web site (see Figure 9.11). I planned a cybertour for Dr. Roizen to talk about his book and quiz. The tour was supposed to follow his real-

Figure 9.11 The RealAge test is a sophisticated diagnostic tool developed by Michael F. Roizen and a team of computer programmers. The test became the central feature of an online promotion for the book *RealAge* (HarperCollins).

world book tour, but the publication date of the book was delayed, and it turned out that his promotional campaign would start with the chat tour.

When Dr. Roizen was booked onto "The Oprah Winfrey Show" scheduled to air the week *before* his book's publication date, all heaven broke loose. We should all have such problems. The main problem was that the Web site was not ready, and most importantly, the programming for the online version of the quiz wasn't finished. Dr. Roizen's team scrambled madly to get everything together, and it seemed like they had a reasonable version of the test at the Web site the day before Oprah aired. The remaining bugs didn't really matter, however, because the traffic generated by Oprah completely shut down the site for three days. No one could tell how defective the test was.

Thanks to Dr. Roizen's PR team and HarperCollins' publicity department, who together engineered the Oprah appearance, my online campaign was a great success. Everyone wanted to know about this man and his book, and people were clamoring to take the test. The book debuted on *The New York Times* bestseller list and was the number one title at Amazon.com. It was an impressive launch and provided my only backroom experience with the power of Oprah Winfrey to move the consumer market. But it could have been much better.

When Roizen first learned about the Oprah appearance, some clear-thinking person should have sensed that the response could overwhelm the Web team's resources. Roizen had a hot property on his hands and a chance to work with a powerful partner to solve some of his own problems and increase his exposure. There's a good chance that America Online would have paid dearly to get the RealAge test onto their service in time for the Oprah appearance. AOL could have put programmers on the job to help finish the interactive version of the test. AOL would have given the test much greater exposure than the RealAge site could hope for. At that time, Oxygen hadn't started, and Oprah's only Internet presence was on America Online, so there was synergy all around waiting for someone to broker the deal. The RealAge Web site suffered with traffic problems for months after Oprah, and the gremlins in the online version of the test were persistent.

Today, the RealAge site has perfected the online test and has branched out into diagnostic software for specific medical conditions. The site now hosts dozens of tests. When I look at all that content, I salivate over potential deals with WebMD, the Mayo Clinic, or once again, AOL. It's so much harder to make a dent online when you hoard the content. And there's such a large market where branded content like this would be welcome and could generate many times the revenue that can be reaped from a standalone site. In October 2000, RealAge cut a deal with MyFamily.com to share content in exchange for promotion. I hope it's just the beginning of an online syndicate for this intelligent software maker.

Traffic Builders

At the extremes of online promotion, there's the high road—partnering with educational and charitable organizations to create something of value while making the world a better place—and then there's the low road: partnering with porn merchants to get some naked people on your site and boost the hit count while increasing your "stickiness." Somewhere in-between, but definitely at the low end of the scale, are traffic builders (or what I like to call Stupid Web Tricks).

Sometimes traffic is really all you need. If your site is dependent upon advertising and that ad revenue is tied strictly to traffic, then stupid Web tricks can give you a quick boost. In the hallucinogenic days of dot.com startups, traffic builders were used not so much to raise ad revenue as capital. Venture funding often came with traffic goals, and sites would use stupid Web tricks to pad their logs and hit their targets. But this traffic is fleeting—the great Internet herd moving in unison to see the hot new thing and then departing just as quickly in search of another cheap thrill. Still, traffic by itself has some merits, especially if you are launching a new site or new product and just want to get eyeballs and learn whether you have a hit on your hands or need to go back to the drawing board.

One of the original Stupid Web Tricks was the Internet Coffee Pot (Figure 9.12). The story of the Internet coffee pot is now a well-worn legend. Some programmers got tired of going to the break room only to find the coffee pot empty. They decided to hook a camera up to their network, then wrote software to deliver updated images of the coffee pot to their computer screens every 20 seconds. Now, they could check the coffee level before embarking on a journey to the break room.

As rumors of the coffee server percolated through the online community, the camera was eventually hooked up to the Web. Hundreds of thousands of people visited the site—probably millions before this wonder of the webbed world ceased operation in August of 2001.

The Internet Coffee Pot generated a lot of traffic, but at whose expense? The traffic from a popular promotion can overload a server and overwhelm a Web site. Of course, if you are a coffee roaster or appliance maker, wouldn't you want to sponsor the Internet Coffee Pot and get all that brand recognition? You bet!

Let's look at some other examples of traffic builders you might want to employ at your site.

Adding Humor to Your Site

Comics are sure-fire traffic builders. InfoSeek used to license the Dilbert comic strip created by Scott Adams (Figure 9.13). Then, InfoSeek was bought by Go.com, and now Go is gone. But you can license Dilbert or dozens of other United Media comics (including Peanuts) for your own site. For more information, contact United Media

The Trojan Room Coffee Machine

 Click here for an up to date picture of the Trojan Room coffee machine.

Figure 9.12 The Trojan Room Coffee Pot, tucked away in a computer lab at Cambridge University, is one of the wonders of the webbed world.

Figure 9.13 Many comic strips can be licensed from major syndicates such as United Media and King Features. The Dilbert strip was licensed by InfoSeek for years to build traffic and to hold traffic at the search engine's site.

Online Sales and Syndication, 1-800-221-4816, or at www.unitedmedia.com. King Features is another purveyor of dozens of comic strips and editorial cartoons. You'll find licensing information at the Web site, www.kingfeatures.com.

The Hot 100 Web site at www.100hot.com added a Jokes section to its site, and it quickly became a hit. Users contribute their own jokes and rate the jokes they read so that the "best" jokes rise to the top. The nice thing for The Hot 100 is that it doesn't have to pay anything for this content. Of course, the down side is that people contribute jokes they've *heard*—not jokes they *created*—and many of these jokes are in fact copyrighted properties of comedians. I'll talk more about copyright considerations in just a moment.

One of my favorite traffic builders was The Kurt Cobain Magic Talking 8-Ball (Figure 9.14). You can ask the late rock star a question and he responds from the great beyond. You can add more humor to your site by running columns written by freelance and syndicated humorists. You'll find dozens of them listed at Yahoo! The syndicated "Word of the Day" inspired one of my clients to develop "Dirty Word of the Day" as a protest against Internet censorship. It featured a new euphemism every day that one could use in place of a common cuss word.

Web Site Animations

You can generate a lot of staying power for your site by adding clever little animations. I'm not recommending this tactic as a marketing strategy, but I've got to admit that a stupid animation loop is a lot more interesting than most of what passes for content online. The only problem with these animations is that they're funny the first time and pretty annoying thereafter. So, if you use an animation, for everyone's sake either change it regularly or use it only for a special promotion such as an online event or open house.

Animation Express at Lycos/HotWired, http://hotwired.lycos.com/animation, is a good source of both animations and ideas for traffic builders. Animations are offered in Shockwave, Flash, and QuickTime formats and include stop motion, 3D, interactive animations, and music videos. Some of the animations can be used for free, and others must be licensed. A source for some *really* stupid content is Yuckles.com, where you'll

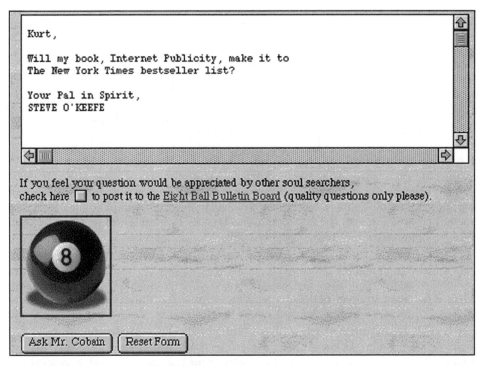

Figure 9.14 Kurt Cobain answers your questions from the comfort of his eternal resting place using this knock-off of the famous Magic 8-Ball.

find silly, repetitive animations accompanied by horrible soundtracks, including Dolly the Amazing Cloned Sheep, dancing snakes, shimmying hula girls, and more tacky stuff.

Perhaps the reigning king of online animation is JoeCartoon.com. Joe has created some Internet classics in his day, especially the Frog in the Blender (Figure 9.15). Like some psych test to determine just how evil you are, Joe gives you a frog floating in a blender and control over 10 speed buttons that determine little froggy's fate. Of course, it doesn't help that the frog taunts you with insults, encouraging you to turn up the speed.

Joe's other creative assets include Shoot the Singer, which he calls the easiest online game to play of all, and MicroGerbil, where our furry friend faces a similar fate as Joe's frog, only this time the torture device is a microwave oven. What sets JoeCartoon's content apart (other than appealing to pent-up frustration) is the quality of the crafts-manship. His colors are great, the interactive features are well thought-out, and the sound effects are a cut above. JoeCartoon has links from his site to many other Web animators doing quality work. All the animations are available for licensing, or you might be able to get Joe to build you a custom cartoon.

Copyright Considerations

I don't mean to put a damper on your fun, but anything really funny or clever that you find online is probably owned by someone else. People seem to think that any image

Figure 9.15   Frog in the Blender is just one of the popular interactive animations available for licensing from JoeCartoon.com.

they encounter online, any audio track, graphic, or gimmick, is fair game to be lifted, looted, and placed on their own Web sites. And there is a pirate spirit online that not only tolerates this behavior but encourages it. Frankly, a lot of creative people don't mind. As long as you aren't selling their work and they get branding and recognition, they don't get too bent out of shape. I know that articles I've written are used several places online without permission, and one fellow even had the chutzpa to pirate the entire companion site to my last book. But I'm personally not a fan of copyright laws, and I'm not going to make a stink, although my publisher probably has a different point of view.

Whether or not there is a spirit of free sharing online, you are taking risks when you steal other people's work, and it's against the law. Sites that accept content generated by the people who visit run the risk that the work is protected by copyright and the site could be sued (and will lose in court). Even something as innocent as Kurt Cobain's Magic Talking 8-Ball, shown in Figure 9.14, is probably trademark infringement. There used to be a lot of Magic 8-Ball sites online, but now you'll be hard-pressed to find any. I suspect that the trademark is being enforced.

So, if you use traffic builders on your site, make sure that you own the right to do so. And if you license traffic builders from others, you might make a few inquiries to ascertain whether the vendor owns what is being sold or get a contract that protects you if the transaction involves a fair amount of money. If you build a device to bring the online hordes clicking to your site, be sure you aren't infringing a registered trademark or you might find that most of the traffic originates from legal domains.

Case Study: Dancing Baby

The story of the Dancing Baby animation provides an amazing study in the spread of popular culture and the power of Internet traffic builders. Unraveling this story is no small task. The articles about the baby are thin, full of wrong information and dead links. But I'll give it a try because it's such an interesting example of group dynamics.

The Dancing Baby goes by the names Baby chat, Oogachaka, and several other monikers (Figure 9.16). In its most common form, the baby is an animated 3D video accompanied by a soundtrack. The music, known as the "Oogachaka Song," is from "Hooked on a Feeling" by the '70s group Blue Swede. The baby does a variation of the ChaCha dance step, which accounts for some of the names it has gone by.

The baby's genealogy is quite convoluted, so you'll have to follow me closely. The parents are Michael Girard and his wife, Susan Amkraut, with assistance from John Chadwick—all partners in the firm Unreal Pictures, Inc. This team took a stock 3D image of a baby that was based on a plastic doll and added dance steps to it. Animator Robert Lurye then modified some of the baby's slick moves before the animation was included as a demo in the software package Character Studio, made by San Francisco firm Kinetix, a division of software giant AutoDesk. Character Studio is a plug-in for 3D Studio Max, which is manufactured by AutoDesk. Girard was disturbed by the Dancing Baby, according to *The New York Times*, and the animation was removed from Character Studio, although the choreography for the dance was still included in the package.

At that point, Ron Lussier, who worked at Kinetix, rescued the baby, reuniting the choreography with the 3D stock image of the baby, then tweaking the animation and adding details. The baby was put back into the Character Studio demo files shipped with the software, and Ron posted the finished AVI file to a forum on CompuServe in 1996 under the name BabyCha2. From there, the baby spread all over the Internet,

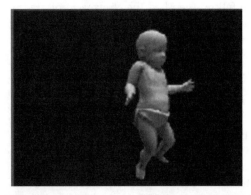

Figure 9.16 Dancing Baby is one of the great traffic builders of all time, spreading across thousands of Web sites, millions of e-mail messages, onto television programs, and into the pop culture psyche of the global village.

attached to e-mail and posted to Web sites. In late 1997, the Dancing Baby appeared on the *Ally McBeal* television program, catapulting the animation to pop stardom. An article in the *Detroit News* in early 1998 quotes Kinetics production manager Jeff Yates as saying the Dancing Baby is in the public domain.

After *Ally McBeal* aired, the Dancing Baby spread like wildfire. Probably thousands of sites displayed the animation, and millions of e-mails carried it to every corner of the globe. Animators quickly morphed the baby into dozens of different themed animations, and multiple soundtracks were attached to its wiggling frame. Blockbuster used the baby in an advertising campaign in spring of 1998. Soon, you could purchase Dancing Baby gear at Web sites, including screen savers, T-shirts, pajamas, and dolls. The money circulating around Dancing Baby grew huge, but the animation (sans the soundtrack) was still available for free reproduction with the purchase of the Character Studio software.

The Dancing Baby story has taken a turn in recent years. I'm not a good enough investigative journalist to figure out exactly what has happened, but I can read between the lines. Kinetix was merged with a company called Discreet Logic after the later firm was acquired by AutoDesk in 1999. A search of trademarks at the AutoDesk site reveals listings for The Dancing Baby (both the name and the image) and the name "Ooga-Chaka." Suddenly, most of the thousands of links to Dancing Baby animations on the Web have gone dead. And the Dancing Baby now has an agent, represented by licensing giant Logotel.

What lessons can we get from the Dancing Baby story? For starters, how fast a simple, cute traffic builder can spread into popular culture thanks to the Internet. Secondly, the incredible amount of sharing that takes place online, much of it without regard to copyright. The Dancing Baby animation can still be legally used by purchasers of the Character Studio software as long as it is modified and kept in a digital format. But the soundtracks so often attached to the animation are not public domain. Using a traffic builder like this one is a great way to build a brand, as Kinetix realized, but you also risk losing control of a potentially lucrative company asset.

Another lesson is the importance of proper trademarking, copyrighting, and branding. You have to dance between viral marketing that spreads your brand far and wide and enforcing ownership, which restricts the reach of your brand but helps preserve the value of your assets. One has to wonder what Blockbuster was thinking, hitching a major advertising campaign to an image that could legally be used by almost anyone. Another lesson is the difficulty of retroactively attaching ownership to something that has been freely available for years. CompuServe learned this lesson when it first tried to generate royalties from the GIF file format for online images. It caused a public relations nightmare, and although CompuServe backed off, the freely available JPEG format replaced GIF as the online leader.

We'll see many more brand babies dancing across the Internet in the coming years. One trick is to recognize when you have a winner and move to capitalize on it before it loses value through cloning or when the public gets tired of it.

Major Events

When I wrote *Publicity on the Internet* in 1996, the biggest event to hit the wired world was the Michael Jackson *SimulChat*, featuring simultaneous appearances on MTV, America Online, CompuServe, and Prodigy. Today, that lineup wouldn't event warrant a yawn from the media. In the good old days, you could mount an online promotion for a few thousand dollars that would ripple through the mainstream press. Today, the bar has been lifted considerably, and major online events such as Oscar Night can take months of preparation and cost millions of dollars to pull off.

Major events today usually span all media formats and include promotions in print, broadcast, online, and at live events. They involve major high-traffic Web sites, promotional partners, and lots of money. You'll find elements of all the campaigns discussed in this chapter in major events—contests, games or quizzes, and traffic builders—along with Web site promotion, chats, and online seminars or conferences. Any project this large has numerous opportunities to fail, whether due to partnership delays, legal problems, or technical glitches. But when it all comes together, it can be a thing of beauty.

One of the most successful online campaigns in recent years was a promotion for the movie "The Blair Witch Project." The main hook for the movie was the issue of whether it was real or fiction. The Web site added to the confusion, and thus the fun, by providing detailed background information for the movie (seemingly supporting its authenticity). The site was marketed mostly through word of mouth and viral techniques instead of ad banners, broadcast, or print advertising. The campaign is hailed as showing the power of the Web to propel an independent film into a box-office superstar. But is that really the case?

"The Blair Witch Project" certainly qualifies as an independent film, having been made for the sum of $65,000, which is less than most major films spend on their credits. But the marketing campaign was not such a low-budget affair. Based on a strong showing at the Sundance Film Festival, the Blair Witch team was able to put $1.5 million into pre-launch marketing. The Web site was an elaborate construction, probably costing more to make than the movie. Once the film opened nationally and showed that it had blockbuster potential, millions of dollars more were spent marketing the movie and the Web site through broadcast media and print ads. The film went on to earn nearly $100 million in theatrical release and spawned the lie that you could promote a major movie with just a Web site and good viral marketing techniques.

Coordinating Big Events

Producing major events takes a lot more than a Web site. If you are in charge of promoting a product launch or an annual extravaganza such as an awards program, you need to gather resources in all media to pull it off. Here's a checklist of the elements found in most major media events:

Direct mail. Invitations, news releases, press kits, solicitations

Print media. Advertisements and publicity blitzes

Broadcast. Advertisements, celebrity interviews, sneak previews

Online. Support site, background materials, fan club, live events

Real world. News conferences, public appearances, live events

Promotion. Merchandise, contests, endorsements, sponsorships

The focus of this book is online promotions, so let's see how you can use the tools and techniques described in this book to put together the online component of a major event.

The Media

You can start by assembling a list of those media contacts who are likely to cover not only the event itself but the preparations leading up to it. This list should be a short, manageable list of a few hundred contacts. Using an e-mail news release, you can introduce the public relations contacts for the event, provide the schedule leading up to the big day, and explain what goodies you hope to share with the media. As described in the News Releases chapter, I don't recommend asking the media to opt-in to this little wire service, but you can certainly let them opt-out upon request. Setting up the media operation in advance gives you ready access to the media as the promotion progresses.

Next, you can query the media about what format they prefer to get materials. Some will want news releases faxed, and others will prefer e-mail. Some will need high-resolution still images, and others will want video. A good publicist can anticipate these needs even without a survey, and an online newsroom can be set up as described earlier in this book to facilitate transfers with the press. The media like to be let in on news before the public gets it and can resent attempts to go around them and directly to the public. One suggestion is to host a restricted-access open house at the Web site exclusively for the media in advance of publicly launching the site. Using a chat interface or instant messaging software, you can answer questions and offer guided tours of the site or even make a celebrity available for interviewing. Hosting an open-house night for the press will help make them aware of what is available at the site while giving you feedback about what's missing.

You can expand beyond your core media list as necessary. E-mail is an excellent way to canvas a large group of journalists to find those who are interested in your story. If you are hosting local activities around the country related to your major event, you can use e-mail releases targeting local journalists to generate grass-roots coverage. Another tactic I've used is to branch off from the major attraction and try to get media play for behind-the-scenes work. For example, you could consider offering interviews or op-ed pieces with a Web site designer about his or her experiences building the site or getting coverage in the business press with a senior executive discussing the planning and logistics of the project. The PR team can even turn the spotlight on itself, syndicating a daily log of its activities to marketing Web sites. Everyone involved in the project is media bait for niche outlets—you don't have to focus only on the headliners.

The Web Site

The Web site can obviously be as grand or as simple as your budget allows. One of the key elements will be to involve the public in some way, which doesn't have to be expensive. Opt-in newsletters are a first level of involvement, and it's great to make lots of content available at the site (such as artwork, animation, and freebies). But this process is passive marketing. The secret to getting users involved is to give them some say, some control. By providing a mailing list that lets subscribers interact with each other and just listening and encouraging discussion instead of controlling the list, you'd be amazed at what can happen. People will interact and share ideas with each other that they won't share with an authority figure such as a host. If you stay invisible, quietly grooming the list to keep it free of rude or commercial behavior, and implement the constructive ideas that come out of the group, you will be surprised at the ingenuity and vitality that results—without any form of compensation or coercion.

The online audience is sensitive to whether it is being listened to or just marketed to. Many sites pay lip service to building community, but when the issues raised in that community have no visible impact on the host organization, the group quickly evaporates. Fan groups can tell when ideas they developed online are reflected in programming, and they love that. A lot of sites think building community means installing discussion threads or chat rooms, but these outlets mean nothing if they aren't groomed by staff and taken seriously by managers. I honestly believe you could build a whole television series around a single pilot episode and then rely completely on an online community to plot the remaining shows, percolating ideas up to writers who simply go with the best thread to come out of the group. Building online community doesn't mean giving people a place to talk as much as providing someone who will listen.

Online voting and polling are common Web site features that can be used to give the audience a greater sense of control. You might try allowing the online audience to vote on elements of your marketing plan, then demonstrate that their input changes the course of events. There is a risk in ceding control to your audience, but breakthrough events don't happen without taking risks. Can users decide who your keynote speaker should be? Can they decide where an event should be held or what entertainment should be provided? Surveys that gauge audience reaction after a decision or event aren't nearly as interesting as those that alter the decision or event.

Online Events

I don't think a major online event is complete without some form of live interaction with the headline talent for the program. For the most part, that means chats. Chat programming will require a substantial amount of software and hardware. If you don't have the resources to pull it off yourself, you should partner with a site that does. Look at sites such as Yahoo!, America Online, and the Microsoft Network that have great chat facilities, and then find advertisers or sponsors at those sites who will back your chat programming. When I was turned down by Yahoo! for a series of chats on financial planning several years ago, I went around them to the editors of *Money* magazine, who hosted a chat show on Yahoo!, and got *Money* to sponsor the chats. It was a lot easier getting onto Yahoo! with the support of one of their major advertisers and partners. Plus, we then got promotional support from *Money*'s Web site and magazine.

Celebrity chats will draw a big crowd, but the audience experience is not that good because there's little chance of interaction with the guests. Big celebrity events can be supplemented with smaller educational events that don't have the star power to draw a large audience but that provide more value for participants. In the same way you spin out behind-the-scenes stories about what it takes to put on a major event like this one, you can use back-office staff for educational seminars and workshops at the Web site or partner sites. The chapter of this book on Seminars and Workshops has great information about how to produce these events. One nice feature of hosting seminars is that multiple partner sites can participate at the same time—unlike chat, where the audience must come to a single chat venue.

Post-Event Activities

Most major events culminate in a single week, day, or even hour of peak entertainment, and then they're over. The Internet provides an excellent vehicle for keeping the fires burning long after a major event has passed into the history books. Television shows and print magazines will give you coverage, but then they have to keep moving. Air time and print space is precious. But the Internet is not constrained that way. There's plenty of space and time to spin out a story as long as the audience is willing to go along.

Movie companion sites have extended the runs of major releases by adding new wrinkles to the story at the Web site. Celebrities who are busy hyping major releases near the launch date find their schedules opening up in the months that follow. They can fit online appearances into their schedules with greater ease. I like to do cybertours after an author or recording artist finishes their real-world tour; they have more time, I run into fewer scheduling problems, and the product is in stores ready to be purchased. I dislike doing publicity in advance of a major release because it's frustrating for the audience to not be able to instantly buy the products they hear about. Using chats, seminars, and workshops, you can extend the punch of any promotion for months. If you are successful building an active community through the Web site, you can keep the momentum rolling for years.

Case Study: A.I.

It's a bit premature for me to write the case history of an online promotion that hasn't run its course yet, but the events surrounding the launch of the Steven Spielberg film "A.I." (Artificial Intelligence) (Figure 9.17) suggest that the future of online promotion is being made today. The film is a Warner Brothers production released in July 2001. But the very strange online campaign behind it started months earlier.

In April 2001, trailers for the movie began running in theaters. A curious observer noticed a line in the trailer credits for "Sentient Machine Therapist—Jeanine Salla" and ran a search at Google with her name. Up popped a whole series of sites—almost 1,000 matches the day I checked—and the chase was on. The Salla links pulled browsers into a fictional universe of Web sites set in the year 2142, with a mystery at their core: who killed Evan Chang?

Clues to the puzzle are laced throughout the Web sites. One of the seekers started a mailing list to coordinate the effort to crack the "A.I." puzzle. Within weeks, thousands of people were participating on the list and following the leads. An analysis of the film's trailer yielded a phone number embedded in notches in the display type. Phoning the number led into a bizarre voice mail system. Things got stranger when

Figure 9.17   The online promotion for the movie "A.I." has set a new standard for online events. The mystery involves dozens of Web sites, each changing based on the behavior of those trying to solve the puzzle.

the phone calls were returned—by robotic recordings. Then, the family of Web sites started displaying information gleaned from the mailing list. Speilberg had moles tracking the progress of the seekers and was modifying the game as he went.

Talk about encouraging participation! The "A.I." promotion is a fantastic example of viral marketing. And I believe one of the secrets to its success is that the various Web sites involved are being run independently. The Web masters themselves are part of the game, not knowing which other companies are involved in the promotion and learning as much from the seekers as the seekers learn from them. At this writing, no one is sure where the mystery will lead. I believe that not even the game's creators know; they're making it up as they go. The chase is outrageous fun for everyone involved.

I like this promotion, too, because it has integrity with the product it promotes. The Web sites try to speculate about how we got from the present into a future world where the movie is set. They fill in the gaps, building a history of robotic development and introducing us to the people who made this future possible. The sites make us think about artificial intelligence and what it means to be human, and what barriers, if any, ultimately separate man and machine.

I think this kind of clever game playing will become central to future online promotions. People are tired of the standard Web site loaded up with commercial content and want to be challenged. People want to be listened to, to see that they have an impact on the course of events. And the only way to accomplish those goals as a promoter is to relinquish control of the promotion itself, to take a risk, to start the ball rolling, and to then make future decisions based on feedback, observation, and listening. That's not a comfortable ride for all of us who are used to planning outcomes and controlling risk. But it might be the fastest way to develop campaigns that truly resonate with the target audience, engage them, and lead to better products, services, and promotion based on contributions from an unfettered audience.

Top Tips

Give yourself time. Between antagonistic attorneys, paralyzed partners, and technological terrors, it's a miracle that any online promotion launches on time.

You can safeguard your sanity with careful planning, clever design, and realistic expectations. Holding a major annual event instead of smaller, more frequent promotions will help you conserve your budget and your brain cells.

Find partners. Expand your reach and reduce your risks by recruiting partners who have strengths where you are weak. Use prize partners to increase your buy-in, portal partners to augment your audience, tech partners to finesse your functionality, and charity partners for that feel-good kicker.

Loosen up. Keep your promotional plans loose until you recruit partners so that you can design the campaign around their capabilities and needs. Give your partners goals, not instructions, or your promotion will spiral into endless loops of oversight and approval.

Listen up. You need to *engage* your online audience, not just market to them. Building community doesn't mean providing a place for people to talk as much as providing someone who listens. Give your audience a stake in the campaign by relinquishing some control over the process and the outcomes.

Cover up. Reduce your exposure to legal problems by seeking advice *before* you launch a contest. Be careful about copyright violation and trademark infringement. It's easy to stumble into trouble, and it's expensive to get out of it.

Ride the lightning. A great promotion is like a bolt of lightning uniting the product being promoted with the target audience and drawing a crowd of onlookers. Watch for lightning to strike, and if you see it, be prepared to ride it into major partnerships and media coverage.

CHAPTER

10

Syndicating Your Promotions

Many of the campaigns described in this book involve partnerships with high-traffic Web sites. These short-term collaborations give you access to a site's audience in exchange for your content. As more marketers have pursued this strategy, the competition for good placements has increased along with the time that it takes to arrange such deals and the size of a campaign that is needed to attract premium partners. Shifting from short-term deals to long-term partnerships helps spread the startup costs of promotional campaigns over a longer time period. This chapter will show you how to prepare materials for syndication, how to locate and pitch potential partners, and how to maintain long-term programs.

Companies such as iSyndicate have become experts at gathering, formatting, and distributing content across the Internet. An easy approach to syndication is to contract with such a firm. But iSyndicate charges for content, and the paying market is thin. A company that is using syndication for publicity purposes—for exposure rather than revenue—is better off handling the work itself. The target sites are usually well known, and company publicists will understand the needs of the marketplace much better than intermediaries. Content offered free in exchange for promotion will reach a wider audience than content offered for sale.

To me, syndication represents the ultimate online marketing strategy. You partner with the sites that are important to your market, offering something of value in exchange for a promotional presence. You face lower promotion costs than you would when putting the content on your own site and trying to pull an audience to it. You have the flexibility of ending the arrangement at any time and moving the content to more fertile territory. I'll describe several examples of early efforts in online syndication and the perils and pleasures of marketing this way. Topics include the following:

Syndication basics. Successful syndication requires the willingness to loosen control over content in exchange for an audience. To help persuade managers to loosen up, I'll talk about the costs of isolation and the benefits of syndication and will cover the important skills of locating and pitching partners.

Documents, files, and news. The low end of the syndication ladder is a campaign to distribute simple files and news summaries to partner sites. I'll cover how to create the files and feed a network of online libraries.

Chats, seminars, and workshops. The second tier of syndication involves distributing people—experts, that is, who are featured in programs that run on sites important to your target audience. I'll examine extended chat series and seminars, including a campaign to recruit schools into the network.

Your own show. The pinnacle of syndication is having your own show on key partner sites. You'll see why I think this concept is the most valuable marketing idea in this book and how opportunities are available right now that will disappear in a few years if not taken advantage of.

Associate and affiliate programs. Learn how to piggy back on these already-existing e-commerce syndicates by providing display materials for online stores.

Case history: myjobsearch.com. Here I include a detailed examination of a comprehensive and ambitious syndication program that included an article syndicate, a chat network, a news wire service, and a full-fledged site network with more than 1,000 outlets.

Syndication Basics

At first glance, the greatest impediment to a successful syndication program is securing agreements with partner sites to display your content. But there is a larger obstacle, and that is the reflex reaction to use promotions to pull traffic to your own site. Promoters instinctively understand that the best way to hype products by using television, radio, and print media is to attract coverage from major media outlets rather than create your own channel, station, magazine, and so on. But for some reason, when it comes to the Web, promoters are either fixated on generating traffic at their own sites or build a standalone site for the promotion and try to draw traffic to it. The biggest barrier to successful syndication is not external but internal.

This built-in lust for traffic is not easy to overcome. You might be in charge of your company's online promotion strategy, but if your superiors do not understand the benefits of syndication, you might quickly have the budget pulled out from under you. Successful syndication begins with challenging the mindset that measures performance by traffic. When management is convinced of the increased benefits and reduced costs that come from distributed promotions, the resulting syndication mentality will help you continually develop effective campaigns. Allow me to provide you with some ammunition in the battle for the hearts and minds of marketing managers.

The Costs of Isolation

Traffic is bad. More traffic is worse. Commuters understand this language, but it's anathema to online marketers. With traffic comes trouble. You have to build and maintain an infrastructure to support that traffic, including server software and hardware, and that costs money. Your Web site in many ways is similar to a toll-free phone number: The public pays nothing to access your service, but you pay more for each call that comes through. A successful toll-free phone number is not one that generates the most calls but one that delivers the most revenue per dollar spent. Limiting the calls to people who will buy is a good strategy, but how do you know who will buy? TV infomercials almost always tell viewers the price of the product so that most calls will come from likely purchasers. Without broadcasting the price, marketers would have to pay for thousands of pricing inquiries that don't result in sales. Traffic costs money and should be reduced; sales generate money and should be increased.

Increased traffic results in greater resources committed to the Web site and greater expenses maintaining it. If a certain percentage of visitors to your site have problems due to their computer configuration, access speed, or software, then as traffic increases, so do the number of frustrated visitors. More traffic tends to mean more inquiries, and if the traffic is not targeted, handling those inquiries drains resources away from serving good customers or sales prospects. Any Web master will tell you about the hardships of coping with user feedback. There are hundreds of tiresome inquiries to sort through for each important message that arrives. It's no wonder that Southwest Airlines doesn't offer *any* e-mail contact through the company Web site (as of this writing). I wonder what the customer service gurus think about that? Here is a company with legendary customer service that doesn't accept e-mail, period. I think it's great; it keeps down costs, which is Southwest's mantra.

Here are some of the other costs that a company incurs when it runs promotions on its own Web site:

Creative development. Time spent thinking up a good promotion, writing copy, recruiting talent, scheduling, organizing, and legal review.

Programming. This strain is felt most keenly in the IT department and includes everything from coding Web pages to databasing content and formatting streaming media presentations for different access speeds.

Graphic design. Quality promotions require a considerable amount of graphic appeal to satisfy the online audience. Impressive artwork and graphic design don't come cheap.

System upgrades. A Web site that is built to handle a small number of core users will have to be muscled-up to host a substantial promotional campaign. Servers and software will have to be installed to handle live chat, streaming media, or even just the traffic increases that come with a popular promotion.

Security. Security becomes a bigger issue as site traffic increases and the general public is invited to participate in online events. Disgruntled visitors can easily poke holes in off-the-shelf software designed to prevent accidental breaches, not systematic attacks.

Support. Any successful promotion will increase inquiries, including people who for a variety of reasons are having difficulty using the site. Do you have the staff to handle these questions, along with an increase in press inquiries, sales leads, and requests from customers for assistance?

Publicity. What good is a promotion if no one knows about it? You incur expenses publicizing online campaigns which, through syndication, could be amortized over numerous partner sites.

On top of these added costs are accepted risks, such as that the promotion will not work properly, that you will generate negative publicity from a poor showing, that your system will crash, or that you will get sued for anything from copyright violation to poor contest design. Through syndication, you can cut your costs, reduce your risks, and expand your reach, making your marketing budget go farther by recruiting partners who are strong where you are weak.

The Rewards of Syndication

At this point, the advantages of syndicating promotions to high-traffic Web sites should be obvious. Just in case a recalcitrant manager remains unconvinced by my list of the perils of isolation, consider these benefits of syndication:

Larger size. Syndication partners will use their own resources to augment the size of a promotion, increasing the likelihood of drawing an audience and breaking through to media coverage.

Greater exposure. When you secure a deal with a high-traffic site such as Yahoo!, Lycos, or MSNBC, you might increase your audience several thousand fold. Even if your syndicate is formed with several smaller niche sites, you will greatly expand the impact of your promotions.

Easier to find. Your campaign materials will pop up in more Web searches when the materials are on more sites. And, if a major search engine or portal is one of your partners, a search will bring your content to the top of the list.

Long-lasting impact. Syndicated promotions tend to linger online a lot longer than standalone projects. Much of the content I've syndicated has been archived longer on partner sites than on the parent site.

Lower technology costs. You can avoid installing much of the hardware and software required for fancy online promotions by partnering with sites that already have it. You can save your tech budget for serving customers rather than squandering it on entertaining a public that really doesn't want to return to your site regularly.

Lower support costs. If software doesn't work, if a quiz is broken, if a Java script fails, or if graphics are slow to load, who gets the blame? Your partner sites get the blame. More importantly, they have to deal with all those pesky "why doesn't this work" inquiries that come with any big online promotion.

Pre-filtered prospects. You might lose some prospects by partnering on promotions, but most of them are poor prospects. A higher percentage of the people who click through from a partner site to your site will be ready to do business.

Continuous promotion. Most of the syndication campaigns I discuss in this chapter are ongoing—refreshed on a daily, weekly, or monthly basis. Partners tend to promote your content between installations, so there is never any down time for the brand.

Long-term partnerships. Through syndication efforts, you form working relationships with the sites that matter to your target audience. These relationships can bear fruit in numerous ways, online and offline, with co-branding agreements, coverage for your breaking news releases, trade show sponsorships, syndication of a column in printed media, and so on.

With all of these positive benefits and the fact that most sites will not charge you to display your syndicated content, why do so many companies continue to run promotions exclusively on their own sites or on special sites built for this single purpose? It's easier. When you run a promotion on your own site, you can just do it. You can work independently on your own timetable and rise or fall on the basis of your own effort. Partnering and syndicating content imposes a discipline that is not welcome in marketing departments that are used to acting at the very last possible minute.

When you syndicate content, you must first come up with an idea that will captivate partner sites. You can run a stupid promotion on your own site any time, but trying to get someone else to go along will be difficult. Look at the number of poorly designed contests online, and you'll see what I mean. Ninety percent of the contests I've seen would never make it past a partner's scrutiny. Having a syndicate makes you work smarter and work harder, and a lot of folks don't want to do that. Good or bad, they just want to run their promotions and get them over with. That's sad.

Partnerships make promotion more complicated, mostly by slowing things down and requiring added layers of approval. You have to think about things months or years ahead of time, not weeks, and you are dependent upon the kindness of strangers to get your promotions installed on time and promoted properly. Building a syndicate requires team players who can forge a consensus and look for ways to get projects unstuck rather than look for places to lay blame. Partnerships can result in a loss of control over content and the message being communicated. The potential benefits greatly outweigh the risks, however, which can be mitigated by avoiding long-term agreements until a partner has survived a test campaign or two.

Locating and Pitching Partners

Partners can be recruited through a company's existing business relationships. If you've joined with others on marketing campaigns in the past, you have inside connections that will speed up syndication agreements. Don't just look at advertising partners, however—anyone you do business with could provide a valuable outlet for your campaign materials. Vendors, suppliers, wholesalers, retailers, trade associations, unions, government agencies, charities, and special-interest groups all have Web sites. With most syndicates, the costs of adding another outlet are minimal. Many of these industry players will want the kind of content usually distributed through online syndicates: news, help files, articles, and experts.

To build a syndicate, you need to find quality sites that might be interested in your content. This search can be time-consuming work that increases the costs of syndicating content. For an article syndication campaign, I often visit 100 sites to find 25 worth pitching to. Of those 25, only about five will actually install the article. Reducing the amount of time wasted with non-productive sites is an important skill to develop. The linkage chapter of this book has instructions for building a road map to sites that matter in any given field. When looking for syndicate partners, I evaluate sites by these four criteria:

1. *Is the site active?* Don't waste your time pitching to sites that haven't been updated in the past two months. The chances are slim that your scintillating inquiry will rouse the Web master from his or her slumbers.

2. *Does the site belong to a competitor?* This question is harder to answer than you might think. A lot of companies go through pains to obscure ownership of a site. Sometimes even if the site does not compete with you, the parent company of the site owns another business that does. If the site already has a content partnership with a company that competes with yours, you are unlikely to unseat the enemy. It's best to leave these sites alone and keep looking.

3. *Is there a natural place to put the content?* If the site has an article archive, your offer to syndicate articles should be warmly received. If you're syndicating news, does the site run news programming or have a newsletter? If you're syndicating a chat program, you need to find sites with chat facilities. Sites are unlikely to redesign to accommodate your content.

4. *Can you find contact information for a decision maker?* I have never understood why the Web is the only medium where content producers hide their identities. Movies and TV programs have credits, magazines have staff rosters, and newspapers have bylines, but online, the people who create Web sites are often anonymous or hide behind generic e-mail addresses such as *webmaster* and *feedback*. Though the trend is slowly changing, this situation is still the most frustrating aspect of securing syndicate outlets: to whom do you send the pitch? Many sites are maintained by independent technology firms who have no control over content, and the staff at these sites can't be relied upon to pass partnership inquiries up the ladder.

It's faster to pitch sites as you're evaluating them rather than make a list of potential outlets and pitch them later. Your content should be ready ahead of time. As soon as you decide that a site meets the four criteria mentioned earlier, send a pitch letter, bookmark the site, and move on in search of the next outlet.

The pitch letter should stress the value of the content and point decision-makers to a Web page where you have installed a sample. The sample might be an article for syndication, a chat profile, a seminar synopsis, or whatever else you have to offer. *Never attach these files to pitch letters* or you will lose placements and gain enemies. Files should only be sent once a Web master has expressed interest in the placement and you've determined what file formats he or she prefers.

When pitching chat shows, seminar series, or long-term article syndicates, you can be somewhat vague about the exact schedule and content. Loose wording will help you avoid giving the Web master a reason to say no without hearing your full pitch and gives you room to tailor the content to the site's needs. The following is a pitch letter I used to secure syndicate outlets for an online seminar series. I had a Web page describing the program but decided not to mention the URL until I found sites interested in the concept. The seminar structure is difficult to explain in e-mail, and I wanted a chance to discuss it over the phone before sending prospects to a Web page.

```
I am working with John Wiley & Sons to produce an online seminar
series around four books for high-end cooks: professional chefs,
gourmet cooks, restaurateurs, etc. I'm writing to see if you would
like to be involved?
Tenagra will be producing the series. We've already recruited the
authors and set up what I feel is a reasonable format. But we'd pre-
fer to partner with a high traffic site such as <<Insert Site Name>>.
You would get the benefit of lots of additional content for your site
(excerpts, seminars, artwork) and all the revenue from sales; Wiley
would get recognition and awareness for its new releases.
I'd love to discuss the details over the phone, if possible. Is
there a good time for me to call you? Thank you for considering this
request.
Sincerely,
STEVE O'KEEFE
Director of Internet Publicity Services
The Tenagra Corporation
504-529-4344

~~~~~~~~~~~~~~~~~~~~~~~~~~~~~~~~~~~~~~~~~~~~~~~~~~~~~~~~~~~
```

Some sites will be interested only in an exclusive relationship. They don't want to see the same content on a competitor's site. As a publicist, you'll have to weigh the merits of limiting the number of outlets. If a site is big enough and the partnership has potential to grow over time, a single outlet might be all you need. This situation is often the case with chat syndicates, where adding additional outlets increases your production costs proportionally. You can usually get Web sites to agree to let you partner with an AOL forum and vice versa, because the two audiences don't overlap much. Many of my syndication programs run on one high-traffic Web site, one AOL forum, and one CompuServe forum. For seminars, I can add one newsgroup and one mailing list. It's difficult to get multiple Web sites to participate in a syndicate, but it's not impossible.

Documents, Files, and News

A syndication campaign can begin modestly, distributing simple documents to partner sites and libraries online. Documents can include such things as product descriptions and specifications, help files, articles, interviews, op-ed pieces, book excerpts, legal documents, tip sheets, forms, newsletters, and chat transcripts. Let's examine how to prepare these documents and distribute them online.

Text Files

My recommendation for creating text files for distribution is to draft them first in a word processing program. I call this version the "doc" version (for the file extension commonly used on Microsoft Word documents). You can use the doc version for proofreading, spellchecking, and seeking approval of clients and/or supervisors. If you set the typeface to a monospace font, such as Courier, and set the line length to 55 characters, you'll have a document that will convert to a text file with near-universal readability. Once you are happy with the doc version, save it as "text only with line breaks" to preserve your short line length. The text version is now ready for syndication.

The advantages of using a text document for syndication are that the file will open in almost any software program, can be printed on virtually any printer, takes up very little disk space, and is easier to read on a computer screen than a file without a fixed right-hand margin. The disadvantages are that you can't use numerous design elements that make documents attractive and easy to read, such as display fonts, larger point sizes, bold, italics, indents, or graphics. You sacrifice the quality of appearance for the quantity of readers.

Popular alternatives to text files for syndication are Microsoft Word documents and Adobe PDF documents. Microsoft Word is probably the second most popular format online, but it still causes problems for many readers. If you created your document using the latest version of Word, you will have trouble reaching people with older versions or an incompatible word processing program. Even those who have the same version of Word you use might have different default settings, fonts, and other configurations that turn your carefully manicured manuscript into alphabet soup. PDF is more forgiving and will look very close to identical on most computers, but the file sizes are huge. I know one company that built an elaborate database of PDF product descriptions intended for syndication to vendor sites—but the vendors wanted nothing to do with these multi-megabyte files. Months of effort and a substantial cash investment went into creating documents that the market shunned. Word documents and text files can easily be pulled into other formats, but distilling the text out of a PDF file and putting it into another format is an exercise in frustration.

Regardless of the format you use, all documents you create for syndication should contain these essential elements that will help you distribute them online:

Filename and extension. If possible, the filename and extension should follow the old PC rule of 8 and 3; that is, the filename should be eight characters or less and the extension should be three characters or less. The extension should identify the file format: *txt* for text, *doc* for a word processing file, *htm* for a Web page, and so on. I still see files uploaded without extensions, and that's a mistake. People want to know what they're downloading, and you'll lose downloads if you don't include an extension.

Title. Most online libraries give you 25 characters or less for a title for the document. If possible, the title should include the name of the product or company you are promoting so that the file turns up in searches for the product name or company name.

Author. The name of the author of the document; it's not essential to have an author name if the document is produced by a company or other entity.

File description. Prepare a brief description of the contents of the file, usually 250 words or less. Include the company and/or product name, a quick sketch of the content, what software is required to enjoy the file, and a list of the target audiences for the file. It's a good idea to begin all documents with a one paragraph file description.

Copyright notice. If you don't own the electronic rights to the document, you must get permission before you post it online. If you have permission or own the rights, the file should contain a clear copyright notice. You might want to include "pass-along permission" that the file can be duplicated or distributed as long as the copyright notice is intact. This statement will help ease any fears your partners might have about displaying it at their sites.

You can place these files in libraries at online communities that allow members to upload files. Virtually all CompuServe forums have libraries that welcome contributions from members. Figure 10.1 shows the Press Releases library in CompuServe's Recreational Vehicle Forum, containing three user uploads.

There are a couple things worth noting in Figure 10.1. First of all, the RV forum leaders were kind enough to provide a dedicated library for news releases. Contrary to popular opinion, news releases are welcome additions to online forums if the release

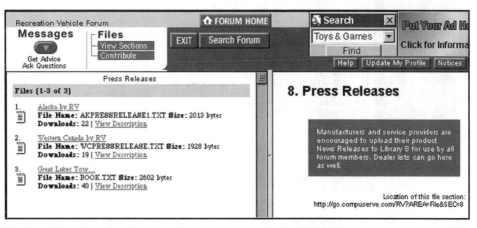

Figure 10.1 The simplest syndication campaign is to upload files into online libraries. This library at CompuServe's RV Forum even has a place for news releases.

fits within the topic of the forum. More and more Web sites are adding places where you can store news releases related to the subjects covered at the site. And these releases do get read. Forty people downloaded the release about a Great Lakes Tour shown in Figure 10.1, perhaps some of them reporters. Notice, too, that in addition to the title and filename, the size for each file is indicated. This situation presents another argument for using text files—the size seldom scares people off.

Figure 10.2 shows the form you fill out when uploading a file into one of CompuServe's libraries. This form is where you add the file description and a list of keywords for indexing the file. You can find similar user-contributed libraries on AOL, although they are getting harder to come by. Rather than searching through forums to find one with a library, you might try searching for files that will generate a list of libraries and then look for a library matching the subject of your file. Using that backdoor approach on AOL should save you some time.

Other Web portals, such as Yahoo!, also let members upload files. Using Yahoo! Groups at http://groups.yahoo.com, you can find a list of special-interest groups devoted to any given topic. Many of these groups allow members to upload files into libraries. You will have to join all these portals and the groups they contain to get

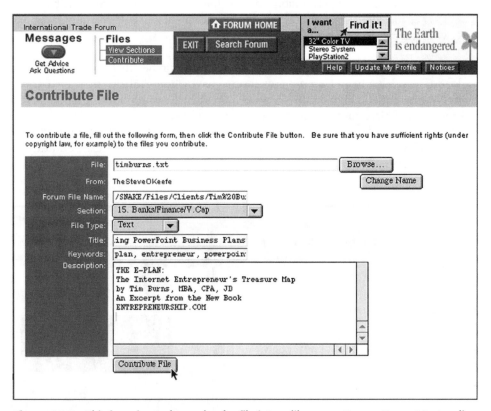

Figure 10.2 This form is used to upload a file into a library on CompuServe. Most online libraries use a similar form with a small space to describe the file and room to list keywords associated with the file.

upload capabilities. You should have a generic username and password ready when you embark on this campaign. Registration is usually instantaneous, although e-mail confirmation of your membership might be required.

Web Pages

Text files are great for user-contributed libraries like those found on CompuServe or Yahoo! Groups, but they don't cut it when you're pitching to Web masters. Unlike text files, Web page uploads require approval, and you're likely to get only a few seconds of attention to make your case. If you send a text file attached to e-mail, chances are that it will never get opened. A better strategy is to create a Web page that quickly communicates the value of the content that you are offering and send the URL to the Web master in a pitch letter.

In designing Web-page syndications, you have to balance between visual appeal and functionality. A sophisticated graphic look might increase your level of interest, but if the page is difficult to weave into someone else's site because of complicated coding, you will lose placements. I use very generic (and boring) coding in HTML files for syndication, recognizing that most Web masters will have to redesign the page to fit the style of their sites. I use simple codes and pile them all at the beginning of the document. Design changes in the middle are harder to excise. Once a Web master has expressed interest in hosting the file, I'll offer a choice of HTML, Word, or text versions. Figure 10.3 shows the top of a document that I syndicated called "A Primer on Digital Literacy." The host site is ibiblio.com, an online public library.

The syndication of the document, A Primer on Digital Literacy, shown in Figure 10.3, is a classic example of the impact of this campaign. Twenty-five sites were approached with the Web feature, and 21 of them used it. The text version was uploaded into libraries on AOL and CompuServe. The bottom of the file included full promotional copy, sales copy, and ordering information. While some sites removed this material or toned it down, most of them ran the article unchanged. This campaign was launched in 1997. Five years later, the feature is still available on more than a dozen Web sites. The document was created in an afternoon, and it took two afternoons to syndicate it with a few follow-up e-mails. The campaign generated an immediate presence for the product on top sites, and the impact has lingered much longer than a chat, workshop, or other event.

Multimedia Files

Beyond text and Web files, you can syndicate a great deal of multimedia content even though the Web is still not an ideal environment for streaming media presentations. For music promotions, distributing an MP3 file has become standard industry practice. For movie promotions, film trailers custom-designed for RealPlayer or Windows Media Player are essential. These files can be distributed far and wide. CD-ROM promotions are tricky, however. If you create a Web demonstration of the CD-ROM, chances are it will work much slower and look worse than it would running native on a user's computer. The online demo will turn off potential users and reduce sales, not

A Primer on Digital Literacy

Adapted from the book

DIGITAL LITERACY

by Paul Gilster

(John Wiley & Sons, 1997)

Introduction

From Promotional Information included with the Primer:

"*Digital Literacy* is essential reading for students, researchers, writers, investors, and anyone who intends to use the bountiful resources available on-line to bolster their work. Teachers and librarians will be particularly pleased with the respect Gilster shows for their professions and the assistance he provides in helping them integrate on-line resources with their existing tools for 'knowledge assembly.'"

For more information about Paul Gilster, *Digital Literacy*, and his other books, please visit the Wiley web site at http://www.wiley.com/compbooks/

Figure 10.3 A syndicated feature article based on the book *Digital Literacy* by Paul Gilster. This feature ran at no charge on more than 20 top Web sites and more than a dozen AOL and CompuServe forums.

increase them. It's a better idea to offer a text or Web page article about the product and to offer to mail a demo CD upon request.

Elsewhere in this book, I cover the production of multimedia promotions that are worthy of syndication. The Online Newsrooms chapter has a section on creating online presentations—streaming PowerPoint slide shows with audio voiceover. These are excellent modules for syndication to Web sites that have Real and Windows media servers. The chapter on Contests has sections on games, animations, and other gimmicks that are very popular on the syndication circuit. You can follow the instructions in those chapters for creating the content files and use the instructions provided here for syndicating them to targeted sites.

News Syndicates

One of the most promising avenues for syndication is the distribution of news items and newsletters to multiple sites. When a company crosses the threshold from distributing news releases to distributing *news*, it will see its profile increase substantially online and will generate many more interview requests than through news releases alone. Developing a news bureau, news feed, or news wire is covered in detail in the chapter of this book about online newsrooms.

If you follow news related to your industry—and who doesn't—you can turn your research into news coverage by distributing your finds in the form of a regular news feed. By providing the media and the public with summaries of important news stories in your field, you get branding and a reputation as an authority on the subjects you cover. You also get a chance to frame these stories, selecting what you feel is the most newsworthy element, calling the attention of journalists and the public to important points that might otherwise be overlooked. By providing a news feed to other sites, you also produce top-quality news items to use on your own site.

A great example of syndicating news feeds is the *Environmental News Service* (ENS) described in Online Newsrooms chapter. Their news briefs are syndicated to Lycos, a top-10 Web site, and other news portals online. Another good example is WorkWire, a news syndicate that I designed for career portal myjobsearch.com. I'll describe this effort in more detail in the case history at the end of this chapter.

Chats, Seminars, and Workshops

Syndicating files, documents, and news is the first step toward building an online network. Step two involves producing programming for syndication in the form of chats, seminars, and workshops. These programs involve interaction with a guest, giving audience members the opportunity to ask questions and to get answers for specific concerns. In the chapter of this book devoted to chat tours, I covered the methods for finding venues and producing a tour. Here I'll look at expanding that concept into a chat series.

Chat Series

As chat venues started to expand in 1996, I switched from booking chats on single sites to booking tours on multiple sites. For a while, it seemed like I had the market to myself and could get guests into chat venues at will. Then, dozens of other publicists discovered the Internet, and soon I was competing with movie stars, top recording artists, and superstar athletes for space in the best chat venues. Tours that I used to book in two days now took two months, and I was forced down into second-tier auditoriums when I had clients that weren't household names. As the workload for putting together a tour increased along with the need to produce more dynamic programming to get into the best venues, I began shifting to chat series.

A chat tour involves one guest doing three to five chats in the course of a week. A chat series involves multiple guests, united by a similar theme, in a program that runs for weeks or months. A typical chat series might involve one new guest each week for four weeks or one new guest each month for four months. Figure 10.4 shows the top of a chat profile for the Personal Finance Chat Series sponsored by Dearborn Publishing, a division of Kaplan. This series ran for six consecutive weeks with a different author each week.

The benefits of chat series over individual chat tours are straightforward. First, there is the reduced booking time. There were six authors featured in the Dearborn Personal Finance Chat Series shown in Figure 10.4. Booking a tour for each author would have taken about a month each. The series was booked in less time than it would have taken for just one author—and at a substantial savings. Second, we were able to secure top venues because of the weight of the series. One of the guests in the

Dearborn, A Kaplan Professional Company

~ is proud to present the ~

Personal Finance
Chat Series

~ featuring ~

Week of September 14th

Blanche Evans

Author of *homesurfing.net*

More than just a guide of cool sites. Evans's book takes consumers step-by-step through the home buying and selling process -- with or without an agent!

Blanche Evans is the editor of *Real Times*, the largest real estate news services on the Internet, which produces consumer, industry, and agent news for Realtor.com, the official web site of the National Association of Realtors, and over 650 other real estate sites. She has written for *The Dallas Morning News*, *The "Homebuyer's Guide*, *The North Texas Relocation Journal*, and is senior editor for *Exclusively Dallas*.

Figure 10.4   The top of a chat profile for the Dearborn Personal Finance Chat Series. The series featured six authors, each described with one paragraph in the chat profile. The profile is used to secure partner sites for the series.

Dearborn series was Gene Walden, author of the bestselling books *The 100 Best Stocks to Own in America* and *The 100 Best Mutual Funds to Own in America*. We could have easily built a chat tour for Walden at top personal finance sites. But booking tours for several of the lesser-known authors would have been difficult. By packaging them with Walden and letting venues know they couldn't get Walden without taking the whole group, we were able to negotiate placements for the rest of the speakers.

One of the very great benefits of chat series over individual tours is the branding boost. Chat tours focus on the guest, not on the company behind the promotion. Series focus on the company, and the company's name is usually embedded into the series name, such as the Dearborn Personal Finance Chat Series or the Dearborn Entrepreneur E-Chat Series. To help reinforce the branding message, a series logo should be created that includes both the sponsoring company's logo and the host venue's logo.

For a chat tour, you can expect to get two weeks worth of promotion at the host venue. For a chat series, the promotion lasts as long as the series, with another promo going up for the next guest as soon as the last one is taken down. For the Dearborn series, we partnered with The Whiz! on AOL and the Investors Forum on CompuServe, where we received around-the-clock promotion for six months.

Booking a chat series is a little different than a regular tour. You create a chat profile and then pitch prospective hosts via e-mail, asking whether they're interested in partnering on the series. But instead of including detailed descriptions of each guest, the chat profile offers just one paragraph per guest. Detailed profiles are created prior to each appearance and then forwarded to the chat hosts who have agreed to participate. Often, when pitching a series I won't know exactly which guests will be available. My pitch letter will say something like, "If you agree to host the series, I will guarantee one guest a month for six months. The exact guests will be worked out once the schedule for the series is known." Or, I might list a pool of guests we expect to draw from, trying to entice hosts without committing to a particular lineup.

Chat series are different for the guests, too. Instead of asking a guest for preferred dates and times, you're slotting guests into an already-fixed schedule. It's a little like musical chairs: When the booking stops, all the guests try to find a seat in the schedule. Chat series are booked far enough in advance that it's usually not a problem to fit the guests into the schedule. Thanks to ghost typists, there are very few demands made of the guests: They simply have to be near a telephone for one hour for each chat. I've never had a problem filling a fixed series schedule, although I've had to do a little juggling.

It's best to run all the chats in a series on the same weeknight at the same time for each venue. For example, a six-week series might run every Thursday at 9 p.m. Eastern time, or a four-month series might run on the first Tuesday of the month at 9 p.m. Eastern time. This repetitive scheduling makes it a lot easier to promote the series and builds regular attendance. Avoid attempts by chat hosts to vary the day or time of the chat.

Chat series can be more intensively promoted than chat tours. The schedule might be known months in advance, allowing you to get coverage from long-lead publications such as magazines and trade newsletters. The series can be promoted with banner advertising, especially if the company sponsoring the series already uses banner ads. Ads can be designed for each guest in the series and mixed in with the rotation of banner ads that the company is already using. Due to the critical mass of a chat series, they get better media coverage. In every series I've been involved with, the sponsor company as well as the venues issued news releases about the series and sought media coverage for the whole program. Chat venues almost never do this for individual guests.

Seminar and Workshop Series

Producing and promoting these programs is covered in the chapter of this book devoted to seminars and workshops. Unlike a chat series, which involves multiple guests, seminars and workshops usually feature a single guest conducting an extended program. For example, a seminar might be held for five consecutive nights or for one night a week for four consecutive weeks. Seminars can be bundled into series, as well. A good example is the Wiley Culinary Seminar Series, which involved four guests with each guest putting in one week of duty and the series running for four months. This ambitious program is described in the seminars chapter of this book.

Many seminars and workshops are not live events. A topic for discussion is distributed in the morning, questions for the guest are collected throughout the day, and then the guest's responses are sent out the next morning with a new topic for discussion. This rather low-tech mechanism actually works quite well, and it has one big advantage over chats: It makes the seminars and workshops easy to syndicate. For a chat series, the guest and the audience meet at a specific place and time for a live event. Chats can be syndicated, but each venue adds to the amount of programming involved and the burdens on the guest. Seminars and workshops, on the other hand, can partner with multiple sites without increasing the programming or the burden on the guest. And partners can include venues that don't have chat facilities or high-powered servers. Seminars and workshops can partner with Usenet newsgroups, Internet mailing lists, newsletters, Web sites, AOL forums, and CompuServe forums.

The biggest difficulty syndicating seminars and workshops is convincing potential hosts that this old-fashioned form of communication will yield a valuable learning experience. I had to be convinced myself, but once I saw the benefits, I was hooked. Venues that have tried these seminars and workshops always want more. In selling seminars and workshops to partner sites, stress the promotional benefits rather than the content to lure them into giving the seminars a try. You shouldn't try anything as ambitious as a multi-guest seminar series until you have experience doing one-shot seminars. After you have established relationships with key venues in your industry, you can leverage them into larger seminar series that will give you a continual promotional presence at those sites.

Case History: Online Classroom Visits

I'm always looking for new ways to tap the potential of the Internet, and I've been fortunate to have clients that fund my experiments, knowing they don't always bear fruit. One of these clients is Random House Children's Publishing (RHCP). I had been putting RHCP authors on chat tours with satisfactory results. It's hard to reach young children through the Internet, and campaigns have to be geared toward parents and teachers (who hold the purchasing power for this demographic). For chat tours, we had been partnering with parenting sites on AOL and CompuServe and with the EduCenter at chat portal Talk City.

In early 1998, Random House asked for a proposal for their Spring line, and I put a new twist on an old campaign. Instead of holding chats, I suggested that we conduct *online classroom visits*. I noticed that many of the children's authors had done tours that included classroom visits. But the authors had become so popular that requests for appearances outstripped their ability to tour. Using the new medium of the Internet, we could pipe authors into multiple classrooms at the same time, reaching a larger audience while requiring a minimal time commitment on the part of the authors.

Another development that drove me to this format was the growing concern over children's safety online. The Internet has predators and a large contingent of idiots who don't mind shouting obscenities in a chat room crowded with kids. The idea for the series was to limit attendance to K-6 classrooms and require preregistration by teachers. The public would be locked out of the chats, and only those with the proper password would enter. I felt that this restriction would protect the integrity of the environment and reassure teachers that the series would be a rewarding experience.

Random House approved the concept, and I worked with Debbie Blailock and other members of the staff at Talk City to plan the project and create the campaign materials.

We also partnered with AOL's Parent Soup forum, although we dropped the classroom visits concept there and just ran it as a standard chat series. Random House provided five authors for the series, including relative newcomer Sally Warner (*Some Friends*) along with veterans Barbara Park (*Junie B. Jones*), Mary Pope Osborn (*Magic Tree House*), and Jack Prelutsky (*A Pizza the Size of the Sun*) and beloved bedtime bards Stan and Jan Berenstain (*The Berenstain Bears*). While we might have had trouble booking Sally Warner into these top venues on a separate chat tour, slipping her into a star-studded lineup assured her acceptance. The chat profile we used to pitch the hosts is shown in Figure 10.5.

Random House got better branding than it would have for a solo chat tour with any one of these authors. Instead of the focus being on an individual author, the marketing revolved around the series, which included the Random House name in its title and the Random House logo. Talk City created a series banner ad, shown in Figure 10.6, which ran not only on its site but elsewhere on the Web. The ad includes the Random

Random House Children's Publishing

~ is proud to present the ~

Children's Author Chat Series

~ featuring ~

Barbara Park

Barbara Park is the author of the well-known "Junie B. Jones" books and several award winning middle-grade books including "Mick Harte Was Here," "My Mother Got Married (And Other Disasters)," "The Kid in the Red Jacket," and "Skinnybones." Barbara was not naturally drawn to reading and writing. About her development as a writer, she says, "Writing books for kids seemed the perfect way I could pretend to be a grownup and still blurt out funny stuff like I did in school."

Mary Pope Osborne

Mary Pope Osborne is the author of the enormously popular "Magic Tree House" series which follows the adventures of the brother-and-sister team of Jack and Annie. Mary has written more than 40 books for young people, including "American Tall Tales," "Favorite Greek Myths," and "One World, Many Religions." She served two terms as president of the Authors Guild -- the leading writers' organization in the United States. She is a frequent classroom visitor, talking with students and teachers about the joys of reading and writing.

Figure 10.5 The top of a chat profile for the Random House Children's Author Chat Series featuring five fantastic writers. This series was syndicated on Talk City's EduCenter and America Online's Parent Soup.

Figure 10.6 Chat series often have enough bulk to warrant banner advertising. This ad, created by Talk City, ran throughout the chat portal and on other sites, taking the Random House brand with it.

House logo, although RHCP was never even asked to make a financial contribution for the ad.

Once the schedule was set, the promotion kicked in. Talk City created a set of instructions for teachers about how to register for the classroom visits, how to connect, and how to use the online chats as a teaching experience. Random House installed these instructions, along with promotions, at its own Web site. We also promoted the events through news releases and discussion group postings, sending the instructions upon request. Prior to the first chat, more than 50 classrooms had registered, and their credentials had been verified by Talk City. Random House was delighted by the prospect of reaching into 50 classrooms with one event. Everyone involved was excited about the series.

Then the first event came, and only two classrooms were connected to the chat. What a disappointment! What happened to keep the other classrooms away from the chat? Debbie Blailock at Talk City personally phoned all the teachers to find out why they didn't attend the chat. A few had forgotten, several planned to attend later chats in the series but not the first one, but the majority of them simply couldn't connect. The connection problems included not being able to get a computer into the classroom on the day of the event, not being able to get the Internet connection working, not being able to log in to Talk City, not having good enough software to participate, dropped connections, crashes . . . On top of the problems, the instructions we had prepared for connecting to the chat were not easy to understand by a lay person and didn't cover many of the contingencies.

I reported the problems to Random House and then got busy with Talk City on a fix. We rewrote the instructions, slashing the length of the document in half and addressing the most common problems. We sent the instructions back out to the teachers, redoubled our publicity efforts, and braced for the second week of the series. Chat time came, and we only had four classrooms connected. We were devastated. We could still reach a lot of children through four classrooms connecting at once, but the fact is that more than 50 other classrooms that had registered were not there. Again, we polled the teachers, and again it was technical problems that separated our star authors from their devoted audience.

At this point, we tried a new strategy. We realized that the teachers had little control over the Internet connection. Most schools had a media department that provided tech support, often consisting of one techie. We realized that the media department was the bottleneck. We asked the teachers to print the instructions and give them to the media person at their school. We also learned that Talk City was locked out of many school systems because the site contained all varieties of chat—including raunchy stuff that earned Talk City a slot on the banned site lists used by many safe-surfing programs.

We included information in our instructions on how to disable this software for the duration of the chats. Then we went out and promoted the third chat aggressively.

When only two classrooms connected for the third chat, I threw in the towel. The series was a disaster, in my opinion—an idea whose time had not arrived. I explained the situation to Random House, and while disappointed, they didn't rub my face in it. We were trying something new, it sounded like a good idea, and if it had worked, it could have revolutionized their author touring process. With two chats to go, we stopped promoting the series, although we honored our commitments to provide guests as planned.

Week four arrived, and lo and behold, 40 classrooms connected for the chat! Perhaps it was the pull of Prelutsky, or maybe the media techs had finally figured out how to get a reliable connection, but the auditorium was full of children asking the most darling questions, gushing about how much they loved characters in the books. What a relief! After the chat, Debbie Blailock told us that she was surprised to see 15 connections to the restricted chat room when she arrived at work that morning. Apparently, the media people hooked the classrooms into the chat in the morning, then left instructions not to touch the computer. Hours later, when the guest appeared, the classrooms were ready to chat.

On the fifth and final week of the series, 25 classrooms logged into the chat. While the number was down from the week before, the volume was satisfactory and told us that we had, indeed, overcome a tech bottleneck. We learned that we had to reach through the Internet to teachers, and through the teachers to technical support people in the schools, if we expected to host successful online classroom visits. I thought Random House would not want to go through this ordeal again, but they signed on for a second series in the fall with six authors.

The following spring, the stakes were raised again. Random House received funding from Target Stores for a promotion built around Read Across America Day, which is sponsored by the National Education Association. We ran another chat series, although this time we lifted the preregistration requirement. Preregistration frustrated teachers who tuned in at the last minute for the chats, and Talk City felt they had enough staff and technical capabilities to quickly lock rude people out of the chat. Target printed flyers with the chat schedule and distributed them in stores. On Read Across America Day, we had more than 130 connections to the chat, many of them representing entire classrooms of students and requiring Talk City to open several overflow chat rooms as capacity was quickly exceeded. The promotion was a rousing success.

There are a lot of lessons to be learned from events like this one, but I think the most important is that it takes experience to get good at programming a series, especially when syndicated to multiple sites. You should never embark on a program like this one until you have enough experience to recognize the likely problems and deal with them quickly. If you work for a public-relations firm or an ad agency, I recommend that you decline grandiose assignments until you've established a good working relationship with a client. When Dearborn Publishing first approached me about doing syndicated series with their authors, I declined until we had been through a few chat tours together. Once they were familiar with the process and documents like the Chat Profile and had realistic expectations about what could be achieved with a series, we went on to construct several programs that resulted in long-term partnerships with key sites in their market.

Your Own Show

The next logical progression from a syndicated chat series or seminar series is to distribute your own show. A show is an ongoing program that gives you a continuous presence on the sites that are most important to your target audience. Producing a show is a major commitment, but it shouldn't be outside the reach of most businesses. In fact, while producing a show will consume substantial resources, the savings in running separate seasonal or product promotions is substantial.

When I produced the Wiley Culinary Seminar Series in 1999, I partnered with four high-traffic cooking sites. Like the online classroom visits format described earlier, the seminar series concept was still in development and I was not confident at all that it would result in a quality experience for the audience. The series is described in the seminars chapter of this book, so I won't go into detail here. The most surprising result of the series was that site users began to meet each other through the series. The series helped foster the first sense of community among visitors to these sites, and this dynamic did not go unnoticed by the host Web masters.

At the end of the Wiley Culinary series, the Web masters asked, "What's next?" They wanted to build on the response and get another series started as soon as possible. I had no control over the process, however, and forwarded these inquiries to Wiley. As time passed, interest waned, and I don't believe Wiley ever extended the program. That's a shame. These sites were willing to dedicate a substantial portion of their real estate and marketing budget to a quality seminar series, but Wiley didn't have the staff in-house to produce the programming and was reluctant to pay the production costs to hire a firm to do the work for them. Then, the Internet crash came and some of the venues disappeared.

Money is an issue in all of these campaigns, but you'll seldom see it addressed in any book about online marketing. It costs money to produce these programs. A typical rate is about $100/hour, an estimate of the hours is worked up, and then a price is put on a comprehensive package. Depending on the complexity of the programming and the number of venues involved, syndicating a chat or seminar series can cost anywhere from $1,000 to $10,000 a program on top of a setup fee of anywhere from $3,000 to $10,000. Expanding the number of venues involved does not increase the costs proportionately, so it's a good idea to involve as many partners as possible. Running the programming for a longer period of time—say, ten weeks instead of two weeks—spreads the startup costs over a greater number of shows. Producing an ongoing program on multiple sites will be expensive but should cost about half of what it would take to run an equal number of standalone campaigns.

Few companies are willing to make a financial commitment to an ongoing show because of the budgeting process. They have a certain budget to spend each quarter, and in the course of a year they will pay twice as much to run quarterly promotions as they would have to fund an annual campaign. One solution to this financial myopia is for companies to hire the in-house staff they need to produce this kind of programming or train existing staff. In a moment, I'll explore some of the specific tasks necessary to produce an ongoing program. But first, I need to deal with another facet of the money issue.

After the dot.com crash of 2000, Web sites needed to generate revenue—not just traffic—in order to stay alive. Many sites started charging for services that they used to give away for free. If you want to host a chat series on Talk City now, you'd better break out the checkbook, because you can't get onto that site free anymore. When you add the hosting fees to the production fees, online programming of this type loses its appeal. Money is funny on the Internet. I remember when AOL announced a $10 million partnership with Monster.com, and none of the news stories bothered to say which way the money was flowing. Was Monster paying AOL, or the other way around? I consulted several people affected by the deal, and none of them could say who was paying whom.

The same Monster/AOL scenario is playing out with chat programming. I have clients who want to license content to venues and collect a fee, and venues think they should be compensated for hosting the content. If I produce a top-notch program for Yahoo!, should Yahoo! be paying to license the program or should I be paying Yahoo! to broadcast it? For years I've been able to tread the middle ground: no money changes hands, the host site gets content that it doesn't pay for, and the client gets promotion it doesn't pay for—except I get my cut in the middle for producing the program. Today, the balance has shifted, and host sites are demanding money to put chat guests on programs or to make files available to their audiences. I think they got it wrong, and the balance will soon shift the other way.

As a rule, guests do not pay to appear on talk shows. When guests pay, it compromises the integrity of the program, and viewership drops. Advertisers or sponsors should pay. And production studios do not pay stations to air their content; rather, the stations pay the studios for producing the content and then collect from advertisers. Advertisers pay the bulk of entertainment costs, and subscribers or end users pay a portion through subscription fees and ticket prices. As Internet entrepreneurs realize that advertisers won't fund all the Web entertainment out there, they are switching to charging subscription fees and pay-per-view, and they've also tried charging the producers for the programming. As weak sites die off, the surviving sites will increase their ability to charge end users and attract advertisers, and the top sites will start paying for content streams again instead of trying to charge content providers.

The upshot is that you face a market where you not only pay to produce programming, but you also pay Web sites to air the programming. That's fine if you're producing infomercials, but by and large people aren't interested in watching infomercials online. If you are absorbing the production costs for programming, you should expect to broadcast that programming at no charge, accompanied by promotional announcements. If the programming is good enough, you should be able to charge the venue to air it, and then the venue can sell through sponsorships or advertising.

Producing an Ongoing Program

There is a real market for quality programming online, and you can exploit the tremendous publicity potential of it by creating your own show. The Internet allows experts to meet with information seekers without the expense of physical relocation. Television does that, too, but the production costs are high and there is precious little interaction between viewers and stars. Radio does it better than TV, allowing some phone-in communication, but the signal is weak. Nothing works better than the Internet for companies that have a niche target audience that is not regionally concentrated.

The strategy that I am laying out here is probably the single most important marketing concept in this book. Look at the history of programming, and you'll see where this market is headed. With broadcast television, there were only a handful of networks competing for huge audiences. Cable made it possible to affordably distribute dozens of specialized networks, each looking for niche audiences. On the Web, every site is a potential station. There are now literally millions of channels to choose from, each of them with global reach and miniscule production costs. Almost no audience is too small to warrant its own channel.

For the most part, Web masters have not awoken to the fact that they're in the TV business—but they soon will. The Web is TV on steroids—programming bulked up with support files, documents, and resources; interactive television with an e-commerce kicker. You can take advantage of the naivete of Web masters by providing the programming that their sites lack and claiming a high-profile position in your niche while your competitors sleep through the revolution. Are you in the accounting profession? Maybe you should consider a program for actuaries running on sites devoted to this arcane science. Do you have a paper mill? Perhaps you could include a program on packaging design for a site devoted to the topic. These programs don't have to be expensive and can bring far higher returns than other advertising expenditures.

Establishing a position as an information authority on the sites that matter to your target audience is a vital new marketing tool. The Web is awash with information, much of which is bad, and it's choking on its own effluent. The quality of most search engines and directories is terrible, with up to 90 percent of search results leading to defunct sites, outdated material, or just plain stupidity. People need assistance getting to the good resources without having to swim through all that crap. They will gravitate to niche sites where intelligent assistance can be found—assistance provided by *you*, in the form of programs, resources, and recommendations. This *friendly guide* strategy is behind many company Web sites—but people do want their information from captive corporate sites, and your company does not have the resources to become a quality information portal. You need to take the content to where the audience is. If the audience moves, you move the content. This strategy has much lower infrastructure costs than building your own niche portal; if the site you're on fails, you simply abandon it without having to kiss off your development costs.

If you survey the sites that cater to your target market and find that they already have programming, help them. Provide support files, guests, or sponsorship dollars. Right now, you can get away with producing whole programs yourself and installing them at target sites. As Web masters wake up to the fact that they're running interactive TV channels, however, they'll begin to assert more control over programming. Then, you'll face the same marketing scenario you do now with radio and TV stations: You'll provide guests for programs, resources, promotions, sponsorships, and ads, but the stations themselves will produce the programming or contract with independent studios to acquire it. Right now, you have the opportunity to become a leading authority on the sites that are most important to your target audience: Are you going to take advantage of this opportunity or keep spinning your wheels and spending your budget trying to turn your corporate site into some kind of entertainment portal?

So, what exactly do you need to become a program producer for this new world of interactive television? Here's the list:

Guests. You need at least one expert. Every organization has someone who is an expert at whatever it is you do, or else how can you stay in business? This expert can be as lightly involved as making a one-hour appearance once a month or as heavily involved as hosting a weekly program that features third-party guests.

Host. In the starting phases, a single guest can also function as a host, but things run more smoothly when there is a separate host. In most cases, the host will be provided by the venue. But if the site is important, you can increase your chances of establishing a program by offering to provide a host as well as a guest.

Typists. If the guest is uncomfortable typing at a conversational speed, having a typist (who can double as a host) will help. A typist is essential if you plan to host a program and cull guests from professionals in the field. You will be able to lure more and better guests if all they have to do is participate in a one-hour phone call.

Schedule. A schedule of topics is essential for promotional purposes. I've tried pitching programs based on the credentials of the guest alone, but a list of topics to be covered builds a lot more interest. You can repeat topics, such as a six-week course that is rerun every two months. A successful program will generate an endless supply of topics tailored to concerns expressed by the audience.

Writer. It helps to have a wordsmith work on the schedule, the topics, descriptions of the programs, introductions for the guests, and promotional copy for news releases and discussion group postings.

Graphics. You'll need a minimal amount of artwork: guest photos, product photos, and banners or buttons for promoting the program. More graphics will be needed depending on the topics covered (painting, for example) or the format used. Many shows include PowerPoint slideshow presentations or Web tours that benefit from a graphic artist's touch.

Support files. For every episode of your program, you'll want to provide some support file, whether it's an article, tip sheet, resource list, case history, or other document that dovetails with the day's topic. These files might get more traffic than the program itself and can build into an important resource library.

Promotion. Every program needs ongoing promotion to attract new audience members and to compensate for attrition. While the launch of a program should include a comprehensive promotional campaign featuring news releases, discussion group postings, and even advertising, subsequent installments can be lightly promoted with calendar listings.

Once you have experience producing chat or seminar programming and you make the decision to expand into your own show, you'll have a pretty good idea of the venues you want to target and who you need to talk with. A good strategy is to prepare a chat profile for the guest, a list of additional guests (if any) who you hope to get for the show, and from four to ten topics you can cover. Then, you can pitch the show to Web masters and ask for a trial period (such as four weeks) and see whether you want to continue based on experience.

As with television programming, it's a good idea to have a termination date for your show so that you can run it quarterly or seasonally, with a major promotional campaign at the beginning of each season. You might want to run the program just once a year, prior to the critical time for decision-making in your industry. Tax preparation firms will want to straddle the year-end, but avoid programming in March and April. Many companies will compete for "air time" in the fall season when Christmas marketing hits its peak. Travel providers should be out in force in the months leading to summer vacations.

Case History: Health for Dummies

In early 1998, I produced a six-month health chat series for publisher IDG Books Worldwide, partnering with THRIVE! on AOL and AHN.COM on the Web. THRIVE! was part of the Oxygen Network, a project involving Oprah Winfrey, and AHN.COM was the Internet arm of the cable television channel America's Health Network. IDG was expanding its popular . . . *For Dummies* series into the health arena. They could hardly have asked for better partners than these two key portals.

To pitch the series, I created a chat profile, the top of which is shown in Figure 10.7. We lifted a chat graphic featuring the Dummies dude from one of the books and used it as a logo for the series. The chat profile provided enough information on the books

Figure 10.7 Chat profile for the "Health for Dummies" chat series sponsored by IDG Books Worldwide. The profile was used to lure partners THRIVE! on AOL (part of the Oxygen Network) and AHN.COM on the Web (the online home of the cable TV channel America's Health Network). The cursor points to the series logo.

and guests, along with graphics, for advance promotion. For each segment in the program, we created a detailed chat profile including promotional copy, introduction, artwork, and sample questions. We also provided a support file for each installment, distributing it to libraries and other sites online while promoting the chat dates.

Both venues were enthusiastic about hosting the series and charged nothing to broadcast it. Both agreed to provide staff resources in the form of a host, on-site promotion, issuing news releases about the program, and calendar listings for the schedule. While I sometimes get in trouble for mentioning dollar costs in a book, I think readers want an idea of what it would cost to get an ad agency to produce a program like this one. A $5,000 setup fee would be reasonable, covering the design of the program, series setup materials and art, pitching the venues, securing the partners, and a substantial promotional campaign. Because the events are one month apart, each installment requires a separate promotional campaign. You might pay around $5,000 each month for promotion and production services, including preparing segment materials and art, coaching the guest, ghost typing, and transcript cleaning. If this series were weekly instead of monthly, the bulk of the promotion would happen up front and individual events would be lightly promoted at a savings of $1,000 to $2,000 per event.

Here is the news release that we used to promote the event. It will give you a good idea of how to spin a series like this one:

```
E-MAIL NEWS RELEASE
Subject Line: Health Chat Series Unites Powerful Partners
FOR IMMEDIATE RELEASE: Thursday, January 13, 1998
Contact Catherine Schmitz, IDG Books Worldwide
Phone: 650-655-3027, mailto:cschmitz@idgbooks.com


IDG Books, Thrive, and AHN.COM Partner on
"Health For Dummies(tm)" Chat Series


Jane Kirby, author of "Dieting For Dummies(r)," kicks off the new
"Health For Dummies" Chat Series sponsored by IDG Books Worldwide in
partnership with THRIVE on America Online and AHN.COM on the web. The
series starts Wednesday, January 27, at 8 pm Eastern on Thrive (AOL
Keyword: Thrive) and 9 pm Eastern on AHN.COM (http://www.ahn.com),
and continues the third Wednesday of each month:
Jan 27: Dieting For Dummies
Feb 17: Family Health For Dummies
Mar 17: Alternative Health For Dummies
Apr 21: Women's Health For Dummies
May 19: Meditation For Dummies
Jun 16: Pregnancy For Dummies
"Online chats increase the value of the ...For Dummies books in the
marketplace by giving readers the chance to have live discussions
about particular and often personal issues with our expert
authors," says Catherine Schmitz, Publicity Manager for Dummies
Press, a division of IDG Books Worldwide. "In our current chat
series, for example, readers can chat with Dr. James Dillard
```

```
("Alternative Medicine For Dummies(r)") about the benefits of accu-
pressure treatment, or with Dr. Joanne Stone ("Pregnancy For Dum-
mies(r)") about having twins. Readers enjoy the opportunity to
interact directly with the person who wrote the book". With over 50
million "...For Dummies" books in print, the Dummies phenomenon is
one of the great publishing stories of all time.
THRIVE is operated by Oxygen Media, Inc., of San Francisco. A
leader in the online community with over 29 million page views per
month, THRIVE offers its 1.6 million users top coverage, resources
and support on healthy living.
AHN.COM is the award-winning web site of America's Health Network,
the 24-hour cable TV channel dedicated to personalized health
information. AHN.COM became famous for broadcasting a live birth
over the Internet, and has continued to pioneer the use of new tech-
nology in the delivery of health-related information.
If you publish a calendar of online events, we hope you will include
listings for the "Health For Dummies" Chat Series. If you're inter-
ested in doing a story related to any of the books or the series,
please let us know. We will provide you with review copies of the
books and interviews with authors and spokespersons. Thank you for
your help.
```

The results of this extended program were mixed. The chats on AHN.COM were lightly attended, with about five to ten people per chat. The chats on THRIVE! drew a more typical crowd of 20 to 50 people, with the exception of the James Dillard chat on Alternative Medicine. This chat was picked up by AOL Live and ran in the site's main auditorium. More than 300 people attended the event, but more importantly, the event was promoted on AOL Live's home page, which at that time was getting half a million hits a day (Figure 10.8).

In reply to the news release, we received several hundred requests for more information from media outlets including the following: *Rolling Stone, Whole Earth, Barrons, Flare,* Avanti News Service, Entertainment Report Syndicate, Senior Wire News Service, Charles Kaye at *CBS News, World & I, Tricycle, FATE, LIFE Magazine, Weight Watchers Magazine, Your Health, Los Angeles Times Book Review,* and The New York Times Syndicate. We received strong coverage in smaller publications devoted to women's interests, parenting, fitness, sports, health, and seniors. Thanks to the long lead time, items about the series appeared in dozens of specialized trade journals including *Telemedicine Journal, Vitamin Retailer, Journal of Clinical Medicine,* and *Family Practice Management.* We also got coverage for the chat schedule from dozens of local daily and weekly newspapers.

More important to my client than the media coverage, I believe, was the online presence at THRIVE! and AHN.COM. The series was continuously promoted for more than half a year at each site with no hosting fees. When the marathon was over, THRIVE! wanted to keep going, having installed chat software at its Web site in addition to its AOL forum. James Dillard, the guest for our breakthrough Alternative Medicine program, has gone on to host his own show on the Oxygen/THRIVE Web site under the name "Holistic Doc." That's a classic example of expanding a program into an ongoing show, partnering with a high-traffic site.

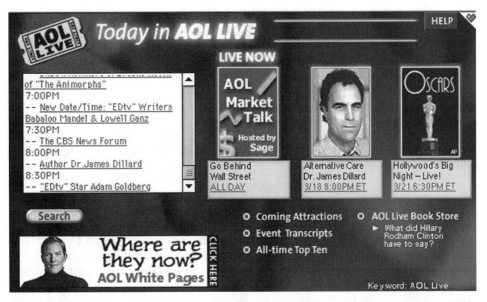

Figure 10.8 A promotion for James Dillard's *Health For Dummies* chat on AOL Live. This home page for AOL Live gets hundreds of thousands of hits a day. Most of the value of an online program comes from the promotional exposure rather than the attendance.

An interesting thing happened at AHN.COM. Producers of programming for the parent cable network noticed what was happening on the Web site and asked me about producing chat programming for their TV programs. They wanted to follow TV shows with live chat opportunities online. This situation is a tremendous example of the benefits of partnership, with online programming leading to print and broadcast opportunities. America's Health Network was purchased by Fox before our discussions got very far, and the opportunity evaporated. Had IDG Books hosted the programming on its own site, it would have incurred a lot of infrastructure costs gearing up for the chat, probably would have drawn audiences even smaller than AHN.COM, and would not have gotten the widespread promotion and other opportunities that came from syndication. In short, they would have paid a lot more for worse results. You make the call.

Associate and Affiliate Programs

Marketing through affiliate and associate programs is an activity largely outside the scope of this book. For people in management and marketing, I recommend the book *Successful Affiliate Marketing for Merchants* by Frank Fiore, Shawn Collins, and James L. Marciano (Que Books, 2001). The research institutes are still weighing the contribution of these partnership arrangements to the e-commerce bottom line. I have some experience setting up affiliate and associate networks (see the case history of myjob-search.com), and I'll share here some insights that pertain to the work of publicists.

Figure 10.9 The Amazon Associates program is one of the great marketing miracles of all time—not for the revenue it generated, but for the brand penetration it gave Amazon.com prior to the company's IPO.

The Amazon Experience

Amazon.com was, of course, the great pioneer in associate programs (Figure 10.9). Begun in 1996, the Amazon Associates program was a marketing campaign—not a revenue-generating operation—and it remains one of the greatest marketing efforts of all time. Jeff Bezos, CEO of Amazon.com, understood intuitively something that millions of online marketers still don't get: The account relationship with consumers is more important than the products being sold. He guessed correctly that people would balk at setting up shopping carts on dozens of different sites and instead would do business with only a handful of sites they trusted with their credit card information. I've watched dozens of publishers try to enable e-commerce on their sites, only to realize that people want to buy books through Amazon where they have an account, a relationship, myriad shipping options, and the ability to pay in a variety of currencies. The associates program appealed to sites that wanted to reap e-commerce revenue without having to install shopping technology. In short, here is a classic example of the power of syndication—partnering with sites who have strengths where you are weak.

The associates program was critical to Bezos's strategy of "get big fast." The program allowed him to lock in relationships with thousands of sites, making it difficult for his sleeping competitors to unseat him. Most importantly of all, it spread the Amazon brand all over the Internet in a hurry, giving Amazon a bigger presence than any other company on the Internet in advance of Amazon's IPO in 1997. Investors all knew about Amazon because they saw Amazon logos everywhere they turned.

The reality of being an Amazon Associate had not caught up with Web masters until after the IPO. The truth is that due to the many facets of how Associate shares are calculated (no cut on special-order books, for example) and the low volume of qualifying sales at associate sites, most Amazon Associates earned almost nothing from their bookstores. Sites that were charging hundreds and thousands of dollars for banner advertising were displaying the Amazon logo for free. Bezos reaped millions of dollars worth of free advertising from the Associates Program while placing a huge hurdle in the way of competitors. It was a brilliant plan, and it worked.

In 1997, I talked with Bezos about the Associates Program, which I thought would turn into a bookkeeping nightmare for him. He had thousands of sites earning less than a dollar in any given royalty period. The accounting burden and the low payments due Associates meant that the checks were literally not worth the paper they were written on. It cost Amazon more to honor its obligations with associates than most associates brought in. But the goal of the campaign was marketing, not money, and the program still looked like a winner from his perspective. I suggested that he partner with charitable institutions so that people setting up associate stores could designate a charity to receive the royalties. It would ease the bookkeeping burden for Amazon, and the royalties of hundreds of stores could add up to a meaningful amount for a charitable organization. Bezos liked the idea but not enough to implement it at his site (as of this writing).

In 1998, I set-up an Amazon Associate store for the @d:tech Convention and got first-hand experience in the process (Figure 10.10). Amazon saved costs—but lost control—by making the associates do-it-yourself projects. To reduce the stigma of greed that accompanies associate stores, all proceeds from the @d:tech store went into the company's scholarship fund. If you are setting up an affiliate or associate program, you should consider partnering with a charitable cause. From a completely cynical point of view, you will generate more goodwill with the gesture than you will revenue for the charity. But, as I say, these revenues can add up for a charitable organization benefiting from hundreds of affiliate and associate programs.

I received the accounting reports for the @d:tech bookstore, and for the first year of operation, the store earned a grand total of $6.75. That's pathetic. Amazon did alter its Associates agreement so that it only had to cut checks if the royalties owed exceeded $100. The cost of check writing is minimal for Amazon, although they still have the burden of bookkeeping, which is highly automated (though not cheap). I'm guessing the vast majority of Associates will never see a penny for their efforts in setting up associate stores. This topic leads to the next problem: Many if not most Amazon Associate stores have been abandoned by their creators. The stores are not maintained, the books are no longer available, and the links no longer work. The Web is littered with Associate corpses, all displaying old Amazon logos, and there is almost nothing Amazon can

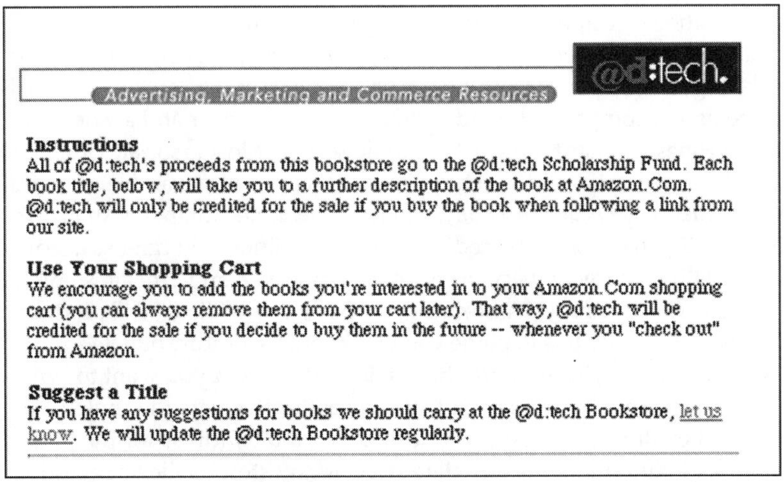

Figure 10.10 An Amazon Associate store set up for a client. Revenues from the store went into the @d:tech Scholarship Fund. The goodwill generated from a charitable associate program will be worth more to most companies than the paltry profits the store generates.

do about it. Visit the showcase of stores featured at http://associates.amazon.com, and you'll see that many of the sites Amazon lists as examples no longer maintain Amazon stores. If Amazon can't be bothered to update its own list of featured stores, you can only imagine how few of the stores themselves are maintained.

Promoting through Affiliate Networks

While associate and affiliate stores seldom generate enough revenue to reward their owners for creating and maintaining them, they still provide a valuable network for syndicating promotional content. Just as Amazon got half a million sites to display the company brand for free, you can piggyback on the installed base of affiliate and associate programs with your own logo and marketing message.

In 1999, I realized that most of the Web sites I was syndicating content to had some sort of affiliate or associate store. These stores added another sales hook to my syndication pitches to Web masters. Not only could I offer them free content for their sites, but they were also free to keep all revenue generated by sales of related products. Because I mostly dealt in book excerpts, associate stores became a back door to getting promotions onto other people's Web sites. If I could no longer get sites to feature an excerpt on the editorial side, I'd try to drop it into the bookstore. I even changed the name of my service from a "syndication campaign" to an "online bookstore display campaign." Publishers understand bookstore displays; it's a terminology they're comfortable with and have shown a willingness to pay for over the years.

Associate and Affiliate programs greatly increased the effectiveness of my syndication efforts. When pitching an article to a Web master, you have to convince them of the merits of the content. But when pitching a store display, the editorial standards are much lower. I would offer to code the display with links to their affiliate or associate programs, thus reducing the amount of work required by the Web master to install the feature. You can take the same approach syndicating your content.

First, determine whether there are any affiliate or associate programs that sell the products you are marketing. Next, try to locate affiliates or associates outlets on the Internet. It would be nice if the parent companies provided you with a list of their affiliate or associate sites, but most businesses guard these lists as trade secrets. Most associate programs use a common URL configuration on purchase links, however. For example, the URL might contain the sequence /storenameassociate/, where "storename" might be Amazon or Egghead or whatever. If you discover the coding used in buy links, you can use a search engine to find these URLs and get a very precise list of associate and affiliate stores. A broader search for terms like "Amazon Associate" or "Hardware Affiliate" will produce a results page with enough quality hits to guide you to potential syndicate outlets.

It's a waste of time to research sites first, then create the content you want to syndicate, and then go back and ask for placements. It's far better to create the content first and then pitch as you explore the sites. Try to locate an e-mail address for the person who is responsible for maintaining the associate store. Many stores solicit suggestions from browsers, and the person who reads this feedback e-mail is most likely the store manager—the person you want to send your pitch to. In your pitch, offer your content as a feature to use in the store, and make sure to say explicitly that "you'll get to keep all the sales revenue the feature generates."

When pitching an article as a feature to Web masters, my success rate averaged between two and five placements for every 25 sites pitched. When pitching an article for use as a store display, the acceptance rate increased to five to 10 placements for every 25 sites pitched. You're not limited to syndicating files to these stores. You can offer chat programming, product reviews, animations, multimedia, software, or even an ongoing show. I have run several seminar programs through a partner's store, rather than locating the content on the editorial side of the site. Syndicating content in this fashion will help you establish relationships with partner sites that can grow into major marketing alliances. Let's look at one extended case history now to see how all of these syndication elements can be combined to create an enormous online presence.

Case History: myjobsearch.com

The short history of myjobsearch.com, a career portal Web site, has lessons for almost any business that is good in a niche but faces a restricted local market. The site was formed in 1999 out of its parent company, The Murdock Corporation. Murdock specializes in career counseling—helping people find jobs for a fee of a few thousand dollars. Located in Salt Lake City, the company had been building for more than 15 years and had a solid formula for success. Experienced career coaches guided job seekers through a process of cataloging their capabilities, defining their goals, locating industry contacts, preparing resumes, securing interviews, and negotiating offers. The program boosted self-esteem and provided encouragement along with ample resources. Proprietary Murdock assets included workbooks, audio tapes, hundreds of articles, and computer banks loaded with leads. The program was successful, but there are only so many job seekers in Salt Lake City.

Murdock set up branches in other cities, but the costs of brick-and-mortar expansion in terms of facilities, staff, and training outran their capital, and the effort was scaled back. Seeing that anything dot.com seemed to be able to draw an unlimited amount of capital, they began porting their operation online with a spin-off company, *myjobsearch.com* (MJS). In early 1999, I was reluctantly pulled into an MJS site promotion effort. When I dug into the site, however (Figure 10.11), I was startled by the tens of thousands of resources that they had assembled in an intelligent, easy-to-use format. The Web site launch was a huge success and helped MJS attract angel investors to build out the site. That's when I took a position on the company's advisory board and began to outline a strategy for expansion.

As you might guess, I recommended a promotional strategy of reaching out to the target audience online and offering them something of value. I set my sights first on building an article syndicate followed by a chat network, a news wire, and finally a site network. I believed it was possible for MJS to create a huge online syndicate, and instead of pulling traffic to its own site, it could push content and revenue opportunities out to hundreds of other sites on the Web. Let's see how the ride went.

An Article Syndicate

In the initial Web site launch campaign for MJS, we distributed an article about using the Internet to find a job. Following on that campaign, we approached the same sites

Figure 10.11 myjobsearch.com is a career portal that grew out of a successful job placement service in Salt Lake City. The challenge was, "Could the company's program be delivered over the Web?"

about featuring a new article each week or each month. MJS had dozens of these articles already written for its in-house career coaching service, so we had a substantial content stream ready to syndicate online.

Several sites took us up on the offer. None was more important, however, than Hoover's. The famous financial information company negotiated a licensing agreement with MJS to use its articles at Hoover's in exchange for online and offline advertising placements. The deal took months to finalize, but eventually the articles started appearing—along with a surge in traffic to the MJS Web site.

A Chat Network

Looking around the Web for opportunities to export myjobsearch.com's content to high-traffic Web sites, I noticed that most of the good real estate had already been gobbled up by Monster.com. Monster offered two great resources: job postings from employers and resumes from job seekers. MJS offered neither of those, instead focusing on the soft skills between: formulating goals, networking, interviewing, salary negotiation, and so on. I also noticed that most of the major portals, such as Yahoo!, Lycos, and Netscape, now had career centers, but no one was offering formal career counseling through chat rooms at those sites. So the plan was to take MJS's career counselors and put them into chat rooms on high-traffic career portals in exchange for the promotional presence and traffic that would result.

I put together a chat profile and queried Web masters at the top portals. My pitch was, "MJS staff will conduct a weekly one-hour Career Coach program at your site. Are you interested?" The starting list of topics was as follows:

- How the Internet has Changed the Job Search
- How Much Are You Worth? Salary Surprises!
- Stupid Resume Tricks: 10 Common Mistakes & Remedies
- How to Land Your Next Job Using the Net
- Getting Off the Roller Coaster: How to *Plan* Your Career
- Tapping the Hidden Job Market -- The Jobs that Never Make it to Monster.com
- Who's Hiring Now? Hot Industries, Hot Companies, Hot Jobs

The first success came from Talk City, the chat portal, which agreed to host the program at its business center. Rather than announce the deal with a news release, we decided to try to lock up a critical mass of such partnerships before going public. Our fear was that if Monster.com got wind of what we were up to, it would use its clout to lock us out from the major portals and start offering coaching itself. We also felt that MJS had a better chance of getting media coverage if it could announce five major deals at once. We rounded up three more deals in short order: CompuServe's Career Management Forum, iVillage's Career Chat, and the Business Center at World Without Borders. Negotiations with our biggest potential partner—Lycos—dragged on for weeks. While booking a chat on a site is an informal process, running an ongoing program often requires a contract. And that means lawyers an delays. Lycos and MJS finally hammered out the boilerplate, and we were ready to launch our chat network.

I hoped for a major chat network announcement in the Internet trade journals, but the media greeted our news release with a yawn. While I had been busy in the trenches, the world of dot.com partnerships had gone supernova, and it took a union as big as AOL and Time Warner to register on the media's radar. Still, the chats gave us a foothold on major portals and resulted in substantially increased site traffic and brand recognition. When MJS showed up in a Jupiter report on career Web sites, we were finally on the map.

Fulfilling the chat obligations was not a major burden. One of the MJS writers kept coming up with topics and preparing articles as support materials for the chats. A ghost typist was employed to keyboard the chats, and it only took a little preparation time plus five hours of chatting a week for MJS's career coach. Still, I could see that expanding the number of outlets would eventually strain our resources. I wanted to broadcast the chats to dozens of sites while letting people participate directly from those sites without having to come to a central location. I dreamed of spending one hour a week and reaching 20 sites. But that would require a technological solution for distributed chat that I had never seen. We stayed with our five-site network while looking for a better solution.

A News Wire

A week after I issued the news release about the MJS chat network that floated like a lead balloon, MJS issued a news release based on an unscientific site poll that 90 percent of resumes submitted in answer to online job postings got no response—not even an acknowledgement. MJS was trying to demonstrate that the reality of online career searching was not living up to the hype. The release was picked up by dozens of media outlets, resulting in both print and TV syndication of stories reaching hundreds more outlets. All of this coverage for a story based on an unscientific Web poll!

A new strategy came out of that release. If the media wanted flashy but unscientific research, we could give them plenty of it. I designed a wire service for MJS called WorkWire to distribute the results of our polls and other news summaries to the media. We learned that we could get more branding by being cited as the source of stories than we could as the subject of stories. The development of WorkWire is described in detail in the newsrooms chapter of this book, so I won't repeat it here. The service went through months of design and testing and was up and running for a few weeks before the dot.com crash of 2000 pulled the funding out from under us.

MJS realized that just by gathering the information it needed to maintain its own site, it could easily generate a news feed for other sites. Examine your own organization and see whether the same isn't true for you. If you are tracking news stories about your industry, monitoring Web sites related to your business, evaluating new sites that appear, and researching statistics about your market, then you have the makings of a wire service. You do the work once but can distribute it to several outlets: the news section of your own site, a newswire for the media, a news feed to other Web sites, an opt-in newsletter delivered via e-mail, and as content for a printed newsletter.

A Site Network

The final element of the MJS online strategy was to create a true network. The parent site itself was so huge it was hard for people to use. Job seekers are interested in mostly two things: jobs in a certain profession or jobs in a specific geographical area. Through sophisticated databasing of MJS's content, users could quickly narrow their search to specific jobs in selected areas. But the same databasing made it possible to export mini career centers to other Web sites.

The idea is a take-off on the Amazon Associates program (with improvements). Amazon's program was designed for branding more than revenue. Associates did all the work building and maintaining their stores for a share of the sales. The MJS syndicate was different in that sites paid an initial fee to get a custom career center, then a monthly fee for maintenance. Fees were based on the content components included in the career center but were far less than what it would cost a site to develop its own center. MJS retained control over the content, look, and feel of the career centers, updating them on a daily basis with fresh content gleaned from the WorkWire and from maintaining the massive MJS database.

If the strategy worked, MJS would be able to build and maintain a network of thousands of sites, each a customized piece of the giant MJS database. Products and services could be sold through the network and advertising pushed through. Revenue sharing arrangements would give network affiliates a rebate on their maintenance fees or even a profit. We felt that we could sell workbooks, audio tapes, and personal career coaching through the network, and we could either push chat programming through the network or charge sites extra to include coaching as part of the Career Center. It was a beautiful idea, and it almost worked.

Professional associations wanted career centers. Schools wanted them, and libraries, welfare agencies, and churches. Newspapers wanted them but didn't want job postings because they competed with the papers' own classified ads. MJS was able to give each of these groups exactly what they wanted: resources related to specific professions, geographical locations, or skill levels. The *Seattle Times* bought a career center, and so did the University of Alabama, the U.S. Armed Forces (Figure 10.12), the NetGodess Web site, the Howard County (Maryland) Library system, Jobs for Texas, and the National Nutritional Foods Association. Before the dot.com crash, MJS had sold more than 1,000 career centers.

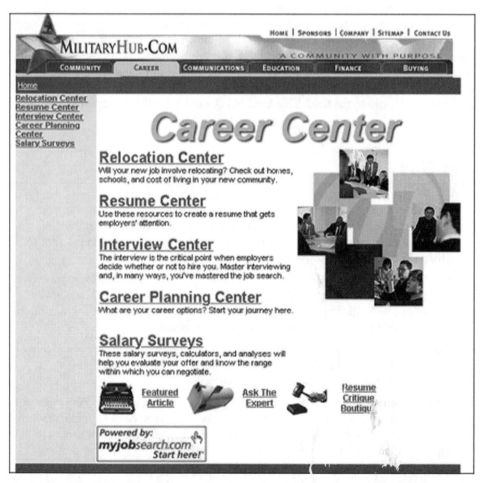

Figure 10.12 This career center was set up by the U.S. government to support the spouses of relocated armed forces members. The career center was built and maintained by myjobsearch.com.

The demise of this beautiful experiment in syndication is difficult to explain. MJS operated too long without a viable revenue stream; when one finally showed up, it was too little, too late. Another problem is that when you are *selling* syndicated content, instead of distributing it in exchange for promotion, you face a whole different set of issues. For-profit syndicates require novel design solutions and constant tinkering. MJS offered a menu of design paradigms for buyers to choose from, but those designs have to be constantly re-evaluated and adjusted based on shifting technology. Trying to deliver a solution that satisfies everyone without having to customize each and every installation is a problem. We never did figure out how to deliver a chat interface through the network, enabling us to syndicate live programming to affiliates. But it was a great experiment that proved the promotional power of syndication. MJS continues to build and maintain career centers today. Someday my stock options might be worth something again, but I'm not holding my breath.

When you are syndicating for publicity, not profit, you face fewer technology problems and associated costs. For most companies, partnering with just one site that is critical to your target market will be enough, giving you a constant presence and a program off which you can hang promotional announcements. The costs are nominal, and the territory is wide open right now. Any business, from the sole proprietor to the huge corporation, is capable of finding a critical target site and securing a premier position as an authority in the field. This kind of relationship will pay dividends for years to come.

Top Tips

It is better to give than to receive. You have more to gain from exporting your content to high-traffic sites than from running promotions on your own site. Management must cultivate a spirit of generosity and cooperation in order to reap the benefits of syndication.

Pitch ideas, not products. For large syndication projects, you need to stay away from details until you have an agreement on the outline. You will face fewer rejections with this approach, and the exact configuration of the program can be more closely tailored to the needs of specific partners.

Pitch on the fly. You have to be prepared to pitch sites while you are researching them. If you try and make a list of target sites, then go back later with a partnership pitch; it will take twice as much time.

Focus on content, not format. Whether you're syndicating a simple Web page or a substantial mini-site, most partners will have to rework the design to fit their sites. By keeping your design light and clean, you make it easy for others to quickly modify and use your content.

Be suspicious of big deals. There's nothing quite so tempting as a major long-term partnership, but you should insist on a smaller trial period until you have experience working with a site. Most of my success has come from building up to major installations, and most of my failures occurred from jumping into the deep end of the pool.

Tune in to the TV of tomorrow. In a few years, once Web masters wake up to the fact that they are running interactive TV stations, most of the good programming slots will be gone. Now is the time to cement a position as a leader in your industry by creating your own show and syndicating it online.

11

Building an Online Publicity
Operation

The Internet has come of age. While the dot.com crash has taken the steam out of Internet startups and online entertainment plays, behind the scenes the Internet is transforming the infrastructures of established companies. The growth market for the Internet isn't the flashy front end but the boring back end, where new technology is reducing costs and increasing productivity by making companies more efficient.

One area benefiting from the new technology is publicity operations. Companies quickly recognized the importance of online publicity, but there just weren't enough people around who understood the tools and techniques to staff a department. So companies purchased these services from ad agencies, PR firms, and high-tech marketing specialists. As the value of these services proved themselves and the cost of leasing them grew, companies looked at bringing these activities in-house. Today, there is an abundance of talent on the market, and companies are in a great position to capitalize on the dot.com crash by hiring experienced online marketers at cents on the dollar.

This chapter will help you ramp-up an in-house online publicity operation. You'll learn what staff positions to create, where to find the people to fill them, and how much work you can expect these people to handle. I'll also cover the tools your staff will need and suggest a training regimen to get them contributing to the bottom line in a hurry. Finally, we'll plumb that bottom line and see how to document and value the results of your very own online publicity operation.

Topics covered include the following:

Organization and budgeting. Where should you stick the online publicity department—in marketing, in PR, or maybe in *information technology* (IT)? Without opening old interdepartmental wounds, I'll suggest a way to put online publicity in its place. And I'll tell you how much various staffing configurations will cost you.

Set-up and training. I begin by dancing around the issues of hardware and software, and then I dig into the details of databases and templates. My suggestions for a publicity boot camp will make potential employees nervous, but my training and testing tips will please PR managers who don't want to practice their crisis-management skills.

Planning campaigns. This planning involves a quick run-down of the tasks involved in campaigns promoting a Web site, a product or service, an event, or a person, including how much time they take. Plus, I'll look at the tricky task of scheduling projects to avoid congestion and smooth the workflow.

Measuring results. How do you know whether this whole operation is worth it? I'll show you how to document the results of a campaign, but placing a value on those results is more difficult than you might think.

Organization and Budgeting

Virtually every modern company needs online publicity capabilities. You can't communicate effectively with the media without it. And the Internet is increasingly a vital tool in marketing. The Internet is used to communicate with customers, prospects, suppliers, and partners and to reach global markets. We aren't saying that you need an online publicity *department*, however. You need the *services* of online publicists, whether you buy them from outside firms or do some or all of the work in-house.

Whether you need an entire department or not depends on your company's size, structure, and resources. It's difficult for me to provide guidance that will be meaningful to the sole proprietor, the Fortune 500 firm, and ad agencies, public relations firms, and marketing communications companies. But I'm going to try. Hopefully, all of you will be able to pick and choose what you need from this chapter to build a solution that makes sense for you. Let's begin our discussion with where inside your organization you want these services to reside.

Organizational Chart

Online publicity is difficult to place in the established hierarchy of departments used by most large organizations. Should it be in marketing, PR, or perhaps even IT? The services provided by an online publicity department are split between two major areas: online media relations (belongs with PR) and online promotion (belongs with marketing). One solution is to eliminate the concept of online publicity altogether and split the functions between online PR and online marketing.

A related issue is whether it makes sense to have departments or job descriptions defined by the technology used to reach the target audience. Do you have a print publicity department, a telephone publicity department, or a face-to-face marketing department? Large corporations might, in fact, have telemarketing operations or direct mail operations, so there is some precedent for this division. It's only because the Internet is so new, and the skills to succeed there are still rare, that job titles include the words "Internet" or "online." Ideally, we'd like all marketing, publicity, and public relations staff to know how to use the Internet. While an ad agency or PR firm should have online specialists, for a corporation it might suffice to include online skills in standard job descriptions.

Let's take a look at some organizational charts and see if we can find approaches that will help you intelligently integrate these services. Table 11.1 shows typical charts for a PR department and a marketing department.

Looking at the organizational charts in Table 11.1, every single division on both charts uses online services. It seems wrong to add a separate online marketing division for the marketing department, or a separate online public relations division for the PR department, or a separate online publicity division for either department. Maybe what we need is an *online services* division for each department—something that reflects the supporting role of technology for all the department's functions?

The problem with that strategy is that *online* is just one component of IT. While computers have been transforming organizations for several decades, the rise of the Internet might be the coin that tips the scales, forcing companies to integrate IT into every department instead of isolating it in a technological ghetto. In five years, do you want to be creating a wireless public relations division or a mobile marketing division? The difficulty placing online services in the organizational chart is just one more illustration that IT needs to be recognized as the vital competitive resource that it is and integrated into every department. Almost everyone working at a company should have computer and Internet skills, and every department with more than five people should have at least one IT person embedded in the department.

I think it will help to look at this discussion from the perspective of job levels for online publicity operations. Basically, there are three job levels: a manager, a writer/creator, and support staff. Both the manager and the writer/creator should remain in each division. For example, a writer/creator in media relations is someone who drafts news releases and interacts with the media. The support staff helps that

Table 11.1 Organizational Charts

MARKETING	PUBLIC RELATIONS
Public Relations	Media Relations
Sales	Investor Relations
Advertising	Community Relations
Promotion	Government Relations
Publicity	Publicity

Typical organizational charts for a marketing department (left) and a public relations department (right). How should online publicity operations be integrated within these two departments?

person send the releases over the Internet. There's no reason to have an *online media relations* person, because virtually all media relations now have an online component. What is needed is for the media relations person to learn how to use the Internet and for the support staff to help set up efficient operations and troubleshoot any problems.

This same scenario is true for sales, advertising, promotion, publicity, public relations, investor relations, community relations, and government relations. We need the people who work in these areas as writers/creators to develop Internet skills. And we need support staff to keep the software up-to-date, to help distribute the work online, to help process responses, to maintain databases, to back up critical work, and to troubleshoot problems. The most elegant strategy I can recommend, then, is to have an IT person in the marketing department and an IT person in the PR department, and these IT people help the departments integrate *all* information technologies while serving as each department's liaison with corporate IT.

I'd like to take one more whack at distributing online publicity services throughout the organizational chart. As I mentioned earlier, I think online media relations belongs mostly to PR. The rest of the work of an online publicist, however, belongs mostly to the marketing department, including such campaigns as Web site promotion, chat tours, seminars, workshops, partnerships, and syndication. I realize there has been a raging battle for decades about whether PR belongs in marketing and over what to do with publicity, which straddles both departments. I come down on the side of publicity being included in marketing, and here's why.

Marketing has all the money. Let's face it, when it comes time to divvy up the budget, marketing always gets way more than PR. Publicity departments that have been stuck in PR are chronically underfunded. I've seen so many companies spend millions of dollars in advertising when thousands of dollars spent on publicity would have generated equal or better results. But because publicity is tucked away in PR, it gets no respect from marketing—and more to the point, gets no money. I think publicity operations need to be compared fairly against advertising, and I don't think that will happen unless publicity is in the marketing department.

I also think there's a major difference in mindset between PR people and marketing people. Most high-level PR managers are defensive. They need to be. They're the ones called upon when a company is in crisis. You don't see marketing people on TV when a plane goes down or product tampering leads to injuries or employees are out on strike. PR gets to deal with these unpleasant tasks. PR works closely with corporate counsel, and PR people tend to have a lawyer's perspective, which helps when you're charged with defending a company but hurts when you're trying to promote one. Marketing people are more offensive, taking the message to the streets, and that's the goal of most publicity operations, too.

Now that I've ruined my chances of getting invited to speak at PR conferences, let me move along to see how online publicity services should be approached by ad agencies (and yes, PR firms).

Ad Agencies and PR Firms

My comments here are directed to advertising agencies, public relations firms, marketing communications companies, and on the periphery, consulting firms. These service companies have good reasons for setting up a separate department focused on the Internet. With the Internet still so new, many of the clients served by these firms aren't ready to handle their own needs in-house. Also, despite the dot.com crash, there still aren't enough skilled people available to fill the online marketing needs of corporations. It will take several years before enough people have gained good Internet skills so that corporations can competently take this work in-house.

You can take the two organizational charts shown in Table 11.1, slap the word "online" in front of every division, and add them to the offerings of ad agencies and PR firms. Just as ad agencies have people or divisions that specialize in television, radio, print, or direct mail, they need to add online specialists or divisions. For the most part, an ad agency won't need people in the creative department to deal exclusively with online issues, because almost all creative work originates on computers and there's a healthy pool of people with computer graphics skills. Media buyers and traffic people can likewise support online and offline campaigns. The positions where the largest changes will be felt will be the *account executives* (AEs) and business development people. Here, you need staff with a deep understanding of how the Internet works and what can and cannot be accomplished there.

In the early days of the Web, many ad agencies were pressed into becoming Web site developers. They hired a few designers, maybe a computer graphics expert, and started pumping out Web sites. As problems crept up and the demand for more and bigger Web sites exploded, ad agencies had to hire technology specialists and started morphing into IT firms. Now, however, much of the Web site development and hosting process has been pulled in-house as companies realize that a Web site isn't just a brochure but has to be integrated with a company's entire infrastructure, including inventory, accounting, internal communications, human resources, purchasing, and so on. While the shift has been wrenching for high-tech ad agencies, in many ways it's a blessing—allowing them to get out of the ugly world of IT and focus on what they do best: marketing.

Instead of building Web sites, ad agencies market them (or market through them). They don't have to worry about the back end any more. They're out in front again, taking a company's message to the target audience and letting the client operate the cash register. With this liberation, hopefully ad agencies will stop building Web sites for every new promotion and return to the tried-and-true method of ramming those ads into whatever content the target audience uses. They will need account executives who know how to locate the target audience online and craft promotions that are welcome at those venues.

Here's one example of the online promotion skills needed at ad agencies. Online newsletter sponsorships are a vastly underused marketing resource. It takes time and patience to gather rates, make buys, deploy the creative, and measure the results. Clients don't have enough recurring need to warrant doing this work themselves. But an ad agency that understands the value of these outlets can make it a specialty, gathering the information in a systematic way, developing working relationships with newsletter editors, and selling this advertising service to dozens of clients. No, it's not as sexy as building a fancy Web site, but the results aren't nearly as disappointing and the service can be sold over and over again.

Ad agencies need AEs who get it. They also need business development people who either get it, too, or are willing to learn from savvy AEs. If I had $10 for every time I've heard a business development person promise a totally ridiculous Web marketing solution, I would be challenging Bill Gates for the richest person in the United States. Some agencies survived for years telling clients who were desperate to get on the Web anything they wanted to hear, building Web sites that produced almost no positive results, losing the account, and moving along to the next desperate client. Only now the tide has turned, everyone's been burned, and it's not so easy to get away with simple solutions such as, "We'll build a Web site," "You just need to promote that site more," or "You need to build a community around your products."

In a period of unlimited demand, ad agencies could get away with murder. But now, in a period of decline, they have to prove results every time. They have to not only *land* a client but *keep* a client and generate recurring business and build trust. This process all starts with business development people who understand the Internet—but not only the Internet. Before, we had business development people who didn't have a clue how the Internet worked and promised solutions they couldn't deliver. Then, we were treated to business development people who know nothing about radio, TV, classified ads, or publicity. If dot.coms really understood the power of the printed word, I'd be getting a lot more offline newsletters and a lot less online newsletters. But their marketing advisors have no experience with printed promotions and don't value them. What a shame.

I think business development positions should go to the most seasoned, veteran people in the trade—not to freshly-minted MBAs. I've seen what happens to print shops that send novices out as estimators; it's not pretty. On an even deeper level, I think AEs should be the business development people. Who better to learn a client's needs, and sell solutions, than the person working the account? But if we must have new business development people, let's make sure they're well rounded and understand not only the Internet but also all the other channels for delivering a client's marketing message.

As for PR firms, I think there are two major areas where they need Internet specialists. The first is in online crisis communications, and the second is in e-mail. I think everyone has realized that the first place people go in a crisis is to a company's Web site. The exact techniques for using a Web site during a crisis have yet to be established, and I will leave that turf for my learned colleagues who specialize in crisis communications. But I do know that planning for online crisis communications is an essential service, and this market will be booming for many years to come. An Internet specialist will not only help develop a crisis plan for a company's Web site but should also know how to syndicate crisis communications to online media outlets. Throughout history, people have been dependent upon the media for news about a company in crisis. For the first time, companies can now communicate directly and continuously with the concerned public. That's a huge change and a major opportunity for PR professionals.

The second area—using e-mail—involves developing better software for integrating contact databases with e-mail. The major area impacted is media relations, but it also pertains to investor relations, government relations, and community relations. E-mail provides an opportunity to communicate directly with the media and also with the public. The press has gone from having no e-mail to being inundated with e-mail to shutting off e-mail contact. It takes a deft hand to navigate e-mail media relations when you realize that press contacts have the ability to filter you out permanently if you are careless in your communications. This statement dovetails nicely with my next topic of discussion, the role of IT.

Interfacing with IT

What role does IT have in positioning online publicity operations? In the arguments I made, I suggested that both marketing and PR should have an IT person in their departments and that everyone on staff should be expected to have some Internet skills. In my opinion, IT builds the infrastructure but should not be building the specific solutions for the marketing or PR departments. If I need to send a message across the hall or across the world, IT should make sure it gets there but should have nothing to do with its content or format. The content should be determined by the writer/creator, and the format should be resolved between that writer/creator and the department's support staff (the IT person in the department).

Here are some examples of the problems with failing to integrate IT people into other departments. I've seen horrible Oracle databases created by IT to integrate e-mail with older contact-management programs. The IT people don't speak the same language as publicists and marketers and don't understand our needs and goals, and it's too hard to teach them to think like promoters. I've seen company Web sites where it's impossible for PR and marketing to put the information they want online. We need crossover artists. We need marketers and publicists who understand IT, who work in the marketing and PR departments, and who make things happen.

Database solutions for marketers have to be designed by marketers. People in marketing and publicity need to control their own piece of the Web site to add content, delete content, and change content at will. Every time I've encountered trouble executing campaigns for a company, I've been warned: *don't call IT*. Can't work with 'em, can't work without 'em. So every department needs an IT person, but that person should not work for IT—they should report to their respective departmental managers.

There are many benefits associated with this solution. If something goes wrong, people in the department call their in-house IT person first. If she or he solves the problem, great, and if not, she or he interfaces with the IT department. That dramatically cuts down on the number of phone calls to IT, while the IT department has the pleasure of communicating with someone that has at least a superficial understanding of the terminology and principles of the technology.

Second, the IT person in the department also has some understanding of the terminology and practices of marketing and publicity. They will help design technology solutions that make sense to marketers and publicists. I would expect an in-department IT person to help design document templates, for example, that communicate well as news releases, memos, position papers, or newsletters—*and* that travel well online.

Third, an in-department IT will help teach a staff of experts in marketing and publicity how to use the Internet better. This concept is part of my theory that you shouldn't have a specialist in online media relations but that everyone in media relations should learn to use the Internet better. I would expect the in-department IT person to show folks how to address bulk e-mail, how to annotate bookmarks, how to set-up filters to process incoming e-mail, and how to put stuff on the Web site.

Some readers are surely shaking their heads thinking, "Of course we want people with crossover skills. But we don't have them, and they're expensive." Ah, but they're not expensive! I see this person as a support person—an entry-level person. Today, you can hire marketing grads out of college who understand enough IT to interface with the IT department. Years of downloading MP3s off Napster, schmoozing in IRC chat, installing upgrades to their media viewers, and wasting hours on role-playing games have given these young people a solid base of skills for helping you communicate better with the press. Thousands of people graduate college every year with hardcore computer skills and only textbook knowledge of marketing and public relations. They're looking for careers in communications and marketing. Your marketing and PR staff gives them a little real-world experience slinging ads or sucking-up to the press, and in return they teach the staff about back doors into Web site contact information. It's a match made in heaven. And it's cheap.

Budgeting

I'm not going to estimate prices for hardware and software. I'll make some recommendations about the computing power and programs you'll need later in this chapter, but any advice on pricing would quickly go out of date. Most companies can work with their existing hardware and software until their budgets allow upgrading. Also, I make specific hardware and software recommendations in other chapters of this book as appropriate. Right now, I want to talk about the cost of staff and the balance between in-house services, using freelancers, and buying services from vendors.

The decision about whether to build your own online publicity operation is mostly a financial one. In pricing services, I have a rule of thumb that many other executives use: price the service at three times staff salaries. For example, if an employee has a salary of $50,000/year, I need to price their services to yield $150,000/year. My casual logic is that one-third of the revenue goes to salaries, one-third to overhead, and one-third as a return on investment. In practice, it's hard to hit that mark, but the 33 percent profit margin can afford to take a hit and still make it worth being in business.

So, if you are deciding whether to bring these functions in-house, look at how much you are spending with outside vendors, divide by three, and see whether you think you can hire people to do the same work for that amount. For example, if you're spending $300,000 a year for these services and you think you can hire staff capable of equal results for $100,000, then you should hire them. Determining exactly what your vendors do for you, and what your own staff would be able to do, is not easy. There's some gut instinct involved based on experience, and whichever way you decide has risks. Hopefully, by the end of this chapter, you'll be able to make a very educated guess.

For someone to manage an online publicity operation, you're looking at a salary in the upper-five figures—between $50,000 and $100,000, depending on a lot of factors. For what I call the writer/creator people, with job titles such as publicist, senior publicist, online publicity specialist, account executive, online marketer, and so on, a starting salary between $25,000 and $50,000 is common (mostly dependent on the number of years of experience in the industry). Support staff, including the in-department IT person mentioned, runs about $15,000 to $25,000 a year. I like using interns in these positions, and I'm also fond of high school graduates with good computer skills. What you save in salary with interns and high school grads you lose in time, because they require a lot of mentoring. In the long run, I think it's a good bargain for the company and for society. But we will talk more about that later.

When buying services from outside vendors, there are of course many factors in pricing. My experience is that I can hire qualified freelancers for about $50/hour. Working with an ad agency, PR firm, marketing firm, and so on, you can expect to pay about $100/hour for the services of line employees, $150/hour for the services of senior staff, and from $150 to $300/hour for the services of a market specialist/guru. Many firms work off retainers or proposals, and these should lower your average hourly costs by as much as 10 percent.

Let's look at some typical staffing configurations and see how the numbers work out. I usually budget one support person for every two middle or upper-staff members. I've had good results using part-time support staff and freelancers until the budget allows additional hiring. You can build a competent online publicity operation within the PR, publicity, or marketing department with just two and a half people—one writer/creator, one tech-savvy support person, and half a manager—for under $100,000 in salaries per year. By "half a manager," I mean a PR, publicity, or marketing manager who understands the Internet but who also oversees other workers.

For a standalone online publicity operation, a good configuration and budget is shown in Table 11.2.

A good estimate for all the other expenses related to the department besides salaries is an amount equal to salaries. This amount would include such things as employee benefits, IT services, accounting services, office space, furniture and fixtures, hardware, software, Internet services, phone service, postage, printing, travel, training, paid promotional placements, and miscellaneous outside services. The two-and-a-half person micro operation mentioned previously might cost a total of $150,000 to $200,000. The four-person-plus standalone department might cost a total of $300,000 to $400,000. By the end of this chapter, you should have a good idea of how much work you can expect to get out of this staff.

Business people in New York City and San Francisco are probably laughing at the salary levels used in my staffing scenarios. At the height of the dot.com boom, when entry-level support persons in hot markets were commanding up to $50,000 a year, those writer/creator types were knocking down $75,000, department managers were starting at $150,000, and everyone was getting stock options and juicy perks. Thank heaven for the crash, which has brought reality back to Internet practices and wages.

Table 11.2 Online Publicity Department

JOB TITLE	ANNUAL SALARY
Online Publicity Manager	$75,000
Senior Writer/Creator	$40,000
Junior Writer/Creator	$30,000
Support Person	$20,000
Freelance Services	$10,000
Total Salaries	**$175,000**

Today, salary levels have dropped to where dot.com companies can hire competent staff at prices they can recoup with profits. One of nice things about the Internet revolution is that you're less dependent on local talent and can bolster your staff with virtual employees working from soft salary markets.

Hiring Practices

Where can you find the people you need to staff an online publicity operation? At the managerial level, a transfer from within is usually easiest. A transferee will understand at least some of the internal politics of your organization. Success in management is related more to people skills than computing skills. I would look for someone who is an experienced publicist and who understands how news is manufactured. Strong media relations skills are important in this job and are not easy to learn from a book. I would look for someone with experience in whatever industry you're working in. The manager's knowledge of how things are done in this business, and his or her industry connections, will be valuable.

For a management position, I wouldn't worry about computer skills beyond basic word processing, spreadsheet, e-mail, and browsing skills. You don't need someone who knows programming or even how to build a Web page. You do need someone who is willing to go back to school a little to learn about the intricacies of online communications, however. If you can't fill the slot from within your organization, then look for someone in the industry. Advertise in trade publications, whether online or offline, and stay away from general-interest job boards or technology job boards.

For what I call writer/creators, I like to hire people with good writing skills and experience. It's a lot easier to teach writers the computer skills they need than to teach computer people how to write. Below is part of a classified ad I used to recruit publicists. You can fill-in the blank with whatever industry:

```
Great Copywriter wanted for online publicity business. Can you slay
me with a few syllables? Are you comfortable, cunning online? Fear-
less in the face of new technology? Do you have _____ industry
experience?
```

I recommend hiring locally unless you are comfortable working with virtual employees. It's not worth relocating someone for this position, so a local ad cuts down on the number of resumes you have to sort through. More than half the responses I've gotten are from recent college grads, and a lot of them cite their work on literary magazines to bolster their writing credentials. Personally, I would avoid anyone with literary ambitions. They frequently have visions of grandeur and take their writing too seriously. On the other hand, a background in journalism is perfect, because it brings not only an understanding of media relations but also a journeyman's attitude toward writing. One person I hired had daily newspaper experience. That's my kind of writer —conditioned to fill-up column inches on command and long over being sensitive about having his writing cut or tweaked.

Another excellent background for a writer/creator is anyone with experience in event production. All advanced online publicity campaigns involve chats, seminars, presentations, workshops, news conferences, grand openings, or other events. Deadlines are usually tight, there are many balls in the air at the same time, scheduling skills are important, and resistance to taking "no" for an answer is essential. I've worked with tech people who accept rejection and are therefore ill-suited to publicity, and I've worked with people who think FTP stands for Fancy Toilet Paper but can talk their way into a chat booking every time. For this job, you need someone with good writing skills, good phone skills, and persistence.

Besides advertising in local and trade publications, you can find good writer/creator people at the Internet sites that are critical to your industry. The linkage chapter of this book has instructions for building a road map to these sites. You can often find under-paid, overworked talent at these sites, working as chat show hosts, message board moderators, Web page designers, content editors, writers, and even Web masters. I've recruited good talent from people I've seen in action at these sites. Once again, stay away from the large Internet job boards, because you'll get flooded with resumes and then sued when you don't hire everyone.

Ideally, you want good computer skills from your writers/creators, too. These skills aren't hard to find anymore, and you should have several applicants who offer a complete package of talents. Knowledge of computer programming is not required, but I like people who have built Web pages, who know how to tease results out of search engines, and who have great e-mail skills. The dream candidate would also have experience with Usenet newsgroups, Internet mailing lists, chat, instant messaging, and know how to scan pictures and create JPEG graphics. The department manager should be able to teach these people how publicity works, how the industry is organized, and how to get things done inside the corporate culture.

For support positions, there are two main types you are looking for. The first is a word processing warrior who can create good-looking documents, handle mailing operations, answer phones competently, process e-mail quickly, and not wear out from repetitive tasks. The second is a "warez dude," someone who knows how to download and install software, what to do if a virus hits, how to use FTP and IRC, how to program function keys on a computer, how to set-up alias e-mail addresses and accounts, how a listserver works, and how to find and post to newsgroups. These two types of support skills don't usually reside in the same person, so if you have a publicist who is a techie, look for a more secretarial support person, and if your publicists are good at handling their own administrative support, hire a hacker.

Warez dudes don't usually attend traditional four-year college programs. You'll often get them as high school grads or from community colleges or tech programs. If they mature and graduate from college, they become IT people and will be too expensive for your department. Warez dudes come in both genders, though females are called "grrrls." You can bring these people in as interns, and it's a great idea to contact the technology teachers at local high schools and colleges for referrals, but you'll soon have to pay them decently because they can make money as Web page builders just about anywhere.

■ As attached as I've grown to my Warez staff over the years, these are revolving door positions. I try to teach them what I can, then help them find bigger and better employment elsewhere. The work involved is simply not worth paying high wages and never will be. Publicists are hopefully building careers and can watch their earnings grow as they move up the ladder into management. But

Warez dudes have nowhere to go inside a publicity department. When I lose the services of these people, I console myself knowing that I was mowing lawns for money at their age and that their annual salary at age 30 will probably exceed my lifetime earnings.

Freelancers

Freelancers are extremely useful for an online publicity operation and are underused by companies on both the client side and the agency side. They give you the capacity to take on more work without having to hire staff. When the overflow work starts getting too expensive, you can hire in and cut back on freelance services. Most freelancers have multiple clients and can take the ebb and flow without the resentment that could sour a relationship. Freelancers provide their own office space, equipment, and communication services. With freelancers, you can hire specialists to fill skill gaps in your own staff.

It takes time to find, evaluate, and hire freelance staff and takes quite a bit of time to train them and build a good working relationship. Managers should budget time accordingly. A typical scenario for me is that I find a freelancer with good experience and references, I teach them to do the work I need, and after a few assignments they either flake out or decide it's not worth the money. I go through roughly two freelance situations that don't work out for every one that does. But when they work, it's beautiful, and they usually last for years. I worked with one freelancer for three years and never met her face-to-face. She handled all my America Online and CompuServe postings. I paid her piece rate, and at first the money wasn't very good. As she gained experience, though, the piecework translated into more than $50/hour, she was happy to get more work, and I was delighted with the quality of the results.

I haven't been able to find freelancers who can handle the writing. The work is too important, I'm painfully obsessive about the details, and it's hard to price. Good assignments for freelancers include discussion group postings, article syndication, chat or seminar coordinator, and especially ghost typists. Ghost typists call chat guests five minutes before a chat, then read questions to the guest and keyboard the guest's answers. Ghost typists and chat coordinators can be recruited from the staff of chat venues. Many Web sites and America Online forums use freelance or volunteer chat staff. You can sometimes get away with posting messages right in the forums or message boards where you're seeking freelance typists or chat coordinators. These people have experience and will almost always jump at a paying gig.

One reason you need freelance ghost typists is that most chats run at night, outside of normal business hours. There might be problems giving employees access to the office at night, both for the safety of your business assets and the safety of your employees. But there are lots and lots of "stay-at-home" parents who have great computing skills, loads of experience chatting online, and want work they can do once the kids are in bed. I've used several freelance chat coordinators. They run the whole operation, from briefing the guests to cleaning the transcripts. But I have to create the chat profile in-house. The same goes with seminar coordinators: They're very good at booking venues and pulling off events, but I wouldn't trust them to write the campaign materials.

Some companies are willing to use freelancers but draw the line at remote employees. I used to be in this camp, too, thinking that critical staff needed to be on site to interact with the team and with clients. But in 1998, all that changed. My wife and I moved to New Orleans, Louisiana, and my staff stayed behind in Port Townsend, Washington. I thought it would be impossible to effectively manage my business from 2,500 miles away, but I was wrong. What a relief it turned out to be. If someone's computer broke, they figured out how to fix it or hired someone to do the job. No more tedious tech support. No more drawn-out staff meetings. No more distractions from work. Although my staff missed me personally, they loved not having the boss around. And I could easily monitor the effectiveness of their work from afar. I didn't care about their habits as long as the work got done on time and up to standards.

Since moving to New Orleans, I've worked with new employees who were interviewed and hired remotely, and whom I have never met in person, despite being their manager for several years. I've never had a client in my hometown—either in Port Townsend or New Orleans—and it hasn't reduced my effectiveness. In fact, I'm able to spend almost 100 percent of my time doing "billable work" because I don't have to attend an endless parade of meetings. If you've been avoiding hiring remote employees, I think you should reconsider. The technology is mature enough to let people work effectively from afar, and the burden they take off the corporation more than compensates for the extra work required to hire, train, and monitor a remote staff.

You can find potential freelancers and remote employees quite easily online. Once again, I recommend you stay away from the big online employment services and look for niche sites, such as trade associations or regional portals. One good service is eLance at www.elance.com, where you can post a project and collect bids. You might have to work with a few vendors until you find someone worth keeping. Many of the sites listed in the Resources section at the companion Web site at www.wiley.com/combooks/okeefe have niche job boards tailored to your specific needs.

Setup and Training

We've covered the personnel issues of setting up a department adequately; now let's talk about the tools and training these people need to perform up to expectations. I'll start with a brief discussion of hardware and software. This book is not an IT manual, and I'm not competent to advise you on IT issues such as what servers to buy. I'm going under the reasonable assumption that companies already have most of the hardware and software they need, and further guidance should be obtained from an IT professional. Then, we'll look at The Big Three: database, templates, and training. I'll conclude with some suggestions for testing the systems you put into place.

Hardware and Software

If your needs are limited, such as managing a database of a few thousand names, you can probably get by with whatever computer you're currently using. A PC running Windows 98 or a Macintosh using System 8 can handle the job nicely as long as your processor speed is higher than 250MHz.

For a small business solution, you'll need personal computers with a Pentium II, 486 processor or better, at least 128MB of RAM, 2 gigs of storage space, and a T1 Internet connection. This equipment will enable you to manage a database in excess of 10,000 contacts and handle a bulk e-mailing of several thousand pieces. For operations this large, it's best to maintain a constant connection to the Internet, 24 hours a day, seven days a week. You can't do that reliably with either a cable modem or DSL—the two high-speed connections available below a T1 level.

Large commercial installations are simply beyond my level of expertise, and you'll have to consult with an IT professional for advice. These systems involve running servers I know nothing about. I know enough about computers to get applications to work for me, but I know very little about setting up complex networks and servers. Sorry.

As far as software goes, most of the people in the department will be able to operate well with the equivalent of the Microsoft Office family of software and a full-featured Web browser. Between them, you'll have software for word processing, spreadsheets, presentations, Web browsing, e-mail, news reading, and file transfer. For e-mail, I recommend paying for a professional, standalone version as opposed to using free versions or those bundled with browsers. You'll want a program with sophisticated filtering capabilities not usually found in free or bundled software.

Other programs helpful for the techies in the department include the following:

- A good Web page building program (for example, PageSpinner)
- Graphics programs (for example, PhotoShop, JPEG View, and graphics converters)
- A dedicated file transfer program (such as Fetch)
- A dedicated Usenet news reader (such as NewsWatcher)

You'll want to have America Online installed on all machines and at least one account, which can be shared as long as two people don't need it at the same time. You should buy an AOL account configuration that includes CompuServe access. AOL Time Warner owns both companies. Publicity work on AOL is important and requires access to features that can be found only on the proprietary service and are unavailable through the Web, even to subscribers. All of your work on CompuServe can be accomplished through the Web interface without having to install special CompuServe software, however.

The most important software decision will be the program in which you decide to keep your contact database. Choices range from no-frills spreadsheets to database programs, contact management programs, specialized packages, or custom-designed networkable solutions, such as Oracle. I recommend upgrading to something at least as powerful as ACT or NowContact. While I caution against spendy solutions such as custom-built Oracle databases, large companies with strong IT departments will need to move this way sooner or later. If you can hold out until package programs come onto the market specifically designed for contact management or publicity operations, you'll save some money and frustration.

I discuss database issues quite a bit in the chapter on news releases, which also includes screen shots of good contact-management templates. There is a new breed of software on the market that combines good contact-management database features with sophisticated e-mailing capabilities (think of ACT merged with Eudora). These programs will not only help you manage your list of media contacts, but they will also automate the use of direct marketing databases and online newsletter subscriptions. They let you e-mail/merge documents with names, send merged documents over the Internet, and process the replies. For companies with good IT support, this software can be nursed into service immediately. For those without confidence in their IT departments, it might be 2003 before this new software is bug-free enough to make it worth abandoning your old, familiar, piecemeal programs.

Finally, I offer a word of caution about the coming multimedia frenzy online. As high-speed Internet access spreads, companies will feel peer pressure to add lots of streaming audio and video to their sites, along with chat services, to accommodate such things as live news conferences. Today, even companies such as Ford and Intel turn to Yahoo! Broadcast Services to handle these events. That should indicate to you that even with the best IT departments, this area is for specialists. Not only will the price of operating a Web site skyrocket when these features are added, but their complexity will require adding expensive IT staff. You are much better off partnering with other sites on these kinds of events than trying to host them at your own site. Resist the pressure to have a Web site with lots of bells and whistles, and when someone snubs you for being a Luddite, just smile and say, "That's *Profitable* Luddite to you."

Databases

A publicist is only as good as his or her contact list, so a major investment and ongoing priority for the publicity department is building and maintaining a good database of media contacts. Chances are, you already have such a database. If it's on a Rolodex, you'll have to join the information age and computerize it. If it's embedded in an old software package, you'll have to upgrade it for multiple users who need to process thousands of contacts quickly. Whatever software you choose, you're going to have to augment that database with a lot more contacts. One of the great advantages of using the Internet in publicity operations is that you can cheaply query thousands of journalists to find out who is interested in a particular story.

The news release chapter covers sources of media contacts. A brief summary is in order here. You start with the ones you know and have in your database already. Then, purchase one or more media databases for sale on the market and merge them with your own. You can buy these from Bacon's, MediaMap, and other vendors. It is completely legal to extract media contact information from these databases and put it into your own database (although some vendors might decline to sell you their databases if they know your intentions). Law regarding databases is under siege right now, so please consult an attorney before undertaking any major merge operation.

The resulting database will have a huge number of contacts—perhaps as many as 20,000 records. But it will contain very few personal e-mail addresses and almost no "new media" contacts. Personal e-mail addresses are essential for your work, and there's really no way to get them other than sleuthing, covered in the news releases chapter. You also need to bolster the database with new media contacts, including online newsletter editors, Usenet newsgroup moderators, Web site content editors, chat show producers, and anyone else who can make your promotions come alive online.

Choosing software, configuring it properly, merging databases, and debugging can be done in about one to two weeks. Pumping up the database with e-mail addresses and new media contacts could occupy a part-time person for a couple months. After that, maintenance chores drop considerably. Using the database often will help keep it clean as contact information is updated, non-working e-mail addresses are deleted, and spam-sensitive folks are weeded off the list. On top of ongoing maintenance, you should have a support person spending at least half a day each week sleuthing new names for the list. This process might involve a weekly trip to a well-stocked library or sifting through a box of old magazines, newsletters, newspapers, and journals looking for media e-mail addresses.

Templates

It took me about three years of running an online publicity operation to realize how important good templates are to efficiency. I used to just revise templates willy-nilly, but now I put them on an annual schedule for review and improvement. I've even borrowed software terminology to help make sure I don't accidentally use old templates. I'm now using stationery version 5.0. You'll find downloadable versions of most of the templates described here at www.wiley.com/compbooks/okeefe.

A quick word on terminology: I call these documents *templates*, but in Microsoft protocol they're *stationery*. When you open a stationery document in Microsoft Word, it makes a copy of the original, and it's impossible to accidentally overwrite the source document. Templates, however, are not as easy to safeguard, and I've accidentally replaced templates with final documents, wasting hours of work. I keep all my templates together in one folder and not in the one Microsoft defaults to for stationery storage. I know that Word warriors can perform miracles with this software, but I don't have their patience for learning how to use all the fancy features. In fact, as you will read throughout this book, a good deal of my time is spent disabling supposedly helpful features in Word, Netscape, AOL, and other software, which are collectively responsible for no small amount of poorly formatted documents online. If anyone at Microsoft is reading this book, here's a tip: Why don't you let users *turn on* features they want in their software instead of forcing them to *turn off* features they don't want. In the "smart house" Bill Gates is building in Seattle, I wonder if all the appliances turn on when he opens the door and he has to go around turning off all the ones he doesn't want to use?

Let's continue with the discussion of templates. Setting up these documents will take a fair amount of time, and the originals should be backed up and safeguarded by a designated document keeper. With a good set of templates in place, your staff will fly. Here's a list of what you need:

- Web site registration form (Word)
- Web site registration report (HTML)
- Web site linkage report (HTML)
- E-mail news release (Word, sent as text)
- Discussion group posting (Word, sent as text)
- Postings report (Word)
- Chat profile (Word and HTML)

- Chat schedule (Word)
- Chat tour guest instructions (Word)
- Seminar pitch page (HTML)
- Seminar welcome letter (Word, sent as text)
- Newsletter (Word sent as text, or Listserver)
- Subscription confirmation (text)
- Syndicated article (HTML and text)

In addition to these templates, you'll want to create several e-mail form letters to use acknowledging replies and dealing with flames. You'll also have your basic office stationery, such as letterhead, envelopes, mailing labels, fax cover sheets, and logos in various sizes and formats. For people working on the agency side, you'll need invoices, purchase orders, contracts, and similar documents. I wouldn't mention these basic items at all except that many of these communications are moving online, and documents need to be reformatted for delivery over the Internet. During your annual stationery upgrade, you might want to start designing online versions of older offline documents and think about how you can deliver this information over the Internet.

As an example of the changing channels of communication, I offer this anecdote for my colleagues on the agency side. I used to send printed packets documenting online campaigns to my clients. You want to send something folks can pass around in a meeting that demonstrates the results of a campaign. But these printed pieces eventually got filed, misplaced, or trashed. At the Tenagra Corporation, we built a password-protected Web site for each client and put every single document for every single campaign on the site. The site functioned as institutional memory for our clients—they could easily locate documents related to any campaign in the past. Our templates had to be retooled so we could draft a document once and as effortlessly as possible convert it into text or HTML. It will take some serious tweaking to get templates that good. I was blessed with the services of Jeremy Hart, a gifted Warez dude, who set up this whole incredible archive, thereby creating one of the most powerful training tools any company could have. Clients used the site lightly, but Tenagra's staff used it all the time.

Training

In 2000, John Wiley & Sons hired me to help set up an online publicity department for them. The department had one manager and four full-time staff. My contract lasted for three months and involved two week-long training sessions in New York. For the first session, I split my time between augmenting their contact database and training sessions with the staff. The second session was split between testing and debugging the database and training sessions with the staff. The goal was to get an actual campaign out the door before I left town—not practice, not a dry run, but real bulk e-mail going to several hundred journalists who might forever hold it against Wiley if we botched it.

I bring this point up because I think the attitude you have to take in training is *zero tolerance for public mistakes*. To err is human, but to really screw up on a global scale requires the assistance of computers. An efficient online publicity operation will involve large mailings to big databases and lots of filtering and automation that makes it possible to make huge mistakes. In learning my craft, I've accidentally sent the wrong document to hundreds of people, I used a contact list from a dairy science campaign for a technology promotion, I sent an unreadable 40-page document to hundreds of journalists, and I used an e-mail filter that sent 80 copies of a document to the same person before I found the bug. Stuff happens. But you want it to happen in-house, to test it, and catch it, because you can do permanent damage to your company's image and your department's effectiveness with a single stupid mistake.

By the end of my training program at Wiley, I think it's fair to say the staff was almost afraid to touch its computers. We drilled on every possible problem I could think of, going over how to avoid the problem, how to detect whether the problem has occurred, and how to remedy the problem. We learned how to handle flames, how you can tell if you're being hacked, and how to treat unhinged Internauts. Wiley's management backed me in this very cautious attitude. The message was that we want results, but not at the expense of trouble.

On my last day at Wiley headquarters, we sent our first live news release. Within minutes, we received the first response from a journalist interested in the story. A cheer went up. By the end of the day, there were something like 16 positive replies and *no complaints*. Within a couple days, the number of positive replies doubled, and still there were no complaints. We all half expected the sky to fall in, but that campaign never generated a single complaint although it used a newly installed contact database. The team has been turning out successful campaigns ever since.

A similar scenario occurred with an insurance company in Seattle where I set up a broadcast e-mail system for media contacts: agonizing training, testing, and fire drills followed by nothing but positive results. So, my advice to you is to put the fear of God into staff concerning anything that leaves the company's offices. The training doesn't take that long, but you have to first cultivate a system of checking and double-checking everything that goes out the door and have materials and procedures in place to quickly handle any complaints that arise.

I like to approach training from three different perspectives. The first is software, getting people familiar with all the programs required for their jobs. In large corporations, in-house mentors are the best way to learn, followed by on-site schooling. Online training, or distance learning, just isn't very effective without some kind of coach in house. You should offer to pay for classes related to an employee's job description, and a generous budget for books helps. If you don't have a corporate account with an online bookseller, consider setting one up and letting staff purchase one book a month. Because you, the employer, will get the bill, it's unlikely that staff will abuse this privilege by purchasing recreational reading.

Books are important, because most of the software used online is poorly documented. Nowadays, a lot of software is purchased online and downloaded, and many software manufacturers have stopped printing manuals, making them available as e-books instead. E-books are not popular with readers, however, and in training they're a poor substitute for a real book. If e-books worked, the computer section of bookstores would be empty. Quite the contrary, it is one of the largest and fastest growing segments in book publishing. Finally, the entire field of online communications is relatively new, and college courses that expose students to the principles and practices involved are just beginning to pop up. Books are the easiest way to tap the minds of experienced practitioners in the field.

After software training, my second approach is to teach the documents. Let the staff fill out the templates and then analyze them in a group setting. Each student will have problems with different aspects of the forms, and they can learn from each other's mistakes. The two focal points are length and format. You have to learn to pare online communications to the bare essentials and flawlessly format them for readability. Many of the formatting difficulties come from transferring between Word, text, and HTML. Training should involve lots of this migrating, so the staff gets familiar with the process and knows where the gremlins like to hide.

The third approach is to teach by task, running through each of the basic campaigns in this book that relate to the person's job description. There are some core skills to focus on that will help with any campaign, and these are as follows:

- How to use search engines effectively
- Figuring out who the decision-makers are at Web sites
- How to find or guess e-mail addresses
- How to annotate bookmarks
- How to research newsgroups and mailing lists
- How to quickly build a list of key sites for any industry
- How to format and address bulk e-mail
- How to design, use, and debug e-mail filters
- How to make and edit screen captures

Any good manager knows that you can't force people into job descriptions. During the training process, people will reveal their strengths and weaknesses. Try to avoid assigning specific duties to the staff in advance so that you can shuffle the responsibilities based on talents and interests. Hopefully, your department will contain an organizer, a writer, a talker, and a techie, and you can match people with tasks regardless of their titles. I've tried pushing techies into writing and pushing writers into sales, and it's never worked well. It's better for everyone concerned to admit that you're only able to do what the staff is capable of, and if the staff can't handle the work, you need to fire and hire to get the right mix.

I've found that it takes three months for someone to learn a job well enough that they are contributing more than they are taking. Any new hire is a drain on management time until they reach this level, and after that they are capable of handling the work without close supervision. I try to keep the assignments light until an employee has crossed that threshold. On the agency side, for example, nothing gets sent to a client that doesn't have my stamp of approval for the first three months. After that, you have to wean your publicists to leave the manager out of the loop and deal directly with the clients unless there is trouble.

Training staff for online publicity operations will get easier every year. Colleges, community colleges, trade associations, and professional development schools are offering more and more courses to prepare people for this kind of work. You should take advantage of these programs. Students are coming out of high schools and college with better computing skills. Lots of students love the Internet, and the skills they learn shopping or chatting or surfing the Web are very relevant to the job skills employers are looking for. I think the biggest problem in the future will be teaching these young people when to use printed promotions or when to put down the mouse and pick up the phone. They think there's a technology solution for everything, and they need managers who understand both the old ways and the new.

Testing

The final phase of setting up a department and training the staff is to test the operation before it goes live. For many tasks, such as posting to newsgroups, you can learn from experience. The systems that really need testing are those capable of blowing up.

Tops on my list for testing are e-mail filters and autobots. E-mail filters examine incoming messages, then take an action based on the content of the message. I use them a lot for sorting e-mail into folders and less so for automatically replying to requests for information. It's useful to set up generic e-mail addresses such as *news*, *info*, or *help* and route these to different staff members. All the generic e-mail addresses need to be checked to be sure they route properly. All the e-mail filters need to be tested to see whether they function as expected. Any time you automate something, there's a double risk. First is that the automation isn't working properly. Second is that there's often no warning signal that something's gone wrong, and the malfunction could go undetected indefinitely.

One tip for anyone in online publicity is to disable automatic sending of e-mail. In the software I use, Eudora, you can set outgoing e-mail so that it *queues* rather than *sends*. Figure 11.1 shows an e-mail that is ready to be dispatched. In the upper right-hand corner, instead of a Send button there's a Queue button. Hitting the button will store the e-mail in my outbox until I'm ready to send it. My e-mail software will hold

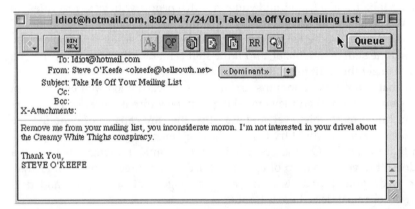

Figure 11.1 This flame mail is ready to be sent, but instead of a Send button in the upper right-hand corner, there's a Queue button. Queuing your e-mail instead of sending it automatically gives you a precious second chance to retrieve any mistakes or ill-advised missives.

the message until I invoke the Send Mail command, or I can program it to send messages every three minutes or every hour (and so on).

Using Queue instead of Send will give you a few minutes after you've finished a message to retrieve it. A lot of mistakes, including errors of judgment, are recognized within a few moments of completing an e-mail. Queuing helps you catch them. Also, I've discovered through experience that about 25 percent of the people requesting information from an auto-responder want or need something other than the auto reply they are going to get. For example, if you offer an article online and provide an address that will automatically send the article upon request, some people using that address might want to interview you or might be asking if you have an article on another subject. Sometimes they're just asking for the article, but if the person's signature reveals that he or she is a producer for *NBC Nightly News*, a phone call might be in order.

When I set up an auto-reply filter, e-mail requests that match the criteria get pulled out of the inbox and filed in a separate e-mail folder. Then, replies are automatically generated and *queued*, not sent. Before I type the `send  mail` command, I quickly skim through the requests looking for any that need special handling. If someone needs special treatment, their reply is removed from the queue before the rest are sent off. This procedure should be required for the first three months of an employee's training and continued thereafter based on results. Browsing the messages will not only help you better process requests, but it's a crash course in the subtleties of online communication. Plus, it's the best way to find bugs in your e-mail filters and learn to design bug-free filters.

Beyond automated functions, the other important area for testing is to view messages using different software. This review is critical when you're setting up a department but doesn't have to become standard operating procedure. Web pages you create should be viewed using Netscape Navigator, Internet Explorer, and AOL. E-mail news releases should be viewed in Outlook Express (Explorer's e-mail module), Netscape Communicator, and AOL's e-mail. Upload discussion group postings to the Usenet newsgroups specifically set up for testing, then view them by using a news reader, Netscape, Explorer, and AOL. Upload Web pages such as Chat Profiles and Feature Articles to your Web site, then view them with different browsers.

This software-compatibility test will usually catch a few problems in your templates that can be fixed once and forgotten. Prudence suggests running a test such as this one about once a year—perhaps as part of your annual template makeover. If you're getting replies to your e-mail and the quoted text or quoted documents have ragged line endings, strange symbols, or anything else that looks less than perfect, you have a formatting problem and need to check your software settings and/or your templates. For managers, one way of discovering formatting problems is to ask your staff to send you the final version of news releases and other documents via e-mail for approval. If you proofread only from printed documents, you might not notice errors that would be obvious in e-mail.

Scheduling Campaigns

At the peak of my activity as director of Internet Publicity Services for the Tenagra Corporation, I was launching four campaigns a week with a staff of three full-time employees, two part-time employees, and freelancers. Scheduling projects became a major undertaking, not only for us but also for clients who needed work faster than we could find holes in the schedule. One of the tricks managers learn is how to balance the workload among employees and across the annual calendar.

I kept two types of calendars, one for the department and one for each publicist or AE. The goal for the departmental calendar was to launch four campaigns a week without launching two campaigns on the same day. Monday morning and Friday are both bad for campaign launches, so on Monday we planned the week's chores and on Friday we cleaned up, documenting all the work, organizing the files, and grooming the infrastructure.

Each publicist or AE should be able to handle one big campaign and one small campaign every week. Big campaigns are chat tours, seminars, online events, and major Web site launches. Small campaigns are news releases, article syndications, linkage campaigns, and registration campaigns. Big campaigns take about three months to organize and execute. Small campaigns take about two weeks. You build the calendar around big campaigns and avoid giving firm launch dates on small campaigns so you can use them to fill gaps in the schedule.

Assignments are added to the annual calendar as far in advance as possible. We typically added items to the calendar six months ahead of the launch date, although our best clients only had to give us three months notice and we could handle emergency work from good clients with little or no notice. You can put a target launch date in a planning calendar, but as that day approaches, the launch will most likely have to be moved. Adjusting the schedule became a weekly process, because publicists had trouble booking tours or campaigns for similar products couldn't be launched in the same week.

Under my system, publicists or AEs were expected to handle 40 to 50 major campaigns a year and 40 to 50 minor campaigns. That's a lot of work. Most of my clients were in the high-volume book publishing industry, some of them releasing hundreds of new titles each season. Most publicists will work for firms with fewer product launches that get larger campaigns. Obviously, the publicity for something like a new automobile or major piece of software will involve a more complex campaign than a mid-list book. So, let's look at the workload from a different perspective.

Billable time is an important measure for ad agencies, PR firms, marketing communications companies, and consulting firms. For a large online publicity department, I would expect 25 percent billable time for the manager and 75 percent billable time for each AE and support staff. For a small department, billable time for the manager should be about 50 percent. You can take the billable time, multiply by hourly rates, and get an annual revenue stream. If you are exceeding the target, you'll need to add staff to handle the workload and remain competitive. Client-side departments can use billable time analysis even if there is no one to bill. Time sheets that clearly differentiate between administrative support activities and campaign activities will help you manage payroll and workload.

I've never been keen on time sheet analysis. If you put too much emphasis on it, employees will simply fudge the figures to give you the numbers you want. For agencies that bill hourly, it's important, but I've noticed that clients like package pricing better than hourly billings, and being able to price by package is a competitive advantage. Time sheet analysis will help you adjust pricing more than it will help you manage employees. If it realistically takes 100 hours to pull off a major chat tour, you will have to price the service or staff the department accordingly rather than browbeat the staff into cutting that to 80 hours.

Measuring Results

Ah, here is the bottom line. How do you know how effective your online promotions are? How do the results compare with alternative uses for company funds? The answers to the questions are at the heart of a raging controversy in the marketing world, which has only been exacerbated by the rise of the Internet and it's increasing commercialization. After all, the Internet holds out the promise of microtuned measurements of ROI, but as with most things online, it has never made good on this promise.

I'm not even going to attempt to present the arguments that have been slung on all sides in this debate. Let me focus first on how you document the results of a campaign; then we'll see whether we can accurately measure their value.

Documentation

At the end of an online promotional campaign, you'll have a number of documents that will demonstrate to superiors and clients exactly what work has been done. To some extent, these documents will also shed light on what results have been accomplished. Here is a list of the documents your project folders should contain:

Registration report. A list of the directories and search engines where information about a Web site was submitted. A quality registration effort will include not only the major online catalogs and search engines but also phone-book style business directories and trade- or industry-specific catalogs and search engines. These listings are an important part of a company's online infrastructure, making a Web site easy for a target audience to locate.

Linkage report. A list of the sites where you requested links back to your site; should include the date of the request, the contact person's name and e-mail address, and the page of the site suggested as a location for the link. The linkage report is an important road map to the Web Sites That Matter in your industry or profession, and the work developing it can pay big dividends in future promotional efforts.

Media inquiries report. When I send news releases, I prepare a report that includes the number of media contacts who were sent the release and all responses, whether thank yous, interview requests, press packet requests, questions, or other feedback. The most important result is not included in the report: How much actual coverage resulted from the news releases? Less important, but valuable, results include the relationships formed or strengthened with media contacts and the correction and updating of contact information.

Postings report. This report is a detailed list of every online discussion group where messages were posted in support of the campaign.

Article syndication report. Like the linkage report, this report is a list of places pitched in an article syndication campaign. It includes information about each site, such as whether they accept outside submission, where they store such documents on their site, and the name and e-mail address of the person responsible for accepting or rejecting such submissions.

Chat schedule. This schedule is a list of the venues for a chat tour, including the date and time for each chat and contact information for chat show producers. The schedule is important in assessing the reach and value of a chat tour, and the contact information is vital in building relationships with chat hosts.

Seminar partners page. This Web page lists the partners for an online seminar or workshop series. It contains capsule descriptions of each partner along with contact names and information. It is used in determining the reach and value of these programs.

Screen captures. These are digital "photographs" made of online coverage of the campaign. They include shots of promotions at chat venues and seminar venues that prove that the event took place and was publicized. They also include shots of article placements, links, or other installations of sufficient merit.

There are other results of the online promotions described in this book that aren't usually recorded as documents. Of great importance are the databases built or augmented. Databases include people registering for online seminars and workshops, registrations as a result of contests or similar promotions, e-mail addresses of people who attended chats, and subscribers to newsletters and opt-in direct mail programs.

Most of these documents demonstrate that the work was performed in a professional manner and give some idea of the reach of a campaign. Clippings services can be used to further measure the impact of campaigns, but anyone who has used these services knows that they only capture a fraction of what is out there. They will find most of the important print pieces that result, but they miss a lot of broadcast coverage, and they're usually terrible at locating online coverage. Still, you have to work with what you can find.

Another way to document results is through Web site traffic log analysis. While there are many ways to look at these numbers, even a cursory analysis should show a bump in traffic related to an online campaign as well as lasting impacts. Analysis of the source of traffic will give a better idea of what is causing any increases. Traffic logs might help you direct resources to more profitable efforts. For example, they might cause you to spend more promoting on AOL and less on search engine optimization. But they don't capture the full value of campaigns run on other people's Web sites, and these sites will almost never share their traffic stats for a particular promotion.

Analyzing Value

Putting a dollar value on all this work is a mystical art at best and a deception at worst. The simplest way of generating a dollar value for this coverage is to find out what it would cost for a similar amount of advertising. Let's say that you get a product review that runs five column inches in a newspaper. You locate the advertising rate card for the paper, see what five inches of display advertising costs in that section of the paper on that day, and put a dollar value on that review. That sounds fairly simple, but multiply that one story by 20, and each newspaper has a different rate structure. Or, you could try and find the circulation of each publication and determine a cost per impression and see how that compares with advertising.

But the measurement problems are enormous, which is why none of my clients has ever attempted this kind of analysis, nor have I offered it. I don't know how many people read each Usenet newsgroup to which I post. Many online newsletters don't reveal the number of their subscribers. Many of the Web sites I work with don't sell advertising or don't have a rate card that tells me how many people view certain pages of the site. What is the value of a strategic partnership built for a chat tour that pays dividends for years to come?

A colleague of mine, John Deveney of Deveney Communication in New Orleans, performed a value analysis on a promotional campaign he did for the Web site, www.mardigras.com. He tallied all the people exposed to his promotional messages, then got the rate cards and determined what it would have cost to buy the same amount of exposure. The result? "Media coverage was valued at more than $7 million, compared to fees of $24,000 (or a 292:1 return ratio) on the client's marketing investment." Wow, that beats the pants off my IRA account.

If we were to believe those numbers, we would have to put the entire marketing budget into publicity instead of advertising—or at least into the hands of John Deveney. But that is exactly the sort of math we are reduced to with ROI calculations. You want ROI, you got it, but can you make decisions based on it? The subject of estimating ROI is worth a detailed look, because many of my colleagues in publicity and public relations have been harassed into generating these numbers in a mistaken attempt to quantify their contributions to the bottom line.

Let's start with media relations. What is the ROI on a news release? Is it simply a matter of finding the coverage that resulted, putting a dollar value on that coverage, and comparing it to the cost? If the cost for delivering a news release via e-mail is zero, why wouldn't you send one to every working journalist in the world? A poorly targeted release like this one would probably generate more coverage—and yield a higher ROI—than one sent to a select group of media. What happens later when your company is in a crisis and you need to get your side of the story out to the press in a hurry, but you have been Bozo-filtered out of the e-mail boxes of key media contacts because of your past indiscretions with news releases? Part of the ROI in sending news releases is opening lines of communication with the press and building relationships based on trust and respect that will help with future promotions. Because the value of these relationships is difficult to calculate, it's not included in ROI. All things being equal, the stupid spamming publicist is going to have a higher ROI than a tactful veteran, because the veteran's wisdom is not included in ROI.

This technique is the sad method that most companies use to calculate ROI: Take the sales that resulted from a promotion and compare them to the costs of the promotion. That's why we have such a problem with spam: If you nuke the Internet with a million messages, and the 50 sales that result cover the cost of the campaign, you've got a winner. That's because ROI does not calculate the damage caused to a company's reputation, let alone the costs of dealing with irate hackers or installing better security software. If you paid a million dollars for a good domain name, and after a mass e-mailing that domain is worthless, the cost side of the ROI equation increases by the million you spent for the domain name and by the cost and inconvenience of shifting to a new one.

There are many other problems with simplistic ROI calculations. What is it worth to a company to have good directory registration throughout the Internet—a backbone of links that will yield traffic for years to come? In 1996, I syndicated an article promoting a book called *Digital Literacy*. I placed the article on 21 Web sites. Six years later, it's still on 17 of those sites. How long would a banner ad campaign for the same book last? How do you value the long-term impact of promotions using ROI? Are we reduced to using campaigns that can be measured in minutes?

If you rule out ROI as a measure of effectiveness, what do you have left? Here's my take: If you have an experienced manager, someone who has been around long enough to have a good idea what happens to sales after good and bad marketing efforts, he or she can make educated guesses about what contributes most to the short-term profits and long-term viability of the organization. The publicity managers I work for have done their jobs long enough that they know when a campaign exceeds expectations or fails to meet them. I can blow smoke about the millions exposed to a message, but they have a sixth sense about whether a campaign was worth it or not—and that sixth sense is more important than ROI.

You pay managers for this educated instinct; if computers could figure it out, you wouldn't need experienced managers. And if a manager's instinct fails often enough, you fire him or her. If you try to replace him or her with someone who knows how to crunch numbers and who shifts the company's resources to high ROI activities, pretty soon you're going to have a 292:1 return on marketing investment and be filing for bankruptcy at the same time.

It's impossible for me to calculate the value of an online promotion to a company's bottom line, just as no one can calculate the return on a display ad in *The New York Times* or a 30-second spot on the Super Bowl. I leave that calculation to my clients. My job here is to help you understand what works and doesn't work in online promotion and to give you detailed instructions for executing these campaigns. As to the value of these campaigns, those with eyes will see and those with ears will listen.

Top Tips

Put an IT tiger in your tank. The easiest way to establish an online publicity operation is to put an IT person in the publicity department. This person doesn't have to be expensive; even entry-level prospects can teach your publicists Internet skills, solve small tech problems inside the department, and interface with IT on major issues.

Use a virtual staff. Virtual employees working out of low-wage markets can reduce your payroll along with your frustration levels. It's stunning how much of their time is billable. Freelancers will help you fill skill gaps while giving you the flexibility to expand or contract quickly without hiring or firing.

The big three: database, templates, training. To set-up an online publicity operation, you need to build a good database of contacts, design great document templates, and train your staff to merge the two.

Debug your bots. Most training comes through trial and error, but autobots and e-mail filters must be thoroughly tested before being used. Switch your e-mail from "send messages" to "queue messages" until you get the hang of designing and debugging bots.

Document, not measurement. When it comes to gauging the effectiveness of campaigns, all forms of measurement have serious problems. Your best bet is to document the results and use the educated instincts of a veteran manager to determine their value.

Companion Web Site

Throughout this book, I have referred to a companion Web site containing Internet publicity resources. Here is a list of what you'll find at the Web site and how to locate it and contact the author. The site is located at

http://www.wiley.com/compbooks/okeefe

Live events related to the book are held at the Online Publicity Group at Yahoo and include programs such as educational chats, training sessions, seminars, and guest appearances. These programs are free of charge and open to the public, although you must become a member of Yahoo and the Online Publicity Group to participate. The group is located at

http://groups.yahoo.com/group/onlinepublicity

The author of this book welcomes your questions, comments, and feedback. You can contact the author directly by sending e-mail to

STEVE O'KEEFE <onlinepublicity@yahoo.com>

Now let's look at all the goodies waiting for you at this book's companion Web site.

Internet Publicity Links

The Links section of the Web site offers an amazing set of time-saving, annotated links to the best online publicity resources available in nine categories. The links are updated monthly and include logo buttons for ease of recognition and navigation. The categories covered include the following:

- Publicity and Marketing SuperSites
- Internet Statistics
- Media Relations (News Releases, News Rooms)
- Discussion Group Postings
- Web Site Registration and Linkage
- Newsletters and Direct E-mail
- Chat Resources
- Contests, Animations, and Stupid Web Ticks
- Online Presentations, Seminars, and Workshops

Document Templates

These templates will help you generate online publicity materials in a hurry. They are designed to help you format documents properly for online delivery. Detailed instructions on how to use the templates are found in the corresponding chapters of this book. Templates available at the Web site include the following:

- Now Contact Database Illustration
- ACT! Database Illustration
- ACT! Layout File
- E-Mail News Release
- Discussion Group Posting
- Discussion Group Postings Report
- Chat Profile in Word
- Chat Profile in HTML
- Chat Schedule
- Web Site Registration Form
- Web Site Registration List
- Linkage Report
- Sample Linkletter
- Article for Syndication in HTML

Job Descriptions

The Web site contains detailed job descriptions for those who want to hire Internet publicity specialists or set up a complete in-house Internet publicity department. The descriptions are written for any company wanting to hire Internet publicity employees, but also contain special notes for marketing firms such as advertising agencies, public relations firms, marketing communications companies, and business consultants. The job descriptions cover the following positions:

Internet Publicity Department Manager

Publicist or Account Executive

Technical and Clerical Support Staff

Index

news releases, 17–19
seminars and workshops online, 220–221
telephone calls to seminars and workshops online, 227
television versus Internet, 11
templates for publicity operations online, 408–409, 419, 426
Tenagra Awards, 323–325
Tenagra Corporation, 291
text based seminars, 222–223, 228–229
text files, syndication of, 362–365
THRIVE site, 380
title tag, 282–283
Topica, 120, 145, 156
trading partners as Web site audience, 271
traditional marketing, 2
traffic analysis, cost of increasing traffic, 357–358
traffic builders, 312, 341–347
training staff for publicity operations online, 394, 409–412, 419
transaction-based nature of Internet, 6
transcripts
chat tours, 214–218
seminars and workshops online, 223, 261

Ulrich's Periodicals Directory, 45
undeliverable e-mail, news releases, 52–53
United Media, 342
universal access, 7–8
Unreal Pictures Inc., 346
unsolicited commercial e-mail (UCE) (See also spam), 15, 31
uppercase or all caps text, 34, 109–110, 112
URLs, 285, 296–297, 299
UUNET newsgroups (See also newsgroups), 115

value-added links, 308–309
value analysis for publicity operations online, 416–418
value sharing, 8
video, 82, 94
virtual employees for publicity operations online, 418

Web site announcement news release, 22–23
Web site design, 5
animations for, 343–344
audience of Web site, 268–269, 309
consumers as Web site audience, 269–270
copyright considerations for, 344–346

customers and prospects as Web site audience, 270
description tag, 282
directories, 273
domain name, 273–274
finding a site versus, 272–277
humor in, 342–343
investors as audience, 271
keywords tag, 280–281, 288–289
linking a Web site, 275, 284–285, 291–309
media as audience as, 271–272
media coverage, 275
META tags, 283–284
promotion, 276
registering a Web site, 285–291
search engines, 273
site traffic analysis, 276–277, 309
spiders, 283
splash pages, 283
stationery for, 274, 309
syndication of Web pages, 365
title tag, 282–283
trading partners as audience, 271
Webby Awards, 323
Welcome letter and instructions, for seminars and workshops, 238–241
Well, The, 124
Windows Media Player, 83
Windows Media Services, 80, 261
Winning PR in the Wired World, 14, 87
wire service type news release, 24–25
Wired News, 72, 162
word processors for news releases, 33–34
WorkWire, 70–71, 75
Write Markets, The, 154–156, 161
writing tips and techniques
for news rooms, 74
for discussion groups, 96, 105–112
for news releases, 25–30

Yack, 198
Yahoo!/Yahoo! Groups, 119–120, 279–280, 303–304
direct e-mail marketing and hosting, 145
newsletters, 156
seminars and workshops online, 231–234, 238, 265
syndication of articles library, 364
Yahoo! Broadcast Services, 81, 86
Yuckles.com, 343